Culture, Mind, and Brain

Recent neuroscience research makes it clear that human biology is cultural biology – we develop and live our lives in socially constructed worlds that vary widely in their structure values and institutions. This integrative volume brings together interdisciplinary perspectives from the human, social, and biological sciences to explore culture, mind, and brain interactions and their impact on personal and societal issues. Contributors provide a fresh look at emerging concepts, models, and applications of the co-constitution of culture, mind, and brain. Chapters survey the latest theoretical and methodological insights alongside the challenges in this area, and describe how these new ideas are being applied in the sciences, humanities, arts, mental health, and everyday life. Readers will gain new appreciation of the ways in which our unique biology and cultural diversity shape behavior and experience, and our ongoing adaptation to a constantly changing world.

LAURENCE J. KIRMAYER is James McGill Professor and Director of the Division of Social and Transcultural Psychiatry at McGill University, where he conducts research on the place of culture in mental health and illness, medical and psychological anthropology, and the philosophy of psychiatry.

CAROL M. WORTHMAN is Samuel Candler Dobbs Professor at the Department of Anthropology at Emory University. She uses a biocultural approach in comparative interdisciplinary research on health and human development in Africa, Asia, and the United States.

SHINOBU KITAYAMA is Social Psychology Area Chair and Robert B. Zajonc Collegiate Professor of Psychology at University of Michigan, where he conducts research on the mutual constitution of mental processes and culture.

ROBERT LEMELSON is President of the Foundation for Psychocultural Research and Adjunct Professor of Anthropology at University of California, Los Angeles. He has been conducting psychological and visual anthropological research in Indonesia yearly for the past twenty years.

CONSTANCE A. CUMMINGS is Project Director of the Foundation for Psychocultural Research, which advances interdisciplinary research on the intersection of brain, mind, and culture. She is coeditor of *Formative Experiences* (2010) and *Re-Visioning Psychiatry* (2015), both with Cambridge University Press.

Current Perspectives in Social and Behavioral Sciences

Current Perspectives in Social and Behavioral Sciences provides thought-provoking introductions to key topics, invaluable to both the student and scholar. Edited by world leading academics, each volume contains specially-commissioned essays by international contributors, which present cutting-edge research on the subject and suggest new paths of inquiry for the reader. This series is designed not only to offer a comprehensive overview of the chosen topics, but to display and provoke lively and controversial debate.

Published titles:
Culture, Mind, and Brain: Emerging Concepts, Models, and Applications edited by Laurence J. Kirmayer, Carol M. Worthman, Shinobu Kitayama, Robert Lemelson, and Constance A. Cummings
Genetics, Ethics and Education edited by Susan Bouregy, Elena L. Grigorenko, Stephen R. Latham and Mei Tan
Global Perspectives on Teacher Motivation edited by Helen Watt, Paul Richardson, and Kari Smith
Nurturing Creativity in the Classroom, 2nd edition edited by Ronald A. Beghetto and James C. Kaufman
Research and Theory on Workplace Aggression edited by Nathan A. Bowling, M. Sandy Hershcovis
Mindfulness and Performance edited by Amy L. Baltzell
Creativity and Reason in Cognitive Development, 2nd edition edited by James Kaufman and John Baer
Reflections on the Learning Sciences edited by Michael A. Evans, Martin J. Packer and R. Keith Sawyer

Culture, Mind, and Brain
Emerging Concepts, Models, and Applications

Edited by

Laurence J. Kirmayer
McGill University

Carol M. Worthman
Emory University

Shinobu Kitayama
University of Michigan

Robert Lemelson
University of California, Los Angeles

Constance A. Cummings
The Foundation for Psychocultural Research

CAMBRIDGE
UNIVERSITY PRESS

University Printing House, Cambridge CB2 8BS, United Kingdom

One Liberty Plaza, 20th Floor, New York, NY 10006, USA

477 Williamstown Road, Port Melbourne, VIC 3207, Australia

314-321, 3rd Floor, Plot 3, Splendor Forum, Jasola District Centre, New Delhi - 110025, India

103 Penang Road, #05-06/07, Visioncrest Commercial, Singapore 238467

Cambridge University Press is part of the University of Cambridge.

It furthers the University's mission by disseminating knowledge in the pursuit of education, learning and research at the highest international levels of excellence.

www.cambridge.org
Information on this title: www.cambridge.org/9781108705967
DOI: 10.1017/9781108695374

© Cambridge University Press 2020

This publication is in copyright. Subject to statutory exception and to the provisions of relevant collective licensing agreements, no reproduction of any part may take place without the written permission of Cambridge University Press.

First published 2020
First paperback edition 2022

A catalogue record for this publication is available from the British Library

ISBN 978-1-108-48414-5 Hardback
ISBN 978-1-108-70596-7 Paperback

Cambridge University Press has no responsibility for the persistence or accuracy of URLs for external or third-party internet websites referred to in this publication, and does not guarantee that any content on such websites is, or will remain, accurate or appropriate.

To Dorothy Lemelson, for her dynamism, vision, deep compassion, and support

The human mind was not designed by evolutionary forces for finding truth. It was designed for finding advantage.

Albert Szent-Györgi

Science sometimes sees itself as impersonal, as "pure thought," independent of its historical and human origins. It is often taught as if this were the case. But science is a human enterprise through and through, an organic, evolving, human growth, with sudden spurts and arrests, and strange deviations, too. It grows out of its past, but never outgrows it, any more than we outgrow our own childhood.

Oliver Sacks, "The Poet of Chemistry"

Le seul véritable voyage ... ce ne serait pas d'aller vers de nouveaux paysages, mais d'avoir d'autres yeux, de voir l'univers avec les yeux d'un autre, de cent autres, de voir les cent univers que chacun d'eux voit, que chacun d'eux est.

The only true voyage ... would be not to visit strange lands but to possess other eyes, to see the universe through the eyes of another, of a hundred others, to see the hundred universes that each of them sees, that each of them is.

Marcel Proust, *Remembrance of Things Past*

Contents

List of Figures	*page* x
List of Tables	xii
List of Contributors	xiii
Preface	xvii
List of Abbreviations	xxi

1 Introduction: Co-constructing Culture, Mind, and Brain 1
   LAURENCE J. KIRMAYER, CAROL M. WORTHMAN, AND SHINOBU KITAYAMA

Part I Dynamics of Culture, Mind, and Brain: Models and Evidence

Section 1 The Co-emergence of Culture, Mind, and Brain
Introduction

2 Culture, Mind, and Brain in Human Evolution: An Extended Evolutionary Perspective on Paleolithic Toolmaking as Embodied Practice 55
   DIETRICH STOUT

3 Mutual Constitution of Culture and the Mind: Insights from Cultural Neuroscience 88
   SHINOBU KITAYAMA AND QINGGANG YU

4 Being There: Foundations, Theory, Method 120
   CAROL M. WORTHMAN

Section 2 The Situated Brain
Introduction

5 Culture in Mind – An Enactivist Account: Not Cognitive Penetration but Cultural Permeation 163
   DANIEL D. HUTTO, SHAUN GALLAGHER, JESÚS ILUNDÁIN-AGURRUZA, AND INÊS HIPÓLITO

viii   Contents

6   The Brain as a Cultural Artifact: Concepts, Actions,
    and Experiences within the Human Affective Niche   188
    MARIA GENDRON, BATJA MESQUITA, AND LISA FELDMAN
    BARRETT

7   Cultural Priming Effects and the Human Brain   223
    SHIHUI HAN AND GEORG NORTHOFF

8   Culture, Self, and Agency: An Ecosocial View   244
    LAURENCE J. KIRMAYER, ANA GÓMEZ-CARRILLO, TIMOTHÉ
    LANGLOIS-THÉRIEN, MAXWELL J. D. RAMSTEAD, AND IAN GOLD

Section 3   How Social Coordination and Cooperation are Achieved
Introduction

9   Neuroanthropological Perspectives on Culture, Mind, and Brain   277
    DANIEL H. LENDE AND GREG DOWNEY

10 The Neural Mechanisms Underlying Social Norms:
    Norm Detection, Punishment, and Compliance   300
    YAN MU AND MICHELE J. GELFAND

11 Ritual and Religion as Social Technologies of Cooperation   325
    CHRISTOPHER KAVANAGH, JONATHAN JONG, AND HARVEY
    WHITEHOUSE

Part II   Applications   *Introduction*

12 The Cultural Brain as Historical Artifact   367
    ROB BODDICE

13 Experience-Dependent Plasticity in the Hippocampus   375
    GREG L. WEST AND VÉRONIQUE D. BOHBOT

14 Liminal Brains in Uncertain Futures: Critical Neuroscience
    and the Cultural Contexts of Neuroeducation   389
    SUPARNA CHOUDHURY AND JOSHUA BERSON

15 The Reward of Musical Emotions and Expectations   402
    BENJAMIN P. GOLD AND ROBERT J. ZATORRE

16 Literary Analysis and Weak Theories   416
    OMRI MOSES

17 Capturing Context Is Not Enough: The Embodied Impact
    of Story and Emotion in Ethnographic Film   426
    ROBERT LEMELSON AND ANNIE TUCKER

18	Social Neuroscience in Global Mental Health: Case Study on Stigma Reduction in Nepal BRANDON KOHRT	438
19	Cities, Psychosis, and Social Defeat FIRRHAANA SAYANVALA, LISA BORNSTEIN, SUPARNA CHOUDHURY, JAI SHAH, DANIEL WEINSTOCK, AND IAN GOLD	450
20	Internet Sociality MORIAH STENDEL, MAXWELL J. D. RAMSTEAD, AND SAMUEL P. L. VEISSIÈRE	461
21	Neurodiversity as a Conceptual Lens and Topic of Cross-Cultural Study M. ARIEL CASCIO	477
22	Epilogue: Interdisciplinarity in the Study of Culture, Mind, and Brain LAURENCE J. KIRMAYER, CAROL M. WORTHMAN, AND SHINOBU KITAYAMA	494

Index   513

Figures

1.1	Networks constitutive of human experience across multiple spatial scales.	*page* 2
1.2	Brain-to-brain synchrony in a couple and a dyad of strangers.	8
1.3	An illustration of hierarchical predictive coding.	10
1.4	Timescales of response in living systems.	13
1.5	Rice terraces in Bali, Indonesia.	32
1.6	Children running in wheat field near Datong, Qinghai, China.	33
2.1	A learning cycle in the helical curriculum.	62
2.2	Species differences in action processing circuitry.	71
3.1	Self-centric motivation for European Americans and East Asians.	96
3.2	Cortical volume of the orbitofrontal cortex.	109
4.1	Timescales of response in living systems (tailored specifically to human life history and evolutionary history).	124
4.2	!Kung San hunter-gatherers out foraging, Kalahari Desert, Botswana.	133
4.3	Dobe !Kung family outside their grass hut, Botswana.	134
4.4	A group of Dobe !Kung women out foraging with their children, Botswana.	135
4.5	The spirit of Soweto, a wall mural in Khayelitsha, Cape Town, South Africa (2008).	137
4.6	Men and children walk a sandy path in a township outside Cape Town, South Africa (2008).	138
4.7	Children with mother hanging laundry outside their home in a township near Cape Town, South Africa (2008).	139
4.8	A poster depicting war experiences, painted by youth in Bandipur, Nepal (2008).	141
4.9	Pedestrian street scene in historic center of Kathmandu, Nepal (2007).	142
4.10	Major street in the town of Jumla, Karnali Province, Nepal.	143

List of Figures

5.1	Examples of stimulus sequences presented in the oddball shape discrimination task.	164
5.2	A schematic illustration of hierarchical predictive coding.	173
6.1	Default mode and salience subnetworks.	192
6.2	A depiction of predictive coding in the human brain.	194
7.1	Illustration of the variation of P1 amplitude in (A) neutral, (B) independent, and (C) interdependent self-construal priming.	232
7.2	Illustration of priming and the face-recognition task.	234
7.3	Modulations of reward activity in the ventral striatum.	236
7.4	Modulation of in-group bias in empathic neural responses.	237
8.1	Brain regions involved in sense of agency and volition.	248
8.2	Predictive processing model of agency and sense of presence.	250
8.3	Multidimensional model of sense of agency.	252
8.4	The rubber hand illusion.	255
8.5	*Dang-ki* healing in Singapore.	262
9.1	Extended, developmental systems model of brain–culture engagement.	290
10.1	Cultural-general N400 effects of social norms violations.	305
10.2	Culture-specific N400 effects of social norm violations.	311
10.3	Cultural modulations of gamma interbrain synchrony during group coordination.	314
14.1	Critical neuroscience and the looping journey of the "brain fact."	395
18.1	Identity threat model of stigmatization in healthcare settings.	442
21.1	Logos for (A) Autistics United Canada and (B) Autistic Self-Advocacy Network.	485
21.2	Logo for Autism Support Network.	485
22.1	The co-construction of culture, mind, and brain on multiple levels.	499

Tables

1.1	Package of care for human young.	*page* 23
1.2	Co-construction of culture, mind, and brain on multiple temporal scales.	30
8.1	Response to outcome mismatch.	264
22.1	Strategies for interdisciplinary collaboration.	500

Contributors

LISA FELDMAN BARRETT, PhD, University Distinguished Professor of Psychology, Department of Psychology, Northeastern University; Research Scientist, Department of Psychiatry and the Athinoula A. Martinos Center for Biomedical Imaging, the Massachusetts General Hospital.

JOSHUA BERSON, PhD, USC Dornsife Berggruen Fellow, Berggruen Institute

ROB BODDICE, PhD, FRHistS, Assistant Professor, Department of History and Cultural Studies, Friedrich-Meinecke-Institut, Freie Universität Berlin; Adjunct Professor, Social Studies of Medicine, McGill University

VÉRONIQUE D. BOHBOT, PhD, Professor of Psychiatry and Researcher, Department of Psychiatry, Douglas Mental Health University Institute, McGill University

LISA BORNSTEIN, PhD, Associate Professor, School of Urban Planning, McGill University

M. ARIEL CASCIO, PhD, Assistant Professor in the Art of Medicine, Central Michigan University College of Medicine

SUPARNA CHOUDHURY, PhD, Assistant Professor, Division of Social and Transcultural Psychiatry, Department of Psychiatry; Co-Director, Culture, Mind, and Brain Program, McGill University

CONSTANCE A. CUMMINGS, PhD, Project Director, Foundation for Psychocultural Research

GREG DOWNEY, PhD, Professor, Department of Anthropology, Macquarie University

SHAUN GALLAGHER, PhD, Lillian and Morrie Moss Professor of Philosophy, Department of Philosophy, The University of Memphis

MICHELE J. GELFAND, PhD, Professor of Psychology, Department of Psychology, University of Maryland, College Park

MARIA GENDRON, PhD, Assistant Professor, Department of Psychology, Yale University

BENJAMIN P. GOLD, PhD, Montreal Neurological Institute, McGill University; Postdoctoral Researcher, Vanderbilt University Medical Center

IAN GOLD, PhD, Professor, Departments of Philosophy and Psychiatry, McGill University

ANA GÓMEZ-CARRILLO, MD, Dr Med, Postdoctoral Fellow, Division of Social and Transcultural Psychiatry, Department of Psychiatry, McGill University

SHIHUI HAN, PhD, Professor, School of Psychological and Cognitive Sciences, Peking University

INÊS HIPÓLITO, MA, PhD Candidate, School of Liberal Arts, University of Wollongong

DANIEL D. HUTTO, PhD, Senior Professor of Philosophical Psychology, School of Liberal Arts, University of Wollongong

JESÚS ILUNDÁIN-AGURRUZA, PhD, Professor and Chair, Department of Philosophy, Linfield College

JONATHAN JONG, PhD, Research Fellow/Assistant Professor and Deputy Director, Brain, Belief, and Behaviour Research Lab, Coventry University; Researcher, Centre for the Study of Social Cohesion, University of Oxford

CHRISTOPHER KAVANAGH, PhD, Associate Professor, Department of Psychology, Rikkyo University; Researcher, Centre for the Study of Social Cohesion, University of Oxford

LAURENCE J. KIRMAYER, MD, FRCPC, FCAHS, FRSC, James McGill Professor and Director, Division of Social and Transcultural Psychiatry, Department of Psychiatry; Co-Director, Culture, Mind, and Brain Program, McGill University

SHINOBU KITAYAMA, PhD, Robert B. Zajonc Collegiate Professor of Psychology, Department of Psychology, University of Michigan

BRANDON KOHRT, MD, PhD, Charles and Sonia Akman Professor of Global Psychiatry; Associate Professor of Psychiatry and Behavioral Sciences and Anthropology, The George Washington University

TIMOTHÉ LANGLOIS-THÉRIEN, BSc, MPhil Candidate and Researcher, Department of History and Philosophy of Science, University of Cambridge; Culture and Mental Health Research Unit, Jewish General Hospital

ROBERT LEMELSON, PhD, President, Foundation for Psychocultural Research; Adjunct Professor, Department of Anthropology, UCLA

DANIEL H. LENDE, PhD, Associate Professor, Department of Anthropology, University of South Florida

BATJA MESQUITA, PhD, Professor of Psychology; Director, Center for Social and Cultural Psychology (CSCP), University of Leuven

OMRI MOSES, PhD, Associate Professor, Department of English, Concordia University

YAN MU, PhD, Professor and Principal Investigator, Institute of Psychology, Chinese Academy of Sciences; Department of Psychology, University of Chinese Academy of Sciences

GEORG NORTHOFF, MD, PhD, Canada Research Chair in Mind, Brain Imaging and Neuroethics, Mind, Brain Imaging & Neuroethics Research Unit, University of Ottawa Institute of Mental Health Research; Royal Ottawa Mental Health Centre

MAXWELL J. D. RAMSTEAD, PhD, Douglas Utting Postdoctoral Fellow, Jewish General Hospital; Division of Social and Transcultural Psychiatry, McGill University

FIRRHAANA SAYANVALA, BSc, MD Candidate, Medical Student, Michael G. DeGroote School of Medicine, McMaster University

JAI SHAH, MD, FRCPC, Assistant Professor, Department of Psychiatry, McGill University

MORIAH STENDEL, MSc, Doctoral Student, Department of Psychology, University of Oregon

DIETRICH STOUT, PhD, Associate Professor, Department of Anthropology, Emory University

ANNIE TUCKER, PhD, Researcher, Elemental Productions

SAMUEL P. L. VEISSIÈRE, PhD, Assistant Professor, Division of Social and Transcultural Psychiatry, Department of Psychiatry; Co-Director, Culture, Mind, and Brain Program, McGill University

DANIEL WEINSTOCK, PhD, Full Professor, James McGill Professor, Director of the McGill Institute for Health and Social Policy; Faculty of Law, McGill University

GREG L. WEST, PhD, Associate Professor, Department of Psychology, University of Montreal

HARVEY WHITEHOUSE, PhD, Professor; Chair of Social Anthropology, Director, Centre for the Study of Social Cohesion, University of Oxford

CAROL M. WORTHMAN, PhD, Samuel Candler Dobbs Professor, Department of Anthropology, Emory University

QINGGANG YU, MS, Graduate Student, Department of Psychology, University of Michigan

ROBERT J. ZATORRE, PhD, Professor, Montreal Neurological Institute and Hospital, McGill University; Co-Director, International Laboratory for Brain, Music, and Sound Research

Preface

We live at a moment when the neurosciences are undergoing a massive expansion yielding fascinating insights into human functioning in health and illness. At the same time, advances in the social sciences and psychology are reshaping understandings of the interplay of culture, mind, and brain in human evolution, cognition, emotion, self, agency, ritual, religion, politics, and other domains of life. The implications of these advances go beyond what can be discerned by any one discipline. Insights in one area can transform work in others, but this requires that we bridge disciplines with developmental and ecological models that link our understanding of the brain, the person, and the social world.

This book has its origin in a 2012 conference of the same name organized by the editors, sponsored by the Foundation for Psychocultural Research (FPR), and hosted by the University of California, Los Angeles. Since its founding in 2000, the FPR has engaged in a wide range of granting and programming to bring together scholars in disparate fields to talk about emerging concepts, methods, and applications in the study of culture, mind, and brain with particular attention to: (1) innovative neuroscience research that successfully engages culture and the social world; (2) the contexts in which methods are used as well as the tacit assumptions that shape research questions; and (3) the kinds of collaboration that can advance interdisciplinary research and training. This was the fifth interdisciplinary conference hosted by the foundation; the previous three had resulted in edited volumes. However, other commitments left this project on the back burner for several years.

In 2016, we returned to the topic with renewed interest and conviction that advances in this arena warranted comprehensive treatment. Powerful new metaphors had emerged, particularly the idea that the brain is a dynamic network of global and regional neural processes, one that actively makes use of prior knowledge, beliefs, and experiences to predict, plan, and implement action programs. At the same time, we have learned more about how closely the brain is coupled with the social world – structurally and dynamically – in processes of co-construction.

Over the past few years, we invited scholars and researchers from many disciplines to join us in taking a fresh look at emerging concepts, models, and applications that provide new ways to think about the interactions of culture, mind, and brain. The book before you is the result of this interdisciplinary exchange. The questions the contributors were invited to address include:

- What are the "cutting-edge" topics in social and cultural neuroscience – the neural, psychological, and social processes underlying human diversity – that have special relevance for efforts to bridge our concepts of culture, mind, and brain?
- Given that the human brain evolved to operate in locally contingent ways within socially constructed environments, an "eco-systemic" approach to mind, brain, and culture may provide a more biologically relevant and richer way to think about "context." But how can concepts of such complexity be studied in a scientifically rigorous fashion?
- What are the clinical and societal implications of current research in neuroscience, including epigenetics, predictive coding, network theories, and our evolving understanding of developmental trajectories through brain–mind–body–environment interactions?
- What are some of the novel transdisciplinary ways to engage human diversity and variation, to think about the mind as embodied and enacted, and to investigate culture as both integral to individual experience, and as a dynamic process at multiple levels of social organization – from family, to community, to society and global networks? How might emerging insights, tools, and frameworks address current challenges to human flourishing and sustainability?

The response to the invitation to address these questions is the rich set of essays in this volume, which explore how neuroscience and social science can be brought together in meaningful conversation to illuminate human nature and experience.

We take this opportunity to thank the speakers, panelists, discussants, and especially our audience at the FPR's Culture, Mind, and Brain 2012 conference for pushing us to consider new theories, methods, and tools. The FPR has played an important role in advancing interdisciplinary training and collaboration in cultural neuroscience and social science since its inception. Founded in 2000 by anthropologist Robert Lemelson, the FPR supports interdisciplinary and integrative research and training on interactions of culture, neuroscience, psychiatry, and psychology, with an emphasis on the central role of cultural processes. The FPR has organized a series of conferences, hosted at UCLA, that reflect its commitment to articulate and support transformative paradigms that address issues of fundamental clinical and social concern: *Posttraumatic Stress Disorder: Biological, Clinical and Cultural Approaches* to Trauma's Effects (2002); *Four Dimensions of Childhood: Brain, Mind, Culture, and Time* (2005); *Seven Dimensions of Emotion: Integrating Biological, Clinical, and Cultural Perspectives on Fear, Disgust, Love, Grief, Anger, Empathy, and Hope* (2007); *Cultural and Biological Contexts of Psychiatric Disorder: Implications for Diagnosis and Treatment* (2010); *Culture, Mind, and Brain: Emerging Concepts, Methods, Applications* (2012); and *A Critical Moment: Sex/Gender Research at the Intersections of Culture, Brain, and Behavior* (2015). This book is the latest volume to emerge from these conferences and represents a stock-taking and capstone project that, we hope, points toward future creative innovation.

The editors wish to thank Irene Sukwandi, director of the FPR, and the foundation's board members – Carole Browner, Marie-Françoise Chesselet, Douglas Hollan, Marjorie Kagawa-Singer, Marvin Karno, Steven López, and Beate Ritz – for their vision, leadership, and support. Additionally, we wish to thank Mamie Wong, FPR program officer, for her sharp insights and skillful editing of the manuscript.

LJK wishes to thank the FPR, his colleagues at the Institute of Community and Family Psychiatry, who have supported his interdisciplinary work for over three decades, and his current collaborators in the McGill-FPR Culture, Mind, and Brain Program for a constant sense of intellectual adventure, excitement, and hope for the future.

CMW wishes to thank the FPR for patiently and presciently fostering the interdisciplinary thought and inquiry reflected in this book, and all those who seek to benefit our common yet diverse struggle to be/come humans together on this small planet.

SK thanks the FPR for its support of the publication of this fabulous collection of essays. It has been instrumental in promoting the science of mind, culture, and the brain. SK is very proud to be part of this effort.

RL wishes to thank both the board and staff of the FPR, all of whom have served for 20 years, for their commitment and deep engagement as we collectively grappled to understand how some of the most complex domains in the social sciences and the neurosciences are related, and creatively designed programs to explore those issues. He feels that he could not have been blessed with a more dedicated, thoughtful, and nice group of employees and colleagues as fellow travelers on this intellectual journey.

Finally, CC thanks her co-editors, the contributors, and Rob Lemelson and the FPR for the opportunity to explore some of this ever-changing terrain with you. CC and her co-editors also wish to thank the highly skilled and thoughtful guidance provided by our CUP team: Stephen Acerra, Matthew Bennett, Rebecca Grainger, Niranjana Harikrishnan, Penny Lyons, and Emily Watton. Finally, CC thanks Erin Hartshorn, Alan Gesek, and Sean Hope Kelly for the superb index and illustrations.

This book goes to press as humanity grapples with a pandemic, attempting to slow the rate of infection and save lives through public health and economic efforts whose profound effects will continue to evolve and ramify well into the future. Our responses highlight both strengths and fault lines in human culture. These include the distinctively human capacity for pro-social cooperative behavior and solidarity on the one hand, and massive global inequalities in the distribution of wealth and opportunity on the other. To meet the myriad challenges, we must call on our capacities for adaptation, collaboration, and creativity. We hope the conceptual tools and research findings presented in this volume – and the larger enterprise of understanding the interplay of culture, mind, and brain – will be useful resources in this ongoing effort as well as for imagining the new configurations of global society that follow.

Abbreviations

4E	embodied, enactive, ecological, extended
4R (allele)	4-repeat allele
5-HTTLPR	serotonin-transporter-linked polymorphic region
7/2-R (allele)	7- and 2-repeat alleles of the *DRD4* gene
7R (allele)	7-repeat allele
ACC	anterior cingulate cortex
ADH1B	gene that regulates the enzyme alcohol dehydrogenase 1B
ADH1B*47His	Polymorphic variant of *ADH1B* associated with alcohol metabolism
ADHD	attention-deficit/hyperactivity disorder
AI	anterior insula
AIDS	acquired immunodeficiency syndrome
AG	angular gyrus
ANI	Autism Network International
APOE2	apolipoprotein E2 allele variant
APOE4	apolipoprotein E4 allele variant
APPS	attenuated positive psychotic symptoms
aSMG	anterior supramarginal gyrus
BA10	Broadman area 10
BDNF	brain-derived neurotrophic factor
BOLD	blood-oxygen-level-dependent
CAAFAG	children associated with armed forces and groups
CMS	cortical midline structures
CREDs	credibility-enhancing displays
CTRA	conserved transcriptional response to adversity
daIns	dorsal anterior insula and includes ventrolateral prefrontal cortex
DLPFC	dorsolateral prefrontal cortex
DMN	default mode network
dmPFC	dorsomedial prefrontal cortex
DNA	deoxyribonucleic acid
DRD4	dopamine D4 receptor gene

EEA	environment of evolutionary adaptedness
EEG	electroencephalography
EES	extended evolutionary synthesis
ENS	empty nose syndrome
ERN	error-related negativity
ERP	event-related potential
ESA	early Stone Age
fMRI	functional magnetic resonance imaging
FOXP2	Forkhead box P2 gene
FRN	feedback-related negativity
GM	gray matter
GPS	Global Positioning System
HCI	human–computer interactions
HIV	human immunodeficiency virus
HPA	hypothalamic–pituitary–adrenal (axis)
HPC	hippocampus
IBH	Interactive Brain Hypothesis
IFG	inferior frontal gyrus
IRL	in real life
ITG	inferior temporal gyrus
LMICs	low- and middle-income countries
LTP	long-term potentiation
M1	primary motor cortex
m/pIns	mid/posterior insula (primary interoceptive cortex)
MC	motor cortex
MCC	midcingulate cortex
MD	medical doctor
mhGAP	mental health Gap Action Programme
MMORPGs	massive multiplayer online role-playing games
MNS	mental, neurological, and substance abuse disorders
MOFC	medial orbitofrontal cortex
mPFC	medial prefrontal cortex
MRI	magnetic resonance imaging
MS	modern synthesis
MSR	Mirror Self-Recognition Test
N400	peak (in milliseconds) of event-related potential
NIMH	National Institute of Mental Health (USA)
NPH	narrative practice hypothesis
NTS	nucleus of the solitary tract
O&M	orientation and mobility
OECD	Organization for Economic Cooperation and Development
OFC	orbitofrontal cortex

List of Abbreviations

P1	ERP component
PACC	perigenual anterior cingulate cortex
PAG	periaqueductal gray
PBN	parabrachial nucleus
PCC	posterior cingulate cortex
PCW	primary care worker
PECMA	perception, emotion, cognition, and motor action
PET	positron emission tomography
pgACC	pregenual anterior cingulate cortex
PHG	parahippocampal gyrus
PLE	power law exponent
PMC	premotor cortex
pMCC	posterior midcingulate cortex
postCG	postcentral gyrus
PPC	predictive processing account of cognition
PPC	posterior parietal cortex
PRIME	Programme for Improving Mental health carE
PTSD	posttraumatic stress disorder
PWLE	persons with lived experience of mental, neurological, and substance use disorders
RCT	randomized control trial
rDLPFC	right dorsolateral prefrontal cortex
REC	radically enactive accounts of cognition
RESHAPE	Reducing Stigma among HealthcAre ProvidErs
rLPFC	right lateral prefrontal cortex
ROI	region of interest
RS	rejection sensitivity
SCS	self-consciousness scale
SES	socioeconomic status
sgACC	subgenual anterior cingulate cortex
SI	primary somatosensory cortex
SII	secondary somatosensory cortex
SLC6A4	serotonin transporter gene
SLFIII	superior longitudinal fasciculus
SMA	supplementary motor area
sMRI	structural magnetic resonance imaging
SRGAP2	SLIT-ROB Rho GTPase-activating protein 2
SSC	somatosensory cortex
SSD	somatic symptom disorder
STS	superior temporal sulcus
tDCS	transcranial direct current stimulation
TIV	total intracranial volume

TL	tightness–looseness
TMS	transcranial magnetic stimulation
TPO	Transcultural Psychosocial Organization (in Nepal)
UN	United Nations
UNICEF	United Nations Children's Fund
V1	primary visual cortex
vaIns	ventral anterior insula
VBM	voxel-based morphometry
vMMN	visual mismatch negativity
vmPFC	ventromedial prefrontal cortex
VNTR	variable number tandem repeat
VS	ventral striatum
WEIRD	Western, educated, industrialized, rich, and democratic
WHO	World Health Organization

1 Introduction
Co-constructing Culture, Mind, and Brain

Laurence J. Kirmayer, Carol M. Worthman, and Shinobu Kitayama

Introduction

The last two decades have seen the emergence of a body of work in the social and cultural neurosciences that is beginning to illuminate the ways in which the nervous system reconfigures itself, in response to diverse sociocultural contexts and lifeworlds, through ongoing dynamic processes of adaptation, plasticity, and learning. This innovative work has benefited from major advances in brain imaging, genomics, and other biotechnologies that are contributing to new ways of studying and thinking about human minds, brains, and cultures. Older brain-centric views are giving way to more integrative pictures, in which the cultural world shapes and reshapes our neural circuitry even as our brains cooperate to produce the social world.

The brain is an adaptive system that is constantly reorganizing itself through dynamic interactions with the larger systems in which it is embedded (the body and the social world), to respond to the challenges and opportunities presented by the environment. In the case of humans, the environments we occupy are always already shaped by culture. All of the adaptive tasks, challenges, and opportunities that we face are organized and made meaningful, both personally and socially, by cultural conventions, practices, traditions, and institutions. We live our lives in and through socially constructed worlds that vary widely in their architecture, sensory qualities, social order, values, ideologies, and aspirations – all of which reflect different histories, institutions, and visions of the future. Human nature, therefore, although grounded in our evolutionary history, is also inescapably cultural and undergoing constant revision. Coming to grips with who we are and who we are becoming requires that we consider not only our biology, but equally the culturally diverse social worlds that shape our experience, psychology, and imagination.

On this view, the brain is the organ of culture; mind and experience are processes located in loops of active engagement of the brain and the body with the social world. This engagement occurs on multiple scales, from evolutionary and coevolutionary adaptation, through the cultural history of communities, to individual developmental trajectories, and moment-to-moment engagement

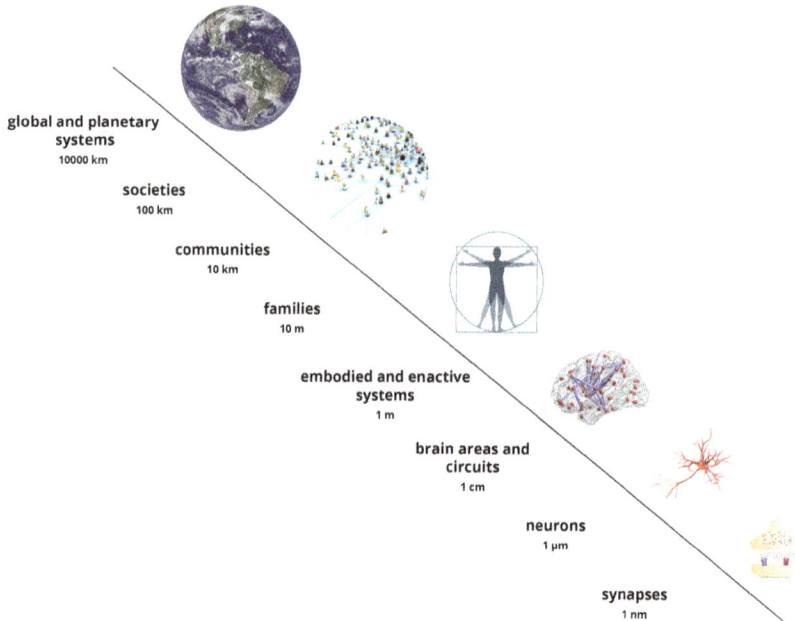

Figure 1.1 Networks constitutive of human experience across multiple spatial scales. The networks that contribute to human behavior and experience are hierarchically organized across multiple spatial scales. Integrating these networks requires a multilevel perspective that includes the brain in its local environment and culturally constructed niche, and extends to family, community, and larger social networks.

with social contexts. Different disciplines have focused on processes at specific spatial and temporal scales. Exciting new work is being done that both reveals the unique dynamics that occur on each of these timescales and captures the interplay among them, allowing us to begin to see the interactions between brain, body, and environment as a complex system that gives rise to our individual experiences and psychological interiority, as well our social worlds. Network theory has emerged in recent years as a valuable tool for describing and quantifying interactions of complex systems that occur across multiple scales (Clauset et al., 2008). In Figure 1.1, these networks are hierarchically organized, and each level (e.g., "whole brain") further subdivides into networks-within-networks. Integrating these networks requires a multilevel perspective that includes the brain in its local environment, cultural niche, and larger social networks, which constitute a kind of ecological system. In this introductory essay, we outline some conceptual building blocks for such an ecosocial view on the co-construction of mind, brain, and culture.

Brain, Mind, and Culture

This book is built around a set of questions about the interplay of three constructs: *brain*, *mind*, and *culture*. Although these are words we all use casually, it is worth pausing for a moment to consider their various meanings.

The brain is an anatomical entity – a three-pound organ, comprised of some 100 billion neurons, nestled within the human skull – that extends its reach throughout the body and into the larger world. Through the autonomic, endocrine, and immune systems, the brain regulates all the other physiological systems of the body. The body, in turn, influences the brain through peripheral neural, endocrine, immune, and circulatory systems, as well as interactions with the trillions of microorganisms that constitute the microbiome of the gut, which itself has upwards of 100 million neurons. Interoception, the perception of the body's internal milieu, is crucial to the regulation and maintenance of healthy functioning, or homeostasis. Through exteroceptive sensory organs and the motor system, the brain and nervous system engage with the world in ways that allow us to survive, meet our basic needs, reproduce, respond to the challenges of a changing environment, and even, at times, to flourish. In addition to these vital regulatory and adaptive functions, which we share with other animals, the human brain subserves consciousness, subjectivity, and agency – our sense of being alive, aware, and able to articulate and pursue our goals. At the same time, the brain is also a discursive object, something we talk about – indeed, references to the brain are increasingly present in the ways we think about ourselves as persons. New ways of talking about human functioning and experience in terms of the brain – which sometimes oversimplify or else go far beyond what neuroscience has actually shown – are having profound impacts in many domains of life including childrearing, education, healthcare, and the law (Choudhury & Slaby, 2012; Rose & Abi-Rached, 2013; Vidal & Ortega, 2017).

The term "mind" stands for our fundamental nature as thinking, feeling, acting beings. The grammar of the English language tends to make us speak of *the* mind as a thing and thus confronts us with the hoary mind–body problem, in which we struggle to explain how to get from the physical machinery of the brain to the complexity of goal-oriented behavior and the qualia of conscious experience. Mind is better thought of not as a thing but as a set of processes. Indeed some philosophers have argued that the mind is what the *brain* does; that is, they argue that what we call the mind can be demystified and ultimately naturalized by identifying it strictly with specific neural processes, all of which are localizable in the brain (e.g., Churchland, 1989). This kind of neuro-reductionism is challenged by evidence for the embodied, enacted, socially embedded, and extended nature of mental processes discussed in many of the contributions to this volume (e.g., see Chapter 5). The term "mind" then remains an important placeholder for the many complex, meaning-centered processes that are the focus of psychology. Taking the social embedding of the person seriously means that mind extends out into the world in ways that include our tools, our social environments, and, crucially, the minds of others, past and present.

The term "culture" stands for the cooperatively constructed, socially shared, transmitted, and enacted knowledge, institutions, and practices that are central to human development and functioning. Culturally shared developmental experiences shape the architecture of our brains, and cultural knowledge and practices stock our minds with the language, models, and metaphors that we use to navigate the world. Culture itself is a hierarchical system with its own dynamics, co-existing in a landscape of diversity with other cultures, and constantly reconfigured in response to new technologies, social processes, and ways of life.

Approaches to studying the role of culture in human experience also are changing to reflect new dynamics. Earlier models analyzed culture and ethnicity (that is, the groups with which people identify, or the particular historical groups, communities, or peoples to which they are assigned by others) in terms of traits or characteristics that were viewed as consequences of particular patterns of childrearing and specific social, ecological, or historical conditions. The focus on shared or collective characteristics has been complemented by work on how individuals make use of culturally mediated and mandated strategies to respond to particular contexts or situations. More recently, both group and individual levels of cultural analysis have been refined by examining how local social contexts interact with global, historical, and ecological conditions. Despite the forces of globalization, humanity continues to exhibit a remarkable efflorescence of cultures and hybrid forms. The great diversity of cultures and ways of life holds keys to understanding human nature and our collective future.

Each of these concepts of culture, mind, and brain has its own social, intellectual, and disciplinary history. While at any point in time, our notions of culture, mind, and brain often are presented as givens, they also can be understood as constructions. The metaphor of construction seems apt when describing social phenomena that we have set in place deliberately through creative invention, cooperative actions, and collective agreement. There are rich traditions of social and cultural constructivism, which study the changing constructs that constitute our social worlds (Hacking, 1999, 2002). Many socially and culturally constructed processes reside in shared discourse, institutions, and practices. But the metaphor of construction can also be applied to the ways that mind, brain, and culture give rise to each other through mutually constitutive processes on multiple timescales.

The Encultured Brain: Genetics, Epigenetics, and Neuroplasticity

The mapping of the human genome was expected to yield immediate insights into how the brain functions. However, behaviors are not produced directly by genes, but instead reflect dynamic, recursive, and multi-layered interactions among genes, cellular machinery, neural circuitry, and the environment over time (Lock & Palsson, 2016). The genome itself is a complex regulatory system, with a large portion of its DNA devoted to its own modulation (Davidson, 2006). A burgeoning field of epigenetics examines the ways in which environmental interactions turn genes on and off through a variety of biochemical mechanisms (Champagne, 2018). The functional genome, then, is not merely given through genetic inheritance but emerges through interactions with an environment – through epigenetic and indeed, *extragenetic* inheritance of cultural and other reliably recurrent environmental factors as well (Griffiths & Stotz, 2013). Brain structures and circuits emerge in neurodevelopment through dense interactions among genetic networks, local regions of tissue, and the larger social and cultural environment. As anatomical structures and circuits emerge, they interact with each other, introducing further levels of complexity.

In current theory, the human brain is viewed as a large-scale network with various, more specialized or modular subnetworks for processing and integrating information at multiple scales (e.g., the synaptic, neuronal, and neural-circuit levels), as well as across distant brain regions. Neuroanatomical connectivity is partially inscribed in our genes, which interact with the environment to produce the brain's basic architecture during early development (Collin & van den Heuvel, 2013), but brain connectivity is also highly dynamic, plastic, and adaptable, shaped by each brain's history of functional activity (Sherwood & Gómez-Robles, 2017; Sporns, 2011), and continuously interacting with the rest of the body (together comprising the *neurome*; Hahn et al., 2019). Neuronal plasticity occurs at many levels: synaptic connections between neurons are modified by their co-activation, allowing neurons to be recruited to join cell assemblies, local networks, or subsystems; neural subnetworks are wired and rewired in response to environmental contingencies; and multiple subnetworks may be recruited to form larger functional assemblies to meet ongoing adaptive challenges (Anderson, 2014).

Recognition of the crucial roles of brain plasticity in structure and function throughout life stands in contrast to earlier views according to which, once developed, brain anatomy remains static, like the hardware of a computer (Martin et al., 2000; Merzenich et al., 2013). Fundamental functions, such as learning and memory, proceed through changes in neuronal structure and connections (e.g., through the formation, strengthening, and pruning of synapses; Tononi & Cirelli, 2014). Previous functions can be restored after trauma and compensatory functions elaborated after sensory loss (e.g., blindness) by rewiring or repurposing cortical areas (Doidge, 2007; Merabet & Pascual-Leone, 2010). The brain is modified by how we use it: for example, occupation (e.g., London taxi drivers; Maguire et al., 2006), skill training (e.g., juggling; Draganski et al., 2004), physical activity (Hillman et al., 2008), rumination or thinking too much (Hamilton et al., 2015), and meditation or attentional practices (Muehsam et al., 2017); all have been associated with shifts in brain structure and function.

Two points merit emphasis here. First, though there are limits to brain plasticity, we now know that the brain's anatomy and activity are dynamically shaped by use and experience from infancy through old age. Second, it follows that brain plasticity represents a critical dynamic through which humans are encultured, not just during early development but throughout the life course. The culturally mediated worlds in which we grow up and live are integral to how our brains achieve their functional capabilities. Culturally informed skills and "habits of mind" reflect neurodevelopmental processes as well as ongoing dynamics of interaction with local environmental niches and the larger social ecologies we inhabit. As a consequence, through everyday activities and social interactions, our individual brain networks become uniquely tuned to aspects of our particular social-cultural niche. It is because of our human capacity to be shaped by, enact, and transmit knowledge, skills, and attitudes – through language, shared intentionality, and other distinctively human attributes (Tomasello, 2019) – that the collaborative workings of many individual brains can achieve the feat of creating, navigating, and reproducing cultural systems (Veissière et al., 2020).

Windows on the Brain

This book is prompted by new theory and findings in neuroscience that have wide implications for the social and behavioral sciences, and for our understanding of what it is to be human. These advances have been stimulated by a range of new technologies that have made it possible to visualize brain activity, connectivity, and dynamic functioning in powerful ways. Earlier generations of research relied on animal models or the study of human brain injury to identify anatomical correlates or localization of particular kinds of brain function (Bennett & Hacker, 2008). This animal work was limited because nonhuman animals do not possess many of the features that define human culture – including language, stories, complex artifacts and technologies, social conventions, institutions, values, and ideologies. At the same time, human research was limited by ethical constraints and by the fact that while studies of brain injury or pathology can shed light on basic processes, the pathology also may obscure normal functioning. The injured brain must jury-rig new ways of functioning, while the person coping with affliction adopts new strategies for adaptation.

Human brain research has benefited enormously from the development of noninvasive neuroimaging techniques at multiple spatial and temporal resolutions, especially electroencephalography (EEG) and functional magnetic resonance imaging (fMRI). EEG techniques involve the use of electrodes attached to the scalp to measure the electrical activity of the brain, particularly the outer cortical layers. The main advantage of this technique is its temporal resolution: it can capture rapid changes (in milliseconds) in brain activity. Its spatial resolution is less impressive. Originally, it could give only a rough measure of cortical activity over a wide area; thanks to new analytic techniques, underlying activity deeper in the brain can be inferred, although still not with extreme precision. That said, EEG is inexpensive and can be done with small, portable equipment allowing studies of activity in more ecologically valid, real-world settings. It can detect synchronous activity among brain networks in the form of specific rhythms that may be associated with particular aspects of brain functioning. EEG can be used to measure event-related potentials (ERPs). ERPs measure electrical activity triggered by specific stimuli and thus can indicate sensory, orienting, attentional, and decision-related responses to a stimulus over the scale of milliseconds. In suitable experimental setups, this allows investigators to unpack the sequence of steps in processing particular kinds of information and build models of attention and cognition.

Magnetic resonance imaging (MRI) can produce detailed pictures of an individual's brain. These can be used to study anatomical differences in the brains of people with different developmental histories, psychological characteristics, or forms of pathology. Functional magnetic resonance imaging examines changes in blood flow to specific regions of the brain, which provides an indirect measure of local metabolic and processing activity. In experiments, fMRI can be used to study dynamic global (whole-brain) and regional neural activity associated with experiential states such as self-related thinking or particular cognitive tasks. Newer methods, such as forms of diffusion MRI, allow us to reconstruct anatomical pathways, taking us a step closer to a comprehensive map of the brain's neural circuitry or "connectome" (Shi & Toga, 2017). This has given rise to a rapidly growing body of work that explores how circuits of the brain subserve particular cognitive functions or behaviors and how neurodevelopment, learning, and experience reconfigure the connectivity of the brain.

The neurodevelopmental processes that give rise to human capacities for language, thought, and creativity extend beyond the brain to include interactions with the environment and, especially, with other people. On a small scale, we can study these interactions in the laboratory by examining brain function in response to socially and ecologically meaningful stimuli. Methods

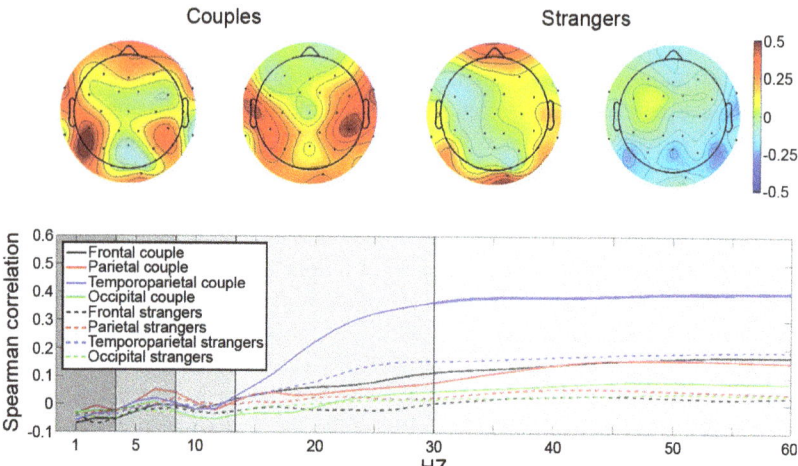

Figure 1.2 Brain-to-brain synchrony in a couple and a dyad of strangers. Kinreich and colleagues simultaneously measured the EEGs of romantic couples and pairs of strangers while the dyads were engaged in a free conversation about a "positive theme." The study found greater neural synchrony in the form of gamma-rhythm correlations in temporal-parietal areas (blue line in graph) among the couples than among the strangers.
From "Brain-to-Brain Synchrony during Naturalistic Social Interactions," by S. Kinreich, A. Djalovski, L. Kraus, Y. Louzoun, and R. Feldman, 2017, *Scientific Reports, 9,* 17060 (https://doi.org/10.1038/s41598-017-17339-5). https://creativecommons.org/licenses/by/4.0/

of hyperscanning, for example, imaging the brains of two or more people while they interact with each other in naturalistic settings, can reveal the processes of coordination, synchrony, and mutual regulation that may underlie crucial aspects of social behavior and help account for aspects of our feelings of empathy and mutual understanding or of strangeness and hostility (Babiloni & Astolfi, 2014; Bilek et al., 2015; Hirsch et al., 2017; Kinreich et al., 2017; Saito et al., 2010). Figure 1.2 illustrates how brain correlates of dyadic interactions can be explored in the laboratory. These new technologies allow us to move beyond theory construction to begin to explore the functional links between the brain and the social world.

4-E Cognitive Science and Predictive Processing as Unifying Frameworks

In each generation, neuroscience has used models and metaphors drawn from contemporary technologies and social arrangements to think about the brain

(Borck, 2012). For Descartes (1649/1989; see also Hatfield, 2007), the brain was the mediator between an immaterial soul and a biological machine. For nineteenth and early twentieth century physiologists such as Sechenov (1863/1965), Sherrington (1906), and Pavlov (1928), the brain was a hierarchy of reflex arcs. The dense forest of neurons revealed under the microscope by the anatomist Ramón y Cajal (1909) was thought to account for the complexity of behavior, but the organizational principles of neural networks have only slowly yielded their secrets (Sporns, 2012). At any historical moment, our most complex artifacts provide us with models and metaphors for brain functioning. Over the course of the twentieth century the brain was successively likened to a telephone switchboard, a cybernetic control system, and a digital computer (Ashby, 1952; Pickering, 2010; Von Neumann, 1958; Wiener, 1948). Each analogy contributed to advancing theory and research, but none is adequate to capture the brain's complexity.

While early work in computational neuroscience revealed that even simple idealized neurons suitably arranged could, in principle, constitute a Turing machine, capable of computing any computable number (McCulloch & Pitts, 1943), the brain is not a single general-purpose digital computer, but a bundle of more specialized mechanisms, organized to enable specific kinds of ecologically meaningful action. The peculiar strengths and limitations of human cognition suggest that brain structures and circuits that emerged for specific adaptive purposes are recruited for new tasks. For example, our visual and linguistic systems did not evolve to read, but have been recruited to serve this cultural practice (Dehaene, 2009).

The reflex arc picture of the brain fits a stimulus–response view of learning and behavior that could be adapted to model the processes of Pavlovian (classical) conditioning and operant (reinforcement) learning. However, during the last century it became increasingly clear that the brain is not usually sitting idle, waiting for environmental stimuli to provoke its response, but is ceaselessly active. Our brains are restless, constantly anticipating potential events, scanning our bodies and the world for news, seeking out novelty, and elaborating imaginative scenarios. Current models of the brain draw from work in artificial intelligence to depict the brain as networks of neurons that are engaged in *active inference*: working constantly to predict their input. On this view, the brain is a prediction machine, anticipating its environment, noticing discrepancies between expectation and reality, and working to refine its predictions to make them more accurate or acting on the environment to make it conform to predictions (Clark, 2015; Friston, 2010; Hohwy, 2013).

Predictive processing models generally propose that the brain is not a diffuse network with neurons interconnected to each other willy-nilly, but is instead structured into layers, with connectivity within each layer distinguished from connections to the layers above and below (Kaiser et al., 2010;

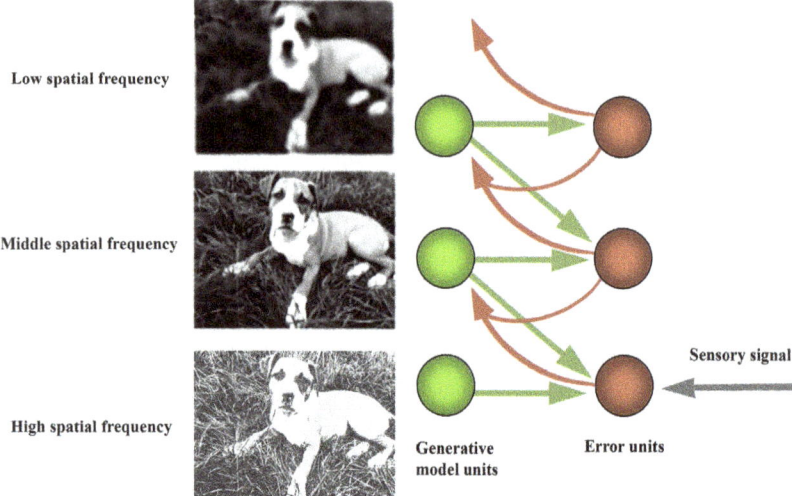

Figure 1.3 An illustration of hierarchical predictive coding. Predictive processing of visual perception involves multiple levels of spatial-temporal resolution. On the left, we see the same image (of a dog) decomposed into high, medium, and low spatial frequency information. High spatial frequency information changes faster than low spatial frequency information (e.g., lips and eyes change more over the course of a conversation than do larger facial features). On the right is a representation of the layers of predictive processing by the brain's neural networks. Layers closer to the sensory periphery (or bottom of the hierarchy), encode fast-changing phenomena that unfold over small spatial ranges. Layers near the top of the hierarchy, encode slower-changing phenomena. In predictive processing models, predictions flow from top to bottom; discrepancies between predictions and what is sensed at any layer ("prediction errors") are sent up the hierarchy. This organization endows the brain with a functional anatomy that enables it to embody context and leverage that context to guide its behavior.
From "Cultural Affordances: Scaffolding Local Worlds through Shared Intentionality and Regimes of Attention," by M. J. D. Ramstead, S. P. L. Veissière, and L. J. Kirmayer, 2016, *Frontiers in Psychology, 7*, 1090 (https://doi.org/10.3389%2Ffpsyg .2016.01090). https://creativecommons.org/licenses/by/4.0/

Park & Friston, 2013). This allows hierarchical processing, in which each layer successively encodes regularities at larger scales (that is, phenomena that extend over longer spans of time and/or larger regions of space) than the layers below, and the brain re-represents the causes of its sensation at all these different scales with dedicated layers (Badcock, Friston, & Ramstead, 2019; Badcock, Friston, Ramstead, Ploeger, et al., 2019; see also Figure 1.3). The hierarchical structure of the brain thus reflects the hierarchically nested spatial and temporal structure of its body and environment.

This hierarchical structure provides the brain with a functional capacity that, under predictive processing, has important implications (Clark, 2015). In effect, each higher layer contextualizes the layer below it by providing predictions about what to expect next; and each lower layer, in turn, sends a prediction error signal upward to the layer above it, which tracks the discrepancy between top-down prediction and reality. This error signal makes its way up the hierarchy, carrying with it whatever remains unexplained by the brain's predictions. The task of the brain is to "explain away" this error signal, either by improving the accuracy of perception – that is, making predictions more like the sensed world – or by taking action to change the world in ways that then make observations of it more like expectations (Clark, 2015). This means that brain literally embodies a hierarchy of knowledge, which it distills from its interactions with the environment; the brain's structure makes its processing inherently context sensitive.

In parallel with changing views of the brain, cognitive science has continued to develop a view of mind as located not in the brain but in loops of active engagement between the person and the world. Drawing on insights from phenomenological philosophy and psychology, this work argues that human cognition and experience must be understood as fundamentally embodied and enacted in specific environments or niches (Varela et al., 1991). A dynamic perspective on mind can provide novel conceptual bridges between our understanding of neural and social processes. This approach has brought together several lines of work under the rubric of 4E cognitive science, emphasizing the embodied, enacted, embedded, and extended nature of cognitive processes (Durt et al., 2017; Fuchs, 2017; Gallagher, 2006, 2017; Newen et al., 2018).

In this formulation, *embodiment* stands for the bodily grounding of cognition and experience. Embodiment has multiple meanings that reflect the different ways in which the body shapes experience: phenomenologically, anatomically, and physiologically. The concept of embodiment thus has one foot in phenomenology and another in the physiological mechanisms of experience. The body's structure and function not only make cognition and experience possible, but also give them a rudimentary structure on which more elaborate forms of meaning can be built up over time through linguistic and cultural practices. Thus, our basic categories and concepts are grounded in particular sensory experiences (Barsalou, 2010) and abstract concepts are elaborated through metaphors based on early bodily sensorimotor experiences (Lakoff & Johnson, 1980; Lakoff, 2012). The use of metaphoric language, in turn, re-evokes the bodily processes from which it was derived. A wealth of experimental work illustrates the two-way traffic between bodily experience and cognition (Gallagher, 2006; Gibbs, 2005).

The body is not simply the medium through which we experience the world, but the way we take hold of it. Enactivist cognitive science puts bodily and communicative action at the center of cognition. Thinking is for action, and – as Wittgenstein (1953) insisted – the meaning of any concept is in its use. Even sensation and perception are always part of loops that include action. The enactive approach to cognition aims to show how many cognitive processes can be clarified when understood in terms of the control of action (Gallagher, 2017; Noë, 2004; Thompson, 2007). This has been well worked out for motor actions, in which the mechanics of the body undergird the kinds of inferences or computations needed to carry out particular actions (Chemero, 2011). But the same emphasis on action applies to more complex cognitive activities, such as narration. We learn to tell stories about ourselves as a social practice and particular modes of narration contribute to our sense of self (Hutto, 2012). Indeed, radical enactivism challenges whether simple and even more complex cognition require internal, brain-based representations of the external world in any conventional sense (Hutto & Myin, 2012). Even seemingly interior processes, such as imagining and remembering, have their origins in – and are enacted through – forms of engagement with the world, through simulation and social practices of narration (Hutto & Myin, 2017).

Enaction thus leads naturally toward an emphasis on the *embedding* of cognition in an environmental setting. Cognition is always situated in particular contexts that evoke particular modes of thinking and acting. In many instances, cognition depends crucially on this setting, relying on resources and reminders that are ready-to-hand to elaborate lines of thought. Learning how to think means knowing how to make use of the information available in particular contexts. Cognition involves external tools, cooperation with others, and social institutions (Clark, 2008). Insofar as cognition depends on context, it may be meaningful to think of mind itself as extended or extensive, residing not in the brain but in the loops that connect brain, body, and environment. Indeed, if cognition is distributed and arises from activities in larger organism–environment networks, we might view it not simply as extended but as extensive – that is, not as an internal process that extends itself outward to engage the world, but as constituted by interactions that intrinsically involve both person and environment.

The environment provides cognitive resources, tools, and opportunities for action. As we engage with these affordances, we lay down traces that become the history of our individual and collective activity, informing the ways we organize or guide our subsequent activity from moment-to-moment choices, on to the longer arcs of life goals and trajectories. Throughout, we constantly think and interact with other people, not only through direct contact or by more distant telecommunication, but also through the built environment, social institutions, routines and practices, and especially our shared language and symbol systems, which not only provide explicit maps of the social world, but also convey implicit knowledge through the meanings sedimented in words, metaphors, and ways of looking at the world (Taylor, 2016). Most of our

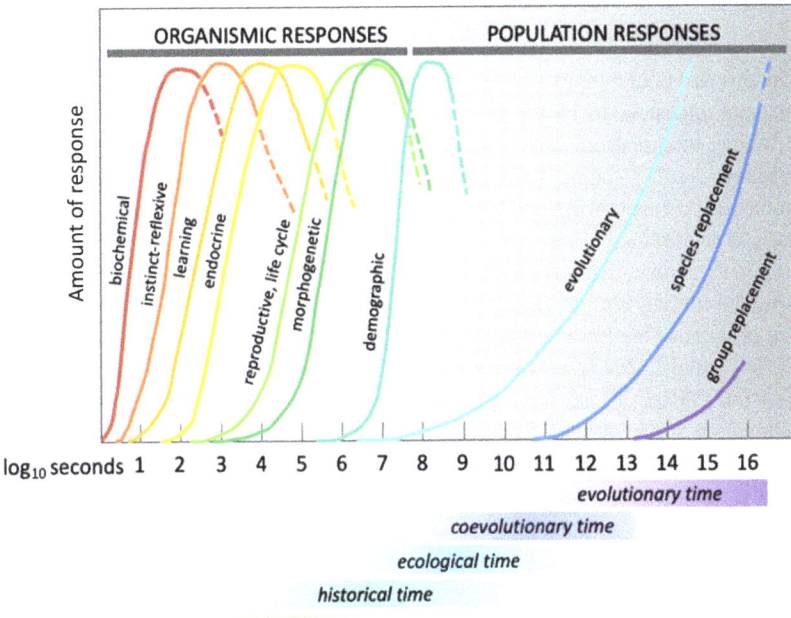

Figure 1.4 Timescales of response in living systems. The curves show time course to attain peak response for each dynamic frame, from the most granular (biochemical) to the most extensive, life's deep evolutionary time. Boxes below the figure indicate the timeframes represented by conventional ways of chunking temporal phenomena. Note that although levels of ongoing phenomena are carved up for analytic purposes, the temporal frames at which the timescales are most operative overlap. Further, the processes operating at each timescale run concurrently, although at different levels of intensity or relevance for the other timescales. So, evolutionary processes are always at work at any timescale, as are biochemical ones.
Response curves drawn from figure 7.2 in E. O. Wilson, 1975, *Sociobiology: The New Synthesis*, Belknap Press

cognition thus depends on other people. In effect, we think through other minds (Veissière et al., 2020).

Taken together, neuroscience, psychology, and social science suggest that culture, mind, and brain co-construct each other on multiple spatial and temporal scales and periods. A rough scheme would distinguish evolutionary, coevolutionary, historical, developmental, biographical, and real-time scales. Each of these timescales involves specific mechanisms (Figure 1.4). In the following sections, we discuss each of these in turn.

The Evolutionary Timescale: Phylogenetic Origins

On the timescale of evolution, the human brain evolved from that of our primate ancestors to be the organ of culture, capable of language, symbolic thinking, imagination, and complex social cooperation. The brain is the vehicle through which social knowledge is stored, accessed, manipulated, and deployed to fashion the environments we inhabit and the tools and strategies we use to survive.

A recent spate of books explores the implications of research for theories of how the human brain and its distinctive particular capacities emerged through the process of evolutionary adaptation (Damasio, 2018; Dunbar, 2016; Heyes, 2018; Laland, 2017; Schwartz, 2018; Tomasello, 2019; Tomlinson, 2018; Wilson, 2019). These accounts reflect ongoing shifts in concepts of both adaptation and evolution. The distinctively human package of an exceptionally large brain (endowed with a unique, disproportionately large neocortex), a protean mind, and a highly elaborate cultural niche has suggested to many that explaining the origins of one will entail accounting for the conjunction of all three. The outsized human brain has posed a particular challenge to evolutionary explanations, given that disproportionately large brains are energetically costly and have evolved very rarely in other species. Early accounts favored a biocultural, coevolutionary scenario in which brain expansion emerged with bipedalism and tool use, driven by adaptive advantages of exploiting new, energy-rich dietary niches via an information- and technology-intensive foraging (hunting plus gathering) strategy. However, the expanding paleoarcheological record indicates a more complex, less linear adaptive radiation, wherein bipedalism (earliest evidence at 6 million years ago) apparently predated tool use (~2.6 million years ago), and the greatest increases in brain size occurred long thereafter (200 000–600 000 years ago). Changes in ecological variability may have shaped the adaptive landscape. Dramatic increases in climate instability in the last half-a-million years apparently generated selection pressure for versatility, the ability to adapt to changing conditions and modify the environment itself (Potts, 1998; Potts & Faith, 2015). Periods of turnover in hominin lineages, technological change, and dispersal coincide with sustained periods of high climate instability.

Consequently, much of the brain's expansion occurred under selective pressures favoring adaptability and the characteristically human sociobehavioral features that supported it, such as cooperative foraging with habitual food sharing, use of fire and habitation, symbolic communication, and the set of social abilities known as *theory of mind* or *mentalization* – that is, the ability to attribute mental states to oneself and others, and to recognize that these may differ from ours (Tomasello et al., 2005; Veissière et al., 2020). Honing of the evolving hominin brains' functional capacities by millennia of tool use, along with the demands of foraging itself, apparently promoted extensive simulation capacities (that is, the capacity to internally simulate or rehearse the likely actions and reactions of others) and also established conditions for language use (see Chapter 2; Kolodny et al., 2015). Moreover, the cognitive demands of living in social groups also act as a source of pressure to develop a "social brain," with the capacity to make more complex inferences about nested levels of social context (e.g., "I think that you think that I think . . ."), and likely drove neocortical expansion (Veissière et al., 2020); among primates, neocortical size is associated (almost linearly) with social group size (Dunbar, 1998). The emergence of the ability of foraging humans to live in fission–fusion social groups, practicing complex forms of reciprocity and operating across shifting ecological conditions, relied on the evolution of greatly expanded inferential capacities for guiding behavior (Worthman, 2009). Even so, processing capacity remains a constraint: effective social network size in humans appears limited to around 150 people (Dunbar, 2008).

Integral to any species' adaptive capacities is a life history strategy, the allocation of resources available in the species' niche for growth, reproduction, and maintenance, which interact to determine body size, growth and fertility rates, and lifespan (Stearns, 1992). Humans pursue a "slow" life history strategy that features highly dependent infants, post-weaning provisioning of young, alloparental care, slow physical growth and delayed maturation, extended pair bonds, and a long life expectancy (Kaplan et al., 2000; Kuzawa & Bragg, 2012). Notably, although human growth and maturation are slowed, brain development is not and achieves 90 percent of adult size by age six (Brown & Jernigan, 2012), imposing energetic demands that require compensatory braking of body growth in childhood (Kuzawa et al., 2014). Prolonged childhood and late maturation opens the window for protracted learning as well.

The field of life history theory has powerfully enriched evolutionary analysis by focusing on the organism and the design constraints in organismic evolution operating across the life course. Hence, life course developmental processes have been incorporated into views of adaptation and evolution. For one, context and the information it provides to guide and modulate development and function increasingly is included as a potent element in processes of biological inheritance and reproduction (Chapter 4). For another, not only can development play a more powerful role than mutation in adaptive evolutionary changes (Baldwin, 1896; West-Eberhard, 2003), but development itself may rely on evolutionary processes, such as overproduction, culling, and selective retention of "what works." This is most powerfully evident in neurodevelopment (Edelman, 1987), particularly in the extraordinarily complex process of building a working brain.

Our penchant to celebrate human exceptionalism has tended to obscure the lessons learned from comparative research. Studies of animals have challenged the claims of our uniqueness and changed the ways we conceptualize culture, mind, and brain (van Schaik, 2016). For example, comparative anatomy among primates of the brain regions involved in human language use show how this capacity is built on gradual structural changes from monkeys to apes to humans (Rilling et al., 2008). Similarly, the capacity for theory of mind had long been considered special to humans, but recent studies have yielded evidence of analogous abilities in species as diverse as great apes, ravens, scrub jays, and dogs (Bugnyar, 2011; Catala et al., 2017; Krupenye et al., 2016). What is distinctively human about these abilities may have more to do with the ways we can reflexively elaborate our theory of mind so that we consider what others think that we think of what they think, and so on (Veissière et al., 2020).

Among the most productive arenas of research in animal cognition is the struggle to define and operationalize what we mean by "mind" – or, for that matter, any mental capacity (Heyes, 2015). Similarly, our understanding of culture – that is, knowledge and behavior shared through social transmission among peers and across generations – which commonly has been considered a distinguishing feature of humans, also has been refined by animal research (Bonner, 1983). Beginning in the 1960s, multiple examples of behavioral innovation and transmission have been documented; first among Japanese macaques (Hirata et al., 2001), then chimpanzees (Whiten et al., 1999) and numerous other species. Cultural transmission is now recognized as widespread among animals, occurring largely through imitation, but also – in rarer cases – through demonstration or teaching (Aplin et al., 2015; Helfman & Schultz, 1984; Rendell & Whitehead, 2001). Thus, nonhuman animals, like humans, also leverage exogenetic inheritance pathways. Again, what makes human cultural transmission unique is the extent to which it uses linguistic and symbolic forms and practices to elaborate complex scripts and knowledge structures that can be directly communicated and installed high up in the hierarchy of cognitive organization (Bengio, 2014; Pinker, 2010; Taylor, 2016) – allowing humans to engage in top-down control of their own actions and in "top-top" control of the actions of others (Roepstorff & Frith, 2004).

Investigations of the phylogenetic origins of brain, mind, and culture have yielded stimulating – and often surprising – insights. This work has begun to engage with the challenging problem of the origins and adaptive value of consciousness itself (Bateson, 1991). Because a dominant paradigm in philosophy and neuroscience views consciousness as an epiphenomenon of, or reducible to, material phenomena occurring in brain and body (Churchland, 1984; Dennett, 1991), evolutionary accounts have focused on the forces that shaped the physical substrate for complex cognition and language (Konner, 2002). But studies also have begun to explore the adaptive value of self-awareness, which may be linked to the salience of affective meaning, the need for self-referentiality, and the capacity to imagine future scenarios of self and other (Feinberg & Mallatt, 2016).

The Coevolutionary Timescale: Adapting to the Cultural Niches We Build

Our capacity to build and occupy our own niches changed the dynamics of evolution. In effect, we have been adapting to environments of our own design for the last 50 000 years and more. Once humans began to live in environments largely of their own construction, adaptation began to include a process of *coevolution* between individuals and their collective niches, communities, or societies. Specific configurations of the social world enable and demand specific modes of brain functioning. Consequently, longstanding patterns of social life may select for particular kinds of neural capacities and account for some differences and diversity across populations.

Perhaps the best-studied example of culture–gene coevolution among humans concerns the lactase enzyme. This enzyme allows infants to digest lactose, the sugar found in milk, and generally its production is switched off by adulthood, resulting in lactose intolerance. The exception occurs in populations that are the descendants of cattle herders and derive much of their adult nutrition from milk. In cattle-raising, pastoral regions (e.g., Sub-Saharan Africa and Northern Europe), genetic mutations were retained that enabled the persistence of lactase production and hence lactose digestion. These mutations were positively selected in these populations over the last several thousand years (Tishkoff et al., 2007), so that the majority of people from these regions show lactose tolerance. Intriguingly, the particular mutations that keep the gene turned on differ across geographic regions. Thus, this genetic adaptation to cattle herding occurred several times independently where this mode of subsistence was culturally adopted over a substantial period. The effects of such coevolution are circular and self-sustaining: Cultural practices selected for a random genetic change in the population that modified digestion, which in turn enabled the cultural practice to persist.

Another, more speculative, example of coevolution concerns the so-called Asian flush response, in which the faces of many individuals of Asian descent turn red after consuming alcohol. This effect occurs because, in these individuals, ethanol (the main molecule that constitutes drinking alcohol) is broken down very rapidly into acetaldehyde. Acetaldehyde is toxic and causes the blood vessels to dilate, resulting in a red flush on the face and upper body along with feelings of discomfort. This response tends to limit drinking and may thus protect affected individuals from alcohol abuse (Edenberg, 2007).

The flushing response occurs in many populations, but is especially common among East Asians (Wall et al., 2016). This elevated prevalence may be due to an intriguing form of gene–culture coevolution (Dudley, 2014). Peng et al. tested more than 2000 people who belonged to 38 different ethnic groups in China (Peng et al., 2010). Their focus was on a gene called *ADH1B*, which regulates the enzyme alcohol dehydrogenase 1B, which in turn breaks down ethanol to acetaldehyde. One polymorphic variant, called *ADH1B*47His*, is known to be associated with increased alcohol metabolism. The researchers measured the frequency of this allele in each of the 38 ethnic groups and used historical records to determine when rice farming had started for each of the groups over the last several thousand years. They found a strong correlation between the frequency of the *ADH1B*47His* allele and the time of onset of rice farming.

Why rice farming might select for individuals with a greater propensity for physiological discomfort from drinking alcohol is a matter of speculation. Alcohol production and consumption may have arisen from our capacity to enjoy eating overripe fruit that has spontaneously fermented (Dudley, 2014). But this widespread cultural practice gave rise to the communal problem of excessive intoxication. One possibility is that alcohol consumption was especially negatively valued in tightly knit rice-farming communities that required close and intense cooperation. Hence, those who tended to avoid alcohol because they experienced the ill effects of its rapid metabolism may have been more productive rice farmers and preferred as mates, thereby achieving better chances of leaving their children (and genes) behind for future generations.

There are many other examples of possible gene–culture coevolution, which range from very plausible to wildly speculative (Henrich, 2015; Laland et al., 2010; Richerson & Boyd, 2005). In each of these accounts, culture provides a basis for the selection of genetic variants on the basis of their effects on the reproductive fitness of the individual or the group. The resultant increase in the frequency of the selected genes, in turn, reinforces the original cultural practices, which then continue to exert selective pressure, in an ongoing cycle of gene–culture coevolution.

Most of the examples of gene–culture coevolution involve the direct effect of genetic variants on specific physiological or behavioral outcomes. Recent work suggests that more complex traits also may reflect gene–culture coevolution, but the mechanisms involved may be more indirect. Much of this work has focused on the dopamine receptor gene, *DRD4*. Evidence is growing that variations in *DRD4* moderate the influence of the environment on many psychological processes, including personality, resilience, and vulnerability to illness (Belsky & Pluess, 2009; van IJzendoorn et al., 2011). This moderating effect extends to the impact of the cultural environment (Kitayama et al., 2016). For example, Asians tend to be more interdependent, and European Americans tend to be more independent (see Chapter 3). These cultural traits appear to be more pronounced for people who carry certain variants of *DRD4* (the 7- and 2-repeat alleles; 7/2-R) compared to those who do not carry these genetic variants (Kitayama et al., 2014). Thus, rather than affecting a specific behavioral trait, *DRD4* is putatively involved in the tendency to acquire normative patterns of behavior, which may differ in each culture.

What does the influence of *DRD4* on cultural acquisition tell us about the coevolution of genes and culture? The 7/2-R allele of *DRD4* may increase the efficiency of reward processing, which in turn could increase the fidelity of reinforcement learning, which we know underlies the acquisition of culturally normative patterns of behavior (Kitayama et al., 2016). Allele carriers would be more likely than noncarriers to acquire such patterns of behavior, acting in accordance with their culture's norms and values. Although this capacity to learn to act in accordance with cultural norms is useful in any culture, there may be cultural differences that make the uniformity of such learning more or less important. Other genetic polymorphisms may also modulate cultural learning and the effects of specific social factors on health and well-being leading to three-way gene × culture × context interactions (Kwon & Sasaki, 2019).

As is the case with our discussion of a putative link between Asian flush and rice farming, the "why" question is difficult to address with solid evidence. Nonetheless, it may be reasonable to suppose that any cultural group or community requires people who differ in the extent to which they adhere to cultural norms. First, many people must acquire their culture's norms and conventions faithfully, internalize them fully, and enact them to maintain the culture. However, all cultures also may benefit from the novelty-seeking, rule-breaking, creativity, and innovation of people who are less influenced by current cultural norms and conventions. If more conservative, norm-following persons are needed to maintain the culture through social conformity (Constant et al., 2019), more unconventional persons are needed when environmental contexts surrounding the culture change, demanding new strategies of adaptation. Only those cultures with a mix of such people may have survived and flourished, but variation among populations in the distribution of individuals on the conservative–unconventional spectrum might reflect the varying demands of particular cultures and contexts. This speculation might serve as a working hypothesis for further exploration of gene–culture coevolution in relation to *DRD4* and other genetic variations that contribute to novelty-seeking or exploratory behavior. The larger implication is that social coevolutionary processes may operate not simply by selecting for individual traits but also by frequency-dependent selection on traits that are valuable when they are part of a larger population – a kind of group selection (Henrich, 2015).

The Historical Timescale

The human capacity for memory and the ability to record events in ways that can be transmitted across generations gives rise to a new time scale for brain–culture interaction (Boyer & Wertsch, 2009). Language and self-representation make possible another order of temporality associated with history, the explicit recollection, organization, and study of the past. Human history is a record of cumulative knowledge, trial and error, and commitments to tradition that result in particular shared memories, collective identities, and ways of life. This history depends not simply on the sequence of events but on our encoding and representations of the past both individually and collectively in narratives (see Chapter 12). In giving explicit accounts of past events, we add a symbolic dimension to our adaptive niche that determines collective identity, draws boundaries around communities, and identifies lines of affiliation through descent. History also is sedimented in the languages that we use to lay down traces in individual memory and collective institutions and archives of past experience, which then become a foundation for building more elaborate forms of social organization and individual cognition; this capacity to "bind time" through mnemo-technologies, such as writing and image making, is a central part of what makes us human. These technologies have changed over time – and with that, so have the ways in which we use our neurocognitive machinery (Danziger, 2009).

Cultures produce systems of knowledge, institutions, and discursive practices that both enlarge and constrain our possibilities for action. These cultures change over time, and their histories are displayed in material artifacts, memorialized in art and architecture, and written down in everyday documents and formal archives (Burke, 2019). In less obvious ways, history is sedimented in the etymology of words, "dead" metaphors, and customary or conventional ways of doing things that only can be understood in terms of their historical origins. Historical traditions are highly contingent, reflecting both the vagaries of local events and larger structures of power and domination that authorize particular versions of the past. As a result, tradition can be both a distillation of empirical knowledge and a repository of seemingly arbitrary and idiosyncratic practices that have their origins and justification in particular definitions of identity and community.

The ways of life that communities create have their own inertia. Cultural institutions and practices persist not only because they have passed the test of time, having proved useful, but because they are perceived as valuable because they are traditional, a living inheritance from our forebears, whether human or divine. Often, such histories are both naturalized and viewed as constitutive of identity: We do things this way because it is natural, the right way, *and* the way that defines us as a people or community.

As a result, much of what we do may not be optimal or adaptive, but instead follows from the historical trajectory of a community and its relationship to other communities, both locally and, increasingly, across larger scales. Humans are a migratory species. The archeological and genetic records indicate that we came out of Africa and spread to the farthest reaches of the planet (Cavalli-Sforza et al., 1994). This migration began in prehistory but has continued up to the present with dramatic effects on our social worlds and predicaments. Local communities or regional peoples adopted ways of life adapted to the particular geography and ecology; and along with material technology came myths and stories that served to transmit, guide, and rationalize social institutions and practices. Although cultural creativity within communities may be driven by iconoclastic "trickster" figures (Hyde, 1998), in many instances, culture is created through encounters between peoples, which lead to boundary making and breaking, conflict, and hybridity (Burke, 2009; Niedenthal et al., 2019).

Often, the historical encounter between peoples has been violent, contributing both to cultural production and destruction. For example, the great diversity of Indigenous Peoples in the Americas prior to European conflict reflected both their long process of adaptation to local ecologies as well as exchange between neighboring and sometimes distant groups. The European invasion and colonization of the Americas was associated with the displacement, extermination, appropriation, and forced assimilation of Indigenous Peoples (Benvenuto et al., 2014). This violence has affected every aspect of Indigenous lives. In particular, the transmission of oral history across the generations was disrupted and deliberately suppressed, which created profound dilemmas for current generations who seek to recover from the cultural genocide and ongoing structural violence. Contemporary Indigenous cultures take many creative forms that reflect tradition, awareness of this history, and active engagement with current sociopolitical predicaments. While some have argued that current problems faced by these communities, such as the high rate of suicide among Indigenous youth in Canada, can be understood in terms of the epigenetic effects of such historical trauma, ongoing social structural and political processes are central to the health and well-being of Indigenous Peoples (Kirmayer et al., 2014; Seligman et al., 2015). These processes are mediated and maintained by particular forms of historical memory within Indigenous communities, in the larger societies they inhabit, and in the transnational networks that have advanced global recognition of indigeneity and the rights of Indigenous Peoples for self-determination (Niezen, 2003).

Historical processes define the groups and communities we live in, and the kinds of identities and social positions we occupy within those communities. Constructs like race, ethnicity, and religion, which shape how people think about themselves, each other, and the world, are based on collective knowledge and traditions transmitted across generations, independently of genetic or epigenetic processes. These constructs form the basis for distinctions between groups and often are essentialized as intrinsic to all members of the group, giving rise to stereotypes and discrimination. Thus, the history of the Atlantic slave trade, which brought some 12 million people from Africa, resulted in the structural inequalities that continue to shape identity, health, and well-being in North, Central, and South America (Black, 2015). The racialized categories that are assigned to people on the basis of skin color or origins are powerful determinants of their life course; they are unrelated to any direct biological or physical correlates, but due instead to how others within the same society treat one another (Gravlee, 2009). As a result, it is not the cultural construct of race, but the consequences of racism – including structural disadvantage and everyday discrimination – that have the most powerful health and social effects. Although race is a cultural construction, with no clear basis in genetics, it marks social distinctions that can be matters of life and death. In other societies, culturally constructed categories of lineage, clan, caste, or religion similarly serve to mark off social groups and confer advantage or disadvantage. These distinctions can be decisive both for brain development and everyday functioning.

The Developmental Timescale

Biologists describe humans as exhibiting *neoteny*, being born comparatively immature and therefore requiring intensive parental care to survive and mature. This developmental pattern involves constant interaction between the brain and the culturally shaped social environment. Humans are, by nature, nurtured creatures; their very survival and development depend on reliable provision of the resources, experiences, and conditions created by the sociocultural world into which they are born (Worthman, 2010). From earliest development, beginning *in utero* and continuing through infancy, humans depend on interactions with others to build physical, socioemotional, and behavioral competence, acquiring a rapidly growing fund of cultural knowledge comprised of language, communicative codes, skills, and behavioral repertoires that tune neural circuitry and ways of processing information to the opportunities or affordances of the local environmental niche.

Consequently, human development is a biocultural project that requires a "package of care" comprising social, affective, cognitive, and physical features to meet the developmental needs of the young (Table 1.1). Via a built-in suite of characteristics and dispositions, children both actively and passively engage and learn from their environment at multiple levels (social, affective, cognitive, and physical; see Hrdy, 2009). Infants and children are intensely social: They quickly acquire essential skills through observation, imitation, and multiple forms of learning, through engaging and bonding with caregivers, and by actively, iteratively co-constructing their social niches *in situ* (Konner, 2010).

Table 1.1 *Package of care for human young*

Domain	Infant/child characteristics: life history strategy	Key components of the package of care	Cultural elements: developmental niche
Social	Intense prolonged dependency Neoteny, cuteness Late social independence Attachment behaviors Social niche co-construction	Member of social group Family and kin Caregiving, alloparenting Sharing, cooperation Multi-generational care	Beliefs and practices about child development, life course appropriate caregiving Social structure, power dynamics Marital and residence patterns
Affective	Attachment, affiliation Predisposed to share and care Smiling, playfulness Affective niche construction	Responsive prolonged care Shared attention Emotional security, belonging	Social relationships Goals for social competence
Cognitive	Extended brain development Extensive simulation Reliance on social learning Exploration, inquisitiveness	Embedded in daily life Inbuilt learning opportunities Bases in symbolism, meaning	Goals for adult competence Subsistence/labor patterns Niche availability Opportunity structure
Physical	Environmental expectancy Cue sensitivity Neoteny Slow growth, long childhood Puberty, late maturation	Extended postnatal provisioning Resource sharing, reciprocity Physical protection, shelter Physical, material security	Subsistence strategy Resource management Sharing, reciprocity norms Residence patterns

Key components of the package of care listed in Table 1.1 must be in place for healthy development to proceed (Stevenson & Worthman, 2014). These components play essential roles in producing viable offspring; and hence, they are critical in human reproduction, and typically present in all human social groups. Nevertheless, specific configurations of the envelope of care vary across societies, which create culture-specific developmental niches based on particulars, such as local beliefs and practices regarding child development and caregiving, goals for social competence and maturity, social structure and relationships, and subsistence and life conditions (Harkness & Super, 1994).

Thus, humans are forged in culturally constructed developmental niches that shape variation between – and indeed within – societies. Recognition of dynamics behind this process constitutes one of the great advances of late twentieth-century science. After protracted battles over the roles of nature or nurture in ontogeny, it is clear that any meaningful account requires both, operating in tandem (Lock & Palsson, 2016).

Culture acquisition begins in utero; for example, the developing auditory system becomes tuned to phonemes of ambient language (Ruben, 1997). This phenomenon reflects a more general process of experiential canalization, in which development is scaffolded by reliable inputs from expectable environments. Experiential canalization was demonstrated by an early series of elegant studies which revealed that newly hatched ducklings' ability to recognize others of their species depends on the vocalizations they hear during gestation (Gottlieb, 1991). Both environmental and internal signals influence gene activation patterns during development in a process of "probabilistic epigenesis" that introduces variability – and indeterminacy – in the relationship between genotype and phenotype (Gottlieb, 1998, 2007).

More recently, work on the impact of early experience on regulation of stress response systems in rodents revealed that early maternal caregiving behavior can mediate intergenerational transmission of phenotypes, namely daughters' maternal behavior and offspring stress reactivity (Caldji et al., 2000; Champagne & Meaney, 2001). Further research identified the specific pathway mediating this effect: maternal licking and grooming behavior in the first week influences hippocampal methylation patterns and alters glucocorticoid receptor expression in offspring, thereby changing central regulation of stress reactivity with long-term effects on behavioral stress responses (Weaver et al., 2004; Zhang et al., 2013). Cumulative work stimulated by these findings has extended to humans, and consistently has linked parental stress and early life adversity to glucocorticoid receptor methylation (McGowan et al., 2009; Turecki & Meaney, 2016).

These discoveries have profoundly influenced developmental science by definitively demonstrating that variation in experience can alter the course of development via its impact on endogenous regulatory systems at the molecular level. They also have drawn attention to critical or sensitive periods when development is particularly open to environmental conditions or inputs, creating pathways for biological embedding of experience with long-term effects (Hertzman & Boyce, 2010), with important implications for health promotion policy and intervention (Shonkoff & Garner, 2012).

Development, then, occurs through interactions among genes and environment that propel trajectories across the life course (Worthman et al., 2010). These interactions drive needs for, access to, and allocation of energy, information, and social resources (Gettler et al., 2015; Worthman, 2009), open windows of risk, opportunity, and vulnerability (Costello et al., 2007; Ellis et al., 2009; McDade et al., 2017), and shape capacities for growth, learning, and resilience (Boyce, 2019; Kohrt et al., 2015; Kwon & Sasaki, 2019). Similarly, neurodevelopment results from an ongoing interaction of biological, behavioral, and social processes that are informed by genes but are equally dependent on molecular, cellular, physiological, organismic, and environmental conditions that regulate whether, when, and precisely how genetic information is used to enable development (Allis & Jenuwein, 2016; Gottlieb, 1998; Jablonka & Raz, 2009; Klemm et al., 2019). Thus, over the course of each individual's development, the nervous system becomes shaped and attuned to, and entrained by, the opportunities and demands of the local environment (Hertzman & Boyce, 2010; Nelson et al., 2016; Schulz & Sisk, 2016). Moreover, given the role of extragenetic influences, both current social environments and past history are essential to understand the development of each individual's brain. Even conditions experienced by ancestors two or three generations earlier have been found to affect developmental outcomes (Vågerö et al., 2018), and current work in epigenetics points to potential pathways for the inheritance of some acquired characteristics (Chen et al., 2016).

The Autobiographical Timescale: Memory, Narrativity, and the Self

Our capacity for narrative thinking and storytelling opens up another timescale that runs the length of a human life and can link that life story to the scales of historical and developmental time (Boyd, 2018; McAdams, 2019; Schechtman, 1996). The developmental trajectory of the individual interacts with a specifically human dimension based on our own self-understanding and self-representation through narrative (Fivush & Haden, 2003; Freeman, 2015). Over our lifespans, we learn to interpret experiences in terms of available cultural models and integrate this understanding into memory, identity, and autobiographical narratives that shape our plans, actions, and responses to events. In particular, we may strive to be consistent with our own internalized values and goals and experience dissonance and distress when our actions or their outcomes do not fit our self-image. This self-fashioning through autobiography adds a distinctive dimension to human functioning that bridges individual and collective stories.

On the biographical timescale, we are engaged with the way we understand our own life story and those of others. To do this, we draw from cultural scripts and templates to learn to create coherent narratives for our everyday actions and the longer trajectories of our lives. As part of the social process of giving reasons and explanations for our actions to others, we learn to use particular notions of self and other to interpret experiences and events (Fivush & Haden, 2003; Hutto, 2012). These modes of self-explanation depend on specific cultural ontologies and notions of personhood. For example, egocentric models of the self emphasize – and perhaps exaggerate – the individual's own agency and choice in directing behavior. A more sociocentric view would highlight the determining influence of family and community. Both views capture aspects of reality, but each emphasizes those elements that are especially important in societies where individualism or familism are core values.

In other cultural settings, people may employ modes of self-understanding that stem from other ontologies. For example, in many cultures, actions and events are seen as influenced by the agency or spirits or ancestors. For many Indigenous Peoples, the land and nonhuman beings are important elements in life narratives. The ways that we construe the causes of our own or others' actions have obvious importance for ascriptions of moral significance. But such explanations may also influence our experiences of agency and subjectivity (see Chapter 8). These modes of explanation influence everyday attributions of causality and control and, in turn, set us on certain trajectories that constitute our sense of selfhood.

Over the course of childhood, we learn to narrate our experiences using templates and modes of self-construal consistent with such overarching cultural values. In the process, we elaborate our sense of agency and interiority, confer meaning on life events, organize the vagaries of life experiences into a coherent story with a clear narrative arc, and assign moral significance to our own and others' actions. In effect, we acquire a folk psychology through narrative practices (Hutto, 2012).

Considering the ways in which we use narratives of the self can provide a bridge between work in cross-cultural psychology on modes of self-construal and studies of the cultural construction of the self in social science and comparative literature. The construction and deployment of a narrative self serves to regulate attention, emotion, and cognition. Cultural and historical templates provide us with scripts for how to live a good life. We can imagine and articulate possible and ideal selves and elaborate our goals and assess our successes and failures in terms of these narrative frameworks. Our moral personhood has to do with managing the tensions and reconciling the contradictions between our ideals and our actual behavior (Taylor, 1989).

The Scale of Real-Time Engagement with Context

Timescales of everyday context reflect moment-to-moment interactions with social and cultural affordances. The culturally constructed niches in which we live include the social contexts of family, community, and institutional settings, which afford specific opportunities for action and elicit or demand specific kinds of performance from moment to moment. We perform our daily roles and tasks in particular places, with corresponding resources and constraints. We improvise performances in ways that draw from these resources using a repertoire that is both cultural and idiosyncratic. We may experience our actions as immediate, natural or given, as if things could not be any other way. Yet this obscures the role of particular social and cultural affordances that reflect our past learning, skills, and expectations and determine how we perceive and respond to the world. The same environment, whether a city street, a home, a classroom, or a park, will be perceived differently and afford different possibilities for action according to our individual histories and the motivations or expectations we bring to that moment. That environment and our past cultural learning shape experiences and responses in the moment.

Other people are often the most salient aspects of any context, and their mere presence is enough to change our awareness, experience, and behavior. However, people also actively communicate through facial expression, gesture, and language, which powerfully influences how we attend to, perceive, and respond to any given context. One widely accepted view proposes that emotions are constructed through active appraisals of the significance of an event on various dimensions (Smith & Ellsworth, 1985). Thus, the emotions experienced in any particular context are thought to depend in large part on how we construe the situation, and that construal can be influenced by the behavior of others (Sinclair et al., 1994; see Chapter 6). As a result, contextual effects on social cognition and social behavior are ubiquitous.

One illustration of this context sensitivity comes from work on cultural differences in self-construal. As discussed earlier, a body of work in cultural psychology has shown how people from different cultural backgrounds tend to differ in how they conceive of the self as relatively independent, with behavior driven by individual choice, or interdependent, with behavior emerging from a web of relationships (Markus & Kitayama, 1991; See Chapter 3). Although these differences in ways of conceiving the self may be general "traits" inculcated by culturally shaped modes of childrearing, they also are influenced by the immediate context. Contextual factors, including a dominant narrative and salient linguistic practices, may bring to mind, or "prime," one or the other mode of construal (Chapter 7).

Oyserman and Lee (2008) reviewed many studies showing that when interdependence (vs. independence) is primed, attention becomes more holistic (that is, the person focuses more on context) across an array of cognitive tasks. These effects have been observed not only among different ethnic groups (i.e., individuals with African, European, and Asian cultural heritage) in North America, but also in Europe and Asia (Kühnen & Oyserman, 2002; Oyserman et al., 2009). Similar effects have been found when interdependence (vs. independence) is indirectly primed with cultural symbols (e.g., Chinese dragon vs. Statue of Liberty; Hong et al., 2000).

The effects of priming independence or interdependence extend beyond the realm of cognition to affect social behavior. In one study, Lakin and Chartrand (2003) found that after subliminal relational priming, individuals imitated their interaction partners more and increased cooperative behavior (Bargh et al., 2001; Chartrand et al., 2005). Moreover, Kimel et al. (2012) reported that after such priming, Americans experienced dissonance for a choice they had made for their friends (Kimel et al., 2017).

An interdependent mindset has been associated with a sense of safety and security. People who are high in interdependent self-construal have been found to be more resilient (Over & Uskul, 2016; Ren et al., 2013; Uskul & Over, 2014). These results may reflect that persons high in interdependent self-construal have more social resources. If so, the threat-buffering effect of interdependent self-construal could be specific to threats that are social in nature. However, other evidence suggests that the buffering effect of interdependent self-construal may be more general. For instance, physiological responses to physical pain are less strong among those who feel they have social support (Eisenberger et al., 2007). Indeed, growing evidence suggests that the presence of close others can mitigate neural reactions to physical pain (Coan et al., 2006). People primed to feel interdependent show similar reductions in pain response (Wang et al., 2014).

Even the effects of chemical substances on the brain depend on context and can be influenced by expectations conveyed through framing and setting. For example, the experience of hallucinogens such as ayahuasca is shaped by the ritual context in which they are ingested. In the Santo Daime church, which emerged in Brazil but has spread worldwide, ayahuasca is regarded as a sacrament and participants anticipate meaningful experiences that will contribute to their spiritual development (Lifshitz et al., 2018). Although the mix of psychoactive plant substances in ayahuasca exerts complex effects on the brain, the experiences of Santo Daime congregants commonly follow the broad outlines of cultural scripts. In effect, the brain is primed to respond to the chemicals in specific ways, and the ongoing intervention of participants in the service contributes to those experiences. In this example, as in everyday life, brain function is constantly modulated in real-time by interactions with others, so that it is not possible to give an account of the impact of the drug on the brain without taking social context into account.

Cultural influences, then, come to us not only through our developmental experiences and personal history but through moment-to-moment interactions with the social contexts we traverse in daily life. These contexts demand that we perform in certain ways, and this, in turn, requires that we use our brains in particular ways. These interactions, in turn, will have enduring effects on how our brains habitually process social information. However, changes in context mandate different modes of processing, and our capacity to adapt flexibly to new contexts is essential both for coping with everyday events and for navigating the more profound changes that come with adopting a new lifestyle, social role, or with migration.

People are generally very responsive to social cues and contexts. Western individualists who value self-direction tend to exaggerate their consistency across different situations (Ross & Nisbett, 1991). However, social norms and self-schemas can provide anchors for momentary cognitions and emotions. As such, the self-narratives or models may themselves function as contexts for cognitive and emotional response. This possibility is suggested by a variety of egocentric biases in social perception and cognition. People often project that others have similar attitudes (Ross et al., 1977), beliefs (Gilovich, 1990), and emotions (Silani et al., 2013) to their own. Intriguingly, these effects extend to physiological states (O'Brien & Ellsworth, 2012; Van Boven & Loewenstein, 2003). For example, when feeling thirsty, people intuitively assume that others want to drink water (Van Boven & Loewenstein, 2003). Similarly, people standing outside in sub-zero temperature find it difficult to imagine what it might be like to be in a warm temperature (O'Brien & Ellsworth, 2012). Hence, cultural models of self and moment-to-moment expectations of others interact to give rise to embodied experience.

Thinking about Culture in the Brain: The Interplay of Multiple Timescales

Although we have considered them separately for the sake of exposition, the multiple timescales outlined in this chapter can all contribute to understanding any human behavior or experience. Focusing on each timescale individually allows us to explore models and mechanisms with specific methods, but they need to be put together to build a more comprehensive picture of culture–mind–brain dynamics. The chapters in this volume each provide distinctive integrative analyses across a range of domains, from emotion and the self to music and narrativity (Table 1.2). Here, we illustrate the interactions of processes on multiple timescales through two examples, the extended evolutionary synthesis and the cultural ecology of self.

The contributions of development, plasticity, and behavior to the central processes of evolution – variation, selection, and intergenerational transmission – are at the core of the modern view known as the *extended evolutionary synthesis* (EES; Laland et al., 2015; see also Chapter 2). The EES highlights the contributions of development to the production of variation through developmental bias, whereby selective pressures on differences in fitness afforded

Table 1.2 *Co-construction of culture, mind, and brain on multiple temporal scales*

Timescale/Time span	Examples	Mechanisms	Chapters in this book
Evolutionary 2.6 mya (Early Stone Age) to Present	• Larger/social brain necessitates slower life history strategy • Stone tool use • Language evolution • Shared intentionality, cooperation, reciprocity • Living in groups • Theory of mind	• Mutations and selective forces and constraints • Adaptation • Cognitive plasticity • Cultural transmission • Helical curriculum • EES (constructive development & reciprocal causation) • Niche construction theory	2–4, 11
Coevolutionary 1 mya to Present	• Lactose intolerance • Asian flus • Rice and wheat farming • Population-level differences in independence/ interdependence	• Culture–gene interactions and coevolution • Selections for genetic polymorphisms and epigenetic pathways • Neuroplasticity	3, 10
Historical 5 kya to Present	• Values, norms • Archeological record • Technologies (writing, image making) • Oral histories • Institutions (school, religion) • Built environment, settlement patterns	• Genetic and epigenetic interactions • Neuroplasticity • Brain network structure, dynamics • Habituation	3, 4, 8, 12, 14–17, 19
Developmental/ ontogenetic <100 years	• Experience-expectant and experience-dependent changes • Language acquisition • Trauma and resilience	• Genetic and epigenetic interactions • Neuroplasticity • Sensitive periods • Sensitization/ habituation	4, 6, 7, 13, 14
Autobiographical <100 years	• Self-understanding and representation • Experiences as interpreted by available cultural	• Genetic and epigenetic interactions • Neuroplasticity	8, 13, 18–21

Table 1.2 *(cont.)*

Timescale/Time span	Examples	Mechanisms	Chapters in this book
	models and integrated into memory • Identity • Autobiographical narratives • Contemplative practices	• Brain network structure, dynamics	
Real-time/contextual Moment-to-moment/real time	• Engagement with immediate environment • Interactions in family, community, institutional settings	• Dynamic brain activity • Neuroplasticity • Contextual affordances and their distribution	5–9

by alternate ontogenetic pathways can influence the direction and pace of trait evolution (West-Eberhard, 2003). The EES emphasizes the integral role of organism–environment interactions in development and in the evolution of phenotypes. Rather than being a source of adaptive pressure or simply "noise" in the system, the environment provides crucial information that supports and guides development suited to the conditions in which the organism lives (Jablonka & Lamb, 2006; Kuzawa & Thayer, 2011). In this process of reciprocal causation, the developing organism's capacity for plasticity permits shifting phenotypic outcomes to meet environmental conditions (Stearns & Koella, 1986; Watson & Szathmáry, 2016).

A key feature of the EES is the emphasis on niche construction, which involves the active role of organisms in creating or modifying their own environments, which in turn, moderate, alter, or even create new selection pressures (Constant et al., 2018; Laland et al., 2016). Finally, the EES recognizes the role of multiple kinds of extra-genomic intergenerational transmission, including the extragenetic inheritance afforded by epigenesis (Jablonka, 2013), cultural transmission (Whiten, 2017), and durable environmental modification in habitats such as cities (Odling-Smee et al., 2003). Taken together, these features of the EES can account for empirical findings concerning ecological and developmental processes and strengthen not only evolutionary theory, but also our understanding of human individual and cultural diversity.

Turning to the more immediate dynamics of cultural ecology, our discussion of studies documenting the significance of context in modulating cognition,

Figure 1.5 Rice terraces in Bali, Indonesia. Rice cultivation requires very high levels of sustained social cooperation and coordination of activity. This practice results in the construction of a particular kind of social niche with corresponding cultural values which, in turn, may select for personality traits conducive to such cooperation. (See Lansing & Fox, 2011; Talhelm, et al., 2014).
Photograph courtesy of L. J. Kirmayer, Ubud, Bali, 2004

emotion, and behavior has only scratched the surface of a large and growing body of research on real-time effects of interaction on brain function. Nevertheless, it makes the point that elements in social situations can influence the moment-by-moment operation of the human mind in highly dynamic ways. This suggests that one reason for group differences in psychological tendencies may relate to differences in the assortment of cues that are available in daily social situations. The notion that psychological tendencies are afforded by cultural constructions of mundane social situations can be extended to understand effects of longer-term, enduring impacts of macro-level ecology. Over the last 10 000 years, humans have taken up sedentary forms of subsistence based on farming crops and herding cattle. The modes of living made possible by local ecologies vary widely and may afford distinct habits of mind, as illustrated by contrasting societies that cultivate rice versus wheat (Figures 1.5 and 1.6).

Rice farming requires far greater social cooperation and intensive labor than wheat farming. Moreover, rice cultivation can provide greater yield to maintain

Figure 1.6 Children running in wheat field near Datong, Qinghai, China. Photograph courtesy of Kelly Dombroski. https://creativecommons.org/licenses/by/4.0/

a larger number of people. Hence, rice farming may be more likely to lead to a society that is oriented toward collectivism (interdependence) and tight normative regulation of behavior. Wheat was initially domesticated in the Fertile Crescent around 9000 years ago, and then spread westward to much of the Western half of the Eurasian Continent. Wheat did not reach the eastern edge of Eurasia because the climate in much of Asia was too hot and humid for the crop. Instead, rice was domesticated in eastern Eurasia and spread to the southern regions of the continent, including parts of India. Domestication of these two different crops arguably was a pivotal development that channeled the formations of social practices, conventions, and institutions. The subsequent unfolding of disparate cultural systems in the two broadly demarcated regions of East and West on the continent may be grounded in this ecocultural dynamic (Talhelm et al., 2014).

Psychologists have identified a cultural emphasis on independence and individualism in the modern West (i.e., Western Europe and its extensions in North America, South Africa, Australia, and so on) in contrast to an emphasis on collectivism and interdependence in Asia (Markus & Kitayama, 1991).

Robust, often sizable cross-cultural differences have been observed between North Americans of European descent and Asians, especially East Asians, regarding forms of the self (Markus & Kitayama, 1991), as well as cognitive (Nisbett et al., 2001), emotional (Tsai et al., 2006), and motivational processes (Heine et al., 1999). Although such cultural differences can be linked to many historical influences, they may have their roots in the ecological conditions and social demands created by the cultivation of specific crops.

Of course, contemporary forms of individualism and collectivism have been shaped by other forces resulting in wide variation in cultural concepts of personhood, models of childrearing, and systems of values that favor particular modes of self-construal and narrative constructions of the self. Moreover, there are other cultural dimensions along which people may differ, including the ways they relate to the environment and to larger realms of ancestors and spirituality. Such differences occur not only in the ways people think about themselves, the developmental trajectories they follow, and the life projects they pursue, but also in the ways their brains are shaped by engagement with particular cultural worlds. Indeed, recent work in cultural neuroscience has documented analogous cultural variation at the level of brain mechanisms (Kitayama & Uskul, 2011; Kitayama et al., 2019; Ma et al., 2014).

In everyday behavior, the tendency to respond in ways consistent with independent or interdependent modes of self-construal will depend on individual traits (which may be more frequent in populations with particular cultural histories and corresponding coevolutionary processes of selection), but will also reflect culturally preferred strategies for recognizing and responding to current contexts. The previously discussed research on priming of independent vs. interdependent modes of self-construal supports the idea that cultural differences in behavior and experience depend on the ways that people respond to specific contexts and expectations (Oyserman et al., 2014). However, it remains that cultural differences also can be observed in relatively enduring structural features of the brain (Yu et al., 2019). Hence, it is likely that some cultural variations in behavior are due not only to situational priming or responding to norms, but also reflect brain-based dispositions acquired across development. Current work on neurodevelopment makes it clear that socialization and enculturation can operate through epigenetic, physiological, and social–psychological mechanisms that give rise to cultural variations both in mentality and in the brain.

Conclusion: Integrating Culture, Mind, and Brain across Multiple Scales

Current scientific evidence and theory are converging on views of evolution and development as mutually constitutive domains that operate synergistically across multiple organizational levels and timescales. The picture of human evolution is changing due in part to the work of developmental and evolutionary biologists who have argued for the active role of the organism in evolutionary change, pointing out that "organisms are constructed in development, not simply 'programmed' to develop by genes. Living things do not evolve to fit into pre-existing environments, but co-construct and coevolve with their environments, in the process changing the structure of ecosystems" (Laland et al., 2014, p. 162). This insight provides a foundation for understanding recursive processes such as constructive development, reciprocal causation, the helical curriculum (see Chapter 2), and the social ecology of mind (Bateson, 1972; Seligman et al., 2015). Shifting combinations of selective forces and constraints – largely ecological adaptive challenges to individuals, partly social cooperative demands – plus organic design constraints and trade-offs drove evolution of brain and life history strategy (Dunbar & Shultz, 2017; González-Forero & Gardner, 2018). Current work in these domains has built in developmental and context-contingent or context-dependent features not considered in the previous century's codification of evolution in the modern synthesis. Comparative and paleoarcheological studies challenge and expand anthropocentric views of culture, mind, and brain.

We are born biologically equipped to acquire culture and, across our lifespan, we become attuned to particular social and cultural environments (Wexler, 2006). The niches we inhabit are cooperatively constructed and presented to us as cultural affordances, that is, potential ways of perceiving and acting on the world that are ordered by culturally mediated goals, scripts, norms, and practices (Ramstead et al., 2016). These environments are part of our cognitive capacities, sense of self, adaptive skills, and meaning-making capacity. The rewiring of circuits in the brain, synaptic plasticity, and underlying changes in gene regulation and expression only make sense in relation to the particular resources, affordances, and adaptive tasks presented to us by these cultural environments. The functions of the brain will become clear only when we consider these resources and adaptive tasks in all their social, cultural, and historical specificity.

Answering the question of what makes us human then turns out to involve not just an evolutionary story in deep time, but also cultural and personal stories in historical, developmental, and biographical time. These in turn underwrite our efforts at self-fashioning through life choices and affiliations. The social and culturally constructed local worlds or niches we inhabit allow us to realize our individual and collective identities even as they present us with new challenges and opportunities for improvisation. As the contributors to this volume show, our views of the co-construction and mutual constitution of culture, mind, and brain must be enlarged to encompass this creative interplay.

REFERENCES

Allis, C. D., & Jenuwein, T. (2016). The molecular hallmarks of epigenetic control. *Nature Reviews Genetics*, *17*(8), 487–500. https://doi.org/10.1038/nrg.2016.59

Anderson, M. L. (2014). *After phrenology: Neural reuse and the interactive brain.* MIT Press.

Aplin, L. M., Farine, D. R., Morand-Ferron, J., Cockburn, A., Thornton, A., & Sheldon, B. C. (2015). Experimentally induced innovations lead to persistent culture via conformity in wild birds. *Nature*, *518*(7540), 538–41. https://doi.org/10.1038/nature13998

Ashby, W. R. (1952). *Design for a brain: The origin of adaptive behaviour.* Chapman & Hall.

Babiloni, F., & Astolfi, L. (2014). Social neuroscience and hyperscanning techniques: Past, present and future. *Neuroscience & Biobehavioral Reviews*, *44*, 76–93. https://doi.org/10.1016/j.neubiorev.2012.07.006

Badcock, P. B., Friston, K. J., & Ramstead, M. J. D. (2019). The hierarchically mechanistic mind: A free-energy formulation of the human psyche. *Physics of Life Reviews*. Advance online publication. https://doi.org/10.1016/j.plrev.2018.10.002

Badcock, P. B., Friston, K. J., Ramstead, M. J. D., Ploeger, A., & Hohwy, J. (2019). The hierarchically mechanistic mind: An evolutionary systems theory of the human brain, cognition, and behavior. *Cognitive, Affective, & Behavioral Neuroscience*. Advance online publication. https://doi.org/10.3758/s13415-019-00721-3

Baldwin, J. M. (1896). A new factor in evolution. *The American Naturalist*, *30*(354), 441–51. www.jstor.org/stable/2453130

Bargh, J. A., Gollwitzer, P. M., Lee-Chai, A., Barndolla, K., & Trötschel, R. (2001). The automated will: Nonconscious activation and pursuit of behavioral goals. *Journal of Personality and Social Psychology*, *81*(6), 1014–27. https://doi.org/10.1037/0022-3514.81.6.1014

Barsalou, L. W. (2010). Grounded cognition: Past, present, and future. *Topics in Cognitive Science*, *2*(4), 716–24. https://doi.org/10.1111/j.1756-8765.2010.01115.x

Bateson, G. (1972). *Steps to an ecology of mind.* Ballantine Books.

Bateson, M. C. (1991). *Our own metaphor: A personal account of a conference on the effects of conscious purpose on human adaptation.* Smithsonian Institution Press.

Belsky, J., & Pluess, M. (2009). Beyond diathesis stress: Differential susceptibility to environmental influences. *Psychological Bulletin*, *135*(6), 885–908. https://doi.org/10.1037/a0017376

Bengio, Y. (2014). Evolving culture versus local minima. In T. Kowaliw, N. Bredeche, & R. Doursat (Eds.), *Growing adaptive machines* (pp. 109–38). Springer-Verlag. https://doi.org/10.1007/978-3-642-55337-0_3

Bennett, M. R., & Hacker, P. M. S. (2008). *History of cognitive neuroscience.* Blackwell.

Benvenuto, J., Woolford, A., & Hinton, A. L., (Eds.). (2014). *Colonial genocide in Indigenous North America.* Duke University Press. https://doi.org/10.1215/9780822376149

Bilek, E., Ruf, M., Schäfer, A., Akdeniz, C., Calhoun, V. D., Schmahl, C., Demanuele, C., Tost, H., Kirsch, P., & Meyer-Lindenberg, A. (2015). Information flow between interacting human brains: Identification, validation, and relationship to social expertise. *Proceedings of the National Academy of Sciences of the United States of America*, *112*(16), 5207–12. https://doi.org/10.1073/pnas.1421831112

Black, J. (2015). *The Atlantic slave trade in world history*. Routledge.

Bonner, J. T. (1983). *The evolution of culture in animals*. Princeton University Press.

Borck, C. (2012). Toys are us: Models and metaphors in brain research. In S. Choudhury & J. Slaby (Eds.), *Critical neuroscience: A handbook of the social and cultural contexts of neuroscience* (pp. 111–33). Wiley-Blackwell. https://doi.org/10.1002/9781444343359.ch5

Boyce, W. T. (2019). *The orchid and the dandelion: Why some children struggle and how all can thrive*. Knopf.

Boyd, B. (2018). The evolution of stories: From mimesis to language, from fact to fiction. *Wiley Interdisciplinary Reviews: Cognitive Science*, *9*(1), e1444. https://doi.org/10.1002/wcs.1444

Boyer, P., & Wertsch, J. V. (Eds.). (2009). *Memory in mind and culture*. Cambridge University Press. https://doi.org/10.1017/CBO9780511626999

Brown, T. T., & Jernigan, T. L. (2012). Brain development during the preschool years. *Neuropsychology Review*, *22*(4), 313–33. https://doi.org/10.1007/s11065-012-9214-1

Bugnyar, T. (2011). Knower-guesser differentiation in ravens: Others' viewpoints matter. *Proceedings of the Royal Society B: Biological Sciences*, *278*(1705), 634–40. https://doi.org/10.1098/rspb.2010.1514

Burke, P. (2009). *Cultural hybridity*. Polity Press.

Burke, P. (2019). *What is cultural history?* (3rd ed.). Polity Press.

Caldji, C., Diorio, J., & Meaney, M. J. (2000). Variations in maternal care in infancy regulate the development of stress reactivity. *Biological Psychiatry*, *48*(12), 1164–74. https://doi.org/10.1016/S0006-3223(00)01084-2

Catala, A., Mang, B., Wallis, L., & Huber, L. (2017). Dogs demonstrate perspective taking based on geometrical gaze following in a Guesser-Knower task. *Animal Cognition*, *20*(4), 581–89. https://doi.org/10.1007/s10071-017-1082-x

Cavalli-Sforza, L. L., Menozzi, P., & Piazza, A. (1994). *The history and geography of human genes*. Princeton University Press.

Champagne, F. A. (2018). Social and behavioral epigenetics: Evolving perspectives on nature-nurture interplay, plasticity, and inheritance. In M. Meloni, J. Cromby, D. Fitzgerald, & S. Lloyd (Eds.), *The Palgrave handbook of biology and society* (pp. 227–50). Palgrave Macmillan. https://doi.org/10.1057/978-1-137-52879-7_10

Champagne, F., & Meaney, M. J. (2001). Like mother, like daughter: Evidence for non-genomic transmission of parental behavior and stress responsivity. In J. A. Russell, A. J. Douglas, R. J. Windle, & C. D. Ingram (Eds.), *Progress in brain research. The maternal brain.* (Vol. 133, pp. 287–302). Elsevier. https://doi.org/10.1016/S0079-6123(01)33022-4

Chartrand, T. L., Maddux, W. W., & Lakin, J. L. (2005). Beyond the perception-behavior link: The ubiquitous utility and motivational moderators of nonconscious mimicry. In R. R. Hassin, J. S. Uleman, & J. A. Bargh (Eds.), *Oxford series in social cognition and social neuroscience. The new unconscious* (pp. 334–61). Oxford University Press. https://doi.org/10.1093/acprof:oso/9780195307696.003.0014

Chemero, A. (2011). *Radical embodied cognitive science*. MIT Press.
Chen, Q., Yan, W., & Duan, E.-K. (2016). Epigenetic inheritance of acquired traits through sperm RNAs and sperm RNA modifications. *Nature Reviews Genetics, 17*(12), 733–43. https://doi.org/10.1038/nrg.2016.106
Choudhury, S., & Slaby, J. (Eds.). (2012). *Critical neuroscience: A handbook of the social and cultural contexts of neuroscience*. Wiley-Blackwell.
Churchland, P. M. (1984). *Matter and consciousness*. MIT Press.
Churchland, P. M. (1989). *A neurocomputational perspective: The nature of mind and the structure of science*. MIT Press.
Clark, A. (2008). *Supersizing the mind: Embodiment, action, and cognitive extension*. Oxford University Press. https://doi.org/10.1093/acprof:oso/9780195333213.001.0001
Clark, A. (2015). *Surfing uncertainty: Prediction, action, and the embodied mind*. Oxford University Press.
Clauset, A., Moore, C., & Newman, M. E. J. (2008). Hierarchical structure and the prediction of missing links in networks. *Nature, 453*, 98–101. https://doi.org/10.1038/nature06830
Coan, J. A., Schaefer, H. S., & Davidson, R. J. (2006). Lending a hand: Social regulation of the neural response to threat. *Psychological Science, 17*(12), 1032–9. https://doi.org/10.1111/j.1467-9280.2006.01832.x
Collin, G., & van den Heuvel, M. P. (2013). The ontogeny of the human connectome: Development and dynamic changes of brain connectivity across the life span. *The Neuroscientist, 19*(6), 616–28. https://doi.org/10.1177/1073858413503712
Constant, A., Ramstead, M. J. D., Veissière, S. P. L., Campbell, J. O., & Friston, K. J. (2018). A variational approach to niche construction. *Journal of the Royal Society Interface, 15*(141), 20170685. https://doi.org/10.1098/rsif.2017.0685
Constant, A., Ramstead, M. J. D., Veissière, S. P., & Friston, K. (2019). Regimes of expectations: An active inference model of social conformity and decision making. *Frontiers in Psychology, 10*, 679. https://doi.org/10.3389%2Ffpsyg.2019.00679
Costello, E. J., Worthman, C., Erkanli, A., & Angold, A. (2007). Prediction from low birth weight to female adolescent depression: A test of competing hypotheses. *Archives of General Psychiatry, 64*, 338–44. https://doi.org/10.1001/archpsyc.64.3.338
Damasio, A. (1995). *Descartes' error: Emotion, reason, and the human brain*. Avon.
Damasio, A. (2018). *The strange order of things: Life, feeling, and the making of cultures*. Pantheon.
Danziger, K. (2009). *Marking the mind: A history of memory*. Cambridge University Press.
Davidson, E. H. (2006). *The regulatory genome: Gene regulatory networks in development and evolution*. Academic Press.
Dehaene, S. (2009). *Reading in the brain: The new science of how we read*. Penguin.
Dennett, D. C. (1991). *Consciousness explained*. Little, Brown and Company.
Descartes, R. (1989). *Passions of the soul*. Hackett Publishing. (Original work published 1649)
Doidge, N. (2007). *The brain that changes itself: Stories of personal triumph from the frontiers of brain science*. Viking Penguin.

Draganski, B., Gaser, C., Busch, V., Schuierer, G., Bogdahn, U., & May, A. (2004). Neuroplasticity: Changes in grey matter induced by training. *Nature, 427*(6972), 311–2. https://doi.org/10.1038/427311a

Dudley, R. (2014). *The drunken monkey: Why we drink and abuse alcohol.* University of California Press.

Dunbar, R. (2016). *Human evolution: Our brains and behavior.* Oxford University Press.

Dunbar, R. I. M. (1998). The social brain hypothesis. *Evolutionary Anthropology, 6*(5), 178–90. https://doi.org/10.1080/03014460902960289

Dunbar, R. I. M. (2008). Cognitive constraints on the structure and dynamics of social networks. *Group Dynamics: Theory, Research, and Practice, 12*(1), 7–16. https://doi.org/10.1037/1089-2699.12.1.7

Dunbar, R. I. M., & Shultz, S. (2017). Why are there so many explanations for primate brain evolution? *Philosophical Transactions of the Royal Society B: Biological Sciences, 372*(1727), 20160244. https://doi.org/10.1098/rstb.2016.0244

Durt, C., Fuchs, T., & Tewes, C., (Eds.). (2017). *Embodiment, enaction, and culture: Investigating the constitution of the shared world.* MIT Press. https://doi.org/10.7551/mitpress/9780262035552.001.0001

Edelman, G. M. (1987). *Neural Darwinism: The theory of neuronal group selection.* Basic Books.

Edenberg, H. J. (2007). The genetics of alcohol metabolism: Role of alcohol dehydrogenase and aldehyde dehydrogenase variants. *Alcohol Research & Health, 30*(1), 5–13. www.ncbi.nlm.nih.gov/pmc/articles/PMC3860432/

Eisenberger, N. I., Taylor, S. E., Gable, S. L., Hilmert, C. J., & Lieberman, M. D. (2007). Neural pathways link social support to attenuated neuroendocrine stress responses. *NeuroImage, 35*(4), 1601–12. https://doi.org/10.1016%2Fj.neuroimage.2007.01.038

Ellis, B. J., Figueredo, A. J., Brumbach, B. H., & Schlomer, G. L. (2009). Fundamental dimensions of environmental risk: The impact of harsh versus unpredictable environments on the evolution and development of life history strategies. *Human Nature, 20*(2), 204–68. https://doi.org/10.1007/s12110–009-9063-7

Feinberg, T. E., & Mallatt, J. M. (2016). *The ancient origins of consciousness: How the brain created experience.* MIT Press.

Fivush, R., & Haden, C. A. (Eds.). (2003). *Autobiographical memory and the construction of a narrative self: Developmental and cultural perspectives.* Lawrence Erlbaum.

Freeman, M. (2015). *Rewriting the self: History, memory, narrative.* Routledge.

Friston, K. (2010). The free-energy principle: A unified brain theory? *Nature Reviews Neuroscience, 11*(2), 127–38. https://doi.org/10.1038/nrn2787

Fuchs, T. (2017). *Ecology of the brain: The phenomenology and biology of the embodied mind.* Oxford University Press.

Gallagher, S. (2006). *How the body shapes the mind.* Clarendon Press.

Gallagher, S. (2017). *Enactivist interventions: Rethinking the mind.* Oxford University Press.

Gettler, L. T., McDade, T. W., Bragg, J. M., Feranil, A. B., & Kuzawa, C. W. (2015). Developmental energetics, sibling death, and parental instability as predictors of maturational tempo and life history scheduling in males from Cebu, Philippines. *American Journal of Physical Anthropology*, *158*(2), 175–84. https://doi.org/10.1002/ajpa.22783

Gibbs, R. W., Jr. (2005). *Embodiment and cognitive science*. Cambridge University Press.

Gilovich, T. (1990). Differential construal and the false consensus effect. *Journal of Personality and Social Psychology*, *59*(4), 623–34. https://doi.org/10.1037/0022-3514.59.4.623

González-Forero, M., & Gardner, A. (2018). Inference of ecological and social drivers of human brain-size evolution. *Nature*, *557*(7706), 554–7. https://doi.org/10.1038/s41586-018-0127-x

Gottlieb, G. (1991). Experiential canalization of behavioral development: Results. *Developmental Psychology*, *27*(1), 35–9. https://doi.org/10.1037/0012-1649.27.1.35

Gottlieb, G. (1998). Normally occurring environmental and behavioral influences on gene activity: From central dogma to probabilistic epigenesis. *Psychological Review*, *105*(4), 792–802. https://doi.org/10.1037/0033-295X.105.4.792-802

Gottlieb, G. (2007). Probabilistic epigenesis. *Developmental Science*, *10*(1), 1–11. https://doi.org/10.1111/j.1467-7687.2007.00556.x

Gravlee, C. C. (2009). How race becomes biology: Embodiment of social inequality. *American Journal of Physical Anthropology*, *139*(1), 47–57. https://doi.org/10.1002/ajpa.20983

Griffiths, P., & Stotz, K. (2013). *Genetics and philosophy: An introduction*. Cambridge University Press. https://doi.org/10.1017/CBO9780511744082

Hacking, I. (1999). *The social construction of what?* Harvard University Press.

Hacking, I. (2002). *Historical ontology*. Harvard University Press.

Hahn, J. D., Sporns, O., Watts, A. G., & Swanson, L. W. (2019). Macroscale intrinsic network architecture of the hypothalamus. *Proceedings of the National Academy of Sciences of the United States of America*, *116*(16), 8018–27. https://doi.org/10.1073/pnas.1819448116

Hamilton, J. P., Farmer, M., Fogelman, P., & Gotlib, I. H. (2015). Depressive rumination, the default-mode network, and the dark matter of clinical neuroscience. *Biological Psychiatry*, *78*(4), 224–30. https://doi.org/10.1016/j.biopsych.2015.02.020

Harkness, S., & Super, C. M. (1994). The developmental niche: A theoretical framework for analyzing the household production of health. *Social Science & Medicine*, *38*(2), 218–26. https://doi.org/10.1016/0277-9536(94)90391-3

Hatfield, G. (2007). The passions of the soul and Descartes's machine psychology. *Studies in History and Philosophy of Science Part A*, *38*(1), 1–35.

Heine, S. J., Lehman, D. R., Markus, H. R., & Kitayama, S. (1999). Is there a universal need for positive self-regard? *Psychological Review*, *106*(4), 766–94. https://doi.org/10.1037/0033-295X.106.4.766

Helfman, G. S., & Schultz, E. T. (1984). Social transmission of behavioural traditions in a coral-reef fish. *Animal Behaviour*, *32*(2), 379–84. https://doi.org/10.1016/s0003-3472(84)80272-9

Henrich, J. (2015). *The secret of our success: How culture is driving human evolution, domesticating our species, and making us smarter*. Princeton University Press.

Hertzman, C., & Boyce, T. (2010). How experience gets under the skin to create gradients in developmental health. *Annual Review of Public Health, 31*, 329–47 3p following 347. https://doi.org/10.1146/annurev.publhealth.012809.103538

Heyes, C. (2015). Animal mindreading: What's the problem? *Psychonomic Bulletin & Review, 22*(2), 313–27. https://doi.org/10.3758/s13423-014-0704-4

Heyes, C. (2018). *Cognitive gadgets: The cultural evolution of thinking.* Harvard University Press.

Hillman, C. H., Erickson, K. I., & Kramer, A. F. (2008). Be smart, exercise your heart: Exercise effects on brain and cognition. *Nature Reviews Neuroscience, 9*(1), 58–65. https://doi.org/10.1038/nrn2298

Hirata, S., Watanabe, K., & Kawai, M. (2001). "Sweet-potato washing" revisited. In T. Matsuzawa (Ed.), *Primate origins of human cognition and behavior* (pp. 487–508). Springer-Verlag. https://doi.org/10.1007/978-4-431-09423-4_24

Hirsch, J., Zhang, X., Noah, J. A., & Ono, Y. (2017). Frontal temporal and parietal systems synchronize within and across brains during live eye-to-eye contact. *NeuroImage, 157*, 314–30. https://doi.org/10.1016/j.neuroimage.2017.06.018

Hohwy, J. (2013). *The predictive mind.* Oxford University Press. https://doi.org/10.1093/acprof:oso/9780199682737.001.0001

Hong, Y. Y., Morris, M., Chiu, C. Y., & Benet-Martínez, V. (2000). Multicultural minds: A dynamic constructivist approach to culture and cognition. *American Psychologist, 55*(7), 709–20. https://doi.org/10.1037/0003-066X.55.7.709

Hrdy, S. B. (2009). *Mothers and others: The evolutionary origins of mutual understanding.* Harvard University Press.

Hutto, D. D. (2012). *Folk psychological narratives: The sociocultural basis of understanding reasons.* MIT Press.

Hutto, D. D., & Myin, E. (2012). *Radicalizing enactivism: Basic minds without content.* MIT Press.

Hutto, D. D., & Myin, E. (2017). *Evolving enactivism: Basic minds meet content.* MIT Press.

Hyde, L. (1998). *Trickster makes this world: Mischief, myth, and art.* Farrar, Straus and Giroux.

Jablonka, E. (2013). Epigenetic inheritance and plasticity: The responsive germline. *Progress in Biophysics and Molecular Biology, 111*(2–3), 99–107. https://doi.org/10.1016/j.pbiomolbio.2012.08.014

Jablonka, E., & Lamb, M. J. (2006). *Evolution in four dimensions: Genetic, epigenetic, behavioral, and symbolic variation in the history of life.* MIT Press.

Jablonka, E., & Raz, G. (2009). Transgenerational epigenetic inheritance: Prevalence, mechanisms, and implications for the study of heredity and evolution. *Quarterly Review of Biology, 84*(2), 131–76. https://doi.org/10.1086/598822

Kaiser, M., Hilgetag, C. C., & Kötter, R. (2010). Hierarchy and dynamics of neural networks. *Frontiers in Neuroinformatics, 4*, 112. https://doi.org/10.3389%2Ffninf.2010.00112

Kaplan, H., Hill, K., Lancaster, J., & Hurtado, A. M. (2000). A theory of human life history evolution: Diet, intelligence, and longevity. *Evolutionary Anthropology, 9*(4), 156–85. https://doi.org/10.1002/1520-6505(2000)9:4<156::aid-evan5>3.0.co;2-7

Kimel, S. Y., Grossman, I., & Kitayama, S. (2012). When gift-giving produces dissonance: Effects of subliminal affiliation priming on choices for one's self versus others. *Journal of Experimental Social Psychology*, 48(5), 1221–4. https://doi.org/10.1016/j.jesp.2012.05.012

Kimel, S. Y., Grossman, I., & Kitayama, S. (2017). When gift-giving produces dissonance: Effects of subliminal affiliation priming on choices for one's self versus others [Corrigendum]. *Journal of Experimental Social Psychology*, 71, 153. https://doi.org/10.1016/j.jesp.2017.02.002

Kinreich, S., Djalovski, A., Kraus, L., Louzoun, Y., & Feldman, R. (2017). Brain-to-brain synchrony during naturalistic social interactions. *Scientific Reports*, 7(1), 17060. https://doi.org/10.1038/s41598-017-17339-5

Kirmayer, L. J., Gone, J. P., & Moses, J. (2014). Rethinking historical trauma. *Transcultural Psychiatry*, 51(3), 299–319. https://doi.org/10.1177%2F1363461514536358

Kitayama, S., King, A., Hsu, M., Liberzon, I., & Yoon, C. (2016). Dopamine-system genes and cultural acquisition: The norm sensitivity hypothesis. *Current Opinion in Psychology*, 8, 167–74. https://doi.org/10.1016/j.copsyc.2015.11.006

Kitayama, S., King, A., Yoon, C., Tompson, S., Huff, S., & Liberzon, I. (2014). The dopamine D4 receptor gene (*DRD4*) moderates cultural difference in independent versus interdependent social orientation. *Psychological Science*, 25(6), 1169–77. https://doi.org/10.1177/0956797614528338

Kitayama, S., & Uskul, A. K. (2011). Culture, mind, and the brain: Current evidence and future directions. *Annual Review of Psychology*, 62, 419–49. https://doi.org/10.1146/annurev-psych-120709-145357

Kitayama, S., Varnum, M. E. W., & Salvador, C. (2019). Cultural neuroscience. In D. Cohen & S. Kitayama (Eds.), *The handbook of cultural psychology* (2nd ed., pp. 79–118). Guilford Press.

Klemm, S. L., Shipony, Z., & Greenleaf, W. J. (2019). Chromatin accessibility and the regulatory epigenome. *Nature Reviews Genetics*, 20(4), 207–20. https://doi.org/10.1038/s41576-018-0089-8

Kohrt, B. A., Jordans, M. J. D., Koirala, S., & Worthman, C. M. (2015). Designing mental health interventions informed by child development and human biology theory: A social ecology intervention for child soldiers in Nepal. *America Journal of Human Biology*, 27(1), 27–40. https://doi.org/10.1002/ajhb.22651

Kolodny, O., Edelman, S., & Lotem, A. (2015). Evolution of protolinguistic abilities as a by-product of learning to forage in structured environments. *Proceedings of the Royal Society B: Biological Sciences*, 282(1811), 20150353. https://doi.org/10.1098/rspb.2015.0353

Konner, M. (2010). *The evolution of childhood: Relationships, emotion, mind.* Belknap Press.

Konner, M. J. (2002). *The tangled wing: Biological constraints on the human spirit* (2nd ed.). Henry Holt.

Krupenye, C., Kano, F., Hirata, S., Call, J., & Tomasello, M. (2016). Great apes anticipate that other individuals will act according to false beliefs. *Science*, 354 (6308), 110–14. https://doi.org/10.1126/science.aaf8110

Kühnen, U., & Oyserman, D. (2002). Thinking about the self influences thinking in general: Cognitive consequences of salient self-concept. *Journal of Experimental Social Psychology*, 38(5), 492–9.

Kuzawa, C. W., & Bragg, J. M. (2012). Plasticity in human life history strategy: Implications for contemporary human variation and the evolution of genus *Homo*. *Current Anthropology*, *53*(S6), S369–S382. https://doi.org/10.1086/667410

Kuzawa, C. W., Chugani, H. T., Grossman, L. I., Lipovich, L., Muzik, O., Hof, P. R., Wildman, D. E., Sherwood, C. C., Leonard, W. R., & Lange, N. (2014). Metabolic costs and evolutionary implications of human brain development. *Proceedings of the National Academy of Sciences of the United States of America*, *111*(36), 13010–15. https://doi.org/10.1073/pnas.1323099111

Kuzawa, C. W., & Thayer, Z. M. (2011). Timescales of human adaptation: The role of epigenetic processes. *Epigenomics*, *3*(2), 221–34. https://doi.org/10.2217/epi.11.11

Kwon, H., & Sasaki, J. Y. (2019). *Gene–Culture Interactions: Toward an Explanatory Framework*. Cambridge University Press.

Lakin, J. L., & Chartrand, T. L. (2003). Using unconscious behavioral mimicry to create affiliation and rapport. *Psychological Science*, *14*(4), 334–9. https://doi.org/10.1111/1467-9280.14481

Lakoff, G. (2012). Explaining embodied cognition results. *Topics in Cognitive Science*, *4*(4), 773–85. https://doi.org/10.1111/j.1756-8765.2012.01222.x

Lakoff, G., & Johnson, M. (1980). *Metaphors we live by*. University of Chicago Press.

Laland, K. N. (2017). *Darwin's unfinished symphony: How culture made the human mind*. Princeton University Press.

Laland, K., Matthews, B., & Feldman, M. W. (2016). An introduction to niche construction theory. *Evolutionary Ecology*, *30*(2), 191–202. https://doi.org/10.1007/s10682-016-9821-z

Laland, K. N., Odling-Smee, J., & Myles, S. (2010). How culture shaped the human genome: Bringing genetics and the human sciences together. *Nature Reviews Genetics*, *11*(2), 137–48. https://doi.org/10.1038/nrg2734

Laland, K. N., Uller, T., Fellman, M. W., Sterelny, K., Müller, G. B., Moczek, A., Jablonka, E., & Odling-Smee, J. (2015). The extended evolutionary synthesis: Its structure, assumptions and predictions. *Proceedings of the Royal Society B: Biological Sciences*, *282*(1813), 20151019. https://doi.org/10.1098/rspb.2015.1019

Laland, K., Uller, T., Feldman, M., Sterelny, K., Müller, G. B., Moczek, A., Jablonka, E., Odling-Smee, J., Wray, G. A., Hoekstra, H. E., Futuyma, D. J., Lenski, R. E., Mackay, T. F. C., Schluter, D., & Strassman, J. E. (2014). Does evolutionary theory need a rethink? *Nature*, *514*(7521), 161–4. https://doi.org/10.1038/514161a

Lansing, J. S., & Fox, K. M. (2011). Niche construction on Bali: The gods of the countryside. *Philosophical Transactions of the Royal Society B: Biological Sciences*, *366*(1566), 927–34. https://doi.org/10.1098/rstb.2010.0308

Lifshitz, M., Sheiner, E., & Kirmayer, L. J. (2018). Cultural neurophenomenology of psychedelic thought: Guiding the "unconstrained" mind through ritual context. In K. Christoff & K. C. R. Fox (Eds.), *The Oxford handbook of spontaneous thought: Mind-wandering, creativity, and dreaming* (pp. 573–94). Oxford University Press. https://doi.org/10.1093/oxfordhb/9780190464745.013.4

Lock, M., & Palsson, G. (2016). *Can science resolve the nature/nurture debate?* Polity Press.

Ma, Y., Bang, D., Wang, C., Allen, M., Frith, C., Roepstorff, A., & Han, S. (2014). Sociocultural patterning of neural activity during self-reflection. *Social Cognitive and Affective Neuroscience*, *9*(1), 73–80. https://doi.org/10.1093/scan/nss103

Maguire, E. A., Woollett, K., & Spiers, H. J. (2006). London taxi drivers and bus drivers: A structural MRI and neuropsychological analysis. *Hippocampus*, *16*(12), 1091–1101. https://doi.org/10.1002/hipo.20233

Markus, H. R., & Kitayama, S. (1991). Culture and the self: Implications for cognition, emotion, and motivation. *Psychological Review*, *98*(2), 224–53. https://doi.org/10.1037/0033-295X.98.2.224

Martin, K. C., Bartsch, D., Bailey, C. H., Kandel, E. R., Lynch, G., Levine, E. S., McEwen, B. S., Katz, L. C., Weliky, M., Crowley, J. C., Zhou, R., Black, I. B., Kaas, J. H., & Recanzone, G. H. (2000). Plasticity. In M. S. Gazzaniga (Ed.), *The new cognitive neurosciences* (2nd ed., pp. 121–247). MIT Press.

McAdams, D. P. (2019). "First we invented stories, then they changed us": The evolution of narrative identity. *Evolutionary Studies in Imaginative Culture*, *3*(1), 1–18. https://www.jstor.org/stable/10.26613/esic.3.1.110

McCulloch, W. S., & Pitts, W. (1943). A logical calculus of the ideas immanent in nervous activity. *Bulletin of Mathematical Biophysics*, *5*(4), 115–33. https://doi.org/10.1007/BF02478259

McDade, T. W., Ryan, C., Jones, M. J., MacIsaac, J. L., Morin, A. M., Meyer, J. M., Borja, J. B., Miller, G. E., Kobor, M.S., & Kuzawa, C. W. (2017). Social and physical environments early in development predict DNA methylation of inflammatory genes in young adulthood. *Proceedings of the National Academy of Sciences of the United States of America*, *114*(29), 7611–16. https://doi.org/10.1073/pnas.1620661114

McGowan, P. O., Sasaki, A., D'Alessio, A. C., Dymov, S., Labonté, B., Szyf, M., Turecki, G., & Meaney, M. J. (2009). Epigenetic regulation of the glucocorticoid receptor in human brain associates with childhood abuse. *Nature Neuroscience*, *12*(3), 342–8. https://doi.org/10.1038/nn.2270

Merabet, L. B., & Pascual-Leone, A. (2010). Neural reorganization following sensory loss: The opportunity of change. *Nature Reviews Neuroscience*, *11*(1), 44–52. https://doi.org/10.1038/nrn2758

Merzenich, M. M., Nahum, M., & Van Vleet, T. M. (2013). Introduction. In M. M. Merzenich, M. Nahum, & T. M. Van Vleet (Eds.), *Progress in brain research. Changing brains: Applying brain plasticity to advance and recover human ability* (Vol. 207, pp. xxi–xxvi). Elsevier. https://doi.org/10.1016/B978-0-444-63327-9.10000-1

Muehsam, D., Lutgendorf, S., Mills, P. J., Rickhi, B., Chevalier, G., Bat, N., Chopra, D., & Gurfein, B. (2017). The embodied mind: A review on functional genomic and neurological correlates of mind-body therapies. *Neuroscience & Biobehavioral Reviews*, *73*, 165–81. https://doi.org/10.1016/j.neubiorev.2016.12.027

Nelson, E. E., Jarcho, J. M., & Guyer, A. E. (2016). Social re-orientation and brain development: An expanded and updated view. *Developmental Cognitive Neuroscience*, *17*, 118–27. https://doi.org/10.1016/j.dcn.2015.12.008

Newen, A., de Bruin, L., & Gallagher, S. (Eds.). (2018). *The Oxford handbook of 4E cognition*. Oxford University Press.

Niedenthal, P. M., Rychlowska, M., Zhao, F., & Wood, A. (2019). Historical migration patterns shape contemporary cultures of emotion. *Perspectives on Psychological Science*, *14*(4), 560–73. https://doi.org/10.1177/1745691619849591

Niezen, R. (2003). *The origins of indigenism: Human rights and the politics of identity.* University of California Press.

Nisbett, R. E., Peng, K., Choi, I., & Norenzayan, A. (2001). Culture and systems of thought: Holistic versus analytic cognition. *Psychological Review*, *108*(2), 291–310. https://doi.org/10.1037/0033-295X.108.2.291

Noë, A. (2004). *Action in perception.* MIT Press.

O'Brien, E., & Ellsworth, P. C. (2012). More than skin deep: Visceral states are not projected onto dissimilar others. *Psychological Science*, *23*(4), 391–6. https://doi.org/10.1177/0956797611432179

Odling-Smee, F. J., Laland, K. N., & Feldman, M. W. (2003). *Niche construction: The neglected process in evolution.* Princeton University Press. http://www.jstor.org/stable/j.ctt24hqpd

Over, H., & Uskul, A. K. (2016). Culture moderates children's responses to ostracism situations. *Journal of Personality and Social Psychology*, *110*(5), 710–24. https://doi.org/10.1037/pspi0000050

Oyserman, D., & Lee, S. W. S. (2008). Does culture influence what and how we think? Effects of priming individualism and collectivism. *Psychological Bulletin*, *134*, 311–42. https://doi.org/10.1037/0033-2909.134.2.311

Oyserman, D., Novin, S., Flinkenflögel, N., & Krabbendam, L. (2014). Integrating culture-as-situated-cognition and neuroscience prediction models. *Culture and Brain*, *2*(1), 1–26. https://doi.org/10.1007/s40167-014-0016-6

Oyserman, D., Sorensen, N., Reber, R., & Chen, S. X. (2009). Connecting and separating mind-sets: Culture as situated cognition. *Journal of Personality and Social Psychology*, *97*(2), 217–35. https://doi.org/10.1037/a0015850

Park, H.-J., & Friston, K. (2013). Structural and functional brain networks: From connections to cognition. *Science*, *342*(6158), 1238411. https://doi.org/10.1126/science.1238411

Pavlov, I. P. (1928). *Lectures on conditioned reflexes: Twenty-five years of objective study of the higher nervous activity (behaviour) of animals* (W. H. Gantt, Trans.). Liverwright Publishing Corporation. https://doi.org/10.1037/11081-000

Peng, Y., Shi, H., Qi, X.-b., Xiao, C.-j., Zhong, H., Ma, R.-l. Z., & Su, B. (2010). The ADH1B Arg47His polymorphism in East Asian populations and expansion of rice domestication in history. *BMC Evolutionary Biology*, *10*(1), 15. https://doi.org/10.1186/1471-2148-10-15

Pickering, A. (2010). *The cybernetic brain: Sketches of another future.* University of Chicago Press.

Pinker, S. (2010). The cognitive niche: Coevolution of intelligence, sociality, and language. *Proceedings of the National Academy of Sciences of the United States of America*, *107*(Supplement 2), 8993–9. https://doi.org/10.1073/pnas.0914630107

Potts, R. (1998). Environmental hypotheses of hominin evolution. *American Journal of Physical Anthropology*, *107*(S27), 93–136.

Potts, R., & Faith, J. T. (2015). Alternating high and low climate variability: The context of natural selection and speciation in Plio-Pleistocene hominin evolution. *Journal of Human Evolution*, *87*, 5–20. https://doi.org/10.1016/j.jhevol.2015.06.014

Ramón y Cajal S. (1909). *Histologie du système nerveux de l'homme et des vertébrés*. Maloine.

Ramstead, M. J. D., Veissière, S. P. L., & Kirmayer, L. J. (2016). Cultural affordances: Scaffolding local worlds through shared intentionality and regimes of attention. *Frontiers in Psychology*, 7, 1090. https://doi.org/10.3389%2Ffpsyg.2016.01090

Ren, D., Wesselmann, E. D., & Williams, K. D. (2013). Interdependent self-construal moderates coping with (but not the initial pain of) ostracism. *Asian Journal of Social Psychology*, *16*, 320–6. https://doi.org/10.1111/ajsp.12037

Rendell, L., & Whitehead, H. (2001). Culture in whales and dolphins. *Behavioral and Brain Sciences*, *24*(2), 309–24. https://doi.org/10.1017/s0140525x0100396x

Richerson, P. J., & Boyd, R. (2005). *Not by genes alone: How culture transformed human evolution*. University of Chicago Press.

Rilling, J. K., Glasser, M. F., Preuss, T. M., Ma, X., Zhao, T., Hu, X., & Behrens, T. E. J. (2008). The evolution of the arcuate fasciculus revealed with comparative DTI. *Nature Neuroscience*, *11*(4), 426–8. https://doi.org/10.1038/nn2072

Roepstorff, A., & Frith, C. (2004). What's at the top in the top-down control of action? Script-sharing and 'top-top' control of action in cognitive experiments. *Psychological Research*, *68*(2–3), 189–98. https://doi.org/10.1007/s00426-003-0155-4

Rose, N., & Abi-Rached, J. M. (2013). *Neuro: The new brain sciences and the management of the mind*. Princeton University Press.

Ross, L., Greene, D., & House, P. (1977). The "false consensus effect": An egocentric bias in social perception and attribution processes. *Journal of Experimental Social Psychology*, *13*(3), 279–301. https://doi.org/10.1016/0022-1031(77)90049-X

Ross, L., & Nisbett, R. E. (1991). *The person and the situation: Perspectives of social psychology*. McGraw-Hill.

Ruben, R. J. (1997). A time frame of critical/sensitive periods of language development. *Acta Oto-Laryngologica*, *117*(2), 202–5. https://doi.org/10.3109/00016489709117769

Saito, D. N., Tanabe, H. C., Izuma, K., Hayashi, M. J., Morito, Y., Komeda, H., Uchiyama, H., Kosaka, H., Okazawa, H., Fujibayashi, Y., & Sadato, N. (2010). "Stay tuned": Inter-individual neural synchronization during mutual gaze and joint attention. *Frontiers in Integrative Neuroscience*, *4*, 127. https://doi.org/10.3389/fnint.2010.00127

Schechtman, M. (1996). *The constitution of selves*. Cornell University Press.

Schulz, K. M., & Sisk, C. L. (2016). The organizing actions of adolescent gonadal steroid hormones on brain and behavioral development. *Neuroscience & Biobehavioral Reviews*, *70*, 148–58. https://doi.org/10.1016/j.neubiorev.2016.07.036

Schwartz, J. H. (Ed.). (2018). *Rethinking human evolution*. MIT Press.

Sechenov, I. M. (1965). *Reflexes of the brain by I. Sechenov* (S. Belsky, Trans.). K. Koshtoyants (Ed., Russian) & G. Gibbons (Ed., English). MIT Press. (original work published 1863)

Seligman, R., Choudhury, S., & Kirmayer, L. J. (2015). Locating culture in the brain and in the world: From social categories to the ecology of mind. In J. Y. Chiao, S.-C. Li, R. Seligman, & R. Turner (Eds.), *The Oxford handbook of cultural neuroscience* (pp. 3–20). Oxford University Press. https://doi.org/10.1093/oxfordhb/9780199357376.013.3

Sherrington, C. S. (1906). *The integrative action of the central nervous system.* Yale University Press.

Sherwood, C. C., & Gómez-Robles, A. (2017). Brain plasticity and human evolution. *Annual Review of Anthropology, 46,* 399–419. https://doi.org/10.1146/annurev-anthro-102215-100009

Shi, Y., & Toga, A. (2017). Connectome imaging for mapping human brain pathways. *Molecular Psychiatry, 22*(9), 1230–40. https://doi.org/10.1038/mp.2017.92

Shonkoff, J. P., & Garner, A. S.; The Committee on Psychosocial Aspects of Child and Family Health, Committee on Early Childhood, Adoption, and Dependent Care, Section on Developmental and Behavioral Pediatrics. (2012). The lifelong effects of early childhood adversity and toxic stress. *Pediatrics, 129*(1), e232–e246. https://doi.org/10.1542/peds.2011-2663

Silani, G., Lamm, C., Ruff, C. C., & Singer, T. (2013). Right supramarginal gyrus is crucial to overcome emotional egocentricity bias in social judgments. *Journal of Neuroscience, 33*(39), 15466–76. https://doi.org/10.1523/JNEUROSCI.1488-13.2013

Sinclair, R. C., Hoffman, C., Mark, M. M., Martin, L. L., & Pickering, T. L. (1994). Construct accessibility and the misattribution of arousal: Schachter and Singer revisited. *Psychological Science, 5*(1), 15–19. https://doi.org/10.1111%2Fj.1467-9280.1994.tb00607.x

Smith, C. A., & Ellsworth, P. C. (1985). Patterns of cognitive appraisal in emotion. *Journal of Personality and Social Psychology, 48*(4), 813–38. https://doi.org/10.1037/0022-3514.48.4.813

Sporns, O. (2011). The human connectome: A complex network. *Annals of the New York Academy of Sciences, 1224*(1), 109–25. https://doi.org/10.1111/j.1749-6632.2010.05888.x

Sporns, O. (2012). *Discovering the human connectome.* MIT Press.

Stearns, S. C. (1992). *The evolution of life histories.* Oxford University Press.

Stearns, S. C., & Koella, J. C. (1986). The evolution of phenotypic plasticity in life-history traits: Predictions for norms of reaction for age- and size-at-maturity. *Evolution, 40*(5), 893–913. https://doi.org/10.1111/j.1558-5646.1986.tb00560.x

Stevenson, E. G. J., & Worthman, C. M. (2014). Child well-being: Anthropological perspectives. In A. Ben-Arieh, F. Casas, I. Frønes, & J. E. Korbin (Eds.), *Handbook of child well-being. Theories, methods and policies in global perspective* (pp. 485–512). Springer. https://doi.org/10.1007/978-90-481-9063-8_20

Talhelm, T., Zhang, X., Oishi, S., Shimin, C., Duan, D., Lan, X., & Kitayama, S. (2014). Large-scale psychological differences within China explained by rice versus wheat agriculture. *Science, 344*(6184), 603–8. https://doi.org/10.1126/science.1246850

Taylor, C. (1989). *Sources of the self: The making of modern identity.* Harvard University Press.

Taylor, C. (2016). *The language animal.* Harvard University Press.

Thompson, E. (2007). *Mind in life: Biology, phenomenology, and the sciences of mind.* Belknap Press.

Tishkoff, S. A., Reed, F. A., Ranciaro, A., Voight, B. F., Babbitt, C. C., Silverman, J. S., Powell, K., Mortensen, H. M., Hirbo, J. B., Osman, M., Ibrahim, M., Omar, S. A.,

Lema, G., Nyambo, T. B., Ghori, J., Bumpstead, S., Pritchard, J. K., Wray, G. A., & Deloukas, P. (2007). Convergent adaptation of human lactase persistence in Africa and Europe. *Nature Genetics*, *39*(1), 31–40. https://doi.org/10.1038/ng1946

Tomasello, M. (2019). *Becoming human: A theory of ontogeny*. Belknap Press.

Tomasello, M., Carpenter, M., Call, J., Behne, T., & Moll, H. (2005). Understanding and sharing intentions: The origins of cultural cognition. *Behavioral and Brain Sciences*, *28*(5), 675–91. https://doi.org/10.1017/S0140525X05000129

Tomlinson, G. (2018). *Culture and the course of human evolution*. University of Chicago Press.

Tononi, G., & Cirelli, C. (2014). Sleep and the price of plasticity: From synaptic and cellular homeostasis to memory consolidation and integration. *Neuron*, *81*(1), 12–34. https://doi.org/10.1016/j.neuron.2013.12.025

Tsai, J. L., Knutson, B., & Fung, H. H. (2006). Cultural variation in affect valuation. *Journal of Personality and Social Psychology*, *90*(2), 288–307. https://doi.org/10.1037/0022-3514.90.2.288

Turecki, G., & Meaney, M. J. (2016). Effects of the social environment and stress on glucocorticoid receptor gene methylation: A systematic review. *Biological Psychiatry*, *79*(2), 87–96. https://doi.org/10.1016/j.biopsych.2014.11.022

Uskul, A. K., & Over, H. (2014). Responses to social exclusion in cultural context: Evidence from farming and herding communities. *Journal of Personality and Social Psychology*, *106*(5), 752–71. https://doi.org/10.1037/a0035810

Vågerö, D., Pinger, P. R., Aronsson, V., & van den Berg, G. J. (2018). Paternal grandfather's access to food predicts all-cause and cancer mortality in grandsons. *Nature Communications*, *9*, 5124. https://doi.org/10.1038/s41467-018-07617-9

Van Boven, L., & Loewenstein, G. (2003). Social projection of transient drive states. *Personality and Social Psychology Bulletin*, *29*(9), 1159–68. https://doi.org/10.1177/0146167203254597

van IJzendoorn, M. H., Bakermans-Kranenburg, M. J., Belsky, J., Beach, S., Brody, G., Dodge, K. A., Greenberg, M., Posner, M., & Scott, S. (2011). Gene-by-environment experiments: A new approach to finding the missing heritability. *Nature Reviews Genetics*, *12*(12), 881. https://doi.org/10.1038/nrg2764-c1

van Schaik, C. P. (2016). *The primate origins of human nature*. John Wiley & Sons.

Varela, F. J., Thompson, E., & Rosch, E. (1991). *The embodied mind: Cognitive science and human experience*. MIT Press.

Veissière, S. P. L., Constant, A., Ramstead, M. J. D., Friston, K. J., & Kirmayer, L. J. (2020). Thinking through other minds: A variational approach to cognition and culture. *Behavioral and Brain Sciences*, *43*, e90: 1–75. https://10.1017/S0140525X19001213

Vidal, F., & Ortega, F. (2017). *Being brains: Making the cerebral subject*. Fordham University Press.

von Neumann, J. (1958). *The computer and the brain*. Yale University Press.

Wall, T. L., Luczak, S. E., & Hiller-Sturmhöfel, S. (2016). Biology, genetics, and environment: Underlying factors influencing alcohol metabolism. *Alcohol Research: Current Reviews*, *38*(1), 59–68. www.ncbi.nlm.nih.gov/pmc/articles/PMC4872614/

Wang, C., Ma, Y., & Han, S. (2014). Self-construal priming modulates pain perception: Event-related potential evidence. *Cognitive Neuroscience*, *5*(1), 3–9. https://doi.org/10.1080/17588928.2013.797388

Watson, R. A., & Szathmáry, E. (2016). How can evolution learn? *Trends in Ecology & Evolution*, *31*(2), 147–57. https://doi.org/10.1016/j.tree.2015.11.009

Weaver, I. C. G., Cervoni, N., Champagne, F. A., D'Alessio, A. C., Sharma, S., Seckl, J. R., Dymov, S., Szyf, M., & Meaney, M. J. (2004). Epigenetic programming by maternal behavior. *Nature Neuroscience*, *7*(8), 847–54. https://doi.org/10.1038/nn1276

West-Eberhard, M. J. (2003). *Developmental plasticity and evolution.* Oxford University Press.

Wexler, B. E. (2006). *Brain and culture: Neurobiology, ideology, and social change.* MIT Press.

Whiten, A. (2017). A second inheritance system: The extension of biology through culture. *Interface Focus*, *7*(5), 20160142. https://doi.org/10.1098/rsfs.2016.0142

Whiten, A., Goodall, J., McGrew, W. C., Nishida, T., Reynolds, V., Sugiyama, Y., Tutin, C. E. G., Wrangham, R. W., & Boesch, C. (1999). Cultures in chimpanzees. *Nature*, *399*(6737), 682–5. https://doi.org/10.1038/21415

Wiener, N. (1948). *Cybernetics: Or control and communication in the animal and the machine.* MIT Press.

Wilson, D. S. (2019). *This view of life: Completing the Darwinian revolution.* Pantheon Books.

Wittgenstein, L. (1953). *Philosophical investigations* (G. E. M. Anscombe, Trans.). Basil Blackwell.

Worthman, C. M. (2009). Habits of the heart: Life history and the developmental neuroendocrinology of emotion. *American Journal of Human Biology*, *21*(6), 772–81. https://doi.org/10.1002/ajhb.20966

Worthman, C. M. (2010). The ecology of human development: Evolving models for cultural psychology. *Journal for Cross-Cultural Psychology*, *41*(4), 546–62. https://doi.org/10.1177%2F0022022110362627

Worthman, C. M., Plotsky, P. M., Schechter, D. S., & Cummings, C. A. (Eds.). (2010). *Formative experiences: The interaction of caregiving, culture, and developmental psychobiology.* Cambridge University Press.

Yu, Q., Abe, N., King, A., Yoon, C., Liberzon, I., & Kitayama, S. (2019). Cultural variation in the gray matter volume of the prefrontal cortex is moderated by the dopamine D4 receptor gene (DRD4). *Cerebral Cortex*, *29*(9): 3922–31. https://doi.org/10.1093/cercor/bhy271

Zhang, T.-Y., Labonté, B., Wen, X. L., Turecki, G., & Meaney, M. J. (2013). Epigenetic mechanisms for the early environmental regulation of hippocampal glucocorticoid receptor gene expression in rodents and humans. *Neuropsychopharmacology*, *38*(1), 111–23. https://doi.org/10.1038/npp.2012.149

Part I

Dynamics of Culture, Mind, and Brain

Models and Evidence

Section 1

The Co-emergence of Culture, Mind, and Brain

Introduction

Humans are storytellers, narrating the world for themselves and others. As the title of this section suggests, there are several stories to tell about the intertwined histories of culture, mind, and brain. Narratives that offer possible answers to basic existential questions are ubiquitous among human societies, and the backstory of how we became human is perhaps the biggest story of all. The chapters in this section deploy evidence from different perspectives to delineate the evolutionary, historical, and ecological origins of and biocultural variation in our species.

Accounts of human evolution emerge from painstaking research and brilliantly illuminate how scientific ingenuity, persistence, and rigorous attention to patterns and details can extract meaning across deep time and space. Indeed, dead men tell tales and our past is pieced together as paleoarchaeologists parse ancient ecologies and metaphorically squeeze blood from stone to infer phenomena as evanescent as cognition and behavior. Stout (see Chapter 2) applies neuroscientific theory, evolutionary theory, and neuroimaging methods to ancient stone tool production to open a window onto the evolution of human cognition and language. Current denigration of manual labor is given pause by evidence that selective pressures on the cognitive capacities and collaborative social context required for tool production (planning, control, imagination, reflexivity), and the subsistence options it unleashed, may have played a long-term role in evolving brain size and structure, emergence of a planful, creative mind, and the eventual leap to language and elaborated culture. This compelling work illustrates the synergistic power of theory and method to tackle interactions of culture, mind, and brain even across deep time.

A widely shared notion that culture took over and evolution ceased to be relevant once our species emerged overlooks the potentially powerful selection forces unleashed by the lifestyles (subsistence strategies, social structures, practices) generated by cultural historical configurations (see Chapter 3). Research in cultural neuroscience and human development has leveraged a radical shift from historical views of culture as a mantle that tames a

53

"primitive" animal. Accumulating evidence demonstrates that culture is not simply a civilizing overlay; rather, it is integral to our species' adaptive strategy, "baked in" to how we develop, think, feel, and behave. Relatedly, mind is both formed and informed by culture–brain dynamics. These insights suggest new approaches to the old question of how deep and wide cultural differences might go. On the one hand, culture may operate ecologically through powerful selective pressures that affect population gene frequencies. On the other hand, culture may exert potent direct effects on brain and mind via evolved facultative capacities for plasticity and context-responsiveness built in to human adaptability. The former operates over long periods of time, while the latter permits rapid adaptive shifts to altered conditions (Figure 1.4). In Chapter 3, Kitayama and Yu trace the impact of cultural constructions of self on both mind and brain, contrasting populations in broadly defined – interdependent versus independent – cultural formations of self and society.

Such observations raise the stakes for understanding just how culture works. Crucially, culture is not just in the mind, it is in the world, realized through human actions that create the conditions of everyday life. Moreover, it is not quite accurate to say that we *became* human over the course of evolution, for each one of us must *become* human in the crucible of culture, mind, and brain. Without the necessary, expectable environments of rearing and living, we cannot survive, much less become or be recognizable as human. Such dependency on and sensitivity to cultural ecology contributes to differences in body, brain, and mind that, in turn, inform what people do, creating a loop of cultural re/production. Consequently, a strong ecological thread runs through anthropological understandings of human diversity and culture's role in its production (see Chapter 4). An ecological perspective undergirds anthropology's emphasis on "being there," its devotion to on-the-ground fieldwork and systematic engagement with the lives of people in distinct times and places. Additionally, the integral role that cultural ecology plays in human development, adaptation, and well-being bears a strong methodological imperative for the study of human diversity.

Experimental research in the biological and social sciences has yielded rapidly expanding knowledge about brain and mind, less so of culture. Nevertheless, in order to deeply understand humans and their diversity, research must engage people "in the wild," centering inquiry on the conditions they inhabit. Yet the medical and social sciences are based largely on work with a very narrow slice of humanity, observed under narrowly defined conditions. This limitation is widely recognized and the de-colonization of understanding humanity has gotten underway, albeit slowly. Narratives about the causes and consequences of human diversity necessarily will expand and shift in the process. It will be exciting to see what stories a book on culture, mind, and brain will have to tell twenty years from now.

2 Culture, Mind, and Brain in Human Evolution
An Extended Evolutionary Perspective on Paleolithic Toolmaking as Embodied Practice

Dietrich Stout

Introduction

Ancient stone tools provide a unique source of empirical evidence for reconstructing the evolutionary origins of human culture, mind, and brain. Although it may appear esoteric in the modern world, stone toolmaking was practiced in one form or another by virtually every human society until the development of metallurgy a mere ~6000 years ago. The Early Stone Age (ESA) alone encompasses roughly 90 percent (2.6–0.25 mya) of human prehistory and charts a technological progression from simple Oldowan stone chips to large, skillfully shaped Acheulean cutting tools. During this period hominid brain size nearly tripled, from the high end of the chimpanzee range to the low end of the modern human range. It is reasonable to conjecture that many distinctive aspects of modern human brain structure and function evolved during this period of massive brain expansion. As a key component of hominid adaptations throughout the Paleolithic, stone tools not only document this critical transition but likely helped to shape it.

Whereas thoughts and actions unfortunately do not leave a fossil record, stone artifacts endure as a concrete trace of past activities. They have even been referred to as a form of "fossilized behavior" (Holloway, 1974, p. 108) although the reconstruction of actions and intentions from mute stones is seldom so straightforward. In practice, archeologists rely heavily on modern ethnographic (David & Kramer, 2001), experimental (Eren et al., 2016), and even ethological (e.g., Whiten, 2015) evidence in order to interpret the past (Wylie, 1985). Such evidence reveals stone toolmaking as a prototypical human skill integrating demands for planning, problem solving, and perceptual-motor coordination within a pragmatic, collaborative context (Nonaka et al., 2010; Roux et al., 1995; Stout, 2002; Stout et al., 2015). Furthermore, this skill is socially reproduced, potentially implicating a wide range of distinctive human capacities for imitation, teaching, and cultural accumulation that have been seen by many as "the secret of our success" (Henrich, 2016).

For these reasons, my colleagues and I have spent years advocating and developing the study of Paleolithic technology as a window on the evolution of human culture, mind, and brain (e.g., Hecht et al., 2014; Stout 2002; Stout & Chaminade, 2007, 2012; Stout & Hecht, 2017; Stout et al., 2019). Here I take the opportunity to frame this research program within the larger theoretical context afforded by an extended evolutionary perspective on Paleolithic toolmaking as embodied practice.

An Extended Theoretical Framework

Until recently, mainstream scientific conceptions of mind and evolution have been rooted in two major intellectual events of the mid-twentieth century: the cognitive revolution in psychology (Crowther-Heyck, 1999; Miller, 2003) and the modern synthesis of evolutionary biology (Pigliucci, 2009). A full intellectual history is obviously beyond the scope of this chapter, but it is fair to say that both of these events were themselves powerfully impacted by the development of computer science (Turing, 1950) and information theory (Shannon & Weaver, 1949). These exciting new intellectual tools encouraged explanation of diverse phenomena in terms of abstract representation and symbol manipulation (Barsalou, 2008), leading, for example, to the pervasive "computer metaphor of mind" in cognitive science as well as the prevailing view of evolution as defined by the intergenerational transmission of information encoded by DNA (Smith, 2000). These influences can also be seen in various approaches to the study of culture as an abstract symbol system, perhaps most obviously in the cultural evolution of gene-like informational "memes" envisioned by Dawkins (1976), but also indirectly (e.g., through linguistics) in symbolic anthropological approaches to culture as knowledge (D'Andrade, 1982).

Over the past several decades, however, reactions to the perceived excesses of this abstract and symbolic approach to mind, culture, and evolution have been gaining ground in the form of "grounded" (Barsalou, 2008), "praxic" (Roepstorff et al., 2010), and "extended" (Laland et al., 2015) perspectives, respectively. Broadly speaking, these newer approaches are distinguished by a common concern with context and materiality that stands in contrast to the drive toward disembodied abstraction characteristic of the cognitive revolution and modern synthesis. This move has profound implications for the study of human cognitive evolution, ranging from what exactly we think was evolving to the diversity of evolutionary processes potentially involved, the kinds of evidence we consider relevant, and the methods we use to study it.

Mind

In the early twentieth century, "mind" was widely considered to be a mystical concept unsuitable for study in a properly scientific discipline of psychology

(Barsalou, 2008; Crowther-Heyck, 1999; Miller, 2003). Many would trace the fall of this behaviorist orthodoxy to seminal contributions by such theoreticians as Lashley (1951), Miller (Miller et al., 1960), and, especially, Chomsky (1957), who explicitly established linguistic syntax as a model for thinking about human cognition. In this view, both language specifically and cognition generally are hierarchically structured, rule-based, computational systems for symbol manipulation. Indeed, the same description applies to the programming languages of computers, and it was this analogy between the mystical-sounding "mind" and the concretely observable computer program that really established the validity of internal cognitive processes as a topic of study (Crowther-Heyck, 1999). Like language, whose symbols are classically thought to display an arbitrary relationship between form and meaning (Saussure, 1916/1966), this led to a vision of cognition as a separate, nonperceptual system – a kind of internal "language of thought" (Fodor, 1975) – which operates through the manipulation of "amodal" symbols (Barsalou, 1999) not directly related to sensory-motor "modes" of experience, such as vision, movement, and internal body states.

This approach generated a huge body of productive research, but has also drawn criticism on a number of points (Barsalou, 2008), including (1) lack of empirical evidence for the recruitment of amodal symbols in cognition, (2) difficulty in relating amodal symbols back to perception and action (the symbol grounding problem), and (3) incompatibility with current understandings of brain function and organization. The second and third points are particularly problematic for investigations into the evolution of mind, as they indicate serious challenges in relating the object of study to the physical evidence for human evolution, such as archeological traces of externalized behaviors and paleontological and comparative evidence of brain size and structure. Perhaps for these reasons, attempts to reconstruct human cognitive evolution have attracted skepticism from many researchers (e.g., Lewontin, 1998). Others have adopted a radically functionalist evolutionary psychology approach, which explicitly dismisses the relevance of the actual neural "hardware" that runs "cognitive programs." Instead, the objective is to identify modular information processing adaptations designed by natural selection to solve problems that a species is thought to have faced in the past (Barkow et al., 1992). This logic was exemplified by Pinker and Bloom (1990) in an influential article on language origins, which argued that language "shows signs of complex design for the communication of propositional structures, and the only explanation for the origins of organs with complex design is the process of natural selection" (p. 726). Although an evolutionary psychology approach typically makes reference to a past environment of evolutionary adaptedness (EEA), there is generally little attempt to ground the details of EEA in actual archeological evidence and little recognition of the diversity of environments and niches that far-flung populations of human ancestors encountered over millions of years.

Alternative approaches to mind as contextually situated and concretely embodied would seem to offer a more promising direction for researchers seeking to ground evolutionary accounts in empirical details of the human past. These approaches, grouped together by Barsalou (2008) under the heading "grounded cognition," are generally unified by an emphasis on simulation rather than amodal symbol manipulation as a basis for cognition. Thus, Barsalou's (1999) theory of perceptual symbol systems implements traditional symbolic operations using simulation and dynamic systems in place of the manipulation of amodal concepts, types, and tokens. Reliance on simulation within the brain's "modal" systems of perception and action naturally grounds cognition with respect to lived experience in the world, affirming the relevance of physical evidence of embodiment and context to an understanding of mind. It is also consistent with current understandings of brain function, including the construction of semantic knowledge through perceptual abstraction (Patterson et al., 2007) and an emerging "predictive brain" framework (Allen & Friston, 2016; Barrett & Simmons, 2015; Clark, 2013) in which the brain does not simply await inputs and produce outputs, but rather maintains a dynamic and generative model of the world that anticipates sensory experience and responds to unexpected discrepancies.

Although such a model can be conceived in purely internal, "cognitivist" terms, it also provides a coherent theoretical framework for a deeper coupling of brain, body, and environment (Allen & Friston, 2016) in the maintenance of allostasis (Barrett & Simmons, 2015; see Chapter 6) and, more broadly, autopoiesis ("self-creation"; Varela et al., 1974). Thus, organisms act in ways that structure the sensory feedback they receive (cf. active perception; Gibson, 1979), leading to what Clark (2013) refers to as "self-structuring of information flows." Such dynamic coupling blurs the classic Cartesian distinction between the mental and the physical, distributing cognition (Clark, 1997) across an integrated organism–environment system. This framework also lends itself naturally to extension through time (Clark, 2013), yielding an integrated view of interacting dynamics across behavioral, developmental, historical, and evolutionary time-scales (Byrge et al., 2014; Cole, 1996; Flynn et al., 2013; Laland et al., 2015; Roepstorff et al., 2010).

This materially and temporally extended view of mind has obvious attractions for cognitive archeology (e.g., Malafouris, 2013). Archeologists have little choice but to focus on artifacts, but they have made a virtue of this necessity by thinking deeply on the role of materiality in human culture and cognition (Hodder, 2012). Schiffer (1999) goes so far as to contend that this material engagement is in fact the most distinctive characteristic of our species and that "what makes humans unique is that we take part in diverse interactions with innumerable kinds of artifacts in the course of daily activities" (p. 2). To the extent that archeologists are able to reconstruct these material interactions and the ways in which they change through time, they can provide insight into the contingencies of timing and context that defined the path of human cognitive evolution (Stout et al., 2019).

Culture

Perhaps the most widely cited definition of "culture" is that of E. B. Tylor (1871), who refers to "that complex whole which includes knowledge, belief, art, morals, law, custom, and any other capabilities and habits acquired by man as a member of society" (p. 1). Although this list is fairly inclusive (an archeologists might note the absence of material culture apart from, possibly, "art"), various theoretical approaches have emphasized different aspects of the definition. According to D'Andrade (1982), the demise of behaviorism and ascendance of the computer metaphor of mind led to a similar shift in anthropology from an emphasis on cultural "habits" (i.e., behavior patterns) to a view of culture as shared knowledge and rules for action, essentially describing a cultural "program" (e.g., Goodenough, 1957). Thus, "culture came to be seen as an information-holding system with functions similar to that of cellular DNA. For individual cells, DNA provides the information needed for self-regulation and specialized growth. For humans, the instructions needed for coping with the environment and performing specialized roles is provided in learned information, which is symbolically encoded and culturally transmitted" (D'Andrade, 1982, p. 198).

Although D'Andrade also notes that there was an almost immediate reaction within anthropology to apparent shortcomings with this conception (see also Turner, 1975), it has been largely maintained in comparative and evolutionary approaches to culture as a form of information transmission (e.g., Bonner, 1980; Cavalli-Sforza & Feldman, 1981). The genetic analogy is, of course, quite explicit in the concept of a meme (Dawkins, 1976), and while the study of cultural evolution has moved substantially beyond any expectation of exact correspondence with biological evolution (Henrich et al., 2008), it remains grounded in a conception of culture as information stored in human brains and transmitted through social learning. Although this has clearly been a useful and productive heuristic, especially to the extent that it supports formal modeling of cultural evolutionary processes (e.g., Kolodny et al., 2016; Powell et al., 2009), it is nevertheless worthwhile to consider the perceived limitations of an "information transmission" view of culture that have so concerned many anthropologists.

Chief among these is the conviction that culture is not limited to knowledge held in the minds of individuals, but includes concrete and durable extensions into the world of actions, people, and objects. In many ways, this critique anticipated the later psychological reactions and alternatives to the computational view of mind discussed above. Geertz (1973, p. 17), for example, stressed the enactive nature of culture, arguing that "it is through the flow of behavior – or, more precisely, social action – that cultural forms find articulation." Such enactive culture naturally extends beyond the transmission of information to the concrete instantiation of social institutions as repeated patterns of activity, structured relations between people, and constructed environments. Thus, Giddens (1976) described a dialectical process of "structuration" in which the actions of individual agents simultaneously create and are constrained by emergent social structures in a manner reminiscent of the diachronic organism–environment coupling and self-structuring information flows described above. Bourdieu (1972) similarly underlined the role of embodied practice in reproducing culture, using the term *habitus* to describe nondiscursive dispositions of thought and action that emerge from repeated participation in structured activity. Explicitly closing the loop from culture back to mind and brain, Roepstorff et al. (2010) discussed the ways in which such patterned practices might help structure the generative world models envisioned by the predictive brain framework and contribute to the interindividual alignment that makes communication and collaboration possible (Hasson & Frith, 2016; Pickering & Garrod, 2013).

The implications of all this for the study of human evolution are most clearly seen in the treatment of technology. As the name implies, early Paleolithic evidence of behavior is dominated by stone tools, and understanding these "technological" artifacts is critical to the reconstruction of human evolution. For the most part, Paleolithic archeologists have tended to view these tools as narrowly utilitarian and ecological, as an extrasomatic means of adaptation. This is consistent with an informational conception of culture in which technology is identified as that restricted domain of knowledge related to utilitarian interactions with the environment (e.g., obtaining food and shelter). This circumscription emphasizes continuity with the tool-use traditions of animals, and implies that Paleolithic technological adaptations can be studied without reference to such problematic topics as the emergence of mind, meaning, and human-like (i.e., symbolic) culture. It stands in stark contrast to the treatment of putative Paleolithic "art," which is identified by its apparently nonutilitarian nature and is seen as inherently social and meaningful, with its appearance heralding the emergence of fully modern cognition in the form of abstract symbol manipulation (e.g., Henshilwood & D'Errico, 2011). A more extended and enactive concept of culture, however, questions this distinction between art and technology (Heidegger, 1954/1977; Ingold, 2001) by emphasizing the material and social constitution of technological systems (Hodder, 2012).

From this perspective, "technology" can be a hazardous concept because its common usage tends to cement a distinction between (high-status) concept and (menial) execution that is peculiar to industrial systems, while simultaneously obscuring the complex web of materials, social and economic relations, institutions, and regulations that constitute the apparently unitary "thing" we call technology (Marx, 1997). This is seen, for example, in the abstract quantification of technological complexity in terms of number of discrete procedural operations (Perreault et al., 2013) or physical components (Oswalt, 1976) involved in tool production, without considering the embodied skills required for actual production and use (Ingold, 1997) and the necessary social conditions for their acquisition. Although technological learning is commonly called social "transmission," this is misleading if it is taken to imply passive reception of information in the form of rules or recipes for action. For real technological proficiency, what is actually learned is a flexible skill rather than an invariant formula. Such learning requires an extended interaction between social inputs and motivated individual practice (Stout, 2013; Stout & Hecht, 2017) better described as social *reproduction* (cf. "guided rediscovery"; Ingold, 1998) rather than transmission (Nonaka et al., 2010).

This dialectic process, exemplified by coaching or apprenticeship, has recently been described by Whiten (2015) as a *helical curriculum*. In such a curriculum, the physical and social environments sustained by the patterned technological practices of other individuals are critical, including incidental availability of materials, situations, and behavioral models for practice (Fragaszy, Biro, et al., 2013; Fragaszy et al., 2017), motivation and structure provided by social norms, values, and identity (Boyette & Hewlett, 2017; Horner et al., 2010; Stout, 2002), active intervention in the form of affective feedback, attention direction, and practice opportunity scaffolding (Hewlett & Roulette, 2016; Musgrave et al., 2016), and intentional teaching through demonstration and instruction (Figure 2.1). These complexities are increasingly recognized in more diverse and inclusive conceptions of teaching and its evolutionary origins (e.g., Burdett et al., 2018; Gärdenfors & Högberg, 2017; Kline, 2015), offering the possibility for a more gradual and detailed account of the emergence of key teaching-related traits such as theory of mind and language.

The complexity of interactions and relationships involved in this view of culture and technology may appear daunting, but it also offers new and exciting prospects for insight into aspects of human evolution long considered inaccessible to empirical inquiry (e.g., Lewontin, 1998). As noted above, the real promise of "extended" conceptions of mind and culture lies in the fact that they are simultaneously grounded in the physical world and capable of seamlessly integrating dynamic interactions across multiple levels of spatio-temporal organization. Thus, neural activity drives behaviors that evoke further neural activity which, over time, will alter the patterns of functional and anatomical brain

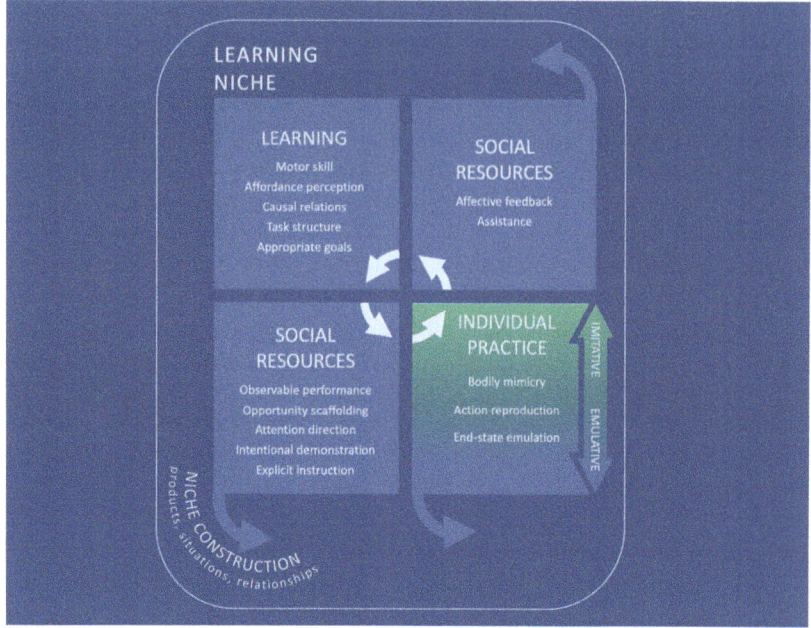

Figure 2.1 A learning cycle in the helical curriculum. Diverse social resources situated in constructed learning contexts support and structure individual practice, which can range from trial-and-error reverse-engineering of products, to the reproduction of actions at various levels of abstraction from overall "program-level" organization (Byrne, 2016), to detailed mimicry of body movement.
Figure adapted from "Evolutionary Neuroscience of Cumulative Culture," by D. Stout and E. E. Hecht, 2017, *Proceedings of the National Academy of Sciences of the United States of America*, 114(30), p. 7863 (https://doi.org/ 10.1073/pnas.1620738114)

connectivity that help to shape behavior (Byrge et al., 2014). This constructive process unfolds over developmental time in a context of patterned practices and structured environments that shapes individual behavior (Flynn et al., 2013) and is itself reproduced on historical time-scales by the accumulated action of individuals. At an even larger scale, these unfolding developmental, social, and environmental dynamics help to shape both the variation and the selective pressures that drive evolutionary change (Laland et al., 2015) to the biological systems that, in turn, constrain development and behavior.

Evolution

Darwin famously lacked a mechanism of inheritance for his theory of evolution by natural selection. Although from a modern perspective this might seem like a relatively minor concern soon to be rectified by the march of scientific progress, in the early twentieth century, natural selection was a theory in crisis. As reviewed by Pigliucci (2009), this crisis was precipitated by the apparent impossibility of reconciling the discrete inheritance of Mendelian characters with natural selection's requirements for continuous variation and gradual change. The solution to this problem ultimately came from the development of population-statistical genetics, which showed how combinations of discrete genes could produce continuous phenotypic variation. This key insight provided the foundation for a gene-centered modern synthesis (MS) of evolutionary biology, which defined evolution in terms of changing gene frequencies and recognized natural selection on these genes as the sole source of adaptation.

By the 1930s and 1940s the MS had firmly established evolutionary biology as a mathematical and statistical enterprise dealing in abstract genetic units. By the time the physical structure and replication mechanisms of DNA were established in the 1950s, the influence of computer science and information theory made a computational interpretation of the genetic "code" essentially inevitable. As Maynard Smith (2000, p. 183) succinctly put it: "The analogy between the genetic code and human-designed codes such as Morse code or the ASCII code is too close to require justification." It thus seemed quite natural and unproblematic for molecular biologists to discuss DNA using informational terms such as transcription, translation, and editing and for evolutionary biologists to think of the encoding and transmission of genetic programs. This computational metaphor became so fundamental that Mayr (1961, p. 1504) used it to define goal-oriented behavior (teleonomy) in biology as "systems acting on the basis of a program" and D'Andrade (1982) took it for granted that DNA was the paradigm example of a symbolic "information-holding system" to be contrasted with culture. The full scope of this conception is conveyed by the conclusion to a review published in *Nature* ("The Major Evolutionary Transitions") by Szathmáry and Smith (1995, p. 231):

A central idea in contemporary biology is that of information. Developmental biology can be seen as the study of how information in the genome is translated into adult structure, and evolutionary biology of how the information came to be there in the first place. Our excuse for writing an article concerning topics as diverse as the origins of genes, of cells, and of language is that all are concerned with the storage and transmission of information.

Not only does DNA provide a program for building an organism, but the very process of evolution by natural selection that generates these programs is itself an algorithm for fitting genomes to environments.

Combined with the so-called central dogma of molecular biology (Crick, 1970) that information travels only from the genes to the body, and never the reverse, this leads to the "selfish gene" concept so influentially advanced (and extended to culture as the selfish meme) by Dawkins (1976). Thus, actual organisms are reduced to the status of vehicles for replicating genes through which the algorithmic process of selection produces adaptation. However, this somewhat extreme view has drawn extensive criticism. Particularly prominent was Ernst Mayr (e.g., Mayr, 1997), who argued that selection acts on whole organisms and only indirectly affects genes because: (1) the fitness value of individual genes is contingent on interactions with the rest of the genome; and (2) there is a stochastic relationship (developmental "reaction norm") between genotype and phenotype that is contingent on environmental inputs. This amounts to a situation in which many different gene combinations can produce the same phenotypic result, whereas the same genes will produce different results in different (genomic, organismal, environmental) contexts (Edelman & Gally, 2001). Consequently, it must be recognized that what is evolving is not symbolic information encoded in nucleotide sequences, but rather the emergent properties of developing systems – what Mayr (1994) called a "somatic program."

Others have taken these critiques further, calling for an extended evolutionary synthesis (EES) to augment the MS (Laland et al., 2015). In a move that will seem familiar from the preceding discussions of "mind" and "culture," advocates of an EES seek to more firmly ground evolutionary theory in the concrete details of developing and behaving organism–environment systems. In much the same way we saw this move blur mental/physical and culture/behavior dualities in psychology and anthropology, the EES questions the established (Mayr, 1961) dichotomy between proximate (immediate mechanisms, i.e., "how") and ultimate (evolutionary history, i.e., "why") causes in biology (Laland et al., 2013). This critique can be summarized around two unifying conceptual themes: *constructive development* and *reciprocal causation* (Laland et al., 2015). Constructive development sees development, not as the execution of a genetic (or even somatic) program, but as an adaptive process in its own right. Thus, "the developmental system responds flexibly to internal and external inputs" so that "organisms are not built from genetic 'instructions' alone, but rather self-assemble using a broad variety of interdependent resources" (p. 6). Reciprocal causation is aptly named, and simply refers to feedback relations in which two processes exert causal influences on each other. Reciprocal causation is actually a feature of constructive development, but also includes causal loops with the environment as in the case of the *niche construction* that occurs when the activities of organisms modify the selective environment of subsequent generations. Together, these concepts effectively de-center the MS emphasis on genes as the sole (proximate) cause of phenotypes and (ultimate) medium of evolutionary change. In so doing, they open the door to considering multiple nongenetic forms of inheritance, ranging from epigenetic and parental effects to physical and cultural environments (Danchin et al., 2011).

For current purposes, an EES perspective is most usefully exemplified by the case of brain evolution. In fact, the brain provides a particularly stark illustration of the difficulties confronting a gene-centered MS account of evolution by random mutation and natural selection (Deacon, 1997). How could random changes to such a complex, integrated system be anything other than catastrophic, let alone produce fitness benefits? The EES answer is that brain development is itself an evolutionary process of remarkable flexibility and adaptability (Buckner & Krienen, 2013; Edelman, 1987; Rakic, 2009). Briefly, multiple rounds of cell division in embryonic proliferative zones produce an overabundance of neurons that must then migrate along a transient system of radial glial cells to form the various regions of the developing cortical sheet. This complex process of proliferation, migration, differentiation, and nerve tract formation is regulated by the local environment of cells, which includes chemical gradients of signaling molecules produced by local patterning centers, as well as chemical and mechanical interactions between neighboring cells. The result is an overproliferation of neurons with highly promiscuous connections between them, which are then carved into functional systems through a process of developmental selection that eliminates elements that have failed to become part of viable, active networks. This adaptive process can generate functional systems in the face of quite significant perturbations as seen, for example, when the disused occipital "visual" cortex of congenitally blind individuals becomes co-opted for high-level linguistic functions previously thought to be the exclusive province of specially evolved language regions (Bedny et al., 2011). Evolutionarily, such constructive development may be essential to the evolvability of complex brains through mechanisms such as the expansion or duplication of cortical areas or peripheral changes in body proportions and sense organs, without requiring the simultaneous appearance of an intricate array of complementary mutations across numerous interacting structures (Deacon, 1997). It is also expected to provide an especially fertile substrate for the behavior-led evolution (West-Eberhard, 2005) of new cognitive capacities, as illustrated experimentally by plastic brain responses to extensive tool-use training in macaques (Iriki & Sakura, 2008).

As an example of reciprocal causation, these developmental processes both respond to and help shape evolutionary change. Conserved developmental sequences of neuron proliferation make it likely that any selection on brain size will tend to produce a disproportionate increase in the size of the cerebral cortex (Yopak et al., 2010). The *tethering hypothesis* of Buckner and Krienen (2013) proposes that the disproportionate expansion of the cortical mantle during evolutionary brain enlargement will increasingly lead to gaps between the chemical signaling gradients that pattern cortical differentiation.

Developmental selection in these gaps would then foster the emergence of "non-canonical" association networks primarily interconnected with each other rather than with more developmentally constrained peripheral sensorimotor systems. Thus, the emergence of many distinctive features of human cognition and behavior rooted in increasingly rich and flexible internal simulation and sensitivity to cultural and environmental influences may have been facilitated by reciprocal evolutionary–developmental causation.

In keeping with this, human association cortices are also relatively late developing (Hill et al., 2010; Power et al., 2010) and variable in connectivity across individuals (Mueller et al., 2013). Indeed, comparative evidence indicates human-specific changes in the rate and timing of synaptogenesis, synapse elimination, and cortical myelination resulting in increased plasticity into adulthood (Preuss, 2012; Somel et al., 2013). That nonspecific selection for increased brain size in the human lineage might have indirectly driven increased plasticity is suggested by evidence of low heritability for cortical morphology (sulcal dimensions) vs. overall brain size in humans, a pattern that contrasts with high heritability of both in chimpanzees (Gómez-Robles et al., 2015). In any case, human association cortex appears particularly sensitive to environmental and behavioral influences, providing a potent evolutionary feedback mechanism between organism and environment.

Such phenotypic flexibility is useful but may come at a cost (e.g., investments in learning or temporary phenotype–environment mismatches). Where possible, natural selection is expected to reduce costs by "canalizing" plastic responses to recurring environmental situations as automatic parts of normal development (Murren et al., 2015). The tethering hypothesis suggests that such innate specializations are most likely to be found in relatively heritable sensorimotor systems and with respect to behaviors/stimuli that have been relatively invariant over long periods of time. Because humans' expanded association areas remain relatively plastic (Mueller et al., 2013) and are both late developing (Power et al., 2010) and phylogenetically recent (Mantini et al., 2013), their derived cognitive features are less likely to be directly shaped by natural selection (*phylogenetically constructed*) and more likely to result from developmental side effects (*developmental construction*) and modifications to the structure of inputs they receive from more peripheral systems (*phylogenetic* and/or *developmental inflection*; Heyes, 2003). In theory, such modifications could arise through environmental as well as genetic inheritance, including persistent changes to the physical and social context of development brought about through niche construction (Flynn et al., 2013; Fragaszy et al., 2013). For example, there is widespread agreement that the human brain lacks specific genetic adaptations for literacy, and yet learning to read reliably produces functional specialization for script perception in a particular region of the left ventral occipitotemporal cortex known as the visual word form area (Dehaene et al., 2015).

In contrast to the MS, an EES thus provides an excellent framework for the integration of "problematic" topics like mind and culture into evolutionary theory without reducing either to a form of disembodied information processing. Indeed, there is a striking intellectual convergence between concepts such as grounded and distributed cognition, cultural structuration and patterned practice, and the constructive development and reciprocal causation of the EES. As noted above, this emerging, cross-disciplinary perspective has great promise for the investigation of human cognitive evolution. What it calls for is a particularistic and mechanistic approach to the comparative, archeological, paleontological, and paleo-environmental evidence of human evolution that avoids "blackboxing" proximate cognitive, cultural, and developmental mechanisms.

The Human Technological Niche

It is useful to begin, as did Darwin (1871, p. 136), with the observation that humans are a highly successful species. Even without agriculture, it has been estimated that *Homo sapiens* would have attained a global population of more than 70 million and a total biomass greater than any other large vertebrate (Hill et al., 2009). Such demographic potential seems paradoxical in a large-brained primate known for its slow and costly development. A growing consensus finds the solution to this paradox in a human strategy of alloparenting (Hrdy, 2009; Kramer, 2010) or "biocultural reproduction" (Bogin et al., 2014), in which individuals other than the parents donate resources to help support offspring. This allows human mothers to produce large-brained children (Isler & van Schaik, 2012) with the shortest interbirth interval of any ape and a total fertility rate three times that of chimpanzees (Kramer, 2010), all funded by the surplus production of helpers. How is it that Pleistocene human foragers, in contrast to other apes, were able to reliably produce the surpluses that fueled their demographic success?

Embodied capital theory (Kaplan et al., 2000, 2010) proposes that humans have evolved a tightly integrated strategy in which a focus on high-value, difficult-to-acquire food resources provides the surpluses needed to fund growth, survival, and reproduction and is, in turn, enabled by the increased longevity and brain size that allow learning of the requisite foraging skills. Cognitive and affective adaptations for prosociality (Hill et al., 2009), which are necessary for biocultural reproduction, also provide a venue for social learning and teaching. Integrating these various theoretical strands leads to a picture of a distinctly human way of life reliant on cognitive, affective, and life-history adaptations supporting the intergenerational reproduction and accumulation of foraging skills (Shennan & Steele, 1999), including the production and use of tools. In our own work (Stout & Hecht, 2017; Stout & Khreisheh, 2015), we have previously referred to this integration of embodied capital and cultural evolutionary theory as describing a specifically *technological* (as opposed to broadly "cultural"; Boyd et al., 2011) niche in order to highlight the critical interaction of embodied skill, material production, and social organization.

Such interactions are also increasingly recognized by comparative studies of brain evolution, which employ variation across extant species to reconstruct the likely characteristics of shared ancestors and identify recurring evolutionary cause–effect relationships. The most comprehensive account currently available is that of van Schaik et al., which effectively grounds the *technological niche* concept by integrating economic and cultural elements under the headings of "expensive" (Isler & van Schaik, 2014) and "cultural" (van Schaik et al., 2012) brain hypotheses. The underlying assumption is that, all else being equal, bigger brains are generally advantageous. The expensive brain framework, thus, seeks to explain interspecific variation in brain size in terms of *net* fitness effects that also take energetic and life history constraints into account. Larger brains can only evolve if mortality is low enough to reward investments in such embodied capital and a sufficient energy budget can be found through increased intake and/or reallocation. Critically, these relationships are inherently bidirectional, as enlarging the brain may also lower mortality (e.g., through predation avoidance) and increase energy intake (foraging productivity). The "cultural brain" (van Schaik & Burkart, 2011; van Schaik et al., 2012) element then adds the possibility of gene–culture coevolution. Modeling indicates that, if baseline conditions of frequency, learning ability, and skill complexity are met, social learning can increase the mean fitness of a population and lead to cumulative cultural evolution (Henrich & McElreath, 2003). This generates yet another potential feedback relationship, in which increasingly complex, socially learned skills both fund and require greater investment in neural tissue, as well as requiring/promoting social tolerance, slower life histories, and extensive resource transfers.

The strength of these comparative and modeling approaches is that they generalize possible evolutionary relationships, interactions, and outcomes, allowing for the identification of recurring patterns and causal relations (cf. evolutionary "laws"; Cartmill, 2002). However, such methods cannot reveal the actual contingencies of timing and context that defined the particular path of human evolution (Stout et al., 2019). Reconstructing the origins of human cumulative culture will require archeological and paleontological evidence of what actually occurred in human evolution, combined with the ethnographic, ethological, and experimental analogies needed to interpret this evidence (Stout & Hecht, 2017).

An Evolutionary Neuroscience of Technology

The archeological record of stone toolmaking encompasses an evolutionary continuum from early Paleolithic skills at or just beyond the limits of modern apes (Toth & Schick, 2009) to the virtuoso craftsmanship of later prehistory (Apel & Knutsson, 2006). The study of knapping skill acquisition and social reproduction is thus a promising avenue for investigating the evolution of the human technological niche. To be clear, knapping is but one of many technological skills that might be studied. Others include fire (Twomey, 2013), hunting and butchery (Stiner et al., 2009), hafting (Wadley et al., 2009), toolmaking in non-lithic materials (d'Errico et al., 2003), and signaling technologies such as pigments and personal adornment (Kuhn, 2014). However, knapping is a skill for which we have a relatively good archeological record and which may reasonably be hoped to be representative of broader trends. Before this evidence can be used to develop or test evolutionary scenarios, however, it must be interpreted. The stones do not speak for themselves.

The Experimental Method

Experimental archeology seeks to recreate past processes in order to test hypotheses about their causal relations to material remains. For example, researchers might test the influence of furnace temperature on the chemical composition of slag left behind by ore smelting or the effect of angle and force of percussion on stone fracture during knapping. This experimental approach, complemented by ethnographic and ecological observations, has been a critical component of archeological inference for many decades. Experimental studies of skill and cognition are a straightforward extension of this endeavor using new methods to collect previously unavailable behavioral data regarding, for example, bodily movements (Nonaka et al., 2010) and neurophysiological responses (Stout et al., 2015). As with any attempt to use modern observations to reason about the past, this involves analogical arguments that must be justified (Wylie, 1985). No experiment will ever be a perfect "replication" of the past; instead, the aim is to model particular variables relevant to the question at hand. The strength of the experimental model can then be tested by using it to make predictions about features that should be present in actual archeological materials.

Paleolithic experimental archeology faces the added challenge of modeling the behavior of extinct hominin species with modern humans (and other primate subjects; Toth & Schick, 2009). Limited reflection might make this appear as a fatal difficulty for experimental "neuroarcheology": how can modern brains and cognition inform us about their prehistoric precursors? However, this is simply another example of the need to develop appropriate analogical arguments. Consider, for comparison, experimental studies of toolmaking and hand morphology (Marzke, 2013). Modern human experiments are used to identify morphological features supporting modern human tool making. These are compared with the morphology of extant primates to identify derived elements of the human pattern, the emergence of which can then be traced in the fossil record and interpreted in terms of functional capacities for toolmaking. A similar logic applies to experimental neuroarcheology. Imaging studies (Figure 2.2B) have shown that stone toolmaking relies on an evolutionarily ancient frontoparietal action system that also supports tool use in monkeys (e.g., Obayashi et al., 2001). It may be concluded that this system was shared with Pleistocene hominins and was a likely target of selection acting on toolmaking ability. In fact, comparative evidence (Figure 2.2A) reveals derived human modifications to this system that are directly relevant to distinctive human tool-use abilities (Hecht, Gutman, et al. 2013; Hecht et al., 2015; Orban & Caruana, 2014), and parallel plastic changes in neuroanatomy induced by stone toolmaking training in modern human subjects. These findings have broader implications for understanding the evolution of human culture, mind, and brain. As with any experimental archeology, neuroarcheological experiments should not be thought of as straightforward "replications" of the past, but rather as contributing to an inferential framework linking variation in brain systems, cognitive processes, and archeologically observable behaviors (Stout et al., 2015).

Learning to Knap Stone

Knapping is a "reductive" technology involving the sequential detachment of *flakes* from a stone *core* using precise ballistic strikes with a hand-held *hammer* (typically stone, bone, or antler) to initiate controlled and predictable fracture. This means that small errors in strike execution can have catastrophic, un-reversible effects. Experiments by Bril et al. have shown that fracture prediction and control is a demanding perceptual-motor skill reliably expressed only in expert knappers (Nonaka et al., 2010; Roux et al., 1995). Building on this work, Stout et al. (Hecht et al., 2014; Stout et al., 2015; Stout & Khreisheh, 2015) found that even twenty-two months ($\bar{x} = 167$ hours) of knapping training produced relatively little evidence of perceptual-motor improvement, in contrast to clear gains in conceptual understanding.

The key bottleneck in learning to knap is thus the extended practice required to achieve perceptual-motor competence. This requires mastery of relationships – for example, between the force and location of the strike and the morphology, positioning, and support of the core (Faisal et al., 2010; Magnani et al., 2014; Nonaka et al., 2010) – that are not perceptually available to naïve observers. Observing an expert can help point learners in the right direction,

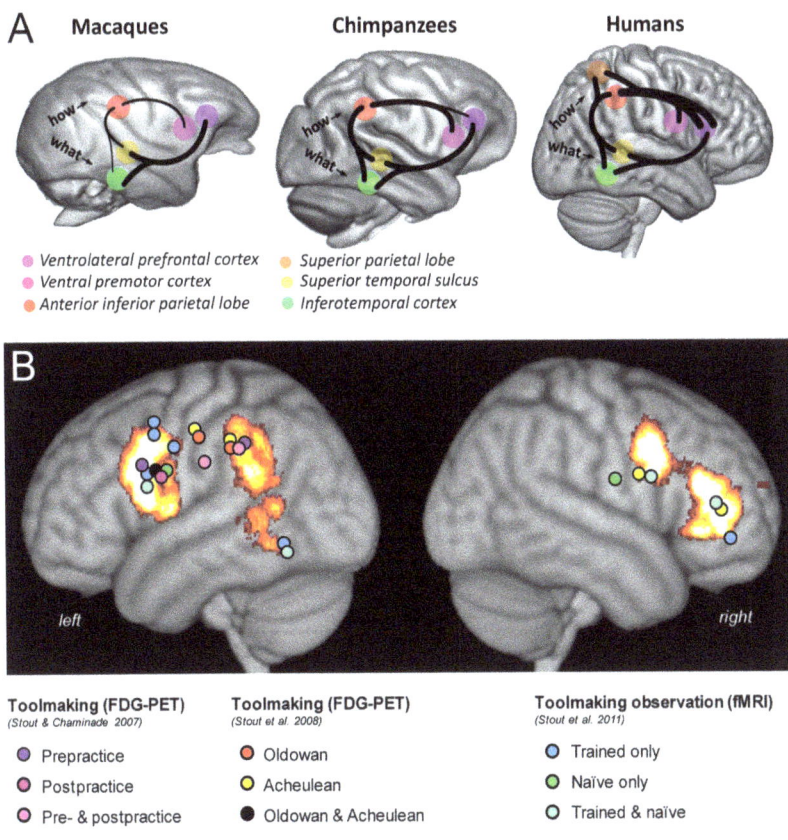

Figure 2.2 Species differences in action processing circuitry (A) compared with the results of neuroimaging studies of structural and functional responses to stone tool-making (B). Circles in (B) indicate functional activations from various paradigms; clusters indicate regions of white matter change associated with tool-making training.
(A) Adapted from "Evolutionary Neuroscience of Cumulative Culture," by D. Stout and E. E. Hecht, 2017, *Proceedings of the National Academy of Sciences of the United States of America*, *114*(30), p. 7865 (https://doi.org/10.1073/pnas.1620738114). (B) Adapted by permission from Springer Nature Customer Service Centre GmbH: Springer Nature, *Brain Structure and Function*, "Acquisition of Paleolithic Toolmaking Abilities Involves Structural Remodeling to Inferior Frontoparietal Regions," E. E. Hecht et al. (https://doi.org/10.1007/s00429-014-0789-6). Copyright 2014

but here the challenge is to translate visual and auditory information of another's actions to appropriate motor commands for one's own body.

Skilled actions, such as the ballistic strikes involved in stone toolmaking, often unfold too quickly to be guided by online sensory feedback and error correction. This limitation can be overcome through the use of internal models that predict movements and outcomes in advance (Wolpert et al., 2003), a simulation process supported by sensorimotor and attentional systems of a dorsal, "how" (Figure 2.2A) stream of perception for action (Milner & Goodale 1995). This simulation likely also forms the basis for understanding and copying the observed actions of others through a process of matching, often referred to as "motor resonance" (Cook et al., 2014). Whether stimulated by social observation or individual exploration, however, novel behaviors must initially be approximated using existing internal models of familiar action elements. When motor precision is not needed (e.g., solving an experimental puzzle box using familiar lift, slide, and turn manipulations) such learning can be quite quick, and is more reliant on a cognitive ability to recognize and reproduce the programmatic structure of goal-oriented action sequences (Byrne, 2016), which is thought to be supported by a *frontoparietal control network* associated with "fluid" or general intelligence (Duncan, 2010). However, for skills like stone knapping, subtle details of execution do matter. Learners must thus embark on a lengthy process of behavioral exploration to discover relevant task constraints and develop corresponding internal models through a self-conscious process of deliberate practice (cf. Ericsson et al., 1993). In the context of the helical curriculum, such learning is greatly facilitated by social and environmental resources, ranging from the availability and spatial association of relevant materials, to observable behavior, and explicit instruction, that channel exploration in productive directions.

Evolving Brains

A predictive account of skilled action control using internal models strongly suggests that the cognitive mechanisms and neural systems supporting social and asocial learning overlap substantially (Cook et al., 2014). Both depend on simulation in sensorimotor systems of the dorsal stream regulated by the more general hierarchically structured sequencing capacities of the frontoparietal control network. This fits well with the close integration of individual and social learning processes in real-world skill acquisition as envisioned by the helical curriculum, and leads to the expectation that social and asocial learning capacities should tend to evolve together (van Schaik et al., 2012) with different patterns of expression across species being driven by behavioral and developmental contexts.

We have thus argued (Stout & Hecht, 2017) that a series of evolutionary changes (Figure 2.2A) to the primate dorsal stream that enabled integration of increasingly fine action details and complex goals during behavior observation and execution are critical to understanding the emergence of human culture and cognition. This includes both changes within the dorsal stream and its enhanced integration with a ventral, "what" stream involved in the recognition of objects, individuals, and body parts. For example, comparative fMRI studies with macaques and humans have identified portions of human intraparietal sulcus with novel sensitivity to 3D form-from-motion stimuli as well as a patch of human anterior supramarginal gyrus (aSMG) specifically responsive to observed tool use (Orban & Caruana, 2014). Both regions are likely implicated in a wide array of evolutionarily relevant object manipulation behaviors, and both are known to be recruited by stone toolmaking activities in modern humans (Stout & Chaminade, 2007; Stout et al., 2011). Anterior SMG, in particular, is believed to support a confluence of object-information from the ventral stream with dorsal stream kinematics in order to manage the novel action possibilities afforded by hand-held tools (Orban & Caruana, 2014).

Enhanced aSMG connectivity between dorsal and ventral steams is just one aspect of a broader pattern of changes in action circuitry over ape and human evolution (Hecht, Gutman, et al., 2013). From macaques, to chimpanzees and then humans, there is a clear trend toward dorsal stream enhancement that may underlie the progressive elaboration of action parsing capacities across the three species (Hecht, Gutman, et al., 2013; Hecht, Murphy, et al., 2013). In humans but not chimpanzees or macaques, the core action circuitry includes a prominent projection to the superior parietal lobule, a region associated with awareness of one's body in space (Hecht, Gutman, et al., 2013). Furthermore, dorsal stream connections (via the third branch of the superior longitudinal fasciculus (SLFIII)) from the inferior parietal cortex extends into more anterior regions of ventral prefrontal cortex in humans, particularly in the right hemisphere (Hecht et al., 2015). Right ventral prefrontal cortex is an element of the frontoparietal control network thought to support the assembly of complex, multi-step action plans. The observed extension of human SLFIII thus would provide an anatomical substrate for the integration of kinematic details into complex action goals and sequences as required for skill learning in a helical curriculum.

Such learning in humans requires a degree of bodily awareness sufficient to match variations in kinematic detail with desired outcomes during deliberate practice. A measure of such awareness that has been applied to other animals is the Mirror Self-Recognition (MSR) Test (Anderson & Gallup, 2015). Unlike enculturated humans, mirror-naïve animals must discover *de novo* that the visual perception of their reflection corresponds to the sensorimotor representations of their own movements. Intriguingly, chimpanzee MSR performance is predicted by individual variation in the degree of right-lateralization of SLFIII projections into the ventral prefrontal cortex. In other words, chimpanzees with more human-like SLFIII connectivity show more human-like MSR behavior (Hecht et al., 2017). This is especially provocative because it has been proposed that such attention to one's own movements plays a key role in the developmental construction of *mentalizing*, or theory of mind, from motor resonance (Heyes & Frith, 2014), thus suggesting further links between dorsal stream evolution, technological reproduction, and the emergence of human culture and mind.

Constructing Minds

Although mentalizing is commonly thought of as a human specialization depending on phylogenetically constructed neurocognitive mechanisms, Heyes and Frith (2014) have recently argued that it is largely a product of developmental inflection and cultural evolution. On this account, low-level, or "implicit," mentalizing capacities emerge directly from motor resonance properties of the action control system discussed above. Specifically, motor resonance provides the input needed to identify recurring relations between actions, outcomes, and internal states and, thus, to predict behavior and infer intent. Insofar as such abilities have been seen as critical to the joint attention and intentional teaching characteristic of human cultural reproduction (Tomasello, 1999) and skill learning in a helical curriculum (Stout & Hecht, 2017), this implies extensive potential for reciprocal causation between changing dorsal stream structure and function, increasingly complex technologies, novel forms of social organization, and enhanced mechanisms for cultural learning in an evolving human technological niche.

In keeping grounded and enactive approaches to mind and culture, this account highlights the importance of embodied skills for action in the world. Dorsal stream action systems constitute a critical substrate for the evolutionary–developmental cascade that constructs the action parsing and mentalizing capacities needed for cumulative culture. These systems are themselves sensitive to inflected input from more peripheral somatic or sensorimotor adaptations and constructed niches that shape early object manipulation and visual experiences (Byrge et al., 2014). Object manipulation and modification contribute to the construction of learning niches populated by the residues of past action (Fragaszy et al., 2013), and provide a persistent external medium scaffolding production of the more complex and protracted action goals and sequences (Stout, 2013) that both require and reward cultural learning through a helical curriculum. Commitment to an increasingly learning-intensive technological niche requires social affiliative mechanisms that support extended interaction and motivate investment by teachers. These mechanisms in turn derive from dorsal stream motor resonance and control processes enabling the interactive behavioral alignment crucial to human social learning, communication, cooperation, and affiliative bonding (Feldman, 2016; Hasson & Frith, 2016).

While behavioral alignment promotes social affiliation across many species (Feldman, 2016), human affiliation routinely extends to include "ultrasocial" cooperation and sharing enabled by the use of language to create social norms and identities, including affinal and fictive kinship ties (Bogin et al., 2014; Hill et al., 2009). It has similarly been proposed that linguistic instruction is required for the acquisition of explicit mentalizing concepts such as false belief, knowledge vs. ignorance, and difference of opinion (Heyes & Frith, 2014), and that human social learning strategies are shaped by explicit metacognitive rules (Heyes, 2016) heavily reliant on linguistic representation.

Of course, it is nothing new to note the importance of language to human cognitive evolution, and a substantial body of research has linked language evolution to exaptation of the same action control systems discussed here (e.g., Arbib, 2012) often with an emphasis on gesture production and action "syntax" in the dorsal stream (Stout & Chaminade, 2012). Less emphasized has been the critical role that the increasingly intricate action production (whether manual, vocal, or artifact-mediated) supported by this system might play in grounding semantic meaning (Clark, 2006). This question is particularly salient given the recent "lexical turn" in linguistics (Christiansen & Chater, 2016, p. 47) that views the combinatorial possibilities of words as lexically specified (and thus retrieved from memory) rather than defined by a separate set of generally applicable syntactic rules or operations. In fact, it has recently been argued that human words and concepts are so distinct from anything seen in other animals that there remains "scant evidence on which to ground an evolutionary account for words" (Berwick et al., 2013, p. 93).

This view initially seems inconsistent with the idea that human cognition in general (Barsalou, 2008), and linguistic meaning in particular (Pulvermüller & Fadiga, 2010), is grounded in perceptual-motor simulation. This might be taken to suggest that there is nothing "special" about the symbolic meaning of words. For example, it has been argued that perceptual abstraction (e.g., moving from elementary auditory features to recognition of conspecific calls) in the ventral stream of monkeys is evolutionarily/computationally continuous with the human capacity for "binding together perceptually based semantic representations into coherent concepts" and, thus, the ability to learn word meanings (Bornkessel-Schlesewsky et al., 2015). However, such an account fails to recognize that words are not in fact internal concepts – they are externalized tokens. Although it has been argued that perceptual symbol systems support internal type-token interpretations (e.g., this particular car I am seeing belongs to the class, CAR) for cognitive processing (Barsalou, 2003), this is clearly not the same as associating concepts with a particular perceptual-motor "object" (e.g., gesture, vocalization) that then acts as a token (e.g., the concept CAR with the word "car"). This may not seem like a big deal, insofar as it can be accomplished through simple repetition and associative learning. As Deacon (1997) has pointed out, however, the symbolic nature of words does not rest in such "indexical" associations between (perceptually abstracted) utterances and objects/events but rather on the relationships between words. Put another way, symbolic meaning is inherently combinatorial and generative and thus can only emerge when a sufficient number of tokens have accumulated in the system. For example, language users are clearly able to rapidly formulate generalizations about the combinatorial possibilities of words they have never heard before based on abstract lexical features such as grammatical class (noun, verb, etc.). Although opinions differ, the preponderance of evidence indicates that such roles are not fully reducible to semantic distinctions between, for example, actions and objects, but additionally depend on distributional cues from the actual occurrence of words in sentences (Vigliocco et al., 2011).

Thus, the actual combinatorial and generative potential of language appears at least in part to rely on actual externalization of concepts as physical (perceptual-motor) tokens and the incorporation of these tokens into a culturally evolving symbol-system shaped by the demands of efficient communication in a serially ordered medium. Whereas we might envision a fairly clear continuity of quantitative enhancements to ventral stream perceptual-abstraction and concept formation capacities across monkeys, apes, and humans, this critical external component to language evolution seems to have relied on more substantial shifts to the basic organization and/or computational capacities of the dorsal stream for the production and parsing of token strings.

The implications of all this for human cognition more generally remain to be fully specified (Clark, 2006), but there is an interesting analogy to be made with numerical cognition. Humans and other animals apparently have perceptually based systems for judging approximate numeracy, but it is only with the tokenization of numbers (i.e., one-to-one correspondence between a quantity and a physical token such as a word or a marking) that exact counting and mathematical reasoning become possible (Dehaene, 1997). As is the case with reading, portions of human cortex appear specialized for mathematical cognition despite the scant time that has passed to imagine genetic adaptations to this behavior, providing another example of constructive development in human brains (Dehaene & Cohen, 2007).

Conclusion

Comparative methods in psychology and biology are essential to identify recurring patterns and processes of evolutionary change, but are limited in their ability to resolve the particular contingencies that have shaped each unique species. A truly evolutionary approach to understanding distinctively human culture, mind, and brain must thus combine a comparative understanding of these broader evolutionary forces with the narrative details provided by the historical sciences of archeology and paleontology (Heyes, 2018; Stout, 2018). An extended evolutionary perspective on Paleolithic toolmaking as embodied practice can help us to appreciate the potential interaction of evolutionary and behavioral processes unfolding across multiple timescales, and to relate these dynamics to the concrete traces left in the archeological record. However, a great deal of empirical work remains to be done in order to realize this promise.

It is fair to say that we still have relatively little idea of how various genetic, developmental, and cultural processes actually did interact over the course of human brain evolution. For example, the extent to which any or all neural differences between species discussed in this chapter are classic "adaptations" in the sense of being canalized products of phylogenetic construction as opposed to developmental construction in a culturally evolved niche is largely unknown. Even in macaques, there is evidence that extensive tool-training can produce plastic alterations in dorsal stream connectivity (Hihara et al., 2006). Enlarged ape and human brains are expected to be more developmentally plastic and subject to inflection by somatic (e.g., bipedal locomotion, hand morphology; Kivell, 2015) and sensorimotor adaptations and/or developmental niche construction (Flynn et al., 2013). In fact, our own work with modern humans has shown that the acquisition of Paleolithic toolmaking skills elicits plastic remodeling of dorsal stream white matter connections, including SLFIII's projection into right prefrontal cortex, even in adults (Hecht et al., 2014). Functionally, the gray matter targeted by this projection is recruited by execution (Stout et al., 2008) and observation (Stout et al., 2011) of relatively complex toolmaking sequences of the kind that appeared with Late Acheulean handaxe technology after about 0.7 million years ago (Stout, 2011).

Such findings are suggestive of evolutionary relations, but remain far from demonstrating the existence or direction of causality. Moving forward will require progress on multiple fronts, including (1) continued fieldwork to refine the narrative details of human evolution history (Antón et al., 2014); (2) experimental archeology studies to aid the interpretation of this evidence (Eren et al., 2016; Stout & Khreisheh, 2015), including especially research on neurocognitive substrates (Stout & Hecht, 2017) and processes of cultural reproduction (Stout et al., 2019); and (3) comparative and developmental research to better understand the interaction of genetic and environmental contributions in the development of individual- and species-level phenotypic variation (Heyes, 2018). This is an ambitious project, but the promised reward is a more complete understanding of the evolutionary origins and current nature of human culture, mind, and brain.

REFERENCES

Allen, M., & Friston, K. J. (2016). From cognitivism to autopoiesis: Towards a computational framework for the embodied mind. *Synthese*, *195*(6), 1–24. https://doi.org/10.1007/s11229-016-1288-5

Anderson, J. R., & Gallup, G. G., Jr. (2015). Mirror self-recognition: A review and critique of attempts to promote and engineer self-recognition in primates. *Primates*, *56*(4), 317–26. https://doi.org/10.1007/s10329-015-0488-9

Antón, S. C., Potts, R., & Aiello, L. C. (2014). Evolution of early *Homo*: An integrated biological perspective. *Science*, *345*(6192), 1236828. https://doi.org/10.1126/science.1236828

Apel, J., & Knutsson, K. (2006). *Skilled production and social reproduction: Aspects of traditional stone-tool technologies: Proceedings of a symposium in Uppsala, Sweden, August 20–24, 2003*. Societas ologica Upsaliensis.

Arbib, M. A. (2012). *How the brain got language: The mirror system hypothesis*. Oxford University Press.

Barkow, J. H., Cosmides, L., & Tooby, J. (1992). *The adapted mind: Evolutionary psychology and the generation of culture*. Oxford University Press.

Barrett, L. F., & Simmons, W. K. (2015). Interoceptive predictions in the brain. *Nature Reviews Neuroscience*, *16*(7), 419–29. https://doi.org/10.1038/nrn3950

Barsalou, L. W. (1999). Perceptual symbol systems. *Behavioral and Brain Sciences*, *22*(4), 577–660. https://doi.org/10.1017/S0140525X99002149

Barsalou, L. W. (2003). Abstraction in perceptual symbol systems. *Philosophical Transactions of the Royal Society B: Biological Sciences*, *358*(1435), 1177–87. https://doi.org/10.1098/rstb.2003.1319

Barsalou, L. W. (2008). Grounded cognition. *Annual Review of Psychology*, *59*, 617–45. https://doi.org/10.1146/annurev.psych.59.103006.093639

Bedny, M., Pascual-Leone, A., Dodell-Feder, D., Fedorenko, E., & Saxe, R. (2011). Language processing in the occipital cortex of congenitally blind adults. *Proceedings of the National Academy of Sciences of the United States of America*, *108*(11), 4429–34. https://doi.org/10.1073/pnas.1014818108

Berwick, R. C., Friederici, A. D., Chomsky, N., & Bolhuis, J. J. (2013). Evolution, brain, and the nature of language. *Trends in Cognitive Sciences*, *17*(2), 89–98. https://doi.org/10.1016/j.tics.2012.12.002

Bogin, B., Bragg, J., & Kuzawa, C. (2014). Humans are not cooperative breeders but practice biocultural reproduction. *Annals of Human Biology*, *41*(4), 368–80. https://doi.org/10.3109/03014460.2014.923938

Bonner, J. T. (1980). *The evolution of culture in animals*. Princeton University Press.

Bornkessel-Schlesewsky, I., Schlesewsky, M., Small, S. L., & Rauschecker, J. P. (2015). Neurobiological roots of language in primate audition: Common computational properties. *Trends in Cognitive Sciences*, *19*(3), 142–50. https://doi.org/10.1016/j.tics.2014.12.008

Bourdieu, P. (1972). *Outline of a theory of practice*. Cambridge University Press.

Boyd, R., Richerson, P. J., & Henrich, J. (2011). The cultural niche: Why social learning is essential for human adaptation. *Proceedings of the National Academy of Sciences of the United States of America*, *108*(Supplement 2), 10918–25. https://doi.org/10.1073/pnas.1100290108

Boyette, A. H., & Hewlett, B. S. (2017). Autonomy, equality, and teaching among Aka foragers and Ngandu farmers of the Congo Basin. *Human Nature*, *28*(3), 289–322. https://doi.org/10.1007/s12110–017-9294-y

Buckner, R. L., & Krienen, F. M. (2013). The evolution of distributed association networks in the human brain. *Trends in Cognitive Sciences*, *17*(12), 648–65. https://doi.org/10.1016/j.tics.2013.09.017

Burdett, E. R. R., Dean, L. G., & Ronfard, S. (2018). A diverse and flexible teaching toolkit facilitates the human capacity for cumulative culture. *Review of Philosophy and Psychology*, 807–18. https://doi.org/10.1007/s13164–017-0345-4

Byrge, L., Sporns, O., & Smith, L. B. (2014). Developmental process emerges from extended brain-body-behavior networks. *Trends in Cognitive Sciences*, *18*(8), 395–403. https://doi.org/10.1016/j.tics.2014.04.010

Byrne, R. W. (2016). *Evolving insight: How it is we can think about why things happen*. Oxford University Press.

Cartmill, M. (2002). Paleoanthropology: Science or mythological charter? *Journal of Anthropological Research*, *58*(2), 183–201. https://doi.org/10.1086/jar.58.2.3631035

Cavalli-Sforza, L. L., & Feldman, M. W. (1981). *Cultural transmission and evolution: A quantitative approach*. Princeton University Press.

Chomsky, N. (1957). *Syntactic structures*. Mouton.

Christiansen, M. H., & Chater, N. (2016). *Creating language: Integrating evolution, acquisition, and processing*. MIT Press.

Clark, A. (1997). *Being there: Putting brain, body, and world together again*. MIT Press.

Clark, A. (2006). Language, embodiment, and the cognitive niche. *Trends in Cognitive Sciences*, *10*(8), 370–4. https://doi.org/10.1016/j.tics.2006.06.012

Clark, A. (2013). Whatever next? Predictive brains, situated agents, and the future of cognitive science. *Behavioral and Brain Sciences*, *36*(3), 181–204. https://doi.org/10.1017/S0140525X12000477

Cole, M. (1996). *Cultural psychology: A once and future discipline*. Belknap Press.

Cook, R., Bird, G., Catmur, C., Press, C., & Heyes, C. (2014). Mirror neurons: From origin to function. *Behavioral and Brain Sciences*, *37*(2), 177–92. https://doi.org/10.1017/S0140525X13000903

Crick, F. (1970). Central dogma of molecular biology. *Nature*, *227*(5258), 561–3. https://doi.org/10.1038/227561a0

Crowther-Heyck, H. (1999). George A. Miller, language, and the computer metaphor and mind. *History of Psychology*, *2*(1), 37–64. https://doi.org/10.1037/1093-4510.2.1.37

D'Andrade, R. G. (1982). Cultural meaning systems. In R. M. Adams, N. J. Smelser, & D. J. Treiman (Eds.), *Behavioral and social science research: A national resource. Part II* (pp. 197–236). National Academy Press.

D'Errico, F., Henshilwood, C., Lawson, G., Vanhaeren, M., Tillier, A.-M., Soressi, M., Bresson, F., Maureille, B., Nowell, A., Lakarra, J., Backwell, L., & Julien, M. (2003). Archaeological evidence for the emergence of language, symbolism, and music: An alternative multidisciplinary perspective. *Journal of World Prehistory*, *17*(1), 1–70. https://doi.org/10.1023/A:1023980201043

Danchin, É., Charmantier, A., Champagne, F. A., Mesoudi, A., Pujol, B., & Blanchet, S. (2011). Beyond DNA: Integrating inclusive inheritance into an extended theory of evolution. *Nature Reviews Genetics*, *12*(7), 475–86. https://doi.org/10.1038/nrg3028

Darwin, C. (1871). *The descent of man, and selection in relation to sex*. John Murray.

David, N., & Kramer, C. (2001). *Ethnoarchaeology in action*. Cambridge University Press.

Dawkins, R. (1976). *The selfish gene*. Oxford University Press.

Deacon, T. W. (1997). *The symbolic species: The co-evolution of language and the brain*. W.W. Norton.

Dehaene, S. (1997). *The number sense: How the mind creates mathematics*. Oxford University Press.

Dehaene, S., & Cohen, L. (2007). Cultural recycling of cortical maps. *Neuron*, *56*(2), 384–98. https://doi.org/10.1016/j.neuron.2007.10.004

Dehaene, S., Cohen, L., Morais, J., & Kolinsky, R. (2015). Illiterate to literate: Behavioural and cerebral changes induced by reading acquisition. *Nature Reviews Neuroscience*, *16*(4), 234–44. https://doi.org/10.1038/nrn3924

Duncan, J. (2010). The multiple-demand (MD) system of the primate brain: Mental programs for intelligent behaviour. *Trends in Cognitive Sciences*, *14*(4), 172–9. https://doi.org/10.1016/j.tics.2010.01.004

Edelman, G. M. (1987). *Neural Darwinism: The theory of neuronal group selection*. Basic Books.

Edelman, G. M., & Gally, J. A. (2001). Degeneracy and complexity in biological systems. *Proceedings of the National Academy of Sciences of the United States of America*, *98*(24), 13763–8. https://doi.org/10.1073/pnas.231499798

Eren, M. I., Lycett, S. J., Patten, R. J., Buchanan, B., Pargeter, J., & O'Brien, M. J. (2016). Test, model, and method validation: The role of experimental stone artifact replication in hypothesis-driven archaeology. *Ethnoarchaeology*, *8*(2), 103–36. https://doi.org/10.1080/19442890.2016.1213972

Ericsson, K. A., Krampe, R. T., & Tesch-Römer, C. (1993). The role of deliberate practice in the acquisition of expert performance. *Psychological Review*, *100*(3), 363–406. https://doi.org/10.1037/0033-295X.100.3.363

Faisal, A., Stout, D., Apel, J., & Bradley, B. (2010). The manipulative complexity of Lower Paleolithic stone toolmaking. *PLoS ONE*, *5*(11), e13718. https://doi.org/10.1371/journal.pone.0013718

Feldman, R. (2016). The neurobiology of human attachments. *Trends in Cognitive Sciences*, *21*(2), 80–99. https://doi.org/10.1016/j.tics.2016.11.007

Flynn, E. G., Laland, K. N., Kendal, R. L., & Kendal, J. R. (2013). Target article with commentaries: Developmental niche construction. *Developmental Science*, *16*(2), 296–313. https://doi.org/10.1111/desc.12030

Fodor, J. A. (1975). *The language of thought*. Thomas Y. Crowell.

Fragaszy, D. M., Biro, D., Eshchar, Y., Humle, T., Izar, P., Resende, B., & Visalberghi, E. (2013). The fourth dimension of tool use: Temporally enduring artefacts aid primates learning to use tools. *Philosophical Transactions of the Royal Society B: Biological Sciences*, *368*(1630), 20120410. https://doi.org/10.1098/rstb.2012.0410

Fragaszy, D. M., Eshchar, Y., Visalberghi, E., Resende, B., Laity, K., & Izar, P. (2017). Synchronized practice helps bearded capuchin monkeys learn to extend attention while learning a tradition. *Proceedings of the National Academy of Sciences of the United States of America*, *114*(30), 7798–7805. https://doi.org/10.1073/pnas.1621071114

Gärdenfors, P., & Högberg, A. (2017). The archaeology of teaching and the evolution of *Homo docens*. *Current Anthropology*, *58*(2), 188–208. https://doi.org/10.1086/691178

Geertz, C. (1973). *The interpretation of cultures*. Basic Books.

Gibson, J. J. (1979). *The ecological approach to visual perception*. Houghton Mifflin.

Giddens, A. (1976). *New rules of sociological method: A positive critique of interpretative sociologies*. Basic Books.

Gómez-Robles, A., Hopkins, W. D., Schapiro, S. J., & Sherwood, C. C. (2015). Relaxed genetic control of cortical organization in human brains compared with chimpanzees. *Proceedings of the National Academy of Sciences of the United States of America*, *112*(48), 14799–804. https://doi.org/10.1073/pnas.1512646112

Goodenough, W. H. (1957). Cultural anthropology and linguistics. In P. L. Garvin (Ed.), *Report on the seventh annual round table meeting on linguistics and language study* (pp. 167–73). Georgetown University Press.

Hasson, U., & Frith, C. D. (2016). Mirroring and beyond: Coupled dynamics as a generalized framework for modelling social interactions. *Philosophical Transactions of the Royal Society B: Biological Sciences*, *371*(1693), 20150366. https://doi.org/10.1098/rstb.2015.0366

Hecht, E. E., Gutman, D. A., Bradley, B. A., Preuss, T. M., & Stout, D. (2015). Virtual dissection and comparative connectivity of the superior longitudinal fasciculus in chimpanzees and humans. *NeuroImage*, *108*, 124–37. https://doi.org/10.1016/j.neuroimage.2014.12.039

Hecht, E. E., Gutman, D. A., Khreisheh, N., Taylor, S. V., Kilner, J., Faisal, A. A., Bradley, B. A., Chaminade, T., & Stout, D. (2014). Acquisition of Paleolithic toolmaking abilities involves structural remodeling to inferior frontoparietal regions. *Brain Structure and Function*, *220*(4), 2315–31. https://doi.org/10.1007/s00429-014-0789-6

Hecht, E. E., Gutman, D. A., Preuss, T. M., Sanchez, M. M., Parr, L. A., & Rilling, J. K. (2013). Process versus product in social learning: Comparative diffusion tensor imaging of neural systems for action execution-observation matching in macaques, chimpanzees, and humans. *Cerebral Cortex*, *23*(5), 1014–24. https://doi.org/10.1093/cercor/bhs097

Hecht, E. E., Mahovetz, L. M., Preuss, T. M., & Hopkins, W. D. (2017). A neuroanatomical predictor of mirror self-recognition in chimpanzees. *Social Cognitive and Affective Neuroscience*, *12*(1), 37–48. https://doi.org/10.1093/scan/nsw159

Hecht, E. E., Murphy, L. E., Gutman, D. A., Votaw, J. R., Schuster, D. M., Preuss, T. M., Orban, G. A., Stout, D., & Parr, L. A. (2013). Differences in neural activation for object-directed grasping in chimpanzees and humans. *Journal of Neuroscience*, *33*(35), 14117–34. https://doi.org/10.1523%2FJNEUROSCI.2172-13.2013

Heidegger, M. (1977). *The question concerning technology, and other essays* (W. Levitt, Trans.). Harper & Row. (Original work published 1954)

Henrich, J. P. (2016). *The secret of our success: How culture is driving human evolution, domesticating our species, and making us smarter*. Princeton University Press.

Henrich, J., Boyd, R., & Richerson, P. J. (2008). Five misunderstandings about cultural evolution. *Human Nature*, *19*(2), 119–37. https://doi.org/10.1007/s12110–008-9037-1

Henrich, J., & McElreath, R. (2003). The evolution of cultural evolution. *Evolutionary Anthropology: Issues, News, and Reviews*, *12*(3), 123–35. https://doi.org/10.1002/evan.10110

Henshilwood, C. S., & d'Errico, F. (Eds.). (2011). *Homo symbolicus: The dawn of language, imagination and spirituality*. John Benjamins Publishing Company.

Hewlett, B. S., & Roulette, C. J. (2016). Teaching in hunter-gatherer infancy. *Royal Society Open Science*, *3*(1), 150403. https://doi.org/10.1098/rsos.150403

Heyes, C. (2003). Four routes of cognitive evolution. *Psychological Review*, *110*(4), 713–27. https://doi.org/10.1037/0033-295X.110.4.713

Heyes, C. (2016). Blackboxing: Social learning strategies and cultural evolution. *Philosophical Transactions of the Royal Society B: Biological Sciences*, *371*(1693), 20150369. https://doi.org/10.1098/rstb.2015.0369

Heyes, C. (2018). *Cognitive gadgets: The cultural evolution of thinking*. Harvard University.

Heyes, C. M., & Frith, C. D. (2014). The cultural evolution of mind reading. *Science*, *344*(6190), 1243091. https://doi.org/10.1126/science.1243091

Hihara, S., Notoya, T., Tanaka, M., Ichinose, S., Ojima, H., Obayashi, S., Fujii, N., & Iriki, A. (2006). Extension of corticocortical afferents into the anterior bank of the intraparietal sulcus by tool-use training in adult monkeys. *Neuropsychologia*, *44*(13), 2636–46. https://doi.org/10.1016/j.neuropsychologia.2005.11.020

Hill, J., Inder, T., Neil, J., Dierker, D., Harwell, J., & Van Essen, D. (2010). Similar patterns of cortical expansion during human development and evolution. *Proceedings of the National Academy of Sciences of the United States of America*, *107*(29), 13135–40. https://doi.org/10.1073/pnas.1001229107

Hill, K., Barton, M., & Hurtado, A. M. (2009). The emergence of human uniqueness: Characters underlying behavioral modernity. *Evolutionary Anthropology: Issues, News, and Reviews*, *18*(5), 187–200. https://doi.org/10.1002/evan.20224

Hodder, I. (2012). *Entangled: An archaeology of the relationships between humans and things*. Wiley-Blackwell.

Holloway, R. L. (1974). The casts of fossil hominid brains. *Scientific American*, *231*(1), 106–15. http://www.jstor.org/stable/24950124

Horner, V., Proctor, D., Bonnie, K. E., Whiten, A., & de Waal, F. B. M. (2010). Prestige affects cultural learning in chimpanzees. *PLoS ONE*, *5*(5), e10625. https://doi.org/10.1371/journal.pone.0010625

Hrdy, S. B. (2009). *Mothers and others: The evolutionary origins of mutual understanding*. Harvard University Press.

Ingold, T. (1997). Eight themes in the anthropology of technology. *Social Analysis*, *41*(1), 106–38. http://www.jstor.org/stable/23171736

Ingold, T. (1998). From complementarity to obviation: On dissolving the boundaries between social and biological anthropology, archaeology and psychology. *Zeitschrift für Ethnologie*, *123*(1), 21–52. http://www.jstor.org/stable/25842543

Ingold, T. (2001). Beyond art and technology: The anthropology of skill. In M. B. Schiffer (Ed.), *Anthropological perspectives on technology* (pp. 17–31). University of New Mexico Press.

Iriki, A., & Sakura, O. (2008). The neuroscience of primate intellectual evolution: Natural selection and passive and intentional niche construction. *Philosophical Transactions of the Royal Society B: Biological Sciences*, *363*(1500), 2229–41. https://doi.org/10.1098/rstb.2008.2274

Isler, K., & van Schaik, C. P. (2012). How our ancestors broke through the gray ceiling: Comparative evidence for cooperative breeding in early *Homo*. *Current Anthropology, 53*(S6), S453–S465. https://doi.org/10.1086/667623

Isler, K., & van Schaik, C. P. (2014). How humans evolved large brains: Comparative evidence. *Evolutionary Anthropology: Issues, News, and Reviews, 23*(2), 65–75. https://doi.org/10.1002/evan.21403

Kaplan, H., Gurven, M., Winking, J., Hooper, P. L., & Stieglitz, J. (2010). Learning, menopause, and the human adaptive complex. *Annals of the New York Academy of Sciences, 1204*(1), 30–42. https://doi.org/10.1111/j.1749-6632.2010.05528.x

Kaplan, H., Hill, K., Lancaster, J., & Hurtado, A. M. (2000). A theory of human life history evolution: Diet, intelligence, and longevity. *Evolutionary Anthropology: Issues, News, and Reviews, 9*(4), 156–85. https://doi.org/10.1002/1520-6505(2000)9:4<156::AID-EVAN5>3.0.CO;2-7

Kivell, T. L. (2015). Evidence in hand: Recent discoveries and the early evolution of human manual manipulation. *Philosophical Transactions of the Royal Society B: Biological Sciences, 370*(1682), 20150105. https://doi.org/10.1098/rstb.2015.0105

Kline, M. A. (2015). How to learn about teaching: An evolutionary framework for the study of teaching behavior in humans and other animals. *Behavioral and Brain Sciences, 38*, e31. https://doi.org/10.1017/S0140525X14000090

Kolodny, O., Creanza, N., & Feldman, M. W. (2016). Game-changing innovations: How culture can change the parameters of its own evolution and induce abrupt cultural shifts. *PLoS Computational Biology, 12*(12), e1005302. https://doi.org/10.1371/journal.pcbi.1005302

Kramer, K. L. (2010). Cooperative breeding and its significance to the demographic success of humans. *Annual Review of Anthropology, 39*, 417–36. https://doi.org/10.1146/annurev.anthro.012809.105054

Kuhn, S. L. (2014). Signaling theory and technologies of communication in the Paleolithic. *Biological Theory, 9*(1), 42–50. https://doi.org/10.1007/s13752-013-0156-5

Laland, K. N., Odling-Smee, J., Hoppitt, W., & Uller, T. (2013). More on how and why: Cause and effect in biology revisited. *Biology & Philosophy, 28*(5), 719–45. https://doi.org/10.1007/s10539-012-9335-1

Laland, K. N., Uller, T., Feldman, M. W., Sterelny, K., Müller, G. B., Moczek, A., Jablonka, E., & Odling-Smee, J. (2015). The extended evolutionary synthesis: Its structure, assumptions and predictions. *Proceedings of the Royal Society B: Biological Sciences, 282*(1813), 20151019. https://doi.org/10.1098/rspb.2015.1019

Lashley, K. (1951). The problem of serial order in behavior. In L. A. Jeffress (Ed.), *Cerebral mechanisms in behavior* (pp. 112–36). John Wiley.

Lewontin, R. C. (1998). The evolution of cognition: Questions we will never answer. In D. Scarborough & S. Sternberg (Eds.), *An invitation to cognitive science: Methods models, and conceptual issues* (2nd ed., Vol. 4, pp. 107–32). MIT Press.

Magnani, M., Rezek, Z., Lin, S. C., Chan, A., & Dibble, H. L. (2014). Flake variation in relation to the application of force. *Journal of Archaeological Science, 46*, 37–49. https://doi.org/10.1016/j.jas.2014.02.029

Malafouris, L. (2013). *How things shape the mind: A theory of material engagement.* MIT Press.

Mantini, D., Corbetta, M., Romani, G. L., Orban, G. A., & Vanduffel, W. (2013). Evolutionarily novel functional networks in the human brain? *Journal of Neuroscience, 33*(8), 3259–75. https://doi.org/10.1523/jneurosci.4392-12.2013

Marx, L. (1997). "Technology": The emergence of a hazardous concept. *Social Research, 64*(3), 965–88. http://www.jstor.org/stable/40971194

Marzke, M. W. (2013). Tool making, hand morphology and fossil hominins. *Philosophical Transactions of the Royal Society B: Biological Sciences 368* (1630), 20120414. https://doi.org/10.1098/rstb.2012.0414

Mayr, E. (1961). Cause and effect in biology. *Science, 134*(3489), 1501–6. https://doi.org/10.1126/science.134.3489.1501

Mayr, E. (1994). Recapitulation reinterpreted: The somatic program. *The Quarterly Review of Biology, 69*(2), 223–32. https://doi.org/10.1086/418541

Mayr, E. (1997). The objects of selection. *Proceedings of the National Academy of Sciences of the United States of America, 94*(6), 2091–4. https://doi.org/10.2307/41593

Miller, G. A. (2003). The cognitive revolution: A historical perspective. *Trends in Cognitive Sciences, 7*(3), 141–4. https://doi.org/10.1016/S1364-6613(03)00029-9

Miller, G. A., Galanter, E., & Pribram, K. H. (1960). *Plans and the structure of behavior*. Henry Holt. https://doi.org/10.1037/10039-000

Milner, A. D., & Goodale, M. A. (1995). *The visual brain in action*. Oxford University Press.

Mueller, S., Wang, D., Fox, M. D., Yeo, B. T., Sepulcre, J., Sabuncu, M. R., Shafee, R., Liu, J., & Liu, H. (2013). Individual variability in functional connectivity architecture of the human brain. *Neuron, 77*(3), 586–95. https://doi.org/10.1016/j.neuron.2012.12.028

Murren, C. J., Auld, J. R., Callahan, H., Ghalambor, C. K., Handelsman, C. A., Heskel, M. A., Kingsolver, J. G., Maclean, H. J., Masel, J., Maughan, H., Pfennig, D. W., Relyea, R. A., Seiter, S., Snell-Rood, E., Steiner, U. K., & Schlichting, C. D. (2015). Constraints on the evolution of phenotypic plasticity: Limits and costs of phenotype and plasticity. *Heredity, 115*(4), 293–301. https://doi.org/10.1038/hdy.2015.8

Musgrave, S., Morgan, D., Lonsdorf, E., Mundry, R., & Sanz, C. (2016). Tool transfers are a form of teaching among chimpanzees. *Scientific Reports, 6*, 34783. https://doi.org/10.1038/srep34783

Nonaka, T., Bril, B., & Rein, R. (2010). How do stone knappers predict and control the outcome of flaking? Implications for understanding early stone tool technology. *Journal of Human Evolution, 59*(2), 155–67. https://doi.org/10.1016/j.jhevol.2010.04.006

Obayashi, S., Suhara, T., Kawabe, K., Okauchi, T., Maeda, J., Akine, Y., Onoe, H., & Iriki, A. (2001). Functional brain mapping of monkey tool use. *NeuroImage 14*(4), 853–61. https://doi.org/10.1006/nimg.2001.0878

Orban, G. A., & Caruana, F. (2014). The neural basis of human tool use. *Frontiers in Psychology, 5*, 310. https://doi.org/10.3389/fpsyg.2014.00310

Oswalt, W. H. (1976). *An anthropological analysis of food-getting technology*. John Wiley and Sons.

Patterson, K., Nestor, P. J., & Rogers, T. T. (2007). Where do you know what you know? The representation of semantic knowledge in the human brain. *Nature Reviews Neuroscience, 8*(12), 976–87. https://doi.org/10.1038/nrn2277

Perreault, C., Brantingham, P. J., Kuhn, S. L., Wurz, S., & Gao, X. (2013). Measuring the complexity of lithic technology. *Current Anthropology*, *54*(S8), S397–S406. https://doi.org/10.1086/673264

Pickering, M. J., & Garrod, S. (2013). An integrated theory of language production and comprehension. *Behavioral and Brain Sciences*, *36*(4), 329–47. https://doi.org/10.1017/S0140525X12001495

Pigliucci, M. (2009). An extended synthesis for evolutionary biology. *Annals of the New York Academy of Sciences*, *1168*, 218–28. https://doi.org/10.1111/j.1749-6632.2009.04578.x

Pinker, S., & Bloom, P. (1990). Natural language and natural selection. *Behavioral and Brain Sciences*, *13*(4), 707–27. https://doi.org/10.1017/S0140525X00081061

Powell, A., Shennan, S., & Thomas, M. G. (2009). Late Pleistocene demography and the appearance of modern human behavior. *Science*, *324*(5932), 1298–1301. https://doi.org/10.1126/science.1170165

Power, J. D., Fair, D. A., Schlaggar, B. L., & Petersen, S. E. (2010). The development of human functional brain networks. *Neuron*, *67*(5), 735–48. https://doi.org/10.1016/j.neuron.2010.08.017

Preuss, T. M. (2012). Human brain evolution: From gene discovery to phenotype discovery. *Proceedings of the National Academy of Sciences of the United States of America*, *109*(Supplement 1), 10709–16. https://doi.org/10.1073/pnas.1201894109

Pulvermüller, F., & Fadiga, L. (2010). Active perception: Sensorimotor circuits as a cortical basis for language. *Nature Reviews Neuroscience*, *11*(5), 351–60. https://doi.org/10.1038/nrn2811

Rakic, P. (2009). Evolution of the neocortex: A perspective from developmental biology. *Nature Reviews Neuroscience*, *10*(10), 724–35. https://doi.org/10.1038/nrn2719

Roepstorff, A., Niewöhner, J., & Beck, S. (2010). Enculturing brains through patterned practices. *Neural Networks*, *23*(8–9), 1051–9. https://doi.org/10.1016/j.neunet.2010.08.002

Roux, V., Bril, B., & Dietrich, G. (1995). Skills and learning difficulties involved in stone knapping: The case of stone-bead knapping in Khambhat, India. *World Archaeology*, *27*(1), 63–87. http://www.jstor.org/stable/124778

Saussure, F. (1966). *Course in general linguistics* (W. Baskin, Trans.; C. Bally & A. Sechehaye, Eds.). McGraw-Hill. (Original work published 1916)

Schiffer, M. B. (1999). *The material life of human beings: Artifacts, behavior and communication*. Routledge.

Shannon, C. E., & Weaver, W. (1949). *The mathematical theory of communication*. University of Illinois Press.

Shennan, S. J., & Steele, J. (1999). Cultural learning in hominids: A behavioral ecological approach. In H. O. Box & K. R. Gibson (Eds.), *Mammalian social learning: Comparative and ecological perspectives* (pp. 367–88). Cambridge University Press.

Smith, J. M. (2000). The concept of information in biology. *Philosophy of Science*, *67*(2), 177–94. http://www.jstor.org/stable/188717

Somel, M., Liu, X., & Khaitovich, P. (2013). Human brain evolution: Transcripts, metabolites and their regulators. *Nature Reviews Neuroscience*, *14*(2), 112–27. https://doi.org/10.1038/nrn3372

Stiner, M. C., Barkai, R., & Gopher, A. (2009). Cooperative hunting and meat sharing 400–200 kya at Qesem Cave, Israel. *Proceedings of the National Academy of Sciences of the United States of America*, *106*(32), 13207–12. https://doi.org/10.1073/pnas.0900564106

Stout, D. (2002). Skill and cognition in stone tool production: An ethnographic case study from Irian Jaya. *Current Anthropology*, *45*(3), 693–722. https://doi.org/10.1086/342638

Stout, D. (2011). Stone toolmaking and the evolution of human culture and cognition. *Philosophical Transactions of the Royal Society B: Biological Sciences*, *366*(1567), 1050–9. https://doi.org/10.1098%2Frstb.2010.0369

Stout, D. (2013). Neuroscience of technology. In P. J. Richerson & M. H. Christiansen (Eds.), *Cultural evolution: Society, technology, language, and religion* (pp. 157–73). MIT Press.

Stout, D. (2018). Human brain evolution: History or science? In J. H. Schwartz (Ed.), *Rethinking human evolution* (pp. 297–318). MIT Press.

Stout, D., & Chaminade, T. (2007). The evolutionary neuroscience of tool making. *Neuropsychologia*, *45*(5), 1091–1100. https://doi.org/10.1016/j.neuropsychologia.2006.09.014

Stout, D., & Chaminade, T. (2012). Stone tools, language and the brain in human evolution. *Philosophical Transactions of the Royal Society B: Biological Sciences*, *367*(1585), 75–87. https://doi.org/10.1098/rstb.2011.0099

Stout, D., & Hecht, E. E. (2017). Evolutionary neuroscience of cumulative culture. *Proceedings of the National Academy of Sciences of the United States of America*, *114*(30), 7861–68. https://doi.org/10.1073/pnas.1620738114

Stout, D., Hecht, E., Khreisheh, N., Bradley, B., & Chaminade, T. (2015). Cognitive demands of lower Paleolithic toolmaking. *PLoS ONE*, *10*(4), e0121804. https://doi.org/10.1371/journal.pone.0121804

Stout, D., & Khreisheh, N. (2015). Skill learning and human brain evolution: An experimental approach. *Cambridge Archaeological Journal*, *25*(4), 867–75. https://doi.org/10.1017/S0959774315000359

Stout, D., Passingham, R., Frith, C., Apel, J., & Chaminade, T. (2011). Technology, expertise and social cognition in human evolution. *European Journal of Neuroscience*, *33*(7), 1328–38. https://doi.org/10.1111/j.1460-9568.2011.07619.x

Stout, D., Rogers, M. J., Jaeggi, A. V., & Semaw, S. (2019). Archaeology and the origins of human cumulative culture: A case study from the earliest Oldowan at Gona, Ethiopia. *Current Anthropology*, *60*(3), 309–430. https://doi.org/10.1086/703173

Stout, D., Toth, N., Schick, K. D., & Chaminade, T. (2008). Neural correlates of Early Stone Age tool-making: Technology, language and cognition in human evolution. *Philosophical Transactions of the Royal Society of London B: Biological Sciences*, *363*(1499), 1939–49. https://doi.org/10.1098/rstb.2008.0001

Szathmáry, E., & Smith, J. M. (1995). The major evolutionary transitions. *Nature*, *374*(6519), 227–32. https://doi.org/10.1038/374227a0

Tomasello, M. (1999). *The cultural origins of human cognition*. Harvard University Press.

Toth, N., & Schick, K. (2009). The Oldowan: The tool making of early hominins and chimpanzees compared. *Annual Review of Anthropology*, *38*, 289–305. https://doi.org/10.1146/annurev-anthro-091908-164521

Turing, A. M. (1950). Computing machinery and intelligence. *Mind*, *59*(236), 433–60. https://doi.org/10.1093/mind/LIX.236.433

Turner, V. (1975). Symbolic studies. *Annual Review of Anthropology*, *4*, 145–61. https://doi.org/10.1146/annurev.an.04.100175.001045

Twomey, T. (2013). The cognitive implications of controlled fire use by early humans. *Cambridge Archaeological Journal*, *23*(1), 113–28. https://doi.org/10.1017/S0959774313000085

Tylor, E. B. (1871). *Primitive culture: Researches into the development of mythology, philosophy, religion, art, and custom* (Vol. 2). John Murray.

van Schaik, C. P., & Burkart, J. M. (2011). Social learning and evolution: The cultural intelligence hypothesis. *Philosophical Transactions of the Royal Society B: Biological Sciences*, *366*(1567), 1008–16. https://doi.org/10.1098%2Frstb.2010.0304

van Schaik, C. P., Isler, K., & Burkart, J. M. (2012). Explaining brain size variation: From social to cultural brain. *Trends in Cognitive Sciences*, *16*(5), 277–84. https://doi.org/10.1016/j.tics.2012.04.004

Varela, F. G., Maturana, H. R., & Uribe, R. (1974). Autopoiesis: The organization of living systems, its characterization and a model. *Biosystems*, *5*(4), 187–96. https://doi.org/10.1016/0303-2647(74)90031-8

Vigliocco, G., Vinson, D. P., Druks, J., Barber, H., & Cappa, S. F. (2011). Nouns and verbs in the brain: A review of behavioural, electrophysiological, neuropsychological and imaging studies. *Neuroscience & Biobehavioral Reviews*, *35*(3), 407–26. https://doi.org/10.1016/j.neubiorev.2010.04.007

Wadley, L., Hodgskiss, T., & Grant, M. (2009). Implications for complex cognition from the hafting of tools with compound adhesives in the Middle Stone Age, South Africa. *Proceedings of the National Academy of Sciences of the United States of America*, *106*(24), 9590–4. https://doi.org/10.1073/pnas.0900957106

West-Eberhard, M. J. (2005). Phenotypic accommodation: Adaptive innovation due to developmental plasticity. *Journal of Experimental Zoology Part B: Molecular and Developmental Evolution*, *304*(6), 610–18. https://doi.org/10.1002/jez.b.21071

Whiten, A. (2015). Experimental studies illuminate the cultural transmission of percussive technologies in *Homo* and *Pan*. *Philosophical Transactions of the Royal Society B: Biological Sciences*, *370*(1682), 20140359. https://doi.org/10.1098/rstb.2014.0359

Wolpert, D. M., Doya, K., & Kawato, M. (2003). A unifying computational framework for motor control and social interaction. *Philosophical Transactions of the Royal Society B: Biological Sciences*, *358*(1431), 593–602. https://doi.org/10.1098%2Frstb.2002.1238

Wylie, A. (1985). The reaction against analogy. In M. B. Schiffer (Ed.), *Advances in archaeological method and theory* (Vol. 8, pp. 63–111). Academic Press. https://doi.org/10.1016/B978-0-12-003108-5.50008-7

Yopak, K. E., Lisney, T. J., Darlington, R. B., Collin, S. P., Montgomery, J. C., & Finlay, B. L. (2010). A conserved pattern of brain scaling from sharks to primates. *Proceedings of the National Academy of Sciences of the United States of America*, *107*(29), 12946–51. https://doi.org/10.1073/pnas.1002195107

3 Mutual Constitution of Culture and the Mind
Insights from Cultural Neuroscience

Shinobu Kitayama and Qinggang Yu

Introduction

In a recent book, the neuroscientist Antonio Damasio (2018) argues that feelings of pleasure and pain are at the core of human activities, including inherently cultural activities. In particular, he posits that the biological system that subserves human emotions is designed to maintain homeostatic balance. Accordingly, whenever this balance is disturbed, the system tries to restore it. Building on this premise, he proposes that this homeostatic principle inherent in human emotion can explain human culture. By making this proposal, Damasio puts forward an essential insight that the spontaneous working of the mind, even including the functioning of low-level emotions, such as fear and anger, contributes to the reproduction and change of a higher-order system of culture. But how might this bottom-up process work? Is this process sufficient to give rise to, let alone maintain, the system of culture?

In the present chapter, we propose that Damasio's argument for the central role of homeostasis and emotions in accounting for culture is right on target. However, we add a critical, logical link. We suggest that, primitive as they might seem at first glance, the emotions that contribute to culture may simultaneously be shaped and conditioned by it. Without cultural conditioning, such emotions would be chaotic and nonresponsive, let alone attuned to culture. Only when they have been properly conditioned by culture might they be able to contribute to its maintenance and change. Under such conditions, emotions might acquire the power to undergird the cultural system. Damasio's homeostatic balance works because culture powerfully, if only tacitly, in the background, is constantly modulating the psychological processes, including the low-level emotions – the focus of his analysis. And the argument we make may apply not only to emotion but also to all aspects of human mental processes. In this chapter, we will also explore the possibility that culture may shape the mind.

Our central thesis then, is that culture is not only realized through the functioning of the mind but, equally importantly, culture shapes both mind and brain (Han et al., 2013; Kitayama & Salvador, 2017; Kitayama & Uskul, 2011; Kitayama et al., 2019). Specifically, the spontaneous operation of cognition, emotion, and motivation may converge to produce and reproduce the cultural systems in the case of humans (but not other nonhuman animals, including our primate cousins) because our mind and brain have significant potential to be shaped by culture.

By arguing for the crucial role of culture in shaping the mind and brain, our work can be placed squarely at the intersection of cultural psychology and cultural neuroscience. Over the last three decades, cultural psychologists have established that there are numerous cultural variations in psychological functions, including not only highly deliberate value judgments and related attitudes (Hofstede, 1980; Schwartz, 2006), but also spontaneously enacted behaviors (Kim & Markus, 1999; Nisbett & Cohen, 1996), automatic styles of thought (Na et al., 2010; Nisbett et al., 2001; Rhee et al., 1995), and unconscious motivations of various kinds (Heine et al., 1999; Kitayama & Tompson, 2015; Kitayama et al., 2004). In more recent years, the cultural psychology literature has begun to utilize cutting-edge neuroscience methods to demonstrate that many of the culturally shaped spontaneous psychological tendencies have important anchors in brain processes (Han et al., 2013; Kitayama & Salvador, 2017; Kitayama et al., 2017, 2019). Altogether, this emerging evidence undergirds the hypothesis that the brain is highly plastic and hence subject to systematic cultural influences (Kitayama & Salvador, 2017; Kitayama et al., 2019). The cultural shaping of the brain ensures that not only does our brain activity generate culture, but human culture – both explicitly and behind-the-scenes – also shapes our brain.

This chapter focuses on how and why such cultural feedback might occur. In what follows, we will start with an overarching theoretical framework on culture and the self. We will then present a selective review of empirical evidence for the effect of culture on both brain functioning and brain structure. Throughout, we will argue that culture influences the mind and brain in idiosyncratic, highly "personalized" manners. At the same time, however, when individuals are aggregated in a collective, idiosyncrasies across individuals will tend to cancel one another out. Only those traces of a culture that are common will remain, and as a consequence, culture is reproduced with a high degree of fidelity.

Culture and the Self: A Theoretical Framework

Independence and Interdependence

It has long been hypothesized that cultures vary in the value placed on personal self versus social relationships (Markus & Kitayama, 1991; Shweder & Bourne, 1982; Triandis, 1995). In Western cultures, including Western European countries and the cultures of Americans and Canadians of European origin, a strong value is placed on the independence of the personal self from others (Markus & Kitayama 1991). Internal attributes of the self – such as values, attitudes, and preferences – are considered primary, and as such, they serve as major drivers and motivators of actions (Savani et al., 2008). Social relations are important, but they are typically seen as derivative of personal choice and based on implicit or explicit social contracts. This form of self has been called independent.

In contrast, in many non-Western cultures, including Asian, Middle Eastern, Sub-Saharan African, and Latin American cultures, the primary commitment is to certain relevant social units, such as family, workplace, community, and other groups both small and large (Markus & Kitayama 1991). Each person's identity is defined by their place in the relationship. Moreover, their actions are guided and motivated by perceived duties and obligations defined within it (Miller et al., 1990). The personal self is important, but it is perceived as being in the service of, or subordinated to, the concerns and priorities of the relationship (Morling et al., 2002). This form of self, called interdependent, has substantial overlap with other selves. Moreover, the self's most important attributes (e.g., role, status, and obligation) are defined within each of the relationships. In this sense, the self is highly relational.

Varieties of Interdependence

Over the last 50 000 years, modern humans began spreading out of Africa to inhabit much of the Eurasian continent, and then eventually beyond to other continents. Subsequently, over the last 10 000 years, humans started sedentary forms of living based on farming and herding. Throughout much of this more recent period, humans were likely fully dependent on immediate groups such as families and tribes. Loyalty to the groups was likely of utmost priority. Even more recently, over the last few thousand years, larger social units such as kingdoms and empires commanded authority over individuals. This authority further enforced the need for commitment to higher-order groups. It is fair to assume then, that throughout the last 10 000-year period, humans across the globe were almost always interdependent. They placed a higher priority on certain social units such as family, tribe, and country over the personal (Henrich, 2015). One could even argue that human groups have continued to be interdependent across much of the globe to this day. There is one notable exception, however. As we shall see, over the last several hundred years in Western Europe, the idea of the self as independent emerged as the guiding principle of society at large. This idea undergirds the modern West. It then spread to other regions (e.g., North America, South Africa, and Australia) through migration of Western Europeans.

Given this extremely abbreviated outline of the human history over the last 10 000 years, it appears sensible to make a broad distinction between the West (the modern West established in Western Europe over the last several hundred years and its diasporas) and the rest, with the rest being contrastively less independent or more interdependent. However, this does not mean that the non-Western regions are homogeneous. To the contrary, depending on a variety of factors, including socio-ecological, economic, geographic, and demographic conditions, different areas of the non-Western region of the globe may have developed different forms of interdependence depending on the context.

Kitayama et al. (2019) have proposed that there are four major forms of interdependence across the globe. First, in tightly knit agrarian societies based on farming, particularly labor-intensive rice farming (Talhelm et al., 2014; Uchida et al., 2019), interdependence is typically promoted by avoiding interpersonal conflict. This type of culture encourages cognitive moderation. For example, compromise is appreciated more than argumentation. Emotional suppression is valued more than expression, and self-effacement and modesty are more virtuous than self-assertion and enhancement. The last two decades of research in cultural psychology have focused on comparisons between North Americans and East Asians and provided substantial evidence for this possibility (Heine et al., 1999; Kitayama et al., 1997). This form of interdependence may be called "self-effacing."

Self-effacing interdependence may be contrasted with another form of interdependence that is common in desert environments. In such environments, water and other resources are scarce and thus can support only small tribes. Each tribal group must protect the in-group from other tribes. Intertribal conflicts are widespread, and as a consequence, the prowess and assertiveness of each self are not only tolerated but also strongly valued for the sake of in-group protection (San Martín et al., 2018). This form of interdependence, referred to as "self-assertive interdependence," is thought to be characteristic of psychological profiles common in Arabic cultures today. It may also extend to Central Asia, which historically shares similar, desert-based, nomadic lifestyles. San Martín et al. (2018) have found that Arabs are highly interdependent in the sense of being attuned to others while also relying on them for their own happiness. In this respect, Arabs are very similar to East Asians. However, San Martín et al. (2018) also found that Arabs are quite self-assertive – much more assertive than East Asians and, in fact, just as assertive as Westerners.

In the course of cultural evolution over the last several thousand years, from the Mediterranean through South Asia, one can find many trade routes. Along the trade routes, some prominent city centers emerged. In these highly populated city centers, conflicts in business were also frequent and, unlike in East Asian farming villages, they are inherent in the mode of life and therefore simply unavoidable. Moreover, these conflicts were the kind that must be settled without physical violence or antagonism since trade relations had to be maintained. Under such conditions, another form of interdependence emerged. This interdependence was based on conflict resolution with "mouth" rather than "fist." Argumentation was the primary means by which to achieve interdependence. Along with argumentation, there arose a tradition of logical, analytic thought, which is often attributed to Aristotle and other Greek philosophers. In all likelihood, this form of interdependence extended far beyond Greek city-states to the wide-ranging region including India and Singapore. For example, even today, argumentativeness is seen as a national character of Indians, according to a prominent Indian economist (Sen, 2005). This form of interdependence may be called "argumentative interdependence."

Recent work analyzing genetic ancestry markers (Reich, 2018) shows that from the very beginning of human evolution, peoples have continuously moved across regions of the globe. It stands to reason that there existed numerous multiethnic and multilingual communities. In these communities, there must have been a substantial difficulty in communication with language alone, even within primary groups such as family and workplace. Recent work (Rychlowska et al., 2015; Wood et al., 2016; Kitayama et al., 2019) hypothesized that in these communities, there arose a tradition of para-linguistic communication, which included the use of poetry, dance, and, above all, emotions to achieve interpersonal and social resonance. This form of interdependence is referred to as "expressive interdependence." In the contemporary world, expressive interdependence may most typically be found in Latin America. Several studies that tested Latin Americans found they are highly interdependent. For example, they are attuned to social contexts and dependent on others for their happiness (Sanchez-Burks et al., 2000; Telzer & Fuligni, 2009; Telzer et al., 2010). However, unlike Asians (who devalue strong emotions and often suppress emotions), Latin Americans value strong emotions – just as much as Westerners do (Ruby et al., 2012; Triandis et al., 1984).

In sum, throughout the last several *thousand* years, most of the people who ever existed were likely highly interdependent within their primary groups. They were loyal to certain relevant social units, some large and some small. They used this primordial interdependence as the guiding principle of life, society, and social relations. Despite this commonality, however, individuals may form interdependent relations for different reasons or motivations. Further, they may do so through various means. Which form of interdependence might arise in a given region may depend on the specific socio-ecological conditions of the region. Thus, the forms of interdependence may vary, reflecting specific socio-ecological niches. Our current working assumption is that interdependence may be achieved (1) through conflict avoidance (predominant in East Asia); (2) through in-group protection (predominant in Arab regions); (3) through argumentation (common in major trade centers); or (4) through emotional social resonance (common in multiethnic communities across the continent, predominant in Latin cultures today).

Collective Construction of Culture

Culture matters in psychology because it is instrumental in shaping mental capacities and tendencies. Having delineated major variations in contemporary cultures, we are now ready to discuss how this cultural influence may take place. Following earlier work (Kitayama & Uskul, 2011; Kitayama et al., 2009), we argue that individual members actively engage with their culture and, in so doing, incorporate some aspects of the culture into their own cognition and neurobiology. Specifically, when a person acts, they receive feedback from others around them, who appraise their behavior in light of the norms, values, and conventions of the culture. Hence, if the action is congruous with cultural norms, values, and conventions, it will be praised, and perhaps, they will be included in the in-group. If, however, their behavior is not congruent, such rewards are unlikely. In fact, they may even be punished. When the feedback is positively reinforcing, it will strengthen the neural circuitry recruited to produce the behavior. Through this mechanism, cultural norms, values, and conventions will gradually "permeate" neural circuitry over time.

Cultural feedback is contingent on a person's behavior, which itself depends on a variety of factors (e.g., upbringing, friendship network, education, etc.). Moreover, any feedback will also depend on salient aspects of culture that happen to be available in the situation, as well as how relevant others interpret the specific behavior at issue. Hence, each individual incorporates relevant parts of the culture in a highly idiosyncratic manner. Thus, no single individual is a complete replica of their culture. Nevertheless, when many such individuals are brought together in some collective (e.g., local community, workplace, or larger unit such as ethnicity and country), behaviors produced tend to cohere along with general themes, reflecting those existing in the culture from which they are derived. In this way, whereas there exists a huge individual variation, culture is still transmitted with high fidelity. This is to say that culture is "collectively constructed" (Kitayama et al., 1997).

Cultural Variation in Mental Experiences

So far, we have argued for psychological differences across cultures. Some of the differences are related directly to the goals of independence and interdependence. These differences may be expected to differentiate Western populations from non-Western populations. In this section, we focus on three such features (correlates of happiness, holistic attention, and holistic social cognition). In these features, we may expect a broad divide between the West and the rest. Of course, this does not mean that the rest (that is, the vast area outside of the modern West) is homogeneous. To the contrary, the preceding discussion implies that there ought to be important differences across diverse regions in the non-West. We will return to this possibility in the concluding section.

Predictors of Happiness

Happiness depends importantly on successfully achieving culturally sanctioned goals and values. In Western, independent cultures, people tend to be motivated to identify their internal attributes such as personal goals and desires and to achieve them. Hence, when they have successfully achieved such goals and desires, the experience of happiness may be maximized. In contrast, in many non-Western cultures, people tend to be motivated to be interdependent with others in their significant relations and thus to be part of such relations. We may therefore anticipate that people would maximize their happiness when they have achieved such social, interdependent goal states.

Evidence for the expected cross-cultural difference in correlates of happiness comes from several studies (Kitayama et al., 2000; Uchida & Kitayama, 2009). In one study, Kitayama et al. (2000) asked Japanese and American participants to rate how frequently in daily life they experience (1) general positive feelings of happiness (e.g., happy, elated, relaxed), (2) positive emotions that are socially *engaging* (e.g., feelings of closeness, friendly feelings), which result from achievement of interdependent goals, and (3) positive emotions that are socially *disengaging* (e.g., pride, feelings of superiority), which result from achievement of independent goals. As may be expected, among Japanese the reported frequency of experiencing the general positive emotions was more strongly associated with the reported frequency of experiencing the socially *engaging* positive emotions than with that for the socially disengaging emotions. In contrast, the reversed pattern was found for European Americans, with the association with the general positive emotions being higher for the socially disengaging emotions than for the socially engaging emotions. In another study, Uchida and Kitayama (2009) tested meanings of happiness (Uchida & Kitayama, 2009). American and Japanese participants were asked to write down features and effects of happiness. These features were compiled and given to new groups of both American and Japanese participants, who sorted them into meaningful groups by similarity. By using these data, it is possible to create an index of similarity for every pair of the features (how many participants sort any given pair of features into a single group). This similarity index was submitted to a multidimensional scaling analysis. The result confirmed that the positive hedonic feeling inherent in happiness overlaps with personal achievement (e.g., "getting what I want") among Americans, yet it overlaps with social harmony (e.g., "having good friends") among Japanese.

Similar cross-cultural variation has been observed with an experience sampling method (Kitayama et al., 2006). In one such study, Japanese and

American participants reported the most emotional event on each of fourteen consecutive days. On each day, they reported how strongly they experienced general positive or negative emotions as well as a list of socially *engaging* or *disengaging* emotions. Across the episodes, the general positive feelings ("happiness") were regressed on both the experience of socially engaging positive emotions and the experience of socially disengaging positive emotions. For Japanese, the primary predictor of happiness was the socially engaging positive emotions, but for Americans, it was the socially disengaging positive emotions. Patterns similar to the one observed for Americans have been found for Western Europeans (British and Germans; Kitayama et al., 2009), as well as Israelis of Ashkenazi origin with European backgrounds (San Martín et al., 2018). In contrast, patterns similar to the one observed for Japanese have been found for Arabs (San Martín et al., 2018).

Are the effects reviewed above reflected in brain responses? In one recent study (Kitayama & Park, 2014), both European American and East Asian participants performed a simple cognitive task. They had been told that they would earn points by performing well in the task. Importantly, the points they would earn in some blocks could be exchanged for a gift they would keep for themselves (the self condition), whereas the points they would earn in the remaining blocks could be exchanged for a gift that would be sent to their best friend on campus (the friend condition). The premise was that European Americans may be more motivated when an independent goal (earning points for the self) is at stake than when an interdependent goal (earning points for the friend) is at stake, whereas this effect may be attenuated or even reversed for East Asians.

To investigate this possibility, the researchers monitored brain electrical activity via an electroencephalogram (EEG) while participants performed the task. The brain response of interest was a negative deflection of event-related potential (ERP) that occurs nearly simultaneously with an error response. This negative wave, called the error-related negativity or ERN, is thought to result from a mismatch between the actual response and the representation of the correct response (Gehring et al., 1993; Hajcak et al., 2005). Intuitively, the ERN corresponds to some immediate recognition that one is committing an error at the very moment it is occurring. Importantly, the ERN is coterminous with the response itself; it is therefore highly automatic and hardly possible to inhibit (or augment) intentionally. Prior work shows that the magnitude of ERN increases when the task is more important (Hajcak et al., 2005). Thus, it may be expected that the magnitude of the ERN would vary between the two conditions of the experiment, depending on the motivational significance of working for the self or for the friend.

Figure 3.1A shows the waveforms for European American participants. One can clearly identify an ERN on error trials, which does not exist on

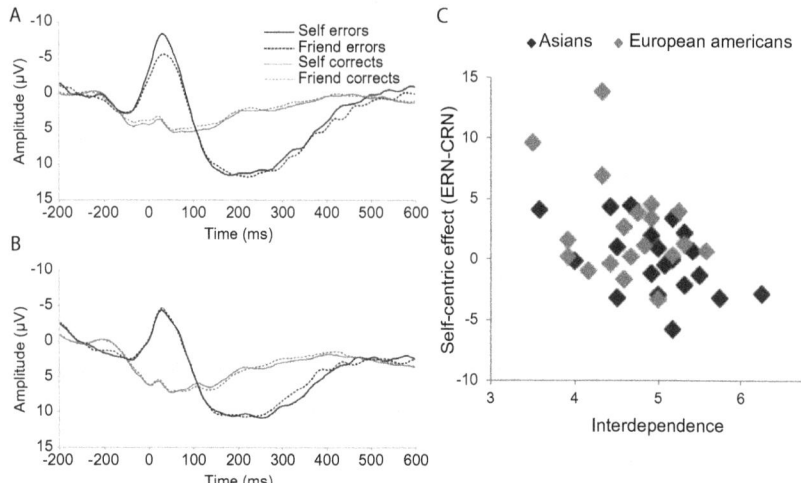

Figure 3.1 Self-centric motivation for European Americans and East Asians. (A) Waveforms for error trials and correct response trials in the self vs. friend condition for European Americans. (B) Corresponding waveforms for East Asians. (C) The self-centric effect as a function of interdependent self-construal. ERN = error-related negativity; CRN = correct-response negativity.
Adapted from "Error-Related Brain Activity Reveals Self-Centric Motivation: Culture Matters" by S. Kitayama and J. Park, 2014, *Journal of Experimental Psychology: General, 143*, pp. 66 and 67 (https://doi.org/10.1037/a0031696.supp). Copyright 2014 by the American Psychological Association

correct-response trials. Importantly, the magnitude of the ERN was significantly greater in the self condition than in the friend condition. This observation suggests that European Americans are motivated more in the task when their self-relevant goals are at stake (relative to the condition in which their goals are for their friend). The result for East Asians was a stark contrast, in that there was no overall difference between the self condition and the friend condition in the ERN magnitude (see Figure 3.1B). The researchers subsequently measured the interdependent self-construal with a standard questionnaire scale and tested whether the magnitude of ERN (relative to the magnitude of the ERP on the correct-response trials) in the self vs. friend condition might vary as a function of this individual difference variable. As can be seen in Figure 3.1C, the magnitude of the ERN in the self (vs. friend) condition decreased systematically as the level of interdependent self-construal increased. Overall, European Americans were less interdependent than East Asians, as may be expected. This cultural difference in the interdependent self-construal statistically accounted for the cultural difference in the ERN magnitude in the self (vs. friend) condition. Importantly, in both cultural groups there was a substantial variation in interdependent self-construal. Moreover, for those who were sufficiently high in interdependence, the ERN tended to be larger in the friend condition than in the self condition. A similar effect favoring interdependent goals has also been demonstrated for Latin Americans in a series of studies conducted by Telzer et al. (2010).

Up to this point, we have focused on cultural variations in the value placed on independence vs. interdependence. However, prior work shows that independent vs. interdependent self-construal can be highlighted temporarily by certain priming procedures (Oyserman & Lee, 2008). For example, individuals may be asked to read a story about a trip to a big city from the perspective of the personal self (as marked by singular pronouns such as "I," "my," and "me") or the social self (as marked by plural pronouns such as "we," "our," and "us"). The singular pronoun priming is known to induce independent self-construal whereas the plural pronoun priming is known to induce interdependent self-construal (Gardner et al., 1999). Using this procedure, two recent studies, both conducted in China with Chinese participants, show that the self-construal priming systematically modulates motivation-related brain responses (Varnum et al., 2014; Zhu et al., 2018).

In one of the studies, Varnum et al. had participants engage in a gambling task while observing their brain activity with functional magnetic resonance imaging (fMRI) (Varnum et al., 2014). On some of the blocks of the experiment, participants gambled on their own behalf whereas on the remaining blocks they gambled on behalf of a close friend. Unbeknownst to the participants, the task was rigged such that they would ultimately win on half the trials under either condition. Moreover, independent of the target manipulation, self-construal was also manipulated. Thus, prior to each of the blocks, participants were asked to read either a singular pronoun story or a plural pronoun story and to circle all the pronouns. The researchers found, first, that the subcortical region of the brain that responds to reward (ventral striatum; VS) was activated more when the participants won the gamble than when they lost it, thus replicating prior work using the same paradigm (Haber, 2011; Knutson & Greer, 2008). Importantly, this effect was stronger when they gambled on their own behalf rather than for a close friend in the independent (singular pronoun) priming condition. However, there was no difference in the VS activity regardless of how they gambled in the interdependent (plural pronoun) priming condition.

In another Chinese study, Zhu et al. (2018) also used a gambling task. As in the Varnum et al. (2014) study, this study was composed of multiple blocks. On some of the blocks participants gambled on their own behalf, whereas on the remaining blocks, they gambled on behalf of a close-other (their mothers). Moreover, some of the blocks were preceded by the induction of the independent self-construal whereas the remaining blocks were preceded by the induction of the interdependent self-construal. Instead of measuring brain activity with fMRI, Zhu et al. tested the degree to which an ERP component responding to positive feedback (called feedback positivity, which is a mirror image of a component responding to negative feedback called feedback-related negativity, or FRN). Consistent with the Varnum et al. findings, the reward positivity (relative to the FRN) was significantly greater in the self condition than in the close-other (mother) condition when the independent self-construal had been primed. However, the difference between the self and close-other condition disappeared when the interdependent self-construal had been primed.

The finding that the motivation-related brain responses can be modulated by self-construal priming reinforces the assumption that the cultural difference shown above may in fact be mediated by self-construal. It is of interest, however, that all the questionnaire-based studies testing predictors of happiness show that among Asians, socially engaged positive emotions (which mark a success in interdependence) are a better predictor of happiness than socially disengaged positive emotions (which mark a success in independence). Extending this pattern to the gambling paradigm used in the neuroscience studies, one might expect that Asians should show stronger brain activities of interest (ERN, VS activation, and reward positivity) in the close-other condition than in the self condition. Further, this effect may be expected to be more pronounced when interdependent self-construal has been primed preceding the gambles that are played. These predictions were not borne out in any of the studies. We wonder if the absence of what might be called the other-centric effect in the experimental paradigms might reflect the fact that very tangible rewards are at stake in this paradigm. These tangible rewards may engage self-interest so strongly that it is hard to overcome this effect even though Asians might otherwise be oriented toward others or this tendency might otherwise be augmented with the priming of interdependence.

Holistic Attention

People with clear personal goals know what they want, and as a consequence, they tend to attend narrowly to objects that are directly relevant to their goals. In contrast, those with more relational, interdependent goals must be attuned to the goals and desires of others in a relationship and, thus, they will attend more holistically to a variety of contextual cues. This possibility was tested earlier on in the context of comparative research between Asians (who are thought to be more interdependent and, thus, more holistic) and European Americans (who are thought to be more independent and, thus, more focused).

In one of the first studies testing this possibility, Masuda and Nisbett (2001) had both Japanese and European American subjects watch various video vignettes (e.g., an underwater scene composed of both focal objects and various contextual elements) and then afterward narrate what they saw.

Whereas European Americans tended to recall the focal objects first and then gradually moved on to report various contextual elements, Japanese showed the opposite tendency, with contextual elements described first to "set the stage" before introducing the focal objects. Moreover, the researchers also tested recognition memory of the focal objects while presenting them in the context in which they had originally been shown, without any context, or in a new context. This manipulation of context during the recognition test significantly influenced the recognition performance of Japanese. The performance was significantly better if the objects were shown in the old context than in the novel context, with the no-context condition falling in between. This demonstrates that Japanese bound the focal objects to the surrounding context while observing the video vignettes. In contrast, the context effect was negligible for European Americans, indicating that these individuals did not associate the objects to the context while observing the video vignettes.

Subsequent studies have extended the initial demonstrations in several directions. For example, one line of work tested whether a similar cross-cultural difference could be found with minimal real-life elements using geometric figures. Specifically, Kitayama et al. presented subjects with a square frame with a vertical line in the frame (Kitayama et al., 2003). Immediately afterward, subjects were shown another square frame of a different size and asked to draw a line identical in either absolute length or proportion to the height of the surrounding square frame.

The researchers observed for European Americans that the performance in the task (assessed with the amount of an error in the line drawing task) was worse in the relative judgment condition than in the absolute judgment condition, suggesting that these individuals were so focused on the line itself that they found it hard to allocate sufficient attention to the square frame, which was also required in order to perform the relative task. In contrast, for Japanese the performance was worse in the absolute task than in the relative task, indicating that their attention extended to the contextual frame even when the task required them to ignore it, and as a consequence, they were thrown off in the absolute judgment condition. Other studies have used brain imaging methods to show that more attentional resources are used when people are asked to perform culturally incongruous tasks (i.e., the absolute task for Asians and the relative task for European Americans; Hedden, Ketay et al., 2008; Murata et al., 2015).

In another line of research, researchers used a much simpler cognitive task that involves classification of objects by either semantic category or thematic relatedness (Ji et al., 2004). For example, the target could be "glove." Subjects were asked to decide whether the target would fit better with either "scarf" or "hand." If people are holistic, they ought to attend to the relatedness, and as a consequence, "hand" ought to be chosen more frequently than "scarf" as a better match. In fact, prior work has shown that the relational choice is more common among Asians than among European Americans.

The same conclusion has been suggested in research utilizing brain indices. For example, Goto et al. tested the degree to which contextual information is automatically taken into account even when there is no need to do so (Goto et al., 2010). Specifically, subjects were shown a contextual scene (parking lot or beach) first. Then, a target object (crab) was superimposed on the scene. Note that the initial context was chosen such that the object (the crab) was either congruous (the beach) or incongruous (the parking lot). Subjects were asked to report whether the target was animate or inanimate while ignoring the context. The researchers tested an ERP component called N400 – a negative deflection that occurs approximately 400 milliseconds poststimulus in response to a violation of semantic expectations. To the extent that subjects pay attention to the context, there would be a stronger N400 in the incongruous condition than in the congruous condition. This pattern, in fact, was found for Asians, suggesting that these individuals inadvertently paid attention to the context despite the fact that doing so was completely irrelevant to the task. In contrast, there was no difference between the congruous and incongruous conditions for European Americans. The study has since been conceptually replicated (Goto et al., 2013).

Altogether, Asians are consistently more holistic relative to European Americans. How about people from other cultures? By using the framed line test, San Martín et al. (2018) find that Arabs are highly holistic – at least equally as much as Asians. Another study showed the same for Latin Americans using a version of the Masuda and Nisbett task (de Oliveira & Nisbett, 2017).

Holistic Social Cognition

If people are holistic in terms of basic attentional processes, they may also be holistic in social inferences. Conversely, if they are more focused in terms of basic attentional processes, they may also be more focused in social inferences. For example, if people are attentive to a focal person and the context in which they are embedded, then they may consider both factors linked directly to the person and those related to the context relatively equally when making inferences about the person. However, if people are more narrowly focused on the person, they may fail to take the context into full account when making inferences about the person. These predictions have been borne out in a voluminous literature on culture and causal attribution (Choi et al., 1999; Miller, 1984; Morris & Peng, 1994).

In a typical study, subjects are shown a vignette describing another person acting in either socially desirable or undesirable ways. They are then asked to explain the person's behavior either by their personality, temperament, or other dispositional attributes or by norms, atmosphere, or other factors in the surrounding situation. Initial studies show a clear cultural difference between European Americans and Asians (Japanese in particular). To begin with, European Americans place a greater weight on dispositional (vs. situational) factors, consistent with prior work in social psychology demonstrating the fundamental attribution error (a bias to focus on a focal person while ignoring the context in which the person is embedded; Gilbert & Malone, 1995; Ross, 1977). In contrast, Asians did not show this bias, rating the involvement of both dispositional and situational factors equally (Kitayama et al., 2009, 2006).

In another related line of research, scholars have investigated ways in which people infer attitudes, personality traits, and other dispositions of a target person while knowing the person's behavior is under certain social constraints. If people are oblivious to the surrounding social context, they may make strong dispositional inferences (inferring the dispositions that correspond to the behavior) even when the behavior is strongly socially constrained. One early study investigated this potential bias in one extreme fashion (Gilbert & Jones, 1986). Subjects were instructed to ask another person to act in one way or another, say, to endorse capital punishment or not. They were then asked to infer the real attribute of the target person. In this case, the subjects themselves are imposing a social constraint and, to the extent that they were at least minimally attentive to this social constraint, they ought to discount the target's behavior in making this inference. Nevertheless, in studies with American subjects, the results were quite clear, indicating that individuals made strong inferences about the target person's real attitude (i.e., ascribing the behavior to an actual attitude of target person rather than the explicit request they made).

Masuda and Kitayama (2004) repeated a similar procedure and replicated the original finding among Americans, showing a strong tendency to narrowly focus on the focal person while ignoring the self-generated social constraint (Masuda & Kitayama, 2004). Importantly, however, in this study, the researchers also tested Japanese. Consistent with the hypothesis that Japanese are more holistic and, thus, prepared to pay close attention to social, contextual constraints, these individuals inferred no correspondent attitudes when they were asked to impose the social constraint on the target person. Similar differences have been replicated in cross-cultural studies (Miyamoto & Kitayama, 2002).

All this is not to say that Asians do not draw any dispositional inferences. To the contrary, they do. For example, when shown someone giving a seat to an old person in a crowded train, Asians do infer that the person must be "kind." However, the studies reviewed above suggest that when there is a blatantly clear situational constraint on the behavior, Asians readily discount the behavior in the trait inference. But European Americans typically fail to discount the focal person's behavior.

Moreover, recent evidence has begun to suggest that even when making trait inference (especially in the absence of any obvious situational constraint),

Asians do not draw this inference automatically (Na & Kitayama, 2011). Na and Kitayama (2011) asked subjects to memorize many pairs of a face and a behavior (e.g., "Checking a fire-alarm before going to bed"). Prior evidence showed that European Americans would infer a corresponding trait (e.g., cautious) from the behavior spontaneously and attach the inferred trait to the target person (Uleman et al., 2008). Drawing on this evidence, Na and Kitayama (2011) hypothesized that among European American subjects when each of the faces used in the memorization task was later presented to the subjects, the face would automatically activate the trait (e.g., "cautious") linked to the paired behavior. To test this possibility, during the second phase of the study, the subjects were given a lexical judgment task such that the face was used as a fixation, followed by a target word (or non-word). The target word was either the corresponding trait ("cautious") or its antonym ("careless"). EEG was monitored throughout. As in the Goto et al. (2010) study reviewed earlier, N400 – a brain signal indicating the detection of semantic incongruity – was tested. As predicted, it was significantly greater in magnitude in the antonym condition than in the corresponding trait condition. This shows that mere exposure to the face was sufficient to activate the corresponding trait ("cautious") in memory. Of importance, and consistent with the proposed cultural difference in trait inference, this effect was negligible for Asians.

How about other cultural groups? Evidence is very clear that Europeans as well as Israelis with European backgrounds tend to be highly dispositional in person perception and person inference. In contrast, non-Westerners including Arabs (San Martín et al., 2018) and Latin Americans (de Oliveira & Nisbett, 2017; Zárate et al., 2001) are similar to Asians.

Culture and Brain Structure

Does Culture Influence Brain Structure?

Evidence reviewed so far has established, first, that there is systematic cultural variation in three features of interdependence (vs. independence). Interdependence entails happiness that is linked more to social engagement (vs. disengagement), holistic attention, and holistic social cognition. With this criterion, Asians are more interdependent as compared to Americans with Western European backgrounds. Moreover, available evidence is consistent with the possibility that in terms of this criterion, various non-Western cultural groups other than Asians also tend to be interdependent. Last, but not least, the cultural variation is also revealed in functional characteristics of the brain as assessed with fMRI and EEG.

The fact that cultural variations can also be identified in brain functioning shows that culture gets under the skin, influencing neural connections and organization. One rather common view of culture would argue that culture is an overlay placed over underlying basic psychological processes. In this view, overt responses could vary across cultures, but the cultural influence may not "go deep" enough to impact the brain. Indeed, when the field of cultural neuroscience was launched over a decade ago, the primary goal was to challenge this assumption (Han et al., 2013). Researchers therefore tested the extent to which these cultural variations could be revealed in specific indices of the brain. The field has so far been very successful in achieving this initial goal.

In our view, the field is now poised to expand its scope to investigate the possibility that culture's influences extend beyond functions of the brain to include more enduring structural features of the brain. When people act in ways that are in line with cultural norms or expectations of others, the relevant neural circuitry will be consolidated and possibly expanded. This change will eventually manifest at the macrostructural level as increases in gray matter volume or cortical thickness (Lövdén et al., 2013).

The possibility that the structure of the brain may change through engagement with culture is consistent with earlier evidence that structural properties of the brain can be modified by mental demands imposed by a variety of tasks (Maguire et al., 2000; Rosenzweig et al., 1962; Woollett & Maguire, 2011). For example, Maguire et al. (2000) tested cab drivers in London. Back then, when GPS was not available, driving in a complex city like London presented substantial navigational demands. Cab drivers who drove all day everyday thus were expected to show increased gray matter volume in brain regions crucial for spatial navigation. One such region is the hippocampus. Maguire et al. (2000) therefore compared structural brain images from sixteen male taxi drivers in London and fifty age- and sex-matched controls, and they found that taxi drivers showed significantly greater volume in the posterior hippocampus bilaterally, relative to the controls. Moreover, the volume of the right posterior hippocampus increased as a function of time they spent as a taxi driver, providing initial evidence that the change in the gray matter volume is likely caused by the use of the navigational capacity. Similar evidence was found thereafter for professional keyboard players and the brain regions responsible for auditory processing and motor control (Gaser & Schlaug, 2003), as well as for normal individuals going through trainings on classic three-ball cascade juggling and brain regions responsible for visuospatial processing (Draganski et al., 2004).

Since culture is composed of a set of cultural tasks and being enculturated requires repetitive engagement and eventually mastery of those tasks, there may also arise systematic cross-cultural variations in the structural properties (i.e., gray matter volume and thickness) of certain brain regions. As noted earlier, independent cultures promote various independent tasks including self-promotion, personal goal pursuit, and finding and realizing the self. These tasks are characterized by what neuroscientists have called the "prefrontal functions." For instance, certain regions of the prefrontal area, particularly the orbitofrontal cortex (OFC), have been implicated in value-based judgment. It is further assumed to be critical for goal-seeking behaviors based on one's own interests and preferences (O'Doherty, 2011; Rolls & Grabenhorst, 2008). In fact, OFC lesions are often associated with the impairment of the ability to maintain consistent personal preferences (Fellows, 2011). Another critical prefrontal region is the medial prefrontal cortex (mPFC), which has been shown to support self-related processing such as developing a clear sense of the self (Northoff et al., 2006; Sui et al., 2013). The evidence reviewed above indicates that individuals engaged in Western cultures are motivated to carry out these tasks throughout their lives. Thus, to the extent that many of independent cultural tasks recruit these prefrontal regions, the Western individuals may eventually show increased volume or thickness in these areas.

Conversely, cross-cultural evidence implies that Asian cultural tasks such as modesty, self-effacement, and behavioral adjustment to social norms and social expectations may require temporary suppression of one's personal goals and selves. Remember, for example, that compared to Westerners, Asians were more likely to associate happiness with social engagement (e.g., social harmony) than with social disengagement (e.g., personal achievement). Further, evidence indicates that self-serving tendencies, which are quite robust among Westerners, are quite attenuated among East Asians (Heine et al., 1999). This suggests that engagement in East Asian cultures might not encourage the same intensive use of prefrontal regions that would be expected for engagement in Western cultures.

Cultural Variation in the Prefrontal Volume

Initial evidence for cultural variation in prefrontal cortex comes from a cross-cultural study by Chee et al., who compared Singaporean Chinese and European Americans (Chee et al., 2011). Their structural brain images were acquired and analyzed using both voxel-based morphometry (VBM) and surface-based analysis (i.e., Freesurfer). Results from both analyses showed that Americans have greater gray matter volume and thickness in several brain regions compared to Singaporeans, after controlling for age, sex, education, and total intracranial volume (TIV). Two regions that showed a notable cross-cultural difference were the OFC and the mPFC.

From this evidence alone, it is not possible to conclude that cultural tasks result in the observed cross-cultural difference in prefrontal volume or thickness. However, a few recent studies have shown that prefrontal volume may be linked to individual differences in interdependent (vs. independent) self-construal within each culture. Within any given culture, individuals can vary widely on this dimension of self-construal. Thus, it is possible that interdependent individuals are less likely than independent individuals to internalize the habit of carrying out independent tasks and, thus, to recruit the prefrontal regions in carrying out many everyday tasks. We would therefore predict an inverse association between interdependent (vs. independent) self-construal and indices of the prefrontal volume. One study tested this prediction among Japanese living in Japan and found a significant negative association between interdependent self-construal and OFC volume (Kitayama et al., 2017). Another study tested Chinese in China and found a significant negative association between interdependent self-construal and mPFC volume – an area contiguous to OFC (Wang et al., 2017).

The two correlational studies suggest that the cross-cultural variation in the prefrontal volume, demonstrated in the Chee et al. (2011) study, could be due to the self-construal dimension of interdependence. However, correlation never implies causality. Thus, this evidence alone does not demonstrate that engagement in culture gives rise to variations in prefrontal volume. Demonstrating causality might require an experimental intervention to see if increased engagement in independent tasks results in an increase of the prefrontal volume and, at present, no such study has been done. Fortunately, there are alternative methods by which to address this question.

The Dopamine D4 Receptor Gene (DRD4): Seeking Evidence for Environmental Influence

One alternative method for examining cultural effects on the brain draws on recent advances in research on gene–environment interactions. This work suggests that certain genetic polymorphisms can augment an individual's sensitivity to environmental influences, including cultural influences (Belsky & Pluess, 2009; Kim & Sasaki, 2014). These polymorphic variations are commonly called "plasticity alleles." Building on this work, we may expect that if the cultural difference in the prefrontal volume is due to cultural influences, the difference should be more pronounced for those individuals who are genetically predisposed to be more sensitive to cultural influences. If, however, the cultural difference in the prefrontal volume were innate, biologically preprogrammed before birth, there is no reason to expect it to be moderated by plasticity alleles.

Belsky and Pluess have identified up to ten plasticity alleles (Belsky & Pluess, 2009). It is not clear if all of them play a role in modulating each person's sensitivity to cultural influences. Moreover, some studies have proved difficult to replicate (Duncan & Keller, 2011). Hence, it is crucial to undertake careful analysis before deciding on the target of this investigation. We have chosen to focus on the varying-number-tandem-repeat (VNTR) of the dopamine D4 receptor gene (*DRD4*). In particular, two allelic variants of *DRD4*, the so-called 7-repeat and 2-repeat alleles (7/2-R), have been the focus of intensive investigation in recent years. We had three reasons for our decision to focus on this gene.

First, it is known that the 7/2-R allele of *DRD4* is associated with blunted activity of the D4 receptor. It should be acknowledged that some scholars (e.g., Bakermans-Kranenburg & Van IJzendoorn, 2011; Weeland et al., 2015) used this fact to theorize that certain behaviors thought to be linked to this allele (e.g., novelty-seeking and impulsivity) are behavioral means of compensating for the blunted dopamine activity. However, this theory ignores the fact that any receptor activity is embedded in a larger network of molecular- and cellular level processing. Indeed, we know of no evidence that such behavioral compensation of the molecular-level depletion of dopamine occurs. Another plausible mechanism is suggested by the fact that the D4 receptor is inhibitory. Thus, the activation of the D4 receptor is thought to downregulate the cellular level activity of the systems innervated by dopaminergic neurons. The blunted D4 receptor activity, caused by the 7/2-R allele of *DRD4*, may thus disinhibit the cellular activity in the relevant systems. Moreover, dopamine is one of the most prevalent neurotransmitters in both subcortical reward processing regions and prefrontal executive systems (Nikolova et al., 2011; Schultz, 2002). Hence, the 7/2-R allelic variants of *DRD4* may increase one's sensitivity to reward signals while also enhancing one's capability to compute the reward contingencies over a long period – the two cognitive and affective capacities believed to be required to accurately infer cultural norms and rules (Kitayama et al., 2014).

Second, there is evidence that these two allelic variants have been actively selected over the course of the last 50 000 years, particularly across the Eurasian continent – a fact suggesting that these alleles may well have coevolved with culture that unfolded during the period. One plausible reason for this selection might come from the fact that the new variants of this particular gene enhanced both reward processing and executive functions, which in turn may have increased individuals' capability to accurately estimate norms and rules of the larger social units that were emerging around that time. This argument implies that *DRD4* was selected for its ability to regulate preexisting brain systems involved in reinforcement-based learning including striatal reward processing and the computation of reward contingencies. Note that these systems are regulated by a large number of genes. Our analysis then amounts to the hypothesis that *DRD4* serves as a highly interconnected "hub" for networks involved in genetic signaling. This status as a hub gene might help us understand why *DRD4* is not just one of humans' 22 000 genes. It can have a nontrivial effect size on specific aspects of behavior linked to reward processing, including cultural learning.

Third, and equally important, a growing body of literature shows that children carrying one of the plasticity alleles (the 7-repeat variant, which is particularly common in Western populations) are quite sensitive or susceptible to parenting quality. In one of the earliest studies investigating this prediction, Sheese et al. (2007) tested 3- to 4-year-old children (all European Americans), whose behavioral profiles were rated by their parents. Brief parent–child interactions were video-taped and coded for parental quality. They contrasted carriers of the 7-repeat allele of *DRD4* with noncarriers (very few European Americans carry the 2-repeat allele). The researchers observed that low quality of parenting predicted increased impulsivity and activity levels of children. Importantly, this association between parental quality and child behavior was evident only among the children carrying the 7-repeat allele of *DRD4*.

This initial finding has since been replicated (Belsky & Pluess, 2009; van IJzendoorn et al., 2011). Moreover, recent work used an experimental intervention intended to improve parental quality and showed that the beneficial effect of this intervention on child behavior was observed only among the children carrying the 7-repeat allele of *DRD4*, providing additional evidence consistent with our analysis (Bakermans-Kranenburg & van IJzendoorn, 2006; 2011; Bakermans-Kranenburg et al., 2008; van IJzendoorn et al., 2010, 2011). Recent reviews underscore the possibility that actions of the 7-repeat allele of *DRD4* is strongly moderated by environmental conditions (Bakermans-Kranenburg & van IJzendoorn, 2011; Weeland et al., 2015).

DRD4 × *Culture Interaction: I. Behavioral Tendencies*

If 7/2-R allele carriers are more sensitive to reward contingencies than noncarriers, it might be expected that the carriers would be more likely to acquire behavioral patterns that are sanctioned in their local communities. Kitayama et al. tested this prediction in the context of East–West psychological differences (Kitayama et al., 2014). As discussed earlier in this chapter, compared to European Americans, Asians are more interdependent or less independent (Kitayama & Salvador, 2017; Kitayama et al., 2009; Markus & Kitayama, 1991). To the extent that the cultural norms of the self being independent or interdependent are acquired through reinforcement-based learning, this cultural difference should also be more pronounced for people carrying the 7/2-R allele as compared to noncarriers.

A total of 398 college undergraduates at the University of Michigan filled out several scales designed to assess various facets of independence (e.g., independent self-construal, self-efficacy, and valuing of self-expression) or interdependence (e.g., interdependent self-construal and holistic cognition). The participants varied in both backgrounds (European vs. Asian) and *DRD4* status (7/2-R carrier vs. noncarrier). As expected, Asians were relatively more interdependent or less independent than European Americans. Further, this cultural difference was observed only among those carrying the 7/2-R allele of *DRD4*. Among the noncarriers, there was no significant cultural difference in independence or interdependence. The cultural difference was highly reliable and "large" in magnitude (Cohen's $d > 1.00$) among the carriers, but it was negligible among the noncarriers (Cohen's $d < .02$). Recently, Tompson et al. (2018) extended this finding by showing that a cross-cultural difference in emotional experience (European Americans experiencing more positive affect than Asians) is evident among carriers, but not among noncarriers (Tompson et al., 2018).

DRD4 × Culture Interaction: II. Brain Structure

If the key mechanism underlying the effect of *DRD4* involves socially mediated reinforcement, we might further theorize that when certain cognitions, emotions, motivations, and behaviors are reinforced, all neural connections and pathways that support them will also be reinforced. Given the inverse association among Japanese between interdependent self-construal and OFC volume discussed above, we would expect a cultural difference in the OFC volume when comparing Asians and European Americans. Since European Americans are less interdependent than Asians, the OFC volume may be expected to be larger for the former than for the latter. Moreover, to the extent that this cultural difference is mediated by reinforcement-based learning in which *DRD4* is likely to play a key role, we may further anticipate that the cultural difference in the OFC volume (European Americans > Asians) would be more pronounced among carriers of the 7/2-R allele of *DRD4* than among noncarriers. Our recent investigation addressed these possibilities (Yu et al., 2019).

One hundred thirty-two undergraduates were recruited such that half had European American cultural backgrounds while the remaining half had Asian cultural backgrounds. Moreover, approximately half in each cultural group had a 7- or 2-repeat allele of *DRD4*. We drew on the Kitayama et al. (2017) study and identified OFC as an anatomical region of interest (ROI; Figure 3.2A). First, we replicated the Kitayama et al. (2017) finding and showed that the gray matter volume of the OFC ROI decreases as a function of interdependent self-construal (Figure 3.2B). Second, and critically, when we analyzed the gray matter volume of the OFC ROI, the interaction between culture and *DRD4* status proved to be statistically significant. As shown in Figure 3.2C, the OFC volume was significantly greater for European Americans than for Asians, after controlling for total brain volume, age, and gender. Importantly, this cultural difference was significantly larger among carriers of the 7/2-R allele of *DRD4* than among noncarriers.

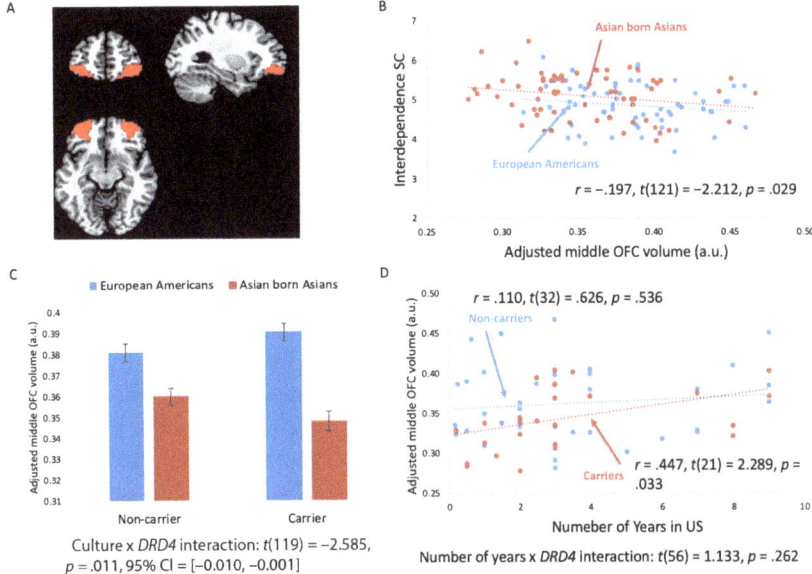

Figure 3.2 Cortical volume of the orbitofrontal cortex. (A) Regions of interest. (B) Inverse association between interdependence self-construal and the OFC volume. (C) Culture × DRD4 status interaction on the OFC volume. (D) The OFC volume among Asians with varying numbers of years in the United States as a function of DRD4 status.

Adapted from Q. Yu et al., "Cultural Variation in the Gray Matter Volume of the Prefrontal Cortex Is Moderated by the Dopamine D4 Receptor Gene (DRD4)," *Cerebral Cortex*, 2018, 29(9), pp. 3925 and 3927 (https://doi.org/10.1093/cercor/bhy271), by permission of Oxford University Press

Further analysis revealed additional evidence for the critical role of experience in modulating OFC volume. Our Asian participants had lived in the United States for varying amounts of time when they were tested. When their OFC volume was analyzed as a function of the time in the United States, there was a clear correlation such that the OFC volume increased as a function of the time in the United States. Moreover, consistent with the role of the 7/2-R alleles of *DRD4* to increase environmental influences, this correlation was larger, albeit non-significantly, for the carriers than for the noncarriers (Figure 3.2D).

Future Directions

We began this chapter with an observation: By spontaneously functioning, the human mind often contributes to the reproduction of the culture in which it is embedded. At the same time, however, we also pointed out that the apparent spontaneity of this process conceals from our view the powerful feedback effect of cultural influences. The mode of human psychological functions is fundamentally cultural – both shaped through culture as well as mediated by it, and as a consequence, it is also equally fundamental to look closely into the "how" of the cultural shaping of the mind.

In seeking to address this question, we examined the evolution of various cultural and ethnic groups over the last 10 000 years. This review identified some reasons to believe in the validity of distinguishing between the West and the "rest." Most human groups over the previous 10 000 years were likely highly interdependent. One important exception to this was the emergence of the modern West in the last several hundred years. Unlike all, or perhaps almost all, previously existent cultures, the modern West was based on a new conception of the self as independent. The newly emerging commitment to the personal self in the modern West was in stark contrast to many non-Western cultures, which is reflected in the cross-cultural evidence reviewed in this chapter. We have shown that interdependent orientations (common in non-Western cultures) are reflected in social happiness, holistic attention, and holistic social cognition. These features are much weaker or otherwise completely reversed to show more personal happiness, focused attention, and social cognition that is anchored in focal objects in Western, independent cultures. This evidence was initially based on various psychological tasks, but it is now extended to include neuroscience evidence (e.g., Figure 3.1). In particular, we reviewed recent evidence that engagement in culture can plastically change regionally specific cortical volume (Figure 3.2).

We are cognizant of a persistent accusation regarding the hypothesized difference between the West and the rest as being no more than the stereotyping of non-Westerners from the West's elitist perspective, which – intentionally or not – patronizes the rest (Said, 1979). This perspective, sometimes called Orientalism, is a depiction of the international power dynamics that can sometimes compromise the validity of analyses of cultures from any single perspective. However, the identification of a non-Western perspective (interdependence) that is distinct from its Western counterpart (independence) could be a useful point of departure that gives fair due to both. Moreover, the thoroughly empirical approach undertaken in the studies summarized in this chapter may serve as an effective, if not perfect, antidote against any elitist, ethnocentric proclivities that might exist in any and potentially all researchers. This antidote is often not readily available, not rigorous enough, or both, in most studies of culture. In addition to these general points, however, we wish to underscore two crucial features of our approach. First, we explicitly underscore the diversity within the non-West. Second, our theoretical approach seeks to integrate individual variability within an analysis identifying a coherent cultural variation. We now turn to each of these two points.

Varying Forms of Interdependence

All the evidence we reviewed in this chapter is limited to the few characteristics of interdependence that are thought to be common to all (or almost all) non-Western cultures, which tend to give greater priority to social relationships over the personal self. As indicated earlier, this does not mean that the non-West is homogeneous. In fact, we pointed out that there are at least four different forms of interdependence, reflecting divergent strategies to achieve the valued state of interdependence.

More research is needed to specify these varying forms of interdependence, which are thought to be related to historically dominant socio-ecologies of the locales. We hypothesize, for example, that East Asian civilization is grounded in the tradition of rice farming, as much as Arab civilization is derived from a nomadic tradition of the living in sparsely populated deserts. This, of course, does not mean that each region is uniform or homogeneous. Nevertheless, the predominant ecology and the way of life in it may often be incorporated into cultural stories and narratives, which in turn become a basis for further development of the cultural groups. The historical development of narratives, or origin myths, that may well be contingent on the ancient social ecology may be an important missing link that can potentially connect the current contemporary cultures and mentalities to those of the ancient times. Clearly, much more work is needed to fill the space in between at the macro, sociohistorical, even evolutionary levels.

Individual Variability and Coherence of Culture

All individuals are unique with idiosyncratic sets of goals, desires, and social networks. Their variability is massive – so much so that it would seem misleading to group them together by any cultural or ethnic categories. Many scholars, especially in the humanities, have taken pains to point out this diversity and have argued that any such genetic or ancestral groupings are no more than unwarranted stereotyping. At the same time, from a cultural psychological perspective, there is no denying that various cultural groups do exist and, moreover, that each of the groups appears distinct enough to warrant careful analysis in their own right. This latter view typically comes from empirical scientists who aggregate individual-level observations and analyze higher-order grouping categories.

In this chapter, we argued that the apparent paradox of variability within culture and the systematic variations across cultures are inherent in how culture is acquired and then reconstructed. Culture as a collective-level reality shapes human brains in a highly idiosyncratic fashion. The culturally shaped brains may then participate in and reproduce parts of the culture. Hence, when focusing myopically on individual behaviors, individuals would appear highly variable and idiosyncratic. However, this variability is a reflection of cultural shaping of the brains. As such, behaviors that are culturally shaped may show systematic patterns when they are aggregated across individuals. This collective-level reality may be reproduced with high levels of fidelity even though there may be great variation at the individual level.

Mutual Constitution of Culture and the Mind

Nearly three decades ago, the anthropologist Richard Shweder (1991) argued that culture and the psyche make each other up. In broad outline, the human mind is constituted by a variety of cultural elements. This process of cultural influence is dynamic, variable, and yet, highly systematic. We have also pointed out that culture is reproduced by the operations of the minds thus constituted. This reproduction is thus mediated by the variable individual behaviors and related brain circuitries. Each individual thus functions in idiosyncratic ways to give rise to novel behaviors and opportunities for cultural change. However, when combined across individuals, individual idiosyncrasies cancel each other out. Culture will have been reproduced with substantial degrees of fidelity, although the individual variability that accompanies the process offers numerous possibilities for cultural change. In this way, culture and the mind are mutually constitutive and, yet, as a whole, they continue to adjust to the ever-changing social, ecological, political, and economic realities that unfold in the world (Shweder, 1991).

To get a better understanding of the dynamic interplay between culture and the mind within the ever-changing and continuously globalizing world is exceptionally challenging as a scientific endeavor. The achievements accomplished over the last three decades of research in both cultural psychology and cultural neuroscience are admittedly limited. However, we believe that they can contribute to a better understanding of this exquisite interplay, which lies at the heart of what it means to be a human being.

REFERENCES

Bakerman`s-Kranenburg, M. J., & van IJzendoorn, M. H. (2006). Gene–environment interaction of the dopamine D4 receptor (DRD4) and observed maternal insensitivity predicting externalizing behavior in preschoolers. *Developmental Psychobiology*, *48*(5), 406–9. https://doi.org/10.1002/dev.20152

Bakermans-Kranenburg, M. J., & van IJzendoorn, M. H. (2011). Differential susceptibility to rearing environment depending on dopamine-related genes: New evidence and a meta-analysis. *Development and Psychopathology*, *23*(1), 39–52. https://doi.org/10.1017/S0954579410000635

Bakermans-Kranenburg, M. J., van IJzendoorn, M. H., Pijlman, F. T. A., Mesman, J., & Juffer, F. (2008). Experimental evidence for differential susceptibility: Dopamine D4 receptor polymorphism (DRD4 VNTR) moderates intervention effects on toddlers' externalizing behavior in a randomized controlled trial. *Developmental Psychology, 44*(1), 293–300. https://doi.org/10.1037/0012-1649.44.1.293

Belsky, J., & Pluess, M. (2009). Beyond diathesis stress: Differential susceptibility to environmental influences. *Psychological Bulletin, 135*(6), 885–908. https://doi.org/10.1037/a0017376

Chee, M. W. L., Zheng, H., Goh, J. O. S., Park, D., & Sutton, B. P. (2011). Brain structure in young and old East Asians and Westerners: Comparisons of structural volume and cortical thickness. *Journal of Cognitive Neuroscience, 23*(5), 1065–79. https://doi.org/10.1162/jocn.2010.21513

Choi, I., Nisbett, R. E., & Norenzayan, A. (1999). Causal attribution across cultures: Variation and universality. *Psychological Bulletin, 125*(1), 47–63. https://doi.org/10.1037/0033-2909.125.1.47

Damasio, A. (2018). *The strange order of things: Life, feeling, and the making of cultures*. Pantheon Books.

de Oliveira, S., & Nisbett, R. E. (2017). Beyond East and West: Cognitive style in Latin America. *Journal of Cross-Cultural Psychology, 48*(10), 1554–77. https://doi.org/10.1177/0022022117730816

Draganski, B., Gaser, C., Busch, V., Schuierer, G., Bogdahn, U., & May, A. (2004). Neuroplasticity: Changes in grey matter induced by training. *Nature, 427*(6972), 311–12. https://doi.org/10.1038/427311a

Duncan, L. E., & Keller, M. C. (2011). A critical review of the first 10 years of candidate gene-by-environment interaction research in psychiatry. *The American Journal of Psychiatry, 168*(10), 1041–9. https://doi.org/10.1176/appi.ajp.2011.11020191

Fellows, L. K. (2011). Orbitofrontal contributions to value-based decision making: Evidence from humans with frontal lobe damage. *Annals of the New York Academy of Sciences, 1239*(1), 51–8. https://doi.org/10.1111/j.1749-6632.2011.06229.x

Gardner, W. L., Gabriel, S., & Lee, A. Y. (1999). "I" value freedom, but 'we' value relationships: Self-construal priming mirrors cultural differences in judgment. *Psychological Science, 10*(4), 321–6. https://doi.org/10.1111/1467-9280.00162

Gaser, C., & Schlaug, G. (2003). Brain structures differ between musicians and non-musicians. *Journal of Neuroscience, 23*(27), 9240–5. https://doi.org/10.1523/JNEUROSCI.23-27-09240.2003

Gehring, W. J., Goss, B., Coles, M. G. H., Meyer, D. E., & Donchin, E. (1993). A neural system for error detection and compensation. *Psychological Science, 4*(6), 385–90. https://doi.org/10.1111/j.1467-9280.1993.tb00586.x

Gilbert, D. T., & Malone, P. S. (1995). The correspondence bias. *Psychological Bulletin, 117*(1), 21–38. https://doi.org/10.1037/0033-2909.117.1.21

Gilbert, D. T., & Jones, E. E. (1986). Perceiver-induced constraint: Interpretations of self-generated reality. *Journal of Personality and Social Psychology, 50*(2), 269–80. https://doi.org/10.1037/0022-3514.50.2.269

Goto, S. G., Ando, Y., Huang, C., Yee, A., & Lewis, R. S. (2010). Cultural differences in the visual processing of meaning: Detecting incongruities between background and foreground objects using the N400. *Social Cognitive and Affective Neuroscience, 5*(2–3), 242–53. https://doi.org/10.1093/scan/nsp038

Goto, S. G., Yee, A., Lowenberg, K., & Lewis, R. S. (2013). Cultural differences in sensitivity to social context: Detecting affective incongruity using the N400. *Social Neuroscience*, *8*(1), 63–74. https://doi.org/10.1080/17470919.2012.739202

Haber, S. (2011). Neuroanatomy of reward: A view from the ventral striatum. In J. A. Gottfried (Ed.), *Neurobiology of sensation and reward*. (pp. 235–62). CRC Press. www.ncbi.nlm.nih.gov/books/NBK92777/

Hajcak, G., Moser, J. S., Yeung, N., & Simons, R. F. (2005). On the ERN and the significance of errors. *Psychophysiology*, *42*(2), 151–60. https://doi.org/10.1111/j.1469-8986.2005.00270.x

Han, S., Northoff, G., Vogeley, K., Wexler, B. E., Kitayama, S., & Varnum, M. E. W. (2013). A cultural neuroscience approach to the biosocial nature of the human brain. *Annual Review of Psychology*, *64*(1), 335–59. https://doi.org/10.1146/annurev-psych-071112-054629

Hedden, T., Ketay, S., Aron, A., Markus, H. R., & Gabrieli, J. D. E. (2008). Cultural influences on neural substrates of attentional control. *Psychological Science*, *19*(1), 12–17. https://doi.org/10.1111/j.1467-9280.2008.02038.x

Heine, S. J., Lehman, D. R., Markus, H. R., & Kitayama, S. (1999). Is there a universal need for positive self-regard? *Psychological Review*, *106*(4), 766–94. https://doi.org/10.1037//0033-295x.106.4.766

Henrich, J. (2015). *The secret of our success: How culture is driving human evolution, domesticating our species, and making us smarter*. Princeton University Press.

Hofstede, G. (1980). *Culture's consequences: International differences in work-related values*. SAGE.

Ji, L.-J., Zhang, Z., & Nisbett, R. E. (2004). Is it culture or is it language? Examination of language effects in cross-cultural research on categorization. *Journal of Personality and Social Psychology*, *87*(1), 57–65. https://doi.org/10.1037/0022-3514.87.1.57

Kim, H., & Markus, H. R. (1999). Deviance or uniqueness, harmony or conformity? A cultural analysis. *Journal of Personality and Social Psychology*, *77*(4), 785–800. https://doi.org/10.1037/0022-3514.77.4.785

Kim, H. S., & Sasaki, J. Y. (2014). Cultural neuroscience: Biology of the mind in cultural contexts. *Annual Review of Psychology*, *65*(1), 487–514. https://doi.org/10.1146/annurev-psych-010213-115040

Kitayama, S., Duffy, S., Kawamura, T., & Larsen, J. T. (2003). Perceiving an object and its context in different cultures: A cultural look at new look. *Psychological Science*, *14*(3), 201–6. https://doi.org/10.1111/1467-9280.02432

Kitayama, S., Ishii, K., Imada, T., Takemura, K., & Ramaswamy, J. (2006). Voluntary settlement and the spirit of independence: Evidence from Japan's 'northern frontier.' *Journal of Personality and Social Psychology*, *91*(3), 369–84. https://doi.org/10.1037/0022-3514.91.3.369

Kitayama, S., King, A., Yoon, C., Tompson, S., Huff, S., & Liberzon, I. (2014). The dopamine D4 receptor gene (DRD4) moderates cultural difference in independent versus interdependent social orientation. *Psychological Science*, *25*(6), 1169–77. https://doi.org/10.1177/0956797614528338

Kitayama, S., Markus, H. R., & Kurokawa, M. (2000). Culture, emotion, and well-being: Good feelings in Japan and the United States. *Cognition and Emotion*, *14*(1), 93–124. https://doi.org/10.1080/026999300379003

Kitayama, S., Markus, H. R., Matsumoto, H., & Norasakkunkit, V. (1997). Individual and collective processes in the construction of the self: Self-enhancement in the United States and self-criticism in Japan. *Journal of Personality and Social Psychology*, *72*(6), 1245–67. https://doi.org/10.1037//0022-3514.72.6.1245

Kitayama, S., Mesquita, B., & Karasawa, M. (2006). Cultural affordances and emotional experience: Socially engaging and disengaging emotions in Japan and the United States. *Journal of Personality and Social Psychology*, *91*(5), 890–903. https://doi.org/10.1037/0022-3514.91.5.890

Kitayama, S., & Park, J. (2014). Error-related brain activity reveals self-centric motivation: Culture matters. *Journal of Experimental Psychology: General*, *143*(1), 62–70. https://doi.org/10.1037/a0031696.supp

Kitayama, S., Park, H., Sevincer, A. T., Karasawa, M., & Uskul, A. K. (2009). A cultural task analysis of implicit independence: Comparing North America, Western Europe, and East Asia. *Journal of Personality and Social Psychology*, *97*(2), 236–55. https://doi.org/10.1037/a0015999

Kitayama, S., & Salvador, C. E. (2017). Culture embrained: Going beyond the nature-nurture dichotomy. *Perspectives on Psychological Science*, *12*(5), 841–54. https://doi.org/10.1177%2F1745691617707317

Kitayama, S., San Martín, Á., & Savani, K. (2019). *Varieties of interdependence and the emergence of the modern West: Toward the globalizing of psychology.* Unpublished manuscript, Department of Psychology, University of Michigan, Ann Arbor, MI.

Kitayama, S., Snibbe, A. C., Markus, H. R., & Suzuki, T. (2004). Is there any "free" choice? Self and dissonance in two cultures. *Psychological Science*, *15*(8), 527–33. https://doi.org/10.1111/j.0956-7976.2004.00714.x

Kitayama, S., & Tompson, S. (2015). A biosocial model of affective decision making: Implications for dissonance, motivation, and culture. In J. M. Olson & M. P. Zanna (Eds.), *Advances in experimental social psychology* (Vol. 52, pp. 72–137). Academic Press. https://doi.org/10.1016/bs.aesp.2015.04.001

Kitayama, S., & Uskul, A. K. (2011). Culture, mind, and the brain: Current evidence and future directions. *Annual Review of Psychology*, *62*(1), 419–49. https://doi.org/10.1146/annurev-psych-120709-145357

Kitayama, S., Varnum, M. E. W., & Salvador, C. M. (2019). Cultural neuroscience. In D. Cohen & S. Kitayama (Eds.), *The handbook of cultural psychology* (2nd ed., pp. 79–118). Guilford Press.

Kitayama, S., Yanagisawa, K., Ito, A., Ueda, R., Uchida, Y., & Abe, N. (2017). Reduced orbitofrontal cortical volume is associated with interdependent self-construal. *Proceedings of the National Academy of Sciences of the United States of America*, *114*(30), 7969–74. https://doi.org/10.1073/pnas.1704831114

Knutson, B., & Greer, S. M. (2008). Anticipatory affect: Neural correlates and consequences for choice. *Philosophical Transactions of the Royal Society B: Biological Sciences*, *363*(1511), 3771–86. https://doi.org/10.1098/rstb.2008.0155

Lövdén, M., Wenger, E., Mårtensson, J., Lindenberger, U., & Bäckman, L. (2013). Structural brain plasticity in adult learning and development. *Neuroscience & Biobehavioral Reviews*, *37*(9, Part B), 2296–310. https://doi.org/10.1016/j.neubiorev.2013.02.014

Maguire, E. A., Gadian, D. G., Johnsrude, I. S., Good, C. D., Ashburner, J., Frackowiak, R. S. J., & Frith, C. D. (2000). Navigation-related structural change in the hippocampi of taxi drivers. *Proceedings of the National Academy of Sciences of the United States of America*, *97*(8), 4398–403. https://doi.org/10.1073/pnas.070039597

Markus, H. R., & Kitayama, S. (1991). Culture and the self: Implications for cognition, emotion, and motivation. *Psychological Review*, *98*(2), 224–53. https://doi.org/10.1037/0033-295X.98.2.224

Masuda, T., & Kitayama, S. (2004). Perceiver-induced constraint and attitude attribution in Japan and the US: A case for the cultural dependence of the correspondence bias. *Journal of Experimental Social Psychology*, *40*(3), 409–16. https://doi.org/10.1016/j.jesp.2003.08.004

Masuda, T., & Nisbett, R. E. (2001). Attending holistically versus analytically: Comparing the context sensitivity of Japanese and Americans. *Journal of Personality and Social Psychology*, *81*(5), 922–34. https://doi.org/10.1037//0022-3514.81.5.922

Miller, J. G. (1984). Culture and the development of everyday social explanation. *Journal of Personality and Social Psychology*, *46*(5), 961–78. https://doi.org/10.1037/0022-3514.46.5.961

Miller, J. G., Bersoff, D. M., & Harwood, R. L. (1990). Perceptions of social responsibilities in India and in the United States: Moral imperatives or personal decisions? *Journal of Personality and Social Psychology*, *58*(1), 33–47. https://doi.org/10.1037//0022-3514.58.1.33

Miyamoto, Y., & Kitayama, S. (2002). Cultural variation in correspondence bias: The critical role of attitude diagnosticity of socially constrained behavior. *Journal of Personality and Social Psychology*, *83*(5), 1239–48. https://doi.org/10.1037//0022-3514.83.5.1239

Morling, B., Kitayama, S., & Miyamoto, Y. (2002). Cultural practices emphasize influence in the United States and adjustment in Japan. *Personality and Social Psychology Bulletin*, *28*(3), 311–23. https://doi.org/10.1177/0146167202286003

Morris, M. W., & Peng, K. (1994). Culture and cause: American and Chinese attributions for social and physical events. *Journal of Personality and Social Psychology*, *67*(6), 949–71. https://doi.org/10.1037/0022-3514.67.6.949

Murata, A., Park, J., Kovelman, I., Hu, X., & Kitayama, S. (2015). Culturally non-preferred cognitive tasks require compensatory attention: A functional near infrared spectroscopy (fNIRS) investigation. *Culture and Brain*, *3*(1), 53–67. https://doi.org/10.1007/s40167–015-0027-y

Na, J., Grossmann, I., Varnum, M. E. W., Kitayama, S., Gonzalez, R., & Nisbett, R. E. (2010). Cultural differences are not always reducible to individual differences. *Proceedings of the National Academy of Sciences of the United States of America*, *107*(14), 6192–7. https://doi.org/10.1073/pnas.1001911107

Na, J., & Kitayama, S. (2011). Spontaneous trait inference is culture-specific: Behavioral and neural evidence. *Psychological Science*, *22*(8), 1025–32. https://doi.org/10.1177/0956797611414727

Nikolova, Y. S., Ferrell, R. E., Manuck, S. B., & Hariri, A. R. (2011). Multilocus genetic profile for dopamine signaling predicts ventral striatum reactivity. *Neuropsychopharmacology*, *36*(9), 1940–7. https://doi.org/10.1038/npp.2011.82

Nisbett, R. E., & Cohen, D. (1996). *New directions in social psychology. Culture of honor: The psychology of violence in the South*. Westview Press.

Nisbett, R. E., Peng, K., Choi, I., & Norenzayan, A. (2001). Culture and systems of thought: Holistic versus analytic cognition. *Psychological Review, 108*(2), 291–310. https://doi.org/10.1037/0033-295X.108.2.291

Northoff, G., Heinzel, A., de Greck, M., Bermpohl, F., Dobrowolny, H., & Panksepp, J. (2006). Self-referential processing in our brain: A meta-analysis of imaging studies on the self. *NeuroImage, 31*(1), 440–57. https://doi.org/10.1016/j.neuroimage.2005.12.002

O'Doherty, J. P. (2011). Contributions of the ventromedial prefrontal cortex to goal-directed action selection. *Annals of the New York Academy of Sciences, 1239*(1), 118–29. https://doi.org/10.1111/j.1749-6632.2011.06290.x

Oyserman, D., & Lee, S. W. S. (2008). Does culture influence what and how we think? Effects of priming individualism and collectivism. *Psychological Bulletin, 134*(2), 311–42. https://doi.org/10.1037/0033-2909.134.2.311

Reich, D. (2018). *Who we are and how we got here: Ancient DNA and the new science of the human past.* Oxford University Press.

Rhee, E., Uleman, J. S., Lee, H. K., & Roman, R. J. (1995). Spontaneous self-descriptions and ethnic identities in individualistic and collectivistic cultures. *Journal of Personality and Social Psychology, 69*(1), 142–52. https://doi.org/10.1037/0022-3514.69.1.142

Rolls, E. T., & Grabenhorst, F. (2008). The orbitofrontal cortex and beyond: From affect to decision-making. *Progress in Neurobiology, 86*(3), 216–44. https://doi.org/10.1016/j.pneurobio.2008.09.001

Rosenzweig, M. R., Krech, D., Bennett, E. L., & Zolman, J. F. (1962). Variation in environmental complexity and brain measures. *Journal of Comparative and Physiological Psychology, 55*(6), 1092–5. https://doi.org/10.1037/h0042758

Ross, L. (1977). The intuitive psychologist and his shortcomings: Distortions in the attribution process. In L. Berkowitz (Ed.), *Advances in experimental social psychology* (pp. 173–220). Academic Press. https://doi.org/10.1016/S0065-2601(08)60357-3

Ruby, M. B., Falk, C. F., Heine, S. J., Villa, C., & Silberstein, O. (2012). Not all collectivisms are equal: Opposing preferences for ideal affect between East Asians and Mexicans. *Emotion, 12*(6), 1206–9. https://doi.org/10.1037/a0029118

Rychlowska, M., Miyamoto, Y., Matsumoto, D., Hess, U., Gilboa-Schechtman, E., Kamble, S., Muluk, H., Masuda, T., & Niedenthal, P. M. (2015). Heterogeneity of long-history migration explains cultural differences in reports of emotional expressivity and the functions of smiles. *Proceedings of the National Academy of Sciences of the United States of America, 112*(19), E2429–E2436. https://doi.org/10.1073/pnas.1413661112

Said, E. W. (1979). *Orientalism.* Vintage Books.

San Martín, A., Sinaceur, M., Madi, A., Tompson, S., Maddux, W. W., & Kitayama, S. (2018). Self-assertive interdependence in Arab culture. *Nature Human Behaviour, 2,* 830–7. https://doi.org/10.1038/s41562-018-0435-z

Sanchez-Burks, J., Nisbett, R. E., & Ybarra, O. (2000). Cultural styles, relational schemas, and prejudice against out-groups. *Journal of Personality and Social Psychology, 79*(2), 174–89. https://doi.org/10.1037/0022-3514.79.2.174

Savani, K., Markus, H. R., & Conner, A. L. (2008). Let your preference be your guide? Preferences and choices are more tightly linked for North Americans than for

Indians. *Journal of Personality and Social Psychology, 95*(4), 861–76. https://doi.org/10.1037/a0011618

Schultz, W. (2002). Getting formal with dopamine and reward. *Neuron, 36*(2), 241–63. https://doi.org/10.1016/s0896-6273(02)00967-4

Schwartz, S. (2006). A theory of cultural value orientations: Explication and applications. *Comparative Sociology, 5*(2–3), 137–82. https://doi.org/10.1163/156913306778667357

Sen, A. (2005). *The argumentative Indian: Writings on Indian history, culture and identity.* Farrar, Straus and Giroux.

Sheese, B. E., Voelker, P. M., Rothbart, M. K., & Posner, M. P. (2007). Parenting quality interacts with genetic variation in dopamine receptor D4 to influence temperament in early childhood. *Development and Psychopathology, 19*(4), 1039–46. https://doi.org/10.1017/s0954579407000521

Shweder, R. A. (1991). *Thinking through cultures: Expeditions in cultural psychology.* Harvard University Press.

Shweder, R. A., & Bourne, E. J. (1982). Does the concept of the person vary cross-culturally? In A. J. Marsella & G. M. White (Eds.), *Cultural conceptions of mental health and therapy culture, illness, and healing* (pp. 97–137). Springer. https://doi.org/10.1007/978-94-010-9220-3_4

Sui, J., Rotshtein, P., & Humphreys, G. W. (2013). Coupling social attention to the self forms a network for personal significance. *Proceedings of the National Academy of Sciences of the United States of America, 110*(19), 7607–12. https://doi.org/10.1073/pnas.1221862110

Talhelm, T., Zhang, X., Oishi, S., Shimin, C., Duan, D., Lan, X., & Kitayama, S. (2014). Large-scale psychological differences within China explained by rice versus wheat agriculture. *Science, 344*(6184), 603–8. https://doi.org/10.1126/science.1246850

Telzer, E. H., & Fuligni, A. J. (2009). Daily family assistance and the psychological well-being of adolescents from Latin American, Asian, and European backgrounds. *Developmental Psychology, 45*(4), 1177–89. https://doi.org/10.1037/a0014728

Telzer, E. H., Masten, C. L., Berkman, E. T., Lieberman, M. D., & Fuligni, A. J. (2010). Gaining while giving: An fMRI study of the rewards of family assistance among White and Latino youth. *Social Neuroscience, 5*(5–6), 508–18. https://doi.org/10.1080/17470911003687913

Tompson, S. H., Huff, S. T., Yoon, C., King, A., Liberzon, I., & Kitayama, S. (2018). The dopamine D4 receptor gene (DRD4) modulates cultural variation in emotional experience. *Culture and Brain, 6*(2), 118–29. https://doi.org/10.1007/s40167-018-0063-5

Triandis, H. C. (1995). *New directions in social psychology. Individualism & collectivism.* Westview Press. https://psycnet.apa.org/psycinfo/1995-97791-000

Triandis, H. C., Marn, G., Lisansky, J., & Betancourt, H. (1984). Simpatía as a cultural script of Hispanics. *Journal of Personality and Social Psychology, 47*(6), 1363–75. https://doi.org/10.1037/0022-3514.47.6.1363

Uchida, Y., & Kitayama, S. (2009). Happiness and unhappiness in east and west: Themes and variations. *Emotion, 9*(4), 441–56. https://doi.org/10.1037/a0015634

Uchida, Y., Takemura, K., Fukushima, S., Saizen, I., Kawamura, Y., Hitokoto, H., Koizumi, N., & Yoshikawa, S. (2019). Farming cultivates a community-level shared culture through collective activities: Examining contextual effects with multilevel analyses. *Journal of Personality and Social Psychology, 116*(1), 1–14. https://doi.org/10.1037/pspa0000138

Uleman, J. S., Saribay, S. A., & Gonzalez, C. M. (2008). Spontaneous inferences, implicit impressions, and implicit theories. *Annual Review of Psychology, 59*(1), 329–60. https://doi.org/10.1146/annurev.psych.59.103006.093707

van IJzendoorn, M. H., Bakermans-Kranenburg, M. J., Belsky, J., Beach, S., Brody, G., Dodge, K. A., Greenberg, J., Posner, M., & Scott, S. (2011). Gene-by-environment experiments: A new approach to finding the missing heritability. *Nature Reviews Genetics, 12*(2), 881. https://doi.org/10.1038/nrg2764-c1

van IJzendoorn, M. H., Caspers, K., Bakermans-Kranenburg, M. J., Beach, S. R. H., & Philibert, R. (2010). Methylation matters: Interaction between methylation density and serotonin transporter genotype predicts unresolved loss or trauma. *Biological Psychiatry, 68*(5), 405–7. https://doi.org/10.1016/j.biopsych.2010.05.008

Varnum, M. E. W., Shi, Z., Chen, A., Qiu, J., & Han, S. (2014). When "Your" reward is the same as "My" reward: Self-construal priming shifts neural responses to own vs. friends' rewards. *NeuroImage, 87*, 164–9. https://doi.org/10.1016/j.neuroimage.2013.10.042

Wang, F., Peng, K., Chechlacz, M., Humphreys, G. W., & Sui, J. (2017). The neural basis of independence versus interdependence orientations. *Psychological Science, 28*(4), 519–29. https://doi.org/10.1177/0956797616689079

Weeland, J., Overbeek, G., de Castro, B. O., & Matthys, W. (2015). Underlying mechanisms of gene-environment interactions in externalizing behavior: A systematic review and search for theoretical mechanisms. *Clinical Child and Family Psychology Review, 18*(4), 413–42. https://doi.org/10.1007/s10567-015-0196-4

Wood, A., Rychlowska, M., & Niedenthal, P. M. (2016). Heterogeneity of long-history migration predicts emotion recognition accuracy. *Emotion, 16*(4), 413–20. https://doi.org/10.1037/emo0000137

Woollett, K., & Maguire, E. A. (2011). Acquiring "the knowledge" of London's layout drives structural brain changes. *Current Biology, 21*(24), 2109–14. https://doi.org/10.1016/j.cub.2011.11.018

Yu, Q., Abe, N., King, A., Yoon, C., Liberzon, I., & Kitayama, S. (2019). Cultural variation in the gray matter volume of the prefrontal cortex is moderated by the dopamine D4 receptor gene (*DRD4*). *Cerebral Cortex, 29*(9), 3922–31. https://doi.org/10.1093/cercor/bhy271

Zárate, M. A., Uleman, J. S., & Voils, C. I. (2001). Effects of culture and processing goals on the activation and binding of trait concepts. *Social Cognition, 19*(3), 295–323. https://doi.org/10.1521/soco.19.3.295.21469

Zhu, X., Zhang, H., Wu, L., Yang, S., Wu, H., Luo, W., Gu, R., & Luo, Y. (2018). The influence of self-construals on the ERP response to the rewards for self and mother. *Cognitive, Affective, & Behavioral Neuroscience, 18*(2), 366–74. https://doi.org/10.3758/s13415-018-0575-7

4 Being There
Foundations, Theory, Method

Carol M. Worthman

Over recent decades, many lines of inquiry have converged on a common, basically ecological view, that the function and development of organisms inherently rely on interactions with context. Put so simply, the notion sounds obvious, intuitive, and scarcely something to have required the efforts of so many working in such diverse fields, from philosophy and anthropology, to developmental neuroscience and evolutionary biology. Yet attainment of this breakthrough has been difficult, slow, and ultimately revolutionary because it runs contrary to fundamental Western existential views that sharply distinguish nature from nurture, body from mind, objective from subjective. These invidious distinctions have impeded and deformed inquiry, particularly regarding humans, until the very mass of evidence itself has overwhelmed and begun to dispel entrenched assumptions. The present volume brings together ideas and findings propelling transformations in thought and research that are reshaping established worldviews and eroding distinctions as they relate to dynamics among culture, mind, and brain, what is referred to here as the culture–mind–brain nexus.

This chapter contributes to that effort by elaborating ecological perspectives and taking up the theme of "being there" in two senses, as existential fact and as corollary method. An ecological framework serves as a point of departure for exploring specific empirical and methodological implications of postdualist science. Phenomenologically, "being there" is a reality of life for any organism, neatly captured by the saying, "everywhere you go, there you are." That inherent person-place, creature-context connection turns out to be a basis for the evolution of context-reliant and context-sensitive features that are built into organic design. Such a fundamental shift in scientific understanding calls for concomitant changes in modes and conduct of research to bring context and person–context interactions more clearly into view. In particular, the characteristic anthropological paradigm of ethnographic participant observation leverages being there to situate the researcher in the thick of things, close to the sites of person–place dynamics in the full flow of social, structural, and physical circumstances.

The following discussion explores these two senses of "being there," ecological and methodological, and discusses their significance at a pivotal moment in which Western thought and inquiry turn toward more grounded and capacious views. It begins with theory and evidence from evolutionary biology, developmental sciences, and anthropology that demonstrate why and how ecological or ecocultural perspectives are particularly valuable for understanding brain, mind, and culture. It then suggests that ecologically grounded theory and methods can inform the culture–mind–brain models and paradigms discussed in this volume, both in research and in application, and points to the value of "being there." Three illustrative case studies are presented and the lessons for evolving engaged, collaborative, mixed method research models are considered.

Being There as Phenomenology

This section presents three lines of theory and evidence suggesting why and how an ecological framework provides an effective approach to unpacking the culture–mind–brain nexus. First, we consider evolutionary processes that conditioned how this nexus evolved, creating the configuration, capacities, and constraints that determine humans' ecological niche, our place in the world. Ecological analysis gains traction by tapping into how the evolutionary history conditioning biology (brain), function (mind), and behavior (culture) plays out in human lives and societies. Second, we discuss the role of ecological forces in development that both have an evolutionary history and drive physical (body/brain), functional (mind), and behavioral (enculturation) development of individuals. Overlapping timelines of organism–environment interaction create nested ecologies of function and behavior through the life course. The first and second sections are linked by a discussion of how considerations of evolutionary design may illuminate the role of ecology in human development. Third, we take up anthropology's approach to culture and its role in becoming and being human, with particular attention to the lines of research and theory that delineate the role of culture in the production of human ecology, essentially constructing the conditions of human existence and thereby our lives, including brain and mind.

Evolutionary Processes and Ecology

The power of applying an ecological frame draws on deep history and the existential fact that living beings always and necessarily are *somewhere*. Hence, context is the constant. It defines resource availability (what is there), niche availability (how it is configured), homeostatic demands (e.g., temperatures), and neighborhood (who is there) through time (in/stability, periodicity).

Aside from functional–structural constraints, the environment therefore is a prime source of selection pressures that affect survival and reproduction. The phenotypes that have evolved as adaptations to meet these selection pressures therefore are finely honed by phenotype–environment interactions in their evolutionary history (Laland et al., 2015; Reeve & Sherman, 1993).

The environment therefore holds a privileged place in evolutionary accounts of organismic design, of what organisms are designed to do and how. An organism's or species' spatial, material, and behavioral uses of a given environment comprise its ecological niche. Contours of the niche depend on the organism's needs and capacities, including its degrees of flexibility, all of which are based on its species' evolutionary history of adapting to a particular set of environmental conditions (Pocheville, 2015). Most species engage in at least some niche construction, modifying the environment to create more favorable conditions (e.g., burrowing, beaver dams; Odling-Smee et al., 1996).

Humans conspicuously rely on niche construction strategies, essentially creating the conditions they inhabit. That sociality and culture drive human niche construction becomes important later in this discussion, but note for now that the human brain is an adaptation essential to both (see Chapters 1 and 2). It forms the primary interface between humans and their world, and as such engages in continuous dialectics with the environment, via internal, sensory, cognitive, and material states.

Development and Context

Developmental sciences have yielded crucial insights into relationships between organism and context (Baldwin, 1896; Bonner, 1974; Changeux & Chavaillon, 1995; West-Eberhard, 2003), and are tied up with questions about reproduction. Production of a viable organism requires sources of information to guide what happens and when. For instance, consider what it takes just to build a human brain, comprising roughly 100 billion neurons with over a thousand times as many synapses. The puzzle of where this information comes from is an essential riddle of reproduction and ontogeny that long preoccupied Western philosophers and scientists, and appeared to have been answered with the discovery of DNA (Gould, 1977). Yet work after the human genome was sequenced in 2001 has pared down the likely number of coding genes to fewer than 20 000, which on its own scarcely suffices as a blueprint for replication (Pertea et al., 2018).

By contrast, context carries immense amounts of information at any organismic scale, from molecular on up: the organism's task is strategically and selectively to use that information in developmental processes as well as in everyday function (Reeve & Sherman, 1993). The surprisingly narrow basis for classic DNA-based replication has motivated intense study of epigenetics, which are the molecules and mechanisms – such as DNA methylation, non-coding RNAs, various histone protein modifications, even "junk DNA" – that alter gene activity without affecting the underlying DNA sequence (Balcerak et al., 2019; Cavalli & Heard, 2019;). Epigenetics comprises a dizzying array of processes operating at the level of cells, systems, and on up to physiologically and/or behaviorally mediated organism–environment interactions that shape phenotypic outcomes (Allis & Jenuwein, 2016; Champagne & Curley, 2009). Epigenetics fills the gap between DNA and translation into ontogeny and function, linking code and context through the contextual information – inputs and conditions – that they instantiate. Hence, epigenetics mediates how the genome is "read" or used, illuminating the importance of dynamics embedded in context to regulate outcomes from DNA information itself.

Furthermore, epigenetic mechanisms, such as DNA methylation, may mediate non-DNA sequence-based heritable effects on phenotypes (Miska & Ferguson-Smith, 2016). Ongoing discoveries have extended notions of biological inheritance and revived views that development also may be guided via somatic transmission of information "through physiological reconstruction of developmental conditions, or through behavior, niche construction, language, etc." (Jablonka, 2017, p. 3). In reconstructive, by contrast to direct replicative, processes, organisms build themselves through recursive context- and condition-responsive mechanisms (Jablonka, 2013). These views are closely congruent with recent constructionist 4E views of mind (cognition is embodied, embedded, enactive, and extended; see Chapter 8), and bioecocultural theory to be discussed later. Becoming human is not simply a matter of physical ontogeny, but a bioecocultural project required to become a viable member of society, to survive and reproduce.

Timelines and Nested Ecologies

Ecology comprises the interactions among organisms and their environment, where environment is considered as extrinsic to the organism. Yet biologists recognize that many existential layers within and outside the organism condition its interactions with its environment. Organismic responses to environmental conditions at play in adaptation occur across a great range of timescales, from immediate biochemical (e.g., neurotransmitter release) or instinctive (e.g., eye-blink) responses, to intermediate ones (e.g., regulation of development or reproduction) at the individual level, on to longer-term responses at the population (demographic) or very long-term evolutionary and taxonomic levels. Figure 4.1 shows Wilson's mapping of organismic responses to environmental challenges, with timescales adjusted to reflect the case of humans. Those that required adjustment lie in the middle ranges

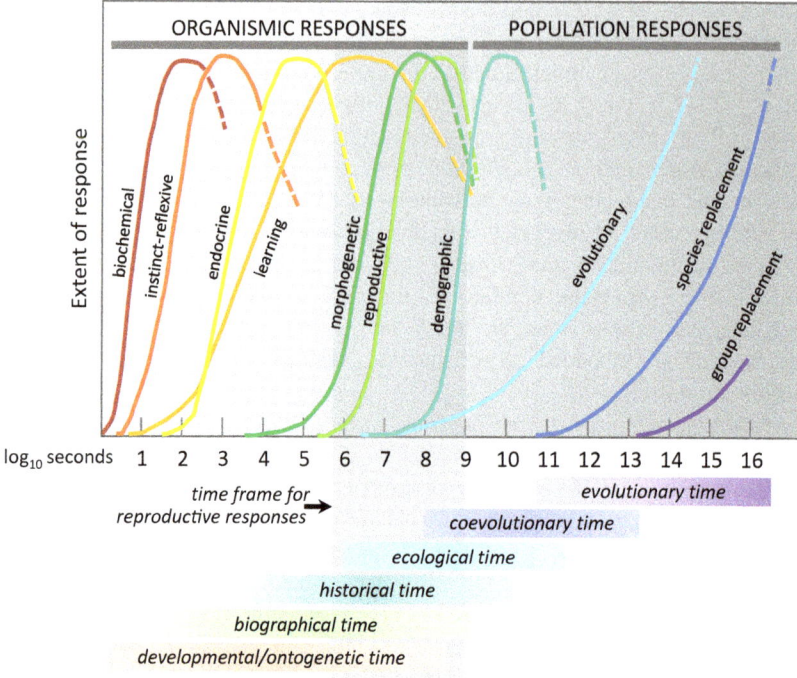

Figure 4.1 Timescales of response in living systems (tailored specifically to human life history and evolutionary history). The curves show time course to attain peak response for each dynamic frame, from the most granular (biochemical) to the most extensive, life's deep evolutionary time. By contrast with the generalized graph for living systems shown in Figure 1.2 (Chapter 1), note here that timelines' morphogenetic, reproductive, and demographic response are shifted right to reflect humans' slow development, late maturation, cooperative breeding with intergenerational resource transfers, long lifespan, and long intergenerational length (30 years for women, 35 years for men). Timeline for learning is greatly expanded to reflect continuous lifetime learning with many years to decades required for highly skilled foraging and other skills required to occupy subsistence and other specialized niches. Boxes below the figure indicate the timeframes represented by conventional ways of chunking temporal phenomena. The shaded rectangle represents the time window over which reproductive response accumulates. Response curves adapted from figure 7.2 in E. O. Wilson, 1975, Sociobiology, Cambridge, MA: Harvard University Press, p. 145

(learning, developmental/morphogenetic, reproductive, and demographic) and reflect humans' life history and culture-based adaptive strategies.

Points of interest in Figure 4.1 include, first, the extent to which the response curves overlap in time, creating graded and continually interactive suites of response. Action at one level also acts as context for other levels, creating a co-constructive dynamic between organism–environment interactions; hence, biochemical cell–cell interactions create the conditions, or proximal environments, for organogenesis, or endocrine dynamics mediate reproduction. Similarly, note the broad overlap among the conventional timelines blocked out below the curves. For the present biologically focused analysis, observe the overlap of ecological time with reproductive response (gray shaded area, center): Ecological conditions exert acute and cumulative effects on reproductive function and career. The field of reproductive ecology investigates this adaptive space where reproductive function and behavior interact with environmental conditions, including availability of material and social resources, environmental qualities (stability, uncertainty, competition), energetic demands (workload, health), and mortality risks. Use of the term "ecology" here refers to the adaptive evolutionary background and the prediction that individual physiological, cognitive, and behavioral responses will be based on that background to shape reproductive outcomes (Ellison, 1994; Vitzthum, 2009).

Relatedly, consider the overlap of developmental/ontogenetic time (Figure 4.1, bottom bar) with reproductive response. Like other primates, humans grow first, then undergo a delayed puberty, and then reproduce. Unlike other primates, timing of reproductive maturation is particularly delayed and varies widely, being highly sensitive to environmental quality at the individual and population level (Worthman & Trang, 2018). Hence, the field of developmental ecology tracks interactions of development and environment through the lens of adaptive design, as will be discussed in the next section.

Developmental Ecology

Viewed in light of these considerations, expectable environments of development become routes for information transfer and thus, intergenerational transmission of phenotypes and sources of plasticity (Stotz, 2014). In the case of humans, those expectable environments are culturally constituted (see Chapter 1, Table 1.1). That human development is designed for reliance on expectable environments of rearing is plainly evident in the process of language acquisition, whereby infants typically acquire the language/s of their social milieu without intervention or instruction (Ruben, 1997). Insofar as language grounds mind and mental experience, this example illustrates how evolved biodesign interacts with culture to shape developing minds (Friederici et al., 2017). The case of literacy offers a telling contrast: Although language forms a core feature of the human adaptive niche, literacy appeared only recently, about 5400 years ago (Dehaene, 2009). Learning to read harnesses the visual system through facultative neuroplasticity and is correspondingly effortful and demanding, exhibiting none of the developmental facilitation evident in language acquisition. Similar to language, acquisition of cognitive-emotional and behavioral requisites for social competence and life skills is supported by the brain's and body's slow development. That puberty comes late in humans lengthens the time for a childhood free of the effects of reproductive hormones, while puberty itself opens a window for further brain maturation and emergence of novel emotional, cognitive, and social capacities (Dahl, 2016). Hence, brain and mind are iteratively shaped through biocultural interaction.

Drawing on evolutionary processes to think about interactions of ecology and organic design has proven effective for formulating testable hypotheses about development. Life history theory arose from comparative analysis of relationships between adaptive niche and life history features (e.g., life span, growth rate, time to maturation, adult size, time to maturation, mortality schedule) that reflect a species' evolved strategy for allocation of scarce resources, energy and time, to growth, reproduction, and maintenance/survival (Charnov, 1993; Stearns, 1992). Differences in the lives of species – mosquitoes versus elephants – embody these evolved strategies. Life history strategies also are informed by constraints on organic design, including those on intergenerational information transmission. As discussed above, meeting this constraint puts a premium on mechanisms that capture pertinent information from the environment to inform development. Such mechanisms often build in plasticity that responds to cues to environmental quality, as well as ones that negotiate trade-offs among competing demands, constraints, and opportunities faced by any organism (Ellis & Del Giudice, 2019). Hence, child growth slows during illness or subnutrition which, if prolonged early in life, may lead to stunting, increased vulnerability to chronic disease, and reduced life expectancy as meeting acute needs is traded off against long-term survivability. Indeed, cues to resource availability or environmental stressors during gestation and infancy have been linked to shifted life history parameters including not only physical (energy allocation, timing of puberty, and life expectancy) but also psychosocial outcomes (mating and parenting strategies, stress reactivity; Del Giudice et al., 2012; Kuzawa & Bragg, 2012).

Testing predictions or interpreting findings based on evolutionary logic have been applied productively not only to development and reproduction, but also to behavior and health in the fields of behavioral ecology (Henrich et al., 2004; Jaeggi et al., 2016), cognition (Gurven et al., 2017), and evolutionary medicine (Kuzawa & Thayer, 2011; Trevathan et al., 2008). In these fields, ecology operates as a key metaphor signaling person–place interactions conditioned by timescales (acute, chronic, developmental, evolutionary). Although it is outside the brief of the present discussion, note that 4E theories also encode similar ecological logics, extending the timescales for response down to momentary mental states, cultural affordances, and a situated, transactional view of mind (Newen et al., 2018; Ramstead et al., 2016).

Human Ecology as Cultural Ecology

With this review of biomaterialist applications of ecological models in mind, we now turn to culture and ecology. From its inception, anthropology has focused on culture as a defining human feature that permeates behavior and experience, and generates diversity (Tylor, 1871; but see Boas, 1911). Formative conceptual advances that propelled the field were, first, a relativistic, pluralistic concept of culture and, second, an ecological–constructivist view of human ecology. Cultural relativism abjured social evolutionary views of societal perfectability along an axis of presumed values. Potential differences in human mind and mental capacities that underlie manifest cultural differences were of central concern. The ecological–constructivist frame offered an account for human variability while conserving basic human unity (especially of mind), by regarding culture as the medium through which people both inhabit and produce the material, social, and psychological conditions of everyday life. In this view, via culture humans become the prime architects of their experience and behavior; hence, cultural variation rather than biological differences was regarded as the primary agent in human diversity (Benedict, 1934; Geertz, 1973).

The primacy of nurture over nature, or cultural mediation over material mediation, became a matter of sharp disagreement among anthropologists. Physical and biological anthropologists largely subscribed to a bio-ecocultural view that privileged the interaction of the two, while a majority of cultural anthropologists shifted to a cultural constructionist view that backgrounded biomaterial forces (Hacking, 1999; Paul R. A., 2015). Correspondingly, the former is more concerned with brain and the latter, more with mind. Previous sections situated the prominent role of ecology in the biological approaches based on evolutionary perspectives. Among culturally focused lines of inquiry, psychological anthropology assumed a more processual than constructivist approach compatible with ecological–materialist views of culture and its role in cognitive, emotional, and social dimensions of human experience and behavior. Boas's early work demonstrating the association of time since immigration with changes in cranial dimensions both established biological sensitivity to environmental conditions and indicated that culture can shape not only cognitive and behavioral variation, but biology as well (Boas, 1912). Ethnographic studies of childhood and adolescence by his student Margaret Mead illuminated interactions of development and culture, and suggested that psychobehavioral variation among societies was attributable in good part to effects of growing up in different cultures (Mead, 1928, 1930; Mead & Macgregor, 1951).

The process of building systematic ecocultural theory began with John Whiting's efforts empirically to track relationships of culture and mind, comparing the course of human development across cultures (Whiting & Child, 1953). With Bea Whiting and their students, the focus turned to the role of cultural ecology on child psychobehavioral development (Whiting et al., 1966). A distinctive hallmark of their collaborative work was model building and hypothesis testing with mixed methods research (reviewed in Worthman, 2010), where the models aimed to trace the processes leading to similarities and differences in developmental outcomes. An assumption that nurture was built in to human nature prompted their focus on the cultural ecology of child development, populated by caregivers and other members of a society and grounded in the culturally constituted social structural and material conditions of childrearing and ontogeny. Together, these dynamics constitute the developmental niche in which the young of a society grow up (Super & Harkness, 1986).

This approach proved to be conceptually powerful and empirically productive, and has fueled decades of research (e.g., Harkness et al., 2013; Hay, 2016; Whiting, 1994; Whiting & Edwards, 1988). The reasons for these successes likely are evident from the previous discussions of adaptation and developmental ecology. For our present purposes they include, first, that the approach was a fairly sound approximation of how development actually works, and, second, that the methods that were used were attentive to determinants, dynamics, and impact of on-the-ground conditions as mediators of culture in human development. But they were not so evident at the time that anthropologists like Boas, the Whitings, and their students formulated their models and pursued an ecological agenda, and for that, they also can be considered pioneers. Moreover, that two quite disparate, largely independent lines of research, in the biosciences and in anthropology, arrived at congruent models and complementary findings bolsters confidence in the value of ecological approaches for understanding complex phenomena, even including the culture–mind–brain nexus.

Being There as Method: What, How, Where, and Who

The opening section discussed the empirical and theoretical bases on which to anticipate that ecologically grounded approaches will yield valuable insights into biology, cognition, and behavior. This section builds directly on that foundation to argue the specific value of being there as method, and a relatively underused one. Many modes of inquiry are required to take on the complex challenge of unpacking the culture–mind–brain nexus, but with all the sophistication of empirical methods at hand, techniques that effectively capture the salient elements of context have lagged behind. This discussion takes a page from anthropology to suggest that modes of being there such as ethnographic inquiry and observant participation may be particularly valuable routes to identify new questions, open new lines of inquiry, refute or validate existing models, and tap dimensions of human experience not readily accessible by other means.

Anthropology and the Ethnographic Method

From its beginnings, anthropology has focused on human diversity (Worthman, 2016). The journey of discovery has been appropriately humbling, tangling with racism, colonialism, and epistemic doubt along the way. Yet the discipline developed a defining approach that has proven invaluable, namely ethnography and its essential requirement of "being there." It is worth analyzing *why* this approach has been so productive. At the outset, studying cultural phenomena from within was a practical requirement rather than a conceptual choice. The sites of anthropological inquiry necessarily were located with the people and place/s they studied, yet those places were geographically removed and culturally remote from the researcher's own accustomed settings. The inevitable physical and cultural dislocation experienced by the investigator induced a disorienting cultural incompetence, inducing inquiry motivated not simply by an intellectual agenda but as or more compellingly, by the urgent need to acquire knowledge, skills, and relationships needed for acceptance and survival. The professional challenge was to engage sincerely in this acculturative project while maintaining distance sufficient to permit reflexivity and "objective" analysis. An existential struggle systematically to probe the requisites of cultural competence while eschewing full acculturation was productive, and generated a liminal space that effectively yielded insights about elements and workings of culture. Moreover, these insights were grounded in and emerged from working within the subject of study, tapping culture in the full flow of operation, a system of systems that would be regarded by complexity theory as comprising "a seamless whole operating simultaneously and complementarily at various levels" (Theise & Kafatos, 2013, p. 11). The ethnographer's stance was one of participant observer, the aim being effacement and minimal perturbation of ongoing conditions and dynamics. The recent turn to calling the approach "observant participation" better recognizes the inevitable and pervasive observer effects.

Early field anthropology initially traveled with colonialism (British Association for the Advancement of Science, 1874) and, following a natural history model, documented difference *per se*, cataloging the "what" of societies and the mainly physical characteristics of their inhabitants (Boas, 1896;

Garson & Read, 1892). Countering innatist and racist logics embedded in this enterprise, Franz Boas's study of US immigrants found that physical differences were driven primarily by life conditions (Boas, 1912; Gravlee et al., 2003). The intellectual and popular stakes lay not in particular physical attributes, but in the qualities they were thought to reflect, such that differences in cranial size or configuration were taken as bases for imputing differences in qualities of mind and the life worlds they supported. Boas and his students refuted these views and went on to identify culture as the major factor shaping those conditions and, hence, in driving human variation (Worthman, 2016). Framing this cultural ecology approach was the notion of fundamental shared humanity, of equivalent claims to be human grounded in shared mental features behind capacities for language and distinctive forms of sociality and behavior (Boas, 1911).

Initially, anthropologists pursued ethnographic fieldwork as a route to understanding the lives of Others. But then they discovered that this process yielded valuable critical insights about anthropologists' own lives and cultures, resulting in two important outcomes. For one, the field discovered its value for critical inquiry, having found that on-the-ground lived realities often do not neatly mesh with or even directly contradict dominant Western cultural assumptions about human nature, mind, or culture (Margaret Mead on Samoa; for example Mead, 1928). Such contradictions challenged ascendant social arrangements, practices, and values, suggesting new possibilities for how humans might live. For another, anthropology shifted from merely documenting difference, to investigating what actual difference those differences make in human lives and well-being. This project spurred deep examination of the workings of power, both within a given society and in wider geopolitical configurations. Accumulating ethnographic inquiry also led to the notion of relativity, that beliefs, values, or practices compatible with or necessary for human flourishing in one cultural time and place may be harmful or repugnant in another (Shweder, 1990; Shweder et al., 2002).

Anthropology's use of ethnography reached a critical juncture in the late 1980s when its grounding in natural history caught up with it and a fundamental flaw became evident. Ironically, ethnography began with the goal to study cultural diversity but largely had ignored subcultural variation across time and space. Specifically, ethnography had treated cultures as categorical types wherein a single specimen could represent the whole such that anthropologists referred to *the* Trobrianders or *the* Nuer. Further, societies were treated as timeless, captured by the ethnographic lens. These assumptions became untenable as colonialism faded with dramatic societal change and emerging globalization. Belatedly, anthropology came to terms with the limits to generalizability in ethnographic inquiry, acknowledging that ethnographic knowledge was *local* and *particular*, grounded in a social milieu at a specific place and time (Rosaldo, 1989). Further, the claim to objective social *science* foundered on the recognition that as texts, ethnographies themselves were partial, necessarily selective representations that are subject to investigator biases, interpretations, and subjectivity (Clifford & Marcus, 1986). These insights intersected with a turn to postmodern critical theory and led to a period of intense reflexivity and critical social analysis (Ortner, 1984, 2016).

Science and Generalizability

As anthropology struggled with epistemological and ethical concerns involved in understanding a diverse humanity, other social and medical sciences retained a notion of a universal modal human being such that phenomena (e.g., human development, brain functioning, disease process, response to medication) found in one population are generalizable to all others. This assumption was challenged in medical anthropology (Simons & Hughes, 1985), but reached wider currency with recognition that ignoring gender or simply studying men might fail to represent either women or gender differences in general (The Women's Health Initiative Study Group, 1998). By 1994, the US National Institutes of Health mandated inclusion gender and ethnicity criteria for inclusion in clinical research (National Institutes of Health, 1994). Concurrently, social psychologists began to explore relationships of culture and psychology, including conceptions of self (Markus & Kitayama, 1991; Triandis, 1989), emotions (Kitayama & Markus, 1994), modes of thought (Nisbett et al., 2001), and subcultures (Nisbett, 1993). This cultural psychology approach proved tremendously productive, yielding empirical insights, methodological advances, and theoretical frameworks that greatly have enriched understandings of culture and social psychology (de Oliveira & Nisbett, 2017; Kitayama & Park, 2017; Markus & Kitayama, 2010).

Despite such pathbreaking efforts, severely skewed representation in behavioral sciences persisted into the early twenty-first century (Arnett, 2008; Henrich et al., 2010), when all but a small fraction of published psychology research came from American or Western, educated, industrial, rich, democratic (WEIRD) authors or societies representing 12 percent of the world's population. Similarly, neuroscience, particularly imaging studies, has suffered acutely from narrow selective samples, given the cost and demanding, immobile technology involved. An ecological perspective suggests that our understanding of brain structure and function will shift, perhaps dramatically, once more populations are tapped. Indeed, that expectation is being met in the emerging field of cultural neuroscience, which has identified neurophysiological patterns associated with cultural differences in many domains, including attention and perceptual processing, experience and perception of affect, social cognition, motivation, and reward processing (reviewed in Kitayama et al., 2019 and Chapter 3).

Why Be There?

Together, recognition of the narrow slice of humanity on which neurosciences and behavioral sciences has been based and accumulating evidence of the value of cross-cultural research have prompted widespread efforts to conduct experimental research in non-WEIRD populations. Even so, rigors of experimental design frequently require that they be conducted in controlled conditions that remove both experimenters and participants from the very settings in which the functions under study have developed and are enacted. Simply moving research to diverse societies overlooks the salient epistemological and methodological challenges involved in navigating the gaps between large questions and local realities.

But what does "being there" mean, and why is it important? This essay argues for the scientific value, even in narrow experimental designs, of characterizing more fully who research participants are and engaging with the ambient culture and settings that they inhabit (Kitayama, 2017). At the very least, venturing forth and being there rehumanizes science, greatly enriching the questions that investigators ask, how they ask them, and how they interpret research results. Indeed, it is essential for conducting research that effectively tracks the line between general shared processes and particular local conditions. In the following sections I present three examples from my own work to illustrate the power of being there for advancing critical inquiry and robust science – breastfeeding and birthspacing, the first 1000 days, and child soldiers.

Case 1 – Roots of a Bioecocultural View: Breastfeeding and Birthspacing The first example takes place in Botswana during the late 1970s, with discovery of the major role that breastfeeding plays in birthspacing. Dramatic increases in global population size, particularly in poor nations, had stimulated intense concern over a "population bomb," and drove efforts to find behavioral and pharmacological means to curtail fertility (Bongaarts, 2009; Bulatao & Lee, 1983; Greenhalgh, 1996). This coincided with a massive ongoing postwar push to develop public health systems for which improvements in life expectancy represented a concrete indicator of success. Mortality in the first 2–5 years of life was the major source of reduced life expectancy and as such, became a prime target for public health interventions such as vaccination. Mobilization for child survival also coincided with promotion of formula feeding as modern, sanitary, and safe, with consequent erosion of

Figure 4.2 !Kung San hunter-gatherers out foraging, Kalahari Desert, Botswana.
Photograph from Harri Jarvelainen Photography

breastfeeding practices and, ironically, exacerbation of infant mortality risk (Stevens et al., 2009).

Meanwhile in the Kalahari of Botswana, a team of anthropologists was pursuing pioneering studies of !Kung San hunter-gatherers as a route to understanding human adaptation to the foraging subsistence niche in which humans evolved (Lee & DeVore, 1976; Figure 4.2).

Interbirth interval among the !Kung was found to be very long, averaging four years (Howell, 1979; Lee, 1972), which was puzzling given their lively sex lives and absence of contraception (Blurton-Jones, 1986; Shostak, 1981). One of the team, Melvin Konner, observed infant care practices and documented that breastfeeding was remarkably intensive (13 minutes between bouts) and prolonged (weaning ~3.5 years; Konner, 1972, 1977; see Figures 4.3 and 4.4). Concurrently, laboratory research on regulation of lactation suggested that breastfeeding has suppressive effects on the regulation of ovarian activity, via its impact on the hypothalamic–pituitary–gonadal axis (Noel et al., 1974; Tyson et al., 1972). This led us to wonder whether the !Kung practice of prolonged intensive breastfeeding might play a role in their surprisingly long interbirth interval. Testing this idea required development of novel field-friendly high-sensitivity assays that needed much smaller blood

Figure 4.3 Dobe !Kung family outside their grass hut, Botswana.
Digitized film original, photograph courtesy of Melvin Konner

samples than usual in clinical studies (Worthman, 1978). Having developed these, we returned to the field and assessed ovarian hormone levels in !Kung women who were and were not currently breastfeeding. Results indicated near-complete 2-year suppression of ovarian activity in nursing mothers and provided strong evidence of a role of sustained frequent breastfeeding in birth spacing (Konner & Worthman, 1980).

Implications of these findings had major global policy effects. On the side of basic biology and public health, first it showed a relationship between a cultural practice and fundamental biological processes, namely lactation and postpartum ovarian activity. This provided early naturalistic evidence that "hard wired" biology may have inbuilt sensitivity to context. Indeed, such biological sensitivity to environmental quality relates to trade-offs between current and future reproduction that evolved with human life history strategy, where reproduction involves intense, prolonged maternal investments before and after birth (Hill & Kaplan, 1999). Second, it suggested how differences in childcare practices may have major demographic and maternal–child health effects, in this case by influencing intervals between births (Howie & McNeilly, 1982). Interbirth interval, in turn, is a well-recognized, powerful predictor of maternal health and child survival (Hobcraft et al., 1983), including among !Kung (Blurton-Jones, 1986). Third, the findings pointed out that

Figure 4.4 A group of Dobe !Kung women out foraging with their children, Botswana.
Digitized film original, photograph courtesy of Melvin Konner

people long have practiced contraception through cultural practices of breastfeeding that can have substantial demographic effects on birth spacing and thence on child survival and maternal health. These insights influenced public health narratives on infant feeding and bolstered support for breastfeeding.

On the side of social science, the findings provided early evidence, first, that culture is not skin deep, by pointing out potential sensitivity of basic biology to behavior and cultural context, with powerful demographic and health consequences. Hence, differences in cultural practices and contexts, in this case infant feeding and care, can be potent factors in populations' variation in function and health. This insight helped to launch the field of reproductive ecology (Ellison, 1994), and opened the door to use of biomarkers in social science resarch. Second, it showed how behavioral–contextual effects on, in this case, biology, health, and demography, may be invisible and thereby become naturalized. Yes, !Kung postpartum ovarian function differed from that of documented Western populations, but the difference was attributable to behavior and lifestyle rather than to genetics or other innate dispositions. Moreover, !Kung infant care practices are oriented to survival and well-being of the young, not consciously toward suppression of mothers' reproductive function and prolonging birth spacing. Historical cases document that populations have been surprised and puzzled by sudden surges in fertility after undergoing lifestyle changes and abandonment of breastfeeding (Schneider & Schneider, 1984). Integration of physiology into study of human cultural and behavioral ecology in the "real world" opened avenues for novel research. The impact of cultural, behavioral, and material ecology on human function and well-being since has become a major focus for biosocial sciences (Bachrach & Abeles, 2004). In terms of the culture–mind–brain focus of the present volume, this early work breached the nature/nurture, body/mind barrier between biological and social sciences by showing an inbuilt linkage between culturally conditioned behavior and a fundamental biological process.

Although we started out to test an idea about birth spacing in a small group of African foragers, the new lines of thought, inquiry, and policy that emerged from the findings illustrate how productive science not only tests existing ideas but also generates discovery. Investigation of the role of breastfeeding in child development and survival has gone on to amass a wealth of evidence for its importance (Rollins et al., 2016; Victora et al., 2016). Yet a part of what initiated all this was on-the-ground observation, being there. Interdisciplinarity added another key ingredient by combining field observations with ongoing experimental, clinical, and social science literatures.

Case 2 – The First Thousand Days For the second example, fast forward to the early twenty-first century and the case of the first thousand days. As discussed in the opening section, understanding the profound developmental effects of early experience was a great achievement of late twentieth century developmental science (Save the Children, 2012; Walker et al., 2011). These effects begin in gestation and proceed most powerfully in the first two years of infancy, propelled in part by the intense pace of neurodevelopment and its sensitivity to context (Fox et al., 2010; Hanson & Gluckman, 2014). Cumulative evidence documented sensitivity of child physical, cognitive, and socio-emotional development to material (nutrition, infection; de Onis et al., 2013; Maternal Child Nutrition Study Group, 2013; Victora et al., 2010) and psychosocial (stressors, quality of care) conditions (Gunnar et al., 2015; Lupien et al., 2009; Petrosini et al., 2009). Impact of environmental conditions, in turn, was firmly linked to health outcomes, both physical and mental, and drew attention to the developmental origins of health and disease (Gluckman & Hanson, 2006). When a set of papers in the *Lancet* compiled the extent of developmental potential lost to either environmental insults or insufficient positive supports during gestation and the first two years of life (Grantham-McGregor et al., 2007; Walker et al., 2007), both developmental scientists and policy makers were mobilized to capitalize on the early gains to be made during the "first thousand days" (Adair et al., 2013; Bhutta et al., 2013; Black et al., 2013).

Figure 4.5 The spirit of Soweto, a wall mural in Khayelitsha, Cape Town, South Africa (2008).
Photograph by author

Stimulated by these ideas, intervention scientist Mary Jane Rotheram-Borus, South African developmental psychologist Mark Tomlinson, South African pediatrician Ingrid Le Roux, and I asked whether an intervention with mothers during and after pregnancy could enhance child outcomes in challenging settings such as the massive immigrant townships in Cape Town (see Figure 4.5). Inspired by successful home visiting programs in the United States (Dodge et al., 2013; Olds et al., 2014), we implemented a randomized controlled trial of a mentor mothers program developed from le Roux's pediatric clinics in the townships (Rotheram-Borus et al., 2011; see Figure 4.6). Mothers from twenty-four township neighborhoods enrolled in the study during the second trimester of pregnancy, and regular home visiting continued thence and through the first six months postpartum. The intervention did improve maternal and infant outcomes at six months postpartum (le Roux et al., 2013), yet the effects were neither as strong nor as durable as anticipated from findings in the USA (Olds et al., 2002; Tomlinson et al., 2015, 2016).

As we considered potential explanations, the anthropologist in me asked: What do parents believe about child development? Beliefs, values, and practices shared by a culture are organized into cognitive schemas that offer affordances for making sense of the world, planning and decision-making,

Figure 4.6 Men and children walk a sandy path in a township outside Cape Town, South Africa (2008).
Photograph by author

and behaving (Shore, 1996; Strauss & Quinn, 1997). Indeed, cultural models of child development and desirable outcomes have been found to inform caregiver behavior, and explain cross-cultural differences in parenting and child outcomes (Harkness et al., 2011, 2007; Super et al., 2008). Consequently, we conducted exploratory interviews with local community leaders and project staff, and focus groups with adult caregivers (parents, grandparents), to discuss understandings of young child development and appropriate parenting (see Figure 4.6). These discussions yielded an unexpected question: At what age or stage can parents most influence their child's development? A cultural consensus study among a sample of caregivers identified a strongly shared answer identifying age 12 as a critical time for parent intervention (Worthman et al., 2016; see Figure 4.7). Respondents cited many reasons for this choice, concerning the risks attending puberty and adolescence (peer pressure, gang violence, school failure, premature pregnancy, substance ab/use) that require parental intervention, as well as adolescents' emerging psychological maturity that caregivers seek to influence toward desirable outcomes.

By comparison, meeting the needs of infants was considered more manageable, simply a matter of providing love and care for them to thrive (Figure 4.7). The long-term effects of early experience on outcomes that motivate interventions in the first 1000 days are by no means as immediate or apparent as are the

Figure 4.7 Children with mother hanging laundry outside their home in a township near Cape Town, South Africa (2008).
Photograph by author

evident risks for adolescents. Moreover, parents' beliefs mesh with current literature on adolescent brain and socioemotional development in adolescence that identifies the second decade as another important maturational period with enduring effects on function and health (Dahl et al., 2018; Sawyer et al., 2018).

Many lessons may be drawn from this case that relate to the culture–mind–brain nexus. First, just because scientists had discovered the importance of the first 1000 days, does not mean it is obvious to everyone else. After all, it took decades of concerted research to map relationships of context and early experience to developmental outcomes with long-term effects on function and health. Translating this insight into changes that benefit children does involve communicating "the facts," but not only that. Intervention is by definition culture change, a shift in how people behave and, behind that, what they feel, believe, and value (Paul B. D., 1955). Existing cultural models and behavioral schemas mesh with many trade-offs faced by actors. In the case of childcare, changes to improve long-term infant outcomes involve reprioritizing existing demands on maternal time and socioemotional budget from other valued or essential goals (Cooper et al., 2014). To be effective and sustainable, an intervention must work through these as well, and "being there" is essential here. Second and relatedly, a risk model may lead to discounting other opportunities across the lifespan. The push for maximizing gains in the first 1000 days may deprioritize other valuable opportunities to enhance developmental outcomes. Findings highlighting important brain development and socioemotional, cognitive, and behavioral advances during the second decade indicate that this period also carries important needs and opportunities (Dahl et al., 2018). Third, local beliefs and behaviors that clash with expert knowledge are not necessarily "irrational" or "ignorant." In this case, parents were clued in to the developmental significance and vulnerabilities of adolescence, and their concerns were legitimate. Realizing developmental gains for brains and minds in these communities means not "quitting early" after the first 1000 days, but persevering to secure further gains during later windows of opportunity.

In sum, interventions represent invaluable learning opportunities to encounter limitations in what we think we know and to discover new phenomena that change our minds, suggesting novel directions to enrich our models of how things work and how better to benefit human welfare. It can change the culture of science, policy, and intervention. In this case, yet again, we had to be there on the ground, in the community, open to observing, asking and listening to many local voices to figure this out.

Case 3 – Trauma and Resilience in Ex-child Soldiers The final case study involves ex-child soldiers who have been drawn or coerced into escalating conflicts, creating widespread concerns about the lasting impact of trauma exposure on these young people (Betancourt et al., 2013; O'Neil & van Broeckhoven, 2018). More accurately characterized as children associated with armed forces and groups (CAAFAG), the United Nations Children's Fund (UNICEF) defines them as "any person below 18 years of age who is or who has been recruited or used by an armed force or armed group in any capacity ... It does not only refer to a child who is taking or has taken a direct part in hostilities" (UNICEF, 2007, p. 7). The prevalent term "child soldiers" is used here, defined according to the United Nations definition criteria. Brandon Kohrt and I were confronted by this issue when the People's War broke out in Nepal and the village site for his long-term research became an epicenter. The war raged over 10 years (1996–2006), during which government security forces and Maoist combatants killed more than 14,000 people. Both sides conscripted child soldiers occupied in a variety of capacities (see Figure 4.8). Soon after peace accords were signed, we conducted a cross-sectional cohort study of repatriated ex-child soldiers and their nonconscripted peers matched on age, gender, ethnicity, and education, to assess the mental health effects of exposure to war.

We found that ex-child soldiers indeed suffered worse mental health outcomes than did their civilian peers, even after controlling for trauma exposure,

Figure 4.8 A poster depicting war experiences, painted by youth in Bandipur, Nepal (2008).
Photograph courtesy of L. J. Kirmayer

but the impact was not borne equally (Kohrt et al., 2008). Both girls and untouchable caste (Dalit) members experienced substantially greater mental health burden and impairment. From the perspective of social ecology, we asked whether community perceptions and treatment played a role in these effects. Indeed, parents and teachers displayed negative stereotypes and fears about returnees in which gender and caste discrimination played some part; moreover, ex-child soldiers in districts with a greater proportion (>40%) of high caste members received less integration support (Kohrt, Jordans, et al., 2010). The question, then, was whether school- and community-level interventions to change the narratives and perceptions around ex-child soldiers could improve their outcomes, and this proved to be the case (Jordans et al., 2010; Kohrt, Perera et al., 2010; see Figure 4.9).

Our measures of social ecology at the individual, family, and community level could explain half the variance in outcomes (mental health, function, and reintegration), but that left another 50 percent unexplained. We then returned for a 5-year postconflict assessment and asked whether an individual psychological factor, resilience, might mitigate the long-term impact of trauma exposure (Stevens & Jovanovic, 2019). Using a biomarker index of stress-related immune activation (the conserved transcriptional response to adversity,

Figure 4.9 Pedestrian street scene in historic center of Kathmandu, Nepal (2007).
Photograph by author

CTRA; Cole, 2014; Uchida et al., 2018), we found that CTRA activation was greater in former child soldiers, and increased linearly with trauma experience and related distress (Kohrt et al., 2016; see Figure 4.10). Yet remarkably, self-reported resilience strongly buffered CTRA activation such that former child soldiers with posttraumatic stress disorder (PTSD) but high personal resilience had low CTRA equivalent to PTSD-free civilians.

This case offers further lessons for thinking about the culture–mind–brain nexus and human well-being. First, it illustrates that trauma and its effects are not just located in individuals, but also reside in communities and society. How returning soldiers were treated greatly affected their outcomes, and such treatment reflected effects of war and trauma on community members and institutions. Therefore, effects of trauma are not inevitable, but can be mitigated during repatriation. Outcomes for child soldiers can be improved by interventions for community, not just individual, healing. Second and relatedly, ongoing social-ecological factors at the household and community-level play significant roles in individual outcomes, signaling the importance of interventions at levels of social ecology beyond the individual (Kohrt, 2013). Third, the body can serve as a window onto the mind and mental suffering. The brain is not wholly separable from the body after all, and the body plays

Figure 4.10 Major street in the town of Jumla, Karnali Province, Nepal.
Photograph by author

essential roles in how we perceive, feel, and think (Damasio, 2009; Damasio & Carvalho, 2013; see Chapter 6). That is, it forms an integral element of mind, *pace* ancient Western body–mind dissociation. Extensive dynamics between mental phenomena (moods, thoughts) and activity of the immune system attest to this relationship (Irwin & Cole, 2011; Miller & Raison, 2016; Murray et al., 2019).

Fourth, biomarkers do not necessarily tell the same story or reflect the same dynamics across different populations, depending on developmental or chronic conditions (Worthman & Costello, 2009). In the case of the CTRA, development and function of the immune system is necessarily guided by contextual input, both material and psychosocial, that provides information about the challenges it must engage (McDade et al., 2017). Given that exposures to pathogens and psychosocial challenges among Nepali youth differ markedly from those among the WEIRD populations where the CTRA had been developed, it was an open question whether the CTRA would be evident or take the same form (Dethlefsen et al., 2007). Hence, conservation of the CTRA among Nepali youth supported the claim of a "conserved" transcriptional response, that sensitivity to social adversity and salience or meaning evolved as an inbuilt feature of immune function. Work in this arena has focused heavily on stress and trauma (Nusslock & Miller, 2016), but our findings that self-reported resilience can counter the CTRA profile of PTSD also point to effects of meaning and emotion processing or social cognitions that buffer stress or may exert effects of their own (Pressman et al., 2019; Stevens & Jovanovic, 2019). Emerging literature identifies cultural differences in links between emotional states and physical health. Whereas Americans consistently manifest associations of negative emotion states with markers of inflammation or CTRA, recent reports find the association is either absent or reversed among Japanese (Kitayama & Park, 2017; Park et al., 2019). Notions of self, norms for affect regulation and expression, and the framework of roles and meanings within which emotions are experienced all may moderate these relationships. Here we see the culture–mind–brain nexus at work in yet another mode via interactions among meaning–inflammation–exposures.

In concluding this case, note that the work entailed a sustained mode of "being there" grounded in ongoing deep collaboration with local residents and professionals, communities, and organizations. Many people, largely Nepali and partly Western, advanced this research through myriad and varied contributions before, during, and after the war. Mutual looking, listening, and acting directed evolving research questions and methods, informed interpretation, and, as importantly, informed processes of intervention (Kohrt, Perera et al., 2010).

Being There as Method: Evolving Research Cultures

Although being there can be the major mode of inquiry for specific forms of research, unpacking the culture–mind–brain nexus involves tackling multiple dimensions with correspondingly diverse models and methods. Methodologically, "being there" is no substitute for other modes of inquiry into mind, brain, and culture, but the case studies have illustrated how it can inspire or complement other modes of research. The observation of long interbirth intervals among !Kung San foragers led to a revelation about culture and fertility regulation, and opened use of biomarkers and fields of inquiry into how culture gets under the skin. Unexpectedly modest effects from an intervention in South Africa designed to boost development in the first thousand days inspired an inquiry into parental beliefs that emphasized the significance of another developmental window, adolescence, and helped spark expansion of global family–child policy. Investigating effects of war trauma on Nepali ex-child soldiers' mental health revealed that how they are treated after coming home is decisive for outcomes, thereby opening new avenues for effective intervention in afflicted populations. Seeing, hearing, participating, and collaborating in the life worlds of participants permit insights not otherwise attainable.

Being there can assume many forms, but involves being present and, so much as possible, embedded in the community and culture spaces where research participants live. Such presence brings possibilities for observation, interaction, inquiry, and experiences outside the frame of a formal research setting. There are advantages and limitations to this approach. It increases connection, insight, and understanding of participants' lives, and the challenges and affordances they encounter. Being there can raise new questions, generate alternate understandings, and identify unanticipated factors that could derail, confound, or reframe ongoing research. It also pushes questions that experimental methods are ill-equipped to address, and thereby incites development of methods for studying people "in the wild." Yet there are limitations to this approach, which is subject to serendipity, to constraints on access and observability, to bias by both observer and observed, and to the limited times and places where one can be present. Furthermore, observers cannot ethically intervene in attempts to test ideas or control conditions.

Thus, informal being there is subject to shortcomings that formal research methods seek to circumvent (Bernard, 2013; Creswell, 2014). Formal methods are less about discovery and more about empirically testing hypotheses and making strong inferences about associations among variables. Research design aims for validity by excluding or systematically testing confounding variables and sources of bias, and in the case of experiments, by controlling the conditions under which observations are made. Furthermore, such designs can deploy methods such as imaging, eye tracking, tasks, or challenges that are not amenable to everyday conditions. On the downside, the inherent artificiality of controlled experiments may reduce ecological validity and limit generalizability to "real life." Moreover, they are subject to multiple sources of error, liable to limitations in construct validity, and vulnerable to what is not observed or controlled, especially the "unknown unknowns." Qualitative research claims a middle ground by systematically inquiring into nonquantitative phenomena comprising modes of thought, meanings and metaphors, working logics, or narrative that may tap subjective experience, reveal the reasons for human behavior or the textures of experience, or suggest how people talk, think, or get things done.

Being there can complement as well as add unique value in identifying and formulating questions and hypotheses, identifying key variables, critically operationalizing constructs, and interpreting observations. Its inherent reflexivity related to issues of bias is particularly useful in conversation with formal research. Investigation of culture, mind, and brain necessarily requires a mix of experimental research, population studies, qualitative inquiry, and being there via observation and ethnography. Ideally, each fuels the other to generate a fluid dialectical process of investigation. Such a fluid, collaborative multimethod dialectical approach is particularly *à propos* as culture–mind–brain research goes global and systematically engages human diversity.

As means of inquiry, being there presses, though not uniquely so, for the need to decolonize inquiry and knowledge production by building local collaborations and capacity rather than simply moving Western research teams and agendas to a wider range of locales. Being there involves a measure of vulnerability, risk taking, and cooperation on the part of researchers, and encourages a hefty commitment to reflexive ethics. As the Nepal case study illustrated most vividly, this requires building reciprocal relations and resource sharing, for local collaboration is integral to such work where collaborators are equal partners, each having unique contributions to make. Moreover, we *know* that immersion in doing research itself builds capacity and human capital. Limitations on materials and funding are common obstacles, but they also have inspired novel techniques or deeply informed questions that step somewhat aside from established lines of work. Hence, the mentor mother program and the collaborative randomized controlled trial were developed, largely led and conducted by South Africans (le Roux, et al., 2010; Tomlinson et al., 2015). Similarly, phases of the child soldiers research variously were led, conducted, or assisted by staff and principals of the Transcultural Psychosocial Organization in Nepal (Jordans et al., 2010; Karki et al., 2009; Kohrt, Perera, etal., 2010; Luitel et al., 2013).

Evolving Models of Science: Complexity and Inclusion

Advances in understanding the mind–brain–culture nexus that is the subject of this book involve not just novel theories and ways of thinking, but also suitably nimble ways of doing, of conducting research and linking to intervention. This essay has surveyed lines of inquiry and related theory that point to the importance of ecological approaches in advancing such work. Ecological analysis gains traction along three foundational axes of the culture–mind–brain nexus, first by bringing the lens of evolutionary design to bear on human biology (brain), function (mind), and behavior (culture). Second, ecological frameworks tap reliance of developmental processes on nested timelines of interaction with context that drive physical (body/brain), functional (mind), and behavioral (enculturation) development across the life course, including effects of historical, ecological, and evolutionary timelines. Third, ecological frameworks hone in on the conditions created by humans' thorough reliance on culture, thereby creating their own ecologies that in turn, generate tremendous human diversity, including in brain and mind.

For historical and geopolitical reasons, dominant natural and social sciences developed cultures and methods of research and bodies of evidence built by and representative of a narrow segment of humanity. Particularly in the case of social sciences, this legacy contributes to underrepresentation of the role of culture in human diversity, and slowed investigation of the culture–mind–brain nexus. Anthropology's focus on human diversity and its use of participant observation suggest that being there can play a valuable role in research, especially as it aims to become more global and inclusive. Three case studies explored that role as it played out in interaction with existing bodies of knowledge, major societal and scientific questions, and studies with novel human cultures and ecologies.

These case histories also sketched an arc of inquiry that progressively has integrated biomarkers and health outcomes with measures of psychosocial dynamics and life course development into population research embedded in community and cultural settings. Being there played an integral role in that trajectory. The contributions to both basic scientific questions and to matters of practical human concern, not just in the case studies but in the many lines of inquiry cited here, suggest the value of a dialectical ecologically informed approach that fluidly deploys diverse modes of research as we tackle the large questions and challenges confronting us.

REFERENCES

Adair, L. S., Fall, C. H., Osmond, C., Stein, A. D., Martorell, R., Ramirez-Zea, M., Sachdev, H. S., Dahly, D. L., Bas, I., Norris, S. A., Micklesfield, L., Hallal, P., & Victora, C. G., for the COHORTS group. (2013). Associations of linear growth and relative weight gain during early life with adult health and human capital in countries of low and middle income: Findings from five birth cohort studies. *Lancet*, *382*(9891), 525–34. https://doi.org/10.1016/S0140–6736(13)60103-8

Allis, C. D., & Jenuwein, T. (2016). The molecular hallmarks of epigenetic control. *Nature Reviews Genetics*, *17*(8), 487–500. https://doi.org/10.1038/nrg.2016.59

Arnett, J. J. (2008). The neglected 95%: Why American psychology needs to become less American. *American Psychologist*, *63*(7), 602–14. https://doi.org/10.1037/0003-066x.63.7.602

Bachrach, C. A., & Abeles, R. P. (2004). Social science and health research: Growth at the National Institutes of Health. *American Journal of Public Health*, *94*(1), 22–8. https://doi.org/10.2105/AJPH.94.1.22

Balcerak, A., Trebinska-Stryjewska, A., Konopinski, R., Wakula, M., & Grzybowska, E. A. (2019). RNA-protein interactions: Disorder, moonlighting and junk contribute to eukaryotic complexity. *Open Biology*, *9*(6), 190096. https://doi.org/10.1098/rsob.190096

Baldwin, J. M. (1896). A new factor in evolution. *American Naturalist*, *30*(354–355), 441–51, 536–53. https://doi.org/10.1086/276428

Benedict, R. (1934). *Patterns of culture*. Houghton Mifflin.

Bernard, H. R. (2013). *Social research methods: Qualitative and quantitative approaches* (2nd ed.). SAGE.

Betancourt, T. S., Borisova, I., Williams, T. P., Meyers-Ohki, S. E., Rubin-Smith, J. E., Annan, J., & Kohrt, B. A. (2013). Psychosocial adjustment and mental health in former child soldiers: A systematic review of the literature and recommendations for future research. *Journal of Child Psychology and Psychiatry, 54*(1), 17–36. https://doi.org/10.1111/j.1469-7610.2012.02620.x

Bhutta, Z. A., Das, J. K., Rizvi, A., Gaffey, M. F., Walker, N., Horton, S., Webb, P., Lartey, A., Black, R. E., The Lancet Nutrition Interventions Review Group, & the Maternal and Child Nutrition Study Group. (2013). Evidence-based interventions for improvement of maternal and child nutrition: What can be done and at what cost? *Lancet, 382*(9890), 452–77. https://doi.org/10.1016/S0140-6736(13)60996-4

Black, R. E., Victora, C. G., Walker, S. P., Bhutta, Z. A., Christian, P., de Onis, M., Ezzati, M., Grantham-McGregor, S., Katz, J., Martorell, R., Uauy, R., & the Maternal and Child Nutrition Study Group. (2013). Maternal and child undernutrition and overweight in low-income and middle-income countries. *Lancet, 382*(9890), 427–51. https://doi.org/10.1016/S0140-6736(13)60937-X

Blurton-Jones, N. (1986). Bushman birth spacing: A test for optimal interbirth intervals. *Ethology and Sociobiology, 7*(2), 91–105. https://doi.org/10.1016/0162-3095(86)90002-6

Boas, F. (1896). The limitations of the comparative method of anthropology. *Science, 4*(3), 901–908. https://doi.org/10.1126/science.4.103.901

Boas, F. (1911). *The mind of primitive man*. Macmillan.

Boas, F. (1912). Changes in the bodily form of descendants of immigrants. *American Anthropologist, 14*(3), 530–62. https://doi.org/10.1525/aa.1912.14.3.02a00080

Bongaarts, J. (2009). Human population growth and the demographic transition. *Philosophical Transactions of the Royal Society B: Biological Sciences, 364*(1532), 2985–90. https://doi.org/10.1098/rstb.2009.0137

Bonner, J. T. (1974). *On development: The biology of form*. Harvard University Press.

British Association for the Advancement of Science. (1874). *Notes and queries on anthropology: For the use of travellers and residents in uncivilized lands*. Edward Stanford.

Bulatao, R. A., & Lee, R. D. (Eds.). (1983). *Determinants of fertility in developing countries* (Vols. 1–2). Academic Press.

Cavalli, G., & Heard, E. (2019). Advances in epigenetics link genetics to the environment and disease. *Nature, 571*(7766), 489–99. https://doi.org/10.1038/s41586-019-1411-0

Champagne, F. A., & Curley, J. P. (2009). Epigenetic mechanisms mediating the long-term effects of maternal care on development. *Neuroscience & Biobehavioral Reviews, 33*(4), 593–600. https://doi.org/10.1016/j.neubiorev.2007.10.009

Changeux, J.-P., & Chavaillon, J. (Eds.). (1995). *Symposia of the Fyssen Foundation. Origins of the human brain*. Clarendon Press. https://doi.org/10.1093/acprof:oso/9780198523901.001.0001

Charnov, E. L. (1993). *Life history invariants: Some explorations of symmetry in evolutionary ecology*. Oxford University Press.

Clifford, J., & Marcus, G. E. (1986). *Writing culture: The poetics and politics of ethnography*. University of California Press.

Cole, S. W. (2014). Human social genomics. *PLoS Genetics, 10*(8), e1004601. https://doi.org/10.1371/journal.pgen.1004601

Cooper, P. J., Vally, Z., Cooper, H., Radford, T., Sharples, A., Tomlinson, M., & Murray, L. (2014). Promoting mother-infant book sharing and infant attention and language development in an impoverished South African population: A pilot study. *Early Childhood Education Journal, 42*(2), 143–52. https://doi.org/10.1007/s10643-013-0591-8

Creswell, J. W. (2014). *Research design: Qualitative, quantitative, and mixed methods approaches* (4th ed.). SAGE.

Dahl, R. E. (2016). The developmental neuroscience of adolescence: Revisiting, refining, and extending seminal models. *Developmental Cognitive Neuroscience, 17*, 101–102. https://doi.org/10.1016/j.dcn.2015.12.016

Dahl, R. E., Allen, N. B., Wilbrecht, L., & Suleiman, A. B. (2018). Importance of investing in adolescence from a developmental science perspective. *Nature, 554*(7693), 441–50. https://doi.org/10.1038/nature25770

Damasio, A. (2009). *The feeling of what happens: Body and emotion in the making of consciousness*. Harcourt.

Damasio, A., & Carvalho, G. B. (2013). The nature of feelings: Evolutionary and neurobiological origins. *Nature Reviews Neuroscience, 14*(2), 143–52. https://doi.org/10.1038/nrn3403

de Oliveira, S., & Nisbett, R. E. (2017). Culture changes how we think about thinking: From 'human inference' to 'geography of thought.' *Perspectives on Psychological Science, 12*(5), 782–90. https://doi.org/10.1177/1745691617702718

de Onis, M., Dewey, K. G., Borghi, E., Onyango, A. W., Blössner, M., Daelmans, B., Piwoz, E., & Branca, F. (2013). The World Health Organization's global target for reducing childhood stunting by 2025: Rationale and proposed actions. *Maternal & Child Nutrition, 9*(S2), 6–26. https://doi.org/10.1111/mcn.12075

Dehaene, S. (2009). *Reading in the brain: The new science of how we read*. Penguin Books.

Del Giudice, M., Hinnant, J. B., Ellis, B. J., & El-Sheikh, M. (2012). Adaptive patterns of stress responsivity: A preliminary investigation. *Developmental Psychology, 48*(3), 775–90. https://doi.org/10.1037/a0026519

Dethlefsen, L., McFall-Ngai, M., & Relman, D. A. (2007). An ecological and evolutionary perspective on human-microbe mutualism and disease. *Nature, 449*(7164), 811–18. https://doi.org/10.1038/nature06245

Dodge, K. A., Goodman, W. B., Murphy, R., O'Donnell, K., & Sato, J. (2013). Toward population impact from home visiting. *Zero to Three, 33*(3), 17–23. www.ncbi.nlm.nih.gov/pmc/articles/PMC3606025/

Ellis, B. J., & Del Giudice, M. (2019). Developmental adaptation to stress: An evolutionary perspective. *Annual Review of Psychology, 70*, 111–39. https://doi.org/10.1146/annurev-psych-122216-011732

Ellison, P. T. (1994). Advances in human reproductive ecology. *Annual Review of Anthropology, 23*, 255–75. https://doi.org/10.1146/annurev.an.23.100194.001351

Fox, S. E., Levitt, P., & Nelson, C. A., III. (2010). How the timing and quality of early experiences influence the development of brain architecture. *Child Development, 81*(1), 28–40. https://doi.org/10.1111/j.1467-8624.2009.01380.x

Friederici, A. D., Chomsky, N., Berwick, R. C., Moro, A., & Bolhuis, J. J. (2017). Language, mind and brain. *Nature Human Behaviour, 1*(10), 713–22. https://doi.org/10.1038/s41562-017-0184-4

Garson, J. G., & Read, C. H. (1892). *Notes and queries on anthropology* (2nd ed.). Harrison and Sons.

Geertz, C. (1973). *The interpretation of cultures: Selected essays*. Basic Books.
Gluckman, P. D., & Hanson, M. A. (Eds.). (2006). *Developmental origins of health and disease*. Cambridge University Press. https://doi.org/10.1017/CBO9780511544699
Gould, S. J. (1977). *Ontogeny and phylogeny*. Belknap Press.
Grantham-McGregor, S., Cheung, Y. B., Cueto, S., Glewwe, P., Richter, L., & Strupp, B. (2007). Developmental potential in the first 5 years for children in developing countries. *Lancet*, *369*(9555), 60–70. https://doi.org/10.1016/S0140-6736(07)60032-4
Gravlee, C. C., Bernard, H. R., & Leonard, W. R. (2003). Heredity, environment, and cranial form: A reanalysis of Boas's immigrant data. *American Anthropologist*, *105*(1), 125–38. https://doi.org/10.1525/aa.2003.105.1.125
Greenhalgh, S. (1996). The social construction of population science: An intellectual, institutional, and political history of twentieth-century demography. *Comparative Studies in Society and History*, *38*(1), 26–66. https://doi.org/10.1017/S0010417500020119
Gunnar, M. R., Doom, J. R., & Esposito, E. A. (2015). Psychoneuroendocrinology of stress: Normative development and individual differences. In M. E. Lamb & R. M. Lerner (Eds.), *Handbook of child psychology and developmental science: Socioemotional processes* (7th ed.,Vol. 3, pp. 106–51). John Wiley & Sons.
Gurven, M., Fuerstenberg, E., Trumble, B., Stieglitz, J., Beheim, B., Davis, H., & Kaplan, H. (2017). Cognitive performance across the life course of Bolivian forager-farmers with limited schooling. *Developmental Psychology*, *53*(1), 160–76. https://doi.org/10.1037/dev0000175
Hacking, I. (1999). *The social construction of what?* Harvard University Press.
Hanson, M. A., & Gluckman, P. D. (2014). Early developmental conditioning of later health and disease: Physiology or pathophysiology? *Physiological Reviews*, *94*(4), 1027–76. https://doi.org/10.1152/physrev.00029.2013
Harkness, S., Super, C. M., & Mavridis, C. J. (2011). Parental ethnotheories about children's socioemotional development. In X. Chen & K. H. Rubin (Eds.), *Socioemotional development in cultural context* (pp. 73–98). Guilford Press.
Harkness, S., Super, C. M., Mavridis, C. J., Barry, O., & Zeitlin, M. (2013). Culture and early childhood development: Implications for policy and programs. In P. R. Britto, P. L. Engle, & C. M. Super (Eds.), *Handbook of early childhood development research and its impact on global policy* (pp. 142–60). Oxford University Press. https://doi.org/10.1093/acprof:oso/9780199922994.003.0007
Harkness, S., Super, C. M., Moscardino, U., Rha, J.-H., Blom, M., Huitrón, B., Johnston, C., Sutherland, M. A., Hyun, O.-K., Axia, G., & Palacios, J. (2007). Cultural models and developmental agendas: Implications for arousal and self-regulation in early infancy. *Journal of Developmental Processes*, *1*(2), 5–39.
Hay, M. C. (Ed.) (2016). *Methods that matter: Integrating mixed methods for more effective social science research*. University of Chicago Press. https://doi.org/10.7208/chicago/9780226328836.001.0001
Henrich, J., Boyd, R., Bowles, S., Camerer, C., Fehr, E., & Gintis, H. (Eds.). (2004). *Foundations of human sociality: Economic experiments and ethnographic evidence from fifteen small-scale societies*. Oxford University Press. https://doi.org/10.1093/0199262055.001.0001

Henrich, J., Heine, S. J., & Norenzayan, A. (2010). The weirdest people in the world? *Behavioral and Brain Sciences*, *33*(2–3), 61–83. https://doi.org/10.1017/S0140525X0999152X

Hill, K., & Kaplan, H. (1999). Life history traits in humans: Theory and empirical studies. *Annual Review of Anthropology*, *28*, 397–430. https://doi.org/10.1146/annurev.anthro.28.1.397

Hobcraft, J., McDonald, J. W., & Rutstein, S. (1983). Child-spacing effects on infant and early child mortality. *Population Index*, *49*(4), 585–618. https://doi.org/10.2307/2737284

Howell, N. (1979). *Demography of the Dobe !Kung*. Transaction Publishers.

Howie, P. W., & McNeilly, A. S. (1982). Effect of breast-feeding patterns on human birth intervals. *Journal of Reproduction and Fertility*, *65*(2), 545–57. https://doi.org/10.1530/jrf.0.0650545

Irwin, M. R., & Cole, S. W. (2011). Reciprocal regulation of the neural and innate immune systems. *Nature Reviews Immunology*, *11*(9), 625–32. https://doi.org/10.1038/nri3042

Jablonka, E. (2013). Epigenetic inheritance and plasticity: The responsive germline. *Progress in Biophysics and Molecular Biology*, *111*(2–3), 99–107. https://doi.org/10.1016/j.pbiomolbio.2012.08.014

Jablonka, E. (2017). The evolutionary implications of epigenetic inheritance. *Interface Focus*, *7*(5), 20160135. https://doi.org/10.1098/rsfs.2016.0135

Jaeggi, A. V., Hooper, P. L., Beheim, B. A., Kaplan, H., & Gurven, M. (2016). Reciprocal exchange patterned by market forces helps explain cooperation in a small-scale society. *Current Biology*, *26*(16), 2180–7. https://doi.org/10.1016/j.cub.2016.06.019

Jordans, M. J. D., Komproe, I. H., Tol, W. A., Kohrt, B. A., Luitel, N. P., Macy, R. D., & de Jong, J. T. V. M.(2010). Evaluation of a classroom-based psychosocial intervention in conflict-affected Nepal: A cluster randomized controlled trial. *Journal of Child Psychology and Psychiatry*, *51*(7), 818–26. https://doi.org/10.1111/j.1469-7610.2010.02209.x

Karki, R., Kohrt, B. A., & Jordans, M. J. D. (2009). Child led indicators: Pilot testing a child participation tool for psychosocial support programmes for former child soldiers in Nepal. *Intervention*, *7*(2), 92–109. https://doi.org/10.1097/WTF.0b013e3283302725

Kitayama, S. (2017). Journal of Personality and Social Psychology: Attitudes and social cognition [Editorial]. *Journal of Personality and Social Psychology*, *112*(3), 357–60. https://doi.org/10.1037/pspa0000077

Kitayama, S., & Markus, H. R. (Eds.). (1994). *Emotion and culture: Empirical studies of mutual influence*. American Psychological Association.

Kitayama, S., & Park, J. (2017). Emotion and biological health: The socio-cultural moderation. *Current Opinion in Psychology*, *17*, 99–105. https://doi.org/10.1016/j.copsyc.2017.06.016

Kitayama, S., Varnum, M. E. W., & Salvador, C. E. (2019). Cultural neuroscience. In D. Cohen & S. Kitayama (Eds.), *Handbook of cultural psychology* (2nd ed., pp. 79–118). Guilford Press.

Kohrt, B. (2013). Social ecology interventions for post-traumatic stress disorder: What can we learn from child soldiers? *British Journal of Psychiatry*, *203*(3), 165–7. https://doi.org/10.1192/bjp.bp.112.124958

Kohrt, B. A., Jordans, M. J. D., Tol, W. A., Perera, E., Karki, R., Koirala, S., & Upadhaya, N. (2010). Social ecology of child soldiers: Child, family, and community determinants of mental health, psychosocial well-being, and reintegration in Nepal. *Transcultural Psychiatry, 47*(5), 727–53. https://doi.org/10.1177/1363461510381290

Kohrt, B. A., Jordans, M. J. D., Tol, W. A., Speckman, R. A., Maharjan, S. M., Worthman, C. M., & Komproe, I. H. (2008). Comparison of mental health between former child soldiers and children never conscripted by armed groups in Nepal. [Erratum appears in *JAMA* (2010), *303*(20), 2034]. *JAMA, 300*(6), 691–702.

Kohrt, B. A., Perera, E., Jordans, M. J. D., Koirala, S., Karki, R., Karki, R., Shrestha, P., Tol, W. A., & Upadhaya, N. (2010). *Psychosocial support model for children associated with armed forces and armed groups in Nepal*. Transcultural Psychosocial Organization-Nepal/UNICEF.

Kohrt, B. A., Worthman, C. M., Adhikari, R. P., Luitel, N. P., Arevalo, J. M. G., Ma, J., McCreath, H., Seeman, T. E., Crimmins, E. M., & Cole, S. W. (2016). Psychological resilience and the gene regulatory impact of posttraumatic stress in Nepali child soldiers. *Proceedings of the National Academy of Sciences of the United States of America, 113*(29), 8156–61. https://doi.org/10.1073/pnas.1601301113

Konner, M. J. (1972). Aspects of the developmental ethology of a foraging people. In N. B. Jones (Ed.), *Ethological studies of child behaviour* (pp. 285–304). Cambridge University Press.

Konner, M. J. (1977). Infancy among the Kalahari Desert San. In P. H. Leiderman, S. R. Tulkin, & A. Rosenfeld (Eds.), *Culture and infancy: Variations in the human experience* (pp. 287–328). Academic Press.

Konner, M., & Worthman, C. (1980). Nursing frequency, gonadal function, and birth spacing among !Kung hunter-gatherers. *Science, 207*(4432), 788–91. https://doi.org/10.1126/science.7352291

Kuzawa, C. W., & Bragg, J. M. (2012). Plasticity in human life history strategy: Implications for contemporary human variation and the evolution of genus Homo. *Current Anthropology, 53*(S6), S369–S382. https://doi.org/10.1086/667410

Kuzawa, C. W., & Thayer, Z. M. (2011). Timescales of human adaptation: The role of epigenetic processes. *Epigenomics, 3*(2), 221–34. https://doi.org/10.2217/epi.11.11

Laland, K. N., Uller, T., Fellman, M. W., Sterelny, K., Müller, G. B., Moczek, A., Jablonka, E., & Odling-Smee, J. (2015). The extended evolutionary synthesis: Its structure, assumptions and predictions. *Proceedings of the Royal Society B: Biological Sciences, 282*(1813), 20151019. https://doi.org/10.1098/rspb.2015.1019

le Roux, I. M., le Roux, K., Comulada, W. S., Greco, E. M., Desmond, K. A., Mbewu, N., & Rotheram-Borus, M. J. (2010). Home visits by neighborhood Mentor Mothers provide timely recovery from childhood malnutrition in South Africa: Results from a randomized controlled trial. *Nutrition Journal, 9*, 56. https://doi.org/10.1186/1475-2891-9-56

le Roux, I. M., Tomlinson, M., Harwood, J. M., O'Connor, M. J., Worthman, C. M., Mbewu, N., Stewart, J., Hartley, M., Swendeman, D., Comulada, W., Weiss, R., & Rotheram-Borus, M. J. (2013). Outcomes of home visits for pregnant mothers and

their infants: A cluster randomized controlled trial. *AIDS, 27*(9), 1461–71. https://doi.org/10.1097/QAD.0b013e3283601b53
Lee, R. B. (1972). Population growth and the beginnings of sedentary life among the !Kung Bushmen. In B. Spooner (Ed.), *Population growth: Anthropological implications* (pp. 329–42). MIT Press.
Lee, R. B., & DeVore, I. (Eds.). (1976). *Kalahari hunter-gatherers: Studies of the !Kung San and their neighbors*. Harvard University Press. https://doi.org/10.4159/harvard.9780674430600
Luitel, N. P., Jordans, M. J. D., Sapkota, R. P., Tol, W. A., Kohrt, B. A., Thapa, S. B., Komproe, I. H., & Sharma, B. (2013). Conflict and mental health: A cross-sectional epidemiological study in Nepal. *Social Psychiatry and Psychiatric Epidemiology, 48*(2), 183–93. https://doi.org/10.1007/s00127–012-0539-0
Lupien, S. J., McEwen, B. S., Gunnar, M. R., & Heim, C. (2009). Effects of stress throughout the lifespan on the brain, behaviour and cognition. *Nature Reviews Neuroscience, 10*(6), 434–45. https://doi.org/10.1038/nrn2639
Markus, H. R., & Kitayama, S. (1991). Culture and the self: Implications for cognition, emotion, and motivation. *Psychological Review, 98*(2), 224–53. https://doi.org/10.1037/0033-295X.98.2.224
Markus, H. R., & Kitayama, S. (2010). Cultures and selves: A cycle of mutual constitution. *Perspectives on Psychological Science, 5*(4), 420–30. https://doi.org/10.1177/1745691610375557
Maternal Child Nutrition Study Group. (2013). Maternal and child nutrition: Building momentum for impact. *Lancet, 382*(9890), 372–5. https://doi.org/10.1016/S0140–6736(13)60988-5
McDade, T. W., Ryan, C., Jones, M. J., MacIsaac, J. L., Morin, A. M., Meyer, J. M., Borja, J. B., Miller, G. E., Kobor, M. S., & Kuzawa, C. W. (2017). Social and physical environments early in development predict DNA methylation of inflammatory genes in young adulthood. *Proceedings of the National Academy of Sciences of the United States of America, 114*(29), 7611–16. https://doi.org/10.1073/pnas.1620661114
Mead, M. (1928). *Coming of age in Samoa: A psychological study of primitive youth for Western civilization*. William Morrow & Company.
Mead, M. (1930). *Growing up in New Guinea: A comparative study of primitive education*. William Morrow & Company.
Mead, M., & Macgregor, F. C. (1951). *Growth and culture: A photographic study of Balinese childhood*. Putnam.
Miller, A. H., & Raison, C. L. (2016). The role of inflammation in depression: From evolutionary imperative to modern treatment target. *Nature Reviews Immunology, 16*(1), 22–34. https://doi.org/10.1038/nri.2015.5
Miska, E. A., & Ferguson-Smith, A. C. (2016). Transgenerational inheritance: Models and mechanisms of non-DNA sequence-based inheritance. *Science, 354*(6308), 59–63. https://doi.org/10.1126/science.aaf4945
Murray, D. R., Haselton, M. G., Fales, M., & Cole, S. W. (2019). Subjective social status and inflammatory gene expression. *Health Psychology, 38*(2), 182–6. https://doi.org/10.1037/hea0000705
National Institutes of Health. (1994). *NIH guidelines on the inclusion of women and minorities as subjects in clinical research*. http://grants.nih.gov/grants/guide/notice-files/not94–100.html

Newen, A., De Bruin, L., & Gallagher, S. (Eds.). (2018). *The Oxford handbook of 4E cognition*. Oxford University Press. https://doi.org/10.1093/oxfordhb/ 9780198735410.001.0001

Nisbett, R. E. (1993). Violence and U. S. regional culture. *American Psychologist*, *48*(4), 441–9. https://doi.org/10.1037/0003-066X.48.4.441

Nisbett, R. E., Peng, K., Choi, I., & Norenzayan, A. (2001). Culture and systems of thought: Holistic versus analytic cognition. *Psychological Review*, *108*(2), 291–310. https://doi.org/10.1037/0033-295X.108.2.291

Noel, G. L., Suh, H. K., & Frantz, A. G. (1974). Prolactin release during nursing and breast stimulation in postpartum and nonpostpartum subjects. *Journal of Clinical Endocrinology and Metabolism*, *38*(3), 413–23. https://doi.org/10.1210/jcem-38-3-413

Nusslock, R., & Miller, G. E. (2016). Early-life adversity and physical and emotional health across the lifespan: A neuroimmune network hypothesis. *Biological Psychiatry*, *80*(1), 23–32. https://doi.org/10.1016/j.biopsych.2015.05.017

O'Neil, S., & van Broeckhoven, K. (Eds.). (2018). *Cradled by conflict: Child involvement with armed groups in contemporary conflict*. United Nations University.

Odling-Smee, F. J., Laland, K. N., & Feldman, M. W. (1996). Niche construction. *American Naturalist*, *147*(4), 641–8. https://doi.org/10.1086/285870

Olds, D. L., Kitzman, H., Knudtson, M. D., Anson, E., Smith, J. A., & Cole, R. (2014). Effect of home visiting by nurses on maternal and child mortality: Results of a 2-decade follow-up of a randomized clinical trial. *JAMA Pediatrics*, *168*(9), 800–806. https://doi.org/10.1001/jamapediatrics.2014.472

Olds, D. L., Robinson, J., O'Brien, R., Luckey, D. W., Pettitt, L. M., Henderson, C. R., Jr., Ng, R. K., Sheff, K. L., Korfmacher, J., Hiatt, S., & Talmi, A. (2002). Home visiting by paraprofessionals and by nurses: A randomized, controlled trial. *Pediatrics*, *110*(3), 486–96. https://doi.org/10.1542/peds.110.3.486

Ortner, S. B. (1984). Theory in anthropology since the Sixties. *Comparative Studies in Society and History*, *26*(1), 126–66. https://doi.org/10.1017/ S0010417500010811

Ortner, S. B. (2016). Dark anthropology and its other: Theory since the eighties. *HAU: Journal of Ethnographic Theory*, *6*(1), 47–73. https://doi.org/10.14318/hau6.1.004

Park, J., Kitayama, S., Miyamoto, Y., & Coe, C. L. (2019). Feeling bad is not always unhealthy: Culture moderates the link between negative affect and diurnal cortisol profiles. *Emotion*. Advance online publication. https://doi.org/10.1037/ emo0000605

Paul, B. D. (Ed.) (1955). *Health, culture, & community: Case studies of public reaction to health programs*. Russell SAGE Foundation.

Paul, R. A. (2015). *Mixed messages: Cultural and genetic inheritance in the constitution of human society*. University of Chicago Press. https://doi.org/10 .7208/chicago/9780226241050.001.0001

Pertea, M., Shumate, A., Pertea, G., Varabyou, A., Breitwieser, F. P., Chang, Y.-C., Madugundu, A. K., Pandey, A., & Salzberg, S. L. (2018). CHESS: A new human gene catalog curated from thousands of large-scale RNA sequencing experiments reveals extensive transcriptional noise. *Genome Biology*, *19*(1), 208. https://doi .org/10.1186/s13059–018-1590-2

Petrosini, L., De Bartolo, P., Foti, F., Gelfo, F., Cutuli, D., Leggio, M. G., & Mandolesi, L. (2009). On whether the environmental enrichment may provide cognitive and brain reserves. *Brain Research Reviews*, *61*(2), 221–39. https://doi.org/10.1016/j.brainresrev.2009.07.002

Pocheville, A. (2015). The ecological niche: History and recent controversies. In T. Hearns, P. Huneman, G. Lecointre, & M. Silberstein (Eds.), *Handbook of evolutionary thinking in the sciences* (pp. 547–86). Springer. https://doi.org/10.1007/978-94-017-9014-7_26

Pressman, S. D., Jenkins, B. N., & Moskowitz, J. T. (2019). Positive affect and health: What do we know and where next should we go? *Annual Review of Psychology*, *70*, 627–50. https://doi.org/10.1146/annurev-psych-010418-102955

Ramstead, M. J. D., Veissière, S. P. L., & Kirmayer, L. J. (2016). Cultural affordances: Scaffolding local worlds through shared intentionality and regimes of attention. *Frontiers in Psychology*, *7*, 1090. https://doi.org/10.3389/fpsyg.2016.01090

Reeve, H. K., & Sherman, P. W. (1993). Adaptation and the goals of evolutionary research. *Quarterly Review of Biology*, *68*(1), 1–32. https://doi.org/10.1086/417909

Rollins, N. C., Bhandari, N., Hajeebhoy, N., Horton, S., Lutter, C. K., Martines, J. C., Piwoz, E. G., Richter, L. M., Victora, C. G., & The Lancet Breastfeeding Series Group. (2016). Why invest, and what it will take to improve breastfeeding practices? *Lancet*, *387*(10017), 491–504. https://doi.org/10.1016/S0140-6736(15)01044-2

Rosaldo, R. (1989). *Culture & truth: The remaking of social analysis*. Beacon Press.

Rotheram-Borus, M. J., le Roux, I. M., Tomlinson, M., Mbewu, N., Comulada, W. S., le Roux, K., Stewart, J., O'Connor, M. J., Hartley, M., Desmond, K., Greco, E., Worthman, C. M., Idemundia, F., & Swendeman, D. (2011). Philani Plus (+): A mentor mother community health worker home visiting program to improve maternal and infants' outcomes. *Prevention Science*, *12*(4), 372–88. https://doi.org/10.1007/s11121-011-0238-1

Ruben, R. J. (1997). A time frame of critical/sensitive periods of language development. *Acta Oto-Laryngologica*, *117*(2), 202–5. https://doi.org/10.3109/00016489709117769

Save the Children. (2012). *Nutrition in the first 1,000 days: State of the world's mothers 2012*. Save the Children.

Sawyer, S. M., Azzopardi, P. S., Wickremarathne, D., & Patton, G. C. (2018). The age of adolescence. *The Lancet Child & Adolescent Health*, *2*(3), 223–8. https://doi.org/10.1016/S2352-4642(18)30022-1

Schneider, J., & Schneider, P. (1984). Demographic transition in a Sicilian rural town. *Journal of Family History*, *9*(3), 245–72. https://doi.org/10.1177/036319908400900305

Shore, B. (1996). *Culture in mind: Cognition, culture, and the problem of meaning*. Oxford University Press.

Shostak, M. (1981). *Nisa, the life and words of a !Kung woman*. Harvard University Press.

Shweder, R. A. (1990). Ethical relativism: Is there a defensible version? *Ethos*, *18*(2), 205–18. https://doi.org/10.1525/eth.1990.18.2.02a00050

Shweder, R. A., Minow, M., & Markus, H. (2002). *Engaging cultural differences: The multicultural challenge in liberal democracies*. Russell SAGE Foundation.
Simons, R. C., & Hughes, C. C. (1985). *The culture-bound syndromes: Folk illnesses of psychiatric and anthropological interest*. D. Reidel. https://doi.org/10.1007/978-94-009-5251-5
Stearns, S. C. (1992). *The evolution of life histories*. Oxford University Press.
Stevens, E. E., Patrick, T. E., & Pickler, R. (2009). A history of infant feeding. *Journal of Perinatal Education*, *18*(2), 32–9. https://doi.org/10.1624/105812409X426314
Stevens, J. S., & Jovanovic, T. (2019). Role of social cognition in post-traumatic stress disorder: A review and meta-analysis. *Genes, Brain, & Behavior*, *18*(1), e12518. https://doi.org/10.1111/gbb.12518
Stotz, K. (2014). Extended evolutionary psychology: The importance of transgenerational developmental plasticity. *Frontiers in Psychology*, *5*. https://doi.org/10.3389/fpsyg.2014.00908
Strauss, C., & Quinn, N. (1997). *A cognitive theory of cultural meaning*. Cambridge University Press. https://doi.org/10.1017/CBO9781139167000
Super, C. M., Axia, G., Harkness, S., Welles-Nyström, B., Zylicz, P. O., Parmar, P., Bonichini, S., Bermúdez, M. R., Moscardino, U., Kolar, V., Palacios, J., Andrzej, E., & McGurk, H. (2008). Culture, temperament, and the "difficult child": A study in seven Western cultures. *European Journal of Developmental Science*, *2*(1–2), 136–57. https://doi.org/10.3233/DEV-2008-21209
Super, C. M., & Harkness, S. (1986). The developmental niche: A conceptualization at the interface of child and culture. *International Journal of Behavioral Development*, *9*(4), 545–69. https://doi.org/10.1177/016502548600900409
The Women's Health Initiative Study Group. (1998). Design of the Women's Health Initiative clinical trial and observational study. *Controlled Clinical Trials*, *19*, 61–109. https://doi.org/10.1016/S0197-2456(97)00078-0
Theise, N. D., & Kafatos, M. C. (2013). Complementarity in biological systems: A complexity view. *Complexity*, *18*(6), 11–20. https://doi.org/10.1002/cplx.21453
Tomlinson, M., Rotheram-Borus, M. J., Harwood, J., le Roux, I. M., O'Connor, M., & Worthman, C. (2015). Community health workers can improve child growth of antenatally-depressed, South African mothers: A cluster randomized controlled trial. *BMC Psychiatry*, *15*, 225. https://doi.org/10.1186/s12888-015-0606-7
Tomlinson, M., Rotheram-Borus, M. J., le Roux, I. M., Youssef, M., Nelson, S. H., Scheffler, A., Weiss, R. E., O'Connor, M., & Worthman, C. M. (2016). Thirty-six-month outcomes of a generalist paraprofessional perinatal home visiting intervention in South Africa on maternal health and child health and development. *Prevention Science*, *17*(8), 937–48. https://doi.org/10.1007/s11121-016-0676-x
Trevathan, W. R., Smith, E. O., & McKenna, J. J. (2008). *Evolutionary medicine and health: New perspectives*. Oxford University Press.
Triandis, H. C. (1989). The self and social behavior in differing cultural contexts. *Psychological Review*, *96*(3), 506–20. https://doi.org/10.1037/0033-295X.96.3.506
Tylor, E. B. (1871). *Primitive culture: Researches into the development of mythology, philosophy, religion, art, and custom* (Vol. 1). John Murray.
Tyson, J. E., Friesen, H. G., & Anderson, M. S. (1972). Human lactational and ovarian response to endogenous prolactin release. *Science*, *177*(4052), 897–900. https://doi.org/10.1126/science.177.4052.897

Uchida, Y., Kitayama, S., Akutsu, S., Park, J., & Cole, S. W. (2018). Optimism and the conserved transcriptional response to adversity. *Health Psychology, 37*(11), 1077–80. https://doi.org/10.1037/hea0000675

UNICEF. (2007). *Paris principles: Principles and guidelines on children associated with armed forces and armed conflict.* United Nations International Children's Emergency Fund.

Victora, C. G., Bahl, R., Barros, A. J. D., França, G. V. A., Horton, S., Krasevec, J., Murch, S., Sankar, M. J., Walker, N., Rollins, N. C., & The Lancet Breastfeeding Series Group. (2016). Breastfeeding in the 21st century: Epidemiology, mechanisms, and lifelong effect. *Lancet, 387*(10017), 475–90. https://doi.org/10.1016/S0140-6736(15)01024-7

Victora, C. G., de Onis, M., Hallal, P. C., Blössner, M., & Shrimpton, R. (2010). Worldwide timing of growth faltering: Revisiting implications for interventions. *Pediatrics, 125*(3), e473–e480. https://doi.org/10.1542/peds.2009-1519

Vitzthum, V. J. (2009). The ecology and evolutionary endocrinology of reproduction in the human female. *American Journal of Physical Anthropology, 140*(S49), 95–136. https://doi.org/10.1002/ajpa.21195

Walker, S. P., Wachs, T. D., Grantham-McGregor, S., Black, M. M., Nelson, C. A., Huffman, S. L., Baker-Henningham, H., Chang, S. M., Hamadani, J. D., Lozoff, B., Gardner, J. M. M., Powell, C. A., Rahman, A., & Richter, L. (2011). Inequality in early childhood: Risk and protective factors for early child development. *Lancet, 378*(9799), 1325–38. https://doi.org/10.1016/S0140-6736(11)60555-2

Walker, S. P., Wachs, T. D., Gardner, J. M., Lozoff, B., Wasserman, G. A., Pollitt, E., & Carter, J. A. (2007). Child development: Risk factors for adverse outcomes in developing countries. *Lancet, 369*(9556), 145–57. https://doi.org/10.1016/S0140-6736(07)60076-2

West-Eberhard, M. J. (2003). *Developmental plasticity and evolution.* Oxford University Press.

Whiting, J. W. M. (1994). *Culture and human development: The selected papers of John Whiting.* E. H. Chasdi (Ed.). Cambridge University Press. https://doi.org/10.1017/CBO9780511598340

Whiting, B. B., & Edwards, C. P. (1988). *Children of different worlds: The formation of social behavior.* Harvard University Press.

Whiting, J. W. M., & Child, I. L. (1953). *Child training and personality: A cross-cultural study.* Yale University Press.

Whiting, J. W. M., Child, I. L., Lambert, W. W., & the Field Teams for the *Six Cultures* series. (1966). *Field guide for a study of socialization.* John Wiley & Sons.

Worthman, C. M. (1978). *Psychoneuroendocrine study of human behavior: Some interactions of steroid hormones with affect and behavior in the !Kung San* [Unpublished doctoral dissertation]. Harvard University.

Worthman, C. M. (2010). The ecology of human development: Evolving models for cultural psychology. *Journal for Cross-Cultural Psychology, 41*(4), 546–62. https://doi.org/10.1177/0022022110362627

Worthman, C. M. (2016). Ecocultural theory: Foundations and applications. In M. C. Hay (Ed.), *Methods that matter: Integrating mixed methods for more effective social science research* (pp. 13–38). University of Chicago Press. https://doi.org/10.7208/chicago/9780226328836.003.0002

Worthman, C. M., & Costello, E. J. (2009). Tracking biocultural pathways in population health: The value of biomarkers. *Annals of Human Biology*, *36*(3), 281–97. https://doi.org/10.1080/03014460902832934

Worthman, C. M., Tomlinson, M., & Rotheram-Borus, M. J. (2016). When can parents most influence their child's development? Expert knowledge and perceived local realities. *Social Science & Medicine*, *154*, 62–9. https://doi.org/10.1016/j.socscimed.2016.02.040

Worthman, C. M., & Trang, K. (2018). Dynamics of body time, social time and life history at adolescence. *Nature*, *554*(7693), 451–7. https://doi.org/10.1038/nature25750

Section 2

The Situated Brain

Introduction

Once upon a time, not so long ago, the brain was regarded as a machine, albeit an extraordinary one. It appeared to have stable "wiring," involved electricity, and eventually wore out: once off the developmental assembly line, the brain was thought to possess a fixed number of neurons and went downhill from there as 25–30 percent of its neurons were irreplaceably lost with age. This model began to crumble with the discovery that learning is based on neuroplasticity, eroded further with documentation of neurogenesis in the adult brain, and finally collapsed beneath overwhelming evidence of continuous brain changes throughout the life span. Recent revolutionary models view brain structure and function as anatomically dynamic and operationally proactive, predictive, and probabilistic rather than reactive, reductive, and linear. Relatedly, an integrated brain–mind–body view of cognition as embedded, embodied, extended, and enacted (see Chapter 5) has emerged from convergent theory and evidence that bridge entrenched dualisms.

The brain-as-machine metaphor reflected Western mind–body dualism distinguishing an inherently rational mind from the body and its irrational products, emotions. The rationalist view of mind underpinned notions of free will and agency based on orderly mental processes. Emotion was "noise" arising from the "primitive brain," intruding into and perturbing these processes. This logic has unraveled under insights from Nobel prize-winning work by Tversky and Kahneman showing systematic biases in human rationality (Kahneman, 2011), accumulating evidence that emotions fuel thought and play crucial roles in "rational" processes such as decision-making (Damasio, 2006), and extensive imaging research delineating nonlinear distributed and demand-sensitive, network-based processing in the brain (Sporns, 2012). The rise of neuroscience prompted a turn to positing mind or consciousness as an emergent property of brain. Emotions are integral processes in 4E cognition (embodied, embedded, enactive, and extended; which may be conscious but usually is not) to enable real-time anticipatory adaptation that balances a person's needs and capacities against external demands and affordances (see Chapter 6). These insights cast new light on notions of agency and subjectivity (see Chapter 8).

Meanwhile, the concept of culture also has had its vicissitudes. "Culture" exploded onto the scene of late nineteenth-century social thought embroiled in a struggle to understand how deep and wide human differences could go, and quickly took hold by conveying a sociodynamic population-based vision of distinctive life worlds. Construed as a package of shared beliefs, values, and practices that mediated meeting fundamental human material, social, and spiritual needs, the concept de-naturalized human differences and recast them as sociohistorical products of particular times and places. This view led to cultural relativism, the claim that a society's cultural content and logics and the lives of its members should be evaluated on their own rather than another's terms. Yet for all its appeal, the culture concept was beset with difficulties, including specifying precisely what it is and how it works, and reconciling the stability and transmission of cultural institutions and practices with their obvious porosity and capacity for change. Ecological and structural accounts have proved useful in clarifying these issues by linking the social construction of life conditions, niches, and perceptions to cultural affordances that can account for different developmental trajectories and outcomes within and between societies (Veissière et al., 2020).

Each chapter in this section contributes to an understanding that culture is not an add-on, showing how culture works both inside-out *and* outside-in (see Chapter 5). The continuous rub of living with and through other people both re/produces culture and its associated conditions of living even as these relationships are also products of local culture (see Chapter 6). Cultural dynamics drive patterned recurrent situations, experiences, demands, and affordances that shape brain and cognition (see Chapter 7), while brain–mind drives behavior, relationships, and agency in both pre-conscious and narrativized terms (see Chapter 8). Insights about embodiment have brought fuzzy, abstract notions of "culture" down to earth, for human development relies on the material circumstances and massive, locally tuned inputs from socioculturally structured and populated conditions of growing up. Through context-informed development and adaptation, the body and the brain come to integrate and continually update vast arrays of information about the condition of the local world and how to survive and adapt within it.

We have arrived at an exciting moment, when concepts of brain, mind, and culture each are undergoing radical reformulations distinguished by a focus on multilevel processes. Understanding *how* such complex embedded systems work on interacting timelines, from the molecular on up, has given new traction to efforts to understand individuals and societies. Provocatively, we are led to regard the brain as a cultural artifact tuned to the sociostructural characteristics of its local niche, proactively marshaling mental and physical resources to manage self and others.

The resultant view of mind aligns with observations that culture modulates early sensory processing. Perception of the world is selective and constructed initially by features of our sensory organs and basic sensory processing, all the way from the perception of color, on up to ongoing reflexive processing of sense of self. Our subjectivity arises through sensorimotor feedback for our own actions and engagement with the environment, and interactions with others that confirm our sense of presence, personhood, and agency. This production of self and other through ongoing interactions with local cultural niches gains added scope and amplitude through engagements with telecommunications and social media, contributing to new ecologies of human existence.

REFERENCES

Damasio, A. R. (2006). *Descartes' error*. Random House.
Kahneman, D. (2011). *Thinking, fast and slow*. Macmillan.
Sporns, O. (2012). *Discovering the human connectome*. MIT Press.
Veissière, S. P. L., Constant, A., Ramstead, M. J. D., Friston, K. J., & Kirmayer, L. J. (2020). Thinking through other minds: A variational approach to cognition and culture. *Behavioral and Brain Sciences*, *43*, e90, 1–75. https://doi.org/10.1017/S0140525X19001213

5 Culture in Mind – An Enactivist Account
Not Cognitive Penetration but Cultural Permeation

Daniel D. Hutto, Shaun Gallagher, Jesús Ilundáin-Agurruza, and Inês Hipólito

> We must ... confront the ever-active predictive brain in its proper setting – inextricably intertwined with an empowering backdrop of material, linguistic and sociocultural scaffolding.
>
> Andy Clark, *Surfing Uncertainty*

Culture, apparently, makes a difference to what we think and perceive. A wealth of empirical evidence points in this direction. The question is, how does it do so? We advance the view that patterned sociocultural practices permeate cognition, even the most basic forms of perception. In doing so, we challenge mainstream framework assumptions about perception that have given life to debates about whether or not perception is cognitively penetrable. What is at stake in how we think about these matters?

Consider that there are two words for "blue" in modern Greek – *ghalazio* ("light blue") and *ble* ("dark blue"). There is only one word for "green." Thierry et al. (2009) tested Greek and English speakers, measuring a specific neuronal signal, visual mismatch negativity (vMMN) over the visual cortex using electroencephalography (EEG). The signal occurs approximately 200 milliseconds following the presentation of an oddball stimulus (for example, a square in a series of circles, or a different colored circle in a series of circles; see Figure 5.1).

The signal plays a role in a preattentive, unconscious, and very early stage of visual processing. The vMMN signal was significantly larger for blue than for green contrasts in Greek speakers, but not for English speakers, correlating with faster perceptual discrimination of the blue contrasts in Greek speakers than in English speakers. Hence, the way Greek and English speakers have been enculturated appears to make a difference to the ways their brains respond in early visual processing to different shades of blue (for a more detailed discussion, see Gallagher, 2017).

These sorts of empirical findings raise questions about the universality of color concepts and the impact of linguistic differences on color processing and cognition. Ever since the Sapir–Whorf hypothesis was first advanced this topic has been a central focus in psychology and anthropology (see, e.g.,

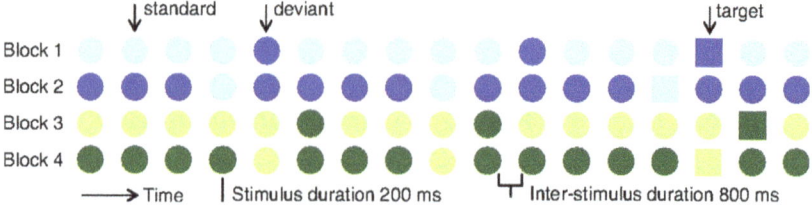

Figure 5.1 Examples of stimulus sequences presented in the oddball shape discrimination task.
From "Unconscious Effects of Language-Specific Terminology on Preattentive Color Perception," by G. Thierry, P. Athanasopoulos, A. Wiggett, B. Dering, and J.-R. Kuipers, 2009, *Proceedings of the National Academy of Sciences of the United States of America*, *106*(11), p. 4567 (https://doi.org/10.1073/pnas.0811155106)

Kay & Kempton, 1984, on the universal semantic constraints on color terminology; Kay, 1999; and Boroditsky, 2001, on the impact of language and metaphors on cognition; also see Cibelli et al., 2016; Dedrick, 2015). In philosophy, as revealed in the section "Cognitivist Options: Contentful Encapsulation, Binding or Adjusting," this debate is played out in terms of cognitive penetration, where it raises questions about whether and how culturally acquired concepts interact with basic perceptual processing.

As understood under the auspices of the classic cognitivist framework, the question is whether the kinds of mental representations that underpin culturally acquired concepts or beliefs can have a top-down influence that informs or biases the processing of the most basic kinds of perceptual content (e.g., Carruthers, 2015).

In contrast, we argue that human cognition is not only shaped but utterly *permeated* by patterned practices embedded in sociocultural contexts within which these practices grow and develop. Sociocultural influences not only operate with respect to our explicitly formed and expressed beliefs and values, but they can also inform and infuse what we see and feel in quite basic ways – as in the cited case of such influences on the early stages of color perceiving for Greek and English speakers. In such cases, the response patterns of the brains of the two sets of speakers have been differently shaped over a protracted developmental timescale.

A radically enactive take on cognition gives us the resources to understand how even the most basic forms of perceiving are permeated by patterned practices. The signature idea of an enactivist account is that cognition is in general best modeled on activities of living systems. So understood, cognition is not restricted to what goes on inside the heads or brains of organisms – cognition is out-in-the-open and found in the interactive, dynamic, relational engagements of organisms and their environments.

Radically enactive accounts of cognition, or REC, are marked out from their more conservative cousins – most prominently O'Regan and Noë (2001) and Noë (2004) – in rejecting the idea that the most basic forms of cognition require, involve, or rest upon the manipulation of representational contents. Contentful forms of cognition represent the world as being in ways that might not obtain – that is, to represent the world contentfully is to represent it in ways that can be true or false, accurate or inaccurate, and so on.

By REC's lights, basic cognition is neither representational nor does it involve picking up and processing contents that are used, stored, and reused to get cognitive work done. In rejecting those mainstream assumptions, REC sets its face, firmly, against a long-established tradition in philosophy of mind and cognitive science.

Thus, according to REC basic perceiving is a form of embodied activity – one that involves an exploration of the world. Yet while this embodied activity may take the forms of honing of sensorimotor skills, REC denies that such mastery is rooted in or best explained by appeal to any mediating, contentful knowledge of the sensorimotor laws mastered at any scale or level.

Accordingly, REC contends that to understand basic perceiving our interest should not rest on a body of knowledge of facts that informs the perceiver, but rather on the facts about the embodied activity of the perceiver and how the perceiver actively explores its environment. How such exploration unfolds is shaped by aspects of a particular environment because of the way the perceiver has interacted with other environments in its previous history. Thus, in some cases, its particular profile of interacting – its specific liabilities and tendencies – will have been shaped by enculturating factors.

Enactivists emphasize not only this kind of direct and non-representationally mediated responsiveness to sensorimotor contingencies but also the way embodied affects and intersubjective interaction shape cognition (Gallagher, 2017; Gallagher & Bower, 2014). The signature enactivist idea is that cognition is a situated organismic activity that takes the form of complex, dynamical processes at multiple levels and on different timescales, where these processes are part of a dynamical engagement or response of the whole organism, living in and materially engaging with structured environments.

For radical enactivists, brains play an important role in the ongoing dynamical attunement of organism to the environment. In social interaction, for example, brain processes integrate into a complex mix of transactions that involve moving, gesturing, and engaging with the expressive bodies of others. These are bodies that, situated in various environments, incorporate artifacts, tools, and technologies, adopt diverse social roles, and engage in various institutional practices. Thus, not only the body, but also physical, social, and cultural environments are important factors both evolutionarily and developmentally for any understanding of neural plasticity (Gallagher et al., 2013).

Brains do not evolve in vitro or floating in a vat. They evolve to function the way they do because they evolve with the body they are part of, and in environments that are coupled in specific ways to those bodies. Brains are not the isolated seat of cognition; they shape and are shaped by non-neural factors. Cognition, even of the most basic sort, involves transactions between body, brain, and environment – and any understanding of cognition thus must consider neural and extraneural elements (Anderson, 2014; Fuchs, 2017; Gallagher, 2017; Hutto & Myin, 2013, 2017; Thompson et al., 2005).

The way environments structure minds and the way minds structure environments involve a plasticity that goes both ways, what Malafouris (2013) calls metaplasticity – brain activity is part of what enables changes to the physical, social, and cultural environments that change brains and vice versa (Malafouris, 2013). Interventions at any point in this self-organizing system of brain–body–environment will incur (sometimes advantageous, sometimes not so advantageous) adjustments to the whole.

REC rejects the classical cognitivist conception of cognition which has enjoyed the status of the received view in the sciences of the mind since the 1950s. Classical cognitivism assumes that "the mind represents and computes" (Branquinho, 2001, xv). It endorses an intellectualist, individualist, and – typically – an internalist vision of minds that regards representationalism and computationalism as defining features of all cognition, even of the most basic kinds.

A signature feature of classical cognitivist attempts to explain behavior is to endorse a methodologically individualistic intellectualism that favors "process" over "context" (Ceci & Roazzi, 1994, p. 74). Accordingly, and in tune with an aspiration to discover universal psychological laws that operate anywhere and everywhere, classical cognitivist approaches have sought to identify narrow, internal properties of individuals – indeed, usually only properties or processes of their brains – that could causally explain how behavior is produced. Such internal factors are portrayed as independent of whatever may be happening in the cognizer's environment. Situationally specific factors are unwelcome in this class of explanations; such explanations "short shrift context" (Ceci & Roazzi, 1994, p. 74).

Fundamentally for classical cognitivists – as Ceci and Roazzi (1994) astutely highlight – the processes that are assumed to constitute cognition – whether these are understood as, say, information processing or neurocomputational activity – are of special explanatory interest. All else, the influences of culture and context included, is treated as a "form of noise" (p. 74). Accordingly, "context is viewed as an adjunct to cognition, rather than a constituent of it" (Ceci & Roazzi, 1994, p. 75).

When thinking about contextual influences, talk of culture is too vague and broad. It is important to focus on specific patterned practices within cultures of interest. Pitched at the right level of grain this leads to a focus on local and specific patterns of practice instead of operating with an abstract notion of culture (see Hutto & Kirchhoff, 2015; Roepstorff et al., 2010).

Going against the standard conceptions of cognition, these authors (along with many others in the embodied cognition or E-cognition movement) called for an approach to cognition that could "integrate the environmental dimensions into a more comprehensive theoretical framework of organism-environment interaction" (Ceci & Roazzi, 1994, p. 76). They sought a framework that would enable us to understand the "intersection in development of an individual's biological background and the sociocultural environment in which the individual grows up" (Ceci & Roazzi, 1994, p. 76).

In what follows, we advance a *radically enactive* account of cognition – just the sort of framework that Ceci and Roazzi (1994) were looking for. We provide arguments in favor of the possibility that cultural factors *permeate* rather than penetrate cognition, such that cognition extensively and transactionally incorporates cultural factors from its inception, rather than there being any question of cultural factors having to break into the restricted confines of cognition.

The section "Cognitivist Options: Contentful Encapsulation, Binding or Adjusting?" reviews the limitations of two cognitivist, modularist accounts of cognition (Carruthers, 2015; Marr, 1982), the idea that perception is modular, and ultimately gives reasons for going beyond the cognitive penetrability debate. Though there is no exact agreement on what a module is in today's literature, modularists of all stripes assume that modules entail at least two features, informational encapsulation and domain specificity. More precisely, it is assumed that modules only have access to the information in the input plus whatever information is available within the module, and that each module is moreover sensitive to a specific domain, for example, the visual module is only activated by visual inputs.

We argue in the section "Cultural Affordances Meet Neurocomputational Models" that there are empirical reasons to prefer predictive processing accounts of cognition (PPC) over their modularist rivals. PPC puts paid to the idea that the basic levels of perceiving are modular, at least in the traditional sense, because cognitive activity, even at the most basic level, is assumed to be informed by and in communication, even if only indirectly[1], with the deliverances of cognitive activity at higher levels. This puts an end to the possibility that basic levels of perceiving are informationally encapsulated or cognitive impenetrable. The section concludes by looking closely at

---

[1] Some suggest that such communication is functionally segregated. More specifically, Bayesian hierarchical levels are paired units encapsulated from other units through a Markov blanket (Hohwy, 2013). This means that each level can only communicate with its adjacent level.

Ramstead et al.'s (2016) attempt to explain how, using the resources of a PPC framework, cultural factors might make a difference to cognition by appealing to our sensitivity to cultural affordances.

While the PPC proposal is *prima facie* promising, the section "Doing Without Neural Models: A Radical Take on Cognition" reveals why committing to a cognitivist interpretation of PPC is problematic. A classical cognitivist reading of PPC assumes that the "predictions" that drive cognition – predictions that operate and are adjusted at every level – are always and everywhere contentful. Thus, for those adherents to PPC who embrace cognitivism even perceivings at the lowest rungs of the cognitive hierarchy represent the world as being one way as opposed to another. This is because on cognitivist renderings PPC assumes that cognition at all levels takes the form of predictions that contentfully represent certain possibilities. Such cognitivist renderings of PPC remain conservatively and problematically attached to the idea of cognitive work that entails the existence of inner models and stored knowledge.

Finally, the section "Culture Permeates Cognition: A Radically Enactive Account" seeks to honor Ramstead et al.'s (2016) motivating insights while avoiding such troublesome theoretical commitments. To achieve this, it offers an alternative, REC account of how cultural factors matter to cognition. Going the radically enactive way requires making an important theoretical adjustment to PPC – abandoning any vestige of the intellectualist idea that cultural factors might possibly inform or influence the contents of basic forms of perception by means of contentful communication. In place of that idea, we promote the possibility that culture instead permeates cognition in enactive and embodied ways.

Pulling all the threads together, we conclude that careful scrutiny of the available theoretical possibilities gives compelling reasons to favor the idea that culture permeates, rather than penetrates, cognition and that a radically enactive approach to cognition gives us the tools to understand how it does so.

Cognitivist Options: Contentful Encapsulation, Binding or Adjusting?

Questions about whether and how deeply cultural and contextual factors might penetrate cognition are only intelligible against the backdrop of particular assumptions about the nature of cognition. This is because how we conceive of cognition determines how we think it is possible that cultural and contextual factors could make a difference to it.

For example, the cognitivist debate about whether or not early vision can be cognitively penetrated assumes that early visual processes are contentful such that it is at least possible, in principle if not in fact, that they might be cognitively penetrated. For only if basic perceiving is contentful would it even be possible that contentful attitudes of belief, desire, knowledge might contentfully inform what we see at the early and elementary stages of visual processing. Conversely, if early vision is contentless, cognitively penetrability will be logically impossible, not just factually so, since there will be no contents to early vision to be contentfully informed by any contentful attitudes that the perceiver may have (Pylyshyn, 1999; Raftopoulos, 2001, 2017).

Importantly, in this light, questions about whether a given cognitive process might possibly be cognitively penetrated turn on the possibility of the process in question being modified "in virtue of the [presumed] content of states of the cognitive system" (Macpherson, 2012, p. 27). Highlighting the importance of this requirement, Macpherson (2012) emphasizes – focusing on the case of early vision – that "there have to be some links between the content of the cognitive state and the content of the perceptual state that is affected of a nature such that the effect on the content of the perceptual experience is made intelligible" (p. 27). To wonder whether early vision might be cognitively penetrated or otherwise only makes sense if it is assumed that early vision can be somehow contentfully informed and not merely causally impacted.[2]

Sensu stricto, cognitive penetrability is only possible if there can be influential contentful communication between the basic perceivings and higher forms of cognition. That cognitive penetration requires the actuality of intelligible links between these two sources of content is a fundamental assumption for all parties in the cognitive penetrability debate (Macpherson, 2012). This assumption operates in the background and goes without notice since anyone embroiled in this debate must subscribe to cognitivism and the assumption that the relevant forms of cognition are contentful.

It is easy to see the importance of these framing assumptions by focusing on the fact that there are at least two senses in which a given process might be cognitively impenetrable: these two senses exhibit different modal forces. The process of, say, digestion of carbohydrates is necessarily cognitively

---

[2] Brogaard and Chomanski (2015) make this point clearly. They write,

Consider the following example of a top-down influence on experience. Izzy is attending a difficult biochemistry lecture on migraines. Her thoughts about the difficult theories about the nature of migraines activate her amygdala, yielding a stress reaction. The activation in the amygdala causes her to develop migraine auras. Her thoughts about migraines thus resulted in an alteration of her visual experience, yet it cannot rightly be considered a case of cognitive penetration. This is because the steps in the chain from the cognitive state to the alterations in her visual experience are not semantically coherent. There is no inferential relation between her thoughts about migraines and her stress reaction or between her stress reaction and her visual experience. So, even though her thoughts of migraines exert some top-down influence on her visual experience, this influence is not an instance of cognitive penetration (p. 471).

impenetrable if it turns out – as we might safely assume – that their digestion does not process any contents that could possibly be penetrated. By contrast, it is widely thought that it is at least an open question of whether early vision might be cognitively penetrated on the assumption that early visual processes are content-involving (Zeimbekis & Raftopoulos, 2015). As such, the contents of early vision would be cognitively impenetrable if it turns out, as a matter of fact, that such contents cannot be informed by other contentful attitudes of perceivers. If, however, the opposite proves to be the case, then the putative contents of early vision would be cognitively penetrable.

Having clarified some of the background philosophical assumptions operating in the debate about cognitive penetrability, it is worth noting that there is a wealth of empirical evidence that points to the existence of top-down effects on early perception (Rauss et al., 2011; Sohoglu et al., 2012). Such findings put great pressure on the modular accounts that assume that contentful attitudes cannot communicate with or inform early perception – viz. that such attitudes do not have any influence on contents at the bottom rungs of cognition since the perceptual processes at that level operate within relatively discrete and independent "modules."

That early perception might be modular in the sense of being informationally encapsulated and isolated from the rest of cognition was first and most prominently advanced by Fodor (1983). If this version of the modularity thesis holds true, then some cognitive systems are informationally encapsulated and are only responsive to a select set of inputs, and insensitive to any other kind of information or content. According to Fodor's account of modules, they are constrained by the information contained in the select set of inputs to which they are responsive and unaffected by whatever other information is available elsewhere in cognition. As such, if the early perception is modular, then it is precluded from communicating with a wider set of contentful attitudes – e.g., expectations, knowledge, and beliefs.

Defenders of traditional modular accounts argue that early perceptual processing is informationally encapsulated from the rest of cognition (Firestone & Scholl, 2016; Raftopoulos, 2015, 2017; Raftopoulos & Lupyan, 2018; Toribio, 2018). Proponents of traditional modular theories assume that the processes of early vision transduce spatiotemporal patterns of light hitting the retina into contentful representations by means of computations that are wholly and solely concerned with such specialized work. Building on the pioneering work of Marr (1982), visual processing is often characterized in terms of computations over contents that lead to specific low-level descriptions of a visual scene, in terms of edges, shadows, and such (Pylyshyn, 1999). For cognitivists about early vision, cognitive impenetrability follows directly: the contents of early visual processing are encapsulated from cognitive states, such as intentions, beliefs, and motivations. This is held to be so on such accounts despite the fact that early vision involves the manipulation of other sorts of contentful representations.

A growing body of evidence suggests that so-called top-down beliefs, desires, emotions, motivations, and intentions do contentfully influence what we see, modifying the presumed contents of low-level perceptual processing, such as brightness, shape, texture, or color (Delk & Fillenbaum, 1965). Goldstone et al. (2001; as cited in Harnad, 1987) report that "one of the largest sources of evidence that concepts influence perceptual descriptions comes from the field of categorical perception" (p. 28). For example, they cite earlier work by Goldstone (1994) regarding the perception of dimensions of brightness and size which revealed that "experience with categorizing objects actually decreased people's ability to spot subtle perceptual differences between the objects, if the objects belonged to the same category" (Goldstone et al., 2001, p. 29). This and much other work provide evidence for extensive top-down influences on even the earliest stages of perception.

This research puts traditional modular accounts that favor the view that early vision is contentfully encapsulated under considerable pressure. The philosophical community has presented strong arguments, based on new experimental evidence, in favor of cognitive penetrability of early vision (Macpherson, 2012; Marchi & Newen, 2015; Newen & Vetter, 2017; Newen et al., 2017; Siegel, 2012; Vetter & Newen, 2014). This new empirical research includes behavioral and neuroimaging evidence that supports the claim that perceptual processes like face and object recognition are directly influenced by several high-level cognitive processes, such as contextual cues, categorical processing, social values, and emotions (O'Callaghan et al., 2017).

Reporting the standard conclusion drawn in the field, Carruthers (2015) tells us that "increasingly it has been argued that perceptual processing is deeply interactive at many different levels simultaneously" (p. 501). One way to accommodate this putative fact within the framework of classical cognitivism without surrendering a modular theory of mind would be to propose, as Carruthers (2015) does, that the products of early perception are not encapsulated from concepts and other contentful attitudes.

The hypothesis is that culturally acquired concepts might be added to basic perceptual processing through a speedy binding process. The conjecture is that conceptual information is transmitted rapidly to areas responsible for early perception; that there is a phase synchrony in the neural activity in the orbitofrontal cortex, temporal cortex, and visual cortex, which, for Carruthers (2015), suggests "meaningful interactions" (p. 502). Culturally acquired concepts might, through this means, inform and become bound up with contents of what is perceived through processes that are fast and online.

Any integration of the sort Carruthers proposes would have to be extremely fast. For example, Thierry et al. (2009) show, in the aforementioned studies concerning Greek and English speakers, that the first, earliest positive peak elicited by visual stimuli revealing differences between the speakers occur in parietooccipital regions at 100–130 milliseconds; 100 milliseconds prior to any indication of visual mismatch negativity (vMMN).

Whatever the exact speed of processing, for Carruthers's proposal to work perceptual and conceptual contents must be integrated by the time what is perceived is broadcast to consciousness. The key idea in this modular–interactionist account is that the nonconceptual contents of basic perception and any culturally acquired conceptual contents start out being quite separate, but they are bound together through neural processes operating on an elemental timescale. Perceiving is thus a mix of the contents served up by early perceptual processing plus an extra step of "adding" conceptual contents before the entire package reaches consciousness. The theory is that even if the early perception is assumed to be modular, it produces nonconceptual contents that are contentfully integrated with conceptual contents in ways that make the final product – the whole package – unencapsulated.

In the end, it is unclear exactly where Carruthers's (2015) account leaves us with respect to the cognitive penetrability debate. On the one hand, do the hypothesized binding processes somehow contentfully infuse early perceptual contents with contents of higher attitudes, such as beliefs? If so, then it would seem that cognitive penetration occurs since the two components are contentfully integrated. On the other hand, does the binding process only attach, say, a believed content to the untouched core of perceptual contents? For if so, then, strictly speaking, the early perceptual contents will remain cognitively unpenetrated.

There is another possibility. There are strong empirical grounds for thinking that perceptual processes are neither linear nor sequentially staged in the way that modular theories, traditional or otherwise, suppose (Rizzolatti & Sinigaglia, 2006/2008). Impressed by these sorts of findings, many researchers have been attracted to predictive processing accounts of cognition, or PPC (Clark, 2016; Friston, 2013; Frith, 2017; Hohwy, 2013). According to PPC, the brain constantly and proactively forms models and hypotheses about what it will perceive in the sensory stream. It corrects its predictions by adjusting to, or acting upon, the incoming sensory stream in an ongoing attempt to minimize error.

Conceiving of perception under the auspices of PPC raises deep questions about the appropriateness of the penetration metaphor that underpins and drives debates about cognitive penetrability. This is because, according to PPC, contentful attitudes – in the form of predictive hypotheses – are assumed to come into play at multiple levels of the perceptual processing hierarchy

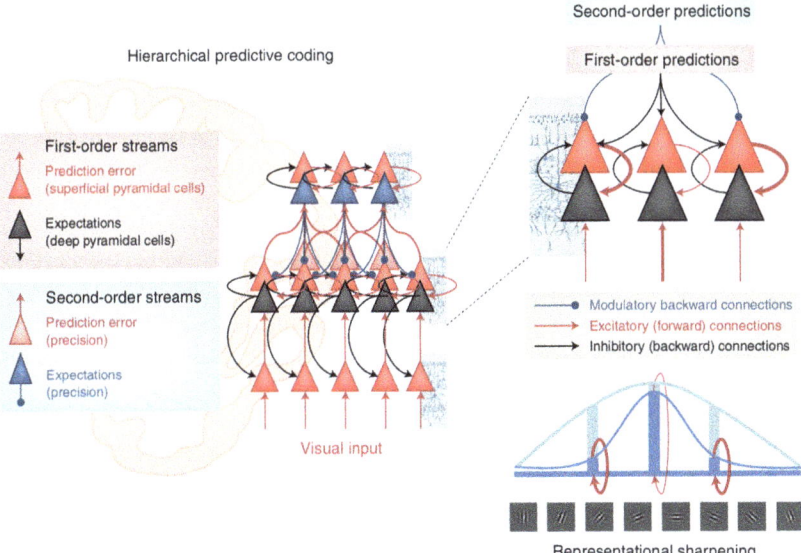

Figure 5.2 A schematic illustration of hierarchical predictive coding. Reprinted by permission from Macmillan Publishers Ltd: *Nature Neuroscience* ("Does Predictive Coding Have a Future?") by Karl Friston, 2018, *21*, p. 1020 (https://doi.org/10.1038/s41593-018-0200-7). Copyright 2018

(Figure 5.2). Communication between and across levels informs and adjusts the content of perceptual hypotheses in an ongoing, dynamic manner at all levels (Clark, 2016; Hohwy, 2013).

For example, according to the PPC, high-level predictions can influence the content of even the most basic of perceptual hypotheses prior to sensory input. On the PPC model, even our most basic perceptual predictions are always one step ahead, poised to act in reply to or actively bring about sensory flows of information. This is why advocates of PPC hold that, "just about every aspect of the passive forward-flowing model is false. We are not passive cognitive couch potatoes" (Clark, 2015, p. 22). Likewise, hypotheses at the higher level are contentfully informed and adjusted by what is conveyed up the line from the lower levels of perceptual processing.

In this way, the contents of perceptual hypotheses at all levels are altered in a dynamic way over time. For example, the precision weightings of specific hypotheses are adjusted in light of everything the perceiver, meta-cognitively, knows about the likelihood of the anticipated possibilities occurring in any given context. According to PPC, perceiving is thus a complex, multi-directional process involving communication across levels in a coordinated attempt to minimize error.

According to PPC, error signals feed into higher levels of processing thereby correcting and adjusting the predictive model. Through further recurrent loops, a better predictive model is generated and fed down again to the sensory input layer until error is minimized. In PPC, then, top-down predictions, expectations, or attitudes play a crucial role – even in early perception – since they contribute directly to the content of what is perceived via their predictions about what is likely to be seen.

Unlike the two modular theories discussed above, PPC requires us to revise thinking about cognitive penetrability quite fundamentally. PPC posits extensive ongoing two-way traffic between levels of the cognitive process. Adoption of a PPC framework renders all modular accounts outmoded, whether they think of the contents of early perception as contentfully encapsulated or contentfully integrated.

There is much that speaks in favor of PPC, but to pursue this line is to embrace a radically revisionary framework that turns a great deal of previous cognitivist thinking on its head. In particular, PPC relinquishes the traditional assumption found in modular theories of perception that we build models of the world in a staged manner based on incoming information (Clark, 2016, pp. 29–37, 51). According to PPC, our prior assumptions and hypotheses about what we expect to perceive in certain circumstances already shape and inform even the most basic perceptual activity. As such, adopting PPC pushes us to abandon asking whether perceiving might be cognitively penetrated or otherwise since, on the PPC account, that question no longer makes sense because perceiving is always already contentful and continually contentfully adjusted in ongoing processes.

Cultural Affordances Meet Neurocomputational Models

Suppose we take PPC seriously as a framework for understanding even the most basic forms of cognition. How, through its lens, ought we to understand the way cultural factors make a difference to what we perceive and think at a fundamental level? According to Clark (2016), PPC contends that cultural factors shape and inform our basic cognitive abilities, skills, and tendencies through interactions occurring not only over the course of each individual's development but also on protracted, multi-generational timescales.

The transformative processes that make our brains receptive to cultural influences involve prolonged exposure to local, socioculturally specific, patterned practices (Hutto & Kirchhoff, 2015; Roepstorff et al., 2010): our basic cognitive capacities are ready to be shaped by sociocultural factors because we repeatedly use them within socioculturally designed environments. Our basic cognitive capacities are scaffolded by being repeatedly deployed in specific ways that conform to established routines, customs, and institutions – and, in some cases, using our basic capacities in such contexts enables the emergence of new forms and varieties of cognition (see Hutto & Myin, 2017; Hutto & Satne, 2015).

A prime example of such sociocultural scaffolding is the way we, arguably, acquire folk psychological capacities to understand the actions of ourselves and others in terms of reasons through the mastery of certain kinds of narrative practice. Hutto (2008) makes a detailed case for the idea that the way we make sense of intentional actions essentially involves the construction of narratives about particular persons. This developmental proposal is known as the narrative practice hypothesis (NPH). The core claim of the NPH is that direct encounters with stories about persons who act for reasons (that is, folk psychological narratives) supply children with both the basic structure of folk psychology and the norm-governed possibilities for wielding it in practice. Accordingly, children acquire their folk psychological competence by being exposed to and engaging in a distinctive kind of narrative practice, where the narrative practices in question are patterned practices that may vary across and within cultures (Hutto & Kirchhoff, 2015).

With the advent of the practices involving external symbols, for example, came the possibility of reading, writing, structured discussion, and schooling in the sociocultural specific forms we are familiar with today. Arguably, that brought certain cognitive capacities into being for the first time – capacities of the sort required for being able to think about the specific subject matter – such as mathematics (Overmann, 2016). The big idea is that through continual exposure to and involvement in patterned sociocultural practices, "Prediction hungry brains ... acquire forms of knowledge that were generally out-of-reach" (Clark, 2016, p. 277).[3]

Clark (2016) maintains that our interaction with material and sociocultural designer environments trains, triggers, and repeatedly transforms our more biologically basic forms of cognition. Some argue, along Gibsonian lines, that perceiving, in general, is always for action and is, thus, a matter of detecting and responding to environmental affordances – where affordances are understood to be perceivable possibilities for action, relative to some creature or creatures (Gibson, 1977).

---

[3] Citing Heyes's (2012) work on how reading and writing act as springboards for the creation of new cognitive capacities, Clark (2016) defends the idea that "many of our capacities for cultural learning are themselves cultural innovations, acquired by social interactions rather than flowing directly from fundamental biological adaptations" (p. 281).

Ramstead et al. (2016) seek to understand how through enculturation we become attuned to special kinds of affordances – cultural affordances – where such attunement is understood as a matter of embodying "shared sets of expectations, reflected in the ability to engage immersively in patterned cultural practices" (p. 7). Harkening back to an idea canvassed by Costall's (1995), who highlighted the social character of many affordances, these authors recognize that, at least for humans, the regularities to which we are sensitive are "densely mediated (and often constituted) by cultural symbols, narratives, and metaphors" (Ramstead et al., 2016. p. 14).

The main hypothesis of Ramstead et al. (2016) is that feedback loops mediating shared attention and shared intentionality are the primary means through which we acquire our special sensitivity to cultural affordances. This is all part and parcel of the individual's history of interactions and the shaping of expectations that history entails.

Despite entertaining the possibility that the whole story about how we are shaped by cultural affordances might be told in contentless, radically enactive terms, Ramstead et al. (2016) cannot imagine how this might be done without appeal to neural models and special kinds of stored knowledge. For example, they are convinced that in order to be sensitive to cultural affordances we "*must have* shared sets of expectations – we *must know* what others expect us to expect" (Ramstead et al., 2016, p. 7, emphasis added).

This insistence – this "musty" thinking – leads them to embrace an intellectualized position; one that stands halfway "in between" enactivist and cognitivist accounts of cognition and tries to marry the two at the altar of PPC (Hutto & Myin, 2017). Thus, these authors, following Clark (2016), endorse a *conservative* enactive account of cognition through which they hope to account for the special knowledge that they think is needed to fill the perceived explanatory gap.

Specifically, Ramstead et al. (2016) maintain that "predictive processing models offer a plausible implementation for the *neural-computational realization* of affordance-responsiveness in the nervous system" (p. 12, emphasis added). Elaborating on this proposal, they tell us that the brain uses generative models which function:

to dynamically extract and encode information about the distal environment as sets of probability distributions. The information involved here can be natural or conventional in kind ... The system uses this generative model to guide adaptive and intelligent behavior by 'inverting' that model through Bayesian forms of (computational, subpersonal) inference. (Ramstead et al., 2016. p. 9)

They are thereby committed to the existence of neurocomputational models – models that exist in cognitive systems – which those systems must call on to explain how they are able to produce and guide "skilled intelligent, context-sensitive, adaptive behavior" (Ramstead et al., 2016, p. 7).

Doing without Neural Models: A Radical Take on Cognition

A long tradition has it that only some organisms – only those that are truly cognitive – learn and deploy models that guide their behavior. Accordingly, those creatures capable of "only model-free responses are, in [a backward-looking sense] condemned to repeat the past, releasing previously reinforced actions when circumstances dictate" (Clark, 2016, p. 254). Such creatures would be behaviorally dumb devices – mechanisms that behave only in accord with blind habit.

By contrast, the cognitively well-equipped creatures make use of models to act on the world intelligently, because having a model is thought to be what enables them "to evaluate potential actions using (as the name suggests) some kind of inner surrogate of the external arena ... [thus they are] able to 'navigate into the future'" (Clark, 2016, p. 254).

It is wildly implausible that any living system could be as simple and stupid as the model-free picture portrays the creatures at what is sometimes deemed to be the bottom rung of animal life. For example, new findings have shown that even bacteria are remarkably sophisticated in the ways in which they adapt, attune, and respond to their environments (Balázsi et al., 2011; Locke, 2013; Losick & Desplan 2008; Perkins & Swain 2009; Tagkopoulos et al., 2008). Thus, in an effort to make the best sense of these findings, Fulda (2017) reports that, "the responsiveness of even the simplest living systems is remarkably flexible ... microbiologists take this responsiveness to be evidence of cognition. After all, it is too supplely adaptive for a machine. Bacteria can respond appropriately to novel conditions, that is, conditions that have no evolutionary or developmental counterpart" (p. 77).

What should we make of this? One natural answer is to deny that there is any model-free behaving. According to that answer, all behavior is model-driven. On such a view, it is models all the way down; models of some kind must drive even the most basic forms of cognition. Any differences in organismic responsiveness would, thus, just be a matter of degree of the sophistication of the model used or how well it is used as opposed to the responsiveness in question being model-driven as opposed to model-free. It seems that this is the sort of answer that Clark (2016) favors: he readily admits that the standard story is "almost certainly over-simplistic" (p. 253). For, despite acknowledging the intuitive pull of the model-based/model-free distinction, he admits that that distinction resonates "with old (but increasingly discredited) dichotomies between habit and reason, between emotion and analytic evaluation" (Clark, 2016, p. 253).

The more fundamental question is why posit any models as the drivers of behavior at all. Some do so because they are persuaded by the following line of argument: "There is a gap between the mind and the world, and (as far as anybody knows) you need to posit internal representations if you are to have a hope of getting across it. Mind the gap. You'll regret it if you don't" (Fodor, 2009, p. 15).

Of course, this cannot be Clark's reason. The idea that inner models are needed to explain behavior has long been challenged by the 4E-movement – embodied, enactive, ecological, extended – in cognitive science that Clark and company embrace. Those attracted to such views are thus happy to propound the roboticist's slogan that, "The world is its own best [model]/representation" (Clark, 1997, p. 46; see also Brooks, 1991). Yet, against this idea, it has been plausibly argued that "the world can't be its own best [model]/representation because the world doesn't [model]/represent anything; least of all itself" (Fodor, 2009, p. 15).

In light of this, for those attracted to the 4E-approaches it seems, at least at first blush, that a better answer would be to hold that an "agent does not have a model of its world – it is a model" (Friston, 2013, p. 213). This obviates having to address the awkward question of how the world, itself, can be a model. But, what exactly might it mean to say the system or agent itself is a model? Friston et al. (2012) advise that, "We must here understand 'model' in the most inclusive sense, as combining interpretive dispositions, morphology, and neural architecture, and as implying a highly tuned 'fit' between the active, embodied organism and the embedded environment." Following through on this logic, we are told that "in essence, [biological/cognitive systems] become models of causal structure in their local environment, enabling them to predict what will happen next and counter surprising violations of those predictions" (p. 6).

This looks like progress. Yet, if we understand models à la Friston's proposal, we face the question of how the system itself can both be a model and, simultaneously, *use* itself as a model to drive its behavior. Is the claim that systems are models descriptive or explanatory?

In this context, it is useful to consider Clark's (2016) discussion of Sokolov's work on habituation and what drives the thought that models are required to explain even very similar forms of psychological behavior and responsiveness. He writes:

One might have thought of [habituation] as some kind of brute physical effect due to some kind of low-level sensory adaption. Sokolov noticed, however, that even a reduction in the magnitude of *some habituated stimulus* could engage 'dishabituation' and *prompted a renewed response*. Sokolov concluded that the nervous system *must learn and deploy a 'neuronal model.'* (Clark, 2016, p. 89, emphases added)

Admittedly, we observe that the system, as a whole, exhibits flexible behavior and is capable of learning. That is a true description of its cognitive capacities. But why *must* it learn a model; how does that explain this flexibility? Does the brain or nervous system learn and deploy a neural model or does the system – as a whole – through its sustained history of worldly engagements – simply become capable of adapted, flexible, and selective responses?

In any case, what might it mean to say that an organism or system learns and deploys a model? Clark (2016) everywhere advances the idea that cognizers acquire knowledge that can be appealed to in order to causally explain their subsequent behavior. Clark (2016) talks of model-driven systems in the following terms: as "using stored knowledge" (p. 6); as "knowledgeable consumers" (p. 6); as acquiring "bodies of knowledge" (p. 68); as something that "learns and deploys a generative model" (p. 22); as building up "the sensory scene using knowledge" (p. 25, p. 17); as "the brain using stored knowledge to predict" (p. 27); of successful perception requiring "the brain to use stored knowledge and expectations" (p. 79); and so on.

To take such talk seriously as part of an explanation, we are owed the details of precisely what changes in the system occur when it acquires a model – when it learns a model – and how such structural changes amount to the acquisition of knowledge that can causally explain and drive the relevant responding. There is a reason to doubt that this can be achieved (Hutto & Myin, 2017, pp. 26–53). Yet without a substantive proposal about how acquired knowledge can causally explain behavior, talk of the system's learning and using models provides no explanation, only the illusion of one.

Here it is useful to compare our compelling need to think that we must explain behavior by reference to systems being guided by neural models with Wittgenstein's (1953/2009, 1956/1983) famous observations about our compelling need to explain rule-following behavior with reference to being guided by our grasp of rules. In the latter case, the grasped rule was meant to be distinct from and to stand, over and above, any actual attempts to apply it. For it seems that if we are to explain our capacity to follow a rule, then there *must be* something – some fact – that determines which rule we are trying to follow and hence which standard we are answerable to. Wittgenstein thinks not; although he recognizes how deep the compulsion to think otherwise can run and its confounding effects on what we imagine is possible and needed to explain such phenomena.

'How can one follow a rule?' That is what I should like to ask. But how does it come about that I want to ask that, when after all I find no kind of difficulty in following a rule? Here we obviously misunderstand the facts that lie before our eyes. (*RFM* VI §38)

But is that all? Isn't there a deeper explanation; or mustn't at least the understanding of the explanation be deeper? – Well have I myself a deeper understanding? Have I got more to give in the explanation? (*PI* §209)

We follow rules, obey orders, and the like. We can describe the circumstances under which we learn to do so, but we cannot give a deeper – philosophically illuminating – explanation of what makes this possible in the terms of grasping the content of the rules in question.

Rather, we are reminded that, "Following a rule is analogous to obeying an order. We are trained to do so; we react to an order in a particular way" (PI §206). As Wright (2007) expounds:

> To say that in basic cases, we follow rules without reason is to say that our moves are uninformed by – are not the rational output of – any appreciation of facts about what the rules require. This is, emphatically, not the claim that it is inappropriate ever to describe someone as, say, knowing the rule(s) for [say] the use of 'red', or as knowing what such a rule requires. Rather it is a caution about how to understand such descriptions – or better: how not to understand them ... In basic cases *there is no such underlying rationalizing knowledge enabling the competence.* (p. 140, emphasis added)

The moral Wright (2007) derives from this is that in basic cases of rule-following, "The knowledge *is* the competence" (p. 140). In this case, we are brought to see something that is already there before our eyes but which is blocked from sight by our attachment to misguided ways of framing the issues. This attachment is philosophical, not scientific in character, and it fuels misplaced explanatory urges of a "musty" variety that have no place in the sciences of the mind.

A similar analysis can be given to claims that we "must" learn and deploy models if we are to explain flexible behaviors on the grounds that only then will we be able to explain how it is the case that such behaviors can be intelligent and flexible. We can avoid this demand by speaking of an organism's or system's embodied know-how or competence, rather than assuming that it must be learning models or using bodies of knowledge. This would be to understand cognition as a kind of acting and interacting. That is what lies at the heart of a radical as opposed to a conservative enactivism (Hutto, 2005). In explaining flexible behavior, radical enactivism makes no appeals to the idea of stored, mediating knowledge.

Culture Permeates Cognition: A Radically Enactive Account

Because enactivists start with different assumptions than cognitivists about the nature of cognition and how to explain adaptive responsiveness, they propose quite a different way of thinking about how culture connects with and influences cognition. The human brain not only evolved along with the human body, and works the way it does because of that; it is also not isolated, but rather dynamically coupled to a body that is in turn dynamically coupled to an environment. The organism operates on the situation itself rather than on a model of the situation inferred by the brain. The complex interactions and transactions of brains, bodies, and environments are structured by the physical aspects of neuronal processes, bodily movements, affects, anatomy and function, and environmental regularities.

We can think of these interactions and transactions as forms of ongoing dynamical adjustments in which the brain, as part of and along with the larger organism, settles into various kinds of attunement with the environment – attuning to physical, social and cultural factors (Gallagher, 2017; Gallagher et al., 2013). Neural accommodation occurs in this larger system. Notions of adjustment and attunement can be cashed out in terms of physical states, or more precisely, physical dynamical processes that involve brain and body, autonomic and peripheral nervous systems, as well as affective and motoric changes.

Many accounts of perception restrict the analysis to questions of recognition. As we have seen, in modular theories the question is often about how the visual system recognizes what is out there in the world given that its access is limited to sensory input (Carruthers, 2006; Fodor, 1983). This leads to the idea that the function of perception is simply to solve a puzzle and what better way to solve a puzzle than to use inferential logic. But perception's function is never purely recognitional; seeing, for example, involves more than recognition and motor control. A full-bodied, richly affective response always involves more than that; there are always ulterior motives in the system. Because the organism desires food or rest or sex or aesthetic enjoyment or understanding, etc., the eye is never innocent.

We saw how enculturation made a difference to the way the brains of Greek and English speakers respond in early visual processing to different shades of blue, revealing that neuronal activity in the earliest of perceptual processing areas, such as the primary visual cortex (V1), is more than simple feature detection. V1 neurons anticipate reward if they have been attuned by prior experience (Shuler & Bear, 2006). This is not a matter of receiving sensory data first, followed by inferential processes that then calculate reward possibility. Rather, it is an intrinsically reward-oriented response or attunement to stimuli due to prior experiences and plastic changes. Indeed, there's no room for or need for inferences in this respect. In the same way that, already attuned by prior experience and enculturation, the visual cortexes of Greek and English speakers differ in how they respond to different shades of blue, V1 is already attuned to reward possibilities.

Furthermore, in synchrony with central perceptual processes, autonomic and peripheral nervous systems are activated generating dynamical patterns that make it unclear what is regulating what. Specifically, along with the earliest perceptual processing, the medial orbital frontal cortex is activated initiating a train of muscular and hormonal changes throughout the body, modulating processes in organs, muscles, and joints associated with prior experience (Barrett & Bar, 2009). Sensory responses are coordinated with, modulate and guide affective and action responses and vice versa. Perceptual stimulation generates not just brain activation, but also specific bodily affective changes that are already integrated with sensory-motor processes tied to the current situation.

Conclusion

There is a long tradition of trying to understand how culture influences cognition. Cognitivist accounts approach culture as something that creates internal representations that exert an effect on cognition and perception. We have argued instead that culture and context are woven into perception and action from their earliest inception.

In sum, rather than wondering if cultural factors might contentfully penetrate or adjust cognition, we defend the idea that cultural factors color or permeate cognition. We have sketched and motivated a radical enactivist way of understanding how this occurs. Going the radical way requires turning one's back on some familiar and deeply ingrained ways of thinking about how best to explain behavior. Thus, when Clark (2016) asks, "Why not simply ditch the talk of inner models and internal representations and stay on the true path of enactivist virtue?" (p. 291), we answer, "Why not, indeed!"

Like those who cannot see how to escape the rule-following paradox, cognitivists are hampered by the limits of their philosophical imaginations. Clark, for example, rhetorically asks: "Could we have told our story in entirely non-representationalist terms, without invoking the concept of a hierarchal probabilistic generative model at all?" (2016, p. 293). In reply, he confesses that "as things stand, *I simply do not see how* this is to be achieved" (p. 293, emphases added).[4] For those whose sight is attuned to a different set of framework commitments, a more rewarding vision of cognitive science – one that carries less unpaid-for metaphysical baggage and avoids intractable philosophical puzzles – is a live possibility.

Acknowledgments

The authors thank the Australian Research Council for funding the Discovery Project "Minds in Skilled Performance" (DP170102987) and for supporting this research.

---

[4] In this passage Clark (2016), like so many others, appears to be offering an inference from lack of imagination argument rather than an inference to the best explanation argument. For further details on the important but often overlooked difference between these two forms of the argument, see Hutto (2008, p. 94).

REFERENCES

Anderson, M. L. (2014). *After phrenology: Neural reuse and the interactive brain*. MIT Press.

Balázsi, G., van Oudenaarden, A., & Collins, J. J. (2011). Cellular decision making and biological noise: From microbes to mammals. *Cell, 144*(6), 910–25. https://doi.org/10.1016/j.cell.2011.01.030

Barrett, L. F., & Bar, M. (2009). See it with feeling: Affective predictions during object perception. *Philosophical Transactions of the Royal Society B: Biological Sciences, 364*(1521), 1325–34. https://doi.org/10.1098/rstb.2008.0312

Boroditsky, L. (2001). Does language shape thought? Mandarin and English speakers' conceptions of time. *Cognitive Psychology, 43*(1), 1–22. https://doi.org/10.1006/cogp.2001.0748

Branquinho, J. (Ed.). (2001). *The foundations of cognitive science*. Oxford University Press.

Brogaard, B., & Chomanski, B. (2015). Cognitive penetrability and high-level properties in perception: Unrelated phenomena? *Pacific Philosophical Quarterly, 96*(4), 469–86. https://doi.org/10.1111/papq.12111

Brooks, R. A. (1991). Intelligence without representation. *Artificial Intelligence, 47*(1–3), 139–59. https://doi.org/10.1016/0004-3702(91)90053-M

Carruthers, P. (2006). *The architecture of the mind: Massive modularity and the flexibility of thought*. Oxford University Press. https://doi.org/10.1093/acprof:oso/9780199207077.001.0001

Carruthers, P. (2015). Perceiving mental states. *Consciousness and Cognition, 36*, 498–507. https://doi.org/10.1016/j.concog.2015.04.009

Ceci, S. J., & Roazzi, A. (1994). The effects of context on cognition: Postcards from Brazil. In R. J. Sternberg & R. K. Wagner (Eds.), *Mind in context: Interactionist perspectives on human intelligence* (pp. 74–101). Cambridge University Press.

Cibelli, E., Xu, Y., Austerweil, J. L., Griffiths, T. L., & Regier, T. (2016). The Sapir-Whorf hypothesis and probabilistic inference: Evidence from the domain of color. *PLoS ONE, 11*(7), e0158725. https://doi.org/10.1371/journal.pone.0158725

Clark, A. (1997). *Being there: Putting brain, body, and the world together again*. MIT Press.

Clark, A. (2015). Embodied prediction. In T. Metzinger & J. M. Windt (Eds.), *Open mind: MIND group*. MIND Group. https://doi.org/10.15502/9783958570115

Clark, A. (2016). *Surfing uncertainty: Prediction, action and the embodied mind*. Oxford University Press. https://doi.org/10.1093/acprof:oso/9780190217013.001.0001

Costall, A. (1995). Socializing affordances. *Theory & Psychology, 5*(4), 467–81. https://doi.org/10.1177%2F0959354395054001

Dedrick, D. (2015). Colour language, thought, and culture. In F. Sharifian (Ed.), *The Routledge handbook of language and culture* (pp. 270–93). Routledge.

Delk, J. L., & Fillenbaum, S. (1965). Differences in perceived color as a function of characteristic color. *The American Journal of Psychology, 78*(2), 290–3. https://doi.org/10.2307/1420503

Firestone, C., & Scholl, B. J. (2016). Cognition does not affect perception: Evaluating the evidence for "top-down" effects. *Behavioral and Brain Sciences, 39*, e229. https://doi.org/10.1017/S0140525X15000965

Fodor, J. (2009). Where is my mind? *London Review of Books, 31*(3), 13–15.
Fodor, J. A. (1983). *The modularity of mind: An essay on faculty psychology*. MIT Press.
Friston, K. (2013). Active inference and free energy. *Behavioral and Brain Sciences, 36*(3), 212–13. https://doi.org/10.1017/S0140525X12002142
Friston, K. (2018). Does predictive coding have a future? *Nature Neuroscience, 21*(8), 1019–21. https://doi.org/10.1038/s41593-018-0200-7
Friston, K., Thornton, C., & Clark, A. (2012). Free-energy minimization and the dark-room problem. *Frontiers in Psychology, 3*(130), 1–7. https://doi.org/10.3389/fpsyg.2012.00130
Frith, C. D. (2017). *Discovering the social mind: Selected works of Christopher D. Frith*. Routledge.
Fuchs, T. (2017). *Ecology of the brain: The phenomenology and biology of the embodied mind*. Oxford University Press.
Fulda, F. C. (2017). Natural agency: The case of bacterial cognition. *Journal of the American Philosophical Association, 3*(1), 69–90. https://doi.org/10.1017/apa.2017.5
Gallagher, S. (2017). *Enactivist interventions: Rethinking the mind*. Oxford University Press. https://doi.org/10.1093/oso/9780198794325.001.0001
Gallagher, S., & Bower, M. (2014). Making enactivism even more embodied. *AVANT. Trends in Interdisciplinary Studies, 5*(2), 232–47. https://doi.org/10.26913/50202014.0109.0011
Gallagher, S., Hutto, D. D., Slaby, J., & Cole, J. (2013). The brain as part of an enactive system. *Behavioral and Brain Sciences, 36*(4), 421–2. https://doi.org/10.1017/S0140525X12002105
Gibson, J. J. (1977). The theory of affordances. In R. Shaw & J. Bransford (Eds.), *Perceiving, acting, and knowing: Toward an ecological psychology* (pp. 67–82). Lawrence Erlbaum.
Goldstone, R. L. (1994). Influences of categorization on perceptual discrimination. *Journal of Experimental Psychology: General, 123*(2), 178–200. https://doi.org/10.1037/0096-3445.123.2.178
Goldstone, R. L., Lippa, Y., & Shiffrin, R. M. (2001). Altering object representations through category learning. *Cognition, 78*(1), 27–43. https://doi.org/10.1016/S0010-0277(00)00099-8
Harnad, S. (Ed.). (1987). *Categorical perception: The groundwork of cognition*. Cambridge University Press.
Heyes, C. (2012). New thinking: The evolution of human cognition. *Philosophical Transactions of the Royal Society B: Biological Sciences, 367*(1599), 2091–6. https://doi.org/10.1098/rstb.2012.0111
Hohwy, J. (2013). *The predictive mind*. Oxford University Press. https://doi.org/10.1093/acprof:oso/9780199682737.001.0001
Hutto, D. D. (2005). Knowing **what**? Radical versus conservative enactivism. *Phenomenology and the Cognitive Sciences, 4*(4), 389–405. https://doi.org/10.1007/s11097-005-9001-z
Hutto, D. D. (2008). *Folk psychological narratives: The sociocultural basis of understanding reasons*. MIT Press.
Hutto, D. D., & Kirchhoff, M. D. (2015). Looking beyond the brain: Social neuroscience meets narrative practice. *Cognitive Systems Research, 34–35*, 5–17. https://doi.org/10.1016/j.cogsys.2015.07.001

Hutto, D. D., & Myin, E. (2013). *Radicalizing enactivism. Basic minds without content*, MIT Press. https://doi.org/10.7551/mitpress/9780262018548.001.0001

Hutto, D. D., & Myin, E. (2017). *Evolving enactivism: Basic minds meet content*. MIT Press.

Hutto, D. D., & Satne, G. (2015). The natural origins of content. *Philosophia*, *43*(3), 521–36. https://doi.org/10.1007/s11406-015-9644-0

Kay, P. (1999). Color. *Journal of Linguistic Anthropology*, *9*(1–2), 32–5. https://doi.org/10.1525/jlin.1999.9.1-2.32

Kay, P., & Kempton, W. (1984). What is the Sapir-Whorf hypothesis? *American Anthropologist*, *86*(1), 65–79. https://doi.org/10.1525/aa.1984.86.1.02a00050

Locke, J. C. W. (2013). Systems biology: How bacteria choose a lifestyle. *Nature*, *503*, 476–7. https://doi.org/10.1038/nature12837

Losick, R., & Desplan, C. (2008). Stochasticity and cell fate. *Science*, *320*(5872), 65–8. https://doi.org/10.1126/science.1147888

Macpherson, F. (2012). Cognitive penetration of colour experience: Rethinking the issue in light of an indirect mechanism. *Philosophy and Phenomenological Research*, *84*(1), 24–62. https://doi.org/10.1111/j.1933-1592.2010.00481.x

Malafouris, L. (2013). *How things shape the mind: A theory of material engagement*. MIT Press.

Marchi, F., & Newen, A. (2015). Cognitive penetrability and emotion recognition in human facial expressions. *Frontiers in Psychology*, *6*, 828. https://doi.org/10.3389/fpsyg.2015.00828

Marr, D. (1982). *Vision: A computational approach*. Freeman. https://doi.org/10.7551/mitpress/9780262514620.001.0001

Newen, A., & Vetter, P. (2017). Why cognitive penetration of our perceptual experience is still the most plausible account. *Consciousness and Cognition*, *47*, 26–37. https://doi.org/10.1016/j.concog.2016.09.005

Newen, A., Marchi, F., & Brössel, P. (2017). Introduction – Cognitive penetration and predictive coding: Pushing the debate forward with the recent achievements of cognitive science. *Consciousness and Cognition*, *47*, 1–5. https://doi.org/10.1016/j.concog.2016.12.001

Noë, A. (2004). *Action in perception*. MIT press.

O'Callaghan, C., Kveraga, K., Shine, J. M., Adams, R. B., Jr., & Bar, M. (2017). Predictions penetrate perception: Converging insights from brain, behaviour and disorder. *Consciousness and Cognition*, *47*, 63–74. https://doi.org/10.1016/j.concog.2016.05.003

O'Regan, J. K., & Noë, A. (2001). A sensorimotor account of vision and visual consciousness. *Behavioral and Brain Sciences*, *24*(5), 939–73. https://doi.org/10.1017/S0140525X01000115

Overmann, K. A. (2016). Beyond writing: The development of literacy in the ancient Near East. *Cambridge Archaeological Journal*, *26*(2), 285–303. https://doi.org/10.1017/S0959774316000019

Perkins, T. J., & Swain, P. S. (2009). Strategies for cellular decision-making. *Molecular Systems Biology*, *5*(1), 326. https://doi.org/10.1038/msb.2009.83

Pylyshyn, Z. (1999). Is vision continuous with cognition?: The case for cognitive impenetrability of visual perception. *Behavioral and Brain Sciences*, *22*(3), 341–65. https://doi.org/10.1017/S0140525X99002022

Raftopoulos, A. (2001). Is perception informationally encapsulated?: The issue of the theory-ladenness of perception. *Cognitive Science, 25*(3), 423–51. https://doi.org/10.1207/s15516709cog2503_4

Raftopoulos, A. (2015). The cognitive impenetrability of perception and theory-ladenness. *Journal for General Philosophy of Science, 46*(1), 87–103. https://doi.org/10.1007/s10838-015-9288-6

Raftopoulos, A. (2017). Pre-cueing, the epistemic role of early vision, and the cognitive impenetrability of early vision. *Frontiers in Psychology, 8*, 1156. https://doi.org/10.3389%2Ffpsyg.2017.01156

Raftopoulos, A., & Lupyan, G. (2018). Pre-cueing effects on perception and cognitive penetrability. *Frontiers in Psychology, 9*, 230. https://doi.org/10.3389%2Ffpsyg.2018.00230

Ramstead, M. J. D., Veissière, S. P. L., & Kirmayer, L. J. (2016). Cultural affordances: Scaffolding local worlds through shared intentionality and regimes of attention. *Frontiers in Psychology, 7*, 1090. https://doi.org/10.3389/fpsyg.2016.01090

Rauss, K., Schwartz, S., & Pourtois, G. (2011). Top-down effects on early visual processing in humans: A predictive coding framework. *Neuroscience & Biobehavioral Reviews, 35*(5), 1237–53. https://doi.org/10.1016/j.neubiorev.2010.12.011

Rizzolatti, G., & Sinigaglia, C. (2008). *Mirrors in the brain: How our minds share actions and emotions* (F. Anderson, Trans.). Oxford University Press. (Original work published in 2006)

Roepstorff, A., Niewöhner, J., & Beck, S. (2010). Enculturing brains through patterned practices. *Neural Networks, 23*(8–9), 1051–9. https://doi.org/10.1016/j.neunet.2010.08.002

Shuler, M. G., & Bear, M. F. (2006). Reward timing in the primary visual cortex. *Science, 311*(5767), 1606–9. https://doi.org/10.1126/science.1123513

Siegel, S. (2012). Cognitive penetrability and perceptual justification. *Noûs, 46*(2), 201–22. https://doi.org/10.1111/j.1468-0068.2010.00786.x

Sohoglu, E., Peelle, J. E., Carlyon, R. P., & Davis, M. H. (2012). Predictive top-down integration of prior knowledge during speech perception. *Journal of Neuroscience, 32*(25), 8443–53. https://doi.org/10.1523/JNEUROSCI.5069-11.2012

Tagkopoulos, I., Liu, Y.-C., & Tavazoie, S. (2008). Predictive behavior within microbial genetic networks. *Science, 320*(5881), 1313–17. https://doi.org/10.1126/science.1154456

Thierry, G., Athanasopoulos, P., Wiggett, A., Dering, B., & Kuipers, J.-R. (2009). Unconscious effects of language-specific terminology on preattentive color perception. *Proceedings of the National Academy of Sciences of the United States of America, 106*(11), 4567–70. https://doi.org/10.1073/pnas.0811155106

Thompson, E., Lutz, A., & Cosmelli, D. (2005). Neurophenomenology: An introduction for neurophilosophers. In A. Brook & K. Atkins (Eds.), *Cognition and the brain: The philosophy and neuroscience movement* (pp. 40–97). Cambridge University Press. https://doi.org/10.1017/CBO9780511610608.003

Toribio, J. (2018). Visual experience: Rich but impenetrable. *Synthese, 195*(8), 3389–406. https://doi.org/10.1007/s11229-015-0889-8

Vetter, P., & Newen, A. (2014). Varieties of cognitive penetration in visual perception. *Consciousness and Cognition*, *27*, 62–75. https://doi.org/10.1016/j.concog.2014.04.007

Wittgenstein, L. (1983). *Remarks on the foundations of mathematics* (G. E. M. Anscombe, Trans.; G. H. von Wright & R. Rhees, Eds.). Blackwell. (Original work published 1956)

Wittgenstein, L. (2009). *Philosophical investigations* (4th ed., G.E.M. Anscombe, P. M. S. Hacker, & J. Schulte, Trans., P. M. S. Hacker, & J. Schulte, Eds.). Blackwell Publishing. (Original work published 1953)

Wright, C. (2007). Rule-following without reasons: Wittgenstein's quietism and the constitutive question. *Ratio*, *20*(4), 481–502. https://doi.org/10.1111/j.1467-9329.2007.00379.x

Zeimbekis, J., & Raftopoulos, A. (Eds.). (2015). *The cognitive penetrability of perception: New philosophical perspectives*. Oxford University Press.

6 The Brain as a Cultural Artifact
Concepts, Actions, and Experiences within the Human Affective Niche

Maria Gendron, Batja Mesquita, and Lisa Feldman Barrett

"Culture" can be defined as a cohesive set of mental representations (ideas, beliefs, and values) and their manifestations (behavioral practices, artifacts, and institutions) shared by a group and acquired by new generations through social learning. This far-reaching definition implies that the worlds that people navigate, and their experiences in those worlds, are *inherently* cultural. Efforts to understand the implementation and generational transmission of human culture can be improved by considering the development, architecture, and dynamics of the human brain: How does the brain wire itself to model and engage with the physical and social surroundings that matter to survival? How does one brain interface with another (each of which is situated within a body)? And how does the brain guide action and create experience in a situated fashion? Attempts to answer these questions lead to the striking insight that human brains are cultural artifacts (e.g., Mithen & Parsons, 2008; Taylor, 2006). Brains implement culture, transmit culture, and are wired by culture.

In this chapter, we discuss the hypothesis that people help to regulate each other's bodies (for better or for worse), and this is a main mechanism through which culture wires a human brain. Specifically, we suggest that the process of regulating a body's internal systems, called *allostasis* (Sterling, 2012; Sterling & Eyer, 1988), drives the bidirectional relationship between the brain as a generator of culture (in concert with other brains) and a product of culture (Barrett, 2017a). This perspective is consistent with the view that culture becomes "embrained" (Kitayama & Salvador, 2017) and considers physiological regulation as a primary driver. That is, throughout a person's life, the brain becomes wired to run a model of the world that will control the body in an efficient manner through *predictive* processes. There is an emerging research consensus that actions, and their accompanying mental events, begin as top-down representations in the brain, fashioned from prior experiences (i.e., priors) that are then tested against the state of the world for correctness (Hutchinson & Barrett, 2019). This emerging internal model will be tuned to the physical and sociocultural features of recurrent situations (and stressors) that an individual encounters. Cultural transmission (in the form of past experiences captured and reimplemented within the brain's wiring) prepares the individual for meeting these recurrent demands, thereby supporting the development of an internal model that is sufficiently tuned to the environment. In a typically developing brain, the result is an internal model that optimizes the balance between cost-effective predictions and more costly learning (i.e., modifying the internal model; Theriault et al., 2019). This hypothesis is informed by a multilevel framework for understanding culture that integrates research and theorizing on predictive physiological regulation (Sterling, 2012; Sterling & Eyer, 1988), predictive processing (Adams et al., 2013; Barrett, 2017b; Barrett & Simmons, 2015; Chanes & Barrett, 2016; Clark, 2013; Friston, 2010), cultural evolution (e.g., Boyd et al., 2011; Henrich et al., 2010; Heyes, 2018), cultural niche construction (Laland et al., 2003), and cultural affordances (Kitayama et al., 2006; Markus & Kitayama, 1991; Ramstead et al., 2016; for a broader discussion, see Barrett, 2017a).

We begin with the insight that humans are social animals because we assist one another with the necessary physiological regulation to meet the changing demands of the physical and social environment – that is, humans help one another to establish and maintain *allostasis*. For humans, allostasis is supported by the physiological dependencies that arise during early social contact. (Of course, humans can also make it harder to maintain allostasis, increasing one another's allostatic burden in various ways related to neglect, adversity, cruelty, power, hierarchy, and marginalization, but these are issues for another chapter). In this chapter, we focus on how humans' extended period of physiological dependency on caregivers provides the necessary conditions for infant brains to wire themselves to their physical and social surroundings. As the infant brain bootstraps a set of experiences into its wiring, it develops a model for how to best regulate its body in a given set of contexts (i.e., within the constraints of their culturally shaped world). The "outside" conditions of this world offer affordances or "possibilities for action" that establish and maintain the brain's internal model, which is inherently culture-dependent.

We then discuss a hypothesis for the workings of a brain's internal model. Specifically, we propose that the brain maintains allostasis by continually engaging in on-the-fly, dynamic concept construction. The brain functions by continually constructing culturally shaped embodied concepts that predictively categorize sensory inputs in a given context, guiding action and creating experience in a highly situated manner. In this view, an internal model is not exclusively "inside" the head of the individual.

Furthermore, we suggest that one brain's internal model guides behavior, which creates a set of affordances that impact others' allostasis, shaping their behavior and experiences in turn. Eventually, allostatic regulation shifts away from primary caregiving relationships, which are supplanted by self-regulation based on a set of learned concepts that are continually reinforced by the social structuring of the environment. This social dependency across the lifespan further ensures the transmission of culture across generations. The particulars of what internal models are generated, and how they are realized in action, language, artifacts, institutions, and so on, are as varied as the ecological and historical contexts that characterize human existence.

We then discuss diversity of conceptual systems for emotion, that is, the psychological representations that are most intimately tied to allostasis, as an example of how profoundly culture tunes internal models to the context. We propose that emotional events, as cultural artifacts, may be learned and transmitted without the need for inherited biological causes such as dedicated emotion circuits. Finally, we consider the profound implications of our framework for the processes that support acculturation, when individuals move from one cultural context to another (including traversing social contexts in the course of a single day).

Social Regulation of the Body

Humans are a social species in many ways – even ultrasocial by some accounts (Tomasello, 2014). We form long-term pair bonds. We live in groups. We care for offspring over an extended period of time. We cooperate with each other and we reciprocate. In this chapter, we integrate the additional hypothesis that members of a social species regulate one another's physiological states in an anticipatory manner (Atzil et al., 2018; Atzil & Gendron, 2017; Barrett, 2017a; Schulkin, 2010), that is, they contribute to one another's *allostasis* (Sterling, 2012).

Allostasis

Allostasis involves continually anticipating the needs of the autonomic nervous system, the immune system, the endocrine system (i.e., the internal milieu), and the motor system – all within a dynamically changing environment (Sterling, 2012; Sterling & Laughlin, 2015). Allostasis meets the body's needs before they arise: It is not a condition of the body, but a set of processes employed by the brain to keep the body's systems in balance, regulating the various systems according to costs and benefits. These continual adjustments promote survival, growth, learning, and reproduction (transferring genes to the next generation). A brain must keep its body in balance in two senses. First, the energy expenditures of all bodily systems must be balanced at any given moment.[1] These expenditures are required to learn, plan, and execute the physical movements necessary to acquire those resources in the first place (and to protect against threats and dangers). Second, resource intake and expenditures must be balanced over the longer term to avoid running a deficit. The latter means that depletion of immediate resources in the short term must be balanced with a long-term return on energy allocation. Animals thrive when they realize a return on their energy allocation, yielding sufficient resources to explore the world. They consolidate the details of experience within the brain's synaptic connections, making those experiences available to guide later decisions about future expenditures and deposits.

The Brain System Implementing Allostasis

It is useful to think of a human brain as a single structure composed of billions of neurons. From a graph-theoretical perspective, neurons cluster into groups (or "nodes") that are strongly interconnected (via "edges") and that themselves interconnect in various arrangements to create broadly distributed sets of nodes or subnetworks (Sporns, 2011; Yeo et al., 2015). Within this structural arrangement, and with the help of other biological agents (such as glial cells, neurotransmitters, neuromodulators, and so on), neurons pass information back and forth to one another with varying degrees of ease, continually shifting from one pattern of information flow to others. Much of this activity occurs in the absence of any inputs from the surrounding world, referred to as "intrinsic activity" (intrinsic activity is very likely related to brain's control of the body, as it is always receiving sensory inputs from the body; e.g., Rebollo et al., 2018). The brain, as a single structure, can take on trillions of different patterns as sensory information from the body and the world modulate its intrinsic activity (Mitra & Raichle, 2016). Intrinsic activity is best described as *an internal model* of a person's body in the world (Barrett, 2017b; Barrett & Simmons, 2015). Modification of intrinsic activity patterns by sensory inputs is best described as *learning* (Hutchinson & Barrett, 2019).

The brain, as a network of neurons, is traditionally parsed into subnetworks of regions that are widely distributed across the brain, two of which are

---

[1] Sometimes allostasis involves dynamically regulating resource allocation (i.e., diverting glucose, electrolytes, water, etc., from one system to another) to meet the body's spending needs. For example, in advance of standing up, the heart beats stronger and faster, blood vessels constrict, and blood pressure raises to ensure that the brain continues to receive the blood (and oxygen). Sometimes allostasis involves signaling the need for resources before the body runs out (e.g., drinking before dehydration occurs) or preparing for the intake of resources in advance of their ingestion. For another example, saliva in humans and some other mammals is made of alpha-amylase, an enzyme that breaks down glucose. When the body needs glucose, saliva is preemptively secreted (even before anything is ingested). Even just imaging food causes glucose secretion.

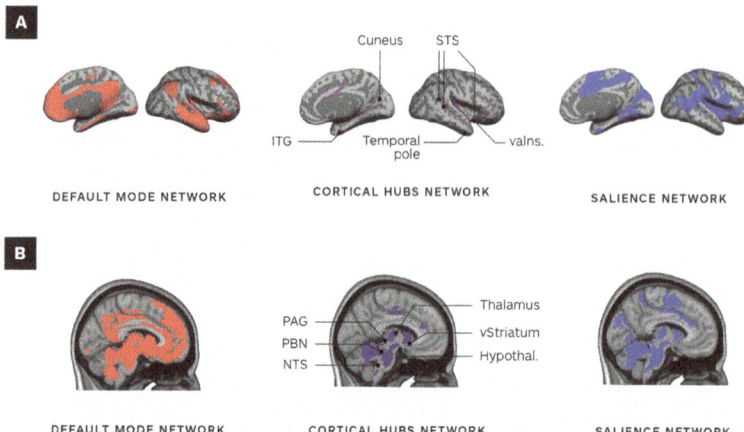

Figure 6.1 Default mode and salience subnetworks. The default mode subnetwork (shown in red) and the salience subnetwork (shown in blue) are interconnected by several "rich club" hubs (i.e., densely connected nodes shown in purple). Hubs belonging to the "rich club" are labeled. vaIns, = ventral anterior insula; MCC = midcingulate cortex; PHG = parahippocampal gyrus; PostCG = postcentral gyrus; PAG = periaqueductal gray; PBN = parabrachial nucleus; NTS = the nucleus of the solitary tract; vStriatum = ventral striatum; Hypothal = hypothalamus.
From L. F. Barrett, "The Theory of Constructed Emotion: An Active Inference Account of Interoception and Categorization," *Social Cognitive and Affective Neuroscience*, 2017, *12*(1), p. 13 (https://doi.org/10.1093%2Fscan%2Fnsw154), by permission of Oxford University Press

important for maintaining allostasis: the "default mode" and "salience" subnetworks (e.g., Buckner, 2012; Seeley et al., 2007; see Figure 6.1). The default mode subnetwork is routinely involved in a variety of psychological tasks such as processing information about the self or any other concept, when mind-wandering, when remembering autobiographical details, during emotion, and during context effects in perception. It has also been implicated in regulating cardiovascular function and other autonomic activity. The default mode subnetwork is thought to be important to the brain's ability to construct an internal model of the world. The salience subnetwork is also routinely involved in a similar range of psychological tasks, including regulating attention, remembering, emoting, integrating multimodal information, and regulating autonomic nervous system activity (for discussions, see Barrett & Satpute, 2013, 2017; Kleckner et al., 2017). Together, these two subnetworks make up an integrated system that implements allostasis, meaning they control the internal organs of the body, called viscera, associated with autonomic, metabolic, and immunological functions. They anticipate the needs of the body and adjust how the internal systems of the body deploy resources to deal with the anticipated sensory world.

Allostatic changes in heart rate, blood pressure, respiration, temperature, and so on cause sensory changes, which are referred to as interoception (Craig, 2014). Several recent papers have suggested that the brain regions concerned with visceromotor regulation of the body within the salience and default mode subnetworks not only maintain and adjust allostasis, but also predict the anticipated interoceptive consequences of the allostatic changes (Barrett & Simmons, 2015; Kleckner et al., 2017; for related discussions, see Pezzulo et al., 2015; Seth, 2013; Seth et al., 2012). These interoceptive predictions are part of the brain's internal model of the world (as we discuss more in the section "Prediction, Concepts, and Categorization"). Regions implementing interoception, in contrast, such as the mid and posterior sections of the insular cortex, ultimately receive interoceptive prediction signals (i.e., the expected sensory consequences of visceromotor commands) and compare them to the actual ascending sensory inputs from the organs and systems within the body's internal milieu, correcting predictions when necessary (Kleckner et al., 2017; discussed in more detail in Figure 6.2). This suggests that the default mode and salience subnetworks are also important for establishing and maintaining the brain's interoceptive representations of the state of the body.

Together, the default mode and salience subnetworks are also important for establishing affective *feelings* (Lindquist et al., 2016). Interoceptive sensations are made available to consciousness as lower dimensional feelings of affect, that is, as feelings of relative activation or deactivation (arousal) and pleasant or unpleasant (valenced) feelings (Barrett & Bliss-Moreau, 2009). The brain is always maintaining (or attempting to maintain) allostasis, and as a consequence interoceptive signals are always being represented, suggesting that affective feelings can be thought of as a general barometer of allostasis. This hypothesis further suggests that affective feelings are not specific to episodes of emotion, but are properties of consciousness. It further suggests that psychological concepts like "stress," "reward," and "motivation" can be understood in terms of allostasis and its temporal dynamics.

As already noted, the default mode/salience system is also at the core of many other psychological phenomena, including memory, decision-making, theory of mind, attention, and a host of others (for discussion, see Kleckner et al., 2017). In fact, the regions that maintain allostasis not only send interoceptive prediction signals, but they also send sensory prediction signals to all sensory systems, in effect helping to establish the brain's internal model (as discussed further, below; see Figure 6.2; see also Chanes & Barrett, 2016; Hutchinson & Barrett, 2019; e.g., Keck et al., 2013). In addition, the network for maintaining allostasis contains more than 50 percent of the most connected

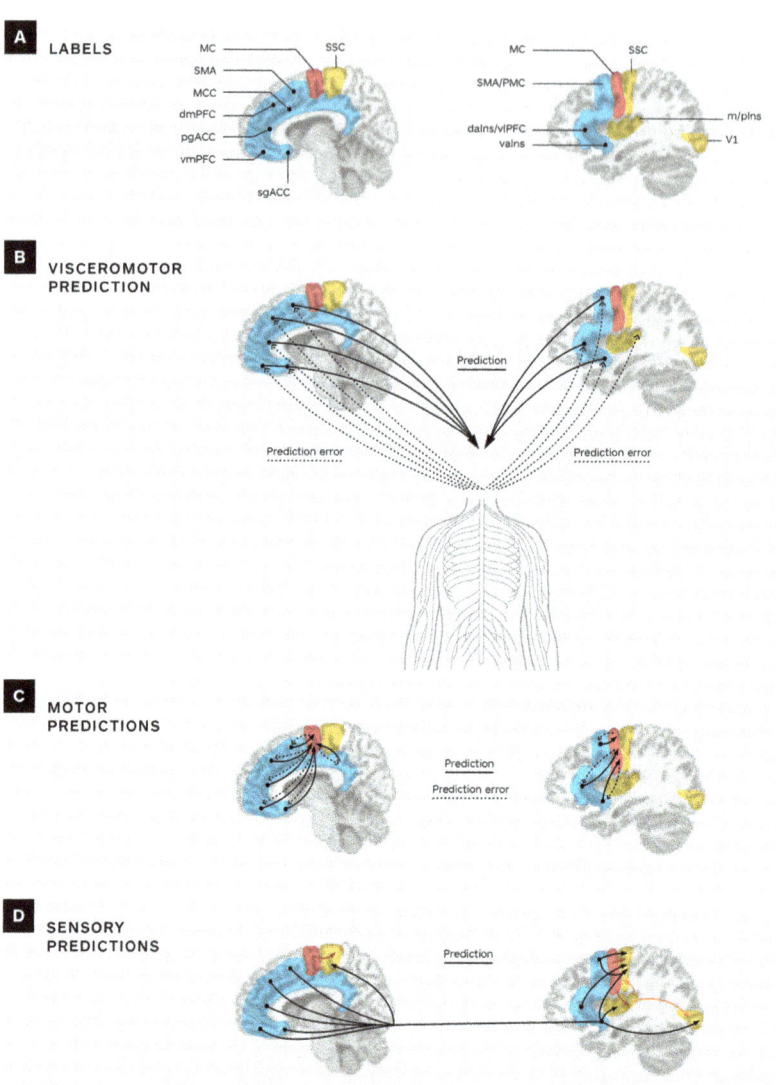

Figure 6.2 A depiction of predictive coding in the human brain. (A) Key limbic and paralimbic cortices (in blue) provide cortical control the body's internal milieu. Primary motor cortex (MC) is depicted in red, and primary sensory regions are in yellow. For simplicity, only primary visual, interoceptive and somatosensory cortices are shown; subcortical regions are not shown. (B) Limbic cortices initiate visceromotor predictions to the hypothalamus and brainstem nuclei (e.g., periacquiductal gray, parabrachial nucleus, nucleus of the solitary tract, etc.) to regulate the autonomic,

cortical regions, called rich-club hubs, that together form a high-capacity backbone for synchronizing neural activity to integrate information across the entire brain (van den Heuvel & Sporns, 2013). This backbone may also be important for establishing and maintaining consciousness (Chanes & Barrett, 2016). These observations prompt the intriguing hypothesis that, whatever else a brain is doing – thinking, feeling, perceiving, preparing for action – it is doing so in the context of regulating the systems of your body (your internal milieu) as energy resources are spent during learning, play, self-protection, reproduction, and when searching for more resources. This balancing act – allostasis – is a fundamental feature of the nervous system (Barrett & Finlay, 2018).

For the purpose of understanding how culture becomes embrained, these insights offer some important hypotheses: the default mode and salience subnetworks, working together as a system for maintaining energy balance, continually anticipate the needs of the body and attempt to meet those needs

---

Figure 6.2 (*cont.*)
neuroendocrine, and immune systems (solid lines). The incoming sensory inputs from the internal milieu of the body are carried along the vagus nerve and small diameter C and Ad fibers to limbic regions (dotted lines). Comparisons between prediction signals and ascending sensory input result in prediction error that is available to update the brain's internal model. In this way, prediction errors are learning signals and therefore adjust subsequent predictions. (C) Efferent copies of visceromotor predictions are sent to MC as motor predictions (solid lines) and prediction errors are sent from MC to limbic cortices (dotted lines). (D) Sensory cortices receive sensory predictions from several sources. They receive efferent copies of visceromotor predictions (black lines) and efferent copies of motor predictions (red lines). Sensory cortices with less well-developed lamination (e.g. primary interoceptive cortex) also send sensory predictions to cortices with more well-developed granular architecture (e.g. in this figure, somatosensory and primary visual cortices, gold lines). For simplicity's sake, prediction errors are not depicted in panel D. sgACC = subgenual anterior cingulate cortex; vmPFC = ventromedial prefrontal cortex; pgACC = pregenual anterior cingulate cortex; dmPFC = dorsomedial prefrontal cortex; vlPFC = ventrolateral prefrontal cortex; MCC = midcingulate cortex; vaIns = ventral anterior insula; daIns = dorsal anterior insula and includes ventrolateral prefrontal cortex; SMA = supplementary motor area; PMC = premotor cortex; m/pIns = mid/posterior insula (primary interoceptive cortex); SSC = somatosensory cortex; V1 = primary visual cortex; and MC = motor cortex.

Figure and caption reprinted from L. F. Barrett, "The Theory of Constructed Emotion: An Active Inference Account of Interoception and Categorization," *Social Cognitive and Affective Neuroscience*, 2017, *12*(1), p. 10 (https://doi.org/10.1093%2Fscan%2Fnsw154), by permission of Oxford University Press

before they arise (i.e., they contribute to allostasis). In so doing, they play a role in predictively regulating action and in constructing the brain's representation of the body's state (as discussed in Barrett, 2017b; Hutchinson & Barrett, 2019). Simultaneously, these subnetworks send signals to other systems in the brain that anticipate the sensory changes consequent to visceromotor and skeletomotor control. These prediction signals constitute the brain's internal model of its body in the world. In this view, a brain does not perceive the world and then act. Instead, seeing, hearing, feeling, and perception as a whole are a consequence of anticipating the needs of the body when preparing to act or learn.

The Infant Brain

To run an internal model of the body in the world that guides efficient allostasis, a brain must contain certain structural connections. But an infant brain is not a miniature adult brain and is not up to the task of allostatically regulating its own body. At birth, most of the long, thick (and metabolically expensive) axon pathways that create the brain's subnetworks are incomplete, such that the connectivity most responsible for allostasis is not yet fully developed (Dubois et al., 2014; Fransson et al., 2007, 2011; Gao, Lin, et al., 2009; Gao et al., 2011, 2017; Gao, Zhu, et al., 2009; Geng et al., 2017; Smyser et al., 2011). As a consequence, a human infant is almost totally dependent on her caregivers to regulate her body, teaching her how to nurse and eventually eat solid food, how and when to put herself to sleep, how to regulate her temperature and so on. As we discuss below, these allostatic activities, along with attention regulation and other social activities, provide opportunities for learning that drive brain development and allow her brain to wire itself to the physical and social realities of her surroundings (see also Atzil et al., 2018; Barrett, 2017a).

This early brain development can be described as growing a contextually relevant model of one's body in the world. Caregivers engage their infants in very different activities across cultures, creating culture-specific opportunities to learn (Greenfield et al., 2003; Shweder et al., 1998). In this way, a human brain, built from one general genetic plan, can become wired to create more than one internal model, depending on the physical and cultural context in which it develops. For example, cultures are highly divergent in the degree to which experiences involving close bodily contact (co-sleeping, continual wearing of infants) are expected. These divergent activities function to shape brain wiring, providing the experiences that eventually equip a person with a culturally tuned, embodied conceptual system within the first years of life. This system, eventually, constitutes the brain's internal model that maintains allostasis, constructs experience, and guides action.

As a consequence of experience, axons grow, myelinate, and organize into fiber tracts, producing a considerable increase in neural connectivity during infancy and childhood (Cao et al., 2017). Neural connections are also pruned, producing substantial changes in neural connectivity (Low & Cheng, 2006), meaning that brain networks develop slowly. The integrated allostatic/interoceptive system (consisting of the default mode and salience subnetworks) remains immature even at two years of age and becomes more developed later in childhood. The human brain does not reach an adult-like structural organization until a person is in their early to mid-20s (Cao et al., 2017; Dosenbach et al., 2010). Correspondingly, from infancy through to adulthood, the brain is able to bear more of its own allostatic burden.

The highly plastic infant brain grows within an extended, dynamic period of allostatic support (Finlay & Uchiyama, 2017) that is culturally prescribed and socially delivered. The long window for brain development in humans allows cultural influences to sculpt brain architecture via the interaction with caregivers and environment. It is now well established that there is tremendous individual variation in the structural aspects of brain development during infancy and childhood, particularly at the front of the brain where circuitry important for allostasis, motor function, and various social functions resides. This anatomical variation is influenced by the epigenetic context (for discussion, see Cao et al., 2017; Gao et al., 2017), including, we hypothesize, social and cultural input. The considerable individual differences and plasticity in brain development in response to environmental factors (including broadly cultural factors like socioeconomic status, SES), coupled with evidence of cultural influences on psychological development, together suggest that cultural practices and structure encourage the infant brain along particular developmental trajectories.

The human brain's structural architecture is the foundation for its complexity, that is, the patterns of information flow within the brain (Deco et al., 2011; Hermundstad et al., 2013; Honey et al., 2009; van den Heuvel & Sporns, 2013). Throughout each day, the human brain rapidly and efficiently shifts its pattern of information flow – that is, its spatiotemporal patterns of neural activity – within this fixed structural architecture. In its adult form, the brain functions as a complex system, able to implement trillions of patterns of information processing; it is also an information-gaining system because it learns from its environment and is able to combine past experiences in novel, generative ways.

The Affective Niche

Early interactions with caregivers and other members of a cultural group, and the way the life of a group is organized, form the basis for learning what aspects of the immediate environment are important to allostasis (the signal) vs. those that are irrelevant to allostasis (the noise). That is, these interactions shape the development of the individual's *affective niche*.

The idea of an affective niche derives from an embodied understanding of how a brain works. A body must be watered, fed, and cared for, so that it can grow, thrive, and ultimately, reproduce and care for its young. Growth, survival, and reproduction (and therefore gene transmission) depend on the near continual intake of energy resources (metabolic and otherwise). Further, the physical movements necessary to move around in the world and acquire those resources in the first place (and protect against threats and dangers) require upfront energy expenditures which in mammals include spending resources such as glucose, water, oxygen, electrolytes, and so on. To flourish, an animal must balance energy expenditures with deposits and see a return on its resource investments, not just in the quality and quantity of resources acquired, but also in having enough surplus energy to encode and consolidate the details of experience, making those experiences available within the brain's synaptic connections to guide future decisions about expenditures and deposits. From the brain's perspective, then, its body and the world beyond are a system within which the body's overall metabolism and energy regulation must be managed. Choices about when and how to move, as well as when and how to encode (learn) new information, are *economic choices* about energetics and other biological resources. All potential actions and learning have an energy cost, and a human's brain (like all animal brains) weighs costs against potential rewards and revenues in the service of balancing its global energy budget via allostasis. Information and the objects/experiences that are obtained with energetic investments (such as movements or learning) are said to have value – they are signal (rather than noise) in the person's niche (i.e., they are parts of the physical environment that are meaningful and relevant to a person's well-being; Barrett, 2017a; Barrett et al., 2016).

An affective niche, therefore, can be said to include everything in the physical (including other social agents and their affective/behavioral repertoire) and psychological environment (including simulations of future, past or imagined events) that is relevant to an individual's allostasis. An affective niche should be considered on a momentary scale, such that anything included has the capacity to have an immediate impact on allostasis. (Note this is distinct from affective niche as defined elsewhere; Colombetti & Krueger, 2015; we conceptualize of an affective niche as anything having the potential to promote *or* disrupt allostasis.) As a result, what is within an organism's affective niche often, but not always, has ramifications for the long-term survival of an organism (individual fitness) or whether their genetic material will be passed on to another generation (inclusive fitness). The implication is that the affective niche of an organism is considerably broader than an organism's ecological niche,[2] which is traditionally defined based on consequences for fitness.

An affective niche is dynamic and constructed. Humans, like all animals, do not merely adapt to or die in a physical environment that they find themselves in. They *create* their environments by selecting and modifying what is inside their affective niche (and what can be safely ignored). Consider this example of niche construction from evolutionary biologist Richard Lewontin's *The Triple Helix* using two songbirds, the phoebe and the thrush (Lewontin, 2000). The phoebe, but not a thrush, builds a grass nest, so grass is part of a phoebe's ecological niche. A thrush uses rocks to crack open seeds, whereas a phoebe does not, so rocks are part of a thrush's ecological niche. Both phoebes and thrushes live in the same physical surroundings filled with grass and rocks within the northeastern United States, but their ecological niches, which are determined by their activities, are different. We would say that grass is important to allostasis in a phoebe and so is part of its affective niche; rocks are important to allostasis in a thrush and so are part of its affective niche.

But the affective niche expands beyond the ecological niche, to include aspects of the environment that may not be relevant to fitness but are relevant to allostasis in the immediate sense.[3] Importantly, affective niche construction is not always beneficial. Just as modifications to the environment can be disruptive and impose new selection pressures on an organism (i.e., negative niche construction; Laland et al., 2000), so, too, affective niche construction can produce novel disruptions to allostasis. All classical conditioning experiments, which pair a neutral object with an object or event of value, so that the originally neutral object takes on value, are examples of niche construction, effectively expanding the affective niche of an animal well beyond what could be considered part of its ecological niche (for discussion, see Barrett, 2017a). For example, Rhesus macaques can learn to distinguish painting styles by Monet, van Gogh, and Dali when they are rewarded with juice or other food, bringing the paintings into their affective niche when otherwise the canvases

---

[2] Similarly, definitions of social and cultural niches also typically emphasize relevance for fitness, typically emphasizing inclusive fitness.

[3] While we can understand the evolution of allostatic mechanisms in terms of their fitness-promoting qualities (i.e., lending necessary flexibility to cope with novel stressors), learning expands the scope of allostatically relevant events well beyond the original conditions under which these mechanisms were originally invoked. For example, it is possible to extend grass to a thrush's affective niche by rewarding the bird with food whenever it, say, picks up a piece of grass in its beak. Various forms of conditioning are, in essence, expanding an animal's affective niche. The consequence is that allostatic mechanisms (the HPA axis, catecholamines, and cytokines) can also lead to "allostatic load" reducing the fitness of an organism, such as when stressors become chronic (McEwen, 2005). That is, the functioning of these same systems that can achieve allostasis can also result in "allostatic overload," the experience of being "stressed out," and, in the long term, to disease and mortality.

would be noise (e.g., Altschul et al., 2017). In humans, this expansion is vast, and largely driven by experiences of social regulation of allostasis and the affordances of the environments that humans construct. We hypothesize that early caregiving experiences help to shape the affective niche of the developing infant, and in so doing create the conditions for a brain to develop a culturally shaped internal model of its body in the world (Atzil et al., 2018).

Caregiving Supports Affective Learning

We hypothesize that early caregiving experiences set the stage for representations of certain "outside" conditions of the physical and social worlds to be wired into the brain as an internal model of that world which, among other things, accomplishes allostasis for the particular body that it regulates. A caregiver's allostatic support is rewarding for an infant (and often the caregiver; Atzil et al., 2018; Barrett, 2017a; Feldman, 2017). While a caregiver is providing nutrition, comfort, and so on, she is, in effect, providing a reinforcement for whatever else is being learned in the moment. Each time a mother feeds her infant is a multisensory event with certain perceptual regularities (how the mother smells, looks, and sounds; the feel of her touch; the taste of her milk or formula; and the infant's interoceptive sensations associated with being fed and cuddled). An infant's brain captures this sensory context (including the interoceptive context), and the more successful the allostatic impact, the more rewarding the event, and therefore the better the learning. Each time an infant brain learns, it takes in a dynamic pattern of sensory inputs from the body and the world: sights, sounds, smells, and so on, and also the sensations from the inner core of the body. Little by little, and with surprising speed, an infant brain learns the regularities in these multisensory associations. This is how changes in light become sights, changes in air pressure become sound, changes in chemicals become smells and tastes, and so on.

Therefore, as a brain learns to represent aspects of the world that impact allostasis, it learns to distinguish those inputs that impact its body's metabolic demands from those that do not in a particular cultural context. This is crucial because brains are metabolically expensive and therefore cannot be frivolous; they do not have the resources to learn about everything. Aspects of the environment that are physically present but irrelevant for allostasis in a particular situation or context are not part of an organism's affective niche. As a result, these environmental features go unnoticed. Learning is a metabolic investment that must produce a return; the energy required to encode and consolidate the details of experience, making those experiences available within the brain's synaptic connections to guide future allostatic decisions, must allow a person to survive and thrive in the cultural context she inhabits.

In effect, an infant brain wires itself to an environment that is shaped by the humans who care for the infant. By supporting allostasis, caregivers shape an infant's affective niche and teach her to construct the environment in which she lives and grows (selecting aspects of the physical environment to attend to or ignore). In this way, the rewarding nature of caregiving provides the reinforcement that encourages the acquisition of behaviors and concepts (i.e., aspects of culture) that are necessary to be a competent member of the culture (Atzil et al., 2018; Atzil & Gendron, 2017; Barrett, 2017a). Ultimately, this allows the brain to bootstrap a set of experiences into its wiring that become its culturally relative internal model of its body in the world.

Prediction, Concepts, and Categorization

An Internal Model Is Predictive, Not Reactive

At the most basic level of description, the brain runs an internal model in order to regulate the body in the world as it uses and replenishes resources.[4] An increasingly popular proposal is that the brain accomplishes this feat by implementing an internal model that is predictive. The proposal is that brains do not simply react to the world; instead they actively predict and test those predictions against incoming sensory evidence. That is, the intrinsic neural activity that implements the brain's internal model functions as prediction signals and incoming sensory input only perturbs this model when there is a mismatch (i.e., prediction error). This idea is called *predictive coding* (e.g., Clark, 2013; Rao & Ballard, 1999; Spratling, 2017), in which prediction signals, as representations constructed from past experiences, are compared with incoming sensory information to form prediction errors; prediction errors can be encoded and learned to update stored experience, which is then available for use in future predictions. Related approaches include *the Bayesian brain* (e.g., Vilares & Kording, 2011), which assumes that the brain performs (approximate) Bayesian inferences when computing predictions and prediction errors, *belief propagation* (e.g., Lochmann & Deneve, 2011), which proposes that predictions are anticipatory causal explanations for sensations that are mapped, inversely, to those sensations, and *active inference* (e.g., Friston et al., 2017), which hypothesizes that the brain's model of how sensations are caused is constrained by the need to minimize the cost of prediction error. Using the various sensations at a given moment in time, the

---

[4] There is a well-known principle of cybernetics: anything that regulates (i.e., acts on) a system must contain an "internal model" of that system (Conant & Ashby, 1970). From a brain's perspective, the "system" in question includes its body and everything in the environment within its niche.

brain predicts what is to happen next; the sights, sounds, and other sensations, including interoceptions that are represented right now (i.e., the present situation) allow the brain to anticipate the physiological state, the specific motor actions, and the sensations (i.e., the demands) that are expected to result a moment from now.

A brain's internal model does not implement one prediction at a time. It is continuously implemented as multiple competing simulations, each of which has some probability of fitting the incoming sensory inputs. In effect, the brain is trying to answer the question, "what is this new, incoming sensory input most similar to, when compared to situated, past experiences?" You can think of a prediction as a partially completed pattern that classifies (categorizes) incoming sensory signals to guide allostasis and action based on prior (culturally constrained) learning.

Based on brain anatomy, physiology, and functional dynamics (Barrett, 2017b; Bassett & Bullmore, 2006; Chanes & Barrett, 2016; Hermundstad et al., 2013), we hypothesize that the default mode and salience subnetworks, also responsible for orchestrating allostasis and interoception (Figure 6.1), initiate prediction signals in the brain. Via cascades of intrinsic activity, these subnetworks modulate the firing of neurons in sensory and motor cortices to implement motor and sensory predictions; these predictions[5] are partial neural patterns that prepare the brain to regulate the autonomic nervous system, the immune system, and the endocrine system; prepare the motor system for a set of muscular movements; and also prepare the sensory systems to perceive the sensory consequences of these upcoming physical changes (see Figure 6.2).

Incoming sensations from the body and the world either confirm these predictions (failing to modulate the intrinsic neural activity) or modify them (by changing the intrinsic neural activity so that the brain learns what it was not able to predict[6]). In this way, the brain uses prior knowledge implemented within its wiring to build representations – predictions –that are similar enough to the current situation for the brain to estimate bodily energy needs and prepare for action (i.e., allostasis). Prediction signals function as conditional, or Bayesian, filters for incoming sensory input, implementing allostasis, driving action, and constructing experience (Barrett, 2017b). Prediction errors, if they are deemed important for allostasis, will be encoded (i.e., learned) and will modify neural firing to modify the brain's internal model. Once prediction errors are minimized, the resulting representations also serve as inferences

---

[5] Prediction signals are also called "simulations," "top-down" or "feedback" signals, "forward models" or memories that continuously anticipate bodily changes, motor actions, and events in the sensory environment.

[6] Unanticipated sense data from the world and the body (prediction errors) function as feedback for predictions, also known as "bottom-up" signals, "feedforward" signals, or simply "learning" signals.

about what caused the sensory events and associated actions (Hohwy, 2013; Lochmann & Denève, 2011).

On the hypothesis that prediction co-opts the same subnetworks, we propose that interoception and allostatic regulation are part of every mental event, whether people are aware or not (Barrett, 2017a). Indeed, interoceptive sensations made available affective feelings, with qualities that scientists describe using various features, such as valence and arousal (Barrett & Russell, 1999; Barrett & Simmons, 2015; Kuppens et al., 2013). These affective properties are not specific to emotion but are basic features of conscious experiences (Damasio, 1999; Dreyfus & Thompson, 2007; Edelman & Tononi, 2000; James, 1890/2007; Searle, 1992, 2004; Wundt, 1896/1897). A brain's internal model predicts not only the relevant sensory regularities in the external environment, but also the statistical regularities of the internal milieu (interoceptions) and their corresponding low-dimensional affective features (Barrett & Simmons, 2015).

Predictions Are Concepts

In every moment, the brain assembles a population of predictions. Each prediction is a partially completed neural pattern that has some probability of being the best fit to the current circumstances (i.e., Bayesian priors). In effect, this population is a concept (Barrett, 2017a, 2017b). A concept is a group of instances that are similar for some purpose (Murphy, 2002). The idea that predictions are concepts is similar to Barsalou's notion of "ad hoc" concepts (Barsalou, 1983) or situated conceptualization (Barsalou, 1999, 2008) – concepts are constructed as needed, using the sensory and motor systems (including those that represent allostatically relevant events; Kan et al., 2003; Kousta et al., 2011; Niedenthal et al., 2009; Wilson-Mendenhall et al., 2011). A concept is a group of distributed activation patterns across some population of neurons. So the human brain can be said to be engaged in dynamic concept construction for the purposes of maintaining allostasis and guiding action. Concept learning, then, is the encoding of sensory and motor prediction errors (i.e., whatever information was not anticipated or anticipated information that did not materialize). Within this framework, we can consider categorization as an instance of "good enough" fit between a given predictive pattern and the observed state of the world.

Of course, not all patterns are equally useful. A conceptual system must be sufficiently complex and context sensitive to maintain allostasis. That is, the conceptual system must support predictions about the upcoming state of the world so the individual can prepare in an efficient and effective manner. Prior knowledge enhances the complexity of a brain, and improves its ability to generate predictions, which in turn improves its efficiency. Culture provides a mechanism for promoting complexity via prior knowledge. Cultural transmission of concepts allows your brain to reconstruct/reassemble the information that has been useful to other people in your cultural context in the past without your having to invest the cost of obtaining that information by trial and error within a single lifetime. Further, building a conceptual system via personal experience alone is not only inefficient, but highly costly. Consider how costly (and dangerous) it is for one person to learn about allostasis in an inductive way, by trial and error. The goal is not to correct mistakes but to prevent them.

Humans have flourished as a species, in part because we can also learn from each other's experience. This arrangement of wiring each other's brains allows humans to expand across the globe, creating livable habitats by feeding, clothing, and learning from each other in otherwise inhospitable physical conditions (Boyd et al., 2011; Henrich et al., 2016; Richerson & Boyd, 2005). We transmit this learning across generations using stories, recipes, and traditions, and also via childrearing practices, shared attention, and other forms of interpersonal interaction (Muthukrishna & Henrich, 2016). This is how each generation shapes the brain wiring of the next, with the ultimate consequence of optimizing prediction within that cultural context. Other individuals in a person's culture(s) fine-tune the conceptual system for maintaining allostasis for a given set of constraints that are of concern to that particular group. That is, people regulate one another's nervous systems using shared concepts.

All social species regulate each other's allostasis, usually by chemical and behavioral means. But humans have this additional way: we influence the development of each other's conceptual systems by the words and expressions we use, the similarities we emphasize, and the ones we ignore. Words are critical elements in the maintenance of allostasis because they fine-tune a conceptual system, allowing it to be more agile and flexible by serving as social invitations to form concepts (Chen & Waxman, 2013; Ferry et al., 2010; Gelman, 2009; Waxman & Gelman, 2010; for an extended discussion, see Barrett, 2017a; Hoemann et al., in press).[7]

---

[7] For example, the English category of *anger* is associated with many goals, one of which involves overcoming an obstacle that someone blameworthy has put in your path. So, when one infant takes a toy away from another, sometimes she will cry, and her parents or caregivers might label this instance as 'anger'. Sometimes, the infant might swat the other child, and, again, her parents or caregivers might label this instance as 'anger'. When the infant spits her food out, or tips a bowl onto the floor, these events might also be labeled as 'anger'. So too when her play is interrupted to get ready for bed, and she stiffens her body as she is picked up. In each situation, the different motor actions are accompanied by different facial movements, different changes in the systems of her body (to support her motor actions) and correspondingly different bodily sensations, different sights, sounds, actions by adults, and so on, but they are all associated with the same goal: to remove an obstruction put there by someone else. We hypothesize that, across these dynamic, multimodal patterns, she also occasionally hears her parents uttering the word

Concepts for Body, Emotion, and Cognition

While all concepts, as instruments of culture, can be conceived of as tools for allostasis (Barrett, 2017a, 2017b), some anchor conceptual knowledge that more directly reflects how human culture organizes and expands the affective niche of the individual. In Western European and North American cultural contexts (comprising much of the psychological literature), allostatically relevant events are perhaps most directly captured by *emotion* concepts, like "sadness" or "disgust." These concepts foreground (and organize the meaning of) disruptions to the internal milieu (i.e., interoceptions), prescribe situation-specific actions, and facilitate communication. Further, emotion concepts serve as critical tools for social coordination and influence, often serving as bids for social regulation of allostasis. Emotion concepts (and the words used to name them) are transmitted early on in development in the context of caregiving relationships (Atzil & Gendron, 2017; Atzil et al., 2018; Xu & Barrett, 2019; Hoemann et al., 2020), and can provide a rich array of information for the individual to leverage or to deal with allostatically challenging situations. For example, conceptualizing a particular pattern of sensory inputs as "anger" guides the brain to prepare specific, situated actions. And indeed, individuals whose brains are able to construct more varied emotion concepts cope better with adverse life events and recover from illness more quickly than those who are less able to construct emotion concepts (for evidence and discussion, see Barrett, 2017a; Kashdan et al., 2015).

Divergent Concepts for Allostasis

Given the importance of the events that emotion concepts like fear and sadness capture, and the functions that they serve, dominant psychological approaches have assumed that such concepts sediment out from inherited biological circuits (what are referred to as *basic emotions*). Yet concepts for allostatically relevant events are not universal. There is remarkable diversity in what these concepts encompass and promote (Heelas, 1996; Lillard, 1998; Mesquita & Frijda, 1992; Russell, 1991). Here, we provide several examples of this diversity to illustrate how concepts likely reflect the wide variety of distinct genetic, environmental, and social contexts that humans inhabit and create (following Boyd et al., 2011). Emotion concepts can be considered a reflection of the tuning of systems of meaning to the context (Mesquita & Boiger, 2014), as well as a means of further reinforcing an affective niche that a culture inhabits.

'angry'. Instances of word usage may be sparse at first (in particular, those directed at the infant; e.g., Beeghly et al., 1986; Dunn et al., 1987), but may help to agglomerate the category over time.

An obvious example of this "tuning" is when concepts for allostatically relevant events are lexically marked (i.e., with a distinct word or phrase) only in some cultural contexts but not others. Concepts that are often assumed to be core/universal are not lexically marked in all languages. For example, a translational equivalent for "sadness" was not noted in Tahitian culture (Levy, 1975; for further discussion, see Russell, 1991). Many terms for emotions also lack adequate translational equivalents in the English language. For example, the term *hygge* from Danish culture is often translated with English language concepts of "cozy," "friendly," and "snug" (Linnet, 2011). Yet these translations do not capture the relational aspect of *hygge* as a concept of social interaction (intimate socialization often involving storytelling, teasing) that promotes niche construction (creating a warm, informal environment) and certain affective consequences (pleasant, low arousal states). Instructively, attempts to export this concept outside of the Scandinavian context have led to simplifications of *hygge* as a décor scheme/lifestyle brand, limiting the potential interpersonal affordances of the concept that derive from *hygge*'s connection to the value systems and consumption patterns of Danish culture (Linnet, 2011). Nevertheless, the popularity of recent popular science compendia of such "untranslatable" emotion terms does highlight the power of language to "spotlight" (Heelas, 1996) aspects of allostatically relevant events (and potentially expand an individual's affective niche), even when those terms are displaced from the original cultural and linguistic context.

Even more striking than variation in individual concepts is that allostatically relevant events are not always organized via concepts that highlight internal, mental experience. For example, distinctions between body states and mental states (Danziger, 1997; Lillard, 1998), or between emotions and other mental or physical states (Russell, 1991), are culture-bound. Little formal research has been undertaken to address the ramifications of making a distinction between emotions, body states, and actions. But evidence from neuroimaging studies reveals that inducing individuals to emphasize interoceptions versus external actions (Oosterwijk et al., 2015) or to experience physical states (more broadly) versus social perspectives (Wilson-Mendenhall et al., 2011) engages both distinct and overlapping circuitry in the brain. These data suggest that in cultural contexts where these distinctions are not made, individuals may routinely engage different sets of distributed neural patterns (potentially resulting in stable differences in subnetwork structure and organization).

While more evidence is needed, we can speculate that emotions are less likely to be treated as a distinct domain when they are not invoked as "causal" mechanisms for actions, experiences, and the grounds for prediction of other's behavior (i.e., essentialism), as they are in the Western folk model of emotion (Lillard, 1998; Lindquist et al., 2013). Consistent with this prediction, in our own research on emotion perception in small-scale societies in Africa where the native languages (Otji-Herero and Hadzane) do not contain a word for the emotion domain, we observed that specific terms for emotional states were used less frequently than by American participants to describe other's non-verbal actions (e.g., a contracted zygomaticus). Instead, participants often generated language for situated *behaviors*, such as laughing at something (Gendron et al., 2018). These findings fit with the observation that multiple forms of categorization (e.g., group membership) are often a more functional means of generating predictions about our social worlds than mental state inferences (Hirschfeld, 2013).

Even when emotion is carved out as a distinct domain in a given language, the tendency to spontaneously use emotion concepts as explanations of allostatically relevant events appears to be culturally variable. Studies of maternal–child talk about impactful events in Chinese culture reveal more action-based language (and less mental state language like emotion term use) than is observed in American mothers (Doan & Wang, 2010). This finding fits more broadly with the observation that individuals from East Asian cultural contexts understand emotions as arising from the relationships between people (Uchida et al., 2009) rather than triggered by events in the environment. The locus of emotion is the roles that define interaction, not a mechanism within an individual, suggesting that emotions are generally less *essentialized* (i.e., defined by an unobservable and unspecified internal property; Medin & Ortony, 1989) in some cultural contexts. As a result, emotions are events that people enact together, such that allostatic regulation is occurring within the context of an interaction, as opposed to regulation at the individual level (Mesquita, 2001).

More broadly, we hypothesize that the cultural tendency to essentialize allostatically relevant events as emotions is related to sources of predictability – for others' behavior and one's own. Many cultures feature more highly scripted behavior that is defined by the situation and relationship between interaction partners (e.g., Gelfand et al., 2011). As a result, concepts will more readily highlight those sources of predictability (i.e., the cultural tasks) rather than internal experiences. Similarly, familiarity with others' action patterns (i.e., their habits) might also make it less likely that emotions are invoked as causal structures for behavior. We speculate that this may be more prevalent in small-scale societies where the range of individuals, situations, and possible behaviors are more constrained due to group size and complexity.

Convergent Concepts for Allostasis

While the discussion thus far has focused on diversity in concepts for allostatically relevant events, there are also clear examples of consistency. Linguistic concepts for "good" and "bad" or "pleasure" and "pain" (what are referred to as concepts for the valence dimension of affect; Barrett & Russell, 1999; Russell, 1980) appear to be one such cultural feature. The ethnographic and linguistic records reveal at least some rudimentary concepts to represent experiences that are "pleasant" and "unpleasant" across cultures (see also Russell, 1991; for discussion of these concepts as "semantic primitives" that are in evidence across languages, see Wierzbicka, 1999).

Consistency in conceptual structures for allostatically relevant events may also be the product of *convergent cultural evolution* (Jablonka & Lamb, 2007; Lipo et al., 2006; Mesoudi et al., 2006; Richerson & Boyd, 2005). That is, different populations may independently develop (and pass on) similar concepts due to shared constraints. This convergence may be due to biological constraints of the human nervous system that make it more likely that certain concepts will "sediment out." For example, it is well documented that robust peripheral physiological changes occur in the context of "emotional" events, evidence of the mechanisms of allostasis at work. Importantly, these "changes" in the body are highly complex and variable both within and across different emotion categories (for meta-analytic evidence; Siegel et al., 2018). We can hypothesize that these properties such as "pleasure" and "displeasure" evolved across cultures to represent these changes, which are experienced as features of conscious experience. The affective features of experience, in this view, are like a simple barometer tied to the general state of the body (i.e., to allostasis). Affect is a core property of the neural architecture for representing viscero-motor changes in the periphery (called interoception; Craig, 2009; Critchley et al., 2004; Kleckner et al., 2017); affective feelings are a low dimensional representation of the interoceptions that arise from allostasis. As a new instance of a concept is learned (i.e., prediction errors are encoded), information from multiple sensory modalities is integrated and compressed (Finlay & Uchiyama, 2015), creating multimodal summaries which are often called "abstractions" (Barrett, 2017a, 2017b). Affect, as an index of allostatic status, is hypothesized to be a universal and fundamental abstraction that human brains make. We hypothesize that valence (pleasure vs. displeasure/comfort vs. discomfort), is a low dimensional representation of the interoceptions that reflect whether an organism is successfully maintaining allostasis. As such, we suggest that affect is a feature of all concepts that the human brain constructs. Consistent with this hypothesis, all human languages have specific words to represent valence (Russell, 1991).

Convergent cultural evolution might explain similarities in concepts for more specific types of disruptions to allostasis due to similar environmental or biological constraints. For example, while we can point out examples of ethnolinguistic groups that lack an exact translational equivalent for an emotion like *sadness*, many ethnolinguistic groups do have highly similar concepts. The prevalence of concepts similar to *sadness* may be related to the experience of loss (i.e., a core theme in English language conceptualizations of sadness; Smith & Lazarus, 1993) as an inevitable biological reality – mortality is a universal. Further, the core neurobiology of attachment includes systems involved in the maintenance of allostasis (i.e., dopamine function within a cortico-striatal-amygdala subnetwork; Atzil et al., 2017) and may be similarly implicated in the experience of broken attachment (Fisher et al., 2010). The experience of loss presents a significant disruption to allostasis across cultures, such that convergent concepts for that disruption, such as sadness and grief, likely evolved to meaningfully construct and regulate the experience of loss. Indeed, cultural systems for loss similarly involve complex forms of affective niche construction, via religious concepts (e.g., afterlife, ancestor worship) and cultural tasks as dictated by rituals (e.g., mourning practices like wearing black, ritualized crying), as well as structural changes in relationships (e.g., levirate marriage).

Emotion Acculturation

If the brain becomes wired with a conceptual system that fits environmental challenges that are specific to its cultural context(s), then moving to a different environment should challenge the maintenance of allostasis. We hypothesize that shifting into a novel cultural context places an enormous burden on the human brain. In the short run, this means that migration would come at a cost to well-being. In the longer run, continual allostatic load would lead to enhanced inflammation, creating a vulnerability to depression and anxiety disorders, along with a host of stress-related metabolic illnesses, including heart disease, diabetes, and cancer (for reviews, see Juster et al., 2010; Korte et al., 2005; see also Doamekpor & Dinwiddie, 2015; Peek et al., 2010).

Immigration is on the rise, and an increasing number of people experience a lack of "fit" between their internal model (and the concepts it enacts) and the environmental context (Mesquita et al., 2019). Consistent with our hypothesis that misfit comes at a cost, immigration has indeed been linked to acculturative stress as manifested by uncertainty, anxiety, and depression (Berry et al., 1987), as well as with problems in social adaptation, including relatively low school/work achievement and social competence (Sam & Berry, 2010). Results on the impact of immigration on physical health problems are not fully consistent (see below).

That it is important for a person to have an internal model that is wired to the physical and social environment is suggested by an increasing number of studies on cultural fit among natives. Natives who fit their culture's average levels of extraversion, promotion focus, emotional responses, and even religiosity were also found to have higher personal well-being and more relationship satisfaction, and even better reported health (De Leersnyder et al., 2014, 2015; Fulmer et al., 2010; Gebauer et al., 2012). A plausible inference from these studies is that the fit between a person's internal model and their sociocultural context offers an advantage to maintaining allostasis.

Research on secondary acculturation of the conceptual system is in its infancy. This is because a tacit assumption in much acculturation research has been that while cultural affiliation and identity change, the 'psyche itself' remains untouched. Our approach challenges this view of acculturation (see also Mesquita et al., 2019). We hypothesize that, as immigrants engage in the new culture, new concept learning will take place to the degree to which concepts learned in the native culture fail to effectively regulate allostasis. For instance, an internal model that cannot predict social rewards in the new culture, or that does not allow for social coordination, will need to be adjusted, or else will come at a high cost. Importantly, when immigrant individuals come to share the conceptual system of the new culture, the majority of others can also help them regulate allostasis. Conversely, lacking social support will tax the person's ability for allostatic regulation.

An emerging body of evidence suggests that contact with a new culture may, in fact, result in a new and changed internal model of the body's relationship to the world (Mesquita et al., 2019; Pavlenko, 2009). In our own research on emotional acculturation, we have found that immigrant minorities' engagement in a new culture leads to better cultural fit of emotions with majority emotions (De Leersnyder, 2017; De Leersnyder et al., 2011; Mesquita et al., 2019). In this research, individuals from immigrant minorities and majority groups were asked to report their emotions in similar emotional situations. Minority emotional patterns were compared to the majority average in the same situation. Compared to first-generation immigrants, we found that second and later generations of immigrants had higher emotional fit with the majority's average emotions in similar situations. Furthermore, within the group of immigrants, the internal emotion models of immigrant minorities who frequently engaged in majority culture (e.g., spoke the majority language, had more majority friends) shifted more toward those of the majority members than the internal models of immigrant minority individuals who had less contact. This is an illustration of shifting internal models. Other research similarly suggests that engaging in a new culture brings about shifts in social cognition, self-esteem, self-concept, personality, and motivation, in the direction of the majority culture (Güngör et al., 2013; Heine & Lehman, 2004; Hong et al., 2000; Pouliasi & Verkuyten, 2012; Savani et al., 2011). Additionally, it seems that learning a language provides new concepts and, thus, itself is a shift in the internal model (Pavlenko, 2014).

Evidence that shifting internal models contribute to regulation of allostasis in the new cultural environment is scarce and inconsistent. Importantly, first-generation immigrants often have been found to be healthier than the general population (and when compared to their natal population), and also healthier than later generations of immigrants, something that has become known under the term "immigrant paradox" (e.g., Hyman, 2004). At first sight, this finding is not consistent with our hypothesis that people with an internal model that cannot predict well in the new culture will fail to achieve allostasis. However, several factors may account for these relatively positive health outcomes for first-generation immigrants, and the research to date does not allow to distinguish among these explanations. One possible explanation for the immigrant paradox is a selection effect, with first-generation immigrants, especially those who voluntarily move, being the healthiest and most educated (Sam & Berry, 2010). It is also possible that many first-generation immigrant minorities live in neighborhoods and communities where their heritage internal models still predict their dealings with others well. Studies specifically connecting minority individuals' shifts in concepts to increases in well-being and health are rare and should be undertaken in future research. In a rare study connecting emotional experience with self-reported health, Consedine et al. found that immigrant women whose emotional experiences were more similar to those reported by their majority counterparts also reported better health (Consedine et al., 2014). One possibility is that healthier people are more able to make the necessary conceptual adjustments (i.e., the conceptual learning may pose less of a burden for the healthy than for those who must allocate resources to health maintenance and/or whose condition impairs capacity to adapt).

It is important to keep in mind that many bi- or multicultural individuals navigate different cultures. To predict their body's relation to each of their cultural worlds, these biculturals will need different internal models, plus the flexibility to apply the models matching the cultural environment at hand. Biculturalism, or the availability of multiple internal models, has been related to higher psychological well-being and better social adaptation (Nguyen & Benet-Martínez, 2013), although this finding may be constrained to those national contexts that favor multi-culturalism. In national contexts that require immigrants to assimilate, and thus fully change their internal models, immigrants seem to be better off if they choose segregation as an acculturation strategy (Mesquita et al., 2019). Segregation would allow immigrant minorities to largely sustain the predictability of their world, without changing their internal models, and to benefit from others from their heritage culture to help regulate allostasis. In a new country or culture, this strategy, while helping to maintain allostasis in the short run, may come at the cost of societal exclusion in the long run.

Immigration, and the shifts in internal models that it may entail, is not only important to study in its own right, but also forms a framework for understanding the predictive complexities with which many individuals in modern life must deal. Individuals traverse cultural boundaries on a daily basis, such as when leaving your family setting at home to enter your cultural context at work, when changing jobs, roles, etc. Even a relationship between two people can be thought of as microculture. A cultural neuroscience approach that offers solutions for the daily challenges of acculturation must consider culture in these broader terms as well.

A Look Ahead

We have outlined a multilevel framework for charting the role that regulation of the body (achieved through allostasis) plays in the acquisition of internal models to organize experience and action within distinct cultural worlds. Neuroscience advances in our understanding of the structure and organization of the human brain (including evolutionary (dis)continuities) strongly suggest that human culture wires the brain with the necessary flexibility and complexity to contend with the expansiveness of the human ecological niche.

More research is necessary to bridge the gap between what we know about variation in internal models (including concepts for allostatically relevant events like "emotions") and how those models function. Questions about what leads a cultural group to develop a set of concepts for certain allostatic challenges and whether those concepts are *functional* for promoting allostasis are complex issues that require more empirical attention at multiple levels of analysis. But the evidence, thus far, suggests that there is a large variety of concepts surrounding allostatically relevant events, and, thus, it is reasonable to posit that a range of internal models are functional, depending on the context. More complex issues that warrant further empirical attention include the role that genetic variation plays in cultural diversity in emotion concepts (and related issues of culture–gene coevolution), how consistent versus divergent representations of emotion are within cultural groups, and how responsive concepts for emotion are within a culture to shifting sociodemographic factors (e.g., from rural to urban, from culturally isolated to interconnected, from subsistence agriculture to commerce, and so on).

REFERENCES

Adams, R. A., Shipp, S., & Friston, K. J. (2013). Predictions not commands: Active inference in the motor system. *Brain Structure and Function*, *218*(3), 611–43. https://doi.org/10.1007/s00429–012-0475-5

Altschul, D., Jensen, G. G., & Terrace, H. S. (2017). Perceptual category learning of photographic and painterly stimuli in rhesus macaques (*Macaca mulatta*) and humans. *PLoS ONE*, *12*(9), e0185576. https://doi.org/10.1371/journal.pone.0185576

Atzil, S., Gao, W., Fradkin, I., & Barrett, L. F. (2018). Growing a social brain. *Nature Human Behaviour*, *2*, 624–36. https://doi.org/10.1038/s41562–018-0384-6

Atzil, S., & Gendron, M. (2017). Bio-behavioral synchrony promotes the development of conceptualized emotions. *Current Opinion in Psychology*, *17*(Supplement C), 162–9. https://doi.org/10.1016/j.copsyc.2017.07.009

Atzil, S., Touroutoglou, A., Rudy, T., Salcedo, S., Feldman, R., Hooker, J. M., Dickerson, B. C., Catana, C., & Barrett, L. F. (2017). Dopamine in the medial amygdala network mediates human bonding. *Proceedings of the National Academy of Sciences of the United States of America*, *114*(9), 2361–6. https://doi.org/10.1073/pnas.1612233114

Barrett, L. F. (2017a). *How emotions are made: The secret life of the brain*. Houghton Mifflin Harcourt.

Barrett, L. F. (2017b). The theory of constructed emotion: An active inference account of interoception and categorization. *Social Cognitive and Affective Neuroscience*, *12*(1), 1–23. https://doi.org/10.1093%2Fscan%2Fnsw154

Barrett, L. F., & Bliss-Moreau, E. (2009). Affect as a psychological primitive. In M. Zanna (Ed.), *Advances in experimental social psychology* (Vol. 41, pp. 167–218). Academic Press. https://doi.org/10.1016/S0065-2601(08)00404-8

Barrett, L. F., & Finlay, B. L. (2018). Concepts, goals and the control of survival-related behaviors. *Current Opinion in Behavioral Sciences*, *24*, 172–9. https://doi.org/10.1016/j.cobeha.2018.10.001

Barrett L. F., Quigley, K. S., & Hamilton P. (2016). An active inference theory of allostasis and interoception in depression. *Philosophical Transactions of the Royal Society B: Biological Sciences*, *371*(1708), 20160011. https://doi.org/10.1098/rstb.2016.0011

Barrett, L. F., & Russell, J. A. (1999). Structure of current affect: Controversies and emerging consensus. *Current Directions in Psychological Science*, *8*(1), 10–14. https://doi.org/10.1111/1467-8721.00003

Barrett, L. F., & Satpute, A. B. (2013). Large-scale brain networks in affective and social neuroscience: Towards an integrative functional architecture of the brain. *Current Opinion in Neurobiology*, *23*(3), 361–72. https://doi.org/10.1016/j.conb.2012.12.012

Barrett, L. F., & Satpute, A. B. (2017). Historical pitfalls and new directions in the neuroscience of emotion. *Neuroscience Letters*, *693*, 9–18. https://doi.org/10.1016/j.neulet.2017.07.045

Barrett, L. F., & Simmons, W. K. (2015). Interoceptive predictions in the brain. *Nature Reviews Neuroscience*, *16*(7), 419–29. https://doi.org/10.1038/nrn3950

Barsalou, L. W. (1983). Ad hoc categories. *Memory & Cognition*, *11*(3), 211–27. https://doi.org/10.3758/BF03196968

Barsalou, L. W. (1999). Perceptual symbol systems. *Behavioral and Brain Sciences*, *22*(4), 577–609. https://doi.org/10.1017/S0140525X99002149

Barsalou, L. W. (2008). Grounded cognition. *Annual Review of Psychology*, *59*, 617–45. https://doi.org/10.1146/annurev.psych.59.103006.093639

Bassett, D. S., & Bullmore, E. (2006). Small-world brain networks. *The Neuroscientist*, *12*(6), 512–23. https://doi.org/10.1177/1073858406293182

Beeghly, M., Bretherton, I., & Mervis, C. B. (1986). Mothers' internal state language to toddlers. *British Journal of Developmental Psychology*, *4*(3), 247–61. https://doi.org/10.1111/j.2044-835X.1986.tb01016.x

Berry, J. W., Kim, U., Minde, T., & Mok, D. (1987). Comparative studies of acculturative stress. *International Migration Review*, *21*(3), 491–511. https://doi.org/10.1177%2F019791838702100303

Boyd, R., Richerson, P. J., & Henrich, J. (2011). The cultural niche: Why social learning is essential for human adaptation. *Proceedings of the National Academy of Sciences of the United States of America, 108*(Supplement 2), 10918–25. https://doi.org/10.1073/pnas.1100290108

Buckner, R. L. (2012). The serendipitous discovery of the brain's default network. *NeuroImage, 62*(2), 1137–45. https://doi.org/10.1016/j.neuroimage.2011.10.035

Cao, M., Huang, H., & He, Y. (2017). Developmental connectomics from infancy through early childhood. *Trends in Neurosciences, 40*(8), 494–506. https://doi.org/10.1016/j.tins.2017.06.003

Chanes, L., & Barrett, L. F. (2016). Redefining the role of limbic areas in cortical processing. *Trends in Cognitive Sciences, 20*(2), 96–106. https://doi.org/10.1016/j.tics.2015.11.005

Chen, M. L., & Waxman, S. R. (2013). "Shall we blick?": Novel words highlight actors' underlying intentions for 14-month-old infants. *Developmental Psychology, 49*(3), 426–31. https://doi.org/10.1037/a0029486

Clark, A. (2013). Whatever next? Predictive brains, situated agents, and the future of cognitive science. *Behavioral and Brain Sciences, 36*(3), 181–204. https://doi.org/10.1017/S0140525X12000477

Colombetti, G., & Krueger, J. (2015). Scaffoldings of the affective mind. *Journal of Philosophical Psychology, 28*(8), 1157–76. https://doi.org/10.1080/09515089.2014.976334

Conant, R. C., & Ashby, W. R. (1970). Every good regulator of a system must be a model of that system. *International Journal of Systems Science, 1*(2), 89–97. https://doi.org/10.1080/00207727008920220

Consedine, N. S., Chentsova-Dutton, Y. E., & Krivoshekova, Y. S. (2014). Emotional acculturation predicts better somatic health: Experiential and expressive acculturation among immigrant women from four ethnic groups. *Journal of Social and Clinical Psychology, 33*(10), 867–89. https://doi.org/10.1521/jscp.2014.33.10.867

Craig, A. D. (2009). How do you feel – now? The anterior insula and human awareness. *Nature Reviews Neuroscience, 10*(1), 59–70. https://doi.org/10.1038/nrn2555

Craig, A. D. (2014). *How do you feel? An interoceptive moment with your neurobiological self*. Princeton University Press. https://doi.org/10.23943/princeton/9780691156767.001.0001

Critchley, H. D., Wiens, S., Rotshtein, P., Öhman, A., & Dolan, R. J. (2004). Neural systems supporting interoceptive awareness. *Nature Neuroscience, 7*(2), 189–95. https://doi.org/10.1038/nn1176

Damasio, A. R. (1999). *The feeling of what happens: Body and emotion in the making of consciousness*: Harcourt College.

Danziger, K. (1997). *Naming the mind: How psychology found its language*. SAGE. https://doi.org/10.4135/9781446221815

Deco, G., Jirsa, V. K., & McIntosh, A. R. (2011). Emerging concepts for the dynamical organization of resting-state activity in the brain. *Nature Reviews Neuroscience, 12*(1), 43–56. https://doi.org/10.1038/nrn2961

De Leersnyder, J. (2017). Emotional acculturation: A first review. *Current Opinion in Psychology, 17*, 67–73. https://doi.org/10.1016/j.copsyc.2017.06.007

De Leersnyder, J., Kim, H., & Mesquita, B. (2015). Feeling right is feeling good: Psychological well-being and emotional fit with culture in autonomy-versus relatedness-promoting situations. *Frontiers in Psychology, 6*, 630. https://doi.org/10.3389/fpsyg.2015.00630

De Leersnyder, J., Mesquita, B., & Kim, H. S. (2011). Where do my emotions belong? A study of immigrants' emotional acculturation. *Personality and Social Psychology Bulletin*, *37*(4), 451–63. https://doi.org/10.1177/0146167211399103

De Leersnyder, J., Mesquita, B., Kim, H., Eom, K., & Choi, H. (2014). Emotional fit with culture: A predictor of individual differences in relational well-being. *Emotion*, *14*(2), 241–5. https://doi.org/10.1037/a0035296

Doamekpor, L. A., & Dinwiddie, G. Y. (2015). Allostatic load in foreign-born and US-born blacks: Evidence from the 2001–2010 National Health and Nutrition Examination Survey. *American Journal of Public Health*, *105*(3), 591–7. https://doi.org/10.2105/AJPH.2014.302285

Doan, S. N., & Wang, Q. (2010). Maternal discussions of mental states and behaviors: Relations to emotion situation knowledge in European American and immigrant Chinese children. *Child Development*, *81*(5), 1490–503. https://doi.org/10.1111/j.1467-8624.2010.01487.x

Dosenbach, N. U. F., Nardos, B., Cohen, A. L., Fair, D. A., Power, J. D., Church, J. A., Nelson, S. M., Wig, G. S., Vogel, A. C., Lessov-Schlaggar, C. N., Barnes, K. A., Dubis, J. W., Feczko, E., Coalson, R. S., Pruett, J. R., Jr., Barch, D. M., Petersen, S. E., & Schlaggar, B. L. (2010). Prediction of individual brain maturity using fMRI. *Science*, *329*(5997), 1358–61. https://doi.org/10.1126/science.1194144

Dreyfus, G., & Thompson, E. (2007). Asian perspectives: Indian theories of mind. In P. D. Zelazo, M. Moscovitch, & E. Thompson (Eds.), *The Cambridge handbook of consciousness* (pp. 89–114). Cambridge University Press.

Dubois, J., Dehaene-Lambertz, G., Kulikova, S., Poupon, C., Hüppi, P. S., & Hertz-Pannier, L. (2014). The early development of brain white matter: A review of imaging studies in fetuses, newborns and infants. *Neuroscience*, *276*, 48–71. https://doi.org/10.1016/j.neuroscience.2013.12.044

Dunn, J., Bretherton, I., & Munn, P. (1987). Conversations about feeling states between mothers and their young children. *Developmental Psychology*, *23*(1), 132–9. https://doi.org/10.1037/0012-1649.23.1.132

Edelman, G. M., & Tononi, G. (2000). *A universe of consciousness: How matter becomes imagination*. Basic Books.

Feldman, R. (2017). The neurobiology of human attachments. *Trends in Cognitive Sciences*, *2*(21), 80–99. https://doi.org/10.1016/j.tics.2016.11.007

Ferry, A. L., Hespos, S. J., & Waxman, S. R. (2010). Categorization in 3- and 4-month-old infants: An advantage of words over tones. *Child Development*, *81*(2), 472–9. https://doi.org/10.1111%2Fj.1467-8624.2009.01408.x

Finlay B. L., & Uchiyama, R. (2015). Developmental mechanisms channeling cortical evolution. *Trends in Neurosciences*, *38*(2), 69–76. https://doi.org/10.1016/j.tins.2014.11.004

Finlay, B., & Uchiyama, R. (2017). The timing of brain maturation, early experience, and the human social niche. In J. H. Kaas (Ed.), *Evolution of nervous systems* (2nd ed., pp. 123–48). Elsevier.

Fisher, H. E., Brown, L. L., Aron, A., Strong, G., & Mashek, D. (2010). Reward, addiction, and emotion regulation systems associated with rejection in love. *Journal of Neurophysiology*, *104*(1), 51–60. https://doi.org/10.1152/jn.00784.2009

Fransson, P., Åden, U., Blennow, M., & Lagercrantz, H. (2011). The functional architecture of the infant brain as revealed by resting-state fMRI. *Cerebral Cortex*, *21*(1), 145–54. https://doi.org/10.1093/cercor/bhq071

Fransson, P., Skiöld, B., Horsch, S., Nordell, A., Blennow, M., Lagercrantz, H., & Åden, U. (2007). Resting-state networks in the infant brain. *Proceedings of the National Academy of Sciences of the United States of America*, *104*(39), 15531–6. https://doi.org/10.1073/pnas.0704380104

Friston, K. (2010). The free-energy principle: A unified brain theory? *Nature Reviews Neuroscience*, *11*(2), 127–38. https://doi.org/10.1038/nrn2787

Friston, K., FitzGerald, T., Rigoli, F., Schwartenbeck, P., & Pezzulo, G. (2017). Active inference: A process theory. *Neural Computation*, *29*(1), 1–49. https://doi.org/10.1162/NECO_a_00912

Fulmer, C. A., Gelfand, M. J., Kruglanski, A. W., Kim-Prieto, C., Diener, E., Pierro, A., & Higgins, E. T. (2010). On "feeling right" in cultural contexts: How person-culture match affects self-esteem and subjective well-being. *Psychological Science*, *21*(11), 1563–9. https://doi.org/10.1177/0956797610384742

Gao, W., Gilmore, J. H., Giovanello, K. S., Smith, J. K., Shen, D., Zhu, H., & Lin, W. (2011). Temporal and spatial evolution of brain network topology during the first two years of life. *PLoS ONE*, *6*(9), e25278. https://doi.org/10.1371/journal.pone.0025278

Gao, W., Lin, W., Chen, Y., Gerig, G., Smith, J. K., Jewells, V., & Gilmore, J. H. (2009). Temporal and spatial development of axonal maturation and myelination of white matter in the developing brain. *American Journal of Neuroradiology*, *30*(2), 290–6. https://doi.org/10.3174/ajnr.A1363

Gao, W., Lin, W., Grewen, K., & Gilmore, J. H. (2017). Functional connectivity of the infant human brain: Plastic and modifiable. *The Neuroscientist*, *23*(2), 169–84. https://doi.org/10.1177/1073858416635986

Gao, W., Zhu, H., Giovanello, K. S., Smith, J. K., Shen, D., Gilmore, J. H., & Lin, W. (2009). Evidence on the emergence of the brain's default network from 2-week-old to 2-year-old healthy pediatric subjects. *Proceedings of the National Academy of Sciences of the United States of America*, *106*(16), 6790–5. https://doi.org/10.1073/pnas.0811221106

Gebauer, J. E., Sedikides, C., & Neberich, W. (2012). Religiosity, social self-esteem, and psychological adjustment: On the cross-cultural specificity of the psychological benefits of religiosity. *Psychological Science*, *23*(2), 158–60. https://doi.org/10.1177%2F0956797611427045

Gelfand, M. J., Raver, J. L., Nishii, L., Leslie, L. M., Lun, J., Lim, B. C., Duan, L., Almaliach, A., Ang, S., Arnadottir, J., Aycan, Z., Boehnke, K., Boski, P., Cabecinhas, R., Chan, D., Chhokar, J., D'Amato, A., Ferrer, M., Fischlmayr, I. C., ... Yamaguchi, S. (2011). Differences between tight and loose cultures: A 33-nation study. *Science*, *332*(6033), 1100–4. https://doi.org/10.1126/science.1197754

Gelman, S. A. (2009). Learning from others: Children's construction of concepts. *Annual Review of Psychology*, *60*, 115–40. https://doi.org/10.1146/annurev.psych.59.103006.093659

Gendron, M., Crivelli, C., & Barrett, L. F. (2018). Universality reconsidered: Diversity in meaning making about facial expressions. *Current Directions in Psychological Science*, *27*(4), 211–19. https://doi.org/10.1177%2F0963721417746794

Geng, X., Li, G., Lu, Z., Gao, W., Wang, L., Shen, D., & Gilmore, J. H. (2017). Structural and maturational covariance in early childhood brain development. *Cerebral Cortex*, *27*(3), 1795–807. https://doi.org/10.1093/cercor/bhw022

Greenfield, P. M., Keller, H., Fuligni, A., & Maynard, A. (2003). Cultural pathways through universal development. *Annual Review of Psychology*, *54*, 461–90. https://doi.org/10.1146/annurev.psych.54.101601.145221

Güngör, D., Bornstein, M. H., De Leersnyder, J., Cote, L., Ceulemans, E., & Mesquita, B. (2013). Acculturation of personality: A three-culture study of Japanese, Japanese Americans, and European Americans. *Journal of Cross-Cultural Psychology*, *44*(5), 701–18. https://doi.org/10.1177%2F0022022112470749

Heelas, P. (1996). Emotion talk across cultures. In R. Harré & W. G. Parrott (Eds.), *The emotions: Social, cultural and biological dimensions* (pp. 171–99). SAGE. https://doi.org/10.4135/9781446221952.n12

Heine, S. J., & Lehman, D. R. (2004). Move the body, change the self: Acculturative effects on the self-concept. In M. Schaller & C. S. Crandall (Eds.), *The psychological foundations of culture* (pp. 305–31). Lawrence Erlbaum Associates.

Henrich, J., Boyd, R., Derex, M., Kline, M. A., Mesoudi, A., Muthukrishna, M., Powell, A. T., Shennan, S. J., & Thomas, M. G. (2016). Understanding cumulative cultural evolution. *Proceedings of the National Academy of Sciences of the United States of America*, *113*(44), E6724–E6725. https://doi.org/10.1073/pnas.1610005113

Henrich, J., Heine, S. J., & Norenzayan, A. (2010). The weirdest people in the world? *Behavioral and Brain Sciences*, *33*(2–3), 61–83. https://doi.org/10.1017/S0140525X0999152X

Hermundstad, A. M., Bassett, D. S., Brown, K. S., Aminoff, E. M., Clewett, D., Freeman, S., Frithsen, A., Johnson, A., Tipper, C. M., Miller, M. B., Grafton, S. T., & Carlson, J. M. (2013). Structural foundations of resting-state and task-based functional connectivity in the human brain. *Proceedings of the National Academy of Sciences of the United States of America*, *110*(15), 6169–74. https://doi.org/10.1073/pnas.1219562110

Heyes, C. (2018). *Cognitive gadgets: The cultural evolution of thinking*. Belknap Press.

Hirschfeld, L. W. (2013). The myth of mentalizing and the primacy of folk sociology. In M. R. Banaji & S. A. Gelman (Eds.), *Navigating the social world: What infants, children, and other species can teach us* (pp. 101–6). Oxford University Press.

Hoemann, K., Wu, R., LobBue, V., Oakes, L. M., Xu, F., & Barrett, L. F. (2020). Developing an understanding of emotion categories: Lessons from objects. *Trends in Cognitive Sciences*, *24*, 39–51. https://doi.org/10.1016/j.tics.2019.10.010

Hoemann, K., Xu, F., & Barrett, L. F. (2019). Emotion words, emotion concepts, and emotional development in children: A constructionist hypothesis. *Developmental Psychology*, *55*, 1830–49. https://doi.org/10.1037/dev0000686

Hohwy, J. (2013). *The predictive mind*. Oxford University Press. https://doi.org/10.1093/acprof:oso/9780199682737.001.0001

Honey, C., Sporns, O., Cammoun, L., Gigandet, X., Thiran, J.-P., Meuli, R., & Hagmann, P. (2009). Predicting human resting-state functional connectivity from structural connectivity. *Proceedings of the National Academy of Sciences of the United States of America*, *106*(6), 2035–40. https://doi.org/10.1073/pnas.0811168106

Hong, Y.-y., Morris, M. W., Chiu, C.-y., & Benet-Martínez, V. (2000). Multicultural minds: A dynamic constructivist approach to culture and cognition. *American Psychologist*, *55*(7), 709–20. https://doi.org/10.1037/0003-066X.55.7.709

Hutchinson, J. B., & Barrett, L. F. (2019). The power of predictions: An emerging paradigm for psychological research. *Current Directions in Psychological Science*, *28*(3), 280–91. https://doi.org/10.1177%2F0963721419831992

Hyman, I. (2004). Setting the stage: Reviewing current knowledge on the health of Canadian immigrants: What is the evidence and where are the gaps? *Canadian Journal of Public Health*, *95*(3), I4–I8. www.jstor.org/stable/41994328

Jablonka, E., & Lamb, M. J. (2007). Précis of evolution in four dimensions. *Behavioral and Brain Sciences*, *30*(4), 353–65. https://doi.org/10.1017/S0140525X07002221

James, W. (2007). *The principles of psychology* (Vol. 1). Dover and Cosimo. (Original work published 1890)

Juster, R.-P., McEwen, B. S., & Lupien, S. J. (2010). Allostatic load biomarkers of chronic stress and impact on health and cognition. *Neuroscience & Biobehavioral Reviews*, *35*(1), 2–16. https://doi.org/10.1016/j.neubiorev.2009.10.002

Kan, I. P., Barsalou, L. W., Solomon, K. O., Minor, J. K., & Thompson-Schill, S. L. (2003). Role of mental imagery in a property verification task: fMRI evidence for perceptual representations of conceptual knowledge. *Cognitive Neuropsychology*, *20*(3–6), 525–40. https://doi.org/10.1080/02643290244000257

Kashdan, T. B., Barrett, L. F., & McKnight, P. E. (2015). Unpacking emotion differentiation: Transforming unpleasant experience by perceiving distinctions in negativity. *Current Directions in Psychological Science*, *24*(1), 10–16. https://doi.org/10.1177%2F0963721414550708

Keck, T., Keller, G. B., Jacobsen, R. I., Eysel, U. T., Bonhoeffer, T., & Hübener, M. (2013). Synaptic scaling and homeostatic plasticity in the mouse visual cortex in vivo. *Neuron*, *80*(2), 327–34. https://doi.org/10.1016/j.neuron.2013.08.018

Kitayama, S., Mesquita, B., & Karasawa, M. (2006). Cultural affordances and emotional experience: Socially engaging and disengaging emotions in Japan and the United States. *Journal of Personality and Social Psychology*, *91*(5), 890–903. https://doi.org/10.1037/0022-3514.91.5.890

Kitayama, S., & Salvador, C. E. (2017). Culture embrained: Going beyond the nature-nurture dichotomy. *Perspectives on Psychological Science*, *12*(5), 841–54. https://doi.org/10.1177/1745691617707317

Kleckner, I. R., Zhang, J., Touroutoglou, A., Chanes, L., Xia, C., Simmons, W. K., Quigley, K. S., Dickerson, B. C., & Barrett, L. F. (2017). Evidence for a large-scale brain system supporting allostasis and interoception in humans. *Nature Human Behaviour*, *1*, 0069. https://doi.org/10.1038/s41562-017-0069

Korte, S. M., Koolhaas, J. M., Wingfield, J. C., & McEwen, B. S. (2005). The Darwinian concept of stress: Benefits of allostasis and costs of allostatic load and the trade-offs in health and disease. *Neuroscience & Biobehavioral Reviews*, *29*(1), 3–38. https://doi.org/10.1016/j.neubiorev.2004.08.009

Kousta, S.-T., Vigliocco, G., Vinson, D. P., Andrews, M., & Del Campo, E. (2011). The representation of abstract words: Why emotion matters. *Journal of Experimental Psychology: General*, *140*(1), 14–34. https://doi.org/10.1037/a0021446

Kuppens, P., Tuerlinckx, F., Russell, J. A., & Barrett, L. F. (2013). The relation between valence and arousal in subjective experience. *Psychological Bulletin*, *139*(4), 917–40. https://doi.org/10.1037/a0030811

Laland, K. N., Odling-Smee, J., & Feldman, M. W. (2000). Niche construction, biological evolution, and cultural change. *Behavioral Brain Sciences*, *23*(1), 131–46. https://doi.org/10.1017/S0140525X00002417

Levy, R. I. (1975). *Tahitians: Mind and experience in the Society Islands*. University of Chicago Press.

Lewontin, R. (2000). *The triple helix: Gene, organism, and environment*. Harvard University Press.

Lillard, A. (1998). Ethnopsychologies: Cultural variations in theories of mind. *Psychological Bulletin*, *123*(1), 3–32. https://doi.org/10.1037/0033-2909.123.1.3

Lindquist, K. A., Gendron, M., Oosterwijk, S., & Barrett, L. F. (2013). Do people essentialize emotions? Individual differences in emotion essentialism and emotional experience. *Emotion*, *13*(4), 629–44. https://doi.org/10.1037/a0032283

Lindquist, K. A., Satpute, A. B., Wager, T. D., Weber, J., & Barrett, L. F. (2016). The brain basis of positive and negative affect: Evidence from a meta-analysis of the human neuroimaging literature. *Cerebral Cortex*, *26*(5), 1910–22. https://doi.org/10.1093/cercor/bhv001

Linnet, J. T. (2011). Money can't buy me *hygge*: Danish middle-class consumption, egalitarianism, and the sanctity of inner space. *Social Analysis*, *55*(2), 21–44. https://doi.org/10.3167/sa.2011.550202

Lipo, C. P., O'Brien, M. J., Collard, M., & Shennan, S. (2006). *Mapping our ancestors: Phylogenetic approaches in anthropology and prehistory*. New Aldine Transaction.

Lochmann, T., & Denève, S. (2011). Neural processing as causal inference. *Current Opinion in Neurobiology*, *21*(5), 774–81. https://doi.org/10.1016/j.conb.2011.05.018

Low, L. K., & Cheng, H.-J. (2006). Axon pruning: An essential step underlying the developmental plasticity of neuronal connections. *Philosophical Transactions of the Royal Society B: Biological Sciences*, *361*(1473), 1531–44. https://doi.org/10.1098/rstb.2006.1883

Markus, H. R., & Kitayama, S. (1991). Culture and the self: Implications for cognition, emotion, and motivation. *Psychological Review*, *98*(2), 224–53. https://doi.org/10.1037/0033-295X.98.2.224

McEwen, B. S. (2005). Stressed or stressed out: What is the difference? *Journal of Psychiatry and Neuroscience*, *30*(5), 315–18. http://jpn.ca/wp-content/uploads/2014/04/30-5-315.pdf

Medin, D., & Ortony, A. (1989). Comments on part I: Psychological essentialism. In S. Vosniadou & A. Ortony (Eds.), *Similarity and analogical reasoning* (pp. 179–96). Cambridge University Press. https://doi.org/10.1017/CBO9780511529863.009

Mesoudi, A., Whiten, A., & Laland, K. N. (2006). Towards a unified science of cultural evolution. *Behavioral and Brain Sciences*, *29*(4), 329–47. https://doi.org/10.1017/S0140525X06009083

Mesquita, B. (2001). Emotions in collectivist and individualist contexts. *Journal of Personality and Social Psychology*, *80*(1), 68–74. https://doi.org/10.1037/0022-3514.80.1.68

Mesquita, B., & Boiger, M. (2014). Emotions in context: A sociodynamic model of emotions. *Emotion Review*, *6*(4), 298–302. https://doi.org/10.1177%2F1754073914534480

Mesquita, B., De Leersnyder, J., & Jasini, A. (2019). The cultural psychology of acculturation. In S. Kitayama & D. Cohen (Eds.), *Handbook of cultural psychology* (2nd ed.). Guilford Press.

Mesquita, B., & Frijda, N. H. (1992). Cultural variations in emotions: A review. *Psychological Bulletin*, *112*(2), 179–204. https://doi.org/10.1037/0033-2909.112.2.179

Mithen, S., & Parsons, L. (2008). The brain as a cultural artefact. *Cambridge Archaeological Journal*, *18*(3), 415–22. https://doi.org/10.1017/S0959774308000450

Mitra, A., & Raichle, M. E. (2016). How networks communicate: Propagation patterns in spontaneous brain activity. *Philosophical Transactions of the Royal Society B: Biological Sciences*, *371*(1705), 20150546. https://doi.org/10.1098/rstb.2015.0546

Murphy, G. L. (2002). *The big book of concepts*. MIT Press.

Muthukrishna, M., & Henrich, J. (2016). Innovation in the collective brain. *Philosophical Transactions of the Royal Society B: Biological Sciences*, *371* (1690), 20150192. https://doi.org/10.1098/rstb.2015.0192

Nguyen, A.-M. D., & Benet-Martínez, V. (2013). Biculturalism and adjustment: A meta-analysis. *Journal of Cross-Cultural Psychology*, *44*(1), 122–59. https://doi.org/10.1177/0022022111435097

Niedenthal, P. M., Winkielman, P., Mondillon, L., & Vermeulen, N. (2009). Embodiment of emotion concepts. *Journal of Personality and Social Psychology*, *96*(6), 1120–36. https://doi.org/10.1037/a0015574

Odling-Smee, F. J., Laland, K. N., & Feldman, M. W. (2003). *Niche construction: The neglected process in evolution*. Princeton University Press.

Oosterwijk, S., Mackey, S., Wilson-Mendenhall, C., Winkielman, P., & Paulus, M. P. (2015). Concepts in context: Processing mental state concepts with internal or external focus involves different neural systems. *Social Neuroscience*, *10*(3), 294–307. https://doi.org/10.1080/17470919.2014.998840

Pavlenko, A. (2009). Conceptual representation in the bilingual lexicon and second language vocabulary learning. In A. Pavlenko (Ed.), *The bilingual mental lexicon: Interdisciplinary approaches* (pp. 125–60). Multilingual Matters.

Pavlenko, A. (2014). *The bilingual mind: And what it tells us about language and thought*. Cambridge University Press.

Peek, M. K., Cutchin, M. P., Salinas, J. J., Sheffield, K. M., Eschbach, K., Stowe, R. P., & Goodwin, J. S. (2010). Allostatic load among non-Hispanic Whites, non-Hispanic Blacks, and people of Mexican origin: Effects of ethnicity, nativity, and acculturation. *American Journal of Public Health*, *100*(5), 940–5. https://doi.org/10.2105/AJPH.2007.129312

Pezzulo, G., Rigoli, F., & Friston, K. (2015). Active Inference, homeostatic regulation and adaptive behavioural control. *Progress in Neurobiology*, *134*, 17–35. https://doi.org/10.1016/j.pneurobio.2015.09.001

Pouliasi, K., & Verkuyten, M. (2012). Understanding the relational self: An intergenerational study in the Netherlands and Greece. *European Psychologist*, *17*(3), 182–9. https://doi.org/10.1027/1016-9040/a000095

Ramstead, M. J. D., Veissière, S. P. L., & Kirmayer, L. J. (2016). Cultural affordances: Scaffolding local worlds through shared intentionality and regimes of attention. *Frontiers in Psychology*, *7*, 1090. https://doi.org/10.3389%2Ffpsyg.2016.01090

Rao, R. P. N., & Ballard, D. H. (1999). Predictive coding in the visual cortex: A functional interpretation of some extra-classical receptive-field effects. *Nature Neuroscience*, *2*(1), 79–87. https://doi.org/10.1038/4580

Rebollo, I., Devauchelle, A-D., Béranger, B., & Tallon-Baudry, C. (2018). Stomach-brain synchrony reveals delayed-connectivity resting-state network in humans. *eLIFE*, *7*, e33321. https://doi.org/10.7554/eLife.33321.001

Richerson, P. J., & Boyd, R. (2005). *Not by genes alone: How culture transformed human evolution*. University of Chicago Press.

Russell, J. A. (1980). A circumplex model of affect. *Journal of Personality and Social Psychology*, *39*(6), 1161–78. http://psycnet.apa.org/doi/10.1037/h0077714

Russell, J. A. (1991). Culture and the categorization of emotions. *Psychological Bulletin*, *110*(3), 426–50. https://doi.org/10.1037/0033-2909.110.3.426

Sam, D. L., & Berry, J. W. (2010). Acculturation: When individuals and groups of different cultural backgrounds meet. *Perspectives on Psychological Science*, *5*(4), 472–81. https://doi.org/10.1177/1745691610373075

Savani, K., Morris, M. W., Naidu, N. V. R., Kumar, S., & Berlia, N. V. (2011). Cultural conditioning: Understanding interpersonal accommodation in India and the United States in terms of the modal characteristics of interpersonal influence situations. *Journal of Personality and Social Psychology*, *100*(1), 84–102. https://doi.org/10.1037/a0021083

Schulkin, J. (2010). Social allostasis: Anticipatory regulation of the internal milieu. *Frontiers in Evolutionary Neuroscience*, *2*, 111. https://doi.org/10.3389/fnevo.2010.00111

Searle, J. R. (1992). *The rediscovery of the mind*. MIT Press.

Searle, J. R. (2004). *Mind: A brief introduction*. Oxford University Press.

Seeley, W. W., Menon, V., Schatzberg, A. F., Keller, J., Glover, G. H., Kenna, H., Reiss, A. A., & Greicius, M. D. (2007). Dissociable intrinsic connectivity networks for salience processing and executive control. *Journal of Neuroscience*, *27*(9), 2349–56. https://doi.org/10.1523/JNEUROSCI.5587-06.2007

Seth, A. K. (2013). Interoceptive inference, emotion, and the embodied self. *Trends in Cognitive Sciences*, *17*(11), 565–73. https://doi.org/10.1016/j.tics.2013.09.007

Seth, A. K., Suzuki, K., & Critchley, H. D. (2012). An interoceptive predictive coding model of conscious presence. *Frontiers in Psychology*, *2*, 395. https://doi.org/10.3389/fpsyg.2011.00395

Shweder, R. A., Goodnow, J. J., Hatano, G., LeVine, R. A., Markus, H. R., & Miller, P. J. (1998). The cultural psychology of development: One mind, many mentalities. In W. Damon & R. M. Lerner (Eds.), *Handbook of child psychology: Theoretical models of human development* (Vol. 1, 5th ed., pp. 865–937). John Wiley & Sons.

Siegel, E. H., Sands, M. K., Van den Noortgate, W., Condon, P., Chang, Y., Dy, J., Quigley, K. S., & Barrett, L. F. (2018). Emotion fingerprints or emotion populations? A meta-analytic investigation of autonomic features of emotion categories. *Psychological Bulletin*, *144*(4), 343–93. https://doi.org/10.1037/bul0000128

Smith, C. A., & Lazarus, R. S. (1993). Appraisal components, core relational themes, and the emotions. *Cognition and Emotion*, *7*(3–4), 233–69. https://doi.org/10.1080/02699939308409189

Smyser, C. D., Snyder, A. Z., & Neil, J. J. (2011). Functional connectivity MRI in infants: Exploration of the functional organization of the developing brain. *NeuroImage, 56*(3), 1437–52. https://doi.org/10.1016/j.neuroimage.2011.02.073

Sporns, O. (2011). *Networks of the brain*. MIT Press.

Spratling, M. W. (2017). A review of predictive coding algorithms. *Brain and Cognition, 112*, 92–7. https://doi.org/10.1016/j.bandc.2015.11.003

Sterling, P. (2012). Allostasis: A model of predictive regulation. *Physiology & Behavior, 106*(1), 5–15. https://doi.org/10.1016/j.physbeh.2011.06.004

Sterling, P., & Eyer, J. (1988). Allostasis: A new paradigm to explain arousal pathology. In S. Fisher & J. Reason (Eds.), *Handbook of life stress, cognition and health* (pp. 629–49). John Wiley & Sons.

Sterling, P., & Laughlin, S. (2015). *Principles of neural design*. MIT Press.

Taylor, T. (2006). The human brain is a cultural artefact. *Edge: What is your dangerous idea?* www.edge.org/response-detail/11835

Theriault, J. E., Young, L., & Barrett, L. F. (2019). The sense of should: A biologically based model of social pressure. *PsyArXiv*. Advance online publication. https://doi.org/10.31234/osf.io/x5rbs

Tomasello, M. (2014). The ultra-social animal. *European Journal of Social Psychology, 44*(3), 187–94. https://doi.org/10.1002%2Fejsp.2015

Uchida, Y., Townsend, S. S. M., Markus, H. R., & Bergsieker, H. B. (2009). Emotions as within or between people? Cultural variation in lay theories of emotion expression and inference. *Personality and Social Psychology Bulletin, 35*(11), 1427–39. https://doi.org/10.1177/0146167209347322

van den Heuvel, M. P., & Sporns, O. (2013). Network hubs in the human brain. *Trends in Cognitive Sciences, 17*(12), 683–96. https://doi.org/10.1016/j.tics.2013.09.012

Vilares, I., & Kording, K. (2011). Bayesian models: The structure of the world, uncertainty, behavior, and the brain. *Annals of the New York Academy of Sciences, 1224*(1), 22–39. https://doi.org/10.1111/j.1749-6632.2011.05965.x.

Waxman, S. R., & Gelman, S. A. (2010). Different kinds of concepts and different kinds of words: What words do for human cognition. In D. Mareschal, P. C. Quinn, & S. E. G. Lea (Eds.), *Oxford series in developmental neuroscience. The making of human concepts* (pp. 101–30). Oxford University Press. https://doi.org/10.1093/acprof:oso/9780199549221.003.06

Wierzbicka, A. (1999). *Emotions across languages and cultures: Diversity and universals*. Cambridge University Press.

Wilson-Mendenhall, C. D., Barrett, L. F., Simmons, W. K., & Barsalou, L. W. (2011). Grounding emotion in situated conceptualization. *Neuropsychologia, 49*(5), 1105–27. https://doi.org/10.1016%2Fj.neuropsychologia.2010.12.032

Wundt, W. (1897). *Outlines of psychology* (C. H. Judd, Trans.). Wilhelm Engelmann and Gustav E. Stechert. (Original work published 1896)

Yeo, B. T. T., Krienen, F. M., Eickhoff, S. B., Yaakub, S. N., Fox, P. T., Buckner, R. L., Asplund, C. L., & Chee, M. W. L. (2015). Functional specialization and flexibility in human association cortex. *Cerebral Cortex, 25*(10), 3654–72. https://doi.org/10.1093/cercor/bhu217

7 Cultural Priming Effects and the Human Brain

Shihui Han and Georg Northoff

Introduction

Cultural neuroscience aims to investigate how culture modulates the functional organization of the human brain and interacts with our genes (Chiao & Ambady, 2007; Han, 2017; Han & Northoff, 2008; Han et al., 2013). A primary method in this field is cross-cultural brain imaging – mainly magnetic resonance imaging (MRI) and electroencephalography (EEG) – which compares brain activity underlying specific cognitive or affective processes of individuals belonging to different cultural groups. This approach has revealed ample evidence for broad cultural group differences between individuals educated in Western or East Asian societies in brain activity underlying perception, attention, mental causation, self-reflection, emotion, reward, and decision-making (e.g., Hedden et al., 2008; Ma, Wang, et al., 2014; Mu et al., 2015; Zhu et al., 2007; see Han, 2017; Han & Northoff, 2008; Han et al., 2013 for review; Han & Ma, 2014 for a meta-analysis). There is also evidence that both functional brain activity and gray-matter volume are correlated with specific cultural values endorsed by individuals on dimensions such as independence/interdependence (Kitayama et al., 2017; Ma, Wang, et al., 2014; Wang et al., 2017; Kitayama, Chapter 3, *this volume*). In addition, the association between brain activity and specific cultural values can vary between two variants of a specific gene (Luo et al., 2015, 2017; Ma, Wang, et al., 2014). The findings suggest that culture influences brain activities involved in multiple cognitive (e.g., attention) and affective (e.g., empathy) processes and provide support for a neuroscience account of cultural group differences in cognition and behavior.

Thus far, however, research demonstrating cultural group differences in brain activities related to cognitive and affective processes is correlational. In cross-cultural brain imaging studies, the cultural groups being sampled may differ in terms of language, history, physical environment, or other ecological contexts. In addition, the cultural groups may differ in many aspects relating to cultural beliefs or values and behavioral scripts. In such experiments, participants are not randomly assigned to a cultural group and culture is not a manipulated variable. Researchers have therefore been unable to determine which aspects of culture provide the best explanation for cultural group differences in brain activity underlying a specific task.

To examine causal relationships between culture and brain, clarifying whether and how cultural experiences shape the brain, cultural neuroscientists have developed an experimental method known as *cultural priming*, which studies effects on much shorter time frames than developmental, trait, or "long-term" studies. Cultural priming – that is, presenting individuals with cultural cues or symbols and determining their influence on thoughts, behavior, or emotions – integrates the concepts of a dynamic cultural system and neural plasticity and combines brain imaging and various behavioral paradigms. This line of research is opening new avenues for understanding the causal relationships between culture and the brain's functional activity. This chapter explores some of these new avenues and is organized as follows. First, we introduce concepts of culture that emphasize its dynamic properties. We then summarize research that provides evidence for the effects of cultural priming on cognition and brain activity. Finally, we discuss the implications of cultural priming effects on the brain.

Dynamic Culture and Plastic Brain

Although cultural neuroscience studies cultural group differences in brain activity, researchers do not conceptualize "culture" as a static monolithic entity, deeply rooted in a particular social group. Instead, like cultural psychology (Hong et al., 2000; Markus & Hamedani, 2007), we view culture as a dynamic system of values, beliefs, and behavioral scripts shared by individuals belonging to a particular social group. Culture can also be understood as a form of "situated cognition" (Oyserman, 2011), whereby mental processes vary according to environmental influences, and this dynamic determines which information is accessible and how information is processed and interpreted (Oyserman, 2011; Oyserman & Lee, 2007; Oyserman et al., 2014). Long-term cultural learning can contribute to a default cultural mindset (e.g., individualistic or collectivist), which, when activated, facilitates information processing and appropriate decision-making or behavior in a specific cultural environment. This understanding essentially underlies how cultural neuroscientists observe and interpret cultural group differences in brain activity involved in a specific task. Our dynamic view of culture further suggests that every individual's cultural mindset is flexible, inclusive, and modifiable from moment to moment. In other words, this view emphasizes the possibility of short-term changes in cultural values and beliefs.

A dynamic view of culture has several important implications. First, while a child acquires cultural values/beliefs and behavioral scripts through social learning from parents and peers, life experiences (such as emigrating from their native country) can change their values, beliefs, and behavioral scripts. Social learning in a new culture can also serve to "update" an individual's previous cultural system, and this can be extremely important for successful adaptation to a new sociocultural environment (see Chapter 6). Migration is occurring with increasing frequency in contemporary societies, where opportunities for cultural exchange, international education, and employment have expanded. Second, learning ability can vary greatly across individuals from the same social group (e.g., a country, a city, or a local community) and influence how well they acquire cultural values/beliefs and behavioral scripts. Consequently, the degree of endorsement of cultural values and beliefs can vary substantially across social group members. Third, modern societies are becoming increasingly multicultural rather than being monocultural. Both children and adults are exposed to the values/beliefs and behavioral scripts of other cultures through movies, social media, international travel, and education. Such cultural experiences make it highly possible that an individual endorses multiple cultural systems and values. In addition, frequent travel across different cultural environments requires a form of "code-switching" between different cultural meaning systems in order to coordinate with others during social interactions. Consistent with these propositions, behavioral research has provided ample evidence that an individual can switch between their native cultural knowledge systems and a new cultural knowledge system so as to increase flexibility in cognition and behavior when interacting with people from different cultures (Hong et al., 2000, 2007). Thus, culture provides a dynamic framework for cognition that underlies our behavior.

The dynamic model of culture also predicts that brain activity underlying cognitive/affective processes may vary on a short temporal scale as a function of recent exposure to one cultural system or another. That is, on the one hand, the existence of cultural group differences in neural correlates of cognition and emotion suggests potential long-term cultural influences on the brain. On the other hand, the brain as a biological organ is highly flexible in response to environment and experiences (Shaw & McEachern, 2001). Substantial neuroscience findings have demonstrated that the brain's neuroplasticity, an intrinsic property, enables the nervous system to respond to environmental pressures, physiological changes, and individual experiences (Pascual-Leone et al., 2005) and to adapt to social contexts during development (Blakemore, 2008). The neuroplasticity of the human brain allows for functional and structural changes in response to both long-term and short-term experiences.

The concept of neuroplasticity – the brain's ability to form or modify neural connections based on activity – is fundamentally important for cultural neuroscience research. Long-term sociocultural experiences may assign different meanings to the same task (e.g., as a reflection of one's own social identity) in different societies. This context sensitivity can result in the engagement of distinct cognitive strategies or processes in two cultural groups that are mediated by discrete brain activities. Long-term sustained engagement of a brain region in a culturally specific task may even result in associations between cultural values/beliefs and the magnitude of the functional response or change in gray matter volume in a specific brain region (Kitayama et al., 2017; Ma, Bang, et al., 2014; Wang et al., 2017). Neuroplasticity also implicates short-term changes of brain activities involved in a specific task. Short-term cultural experiences such as recent use or temporary activation of specific cultural knowledge may also shift cognitive strategies or processes involved in a specific task and consequently result in changes of brain activity engaged in cognition and emotion.

This hypothesis has been tested by researchers who integrated brain imaging and cultural priming to examine whether and how specific cultural beliefs/values induce subsequent variations in brain activity underlying specific cognitive/affective processes. The cultural priming approach to investigating the relationship between culture and brain typically measures behavior or brain activity in a sample of people from the same cultural group before and after cultural priming. By comparing the same people before and after priming, this approach excludes the influences of language, physical environment, and other potential confounding factors on brain and cognition. Moreover, cultural priming paradigms allow inferences about causal relationships between culture and brain. This is because, in this approach, behavior and brain activity are measured immediately after priming manipulations; researchers therefore can test whether the patterns of variations of behavior and brain activity after the priming fit predictions based on a causal model. Finally, the cultural priming approach allows researchers to examine the effect of a specific cultural belief/value on the dynamic brain activity involved in cognitive and affective processes. Taken together, the findings of cultural neuroscience studies employing cultural group comparison and cultural priming provide converging evidence that culture as shared beliefs/values or situated cognition influences how the brain functions to give rise to specific types of cognition and behavior (Han, 2017; Han et al., 2013; Han & Humphreys, 2016).

Cultural Priming Effects on Cognition

Cultural psychologists have developed several paradigms to prime specific cultural values or cognitive styles (Oyserman & Lee, 2007). For example, Wong and Hong (2005) used pictures of cultural symbols, such as a Chinese dragon or the American flag, as cues to induce a switch between East Asian and Western cultural beliefs/values or frames in bicultural individuals. Early research also developed the Sumerian Warrior Story task and the Similarities and Differences with Family and Friends task to evoke individualistic or collectivistic cultural values or frames (Trafimow et al., 1991). The Sumerian Warrior Story describes a dilemma in which Sostoras, a military general, has to decide which warrior to send to a king. In one version of the story that aims to prime individualism, Sostoras chooses the warrior because his ability and traits qualify him for the job. In another version that aims to prime collectivism, Sostoras chooses the warrior who is a member of his own family and thus the relationship between individuals is emphasized. After reading the story, participants make a judgment about whether or not they admire the general. The Similarities and Differences with Family and Friends task asks participants to think for a short period of time about what makes them different from their family and friends (to prime values of individualism) or else what they have in common with their family and friends (to prime values of collectivism). Participants are then required to write a short essay about their thoughts.

Studies have shown that cultural priming influences social cognitive processes related to both oneself and others. Wong and Hong (2005) first exposed Chinese college students in Hong Kong to slides of Chinese or American cultural icons. Thereafter, participants played a Prisoner's Dilemma game, which assesses the payoffs of cooperating or defecting, with either friends or strangers. In this game, participants had to decide whether to cooperate or to defect and the outcome depended on the strategies that both players choose. Defecting resulted in a better individual outcome for the participant, regardless of whether their partner chose cooperation or defection. However, participants could get a better joint outcome if both partners chose to cooperate. The study found that priming Chinese (vs. American) culture led to more cooperative decisions with friends but fewer cooperative decisions with strangers after both Chinese and American cultural priming. Ng and Lai (2009) showed that the self-concept of bicultural Chinese became more socially connected after Chinese versus Western cultural priming. They examined self-concept in Chinese college students in Hong Kong using a self-reference task consisting of an encoding phase (to judge whether trait adjectives describe oneself and others) and a retrieval phase (to recall the trait adjectives related to oneself and others). Participants performed the self-referential task after being exposed to icons of Chinese culture (e.g., the Great Wall) or Western culture (e.g., the British parliament). The researchers found that Western cultural priming led to recalling more information related to the self than information related to others (including a nonidentified person and a participant's mother). In contrast, priming Chinese culture made participants remember information related to the self and others equally well. Similar results were reported in a study with Chinese college students in Beijing who were primed with Chinese/American cultural icons (Sui et al., 2007).

These paradigms of cultural priming can be understood in terms of the individualism–collectivism framework, which distinguishes two different cultural values that give prominence to individuals or to the social group, respectively (Oyserman & Lee, 2008), and which are also thought to reflect a tendency to employ analytic (individualistic) or holistic (collectivistic) forms of reasoning (Miyamoto, 2013). However, viewing pictures of cultural symbols or reading stories may activate numerous cultural values, beliefs, and known facts. Therefore, researchers have developed priming tasks that activate a culturally specific psychological construct. For example, Utz (2004) primed independence or interdependence by asking German college students to reorganize scrambled sentences that contained words such as "individual," "self-contained," and "independent" to activate the concept of independence or words such as "group," "friendships," and "together" to activate the concept of interdependence. Participants then played a four-coin give-some dilemma game, ostensibly with another participant. At the beginning of each round, each player had four coins worth 1 euro to him/herself but 2 euros to the other person, and had to decide how many (0, 1, 2, 3, or 4) of their four coins to give to the other person. Participants primed with independence (vs. interdependence) gave less money to the other person, indicating lower levels of cooperation. The findings support the claim that priming independence (vs. interdependence) leads to increased focus on one's own benefit with the cost of ignoring the benefit to others.

Self-construal priming is another simple procedure designed specifically for shifting self-construal styles: interdependent (inherently connected to or interrelated with others) or independent (bounded, unique, distinct from others) (Brewer & Gardner, 1996; Gardner et al., 1999). Participants are presented with two versions of short essays that describe a trip or a story. The two versions differ only with respect to pronouns. To prime independent self-construals, participants are asked to read essays in which singular pronouns (e.g., "I," " mine," "my") are used. The procedure to prime interdependent self-construals is the same except for the use of plural pronouns (e.g., "we," "ours," "us"). Participants are asked to read the essays and circle all the pronouns in the essays. Essays used for the control priming task are similar except that no independent or interdependent pronouns appear in an essay. The different versions of priming materials putatively lead participants to focus their attention on the self as an individual or as a member of a social group. Gardner et al. (1999) found that in a social judgment task that measured the extent to which interpersonal norms of helping behavior were seen as objective obligation, persons primed with independence tended to perceive lower obligations to others in their social network whereas those primed with interdependence perceived higher social obligations to others.

Evidence from behavioral research further suggests that self-construal priming influences multiple-level social cognitive and affective processes by testing participants from different sociocultural environments. Early cultural priming research focused on variations in cognitive style with respect to visual perception and attention induced by self-construal priming. For example, Kühnen and Oyserman (2002) tested the hypothesis that priming interdependent self-construals drives individuals to focus on contextual information or the relationship between perceptual objects whereas priming an independent self-construal biases their attention to focal objects. The researchers primed one group of participants with independence and another group with interdependence before all participants were asked to identify either the global or local letters in a compound stimulus made up of a large letter composed of small ones. They found that participants primed with independence responded faster to local letters relative to global letters, whereas participants primed with interdependence tended to respond faster to global than local letters. These effects were observed in a sample consisting of individuals who self-identified as White, Black, Asian, or Hispanic. To further assess whether self-construal priming can produce bidirectional effects on global and local processing, Lin and Han (2009) measured response speeds to global and local letters in compound stimuli after independent and interdependent self-construals had been primed. A control priming condition was also included in which participants read essays that included neither independent nor interdependent pronouns. They found that, relative to the control priming condition, priming interdependence resulted in faster responses to global than local targets whereas a reverse pattern of reaction times was observed after independent self-construal priming. The findings suggest that priming independent or interdependent self-construals can shift cognitive styles toward enhanced attention to a focal object or to contextual information, respectively.

Self-construal priming effects are also evident in social cognition and social behavior. Colzato et al. (2012) examined how priming interdependent or independent self-construals influences corepresentation of actions of oneself and a co-actor using a social Simon task during which two participants sat next to each other and responded to the color (green or blue) of a dot that might appear to the left or right of a central fixation of circles. Each participant responded by pressing one of two keys and had to ignore stimulus locations. The social Simon effect refers to the finding that participants respond faster when the sitting position and the target required to be responded to are spatially correspondent than when they are incongruent. If priming interdependence (vs. independence) draws people's attention to the co-actor, one would expect a greater social Simon effect when interdependence is primed. This is indeed what Colzato et al. (2012) found: participants primed with interdependence showed a larger social Simon effect in reaction times relative to those primed with independence.

Taken together, the findings summarized here indicate that cultural priming, using either pictures of cultural icons or semantic single/plural pronouns, results in changes of multiple cognitive and affective processes involved in perception, memory, and economic decisions. These behavioral findings suggest a causal relationship between cultural values/beliefs (e.g., interdependence or independence) and cognition/emotion. The findings support the proposition that an individual can have two sets of cultural knowledge systems that, under certain circumstances, can be dynamically switched in response to sociocultural environments and experiences in order to adjust social behavior. The findings also implicate potential influences of cultural priming on brain activities underlying cognition and emotion.

Cultural Priming Effects on the Brain

The findings regarding cultural priming effects on cognition and behavior have inspired cultural neuroscientists to examine whether and how cultural priming modulates brain activity underlying cognition and behavior. There are several motives behind this line of research. First, given that cognition and behavior are mediated by the brain, researchers are interested in how cultural priming effects are implemented in the brain (Han, 2015). Clarifying how cultural priming modulates human brain activity related to cognitive and affective processes is important for several reasons. The findings would help researchers to construct theoretical models of brain functional reorganization due to shifts of cultural values/beliefs; these models may enhance prediction of people's behavioral changes in specific sociocultural contexts. Second, if cultural priming induces changes of brain activities underlying cognition and behavior, one may further infer a causal relationship between culture and brain (which, however, cannot be demonstrated by the findings of cross-cultural brain studies). In particular, integration of cultural priming and brain imaging allows researchers to investigate how a specific cultural value or belief modulates brain activity underlying a specific cognitive/affective process. From this point of view, integration of cultural priming and brain imaging goes beyond cross-cultural comparisons of brain imaging results, which are always confronted with the difficulty of explaining which aspects of culture give rise to the results. Third, any findings of cultural priming effects on brain activity would provide direct evidence that cultural beliefs/values provide a mental scaffolding for the brain. This perspective is particularly important for understanding brain functional organization from an evolutionary perspective (Han & Ma, 2015). As physical environments become increasingly similar, particularly for people who live in urban areas (two-thirds of the world's population by 2050; United Nations, 2018), variations in human brain development may be more reflective of cultural contexts than of climate or geography. In sum, integration of cultural priming and brain imaging can provide new and deeper insights into the functional organization of the brain's neural networks.

Cultural neuroscience studies have accumulated evidence that short-term cultural priming can modulate human brain activities engaged in multiple sensory, perceptual, cognitive, and affective processes. For example, to investigate whether and how temporary shifts in self-construals modulate sensory and perceptual processing during physical pain, using electroencephalography (EEG), a method for measuring ongoing electrical brain activity, Wang et al. (2014) recorded event-related potentials (ERPs) in response to painful and nonpainful electrical stimulations administered to Chinese adults. Physical pain is mediated by a neural circuit including the primary and secondary somatosensory cortex (SI and SII, respectively), anterior cingulate, insula, and supplementary motor area (Peyron et al., 2000). ERP studies uncovered electrophysiological responses to painful stimulation, including two early negative deflections that peak at 60 and 130 milliseconds after the onset of stimulation (called N60 and N130; ERP components are labeled N/P for negative/positive polarity), which arise from the contralateral SI/SII and mediate somatosensory processing of physical pain, and a late activity that arises from the anterior cingulate cortex (ACC) and mediates cognitive evaluation of and affective responses to physical pain (Bromm & Chen, 1995; Christmann et al., 2007; Zaslansky et al., 1996). If priming independent (vs. interdependent) self-construal leads to increased self-focus, one would expect enhanced neural activity in response to painful stimulations after independent self-construal priming. Indeed, it was found that painful compared to nonpainful electrical stimulations to the left hand enlarged the amplitudes of the N130 and two positive activities peaking at 90 and 300–400 milliseconds after stimulus onset (i.e., P90 and P300). Moreover, independent compared to interdependent self-construal priming induced larger N130 amplitudes to painful stimulation, which were of larger amplitude over the right central electrodes and originated from the right somatosensory cortex. This result suggests that independent self-construal priming modulates the early sensory processing of physical pain by providing a cognitive frame of enhanced self-focus.

Self-construal priming also affects neural activity involved in perception. Lin et al. (2008) recorded ERPs during a task to discriminate the global/local letters in a compound stimulus (a large letter composed of small ones) from Chinese adults who had been primed with interdependent or interdependent self-construals. This design allows researchers to examine whether the neural activity in the extrastriate cortex underlying the global/local perception of compound stimuli is modulated by self-construal priming. They adjusted the visual angle of the compound stimuli so that, under a control priming

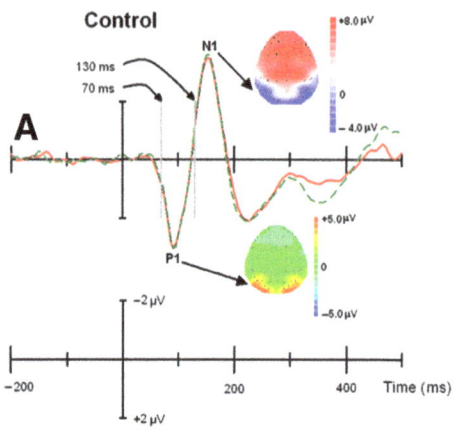
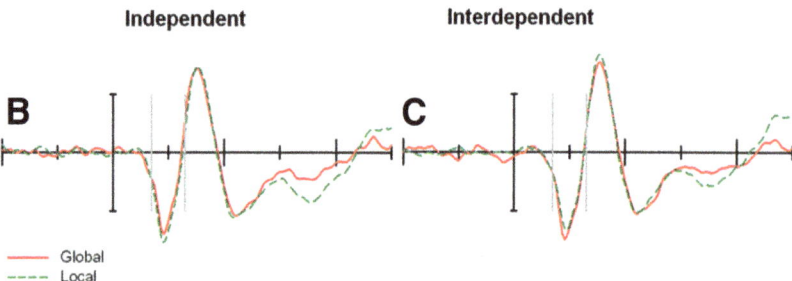

Figure 7.1 Illustration of the variation of P1 amplitude in (A) neutral, (B) independent, and (C) interdependent self-construal priming.
Adapted from *Biological Psychology, 77*(1), Z. Lin, Y. Lin, and S. Han, "Self-Construal Priming Modulates Visual Activity Underlying Global/Local Perception," p. 95 (https://doi.org/10.1016/j.biopsycho.2007.08.002). Copyright 2007, with permission from Elsevier

condition, the amplitude of the P1 component over the occipital cortex, which originates from the extrastriate cortex and underlies early visual perception (e.g., Martínez et al., 1999), was comparable between the global and local task. However, it was found that independent self-construal priming resulted in larger P1 amplitude to local relative to global targets, whereas interdependent self-construal priming led to larger P1 amplitude to global than local targets (Figure 7.1). This finding suggests that self-construal priming influences visual perceptual processing of local and global properties of compound stimuli by modulating the extrastriate activity at an early stage of visual processing.

According to Markus and Kitayama (1991), independent self-construals encourage self-focus, whereas interdependent self-construals emphasize fundamental social connections and attention to others. This proposition predicts that priming independent (vs. interdependent) self-construals should facilitate processing of self-relevant information such as the appearance of one's own face. Sui and Han (2007) tested this hypothesis by scanning twelve neurologically healthy adults whose native language was Chinese using fMRI while they viewed photos of their own faces or of a friend and made judgments about the photo's orientation (left or right) by pressing a button. Prior to the judgment task, participants were primed with independent or interdependent pronouns (e.g., *I* or *we*). If priming independence (vs. interdependence) promotes a mindset of self-focus, one would expect enhanced brain activity in response to one's own face after independent self-construal priming. Both behavioral performance and fMRI results support this prediction. Participants showed faster responses to their own faces than that of a friend after independent self-construal priming but faster responses to a friend's face than their own after interdependent self-construal priming. In addition, the right middle frontal activity in response to their own faces was increased by independent self-construal priming but decreased by interdependent self-construal priming. The behavioral and brain imaging results consistently suggest that in human adults, the neural correlates of self-awareness associated with recognition of one's own face are modulated by short-term self-construal priming (Figure 7.2), suggesting a causal relationship between self-construals and brain responses during self-face recognition.

Cultural priming also modulates brain activity mediating reflection on the personality traits of oneself and others. Ng et al. (2010) integrated cultural priming and a self-referential task that required judgments of this type. They primed Chinese college students in Hong Kong with typical Chinese (e.g., the Great Wall) or Western (e.g., the British parliament) cultural icons before fMRI scanning, during which participants performed personality traits judgments on the self, their mothers, and an unidentified person with whom they would not identify. Because the previous research found overlapping neural representations of the self and mother in the medial prefrontal cortex (mPFC) in Chinese but not Westerners (Zhu et al., 2007), one would predict that priming participants with Western cultural icons would increase the neural differentiation of the self and others while priming with Chinese cultural icons would enhance the neural overlapping of the self and others. Indeed, after Western cultural priming, self-judgments induced increased activity in the mPFC relative to both the unidentified person and the mother, whereas after Chinese cultural priming, the fMRI results failed to show any brain activation in the contrast of self vs. mother and self vs. unidentified person. The effects were produced by the fact that Western (vs. Chinese) cultural priming both increased mPFC activity related to the self and decreased mPFC activity related to others. It appears that Western/Chinese cultural priming modulated neural activity related to both the self and others in order to enhance the neural

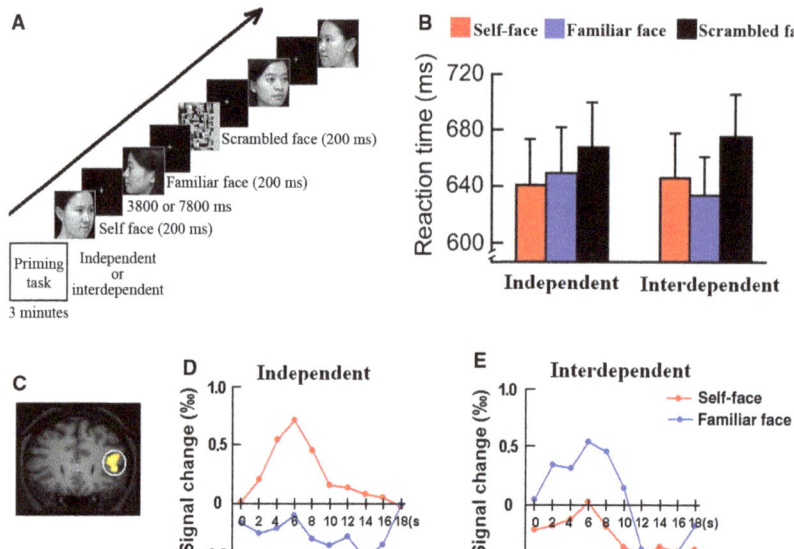

Figure 7.2 Illustration of the self-construal priming procedure and the face-recognition task. After the self-construal priming task (A), participants were scanned while being presented with images of their own face, a familiar face, and scrambled faces, and had to indicate the head orientation of the intact faces and the location of the gray bar next to the scrambled faces by pressing a button with the right index or middle finger. (B) Mean reaction times to self-face, familiar faces, and scrambled faces. (C) Illustration of the right frontal activation in association with self-face. (D) The time courses of the blood-oxygenation-level-dependent (BOLD) signals in the right middle frontal cortex after the independent self-construal priming. (E) BOLD signal in the right middle frontal cortex after the interdependent self-construal priming.
From J. Sui and S. Han, *Psychological Science* (Volume 18, Issue 10), 861–6, pp. 862 and 864 (https://doi.org/10.1111/j.1467-9280.2007.01992.x). Copyright 2007 by SAGE Publications, Inc. Adapted by permission of SAGE Publications, Inc.

differentiation between self and others. The mPFC activity underlying self-reflection is also modulated by other types of cultural priming. Chiao et al. (2009) primed college students living in the United States who self-identified as "bicultural" with individualistic or collectivistic cultural values using the Sumerian Warrior Story task and the Similarities and Differences with Family and Friends task (Trafimow et al., 1991). Chaio et al. (2009) found that participants primed with individualism showed a greater mPFC activity when reflecting on their own general traits relative to their own dispositions in a specific context. By contrast, participants primed with collectivism showed a greater mPFC activity for contextual relative to general self descriptions. These findings provide further evidence for the dynamic influence of temporal shifts of cultural frame on neural representations underlying self-reflection.

There has been evidence that self-construal priming also modulates brain activities involved in social emotion. For instance, Varnum et al. (2014) demonstrated that priming independence or interdependence modulated neural activity in the subcortical structures involved in vicarious reward. In this study, Chinese adults were first primed with independent or interdependent self-construals, then played a card-guessing game to win extra monetary rewards for themselves and their friends. This required them to guess whether the number on the card would be smaller or greater than 5. The authors tested whether priming interdependence compared to independence would increase feedback-induced reward activity in response to a friend's benefit. They found that, while winning compared to losing the monetary reward activated the bilateral ventral striatum, independent self-construal priming led to stronger activity in the ventral striatum in response to winning money for the self than for a friend. Interdependent self-construal priming, however, resulted in comparable reward activity in the striatum when winning money for the self and for a friend (Figure 7.3). It appears that priming the concept of close connection between oneself and others causes similar vicarious feelings of rewards for oneself and a friend, which may in turn motivate altruistic behavior toward close others.

A more recent fMRI study investigated how self-construal priming interacts with in-group/out-group perception to modulate empathic neural responses to others' pain (Wang et al., 2015). Individuals from collectivistic cultures, compared with those coming from individualistic cultures, showed stronger in-group favoritism in empathic neural responses (i.e., greater activity during empathy) for the pain of in-group members than that of out-group members (Cheon et al., 2011; Mathur et al., 2010). One may hypothesize that priming collectivistic culture may augment in-group favoritism in empathy, whereas priming individualistic culture may reduce in-group favoritism in empathy. Wang et al., (2015) tested the effects of self-construal priming on empathic neural responses to perceived pain from in-group or out-group individuals. Because an independent schema of the self results in a weakened sense of in-group/out-group relationship and an interdependent schema of self a significant distinction between in-group and out-group (Markus & Kitayama, 2010), Wang et al. predicted decreased in-group bias in empathic neural responses. During fMRI scanning, Chinese adults were presented with video clips that depicted painful or nonpainful stimulations applied to the faces of in-group and out-group models. Participants showed stronger neural activities in the mid-cingulate, left insula, and supplementary motor areas in response to in-group (vs. out-group) members' pain after being primed with interdependent

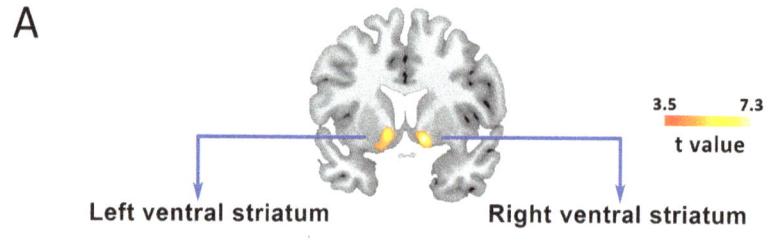
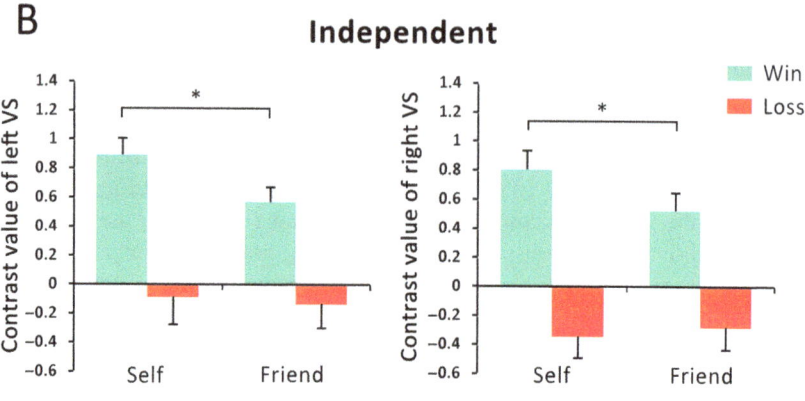
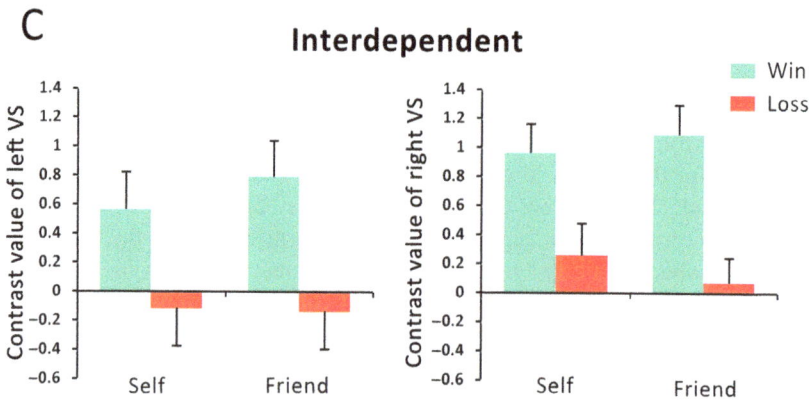

Figure 7.3 Modulations of reward activity in the ventral striatum. The upper panel (A) illustrates the reward activity in the ventral striatum. The middle (B) and lower (C) panels show BOLD responses to a participant's own and a friend's reward. The response to their own reward was stronger than that to a friend's reward after independent self-construal priming, whereas interdependent self-construal priming tended to produce an opposite pattern. Adapted from *NeuroImage, 87,* M. E. W. Varnum, Z. Shi, A. Chen, J. Qui, and S. Han, "When 'Your' Reward Is the Same as 'My' Reward: Self-Construal Priming Shifts Neural Responses to Own vs. Friends' Rewards," p. 168 (https://doi.org/10.1016/j.neuroimage.2013.10.042). Copyright 2013, with permission from Elsevier

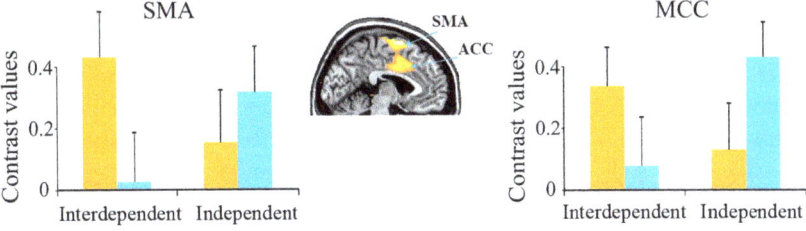

Figure 7.4 Modulation of in-group bias in empathic neural responses. The supplementary motor area (SMA) and anterior cingulate (ACC) activated by perceived painful vs. non-painful stimulations are illustrated in the middle panel. Modulations of the SMA and ACC activity in response to same-race and other-race pain by self-construal priming are illustrated in the left and right panels.
Adapted from C. Wang et al., "Challenging Emotional Prejudice by Changing Self-Concept: Priming Independent Self-Construal Reduces Racial Ingroup Bias in Neural Responses to Other's Pain," *Social Cognitive and Affective Neuroscience*, 2015, *10*(9), p. 1199 (https://doi.org/10.1093/scan/nsv005), by permission of Oxford University Press

self-construals. However, independent self-construal priming significantly reduced the in-group bias in neural responses to others' pain in these brain regions (Figure 7.4). These findings indicate that shifting an individual's self-construal modulates perceived intergroup relationships between onlookers and targets, which in turn modulates empathic neural responses to in-group and out-group pain.

In sum, these findings are consistent with the argument that self-construals provide a cultural framework that constrains brain activity underlying multiple cognitive and affective processes (Han & Humphreys, 2016). Self-construal priming induces transient shifts in the default style of self-continuity that are mediated by the cortical midline structures and provides a framework that constrains brain responses to stimuli during a task. This framework biases the brain to respond in a specific way to guide behaviors that fit a particular sociocultural context.

Conclusion

The behavioral and brain imaging findings summarized in this chapter have significant implications for understanding culture and brain function. First, in most of the previous cultural priming studies, the priming procedure lasted for only a short period of time (e.g., a few minutes) yet it induced significant changes in behavioral performance and related brain activities. These findings demonstrate that individuals can switch temporarily between two cultural value/belief systems. Thus, although individuals' long-term cultural experiences may lead to dominant cultural beliefs/values, short-term exposure to other cultural symbols can override these mindsets and shape individual's behavior and brain function. Cultural priming studies illustrate the plasticity of brain functional organization in response to short-term cultural experiences, which accords well with predictive models of cognition in which the brain continuously generates, tests and corrects models of the world (see Chapter 5).

Second, it is of note that the priming procedures employed in the aforementioned brain imaging studies were very different: reading single/plural first-person pronouns; viewing pictures of cultural symbols; and thinking self–other similarity or differences. Nevertheless, these priming procedures produced effects on behavioral and underlying brain activity that are consistent with previous studies using cross-cultural group comparison and the results fit the dominant theories of culture (e.g., Markus & Kitayama, 1991). This suggests that, although the cultural priming procedures differ in form and language, they activate similar cultural beliefs/values regardless of the different cognitive processes involved. Thus, it appears that it is the cultural beliefs, values, and norms of individualism and collectivism, rather than how these are activated, that is fundamentally important in modulating brain activity underlying self-related processes.

Third, the imaging studies mentioned in this chapter demonstrate that cultural priming influences human brain activity involved in sensory, perceptual, cognitive, and affective processes. The findings strengthen our understanding of a causal relationship between culture and functional organization of the human brain and indicate that, even during adulthood, one's cultural knowledge system can be temporarily changed and that the short-term shift of cultural values/norms similarly modulates cognition, behavior, and underlying brain activity. While long-term cultural learning and experience formulate a sustained and default cognitive frame that guides routine ways of thinking and doing things, cultural priming may provide a transient frame for guiding both brain activity and mental processes in order to choose appropriate behaviors in response to a cognitive task in a specific social context.

To date, the neuronal mechanisms underlying the cultural priming process itself, which is prior to and independent of its effects on cognition and brain, remain unclear. As the effects of cultural priming in most previous studies were closely related to self-construals, Wang et al. (2013) scanned Chinese students during self-construal priming and a following resting-state. It was found that, relative to a calculation task, both interdependent and independent self-construal priming activated the mPFC and posterior cingulate cortex (PCC). The contrast of interdependent vs. independent self-construal priming revealed further increased activity in the dorsal mPFC and left middle frontal cortex. The analysis of the resting-state after the self-construal priming revealed enhanced local synchronization of spontaneous activity in the dorsal mPFC but decreased local synchronization of spontaneous activity in the PCC when contrasting interdependent vs. independent self-construal priming. These findings suggest that self-construal priming may change the resting-state activity along the cortical midline structure that mediates self-consciousness, an area critical for mediating the continuity of the self across time or self-continuity.

In conclusion, the cultural priming approach in cultural neuroscience research provides evidence that cultural influences go beyond behavioral and psychological effects and extend the function of culture to shape the neural basis of behavior and mental processes. Multicultural environments provide the precondition of building both sustained and transient cultural frames that allow individuals to switch between cultural schemas according to the immediate sociocultural context. Both sustained and transient cultural frames influence multiple levels of neural substrates of sensation, perception, attention, emotion, self-reflection, empathy, and mental state inference. The interaction between sustained and transient cultural frames constrains neural strategies and biases the brain's spontaneous and task-evoked activity to respond in specific ways to guide human behavior.

Acknowledgment

This work was supported by the National Natural Science Foundation of China (Projects 91332125, 31421003, 31470986) (S. H.).

REFERENCES

Blakemore, S. J. (2008). The social brain in adolescence. *Nature Reviews Neuroscience*, 9(4), 267–77. https://doi.org/10.11038/nrn2353

Brewer, M. B., & Gardner, W. L. (1996). Who is this 'we'? Levels of collective identity and self representations. *Journal of Personality and Social Psychology*, 71(1), 83–93. https://doi.org/10.1037/0022-3514.71.1.83

Bromm, B., & Chen, A. C. N. (1995). Brain electrical source analysis of laser evoked potentials in response to painful trigeminal nerve stimulation. *Electroencephalography of Clinical Neurophysiology*, 95(1), 14–26. https://doi.org/10.1016/0013-4694(95)00032-T

Cheon, B. K., Im, D.-m., Harada, T., Kim, J.-S., Mathur, V. A., Scimeca, J. M., Parrish, T. B., Park, H. W., & Chiao, J. Y. (2011). Cultural influences on neural basis of intergroup empathy. *NeuroImage*, 57(2), 642–50. https://doi.org/10.1016/j.neuroimage.2011.04.031

Chiao, J. Y., & Ambady, N. (2007). Cultural neuroscience: Parsing universality and diversity across levels of analysis. In: S. Kitayama & D. Cohen (Eds.), *Handbook of cultural psychology* (pp. 237–54). Guilford Press.

Chiao, J. Y., Harada, T., Komeda, H., Li, Z., Mano, Y., Saito, D., Parrish, T. B., Sadato, N., & Iidaka, T. (2009). Dynamic cultural influences on neural representations of the self. *Journal of Cognitive Neuroscience, 22*, 1–11. https://doi.org/10.1162/jocn.2009.21192

Christmann, C., Koeppe, C., Braus, D., Ruf, M., & Flora, H. (2007). A simultaneous EEG-fMRI study of painful electrical stimulation. *NeuroImage, 34*, 1428–37. https://doi.org/10.1016/j.neuroimage.2006.11.006

Colzato, L. S., de Bruijn, E. R., & Hommel, B. (2012). Up to "me" or up to "us"? The impact of self-construal priming on cognitive self-other integration. *Frontiers in Psychology, 3*, 341. https://doi.org/10.3389/fpsyg.2012.00341

Gardner, W. L., Gabriel, S., & Lee, A. Y. (1999). 'I' value freedom, but 'we' value relationships: Self-construal priming mirrors cultural differences in judgment. *Psychological Science, 10*(4), 321–6. https://doi.org/10.1111/1467-9280.00162

Han, S. (2015). Understanding cultural differences in human behavior: A cultural neuroscience approach. *Current Opinion in Behavioral Sciences, 3*, 68–72. https://doi.org/10.1016/j.cobeha.2015.01.013

Han, S. (2017). *The sociocultural brain: A cultural neuroscience approach to human nature.* Oxford University Press.

Han, S., & Humphreys, G. W. (2016). Self-construal: A cultural framework for brain function. *Current Opinion in Psychology, 8*, 10–14. https://doi.org/10.1016/j.copsyc.2015.09.013

Han, S., & Ma, Y. (2014). Cultural differences in human brain activity: A quantitative meta-analysis. *NeuroImage, 99*, 293–300. https://doi.org/10.1016/j.neuroimage.2014.05.062

Han, S., & Ma, Y. (2015). A culture-behavior-brain loop model of human development. *Trends in Cognitive Sciences, 19*(11), 666–76. https://doi.org/10.1016/j.tics.2015.08.010

Han, S., & Northoff, G. (2008). Culture-sensitive neural substrates of human cognition: A transcultural neuroimaging approach. *Nature Reviews Neuroscience, 9*(8), 646–54. https://doi.org/10.1038/nrn2456

Han, S., Northoff, G., Vogeley, K., Wexler, B. E., Kitayama, S., & Varnum, M. E. W. (2013). A cultural neuroscience approach to the biosocial nature of the human brain. *Annual Review of Psychology, 64*, 335–59. https://doi.org/10.1146/annurev-psych-071112-054629

Hedden, T., Ketay, S., Aron, A., Markus, H. R., & Gabrieli, J. D. E. (2008). Cultural influences on neural substrates of attentional control. *Psychological Science, 19*(1), 12–17. https://doi.org/10.1111/j.1467-9280.2008.02038.x

Hong, Y.-y., Morris, M. W., Chiu, C.-y., & Benet-Martínez, V. (2000). Multicultural minds: A dynamic constructivist approach to culture and cognition. *American Psychologist, 55*(7), 709–20. https://doi.org/10.1037//0003-066x.55.7.709

Hong, Y., Wan, C., No, S., & Chiu, C-.y. (2007). Multicultural identities. In S. Kitayama & D. Cohen (Eds.), *Handbook of cultural psychology* (pp. 323–46). Guilford Press.

Kitayama, S., Yanagisawa, K., Ito, A., Ueda, R., Uchida, Y., & Abe, N. (2017). Reduced orbitofrontal cortical volume is associated with interdependent self-construal. *Proceedings of the National Academy of Sciences of the United States of America, 114*(30), 7969–74. https://doi.org/10.1073/pnas.1704831114

Kühnen, U., & Oyserman, D. (2002). Thinking about the self influences thinking in general: Cognitive consequences of salient self-concept. *Journal of Experimental Social Psychology*, *38*(5), 492–9. https://doi.org/10.1016/S0022-1031(02)00011-2

Lin, Z., & Han, S. (2009). Self-construal priming modulates the scope of visual attention. *The Quarterly Journal of Experimental Psychology*, *62*(4), 802–13. https://doi.org/10.1080/17470210802271650

Lin, Z., Lin, Y., & Han, S. (2008). Self-construal priming modulates visual activity underlying global/local perception. *Biological Psychology*, *77*(1), 93–7. https://doi.org/10.1016/j.biopsycho.2007.08.002

Luo, S., Ma, Y., Liu, Y., Li, B., Wang, C., Shi, Z., Li, X., Zhang, W., Rao, Y., & Han, S. (2015). Interaction between oxytocin receptor polymorphism and interdependent culture on human empathy. *Social Cognitive and Affective Neuroscience*, *10*(9), 1273–81. https://doi.org/10.1093/scan/nsv019

Luo, S., Yu, D., & Han, S. (2017). 5-HTTLPR moderates the association between interdependence and brain responses to mortality threats. *Human Brain Mapping*, *38*(12), 6157–71. https://doi.org/10.1002/hbm.23819

Ma, Y., Bang, D., Wang, C., Allen, M., Frith, C., Roepstorff, A., & Han, S. (2014). Sociocultural patterning of neural activity during self-reflection. *Social Cognitive and Affective Neuroscience*, *9*(1), 73–80. https://doi.org/10.1093/scan/nss103

Ma, Y., Wang, C., Li, B., Zhang, W., Rao, Y., & Han, S. (2014). Does self-construal predict activity in the social brain network? A genetic moderation effect. *Social Cognitive and Affective Neuroscience*, *9*(9), 1360–7. https://doi.org/10.1093/scan/nst125

Markus, H. R., & Hamedani, M. G. (2007). Sociocultural psychology: The dynamic interdependence among self systems and social systems. In S. Kitayama, & D. Cohen (Eds.), *Handbook of cultural psychology* (pp. 3–39). Guilford Press.

Markus, H. R., & Kitayama, S. (1991). Culture and the self: Implications for cognition, emotion, and motivation. *Psychological Review*, *98*(2), 224–53. https://doi.org/10.1037/0033-295X.98.2.224

Markus, H. R., & Kitayama, S. (2010). Cultures and selves: A cycle of mutual constitution. *Perspectives on Psychological Science*, *5*(4), 420–30. https://doi.org/10.1177/1745691610375557

Martínez, A., Anllo-Vento, L., Sereno, M. I., Frank, L. R., Buxton, R. B., Dubowitz, D. J., Wong, E. C., Hinrichs, H., Heinze, H. J., & Hillyard, S. A. (1999). Involvement of striate and extrastriate visual cortical areas in spatial attention. *Nature Neuroscience*, *2*(4), 364–9. https://doi.org/10.1038/7274

Mathur, V. A., Harada, T., Lipke, T., & Chiao, J. Y. (2010). Neural basis of extraordinary empathy and altruistic motivation. *NeuroImage*, *51*(4), 1468–75. https://doi.org/10.1016/j.neuroimage.2010.03.025

Miyamoto, Y. (2013). Culture and analytic versus holistic cognition: Toward multilevel analysis of cultural influences. *Advances in Experimental Social Psychology*, *47*, 131–88. https://doi.org/10.1016/B978-0-12-407236-7.00003-6

Mu, Y., Kitayama, S., Han, S., & Gelfand, M. J. (2015). How culture gets embrained: Cultural differences in event-related potentials of social norm violations. *Proceedings of the National Academy of Sciences of the United States of America*, *112*(50), 15348–53. https://doi.org/10.1073/pnas.1509839112

Ng, S. H., Han, S., Mao, L., & Lai, J. C. L. (2010). Dynamic bicultural brains: fMRI study of their flexible neural representation of self and significant others in response to culture primes. *Asian Journal of Social Psychology, 13*(2), 83–91. https://doi.org/10.1111/j.1467-839X.2010.01303.x

Ng, S. H., & Lai, J. C. L. (2009). Effects of culture priming on the social connectedness of the bicultural self: A self-reference effect approach. *Journal of Cross-Cultural Psychology, 40*(2), 170–86. https://doi.org/10.1177/0022022108328818

Oyserman, D. (2011). Culture as situated cognition: Cultural mindsets, cultural fluency, and meaning making. *European Review of Social Psychology, 22*(1), 164–214. https://doi.org/10.1080/10463283.2011.627187

Oyserman, D., & Lee, S. W. S. (2007). Priming "culture": Culture as situated cognition. In S. Kitayama, & D. Cohen. (Eds.), *Handbook of cultural psychology* (pp. 255–79). Guilford Press.

Oyserman, D., & Lee, S. W. S. (2008). Does culture influence what and how we think? Effects of priming individualism and collectivism. *Psychological Bulletin, 134*(2), 311–42. https://doi.org/10.1037/0033-2909.134.2.311

Oyserman, D., Novin, S., Flinkenflögel, N., & Krabbendam, L. (2014). Integrating culture-as-situated-cognition and neuroscience prediction models. *Culture and Brain, 2*(1), 1–26. https://doi.org/10.1007/s40167-014-0016-6

Pascual-Leone, A., Amedi, A., Fregni, F., & Merabet, L. B. (2005). The plastic human brain cortex. *Annual Review of Neuroscience, 28*, 377–401. https://doi.org/10.1146/annurev.neuro.27.070203.144216

Peyron, R., Laurent, B., & García-Larrea, L. (2000). Functional imaging of brain responses to pain. A review and meta-analysis (2000). *Neurophysiologie Clinique, 30*(5), 263–88. https://doi.org/10.1016/S0987-7053(00)00227-6

Shaw, C., & McEachern, J. (Eds.). (2001). *Toward a theory of neuroplasticity*. Psychology Press.

Sui, J., & Han, S. (2007). Self-construal priming modulates neural substrates of self-awareness. *Psychological Science, 18*(10), 861–6. https://doi.org/10.1111/j.1467-9280.2007.01992.x

Sui, J., Zhu, Y., & Chiu, C.-y. (2007). Bicultural mind, self-construal, and self-and-mother reference effects: Consequences of cultural priming on recognition memory. *Journal of Experimental Social Psychology, 43*(5), 818–24. https://doi.org/10.1016/j.jesp.2006.08.005

Trafimow, D., Triandis, H. C., & Goto, S. G. (1991). Some tests of the distinction between the private self and the collective self. *Journal of Personality and Social Psychology, 60*(5), 649–55. https://doi.org/10.1037/0022-3514.60.5.649

United Nations. (2018). *2018 Revision of world urbanization prospects*. New York, NY: Population Division of the United Nations Department of Economic and Social Affairs. https://population.un.org/wup/Publications/Files/WUP2018-Report.pdf

Utz, S. (2004). Self-construal and cooperation: Is the interdependent self more cooperative than the independent self? *Self and Identity, 3*(3), 177–90. https://doi.org/10.1080/13576500444000001

Varnum, M. E. W., Shi, Z., Chen, A., Qiu, J., & Han, S. (2014). When "your" reward is the same as "my" reward: Self-construal priming shifts neural responses to own vs. friends' rewards. *NeuroImage, 87*, 164–9. https://doi.org/10.1016/j.neuroimage.2013.10.042

Wang, C., Ma, Y., & Han, S. (2014). Self-construal priming modulates pain perception: Event-related potential evidence. *Cognitive Neuroscience*, *5*(1), 3–9. http://doi.org/10.1080/17588928.2013.797388

Wang, C., Oyserman, D., Liu, Q., Li, H., & Han, S. (2013). Accessible cultural mindset modulates default mode activity: Evidence for the culturally situated brain. *Social Neuroscience*, *8*(3), 203–16. https://doi.org/10.1080/17470919.2013.775966

Wang, C., Oyserman, D., Liu, Q., Li, H., & Han, S. (2015). Challenging emotional prejudice by changing self-concept: Priming independent self-construal reduces racial in-group bias in neural responses to other's pain. *Social Cognitive and Affective Neuroscience*, *10*(9), 1195–201. https://doi.org/10.1093/scan/nsv005

Wang, F., Peng, K., Chechlacz, M., Humphreys, G. W., & Sui, J. (2017). The neural basis of independence versus interdependence orientations: A voxel-based morphometric analysis of brain volume. *Psychological Science*, *28*(4), 519–29. https://doi.org/10.1177/0956797616689079

Wong, R. Y.-M., & Hong, Y.-y. (2005). Dynamic influences of culture on cooperation in the prisoner's dilemma. *Psychological Science*, *16*(6), 429–34. http://journals.sagepub.com/doi/full/10.1111/j.0956-7976.2005.01552.x

Zaslansky, R., Sprecher, E., Tenke, C. E., Hemli, J. A., & Yarnitsky, D. (1996). The P300 in pain evoked potentials. *Pain*, *66*(1), 39–49. https://doi.org/10.1016/0304-3959(96)03020-5

Zhu, Y., Zhang, L., Fan, J., & Han, S. (2007). Neural basis of cultural influence on self-representation. *NeuroImage*, *34*(3), 1310–16. https://doi.org/10.1016/j.neuroimage.2006.08.047

8 Culture, Self, and Agency
An Ecosocial View

Laurence J. Kirmayer, Ana Gómez-Carrillo, Timothé Langlois-Thérien, Maxwell J. D. Ramstead, and Ian Gold

It is a weekday evening in Singapore and, at a local Taoist temple, a traditional healer or *dang-ki* is preparing to become possessed by a divine spirit. He sits in an ornate chair, quietly listening to his assistants chanting. He begins to rapidly bounce his leg and to retch and vomit onto the newspaper placed on the floor in front of his chair. Suddenly, he jumps up into his chair, crosses his legs in the lotus position and brings his hands together in supplication. He starts moving his head rhythmically from side to side and making a high-pitched humming sound. He is now possessed by a deity. Dressed in a colourful apron by his attendants, he gets up to give his thanks to the gods at a small shrine and then stations himself at a table with his ritual implements to begin his consultations. Over the next three hours, he sees one person after another who has come for advice, help, or healing. When no more clients remain to be seen, he returns to his ceremonial chair and, after a brief ritual that reverses the steps that invited the god in, the god abruptly departs, announced by his assistants' hand claps, and he falls back into the chair exhausted. After he recovers for a few minutes, the healer comes over to those of us watching the proceedings to explain that we are welcome to write about what we have seen but should be careful to get our account right: It was not a spirit but a god who has been present; and it was not the human person who did healing – it was the god.

Lee and Kirmayer (2019)

A refugee girl in Sweden becomes withdrawn, refusing to drink or eat. She lapses into a stupor, is unresponsive and requires tube feeding and coma-care. Soon many other children are affected and a new health problem is described: *resignation syndrome*. Resignation syndrome occurs exclusively among the children of refugee claimants who are facing prolonged uncertainty about their migration status. The children recover when their family's refugee status is resolved. A heated debate erupts among health professionals over whether to understand this syndrome as a neurobiological disorder or simply a form of social protest.

Kirmayer and Gómez-Carrillo (2019)

In a courtroom in the U.S., a lawyer is arguing for a reconsideration of the sentence of a convicted murderer because the original trial never considered evidence that his brain shows abnormalities on a scan that suggest he was not fully in control of his actions. The judge concurs and grants an appeal.

Miller (2016)

Introduction

How do we come to experience ourselves as being in control of our actions? Under what circumstances do we feel that our behavior is guided or controlled by something or someone else – a spirit, a god, an illness, or brain dysfunction? Though the answers to these questions always reflect the local dynamics of power and politics, they also depend on cognitive and cultural interpretive processes. Indeed, the opening vignettes point to the conundrums of agency across diverse cultures and contexts. The wide cultural variation in experiences of agency poses interesting questions which recent neuroscience can help address. However, as we hope to show in this chapter, the picture that emerges from neuroscience is of a brain that is thoroughly entangled with its social and cultural environment, such that any account of agency must be irreducibly ecosocial, understanding brain–person–environment as a dynamic system.

Intentional action and agency are among the most important concepts that we use to characterize our minds, selves, and personhood. Experiences and ascriptions of personal agency have cardinal importance in Western societies because the individualistic notion of the person that is prominent in Western contexts is centered on individual choice and self-direction (Rose, 1998; see Chapter 3). Agency underpins the notion of social and moral responsibility – indeed, free will and moral responsibility have long been bound together in the Western tradition – and thus inform the legal system as well (Frith, 2014). Moreover, health and well-being may be associated with self-efficacy and the ability to pursue one's personal goals (Chirkov et al., 2011).

Much of Western thought construes agency as a capacity that depends largely or even entirely on features of individuals. This conception of agency as a faculty of the will has a long history in the West, which we can trace back as far as Aristotle and Augustine. In this conception, an agent is a person who is able to act intentionally, that is, to form an intention which causes them to act in a particular way. In contemporary Anglo-American philosophy, this process is viewed as being rooted in *reason*: an agent's actions always must have been brought about by virtue of standing in the right kind of connection to the right kind of mental states: a reason for acting, an explicit goal, or a desired outcome. One might expect that cognitive neuroscience would provide support for this internalist account. In fact, neuroscience provides evidence for a more expansive conception of agency as embodied, enacted, and distributed – in ways that make agency dependent not only on internal processes, but also on ongoing social interactions.

Our purpose in this chapter, then, is twofold: First, we want to review work in cognitive neuroscience that shows how agency depends on *situated* sensorimotor loops. In effect, recent neuroscience challenges standard Western accounts of the sources of agency as residing exclusively within the agent.

Second, we will argue that the relational nature of agency extends well beyond sensorimotor loops. Even everyday actions depend on interpretive processes that involve cultural affordances and ontologies as well as social and political structures. Far from being a feature of individual cognition, therefore, agency is dependent on the social world.

Locating Agency

Agency refers to our capacity to choose, initiate, and control our actions to influence events in the world. It is the way that our intentions seamlessly give rise to actions that indicates they belong to us. In individualistic or independent cultural contexts, like those common in Euro-American cultures, resistance to our goals and limitations of our actions may be readily experienced as "other," reflecting some extrinsic force or counter-agency, demarcating limits of the self. Such resistance can also be an indication of inner conflict and this provides the basis for psychodynamic theory, which posits internal dynamics of ambivalence and negotiation among competing desires, drives, affects, and fantasies – but all of this occurs with a sense of presence or immediacy that, under ordinary circumstances, makes it palpably part of the self. Of course, this experience of immediacy does not mean that such experiences are truly unmediated. Indeed, various forms of psychopathology are marked by a sense of self-alienation, detachment from the world, and a destabilization of the taken-for-granted aspects of self and world. This suggests that the experience of self and agency is a dynamic construction, rather than a simple given or developmental achievement that, once achieved, remains stable and in no need of ratification or repair.

The experience of having agency may involve some basic bodily perceptions but usually also involves cognitive processes of attribution and interpretation. Ascriptions of agency to ourselves or to others for our actions depend on a complex web of inferences. Although agency is commonly linked to conscious intentions, in reality, most actions occur without much conscious awareness. When performing familiar routines or deploying well-learned skills, like driving the same way to work every day, we often act more or less automatically (Papies & Aarts, 2016). Even actions that are automatic or habitual, carried out in a "mindless" fashion through non-conscious cognitive processes, may be viewed as agentic because (1) they follow from an overarching plan, goal, attitude, or commitment; (2) they were once intentional but have become automatized, or (3) they simply fit with our notion of appropriate behavior in a specific context. On the one hand, we may disavow as non-agentic, those behaviors that we have never intentionally done and that are inconsistent with our goals, self-narrative, or notions of what is appropriate.

A common moral and psychological meaning of agency in Euro-American cultures has to do with our capacity to deliberately inhibit or control our behavior through "willpower." Greater willpower, in the sense of the ability to delay gratification, is associated with many positive outcomes over the lifespan (Mischel et al., 2010). Willpower reflects both individual personality traits and psychophysiological states. People perform relatively poorly on self-control tasks if they have recently performed another self-control task (Baumeister, 2008). Hence, there seems to be some general resource that subserves self-control and that can be (temporarily) depleted. This extends to making choices: Effortful choice appears to use some of the same resources as self-control. This accords with the folk concept or metaphor of "willpower" as a fixed quantity – which can be plentiful or in short supply. Indeed, Gailliot and Baumeister (2007) found that efforts at self-control caused measurable changes in brain blood glucose utilization, indicating this is a process that requires metabolic energy. Willpower can be depleted, at least temporarily, and behavior may then be driven more by habits and immediate desires than by deliberate choices or aspirations. However, these effects of depleting self-control depend in part on whether one believes that self-control is a limited quantity (Job et al., 2010). This points to the possibility that experiences of willpower depend not only on personality traits, but also on cultural learning and strategies for self-control, which may modulate one's beliefs about the extent to which actions are under one's control.

Another important use of the notion of agency occurs in social and political science, where it refers to the capacity for individuals or groups to act on and through social situations, relations, and institutions to articulate and advance their interests. Social agency is related both to the kind of status or position one has within particular social systems or structures and one's ability or power to influence others (Giddens, 1979). Cultural models and social positioning affect the scope of actions available to individuals, the kinds of actions the environment affords them, the corresponding embodied skills they acquire, and the ways in which they interpret events. Social affordances and constraints on agency exert their influence across the lifespan from earliest development to old age (Ramstead et al., 2016). We might expect the cultural world, then, to influence the ways in which the processes that underwrite agency are developed, embodied, and enacted.

The Cognitive Neuroscience of Agency

The sense of agency is a fundamental building block of our sense of self, is altered in many forms of psychopathology, and has been identified as an important determinant of health (David, 2012; Haggard, 2017). Yet, despite its importance, agency has received sustained neuroscientific attention only in the past two decades.

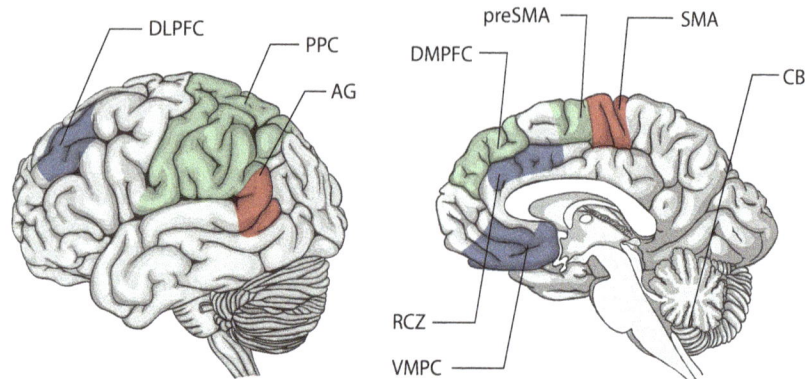

Figure 8.1 Brain regions involved in sense of agency and volition. Medial brain regions include: SMA = supplementary motor area; preSMA = pre-supplementary motor area; RCZ = rostral cingulate zone; DMPFC = dorsomedial prefrontal cortex; VMPFC = ventromedial prefrontal cortex; DLPFC = dorsolateral prefrontal cortex; CB = cerebellum. Lateral brain regions include: AG = angular gyrus; PPC = posterior parietal cortex; AG = angular gyrus.

In cognitive neuroscience research, agency often has been approached as an experience that is measured explicitly, for example, by asking participants to judge their sense of agency following a certain task. While this method has been widely used, it is subject to many cognitive biases. This has led to efforts to develop implicit measures. In some recent experiments, sense of agency is inferred by observing the *intentional binding effect* (Haggard, 2017): When an action is experienced as self-initiated, the time between the action and its outcome is perceived as shorter than the objective time interval. In effect, the brain "binds" action and outcomes more closely as a unit in perception.

Three steps that may contribute to sense of agency have been distinguished: (1) action selection; (2) action preparation; and (3) action-outcome prediction. Each of these steps has been linked to specific brain regions (Brass et al., 2013). Figure 8.1 shows some of the brain regions that appear to contribute to the sense of agency.

Action selection is "the ability to choose between alternative possible actions" (Haggard, 2017). This process is thought to occur in prefrontal areas, mainly the dorsolateral prefrontal cortex (DLPFC), which assembles a "response space" associated with potential actions (Haggard, 2017). Experimental paradigms using subliminal priming show that fluency in action selection (i.e., degree of ease of choice and certainty about which action to take) increases the sense of agency (Chambon et al., 2014).

Action preparation, which involves motor and premotor areas, has been linked to volition, the sense that an action is voluntary rather than involuntary or automatic. Many experiments have focused on the readiness potential, "a characteristic slow negative electroencephalographic potential that occurs before movement," which has been described as a marker of volition – although, as discussed in the next section, this has been challenged (Haggard, 2017). Indeed, the boundaries between selection, preparation, and execution may be fluid.

Action–outcome prediction occurs in parietal areas. The posterior parietal cortex (PPC) and, more precisely, the angular gyrus (AG) is thought to compute prediction-outcome matching discrepancies (Haggard, 2017), mostly between self-produced cues (from motor action) and visual cues (David et al., 2008). The cerebellum has also been implicated in monitoring discrepancies between predicted outcomes and proprioceptive consequences of movements (David et al., 2008).

Taken together, research suggests that the neural correlates of the sense of agency lie not in a specific structure or region but in the connectivity between the frontal and prefrontal motor areas that initiate action and the parietal areas that monitor perceptual events (Haggard, 2017). Frontal regions may assemble a response space and initiate intentional actions, while parietal regions monitor discrepancies between intentions, actions, and outcomes. Three main approaches to modeling this functional connectivity have been developed in the neurocognitive literature: (1) bottom-up comparator models; (2) top-down (mental causation) models; and (3) multidimensional models which attempt to show how multiple top-down and bottom-up processes contribute to the sense of action. Experiments have shown that the relative contribution of different processes varies across contexts and with the type of action (Haggard & Eitam, 2015).

Comparator models hold that the brain computes agency by predicting the effects of ongoing actions, and subsequently comparing these predictions to actual outcome. This model sees the sense of agency as arising from a match between prediction and outcome. When mismatch in this comparison occurs, the sense of agency is disrupted (see Figure 8.2). This comparison process may involve the right temporo-parietal junction. The sense of agency then may emerge in an ongoing way during action.

Top-down theories view the sense of agency as the outcome of higher-order cognitive processes that may be automatic or implicit. For example, the theory of *mental causation* advanced by Wegner (2003), implies that actions and intentions are computed unconsciously and in parallel with action generation. The sense of agency appears as a consequence of cognitive-attributional

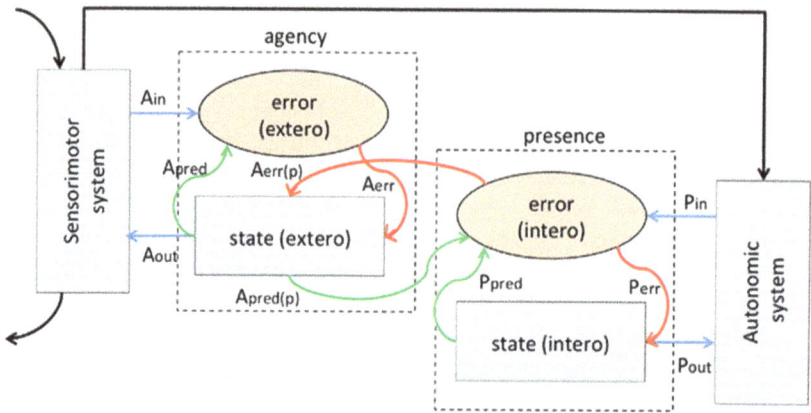

Figure 8.2 Predictive processing model of agency and sense of presence. This figure depicts a predictive processing model of agency and sense of presence, a phenomenological quality which may underwrite the sense of ownership. Presence and agency are modeled as each having a separate component in this account. Each component, in turn, is divided into a state unit and an error unit, which compute the most probable (external and internal) state and the divergence between the current state and the expected one, respectively. The model is hierarchically structured: the agency component is layered upon the presence component, and provides it with beliefs about which interoceptive state to expect next, given the actions that it generates. In this model, the sense of agency results from the successful prediction by the agent of the sensory consequences of actions in the world; whereas the sense of presence is the result of minimizing (or "explaining away") prediction error at the interoceptive level by successfully matching interoceptive predictions to expected inputs. A = agency components; P = presence components; in = input; err = error signal; out = output; pred = prediction.

(From "An Interoceptive Predictive Coding Model of Conscious Presence," by A. K. Seth, K. Suzuki, and H. D. Critchley, 2012, *Frontiers in Psychology, 2*, 395 (https://doi.org/10.3389/fpsyg.2011.00395)

processes that identify the fit with specific criteria of priority, consistency, and exclusivity, that is: "our intention to act happens before we act, is consistent with the action, and is the only plausible cause of the action" (Moore, 2016, p. 4). In this account, the sense of agency depends on a cognitive interpretive or inferential process based on past learning and environmental or social cues. This may also involve meta-cognition: that is, thinking about the role that thinking plays in an action. The sense of agency may then occur both before or after the fact as a consequence of interpretation.

Multidimensional models. While top-down and bottom-up theories differ on the primary drivers of sense of agency, they both hold that sense of agency depends on the outcome of action and hence can only emerge as the outcome of our action is assessed. More recently, in order to account for experimental findings, multifactorial models have been developed which argue that the sense of agency is the product of several contributory elements which are differentially weighted in specific situations (Synofzik et al., 2008). On this account, cues from internal efference, reafference, intention, *and* the environment all interact dynamically to give rise to a sense of agency in a given situation. This view suggests that "both prediction and reconstruction contribute to the sense of agency but that they are differently weighted for some situations compared to others" (David, 2012). The multidimensional approach offers a two-step account of the sense of agency (Figure 8.3), distinguishing the feeling of agency from the judgment of agency (Synofzik et al., 2008). Feelings of agency can prompt the judgment of agency, but the reflective processes underlying the judgment can also phenomenally overwrite the feeling of agency in some situations (Moore, 2016). Indeed, agency experiences may occur on multiple timescales from real-time feedback in the course of performing an action, to longer periods of minutes or hours and even days, weeks, months, and years, the latter based on narratives that interpret actions as agentic.

Sense of agency thus can be understood both in terms of bottom-up processes involving the correlation of sensory or motor signals (afference or efference copy) that indicate an action was self-generated and top-down processes of inference or attribution, which may be based on cognitive maps or models that indicate which kinds of actions are attributable to ourselves, or which actions are related to our goals, plans, and intentions. Each stage in the sequence of choice, plan, initiation, execution, and adjustment of action based on monitoring of outcome contributes to the ascription of agency at the next step in the sequence.

Experiencing actions as being a result of our intentions then appears to involve sensorimotor feedback as well as higher-order processes of attribution and interpretation. The relationship between embodied experience and attribution works in both directions: that is, the embodied experience gives rise to the attribution of agency, but the attribution itself can also alter bodily experience. This link can be seen in studies of intentional binding (Haggard, 2017). The more strongly we believe the outcome is caused by our action or the more we care about the outcome, the closer the binding and the stronger the associated sense of agency (Dogge et al., 2012). Interestingly, this binding is stronger for actions with moral implications (Frith, 2014; Moretto et al., 2011). Moreover, an increase in emotional arousal can increase the sense of binding, while negative emotions like fear and anger can decrease the binding – reflecting a process of disavowal of agency (Christensen et al., 2019). These cognitive, emotional, and contextual effects point to the ways in which sense of agency can be shaped by social and cultural processes.

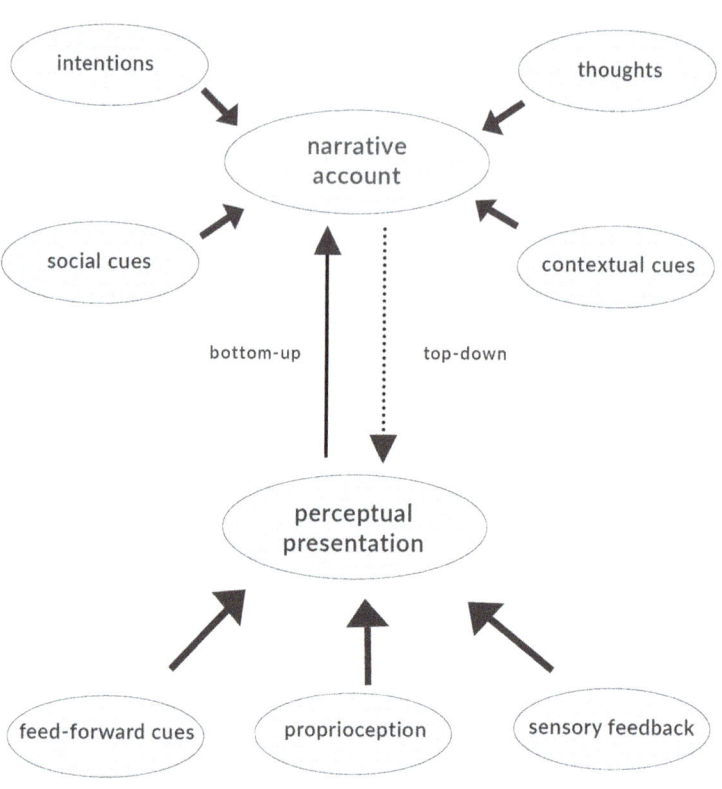

Figure 8.3 Multidimensional model of sense of agency. This model of the sense of agency distinguishes between a basic (bottom-up) pre-conceptual feeling of agency and an explicit (top-down) judgment of agency. The feeling of agency is produced by a subpersonal process of weighing different action-related perceptual and motor cues. This preconceptual core is further processed in relation to concepts and attitudes (e.g., ontologies, intentions, beliefs, desires) to yield an attribution or judgment of agency. The extent to which the feeling and judgment of agency each contribute to the overall sense of agency depends on context and task requirements.
From "Beyond the Comparator Model: A Multifactorial Two-Step Account of Agency," by M. Synofzik, G. Vosgerau, and A. Newen, 2008, *Consciousness and Cognition*, *17*(1), p. 395 (https://doi.org/10.1016/j.concog.2007.03.010)

Agency and the Illusion of Free Will

According to recent accounts of agency based on *prediction* – that is, emulator theories (Grush, 2004) and predictive processing theories (Seth et al., 2012) – the same mechanisms that control the selection of actions underlie the sense of agency and the felt sense of being present in a situation. The basic idea behind prediction-based accounts is that the brain functions by managing its anticipatory engagement with its world (Clark, 2016). In this scheme, the networks of the brain embody expectations (or prior beliefs) about the typical consequences of motor action, which generate predictions about what to sense next; so, the brain essentially *emulates* what it should sense at a given moment, based on what the agent is doing (Grush, 2004). Predictions about the expected sensory consequences of how we act are compared with the sensory data actually registered to compute the discrepancy between prediction and reality – what is known as a *prediction error*. In these frameworks, the brain aims to minimize this discrepancy or error – either by correcting its prediction-generating beliefs (perception and learning) or by acting on its world to make its observations more like its predictions. In predictive processing accounts of agency, the successful suppression of prediction errors by predictions issuing from motor regions corresponds to the internal sense that we have initiated or carried out an action – i.e., it accounts for the felt sense of presence (Grush, 2004; Seth et al., 2012).

For motor action, a major cue facilitating the attribution of agency to oneself is evidence of spatial and temporal contiguity between one's own movement and the movement of an object. By manipulating sensory cues, we easily can be tricked into claiming to have had intentions for outcomes we are made to believe were the result of our actions (Johansson et al., 2005). Indeed, Wegner et al. (2017) have argued that this is generally the case: we readily believe that we choose and control actions that are actually determined by external influences and non-conscious cognitive processes. Indeed, on this view, free will is an illusion.

This position received support from a provocative experiment by Libet et al. (1983), which found that there was specific brain activity, thought to be associated with voluntary motor action, several hundred milliseconds *before* the person recognized that they had made a decision to act. In a laboratory setting in which action was monitored by EEG, a "readiness potential" occurred from 225 to 1200 milliseconds before the person reported they had decided to press a button. This seems to pose a challenge to our intuitive experience (and folk psychology) which assumes that we first (consciously) decide to act and then act. Instead, Libet's study suggested that whatever process was associated with initiating action occurred outside of (and prior to) our conscious awareness. To some, this made it seem not only that consciousness was irrelevant to our actions but that the very notion of autonomy and free will was an illusion (Saigle et al., 2018).

Libet's experiments used a very simple motor task. The sense of the 'urge to move' may be associated with the point in decision-making at which an action has been chosen (rather than initiated). The simple linear causal model of intention leading to action lends itself to a naïve interpretation of the Libet experiment, in which the fact that correlates of action appear before the person is aware of making a decision seems to undermine the reality of choice as a factor in decision-making and with that, subverts the whole idea of free will. But looking at causation on a very short timescale may miss the basic temporal structure of intentionality. There is a longer temporal arc in which voluntary action is embedded: sizing up a situation, developing the intention to do something, choosing an action, initiating the action, carrying out the action, assessing its outcome, and reacting to the outcome, perhaps with further effort to achieve one's goal. These processes occur in a cyclical feedback loop of sensorimotor control that is embedded in larger hierarchical structures of plans and intentions. Moreover, the notion of free will usually is applied not to discrete or punctual situations in which we decide to press a button, but to larger choices of life direction, moral quandaries, and stances that involve choices, goals, and plans over longer stretches of time. As Gallagher (2017) argues, free will applies to this larger planful structure, which at the highest level is concerned with our own goals, biography, and life trajectory. Our free will and moral personhood have to do with our embedding in a particular social world, situation, and predicament.

Interestingly, the notion of free will itself has impact on our behavior. People who believe in free will perform better on self-control tasks in both laboratory and real-world settings. Undermining the belief in free can cause a decrease in prosocial behaviors and an increase in negative social behaviors like cheating, aggression, and expressions of racism (Feldman, 2017). Free will then functions not simply as a description of the relationship between intentionality and voluntary action but as a culturally shaped construct and set of practices that reinforce self-control and sociomoral accountability (Kushnir, 2018).

The Malleability of Ownership, Agency, and Control

Subjectivity, ownership, and agency are at the center of our experience of self. One key facet of our subjectivity is that we experience bodily sensations, emotions, and thoughts as our own. This sense of ownership does not seem to be merely a spatial localization or attribution we make, but comes with experiential qualities of immediacy, intimacy, privacy, and sometimes urgency. Our agency has to do with the sense of being able to choose our

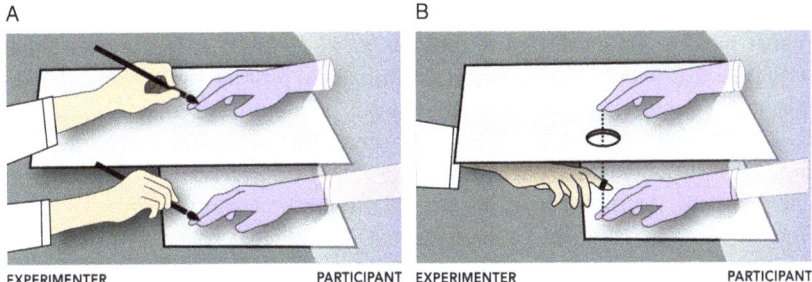

| EXPERIMENTER | PARTICIPANT | EXPERIMENTER | PARTICIPANT |

Figure 8.4 The rubber hand illusion. (A) The classical rubber hand illusion. "The participant's hidden hand (lower shelf) and rubber hand (upper shelf) are synchronously stroked by the experimenter. In most participants this induces an illusory SoO [sense of ownership] over the rubber hand." (B) The active rubber hand illusion. "The participant's index finger and artificial index finger are connected via a small rod (dashed line). As a result, whenever the participant moves his or her own index finger up or down, or alternatively the rod is moved up or down by the experimenter, the artificial hand's index finger moves correspondingly. The occurrence of SoO and SoA [sense of agency] can be systematically investigated by varying the mode of agent (i.e., whether the artificial finger movements are self-generated or generated by the experimenter) and by the positioning of the artificial hand." Figures 8.4A and 8.4B and captions from "The Senses of Agency and Ownership: A Review," by N. Braun, S. Debener, N. Spychala, E. Bongartz, P. Sörös, H. H. O. Müller, and A. Philipsen, 2018, *Frontiers in Psychology*, *9*, 535 (https://doi.org/10.3389/fpsyg.2018.00535)

actions and control them as they are carried out. We are the initiators or originators of behaviors, through which we carry out our intentions or desires; and, crucially, we experience ourselves as the origin of these actions. Again, we usually do not understand agency as simply a post hoc attribution of causality, but experience it as an intrinsic property of certain behaviors that arise from our intentions.

Once achieved developmentally, the senses of ownership of our body and of agency for our actions seem to arise automatically in everyday life (Chambon et al., 2014). However, experimental studies indicate that ownership and agency can be readily dissociated or altered by misleading feedback to produce some surprising illusions. Suitable arrangements of sensorimotor feedback can create illusions like the feeling of owning a rubber hand, being outside one's body, or of having control over external events.

Figure 8.4 illustrates the rubber hand illusion experiment (Botvinick & Cohen, 1998). The participant views a rubber hand placed above or beside their actual hand, which is hidden from view by a screen. The experimenter then repeatedly strokes the hidden hand, while at the same time stroking the visible rubber hand in the same way. Participants quickly experience the rubber hand as an actual part of their body; when asked to locate their hand with their eyes closed, they report it as close to the position of the rubber hand. When confronted with a potentially painful or harmful threat to the rubber hand, they respond with emotional and physiological arousal just as though they were experiencing an actual threat of injury to their body. For all intents and purposes, the rubber hand has temporarily become part of their body. The illusion of ownership can be strengthened by linking a finger of the rubber hand to the participant's own finger so that they move in synchrony (Kalckert & Ehrsson, 2012). Thus, sense of agency reinforces sense of ownership. The same experiment shows that sense of ownership can strengthen sense of agency; but sense of agency can occur even without a sense of ownership, for example, when experimental participants see a robot hand move in synchrony with their own (Ismail & Shimada, 2016). The sense of agency breaks down when there is too long a delay between real and robot hand movements or too much asynchrony.

Sense of ownership and agency also can be manipulated through virtual reality and these alterations can extend from body parts to the body as a whole (Slater et al., 2009). Thus, it is possible to create bodily displacements, in which one feels one's body to be somewhere else, or coterminous with a virtual alter, or out of body experiences, in which one feels one's self to be outside one's body watching from a distance, a kind of induced depersonalization. For example, when participants wear a virtual reality goggle headset and see their body from a camera placed behind them and then see their body double being stroked at the same time that they feel their own body being stroked, their sense of location shifts to the position of the camera, feeling themselves (or their awareness) to be outside their actual body (Lenggengager et al., 2007). Illusory agency can be created when participants are primed to think of a particular action and then experience their virtual body carrying out that action; for example, primed to think of walking and then seeing their virtual body walking, seated subjects may experience themselves walking (Kokkinara et al., 2016). The vividness of virtual reality environments and games depends on these experiences of ownership and agency achieved through synchrony of expectation, action, and sensation – through multiple sensory channels (Gonzalez-Franco & Lanier, 2017).

In summary, several different kinds of self-experience can be readily manipulated in the laboratory creating alterations of self-identity (Is this my body?), body-location (Where is my body?), self-location (i.e., From where do I perceive the world? – which may be separate from where I believe my body is located), and agency (Is this my action?) (Blanke, 2012). In ordinary experience, these facets of self-experience are bound together and mutually reinforced through interoceptive and sensorimotor feedback but with suitable arrangements in the laboratory (and with certain forms of brain lesions or psychopathology) they can be separated out as independent processes.

Many clinical conditions involve disruptions of the sense of ownership and agency. Functional movement disorders, that is, motor problems that have no apparent basis in neurological disease, including involuntary movements, weakness, or paralysis, are characterized by the lack of self-agency for the action of the affected limb (Nahab et al., 2017). Such patients may have decreased functional connectivity between the right temporo-parietal junction and bilateral sensorimotor regions (Maurer et al., 2016). These striking forms of pathology suggest some of the functional processes and components that may contribute to sense of agency. Of course, pathology may have its own unique characteristics with mechanisms distinct from those involved in everyday functioning. And the impact of brain pathology on agency also depends on attributional and interpretive processes (e.g., "It's my body, not me"). However, the experimental work shows how readily the sense of ownership and agency can be modified, even in ways that violate everyday expectations and assumptions. Taken together, this points to potential malleability of the senses of ownership and agency, which are not fixed achievements but produced and maintained by active processes.

Agency, Suggestion, and Dissociation

Another line of research that shows that the sense of agency may be highly malleable among healthy individuals involves hypnotic suggestion. Highly hypnotizable subjects can readily experience suggested actions and experiences as non-agentic, that is, as simply happening (or happening to them) rather than under self-control (Hilgard, 1986). In clinical or laboratory settings, individuals may respond to specific hypnotic suggestions by feeling their arm is moving without their control or that they cannot unclasp their hands. These changes in sense of agency, however, are not a direct result of some hypnotic state but reflect the specific tasks, experiences, and interpretations that are evoked during an individual's experience (Frith, 2014; Polito et al., 2014). A large body of work in hypnosis indicates that the sense of agency can be influenced by expectations, which in turn may reflect past experience, current contexts, and instructional sets.

The phenomenon of hypnotic catalepsy in which a limb floats effortlessly, without conscious will or control, receives two types of explanation in the hypnosis literature: as a misattribution or as a dissociation of control (Lynn et al., 1990). In the first explanation, the phenomenon is essentially attributional, having to do with how movement is explained, that is, whether it is attributed to self or other. In the second explanation, some distinctive change in cognitive control processes is posited: the cataleptic limb is controlled not by a simple motor action plan with feedback from the muscles confirming the execution of the willed movement; instead, it is engendered as an indirect consequence of communication from others or another aspect of the self, less closely allied or fused with a central willing agency. Thus, an image may evoke certain unintentional responses: thinking of a balloon attached to a limb may cause an arm to rise with the feeling that this is happening automatically. For the misattribution theorist, the movement occurs voluntarily but we misattribute it to some effect of the image of the balloon. From the perspective of dissociation theory, the image itself can be the proximate cause of the levitation through the process of ideomotor action. The dissociation model allows for a second type of automaticity in which verbal suggestions or statements may also set in motion motor effects without conscious control. On this view, the experience of involuntariness is not really a misattribution, but a consequence of alternate control mechanisms or an altered hierarchy of control in which action occurs without an immediate or direct link to explicit intention (Hilgard, 1986). A hybrid account, akin to the multidimensional neurocognitive models discussed in the previous section of this chapter, would locate the regulation of control in loops that include cognitive-attributional processes that are influenced by cultural scripts that can influence alternate control mechanisms or hierarchies of control (Seligman & Kirmayer, 2008).

In a study in which highly hypnotizable subjects were given suggestions that their hand movements were being controlled by another person or a machine, they experienced a vivid sense of loss of agency and ownership of their hand (Deeley et al., 2014). The alterations in sense of ownership and agency were associated with changes in brain activity as measured by fMRI; however, the regions of the brain involved varied with the specific suggestion. Compared to subjects told that an impersonal machine was controlling their hand, subjects who were given the suggestion that an alien personal agency (an invisible "Engineer") was controlling their hand movements, either externally (a situation meant to resemble a psychotic delusion of control) or by occupying their body (a suggestion meant to mimic the experience of spirit possession), showed increased connectivity between the primary motor cortex (M1) and a variety of regions associated with social cognition, including attribution of mental states (e.g., BA10) and representing the self in relation to others (cortical midline structures including BA10 and left precuneus). This suggests that experiencing one's body as being controlled by another person or personlike entity involves activation of regions of the brain that serve social cognition.

This and other experiments make it clear that sense depends both on sensorimotor loops and higher order cognition. The picture of agency that emerges from current neuroscience research is of bottom-up processes of sensorimotor synchrony combined with top-down processes of attribution and interpretation, which in turn depend on cultural models and situational expectations.

Cultural Variations in Agency

Although they can be distinguished, both conceptually and experimentally, subjectivity, ownership, and agency are closely related in several ways. In everyday experience, each is a precondition and warrant of the other. We can have agency because we have a sense of our own desires, goals, and intentions, which we can carry out through action. Our ability to articulate and pursue our own plans and choices is usually taken by others as a reflection of our interior thoughts and feelings. Verbal and nonverbal expressions of our intentions are forms of action in themselves. The ways that we explain or reinterpret events to put our actions at the center or to portray ourselves as driven by forces beyond our control varies across cultures and serves to enact particular kinds of self and subjectivity (Markus & Kitayama, 2010).

To the extent that we identify our body as the physical origin and locus of actions, there is a connection between sense of self, ownership, and agency. In everyday life, agency is also linked to the self through social positioning, and through the culturally shaped narratives in which accounts of agency are embedded and expressed. These stories are generated by narrative practices, which we learn across the course of development by participation in particular cultural worlds. This points to one basic way in which accounts of agency can vary: through our efforts to narrate and explain our actions in culturally coherent ways (Frith, 2014). These modes of self-construal vary with social status, gender, education, and many other aspects of our social positioning (Miller et al., 2011). Everyday accounts draw from an implicit ontology (Kirmayer & Ramstead, 2017): Each culture teaches us that the world includes particular kinds of causal agents, and corresponding forms of agency, which may be motivated or capricious and which can account for both desired outcomes and adversity. These causal agents may include ourselves and other persons, but they can also include nonhuman persons (animals or spirits), as well as impersonal agencies. The range of available agents, the scope of their power, and the signs of their influence vary with particular cultural ontologies. When the agents are powerful or omnipotent, and the signs of their presence ubiquitous or readily found, they can always be invoked to explain untoward events (Kpanake, 2018). This is often the case in situations like chronic illness where there may be great pressure to find an explanation to guide the search for help, find meaning, and assign responsibility for suffering (Tilly, 2006).

The relationship between ontology and the experience of agency is complex. We can attribute causality to the kinds of agents we recognize in the world. At the same time, the availability of specific types of attribution, which situate action and events in particular narrative frames, create the possibility for certain types of experience. These experiences are mediated not only by attributions and narrative practices but by cognitive-sensorimotor loops involving embodied sensations, dispositions, or habitus.

The ways that people attribute agency vary with language and culture. For example, while both English and Japanese use similar agentic language to describe events they view as intentional, English speakers are more likely to describe accidental events in terms of their own or other's agency. This difference then influences the ways that English and Japanese speakers recall events (Fausey et al., 2010). The use of specific types of cues in judgments of agency also may vary across cultures. For example, in one study, compared to Austrians, Mongolians were less influenced by changes in temporal contiguity (Bart et al., 2019).

To explore cultural differences in the ways people think about agency, Edge and Suryani (2002) gave a questionnaire on volitional competency to subjects in the United States and Bali. They found similarities in core features, in that "both cultures emphasize the ability to initiate and persist in action" (p. 62), and recognize individuals' sense of confidence or self-efficacy in their ability to initiate and carry out actions to meet their goals, to inhibit or suppress inappropriate acts, and to resist outside influences that would keep them from carrying out the action. However, what differs across cultures is the importance of generating choices autonomously and attribution of success and failure in exercising volition. Drawing from the literature on individualistic and collectivist sense of self (or independent and interdependent, cf. Chapter 4), Edge and Suryani argue that:

[I]n individualistic cultures, the self identifies with itself and the faculty of will, but in collectivist cultures, the self identifies with others, so what needs to be emphasized and valued in such a culture is not control over one's individual will, but the relationship with others. Thus, one difference between individualist and collectivist cultures (or at least the Balinese culture) is that individualist cultures find it natural to talk about exerting the will toward one's [own] end, while collectivist cultures do not. (Edge & Suryani, 2002, p. 65)

Balinese tend to see their lives as directed by a superior power or being. This reduces the tendency to attribute outcomes to individual agency, but not the effort to maintain social norms and strive to achieve spiritual goals in how one lives one's life. This includes efforts to maintain appropriate emotional composure not only for one's own social standing but also to ensure the well-being of others both living and dead (Wikan, 1990). Balinese are more likely than Americans to acknowledge worrying about offending or hurting others. Balinese "act with a firm sense of duty to society ... Thus, a sense of control (of self and the world) is part of their sense of volition, as in the U.S., but their concept of volition differs in that it aims at secondary control, at fitting into the world and adapting to others (out of a sense of duty)" (Edge & Suryani, 2002, p. 67).

Edge and Suryani conclude that while the ability to initiate and persist in action are basic human capacities, recognized in all cultures, that vary with specific personality traits or states, other aspects of volition need to be culturally contextualized. In particular, cultures vary on whether it is useful to think about will as a function of mind or brain, and on whether one mainly seeks to control the social world (primary control), or to adjust one's self to fit in to its demands (secondary control) (Weisz et al., 1984). Of course, the assumption that primary control is more basic is itself a cultural value (Azuma, 1984). Oerter et al. (1996) found that even collectivist cultures value autonomy as basic to having one's own opinion, capacity to make decisions, and economic independence. This underwrites moral responsibility. Thus, the tight links between self, volitional, autonomy, and responsibility are basic to the language and logic of morality.

How Cultural Affordances and Ontology Shape Agency

The experience of agency always occurs in particular social and cultural contexts that shape the meaning of action. This context presents itself to us in terms of *affordances* – that is, as possibilities for particular kinds of action (Kirmayer & Ramstead, 2017; Ramstead et al., 2016). The example of the *dang-ki* healer described at the start of this chapter illustrates this process. In preparation for seeing clients, the healer gives over control of his body to the deity, and it is the deity who then takes action (Lee, 2016). The healers and experience and, indeed, the healing process itself depend on an ontology in which deities have agency. This ontology not only provides explanations for the *dang-ki*'s actions but reaches down into the body and out into the social world to influence the primary experience of agency of the *dang-ki*, his assistants, and, to varying degrees, his clients (Lee & Kirmayer, 2019).

The healer works in a setting rich with symbols related to the shift in agency he invites (Figure 8.5). The temple, the decoration of the room where he works, his ritual clothing, and even the chair he sits in all evoke the potential presence of the deity. Surrounded by his assistants, the *dang-ki* undergoes a ritual in which he focuses on purifying or emptying himself out to invite the deity in. Once the deity arrives, all subsequent action (until the deity departs during a closing ritual) is attributed to the deity by the *dang-ki*, his assistants, and his clients. We can understand this process at a neurocognitive level as closely akin to the functional changes in attention and self-control that occur in hypnosis. But an adequate account must also reference the specific cultural meaning and social interactions in which all participants play a role (Lee, Kirmayer, & Groleau, 2010).

The cultural affordances present in the healing shrine are found not only in the pictures of deities on the walls, the statues in the shrine, or the implements arrayed on the table, but also in the actions, expectations, and beliefs of others who participate in the ritual. The assistants themselves have experienced the healing efficacy of the deity and they reinforce their own commitment through

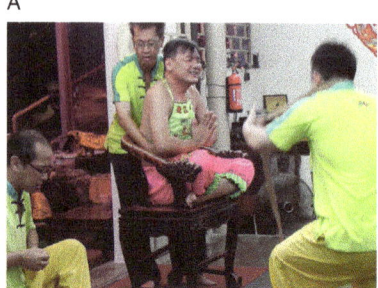 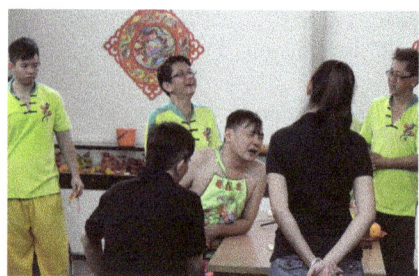

Figure 8.5 *Dang-ki* healing in Singapore. (A) *Dang-ki* becoming possessed by a deity. (B) *Dang-ki* providing advice while possessed.
Photographs courtesy of L. J. Kirmayer with permission of the dang-ki and participants. Singapore, April 24, 2012

regular participation in the practice. The clients of the *dang-ki* come with varying degrees of hope and acceptance of the ontology of deities, but the evidence of the deity's presence seen in the changes in the *dang-ki*'s demeanor and behavior creates or reinforces strong expectations for positive outcomes.

For the *dang-ki*, the assistants, and clients, the ontology of deities confers a special authority and healing efficacy on the subsequent actions. The writing of magical inscriptions on rice paper, the diagnostic assessment, and advice offered by the *dang-ki* are based on this epistemic authority. This authority occurs in the setting of Singapore, a modern, multicultural city with a highly educated population heavily exposed to global media and Western models of self and personhood. The people who consult the *dang-ki* have widely varying degrees of conviction about the potential efficacy of his practice. The survival of this traditional form of healing, rooted in a syncretic Taoist worldview, speaks to how cultural diversity shapes important domains of life, including illness and healing. The fact that the experience of agency is malleable, as revealed by the experiments discussed earlier in this chapter, helps to explain how cultural expectations, even when not based on strongly held beliefs, can lead to compelling experiences that support the reality and authority of the cultural worldview (Kirmayer & Ramstead, 2017).

The practice of *dang-ki* healing also underscores the fact that culture is not entirely a matter of the individual reproduction of collective knowledge and agency. Ritual action like *dang-ki* healing is not simply a matter of the agency of the person whose life trajectory has brought him to this role, but of the expectations and commitments of others – congregants, clients, family, community, historical forbears. The *dang-ki*'s practice reflects the process of "thinking through other minds" (Veissière et al., 2020) – all manner of others who frame one's life and to whom one must answer – and those others are constrained, in turn, by a social system with its history, institutions, exigencies, imperatives, and momentum.

The Politics of Agency

Most of the work in cognitive neuroscience on agency focuses on simple motor acts, which can be closely studied in the laboratory. But everyday action is usually embedded in overarching plans with various goals and subgoals. Indeed, the most important meanings of agency and volition have to do with our choices made in relation to these longer-term plans and life projects. Then too, most work on agency views the experience in dichotomous terms – actions are either agentic or not – although measures that allow for gradations along a given dimension and multidimensional models might point to different varieties of agency.

Voluntary action involves a sequence of steps, including: (1) formulating a goal; (2) developing an overarching plan; (3) action selection; (4) execution; and (5) outcome monitoring. Goals are formulated in terms of personal motivations, developmental trajectories, autobiographical narratives, and sociocultural norms and expectations. Plans are elaborated in relation to overarching goals and may be nested or sequentially discovered. Action selection comes from a repertoire of skills, which allow the individual to recognize and respond to particular affordances. Execution reflects local motor actions regulated by sensorimotor feedback. The process runs in the other direction as well, through feedback loops: (1) feedback from outcome monitoring controls action; (2) when actions fail to converge on an intended outcome, an alternative action may be selected; (3) information about available affordances prompts alternate plans of action; and (4) new plans suggest alternative goals. This organization of action in terms of a hierarchy of feedback loops is central to cybernetic models of mind and behavior (Miller et al., 1960; Powers, 1973) and agency can be situated in relation to these hierarchical control mechanisms (Juarrero, 1999).

What are the links between the minimal forms of agency described in the cognitive models of action and the larger sociomoral and political meanings of agency as having the power and capability to influence events and pursue individual goals and interests? Beyond the simple facts of being able to act physically on one's environment, the small-scale, moment-to-moment experience of agency is related to the larger social meaning in multiple ways: each provides support for the other as a possibility (sense of potential agency, efficacy) – being able to express agency in small-scale actions raises the possibility of being capable of acting to change larger circumstances (and vice versa); each is a warrant of the social and moral meaning of the other – having a sense of agency (or being viewed by others as agentic) at one level inserts

Table 8.1 *Response to outcome mismatch*

Attribution of cause (choice or initiation of action)	Attribution of control (carrying out or completion of action)	
	Self	Other
Self	Dissonance (Irritability)	Reactance (Anger)
	Dissonance reduction	*Opposition, rebellion*
Other	Emotional exacerbation (Anxiety)	Withdrawal (Depression)
	Trying harder	*Avoidance*

Adapted from "Resistance, Reactance, and Reluctance to Change: A Cognitive Attributional Approach to Strategic Interventions" by L. J. Kirmayer, 1990, *Journal of Cognitive Psychotherapy, 4*(2), p. 88 (https://doi.org/10.1891/0889-8391.4.2.83).

one's actions in potential sociomoral consequential frames that operate on the other level as well. These bidirectional influences act at many levels, including through: implicit, embodied experiences and sense of self; meta-cognition (thoughts about self); rhetorical resources and response of others; social positioning and the negotiation of predicaments; and the creation of new social–cultural affordances (Buhrmann & Di Paolo, 2017).

The experience of agency, then, is not simply an internal process of monitoring our ability to choose, initiate, and carry out actions, but is mediated by our interactions with other people. The mere presence of others in a situation can reduce our own sense of agency, and this effect can occur at the level of neural processing rather than through any explicit consideration of the implications (Beyer et al., 2017). Research on *psychological reactance* shows that people are sensitive to constraints on their freedom of choice by others (Brehm & Brehm, 2013). When an option is offered but then taken away, people respond by desiring that option more, trying to actively reassert their freedom to choose that option, and even by aggressing against the person who restricted their freedom of choice. The cognitive-emotional response to constraints on behavior depends on attributions of causality and control (Table 8.1). While these responses may be observed across cultures, they are modulated by explanatory models and culturally prescribed modes of coping, emotion regulation, and interpersonal interaction.

The power of the social world in modulating agency is evident in the example of the refugee children with resignation syndrome, described at the start of this chapter. These children report losing control of their bodies and even their conscious awareness. In their state of obtundation, they are unable to feed or care for themselves and require intensive care. Yet there is no clear neuropathological basis for their illness. Instead, it is the social predicament of the children and their family that appears to instigate the withdrawn behavior and loss of control. The attempts to diagnose the problem in medical or psychiatric terms faced difficulties because of the dichotomous models of agency in everyday moral thinking and psychological theory, but also because of a lack of understanding of the interplay of individual, family, and political agency (Kirmayer & Gómez-Carrillo, 2019). Ironically, a lack of ordinary activity that represented a kind of resolute giving up exerted a powerful influence on others. The syndrome was described by some as a form of protest, while others saw it as an involuntary consequence of social and psychopathological processes. While bringing attention to the plight of their own family, the children's suffering had wider political implications. In effect, the children's experience of loss of agency at the social level led to a behavioral withdrawal with severe physiological effects which, owing to the response of others in the healthcare system, resulted in collective agency on a larger political level.

Moral Agency and Responsibility

The technologies of neuroscience make the brain visible in ways that can advance our scientific understanding of mind, self, and person, but they also increasingly influence ascriptions of agency in many practical domains. Recent years have seen a dramatic increase in the use of neuroscience images in the courtroom. From 2005 to 2015, the number of cases in the United States that included neuropsychiatric information increased fivefold (Greely & Farahany, 2019). The hope in all of this is that criminal acts carried out by individuals who have a reduced capacity to initiate and control their behavior due to brain disorders will be assessed in ways that do not unfairly judge those with diminished capacity. At the same time, many have expressed concern about the potential for juridical abuse, not only because only the wealthy can afford a sophisticated defense that invokes neuroscientific expertise, but also because the very nature of neuroscientific knowledge and what it can explain is misrepresented in the courtroom.

Expert testimony (accompanied by neuroimages) of a brain injury or tumor that has damaged a large anatomical region would seem to be a clear-cut basis for assigning diminished capacity. However, in general, there are only statistical correlates between the size and precise location of a lesion and the resulting decrease in agency. Moreover, in many cases, the effect of a brain lesion is not to entirely preclude self-control but to make it more difficult; so too, of course, for drinking alcohol, smoking cannabis, or becoming enraged because one has been shamed or humiliated. Should we consider that because an act was committed while the person was intoxicated or experiencing a fit of "passion" that they are less morally culpable? These questions antedate our current knowledge of the brain and public opinions and jurisprudence vary in different countries, reflecting cultural differences in notions of moral personhood and explanations of behavior.

The current appeal to neuroscience to refine or resolve this issue raises an additional set of conundrums. The problem is that the neuroimage itself is a statistical fabrication that tells us little. Everything depends on the interpretation and the interpretation involves a long chain of inferences to build up a plausible story; in the cases of individuals' functioning, the links to the generic story are statistical, and, again, those statistics are hidden from view. So the arresting brain image hides all of the complex inferential processes that should cast a long shade on any attempt to derive conclusions. Set this indeterminacy against the backdrop of our dichotomous thinking about agency and we have a setting ripe for miscarriages of justice. Understanding criminal behavior as emerging from neurodevelopmental problems may open the door to strategies for prevention and contribute to a justice system more focused on rehabilitation than punishment (Raine, 2019). However, excessive focus on the brain may serve to undermine or bracket off contextual information that points to the larger social structural determinants of criminal behavior (Fallin et al., 2018). Peering deeper into the brain may blind us to the social world.

Conclusion

Our everyday folk psychology seems to follow a naïve model of agency in which action begins with an idea for that action, followed by its execution. But cognition and action selection always occur as part of an ongoing engagement with the world, including both our local environment and relationships with others. The arrangements of the social world, and the resulting affordances, are crucial determinants of our actions, and the nature and degree of agency should be judged only against the extent to which we have a behavioral repertoire (and an environment) that affords us alternatives.

Agency arises not from a homunculus sitting behind the controls in our forebrain, making moment-to-moment decisions, but from our ongoing participation in extended plans that involve engagement with the environment. In particular, agency resides in iterative loops of intention, action, and response to social and cultural affordances. While our ability to engage with these affordances depends on the brain, and damage to the brain may disrupt our capacity to respond to these affordances, it is a conceptual error to locate these capacities entirely in the brain. Without our developmental experiences of learning to give accounts of our behavior to others, struggling to reconcile our actions with our intentions, and striving to adhere to cultural values and fulfill our ideals, we would not have agency or free will in the specifically human ways that matter. The broader implication of this social–ecological view is that enabling human agency depends not just on ensuring the healthy functioning of the brain but on supporting the social structures and cultural meanings that make moral life possible. There can be no science, medicine, or morality of human volition without equal attention to the brain and the social world.

REFERENCES

Azuma, H. (1984). Secondary control as a heterogeneous category. *American Psychologist*, *39*(9): 970–71. https://doi.org/10.1037/0003-066X.39.9.970

Bart, V. K. E., Sharavdorj, E., Bazarvaani, K., Munkhbat, T., Wenke, D., & Rieger, M. (2019). It was me: The use of sense of agency cues differs between cultures. *Frontiers in Psychology*, *10*, 650. https://doi.org/10.3389/fpsyg.2019.00650

Baumeister, R. F. (2008). Free will in scientific psychology. *Perspectives on Psychological Science*, *3*(1), 14–19. https://doi.org/10.1111/j.1745-6916.2008.00057.x

Beyer, F., Sidarus, N., Bonicalzi, S., & Haggard, P. (2017). Beyond self-serving bias: Diffusion of responsibility reduces sense of agency and outcome monitoring. *Social Cognitive and Affective Neuroscience*, *12*(1), 138–45. https://doi.org/10.1093/scan/nsw160

Blanke, O. (2012). Multisensory brain mechanisms of bodily self-consciousness. *Nature Reviews Neuroscience*, *13*, 556–71. https://doi.org/10.1038/nrn3292

Botvinick, M., & Cohen, J. (1998). Rubber hands 'feel' touch that eyes see. *Nature*, *391* (6669), 756. https://doi.org/10.1038/35784

Brass, M., Lynn, M. T., Demanet, J., & Rigoni, D. (2013). Imaging volition: What the brain can tell us about the will. *Experimental Brain Research*, *229*(3), 301–12. https://doi.org/10.1007/s00221-013-3472-x

Brehm, S. S., & Brehm, J. W. (2013). *Psychological reactance: A theory of freedom and control*. Academic Press.

Buhrmann, T., & Di Paolo, E. (2017). The sense of agency – A phenomenological consequence of enacting sensorimotor schemes. *Phenomenology and the Cognitive Sciences*, *16*(2), 207–36. https://doi.org/10.1007/s11097-015-9446-7

Chambon, V., Sidarus, N., & Haggard, P. (2014). From action intentions to action effects: How does the sense of agency come about? *Frontiers in Human Neuroscience*, *8*, 320. https://doi.org/10.3389/fnhum.2014.00320

Chirkov, V. I., Ryan, R. M., & Sheldon, K. M. (Eds.). (2011). *Human autonomy in cross-cultural context: Perspectives on the psychology of agency, freedom, and people's well-being*. Springer. https://doi.org/10.1007/978-90-481-9667-8

Christensen, J. F., Di Costa, S., Beck, B., & Haggard, P. (2019). I just lost it! Fear and anger reduce the sense of agency: A study using intentional binding. *Experimental Brain Research*, *237*(5), 1205–12. https://doi.org/10.1007/s00221-018-5461-6

Clark, A. (2016). *Surfing uncertainty: Prediction, action, and the embodied mind*. Oxford University Press.

David, N. (2012). New frontiers in the neuroscience of the sense of agency. *Frontiers in Human Neuroscience*, *6*, 161. https://doi.org/10.3389/fnhum.2012.00161

David, N., Newen, A., & Vogeley, K. (2008). The "sense of agency" and its underlying cognitive and neural mechanisms. *Consciousness and Cognition*, *17*(2), 523–34. https://doi.org/10.1016/j.concog.2008.03.004

Deeley, Q., Oakley, D. A., Walsh, E., Bell, V., Mehta, M. A., & Halligan, P. W. (2014). Modelling psychiatric and cultural possession phenomena with suggestion and fMRI. *Cortex*, *53*, 107–19. https://doi.org/10.1016/j.cortex.2014.01.004

Dogge, M., Schaap, M., Custers, R., Wegner, D. M., & Aarts, H. (2012). When moving without volition: Implied self-causation enhances binding strength between involuntary actions and effects. *Consciousness and Cognition*, *21*(1), 501–6. https://doi.org/10.1016/j.concog.2011.10.014

Edge, H., & Suryani, L. (2002). A cross-cultural analysis of volition. *Florida Philosophical Review*, *2* (2), 56–72.

Fallin, M., Whooley, O., & Barker, K. K. (2018). Criminalizing the brain: Neurocriminology and the production of strategic ignorance. *BioSocieties*, 1–25. Advance online publication. https://doi.org/10.1057/s41292-018-0135-y

Fausey, C. M., Long, B. L., Inamori, A., & Boroditsky, L. (2010). Constructing agency: The role of language. *Frontiers of Psychology*, *1*, 162. https://doi.org/10.3389/fpsyg.2010.00162

Feldman, G. (2017). Making sense of agency: Belief in free will as a unique and important construct. *Social and Personality Psychology Compass*, *11*(1), e12293. https://doi.org/10.1111/spc3.12293

Frith, C. D. (2014). Action, agency and responsibility. *Neuropsychologia*, *55*, 137–42. https://doi.org/10.1016/j.neuropsychologia.2013.09.007

Gallagher, S. (2017). *Enactivist interventions: Rethinking the mind*. Oxford University Press. https://doi.org/10.1093/oso/9780198794325.001.0001

Gailliot, M. T., & Baumeister, R. F. (2007). The physiology of willpower: Linking blood glucose to self-control. *Personality and Social Psychology Review*, *11*(4), 303–27. https://doi.org/10.1177/1088868307303030

Giddens, A. (1979). *Central problems in social theory: Actions, structure and contradiction in social analysis*. Palgrave. https://doi.org/10.1007/978-1-349-16161-4_3

Gonzalez-Franco, M., & Lanier, J. (2017). Model of illusions and virtual reality. *Frontiers in Psychology*, *8*, 1125. https://doi.org/10.3389/fpsyg.2017.01125

Greely, H. T., & Farahany, N. A. (2019). Neuroscience and the criminal justice system. *Annual Review of Criminology*, *2*, 451–71. https://doi.org/10.1146/annurev-criminol-011518-024433

Grush, R. (2004). The emulation theory of representation: Motor control, imagery, and perception. *Behavioral and Brain Sciences*, *27*(3), 377–96. https://doi.org/10.1017/S0140525X04000093

Haggard, P. (2017). Sense of agency in the human brain. *Nature Reviews Neuroscience*, *18*(4), 196–207. https://doi.org/10.1038/nrn.2017.14

Haggard, P., & Eitam, B. (Eds.). (2015). *The sense of agency*. Oxford University Press. https://doi.org/10.1093/acprof:oso/9780190267278.001.0001

Hilgard, E. R. (1986). *Divided consciousness: Multiple controls in human thought and action* (Expanded ed.). Wiley.

Ismail, M. A. F., & Shimada, S. (2016). 'Robot' hand illusion under delayed visual feedback: Relationship between the senses of ownership and agency. *PLoS ONE*, *11*(7), e0159619. https://doi.org/10.1371/journal.pone.0159619

Job, V., Dweck, C. S., & Walton, G. M. (2010). Ego depletion – Is it all in your head? Implicit theories about willpower affect self-regulation. *Psychological Science*, *21*(11), 1686–93. https://doi.org/10.1177/0956797610384745

Johansson, P., Hall, L., Sikström, S., & Olsson, A. (2005). Failure to detect mismatches between intention and outcome in a simple decision task. *Science*, *310*(5745), 116–19. https://doi.org/10.1126/science.1111709

Juarrero, A. (1999). *Dynamics in action: Intentional behavior as a complex system*. MIT Press. https://doi.org/10.7551/mitpress/2528.001.0001

Kalckert, A., & Ehrsson, H. H. (2012). Moving a rubber hand that feels like your own: A dissociation of ownership and agency. *Frontiers in Human Neuroscience*, *6*, 40. https://doi.org/10.3389/fnhum.2012.00040

Kirmayer, L. J. (1990). Resistance, reactance, and reluctance to change: A cognitive attributional approach to strategic interventions. *Journal of Cognitive Psychotherapy*, *4*(2), 83–104.

Kirmayer, L. J., & Gómez-Carrillo, A. (2019). Agency, embodiment and enactment in psychosomatic theory and practice. *Medical Humanities*, *45*(2), 169–82. https://doi.org/10.1136/medhum-2018-011618

Kirmayer, L. J., & Ramstead, M. J. D. (2017). Embodiment and enactment in cultural psychiatry. In C. Durt, T. Fuchs, & C. Tewes (Eds.), *Embodiment, enaction, and culture: Investigating the constitution of the shared world* (pp. 397–422). MIT Press. https://doi.org/10.7551/mitpress/9780262035552.003.0021

Kokkinara, E., Kilteni, K., Blom, K. J., & Slater, M. (2016). First person perspective of seated participants over a walking virtual body leads to illusory agency over the walking. *Scientific Reports*, *6*, 28879. https://doi.org/10.1038/srep28879

Kpanake, L. (2018). Cultural concepts of the person and mental health in Africa. *Transcultural Psychiatry*, *55*(2), 198–218. https://doi.org/10.1177/1363461517749435

Kushnir, T. (2018). The developmental and cultural psychology of free will. *Philosophy Compass*, *13*(11), e12529. https://doi.org/10.1111/phc3.12529

Lee, B. O. (2016). Transformation in dang-ki healing: The embodied self and perceived legitimacy. *Culture, Medicine, and Psychiatry*, *40*(3), 422–49. https://doi.org/10.1007/s11013-016-9497-4

Lee, B.-O., & Kirmayer, L. J. (2019). Dang-ki healing: An embodied relational healing practice in Singapore. *Transcultural Psychiatry*. Advance online publication. https://doi.org/10.1177%2F1363461519858448

Lee, B. O., Kirmayer, L. J., & Groleau, D. (2010). Therapeutic processes and perceived helpfulness of dang-ki (Chinese shamanism) from the symbolic healing perspective. *Culture, Medicine, and Psychiatry*, *34*(1), 56–105.

Lenggengager, B., Tadi, T., Metzinger, T., & Blanke, O. (2007). Video ergo sum: Manipulating bodily self-consciousness. *Science*, *317*(5841), 1096–9. https://doi.org/10.1126/science.1143439

Libet, B., Gleason, C. A., Wright, E. W., & Pearl, D. K. (1983). Time of conscious intention to act in relation to onset of cerebral activity (readiness-potential): The unconscious initiation of freely voluntary act. *Brain*, *106*(3), 623–42. https://doi.org/10.1093/brain/106.3.623

Lynn, S. J., Rhue, J. W., & Weekes, J. R. (1990). Hypnotic involuntariness: A social cognitive analysis. *Psychological Review*, *97*(2), 169–84. https://doi.org/10.1037/0033-295X.97.2.169

Markus, H. R., & Kitayama, S. (2010). Cultures and selves: A cycle of mutual constitution. *Perspectives on Psychological Science*, 5(4), 420–30. https://doi.org/10.1177/1745691610375557

Maurer, C. W., LaFaver, K., Ameli, R., Epstein, S. A., Hallett, M., & Horovitz, S. G. (2016). Impaired self-agency in functional movement disorders: A resting-state fMRI study. *Neurology*, 87(6), 564–70. https://doi.org/10.1212/WNL.0000000000002940

Miller, G. (2016, March 1). The brain gets its day in court. *The Atlantic*. www.theatlantic.com/science/archive/2016/03/neurolaw-brain-scans-court/471615

Miller, G. A., Galanter, E., & Pribram, K. H. (1960). *Plans and the structure of behavior*. Holt, Reinhart, Winston. https://doi.org/10.1037/10039-000

Miller, P. J., Koven, M., & Lin, S. (2011). Language socialization and narrative. In A. Durant, E. Ochs, & B. Schieffelin (Eds.), *The handbook of language socialization* (pp. 190–208). Wiley. https://doi.org/10.1002/9781444342901.ch8

Mischel, W., Ayduk, O., Berman, M. G., Casey, B. J., Gotlib, I. H., Jonides, J., Kross, E., Teslovich, T., Wilson, N. L., Zayas, V., & Shoda, Y. (2010). 'Willpower' over the life span: Decomposing self-regulation. *Social Cognitive and Affective Neuroscience*, 6(2), 252–6. https://doi.org/10.1093/scan/nsq081

Moore, J. W. (2016). What is the sense of agency and why does it matter? *Frontiers in Psychology*, 7, 1272. https://doi.org/10.3389/fpsyg.2016.01272

Moretto, G., Walsh, E., & Haggard, P. (2011). Experience of agency and sense of responsibility. *Consciousness and Cognition*, 20(4), 1847–54. https://doi.org/10.1016/j.concog.2011.08.014

Nahab, F. B., Kundu, P., Maurer, C., Shen, Q., & Hallett, M. (2017). Impaired sense of agency in functional movement disorders: An fMRI study. *PLoS ONE*, 12(4), e0172502. https://doi.org/10.1371/journal.pone.0172502

Oerter, R., Oerter, R., Agostiani, H., Kim, H. O., & Wibowo, S. (1996). The concept of human nature in East Asia: Etic and emic characteristics. *Culture & Psychology*, 2(1), 9–51. https://doi.org/10.1177/1354067X9621002

Papies, E. K., & Aarts, H. (2016). Automatic self-regulation: From habit to goal pursuit. In K. Vohs & R.F. Baumeister (Eds.), *Handbook of self-regulation: Research, theory, and applications* (3rd ed., pp. 203–22). Guilford Press.

Polito, V., Barnier, A. J., Woody, E. Z., & Connors, M. H. (2014). Measuring agency change across the domain of hypnosis. *Psychology of Consciousness: Theory, Research, and Practice*, 1(1), 3–19. https://doi.org/10.1037/cns0000010

Powers, W. T. (1973). *Behavior: The control of perception*. Aldine.

Raine, A. (2019). A neurodevelopmental perspective on male violence. *Infant Mental Health* 40(1), 84–97. https://doi.org/10.1002/imhj.21761

Ramstead, M. J., Veissière, S. P., & Kirmayer, L. J. (2016). Cultural affordances: Scaffolding local worlds through shared intentionality and regimes of attention. *Frontiers in Psychology*, 7, 1090. https://doi.org/10.3389/fpsyg.2016.01090

Rose, N. (1998). *Inventing our selves: Psychology, power, and personhood*. Cambridge University Press.

Saigle, V., Dubljević, V., & Racine, E. (2018). The impact of a landmark neuroscience study on free will: A qualitative analysis of articles using Libet and colleagues' methods. *AJOB Neuroscience*, *9*(1), 29–41. https://doi.org/10.1080/21507740.2018.1425756

Seligman, R., & Kirmayer, L. J. (2008). Dissociative experience and cultural neuroscience: Narrative, metaphor and mechanism. *Culture, Medicine and Psychiatry*, *32*(1), 31–64. https://doi.org/10.1007/s11013-007-9077-8

Seth, A. K., Suzuki, K., & Critchley, H. D. (2012). An interoceptive predictive coding model of conscious presence. *Frontiers in Psychology*, *2*, 395. https://doi.org/10.3389/fpsyg.2011.00395

Slater, M., Perez-Marcos, D., Ehrsson, H. H., & Sanchez-Vives, M. V. (2009). Inducing illusory ownership of a virtual body. *Frontiers in Neuroscience*, *3*(2), 214–20. https://doi.org/10.3389%2Fneuro.01.029.2009

Synofzik, M., Vosgerau, G., & Newen, A. (2008). Beyond the comparator model: A multifactorial two-step account of agency. *Consciousness and Cognition*, *17*(1), 219–39. https://doi.org/10.1016/j.concog.2007.03.010

Tilly, C. (2006). *Why? What happens when people give reasons . . . and why*. Princeton University Press.

Veissière, S. P., Constant, A., Ramstead, M. J., Friston, K. J., & Kirmayer, L. J. (2020). Thinking through other minds: A variational approach to cognition and culture. *Behavioral and Brain Sciences*, 43, e90: 1–75. doi:10.1017/S0140525X19001213

Wegner, D. M. (2003). The mind's best trick: How we experience conscious will. *Trends in Cognitive Science*, *7*(2), 65–9. https://doi.org/10.1016/s1364-6613%2803%2900002-0

Wegner, D. M., Gilbert, D., & Wheatley, T. (2017). *The illusion of conscious will*. MIT Press. https://doi.org/10.7551/mitpress/11151.001.0001

Weisz, J. R., Rothbaum, F. M., & Blackburn, T. C. (1984). Standing out and standing in: The psychology of control in America and Japan. *American Psychologist*, *39*(9), 955–69. https://doi.org/10.1037/0003-066X.39.9.955

Wikan, U. (1990). *Managing turbulent hearts: A Balinese formula for living*. University of Chicago Press.

Section 3

How Social Coordination and Cooperation are Achieved

Introduction

Human cooperation has been a great puzzle for biologists, who find no equal among other animals (Fotouhi et al., 2019), and for social scientists, who struggle to figure out how and why it works, or doesn't. The extent and forms of cooperation and reciprocity seen in humans form a crucial element in their adaptive niche. It helps to think of the effect of multiple timelines on this process (see Chapter 1). This section tackles the problem at the level of within-species variation in cooperative behavior among contemporary populations, to identify biocultural factors and evolutionary–historical constraints in cooperation and its culturally diverse manifestations. One approach investigates the effects of cultural practices on cooperative behavior, while another looks at cultural effects on the psychology of cooperation. Ritual and religion feature prominently in every known society and are tied to group behavior, beliefs, and values, suggesting they play an important role in fostering social coordination and cooperation. Kavanagh et al. (Chapter 11) deftly review the literature on these "cultural technologies." Work to characterize the pragmatics and "active" ingredients in ritual and religion that promote cooperation has generated many intriguing hypotheses, but the evidence remains largely inconclusive. Their chapter also traces a welcome surge of multisite, cross-cultural study designs and experimental methods, and describes the insights to be gained by applying mixed methods research to tap cultural, behavioral, cognitive, and biological dimensions. Other recent studies indicate the importance of cues and affordances that condition whether or not cooperative behavior occurs, and point to the possibility that cultures mold cooperation by structuring both the ecology of cues and affordances, and their cognitive-behavioral impact

In related work, cultural psychology has investigated axes along which cultural constructions vary, including modes of self-construal (interdependent–independent), emotional valence (negative–positive, threat–reward), and their psychosocial consequences. In their chapter, Mu and Gelfand (Chapter 10) examine cultural variation along a dimension of loose-to-tight configurations of strength and enforcement of social norms, and link this to ecological–historical threat, brain and behavioral responses to norm violations or threat, and the prevalence of threat- or reward-oriented variants of neuroregulatory genes. This rich vein of research raises many questions about social cognition and behavior, their sociohistorical and coevolutionary roots, and embodiment in members of a society.

Emerging evidence that the brain uses probabilistic predictive algorithms (*predictive processing* or *active inference*, as discussed in Chapters 1, 5, and 6) to guide action shows how "cooperation" may reflect the deep, pervasive effects of shared cultural frames (Veissière et al., 2020). Such frames (belief- and value-saturated models of the world and the action schemas they generate) may play essential cognitive roles in feeding the predictive brain by making the world comprehensible, coherent, and predictable. Lende and Downey (Chapter 9) discuss the literature on cultural consensus and consonance, that is, the extent to which something is shared in a culture, and the individual's ability to enact that shared view. Both consensus and consonance determine the level of "surprisal" or cognitive dissonance that burdens brain processing. Cultural consonance, in turn, has been associated with mental and physical health. Running through the observations and models discussed in this section is the evidence that as culture becomes embodied in brain, the brain then instantiates culture in the world through memory, meaning, and action.

Two unaddressed lines of social neuroscience research should be mentioned here. First are arresting insights into the significance of brain synchrony that are emerging from recent methodological innovations. Imaging has expanded from tracking one brain's responses to stimuli or tasks, to tracking activity during interactions of two people, in increasingly natural or naturalistic settings (Dikker et al., 2014; Redcay & Schilbach, 2019). The brain responds differently to dyadic interaction compared to third-person observation of others. Brain activity becomes synchronized or coupled when people share an experience such as mutual understanding of a narrative (Nguyen et al., 2019), and experiences of shared attention build social memory by being represented and retained in a pair-specific manner (Koike et al., 2016). However, brain responses to the same experience lack synchrony when people do not share the same beliefs and values (Yeshurun et al., 2017).

A second line of important work concerns social neuroscientific findings about cooperation's shadow, which takes the form of in-group–out-group bias, stereotyping, social devaluation, dehumanization, and exclusion. This work is delineating the neural bases of these processes and identifying the implicit cues and situational factors that determine the negative evaluation of others viewed as members of an out-group (Amodio, 2014; Harris et al., 2014;

Leander et al., 2011; Swencionis & Fiske, 2014). Neural activity patterns associated with group membership overlap with those associated with self (Morrison et al., 2012), reflecting the profound importance of both cultural constructions and social relations for personhood.

Many lines of evidence and social analysis converge on the centrality of social cooperation for humans. The forces unleashed by globalization and social media are generating new possibilities for connection and solidarity and unexpected threats to the social webs on which we all rely, raising the stakes for understanding and promoting a central feature of the human adaptive niche essential to our welfare.

REFERENCES

Amodio, D. M. (2014). The neuroscience of prejudice and stereotyping. *Nature Reviews Neuroscience*, *15*(10), 670–82. https://doi.org/10.1038/nrn3800

Dikker, S., Silbert, L. J., Hasson, U., & Zevin, J. D. (2014). On the same wavelength: Predictable language enhances speaker–listener brain-to-brain synchrony in posterior superior temporal gyrus. *Journal of Neuroscience*, *34*(18), 6267–72. https://doi.org/10.1523/jneurosci.3796-13.2014

Fotouhi, B., Momeni, N., Allen, B., & Nowak, M. A. (2019). Evolution of cooperation on large networks with community structure. *Journal of the Royal Society Interface*, *16*(152), 20180677. https://doi.org/10.1098/rsif.2018.0677

Harris, L. T., Lee, V. K., Capestany, B. H., & Cohen, A. O. (2014). Assigning economic value to people results in dehumanization brain response. *Journal of Neuroscience, Psychology, and Economics*, *7*(3), 151–63. https://doi.org/10.1037/npe0000020

Koike, T., Tanabe, H. C., Okazaki, S., Nakagawa, E., Sasaki, A. T., Shimada, K., Sugawara, S. K., Takahashi, H. K., Yoshihara, K., Bosch-Bayard, J., & Sadato, N. (2016). Neural substrates of shared attention as social memory: A hyperscanning functional magnetic resonance imaging study. *NeuroImage*, *125*, 401–12. https://doi.org/10.1016/j.neuroimage.2015.09.076

Leander, N. P., Chartrand, T. L., & Wood, W. (2011). Mind your mannerisms: Behavioral mimicry elicits stereotype conformity. *Journal of Experimental Social Psychology*, *47*(1), 195–201. https://doi.org/10.1016/j.jesp.2010.09.002

Morrison, S., Decety, J., & Molenberghs, P. (2012). The neuroscience of group membership. *Neuropsychologia*, *50*(8), 2114–20. https://doi.org/10.1016/j.neuropsychologia.2012.05.014

Nguyen, M., Vanderwal, T., & Hasson, U. (2019). Shared understanding of narratives is correlated with shared neural responses. *NeuroImage*, *184*, 161–70. https://doi.org/10.1016/j.neuroimage.2018.09.010

Redcay, E., & Schilbach, L. (2019). Using second-person neuroscience to elucidate the mechanisms of social interaction. *Nature Reviews Neuroscience*, *20*(8), 495–505. https://doi.org/10.1038/s41583-019-0179-4

Swencionis, J. K., & Fiske, S. T. (2014). How social neuroscience can inform theories of social comparison. *Neuropsychologia*, *56*, 140–6. https://doi.org/10.1016/j.neuropsychologia.2014.01.009

Veissière, S. P., Constant, A., Ramstead, M. J., Friston, K. J., & Kirmayer, L. J. (2020). Thinking through other minds: A variational approach to cognition and culture. *Behavioral and Brain Sciences*, *43*, e90, 1–75. https://10.1017/S0140525X19001213

Yeshurun, Y., Swanson, S., Simony, E., Chen, J., Lazaridi, C., Honey, C. J., & Hasson, U. (2017). Same story, different story: The neural representation of interpretive frameworks. *Psychological Science*, *28*(3), 307–19. https://doi.org/10.1177/0956797616682029

9 Neuroanthropological Perspectives on Culture, Mind, and Brain

Daniel H. Lende and Greg Downey

Introduction

New research on the brain increasingly shows that human cultural differences – such as native language, models for self-construal, and emotion norms – affect neurological functioning in observable ways (Chiao et al., 2013). Brain scientists and cognitive theorists acknowledge the importance of culture in inflecting some of our most basic neural architecture and dynamics, leading to emerging fields like cross-cultural neuroimaging and cultural neuroscience (Bender & Beller, 2016; Chiao et al., 2016; Han & Northoff, 2008). Research from brain imaging reports how different skill sets, such as learning to use an abacus, play the violin, or navigate London's complicated streets, affect the size, activity, or connectivity of particular brain areas (for review, Downey, 2016; Wexler, 2006). Studies also show that different political inclinations, the depth of one's religious faith, or the linguistic milieu in which we grow up all influence how our nervous system responds to basic stimuli (Chiao et al., 2016; Rule et al., 2013).

While the range of human diversity is no surprise to anthropologists, that these differences have observable neurological correlates may be. Culture becomes "embrained" to a degree greater than most cultural anthropologists realize. The resulting biocultural imbrication demands that neurobiology be given greater consideration as part of cultural research. At present, however, when anthropologists explore medical, psychological, and developmental topics, they generally use theoretical and analytical tools oriented toward social and cultural reduction. Social theorists typically emphasize the social origins of variation while disregarding biology, either because they mistrust claims of innateness or genetic determinism, or they view biology as largely irrelevant because of the determining force of "social construction." For this reason, theorists seldom grapple with evidence of context sensitivity in physiological systems (in particular our nervous system), and how these systems interact with the sociocultural practices, places, and artifacts that make up our local worlds (Pitts-Taylor, 2016). Ironically, this reduction to the social or cultural diminishes anthropologists' ability to understand the variation they seek to explain and disregards evidence that cultural variation has biological consequences.

Neuroanthropology responds to the need to develop integrative approaches to understanding human variation (Lende & Downey, 2012a). This approach emerged out of researchers drawing on neurological and cognitive science to address ethnographic problems that appeared during field research, for example, how balance works across different sports and societies (Downey, 2012). Neuroanthropologists advocate drawing on neurobiology to theorize about ethnographic problems, to interpret data in novel ways, and to do applied work (Duque et al., 2009; Lende & Downey, 2012b). This chapter first examines how neuroanthropologists approach the study of human variation. Then it tackles three examples of bringing together neuroscience and anthropology: (1) understanding habitus, (2) using computational neuroscience to examine cultural consensus and consonance, and (3) the social and interactional context of emerging human capacities.

Understanding Human Variation

Neuroscience research reveals a brain that defies longstanding assumptions: it is more plastic and interconnected, and possesses a potent ability to reuse existing resources to accomplish novel ends (Anderson, 2010). The revelation of deep developmental neuroplasticity undermines the assertion in evolutionary psychology that "our modern skulls house a stone age mind," by Leda Cosmides and John Tooby (1997). Cross-cultural neuroimaging demonstrates that brain structures are susceptible to enculturation (Chiao et al., 2016); the emergence of many features and connections requires activity and external stimulation, often patterned by cultural context in ways that influence their mature configuration. Our biographies, social positions, education, training, perceptions, and experiences leave their traces in our nervous systems (Roepstorff et al., 2010). No longer can anthropological theory assume that underlying a culturally diverse "mind" is a species-general "brain" that assures our "psychic unity" (see Shore, 1996). By exploring "brains in the wild," neuroanthropology addresses how context and culture come together with neural development and function. Just as Margaret Lock (1993) proposed the concept of "local biologies" to capture the integration of social with biological forces, neuroanthropologists examine "local neurologies."

Ecological approaches to human development and niche construction model how person–place interactions produce human similarity and difference (Worthman, 2010). Social and cultural factors, including forms of economic organization, inequality, gender, and other social forces, shape neural diversity by providing ongoing supports for action. The challenge for neuroanthropology is not just to recognize correlations between contextual and neurological features but also to explore the developmental processes that transform context into physiology. Theorizing these connections generally requires "middle-range" concepts and models, exploring person–place interactions in culturally specific forms while also seeking to illuminate mechanisms that will be relevant in other contexts. This middle-range approach can focus, for example, on how "patterned practices" and skill acquisition play a fundamental role in shaping key characteristics of local neurologies (Downey, 2012; Roepstorff et al., 2010).

Middle-range analyses are also required because of the "intersectionality" of neurological development, to borrow a term from feminist theory. Coined by legal scholar Kimberlé Crenshaw (1989), the term highlights the interplay and cumulative effects of forms of discrimination, how, for example, gender and racial discrimination exacerbate each other. We use the term to highlight that different developmental influences – insults and chronic influences, as well as functioning enhanced by education or skill acquisition – are cumulative, interacting influences on brain structures and functions. The "modular" account of the mind, popularized by philosopher Jerry Fodor (1983) and later radicalized as "massive modularity" by evolutionary psychologists (e.g., Carruthers, 2006), holds that the mind is made up of segregated, special-purpose cognitive tools, largely automatic and inaccessible to awareness (p. 12). In contrast, an "intersectional" brain is heavily influenced by its environment, incorporating diverse forces into its structure in complex, interconnected ways.

A neuroanthropological approach contrasts in several ways with most current neurobiological and psychological research, which draws from a narrow range of human potential. The dominant subject population in experimental psychology research is "WEIRD" or Western, educated, industrialized, rich, and democratic, according to an influential paper by Henrich et al. (2010). Without a broader sense of extant and extinct human variation, brain researchers might believe they are exploring a universal "human brain" when they are really mining insights from selected local neurologies: Those variants of humanity who take psychology classes or visit neuroimaging facilities.

As a critique of neuroscience, however, the "WEIRD" characterization presents two problems. First, "WEIRD" as a descriptor ironically flatters these subjects, focusing on traits that Westerners typically highlight to describe themselves in ways that are, however inadvertently, self-congratulatory. Sedentism, social stress, consumerism, isolation, adiposity, pollution, urbanization, industrialized diet, and literacy, for example, all influence neurological development (Panter-Brick et al., 2012; Worthman, 2009). For WEIRD populations, their Occidentalism, economic organization, independence, and political participation may not contribute most to their distinctive profile; they can be neurologically odd for reasons other than being "WEIRD."

Another gap in the WEIRD critique is that it still leaves "the Other" undifferentiated. When it flattens the internal variation in WEIRD populations – for example, average education levels may be higher in the West, but within-group variation is high – it also risks egregiously erasing the greater variation among non-Western populations. That is not a theoretically sophisticated approach to understanding human variation and does not address researchers' tendencies to interpret results from their own preconceived ideas (such as assuming human universality or a West–East dichotomy that risks instantiating a "neural Orientalism"; Downey & Lende, 2012a, p. 35). A more effective approach is to critically reflect on methods, positionality, and academic bias. Anthropologists recognized this problem long before other fields, but the ways to address biases in our research have not extended into most research on culture, mind, and brain (Roepstorff, 2013). For example, replication – while important – is only one safeguard to producing stronger insights into human psychological diversity. Equally important are reflexivity about research and sampling and critical assessments of how one's methods and theories produce the results one anticipates (Muthukrishna & Henrich, 2019).

Habitus and the Production of Local Neurologies

Habitus provides an example of how social theory can be enriched by considering neurobiology. "Habitus" refers to the acquired dispositions that people have based on their social developmental trajectories. Initially developed by Bourdieu (1972/1977, 1979/1984), the habitus concept provides an account of how social divisions such as class become embodied. The habitus concept addresses the question, how do cultural biases and social structures get internalized through behavior and imposed on the world as patterns of action, perception, and thought?

Habitus is intriguing to neuroanthropologists because the definition implies a cluster of non-conscious, embodied processes, such as emotional and perceptual biases, rather than offering a semiotic or symbolic account of socialization. The insistence that the habitus is embodied rather than mental suggests that it is amenable to a combined biocultural account. However, the habitus concept when used by Bourdieu puts to one side human variation and physiology, blackboxing neurodevelopmental processes implicit in the model and paving over the developmental dynamics that might produce neural variation (Downey, 2010a; Roepstorff et al., 2010). Even proponents suggest that the theoretical abstraction demands empirical testing and analytical parsing (Wacquant, 2016, p. 70; Warin et al., 2016). As Crossley (2013, p. 137) writes, habitus is a "question-begging concept," one that uses a language of materiality without engaging biology. Recent developmental research has identified pathways that mediate processes of embodiment in the cumulative formation of patterns like "habitus" both within and across generations, such as neuroendocrine responses to stress (Worthman, 2009) and other biological responses to inequality and hardship (Burbank, 2012; Lende, 2012).

Humans' disproportionate neurological endowment relative to other primates makes us uniquely susceptible to environmental shaping, both the natural settings we encounter and the artificial ones we create. We come into the world neurologically incomplete, and we shape our own and each other's development. This neural susceptibility to environmental influence has allowed us – cumulatively, over many generations – to create developmental niches, which results in a more complex dynamic model than simply assuming that bodily habitus mirrors social position (Fuentes, 2016; Stotz, 2010).

For example, a "habitus" such as a gendered difference in bodily motility can become embodied through a complex combination of procedural learning, sensory bias, learned inhibition, implicit categorization, and physiological canalization; men's and women's bodies may start chromosomally distinct, but they can become more divergent over time through physiological, emotional, and neurological sculpting (Downey, 2010b; Young, 1980). Rather than finding a clear biology–culture distinction between "sex" and "gender" to explain differences in the brain, for example, local gender neurologies emerge from complex "whole body" dynamics that involve other organs and gut ecology, as well as complex social relations (de Vries & Forger, 2015; Fausto-Sterling, 2019). In addition, to gain theoretical traction, habitus is often assumed to be homogeneous within a group; without this assumption, Bourdieu's (1972/1977) notion that members of a class share habitus is incoherent. This assumption obscures a series of deeper investigations into local neurologies and the intersectionality of the brain.

Our neurological endowment gives humans greater autonomy and self-control, albeit constrained by the need to build our capacities through long-term regimens of neurological cultivation. Humans embark on long-term projects of self-determination, such as skill acquisition, that would be impossible without our regulatory capacities bolstered by learned self-management systems, like language used as internal admonition or motivations reinforced by external incentives. Recognizing the complex ways that patterns of experience are biologically embodied allows us to reinterpret physiological differences we find between groups, recognizing that they are biocultural adaptation and not predestination (Gravlee, 2009). Focusing on local neurologies allows us to operationalize habitus, to open the black box, and to ask about the specific behavioral–developmental mechanisms of embodiment that lead an individual to reflect and continually reconstruct a social position. Developmental niche construction, both conscious and unintentional, rebounds back upon behavior and nervous system performance in ways that "habitus" seeks to label without sufficiently describing or accounting for theoretically.

Computational Neuroscience and Cultural Consonance

Advances in computational neuroscience offer one way to operationalize the intersection of local neurologies with specific life trajectories. This section examines how the "predictive brain" approach (Clark, 2013), in particular using Bayesian statistics to model neural function, can be brought into conversation with a prominent computational approach in anthropology: cultural consensus and consonance, an empirical analytical technique to assess sharedness and individual variation in cultural knowledge (Dressler, 2017).

Computational neuroscience increasingly uses statistical models to examine how brains can accurately and rapidly adapt to their environment in real-time. Bayesian statistics estimates the initial probability of events based on prior expectations; in other words, what was known about the probability of some event before current evidence or experience is considered. Bayes's rule is used to combine these priors with likelihoods, which is the probability of events given some evidence. This combination yields an expectation, that is, a "best guess" based on an optimal combination of previous experience with current experience.

When the prediction diverges from what actually happens, the model is updated. For example, early work on dopamine function indicated how "prediction errors" – the difference between an expected input and the actual signal from dopamine neurons – provide a teaching signal to titrate dopamine function during reward-based learning (Schultz et al., 1997). Continued research on dopamine demonstrates how "error-driven learning" can provide feedback to improve prediction and thus function more efficiently neurologically (Keiflin & Janak, 2017).

Recently, Friston has developed the "free energy" variant of Bayesian computational approaches (Friston, 2010; Friston et al., 2018). The free energy view posits that cognition, like all biological functions, uses self-organization against the fundamental law of entropy. For neural function, the minimization of "free energy" provides a computational principle promoting adaptive cognition in the face of the inevitable demands of entropy (Bruineberg et al., 2018; Friston, 2009). In Friston's model, neural function reduces entropy by seeking more efficient alternatives that result in less energy loss. Simplified, free energy "is just the amount of prediction error" (Friston, 2009, p. 293).

Drawing on Friston, some authors interested in the intersection of culture, mind, and brain have found the "active inference" variant of the Bayesian approaches useful to model cultural cognition and human interactions (Ramstead et al., 2016; Veissière & Stendel, 2018). Authors in this tradition (e.g., Friston, 2010; Ramstead et al., 2016, 2018) highlight the importance of considering "surprisal." Surprisal quantifies how unexpected a given state is; that is, how far some sensory outcomes depart from what is typical (or even what is embodied phenotypically). Active inference suggests that organisms evaluate how "surprising" some sensory data are by comparing the data to which they are privy with prior expectations. This difference – between what I expect, given my model of the world, and what I sense – is a quantity called "variational free energy," which is roughly speaking an estimation of surprisal. That is, free energy (and therefore surprise) is high when sensory states do not match what the brain expected (e.g., neural predictions from top-down models). Surprise is reduced when the organism enacts its expectations, that is, makes the world more like its model.

Researchers using the free energy approach have proposed that culture itself extends our brain's ability to avoid surprise, thus sustaining higher levels of self-organization (Ramstead et al., 2016, 2018; Ramstead, Constant, et al., 2019; Ramstead, Kirchhoff et al., 2019). This "free energy" approach has been taken a step further by Constant et al. (2018), who propose that the human environment, which crucially includes other agents and their engagement in shared cultural practices, is also a surprisal-minimizing mechanism. People shape their local developmental niches through activities and the creation of material artifacts; in turn, these changes in the local environment provide ways for developing humans to increase the fit between their internal models and the more precise sensory inputs that come from an altered local environment.

This free energy approach focuses largely on individual cognition in relation to the environment, leaving to one side considerations of biological mechanisms based on experimental and physiological research (see Shipp, 2016, for some useful insights). As Ramstead, Constant, et al. (2019) write, the free energy approach "is not a theory of everything; it does not, on its own, provide an explanation of the systemic processes that constitute living systems" (pp. 3–4).

As a "middle-range" approach, this type of research is also not an examination of the systemic processes of culture. Here, research on how culture shapes cognition can potentially help bridge the gap between abstract statistical models and ethnographic research on how people interact with culturally mediated environments.

Ramstead et al. (2016) argue for the importance of considering "agents" skillfully leveraging explicit or implicit expectations, norms, conventions, and cooperative social practices. Agents have "the ability to correctly infer (implicitly or explicitly) the culturally specific sets of expectations in which they are immersed" (p. 2). We propose here that consideration of expectations and processes of feedback can expand understanding of cultural consensus and whether individuals are consonant (fit in) with local beliefs and standards.

Consonance and the reduction of variational free energy are analogous. Cultural consonance occurs when people's top-down predictive models fit well with their local cultural values; a lack of "fit" or individual consonance is experienced as distressing (Dressler & Bindon, 2000; Dressler et al., 2005). The computational principle to reduce free energy can manifest by reducing cultural dissonance. Drawing on the active inference and free energy approach, humans as cultural beings seek consonance to improve their long-term viability in specific sociocultural settings. To put it another way, cultural learning decreases surprise and stress, and promotes adaptation.

Social interactions help support these matching-and-prediction error processes, for example, through how coordinated behavior models what we are expected to do (say, the "proper way" to eat). Thus, in cultural interactions, we should be sensitive to mismatches and errors, not simply to augment individual learning, but also to promote cultural adaptation (for a similar discussion, see Ramstead et al., 2016). This view implies that in sociocultural interactions, people should attend to those specific sensory inputs that promote error feedback that helps to achieve cultural consensus. Cultural conformity does not come as a given; rather, people figure out where they lack consensus through social interaction. Moreover, people can vary in how distressing they find a lack of consonance; Dressler et al. (2012) found interesting interactions between consonance, particular genotypes, and depressive symptoms.

It is also important to recognize that individuals-as-agents do not benignly promote consensus. Rather, people can work to establish or prioritize what counts as consensus, often in competition or cooperation with others in specific social spaces. For example, elites can control a situation, creating rules that favor them while excluding others. At the same time, individual learning can shape a person's ability to create a shared model and to process feedback when there is a mismatch. For example, someone might recognize the importance of wealth and privilege (a shared model) but be excluded from the opportunities to learn the subtle task demands specific social situations demand to truly "fit in."

At a sociocultural level, consonance arises because an inability to match a cultural ideal (or consensus) can be distressing to individuals. But there are potentially different types of consonance. First, lack of consonance can be stressful for individuals because they realize they cannot match a model, even if they want to; inequality and social barriers block the ability to match valued models. This type of dissonance fits well with political–economic analyses. Jay MacLeod (2018) documented how white, low-income high school students became deeply pessimistic about achieving academic success; they understood the achievement ideology, but felt blocked from fully participating in it and eventually formed a marginalized group in school focused on drinking and doing drugs.

Second, lack of consonance is stressful because people cannot generate the learning to match models that they know are important. A good example can be drawn from Philippe Bourgois's (1995) ethnography, *In Search of Respect:*

Selling Crack in El Barrio, in which he describes how some Harlem drug dealers who desired upward mobility sought opportunities in mainstream endeavors. However, the way they acted in these situations backfired; their models for social interaction were ill-suited to these challenges.

Third, people may continue to rely on models that they realize undercut them, but find it nearly impossible to get off the proverbial treadmill; that is, they keep participating in culture the same way, even though they are aware that their behavior impedes success. For example, for many PhD students, academic precarity is a fact of life; they embrace the culture of academia and keep pursuing excellence in their studies and research even as many of them recognize that they are unlikely to get tenure-track jobs (Peacock, 2016).

This account extends applications of consonance to multiple domains: political–economic, social, and individual. While these often overlap, they are distinguishable at a theoretical level and offer targets for different types of assessment. Put differently, considering the computational processes behind consonance, and the complexities introduced by operation in settings charged by multiple cooperating and competing agents, helps us to better understand how it works. Overall, this neuroanthropological approach proposes that cultural information processing provides a way to adapt computational neuroscience and predictive approaches in cognitive science to study culture, and to show that existing results in anthropology can be repurposed to consider the interactive processes behind specific cultural dynamics like consensus and consonance.

Social Interaction and the "Extended Nervous System"

A primary driver of hominid brain evolution – and one of its products – is our species' complex social life (Downey & Lende, 2012b; Dunbar, 1993; Humphrey, 1976). Animal studies show that increased group size, even within a single species, can lead to neurological refinement, from increases in specific parts of the cortices to tighter functional coupling among cortical areas (Sallet et al., 2011). Research correlating the size of people's social network, measured by number of Facebook friends, with architectural differences in the amygdala suggests that sociality and brain architecture influence each other even in adulthood (Bickart et al., 2011).

Debates about the "social brain" initially sought to map which parts were "social." Brothers (1990) proposed that a circumscribed region, including the amygdala, orbital frontal cortex, and temporal cortex, was dedicated to social cognition. This hypothesis was refined by neural imaging studies (Ochsner & Lieberman, 2001), with experiments showing a set of brain networks recruited when individuals perform social tasks, such as "mentalizing" or reasoning about another person's mental state (Frith, 2007; Frith & Frith, 2000).

Depending upon the experimental task, however, "theory of mind" activities employ overlapping but not identical neurological assemblies (Schurz et al., 2014), including areas not solely dedicated to social cognition (Parkinson & Wheatley, 2015; Spunt & Adolphs, 2017). Complex tasks like cooperation require the orchestration or "soft assembly" of multiple brain systems, including those underwriting "mind-reading," into larger functional networks (Kennedy & Adolphs, 2012). Joint action, for example, demands the perception and pursuit of shared goals (and suppression of self-serving impulses) as well as coordination of timing, judgment, and behavior (Engemann et al., 2012). Cooperation and competition, though both draw on social skills, recruit different neurological resources (Decety et al., 2004), possibly because of increased executive demands or intrinsic rewards to cooperation (Engemann et al., 2012, p. 6).

In addition, the discovery of the "mirror system" in monkeys and humans, parts of the premotor cortex responsive to others' movements (Rizzolatti & Craighero, 2004), demonstrated that social understanding may occur through an alternative mechanism: implicit motor simulation (Catmur et al., 2007). Although often posed as competing accounts of the neurological basis of sociality – whether humans achieve intersubjectivity primarily through "mind-reading" or embodied "simulation" – both are fundamental ways that the human brain engages socially (Van Overwalle & Baetens, 2009).

But mentalizing and mirror systems, for all their diversity, are only two of those involved in or affected by social life. Even with animal models, "social" functions are diverse, resulting in widespread involvement of different brain regions, depending upon task, interaction, or setting (Chen & Hong, 2018). Social functions such as facial recognition (Gobbini & Haxby, 2007), empathy (Hein & Singer, 2008), trust (Bellucci et al., 2017), and perceiving salience in social interaction (Seeley et al., 2007), such as rejection (Wang et al., 2017), are subserved by a variety of systems.

Many forms of interaction arise dynamically without demanding a representation of the internal mental state of others. For example, entrainment with music (Merchant et al., 2015) and turn-taking and movement synchronization (Dumas et al., 2010) are handled by fast, nonmentalizing neurological systems; the mere presence of other individuals affects our attentional mechanisms (Monfardini et al., 2016). Likewise, the ability to follow the gaze of another person, or joint attention, precedes developmentally the capacity to create a representation of another person's internal state (Tomasello, 2014, 2019). Research on shared understanding shows that individuals' brain rhythms and activity of specific regions, such as in the default mode network, synchronize when we share interpretations, engage in joint activity, or are friends (Nguyen et al., 2019; Nummenmaa et al., 2018; Parkinson et al., 2018). Dancing together releases endogenous opioids and affects pain perception (Tarr et al.,

2015), and observing a ritual produces autonomic arousal, especially when loved ones are involved (Xygalatas et al., 2011).

The point is that there are many surfaces of contact between the brain and the outside world; a capacity like joint attention may be bootstrapped from shared action or affective engagement rather than a more cognitively demanding capacity like building a representation of another person's internal state (Racine & Carpendale, 2007). That neural systems do not require attributing "meaning" in a conscious way does not mean they are not subject to enculturation or training (e.g., Calvo-Merino et al., 2004; Kirschner & Ilari, 2014). Even non-conscious, non-representational neurocognitive systems can be induced to perform in a variety of ways, often through social behavioral regimes of canalized development (Downey, 2012). This summary scarcely begins to enumerate the ways in which the brain enmeshes with others, so much so Riitta Hari et al. (2015) argue that social interaction be considered the brain's "default mode" (p. 189).

Philosopher Andy Clark (2015) proposes similarly that, alongside the "predictive brain," an "extended mind" operates in relation to the environment, making our cognition inherently social. According to Clark, a significant portion of cognitive processing happens through systems of "mind" that reach beyond the individual. As anthropologist Edwin Hutchins (2011) describes, cultural practices can "soft assemble" cognitive mechanisms that extend beyond the brain, rather than being isolated internally. For example, shipboard navigation in the US Navy (prior to geographic positioning systems) required multiple people working on separate tasks in coordination while relying on instruments specifically designed for navigation (maps, compasses, and so forth; Hutchins, 1995). Ship navigation – understood as cognition – thus requires the coordination of people, materials, and task components, provided by a history of cultural learning and innovation.

Put more abstractly, navigation requires culture, these shared systems we create, and which then shape what we do and how we think. In this anthropological approach to cognition, computation must include the interaction itself, specifically how people coordinate and create shared meaning and engage skillfully. Viewed this way, culture should be formative to human computational neuroscience: culture helps to solve the computational problems we face as thinking beings. Thus, neural and cultural processing are more intertwined than most neuroscientists or anthropologists typically consider.

Cultural practices like navigation are interactive – they happen between people. In this neuroanthropological approach, information can be processed by the interaction itself with consequences for how the nervous system operates. One example is to recognize that top-down cognition can actually come from the outside through instructions and other verbal interactions (Roepstorff & Frith, 2004). Koban et al. (2017) explicitly tie instructions and social information into pain, directly affecting the generation of sensations and emotion as well as reinforcement learning. Drawing on both verbal interactions and their own ability to train their bodies, for instance, jujitsu fighters learn how to manage pain in specific settings, such as how to deal with choke holds, by sharing experiences and teaching each other, leveraging social interaction into changed perceptual sensitivity (Downey, 2007).

Another example of how interactions process information comes from research on games and joint activity. Research has established that people often synchronize their behavior when working on joint tasks, with the synchrony leading to greater success and satisfaction while working together (Wallot et al., 2016). Behavioral and perceptual synchronization in group activities, such as joint attention, involves brain synchronization as well (Dumas et al., 2010). For example, a recent study of classroom interaction by Dikker et al. (2017) found that brain synchronization predicted student engagement in classroom activities, and that face-to-face interaction prior to group activities primed higher levels of subsequent synchronization.

Many of the tasks studied in this research have been simple; in these cases, behavioral synchronization facilitates the joint processing of information. However, when more complex tasks are presented, for example building model cars together, superior outcomes require coordinated division of labor rather than greater synchrony (Wallot et al., 2016). This research highlights how simple matching (synchronizing) is not enough to understand how social interactions work to process information. Rather, it is crucial to understand the context of what is being done and how individuals match up or not with the expectations and demands of a particular context. Our local neurologies work in the context of social interactions, where cultural computation takes place.

The individual's internal neurological space is strongly influenced by social context and interaction in moment-to-moment ways, but more profound shaping happens cumulatively. Neuroanthropological research suggests that social capacities are not preformed, special-purpose parts of the brain, but rather the outcome of neural development embedded in and open to the social world. The ability to interact socially in the brain does not precede interaction, but arises from it; as Di Paolo and De Jaegher (2012) write: "the practice of social interaction has forged social understanding mechanisms during development." Processes of social interaction are not "spectatorial" but rather "participatory" (p. 2).

Di Paolo and De Jaegher (2012, p. 5) designate these two timescales of social influence "contemporaneous" and "developmental" in their "interactive brain hypothesis" (IBH). The IBH draws on the enactive approach to mind of Varela et al. (1991), which holds that cognitive processes are inherently relational, rather than the product of an internalized mind that manipulates representations of the external world. By implication, if our approach to brain enculturation is "neurodevelopmental" (Westermann et al., 2007), this embedding of the extended nervous system in body and world – and the embedding of brain regions within functional neural networks – will especially affect how the organism functions. Even nonsocial functions, like proprioception and equilibrium, can be influenced by social processes of training and canalized development (e.g., Downey, 2012).

The analytical implication of this developmental and extended nervous system approach is that we need to model the unfolding of extended systems that subserve human functions beyond the encapsulated brain, just as cognitive and brain scientists have traced functional networks of areas within it. The human nervous system is open to different aspects of the world at a variety of surfaces, but not every part is equally open, nor responds on the same time scale. As Rilling (2008, p. 3) writes: "The study of neuro-development ... reveals which aspects of brain development are highly canalized and which are more labile, and in so doing, identifies mechanisms by which brain development can be affected by social and cultural environments to make people in one culture think and act differently from those in another."

The extended nervous system approach encourages us to go beyond conceiving of interaction between brain and culture in a dialectical relationship to be more specific and detailed. Taking a page from complex neurodevelopmental models provided by Westermann et al. (2007), we might model how very specific aspects of the social world – repeated behavior, motivational reinforcement, educational scaffolding, an artifact – engage with particular neurological systems open to social influence to affect the nervous system's capacities. Both brains and cultural niches are complex systems, engaged at a variety of points. For example, the practices, ideas, and interactions that socialize an individual's emotional comportment are distinct than those cultivating sensory skills or repetitive motor patterns. We need an ecological model of enculturation from anthropology as complex as the dynamic model of social brain systems emerging in neuroscience.

In Figure 9.1, we offer an illustrative sketch of how we might think about an extended developmental system, in this case focused on how the capacity to perceive among some blind individuals through echolocation might emerge (or not; Downey, 2016). The nervous system of a vision-impaired person is embedded in a social and cultural milieu, but the specific parts of that cultural milieu (such as social structures and cultural understandings of disability) affect the individual's nervous system through the structuring of a disability education system, which influences an individual's daily activities and immediate environment.

Individuals can fail to develop highly skilled echolocation because parental concern, social stigma, and educational theory affect very specific parts of the nervous system by discouraging (or alternatively encouraging) exploratory

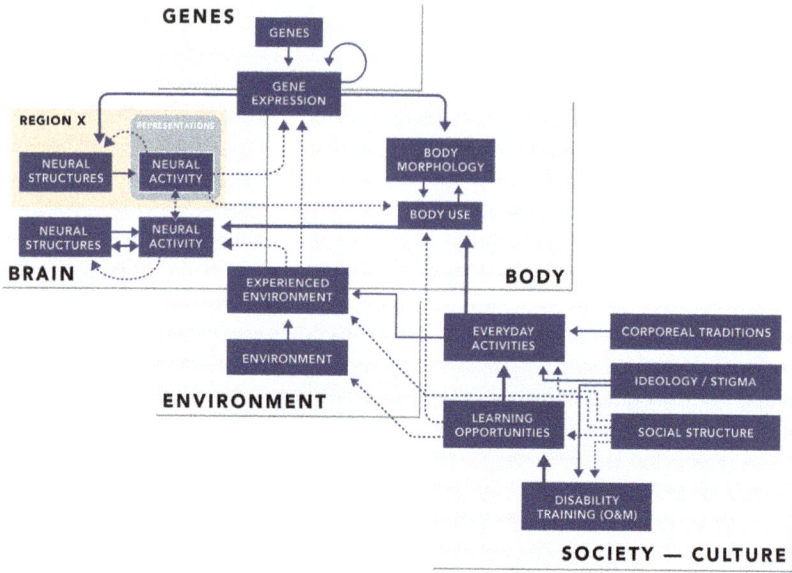

Figure 9.1 Extended, developmental systems model of brain–culture engagement. The model combines neural and biological components with aspects of local social and cultural context in dynamic fashion. In this case, it illustrates how the ability to echolocate or perceive through reflected sound, and the neural resources that subserve that ability, might emerge from the interactions of an individual with their context. The model suggests that a vision impaired individual's nervous system repeatedly engages the environment through the behavior of clicking and listening to echoes, thus cultivating distinctive neurological networks and refinements that enable their distinctive sensory skill (see Downey, 2016). This diagram highlights (with bolded arrows) that the skill development can be stymied (or enabled) by the specific techniques of Orientation and Mobility (O&M) training provided to blind children. If those techniques focus on haptic rather than auditory orientation, for example, and do not acknowledge the possibility of echolocation, learning opportunities will be skewed, and thus the individual's everyday activities will not include using, talking about, or refining the capacity to perceive with echolocation. The resulting pattern of body use will have developmental consequences for the use of the nervous system, including those specific neural regions linked to auditory and spatial perception in a behavioral–developmental spiral.

Adapted from "Neuroconstructivism," by G. Westermann, D. Mareschal, M. H. Johnson, S. Sirois, M. W. Spratling, and M. S. C. Thomas, 2007, *Developmental Science*, *10*(1), p. 80. Copyright 2007 by John Wiley & Sons. Adapted with permission sensory behavior and physical risk taking in movement. Complex models like this one allow us not only to see causal chains and alternative developmental pathways, but also specific links within the system that might allow neuroanthropological knowledge to be applied to real-world problems.

Conclusion

This chapter has laid out several approaches to neuroanthropology. First, a neuroanthropology framework can enrich the study of human variation by selectively drawing from the strengths of the cognitive sciences, neuropsychology, and anthropology. By being reflexive about sample selection, methodologies, and bias, researchers position themselves to better assess and explain patterns in human variation, including brain function. Second and complementarily, development of integrative approaches may be more effective for tackling specific problems. For example, habitus provides a way to understand how social structures become internalized, but this social science analytic is strengthened by considering the underlying mechanisms of human development and brain enculturation that generate both diverse and shared outcomes. Third, neuroanthropology can develop analyses of concrete problems by drawing on both cultural and biological approaches. For instance, the active inference approach from computational neuroscience can inform work on cultural consensus and consonance to develop a better understanding of how social interactions at once support cultural computations while providing individuals with feedback on their fit, or consonance, with local cultural values and practices. Because forms of interaction vary across groups of people, and are patterned within groups by factors like social status, not every interaction will provide the same type of social feedback, nor will every individual be equally sensitive to that feedback. Fourth, combining the sophistication of brain sciences and cultural anthropology can provide more complex holistic models than either alone can provide. As Figure 9.1 illustrates, these models can apply to both theoretical and applied problems.

The patterning of human variation, the embodiment of social and cultural lives into encultured brains and bodies, and the specific intersection of cultural and neural dynamics together cultivate local neurologies. Because our nervous systems are "extended," both in contemporaneous interaction and in long-term developmental unfolding, drawing on and incorporating social and cultural contexts, their enculturation is not the addition of a "cultural" layer to an "uncultured" biology. Rather a holistic neurodevelopmental approach to the cultivation of distinctive forms of human being seeks out the points of contact and extended niches that shape different systems in the brain. That is how humans work, and research should focus increasingly on how local neurologies can better explain specific datasets that come out of neuroscience and place social and cultural theory on a more solid foundation of increased analytical and empirical insight.

One problem we encounter in neuroanthropology when trying to take account of the developmental or long-term consequences of the socially embedded brain is that "culture" and "brain" are both treated in our field as discrete entities that might engage, for example, in a "dialectical" relationship. No matter how subtle or complex the account of this "relationship" is, this approach reifies "culture" or assumes that the brain is a discrete, unified entity that enters into social relations subsequent to its formation. Such an approach poses insoluble intellectual problems for an accurate account of the developmental unfolding of various types of human brains in their developmental niches (Stotz, 2010; Super & Harkness, 1986). That is, "culture" is not distinct from the brain, nor is it a particular layer of "information" contained in the mind. Rather, "culture" is a conceptual way of trying to grasp patterns in the way that human brains perform, conditioned as they are by diverse developmental contexts. "Culture" is not a separate "thing" from brains, but the patterns we perceive in the ways that we interact and jointly produce human life and forms of human being.

REFERENCES

Anderson, M. L. (2010). Neural reuse: A fundamental organizational sprinciple of the brain. *Behavioral and Brain Sciences*, *33*(4), 245–66. https://doi.org/https://doi.org/10.1017/S0140525X10000853

Bellucci, G., Chernyak, S. V., Goodyear, K., Eickhoff, S. B., & Krueger, F. (2017). Neural signatures of trust in reciprocity: A coordinate-based meta-analysis. *Human Brain Mapping*, *38*(3), 1233–48. https://doi.org/10.1002/hbm.23451

Bender, A., & Beller, S. (2016). Current perspectives on cognitive diversity. *Frontiers in Psychology*, *7*, 509. https://doi.org/10.3389/fpsyg.2016.00509

Bickart, K. C., Wright, C. I., Dautoff, R. J., Dickerson, R. J., & Barrett, L. F. (2011). Amygdala volume and social network size in humans. *Nature Neuroscience*, *14*(2), 163–4. https://doi.org/10.1038/nn.2724

Bourdieu, P. (1977). *Outline of a theory of practice* (R. Nice, Trans.). Cambridge University Press. (Original work published 1972). https://doi.org/10.1017/CBO9780511812507

Bourdieu, P. (1984). *Distinction: A social critique of the judgment of taste* (R. Nice, Trans.). Harvard University Press. (Original work published 1979)

Bourgois, P. (1995). *In search of respect: Selling crack in el barrio.* Cambridge University Press.

Brothers, L. (1990). The social brain: A project for integrating primate behavior and neurophysiology in a new domain. *Concepts in Neuroscience*, *1*, 27–51.

Bruineberg, J., Kiverstein, J., & Rietveld, E. (2018). The anticipating brain is not a scientist: The free-energy principle from an ecological-enactive perspective. *Synthese*, *195*(6), 2417–44. https://doi.org/10.1007/s11229-016-1239-1

Burbank, V. K. (2012). Life history and real life: An example of neuroanthropology in aboriginal Australia. *Annals of Anthropological Practice, 36*(1), 149–66. https://doi.org/10.1111/j.2153-9588.2012.01097.x

Calvo-Merino, B., Glaser, D. E., Grèzes, J., Passingham, R. E., & Haggard, P. (2004). Action observation and acquired motor skills: An fMRI study with expert dancers. *Cerebral Cortex, 15*(8),1243–9. https://doi.org/10.1093/cercor/bhi007

Carruthers, P. (2006). *The architecture of the mind: Massive modularity and the flexibility of thought.* Oxford University Press. https://doi.org/10.1093/acprof:oso/9780199207077.001.0001

Catmur, C., Walsh, V., & Heyes, C. (2007). Sensorimotor learning configures the human mirror system. *Current Biology, 17*(17), 1527–31. https://doi.org/10.1016/j.cub.2007.08.006

Chen, P., & Hong, W. (2018). Neural circuit mechanisms of social behavior. *Neuron, 98*(1), 16–30. https://doi.org/10.1016/j.neuron.2018.02.026

Chiao, J. Y., Cheon, B. K., Pornpattananangkul, N., Mrazek, A. J., & Blizinsky, K. D. (2013). Cultural neuroscience: Progress and promise. *Psychological Inquiry, 24*(1), 1–19. https://doi.org/10.1080/1047840X.2013.752715

Chiao, J. Y., Li, S.-C., Seligman, R., & Turner, R. (Eds.). (2016). *The Oxford handbook of cultural neuroscience.* Oxford University Press. https://doi.org/10.1093/oxfordhb/9780199357376.001.0001

Clark, A. (2013). Whatever next? Predictive brains, situated agents, and the future of cognitive science. *Behavioral and Brain Sciences, 36*(3), 181–204. https://doi.org/10.1017/S0140525X12000477

Clark, A. (2015). *Surfing uncertainty: Prediction, action, and the embodied mind.* Oxford University Press. https://doi.org/10.1093/acprof:oso/9780190217013.001.0001

Constant, A., Ramstead, M. J. D., Veissière, S. P. L., Campbell, J. O., & Friston, K. J. (2018). A variational approach to niche construction. *Journal of the Royal Society Interface, 15*(141), 20170685. https://doi.org/10.1098/rsif.2017.0685

Cosmides, L., & Tooby, J. (1997, January 13). *Evolutionary psychology: A primer.* www.cep.ucsb.edu/primer.html.

Crenshaw, K. (1989). Demarginalizing the intersection of race and sex: A black feminist critique of antidiscrimination doctrine, feminist theory and antiracist politics. *University of Chicago Legal Forum, 1989*(1), 139–67. https://chicagounbound.uchicago.edu/uclf/vol1989/iss1/8

Crossley, N. (2013). Habit and habitus. *Body & Society, 19*(2–3), 136–61. https://doi.org/10.1177%2F1357034X12472543

de Vries, G. J., & Forger, N. G. (2015). Sex differences in the brain: A whole body perspective. *Biology of Sex Differences, 6*(1), 15. https://doi.org/10.1186%2Fs13293-015-0032-z

Decety, J., Jackson, P. L., Sommerville, J. A., Chaminade, T., & Meltzoff, A. N. (2004). The neural bases of cooperation and competition: An fMRI investigation. *NeuroImage, 23*(2), 744–51. https://doi.org/10.1016/j.neuroimage.2004.05.025

Dikker, S., Wan, L., Davidesco, I., Kaggen, L., Oostrik, M., McClintock, J., Rowland, J., Michalareas, G., Van Bavel, J. J., Ding, M., & Poeppel, D. (2017). Brain-to-brain synchrony tracks real-world dynamic group interactions in the classroom. *Current Biology, 27*(9), 1375–80. https://doi.org/10.1016/j.cub.2017.04.002

Di Paolo, E., & De Jaegher, H. (2012). The interactive brain hypothesis. *Frontiers in Human Neuroscience*, *6*, 163. https://doi.org/10.3389/fnhum.2012.00163.

Duque, J. F. D., Turner, R., Lewis, E. D., & Egan, G. (2009). Neuroanthropology: A humanistic science for the study of the culture-brain nexus. *Social Cognitive and Affective Neuroscience*, *5*(2–3), 138–47. https://doi.org/10.1093/scan/nsp024

Downey, G. (2007). Producing pain: Techniques and technologies in no-holds-barred fighting. *Social Studies of Science*, *37*(2), 201–26. https://doi.org/10.1177%2F0306312706072174

Downey, G. (2010a). "Practice without theory": A neuroanthropological perspective on embodied learning. *Journal of the Royal Anthropological Institute*, *16*(s1), S22–S40. https://doi.org/10.1111/j.1467-9655.2010.01608

Downey, G. (2010b). Throwing like a Brazilian: On ineptness and a skill-shaped body. In R. Sands & L. Sands (Eds.), *Anthropology of sport and human movement: A biocultural perspective* (pp. 297–326). Lexington Books.

Downey, G. (2012). Balancing across cultures: Sensory plasticity. In D. H. Lende & G. Downey (Eds.), *The encultured brain: Introduction to neuroanthropology* (pp. 169–94). MIT Press.

Downey, G. (2016). Sensory enculturation and neuroanthropology: The case of human echolocation. In J. Y. Chiao, S.-C. Li, R. Seligman, & R. Turner (Eds.), *Oxford handbook of cultural neuroscience* (pp. 41–57). Oxford University Press. https://doi.org/10.1093/oxfordhb/9780199357376.013.23

Downey, G., & Lende, D. H. (2012a). Neuroanthropology and the encultured brain. In D. H. Lende & G. Downey (Eds.), *The encultured brain: An introduction to neuroanthropology* (pp. 23–65). MIT Press. https://doi.org/10.7551/mitpress%2F9219.003.0004

Downey, G., & Lende, D. H. (2012b). Evolution and the brain. In D. H. Lende & G. Downey (Eds.), *The encultured brain: An introduction to neuroanthropology* (pp. 103–37). MIT Press. https://doi.org/10.7551/mitpress/9219.003.0006

Dressler, W. W. (2017). *Culture and the individual: Theory and method of cultural consonance*. Routledge.

Dressler, W. W., Balieiro, M. C., & dos Santos, J. E. (2012). Cultural consonance, consciousness, and depression: Genetic moderating effects on the psychological mediators of culture. In D. H. Lende & G. Downey (Eds.), *The encultured brain: An introduction to neuroanthropology* (pp. 363–88). MIT Press. https://doi.org/10.7551/mitpress/9219.003.0018

Dressler, W. W., & Bindon, J. R. (2000). The health consequences of cultural consonance: Cultural dimensions of lifestyle, social support, and arterial blood pressure in an African American community. *American Anthropologist*, *102*(2), 244–60. https://doi.org/10.1525/aa.2000.102.2.244

Dressler, W. W., Borges, C. D., Balieiro, M. C., & dos Santos, J. E. (2005). Measuring cultural consonance: Examples with special reference to measurement theory in anthropology. *Field Methods*, *17*(4), 331–55. https://doi.org/10.1177/1525822X05279899

Dumas, G., Nadel, J., Soussignan, R., Martinerie, J., & Garnero, L. (2010). Inter-brain synchronization during social interaction. *PLoS ONE*, *5*(8), e12166. https://doi.org/10.1371/journal.pone.0012166

Dunbar, R. I. M. (1993). Coevolution of neocortical size, group size and language in humans. *Behavioral and Brain Sciences*, *16*(4), 681–94. https://doi.org/10.1017/S0140525X00032325

Engemann, D. A., Bzdok, D., Eickhoff, S. B., Vogeley, K., & Schilbach, L. (2012). Games people play: Toward an enactive view of cooperation in social neuroscience. *Frontiers in Human Neuroscience*, *6*, 148. https://doi.org/10.3389/fnhum.2012.00148

Fausto-Sterling, A. (2019). Gender/sex, sexual orientation, and identity are in the body: How did they get there? *Journal of Sex Research*, *56*(4–5), 529–55. https://doi.org/10.1080/00224499.2019.1581883

Fodor, J. A. (1983). *The modularity of mind*. MIT Press.

Friston, K. (2009). The free-energy principle: A rough guide to the brain? *Trends in Cognitive Sciences*, *13*(7), 293–301. https://doi.org/10.1016/j.tics.2009.04.005

Friston, K. (2010). The free-energy principle: A unified brain theory? *Nature Reviews Neuroscience*, *11*(2), 127–38. https://doi.org/10.1038/nrn2787

Friston, K., Fortier, M., & Friedman, D.A. (2018). Of woodlice and men: A Bayesian account of cognition, life and consciousness. An interview with Karl Friston. *ALIUS Bulletin*, *2*, 17–43.

Frith, C. D. (2007). The social brain? *Philosophical Transactions of the Royal Society B: Biological Sciences*, *362*(1480), 671–8. https://doi.org/10.1098%2Frstb.2006.2003

Frith, C., & Frith, U. (2000). The physiological basis of theory of mind: Functional neuroimaging studies. In S. Baron-Cohen, H. Tager-Flusberg, & D. J. Cohen (Eds.), *Understanding other minds: Perspectives from developmental cognitive neuroscience* (2nd ed., pp. 335–56). Oxford University Press.

Fuentes, A. (2016). The extended evolutionary synthesis, ethnography, and the human niche: Toward an integrated anthropology. *Current Anthropology 57*(S13), S13–S26. https://doi.org/10.1086/685684

Gobbini, M. I., & Haxby, J. V. (2007). Neural systems for recognition of familiar faces. *Neuropsychologia*, *45*(1), 32–41. https://doi.org/10.1016/j.neuropsychologia.2006.04.015

Gravlee, C. C. (2009). How race becomes biology: Embodiment of social inequality. *American Journal of Physical Anthropology*, *139*(1), 47–57. https://doi.org/10.1002/ajpa.20983

Han, S., & Northoff, G. (2008). Culture-sensitive neural substrates of human cognition: A transcultural neuroimaging approach. *Nature Reviews Neuroscience*, *9*(8), 646–54. https://doi.org/10.1038/nrn2456

Hari, R., Henriksson, L., Malinen, S., & Parkkonen, L. (2015). Centrality of social interaction in human brain function. *Neuron*, *88*(1), 181–93. https://doi.org/10.1016/j.neuron.2015.09.022

Hein, G., & Singer, T. (2008). I feel how you feel but not always: The empathic brain and its modulation. *Current Opinion in Neurobiology*, *18*(2), 153–8. https://doi.org/10.1016/j.conb.2008.07.012

Henrich, J., Heine, S. J., & Norenzayan, A. (2010). The weirdest people in the world? *Behavioral and Brain Sciences*, *33*(2–3), 61–83. https://doi.org/10.1017/S0140525X0999152X

Humphrey, N. K. (1976). The social function of intellect. In P. P. G. Bateson & R. A. Hinde (Eds.), *Growing points in ethology* (pp. 303–17). Cambridge University Press.

Hutchins, E. (1995). *Cognition in the wild*. MIT Press.

Hutchins, E. (2011). Enculturating the supersized mind. *Philosophical Studies*, *152*(3), 437–46.
Keiflin, R., & Janak, P. H. (2017). Error-driven learning: Dopamine signals more than value-based errors. *Current Biology*, *27*(24), R1321–R1324. https://doi.org/10.1016/j.cub.2017.10.043
Kennedy, D. P., & Adolphs, R. (2012). The social brain in psychiatric and neurological disorders. *Trends in Cognitive Sciences*, *16*(11), 559–72. https://doi.org/10.1016/j.tics.2012.09.006
Kirschner, S., & Ilari, B. (2014). Joint drumming in Brazilian and German preschool children: Cultural differences in rhythmic entrainment, but no prosocial effects. *Journal of Cross-Cultural Psychology*, *45*(1), 137–66. https://doi.org/10.1177%2F0022022113493139
Koban, L., Jepman, M., Geuter, S., & Wager, T. D. (2017). What's in a word? How instructions, suggestions, and social information change pain and emotion. *Neuroscience & Biobehavioral Reviews*, *81*(Part A), 29–42. https://doi.org/10.1016/j.neubiorev.2017.02.014
Lende, D. H. (2012). Poverty poisons the brain. *Annals of Anthropological Practice*, *36*(1), 183–201. https://doi.org/10.1111/j.2153-9588.2012.01099.x
Lende, D. H., & Downey, G. (Eds.). (2012a). *The encultured brain: An introduction to neuroanthropology*. MIT Press.
Lende, D. H., & Downey, G. (2012b). Neuroanthropology and its applications: An introduction. *Annals of Anthropological Practice*, *36*(1), 1–25. https://doi.org/10.1111/j.2153-9588.2012.01090.x
Lock, M. (1993). *Encounters with aging: Mythologies of menopause in Japan and North America*. University of California Press.
MacLeod, J. (2018). *Ain't no makin' it: Aspirations and attainment in a low-income neighborhood*. (3rd ed.). Routledge.
Merchant, H., Grahn, J., Trainor, L., Rohrmeier, M., & Fitch, W. T. (2015). Finding the beat: A neural perspective across humans and non-human primates. *Philosophical Transactions of the Royal Society B: Biological Sciences*, *370*(1664), 20140093. https://doi.org/10.1098/rstb.2014.0093
Monfardini, E., Redouté, J., Hadj-Bouziane, F., Hynaux, C., Fradin, J. Huguet, P., Costes, N., & Meunier, M. (2016). Others' sheer presence boosts brain activity in the attention (but not the motivation) network. *Cerebral Cortex*, *26*(6), 2427–39. https://doi.org/10.1093/cercor/bhv067
Muthukrishna, M., & Henrich, J. (2019). A problem in theory. *Nature Human Behaviour*, *3*, 221–9. https://doi.org/10.1038/s41562-018-0522-1
Nguyen, M., Vanderwal, T., & Hasson, U. (2019). Shared understanding of narratives is correlated with shared neural responses. *NeuroImage*, *184*, 161–70. https://doi.org/10.1016/j.neuroimage.2018.09.010
Nummenmaa, L., Lahnakoski, J. M., & Glerean, E. (2018). Sharing the social world via intersubject neural synchronisation. *Current Opinion in Psychology*, *24*, 7–14. https://doi.org/10.1016/j.copsyc.2018.02.021
Ochsner, K. N., & Lieberman, M. D. (2001). The emergence of social cognitive neuroscience. *American Psychologist*, *56*(9), 717–34. https://doi.org/10.1037/0003-066X.56.9.717
Panter-Brick, C., Lende, D., & Kohrt, B. A. (2012). Children in global adversity: Physical, mental, behavioral, and symbolic dimensions of health. In R. King &

V. Maholmes (Eds.), *The Oxford handbook of poverty and child development* (pp. 603–21). Oxford University Press. https://doi.org/10.1093/oxfordhb/ 9780199769100.013.0033

Parkinson, C., Kleinbaum, A. M., & Wheatley, T. (2018). Similar neural responses predict friendship. *Nature Communications*, *9*(1), 332. https://doi.org/10.1038/ s41467-017-02722-7

Parkinson, C., & Wheatley, T. (2015). The repurposed social brain. *Trends in Cognitive Sciences*, *19*(3), 133–41. https://doi.org/10.1016/j.tics.2015.01.003

Peacock, V. (2016). Academic precarity as hierarchical dependence in the Max Planck Society. *HAU: Journal of Ethnographic Theory*, *6*(1), 95–119. https://doi.org/10 .14318/hau6.1.006

Pitts-Taylor, V. (2016). *The brain's body: Neuroscience and corporeal politics*. Duke University Press. https://doi.org/10.1215/9780822374374

Racine, T. P., & Carpendale, J. I. M. (2007). The role of shared practice in joint attention. *British Journal of Developmental Psychology*, *25*(1), 3–25. https://doi .org/10.1348/026151006X119756

Ramstead, M. J. D., Badcock, P. B., & Friston, K. J. (2018). Answering Schrödinger's question: A free-energy formulation. *Physics of Life Reviews*, *24*, 1–16. https://doi .org/10.1016/j.plrev.2017.09.001

Ramstead, M. J. D., Constant, A., Badcock, P. B., & Friston, K. J. (2019). Variational ecology and the physics of sentient systems. *Physics of Life Reviews*, *31*, 188–205. https://doi.org/10.1016/j.plrev.2018.12.002

Ramstead, M. J. D., Kirchhoff, M. D., Constant, A., & Friston, K. J. (2019). Multiscale integration: Beyond internalism and externalism. *Synthese*. Advance online publication. https://doi.org/10.1007/s11229-019-02115-x

Ramstead, M. J. D., Veissière, S. P. L., & Kirmayer, L. J. (2016). Cultural affordances: Scaffolding local worlds through shared intentionality and regimes of attention. *Frontiers in Psychology*, *7*, 1090. https://doi.org/10.3389%2Ffpsyg .2016.01090

Rilling, J. K. (2008). Neuroscientific approaches and applications within anthropology. *American Journal of Physical Anthropology*, *137*(S47), 2–32. https://doi.org/10 .1002/ajpa.20947

Rizzolatti, G., & Craighero, L. (2004). The mirror-neuron system. *Annual Review of Neuroscience*, *27*, 169–92. https://doi.org/10.1146/annurev.neuro.27.070203 .144230

Roepstorff, A. (2013). Why am I not just lovin' cultural neuroscience? Toward a slow science of cultural difference. *Psychological Inquiry*, *24*(1), 61–3. https://doi.org/ 10.1080/1047840X.2013.768058

Roepstorff, A., & Frith, C. (2004). What's at the top in the top-down control of action? Script-sharing and 'top-top' control of action in cognitive experiments. *Psychological Research*, *68*(2–3), 189–98. https://doi.org/10.1007/s00426-003- 0155-4

Roepstorff, A., Niewöhner, J., & Beck, S. (2010). Enculturing brains through patterned practices. *Neural Networks*, *23*(8–9), 1051–9. https://doi.org/10.1016/j.neunet .2010.08.002

Rule, N. O., Freeman, J. B., & Ambady, N. (2013). Culture in social neuroscience: A review. *Social Neuroscience*, *8*(1), 3–10. https://doi.org/10.1080/17470919 .2012.695293

Sallet, J., Mars, R. B., Noonan, M. P., Andersson, J. L., O'Reilly, J. X., Jbabdi, S., Croxson, P. L., Jenkinson, M., Miller, K. L., & Rushworth, M. F. S. (2011). Social network size affects neural circuits in macaques. *Science*, *334*(6056), 697–700. https://doi.org/10.1126/science.1210027

Schultz, W., Dayan, P., & Montague, P. R. (1997). A neural substrate of prediction and reward. *Science*, *275*(5306), 1593–9. https://doi.org/10.1126/science.275.5306.1593

Schurz, M., Radua, J., Aichhorn, M., Richlan, F., & Perner, J. (2014). Fractionating theory of mind: A meta-analysis of functional brain imaging studies. *Neuroscience & Biobehavioral Reviews*, *42*, 9–34. https://doi.org/10.1016/j.neubiorev.2014.01.009

Seeley, W. W., Menon, V., Schatzberg, A. F., Keller, J., Glover, G. H., Kenna, H., Reiss, A. L., & Greicius, M. D. (2007). Dissociable intrinsic connectivity networks for salience processing and executive control. *Journal of Neuroscience*, *27*(9), 2349–56. https://doi.org/10.1523/JNEUROSCI.5587-06.2007

Shipp, S. (2016). Neural elements for predictive coding. *Frontiers in Psychology*, *7*, 1792. https://doi.org/10.3389/fpsyg.2016.01792

Shore, B. (1996). *Culture in mind: Cognition, culture, and the problem of meaning*. Oxford University Press.

Spunt, R. P., & Adolphs, R. (2017). A new look at domain specificity: Insights from social neuroscience. *Nature Reviews Neuroscience*, *18*(9), 559–67. https://doi.org/10.1038/nrn.2017.76

Stotz, K. (2010). Human nature and cognitive-developmental niche construction. *Phenomenology and the Cognitive Sciences*, *9*(4), 483–501. https://doi.org/10.1007/s11097-010-9178-7

Super, C. M., & Harkness, S. (1986). The developmental niche: A conceptualization at the interface of child and culture. *International Journal of Behavioral Development*, *9*(4), 545–69. https://doi.org/10.1177%2F016502548600900409

Tarr, B., Launay, J., Cohen, E., & Dunbar, R. (2015). Synchrony and exertion during dance independently raise pain threshold and encourage social bonding. *Biology Letters*, *11*(10), 20150767. https://doi.org/10.1098/rsbl.2015.0767

Tomasello, M. (2014). Joint attention as social cognition. In C. Moore & P. J. Dunham (Eds.), *Joint attention: Its origins and role in development* (pp. 103–30). Psychology Press.

Tomasello, M. (2019). *Becoming human: A theory of ontogeny*. Belknap Press.

Van Overwalle, F., & Baetens, K (2009). Understanding others' actions and goals by mirror and mentalizing systems: A meta-analysis. *NeuroImage*, *48*(3), 564–84. https://doi.org/10.1016/j.neuroimage.2009.06.009

Varela, F. J., Thompson, E., & Rosch, E. (1991). *The embodied mind: Cognitive science and human experience*. MIT Press.

Veissière, S. P. L., & Stendel, M. (2018). Hypernatural monitoring: A social rehearsal account of smartphone addiction. *Frontiers in Psychology*, *9*, 141. https://doi.org/10.3389%2Ffpsyg.2018.00141

Wacquant, L. (2016). A concise genealogy and anatomy of habitus. *Sociological Review*, *64*(1), 64–72. https://doi.org/10.1111/1467-954X.12356

Wallot, S., Mitkidis, P., McGraw, J. J., & Roepstorff, A. (2016). Beyond synchrony: Joint action in a complex production task reveals beneficial effects of decreased

interpersonal synchrony. *PLoS ONE, 11*(12), e0168306. https://doi.org/10.1371%
2Fjournal.pone.0168306

Wang, H., Braun, C., & Enck, P. (2017). How the brain reacts to social stress (exclusion): A scoping review. *Neuroscience & Biobehavioral Reviews, 80*, 80–8. https://doi.org/10.1016/j.neubiorev.2017.05.012

Warin, M., Moore, V., Davies, M., & Ulijaszek, S. (2016). Epigenetics and obesity: The reproduction of habitus through intercellular and social environments. *Body & Society, 22*(4), 53–78. https://doi.org/10.1177%2F1357034X15590485

Westermann, G., Mareschal, D., Johnson, M. H., Sirois, S., Spratling, M. W., & Thomas, M. S. C. (2007). Neuroconstructivism. *Developmental Science, 10*(1), 75–83. https://doi.org/10.1111/j.1467-7687.2007.00567.x

Wexler, B. E. (2006). *Brain and culture: Neurobiology, ideology, and social change.* MIT Press.

Worthman, C. M. (2009). Habits of the heart: Life history and the developmental neuroendocrinology of emotion. American Journal of Human Biology, *21*(6), 772–81. https://doi.org/10.1002/ajhb.20966

Worthman, C. M. (2010). The ecology of human development: Evolving models for cultural psychology. *Journal of Cross-Cultural Psychology, 41*(4), 546–62. https://doi.org/10.1177%2F0022022110362627

Xygalatas, D., Konvalinka, I., Bulbulia, J., & Roepstorff, A. (2011). Quantifying collective effervescence: Heart-rate dynamics at a fire-walking ritual. *Communicative & Integrative Biology, 4*(6), 735–8. https://doi.org/10.4161/cib.17609

Young, I. M. (1980). Throwing like a girl: A phenomenology of feminine body comportment, motility and spatiality. *Human Studies, 3*(2), 137–56. https://doi.org/10.1007/BF02331805

10 The Neural Mechanisms Underlying Social Norms
Norm Detection, Punishment, and Compliance

Yan Mu and Michele J. Gelfand

Social norms, or unwritten standards for behavior (Elster, 1989), are a hallmark of the human species. They are omnipresent in our lives, guiding much of our behavior on a daily basis – from dress codes and dining etiquette to conversation customs, classroom rules, and driving regulations. Across the millennia, social norms have served critical functions for human groups. They have enabled coordination among diverse groups of individuals and ultimately produced unprecedented levels of cooperation in human societies (Fehr & Fischbacher, 2004a). Without norms at the macro-level (e.g., punishments for theft, murder, and other forms of societal deviance) and the micro-level (e.g., customs, practices, and rules), human societies could not function.

Given the ubiquity and importance of social norms, scholars from numerous disciplines – psychology, sociology, economics, primatology, political science, and organizational behavior, among others – have sought to understand the mechanisms underlying the development, maintenance, and enforcement of social norms. More recently, cultural neuroscience, an emerging interdisciplinary field that examines the relationships among culture, the brain, and behavior (Chiao, 2009; Han et al., 2013; Kitayama & Uskul, 2011), has begun to contribute unique insights into the function of social norms, their cultural variation, and their underlying neurobiological mechanisms.

In this chapter, we provide a synthesis of the literature on the cultural neuroscience of social norms. We begin with a discussion of whether social norms are unique to humans. We then elucidate how social norms are processed in the brain, with a particular focus on the neuroscience of social norm detection, punishment of violations, and compliance. We explore what might be culturally universal and also culture-specific for each of these processes, and also discuss how culture and genes might interact to produce unique normative psychologies across human groups. We conclude with a discussion of exciting frontiers that await investigation in the cultural neuroscience of social norms.

Are Social Norms Unique to Humans?

Scientists have long pondered the question of whether social norms are unique to humans. Evidence from animal research suggests that the preconditions for the presence and enforcement of social norms indeed exist in other species, such as monkeys (van de Waal et al., 2013), chimpanzees (Whiten et al., 2005), wild birds (Aplin et al., 2015), and Norway rats (Galef & Whiskin, 2008). For example, van de Waal et al. (2013) found that wild vervet monkeys conformed to local eating norms when they moved to a new habitat. Likewise, Aplin et al. (2015) showed that birds disproportionately copy the most commonly used foraging techniques in their groups, and like the vervet monkeys, those that moved between subpopulations switched their preferences to match the behavior of the new group. Norway rats have also been found to ignore their own preferences and copy others who eat food that tasted bad or was even toxic (Galef & Whiskin, 2008). Further observations from primatologists support the notion that nonhuman species show differences in behavioral patterns across geographic populations. For example, nut-cracking behavior has been observed in the westernmost forest chimpanzee population, whereas it has not been observed in those living in forests some 30 km east of the Sassandra River in West Africa or further away (Boesch et al., 1994). Importantly, these group differences also emerge among neighboring communities of chimpanzees who are not genetically differentiated, suggesting that social learning is an important driver of chimpanzee group differences (Luncz et al., 2012).

Nevertheless, social norms among humans are distinct from those in animals in a number of ways. For example, research to date shows that while humans will conform for symbolic reasons (e.g., to signal commitment to a group), nonhuman species conform mainly when it serves an instrumental goal (e.g., getting more food) (Haun et al., 2014). Likewise, relative to nonhuman groups, human groups tend to "overimitate" others' behaviors whose purpose may be unclear in relation to a certain goal (Hoehl et al., 2019; Whiten, 2019). In addition, compared to nonhuman groups, human groups have more complex systems of social norms that enable cooperation at a much larger scale. For example, norms in animals concern limited behavioral patterns, such as foraging techniques, tool use, and eating behavior. By contrast, human norms span a huge variety of written and unwritten rules covering everything from everyday conversations to complex institutions. Moreover, elaborate transmission systems such as language, institutions, and technologies enable human norms to spread across time and space and to create radical improvements over time (Tomasello et al., 1993). Though a few studies show the possibility of cumulative modification of tool use in chimpanzees (e.g., adapting basic tools to make fishing more efficient; Sanz et al., 2009), cumulative cultural evolution is much more sophisticated among human groups.

Variation in Social Norms across Human Groups

While social norms are a human universal, there is great culture specificity in their content and strength. A growing body of cross-cultural research has demonstrated striking differences in social eating norms (Higgs, 2015), marriage and family norms (Dixon, 1971; Reher, 1998), dressing norms (Dellinger, 2002), gender roles (Suitor & Carter, 1999), burial rituals (Balzer, 1980), and norms for obedience to authority (Spring, 2008), among many others. Cultural psychologists have provided unique theoretical frameworks such as independent–interdependent self-construals (Markus & Kitayama, 1991; Singelis, 1994), individualism–collectivism (Triandis, 1989; Triandis & Gelfand, 1998), power distance, uncertainty avoidance, and masculinity (Hofstede, 1980), among other cultural values (Schwartz, 1992) to understand how sociocultural contexts shape the content of social norms.

Aside from their content, social norms also differ in their *strength* (Gelfand et al., 2011, 2017; Pelto, 1968; Triandis, 1989). Cultural variation in the degree to which norms are clearly defined and rigorously imposed was first documented by Pelto (1968) in his observations of over 20 traditional societies. He found that some, such as the Hutterites, Hanno, and Lubara, were "tight" societies with strong norms and severe sanctions for norm violations, whereas others such as the !Kung Bushmen, the Cubeo, and the Skolt Lapps were "loose" and had ambiguous norms and greater permissiveness. Pelto also observed that tight groups often had higher population density and greater dependence on crops as compared to the loose societies.

Gelfand et al. (2011) later advanced a multilevel model of cultural tightness–looseness across modern nations. They found wide variation in the strength of norms, with some nations being very tight (e.g., Japan, Pakistan, Singapore) and others very loose (e.g., New Zealand, Brazil, the Netherlands). They also found that variation in the strength of norms was predicted by the degree of ecological and historical threat that nations experienced. Tight nations have more natural disasters, a greater incidence of territorial threat, higher population density, fewer natural resources, and greater pathogen prevalence compared to loose countries. In this regard, strong norms and punishments for violations serve an important function: They help groups to coordinate and survive in the face of challenging ecologies. Tight nations also have institutions that enforce social order – they are more autocratic, have more media restrictions and fewer civil liberties, make greater use of the death penalty, and have many more constraints in everyday social situations. At the individual level, people in tight cultures have more "felt accountability," exhibiting higher self-monitoring, greater prevention focus, higher impulse control, and a greater need for structure relative to people living in loose countries. By contrast, loose countries have fewer ecological and societal threats, which allows for weaker social norms, more tolerance of deviant behaviors, and a decreased need for sanctioning of deviant behaviors.

Variation in the strength of social norms is also found at the state level of analysis (Harrington & Gelfand, 2014). Consistent with the country-level findings, an analysis of the fifty US states showed wide variation in tightness–looseness and that such variation was related to ecological and historical threat as well. Tight states also have more order: more law enforcement personnel per capita, lower mobility, less social disorganization (e.g., divorce, homelessness), and higher self-regulation (e.g., lower rates of alcohol and drug abuse) as compared to loose states. Yet loose states have more openness than tight states: they are more creative and have far less discrimination.

The strength of social norms also varies by social class. In a series of studies, Harrington and Gelfand (2020) found that the working class, who are exposed to a wide range of potential threats, such as falling into poverty and working in more dangerous jobs, have a higher level of tightness than do the upper class. They also showed similar tightness–looseness "trade-offs" that have been found at the nation and state level, with the working class demonstrating higher conscientiousness, a greater need for structure, more stringent moral beliefs, and a lower tendency to engage in unethical behavior as compared to the upper class. This group, however, was found to be lower in creativity and openness relative to the upper class.

Taken together, cultural differences in the content and strength of social norms have been widely observed in different human groups. However, it is only recently that we have begun to understand the neurological mechanisms underlying social norms within and across cultures. By utilizing various neuroimaging techniques, including functional magnetic resonance imaging (fMRI), electroencephalography (EEG), transcranial direct current stimulation (tDCS), and transcranial magnetic stimulation (TMS), neuroscientists have provided unique insights into the role of brain functions involved in processing social norms. In the next section, we discuss the neurological mechanisms underlying three different norm-related processes: detection of norm violations, norm enforcement, and norm compliance.

Neural Processes Involved in the Detection of Norm Violations

From an evolutionary perspective, the human brain presumably evolved unique neural mechanisms supporting the processing of social norms in order to survive ecological and human threats (Fehr & Fischbacher, 2004a, 2004b). When someone violates a social norm (for example, speaks loudly in the library), we can usually detect it immediately. Until recently, however, we had little understanding of the neural mechanisms that support such processes.

To be sure, there has been research on neural processing involved in detecting unexpected linguistic stimuli (Ceballos et al., 2005; Hagoort et al., 2004; Kutas & Federmeier, 2011; Röder et al., 2000). And research has found that the N400 – a negative shift in event-related potentials (ERPs) around 400 milliseconds – also serves as a potent neural index of the detection of unexpected anomalous stimuli and affective and socially incongruent information (Goto et al., 2009; Na & Kitayama, 2011; Varnum et al., 2012; White et al., 2009). Yet the neural underpinnings of detecting social norms violations has received little attention.

To investigate this, Mu et al. (2015) utilized EEG, a noninvasive method to record electrical activity in the brain with high time resolution. This method is well suited for capturing temporal characteristics of brain activity when humans detect social norm violations (Mu et al., 2015). To operationalize the violation of social norms, the researchers developed a task in which participants were asked to judge whether a certain behavior (e.g., dancing) was appropriate or not in different situations (appropriate, e.g., tango lesson; weakly inappropriate, e.g., subway platform; strongly inappropriate, e.g., art museum). The EEG results showed a prominent N400 component in both the strong and weak violation conditions relative to the appropriate condition at the central and parietal regions that was unrelated to the N400 involved in detecting semantic violations (see Figure 10.1). This study provided the first evidence for the N400 component supporting social norm violation detection.

In recent years, neuroimaging research has used fMRI to understand the brain regions involved in the detection of norm violations. This noninvasive measure of brain activity can help investigate the brain functions underlying perception, cognition, emotion, and social processes. It allows for the measurement of local changes in blood-oxygenation levels in the brain, an indirect measure of neural activity, as a function of cognitive and social operations that participants carry out in different experimental conditions. Unlike EEG, one of the major advantages of fMRI over other imaging techniques is its high spatial resolution, which refers to the degree of accuracy with which brain activity (i.e., hemodynamic responses) can be located in space (Heeger & Ress, 2002).

Using this technique, Berthoz et al. (2002) investigated the neural systems supporting the processing of social norm violations. In particular, the authors compared neural activity while participants read stories either describing social norm violations (e.g., having a bite of food but spitting it back onto the plate) or normative situations (e.g., having a bite of food and keeping it in one's mouth). The neuroimaging data showed that the norm violation stories, relative to the normative ones, led to greater brain activation in the medial and superior

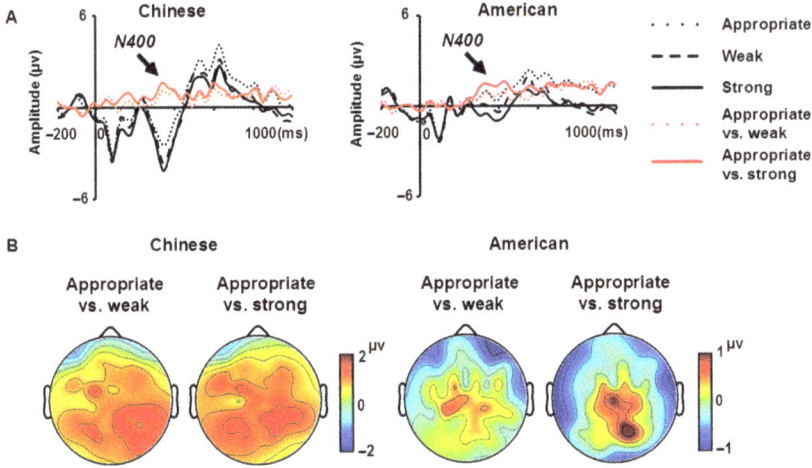

Figure 10.1 Cultural-general N400 effects of social norms violations.
(A) Grand average ERPs (black lines) for the strong violation, weak violation, and appropriate conditions and differential ERPs (red lines) for the contrasts between appropriate and strong/weak violation conditions at the central–parietal regions in Chinese and American. (B) The topographies show the distribution of the N400 effect (appropriate vs. strong/weak violation conditions) at 200–600 ms for Chinese and American, respectively.
From "How Culture Gets Embrained: Cultural Differences in Event-Related Potentials of Social norm Violations," by Y. Mu, S. Kitayama, S. Han, and M. J. Gelfand, 2015, *Proceedings of the National Academy of Sciences of the United States of America, 112* (50), 15350 (https://doi.org/10.1073/pnas.1509839112)

prefrontal cortex, left middle and inferior prefrontal cortex, left orbitofrontal cortex, anterior temporal pole, left temporal–parietal junction, occipital cortex with foci in cuneus, posterior fusiform gyrus, and the brain stem. Among these brain regions, the medial prefrontal and temporal areas are engaged in representing and understanding others' mental states and intentions (Frith & Frith, 2006). The lateral orbitofrontal area is involved in responding to the aversive emotional reactions of others, such as anger (Blair et al., 1999). Furthermore, the authors manipulated whether the story's protagonist violated a social norm intentionally or unintentionally to test whether this evoked different neural activations. The results showed that the detection of intentional social norm violations induced greater activation relative to the unintentional social norm violations in the brain regions involved in representing others' mental states, such as the superior and medial frontal cortex, temporal pole, and left inferior parietal cortex. These increased brain activations reflect the recruitment of the network engaged in mentalizing others, which supports individuals' attempts to determine the protagonist's intention in violating social norms.

Using a different experimental paradigm, Mu, Han, et al. (2020) combined fMRI techniques with a social norm violation task to shed light on the neural circuits recruited in the perception of norm violations and subsequent norm enforcement. In this study, participants were asked to read a set of sentences describing social norm violations from the previous work (Mu et al., 2015) and make judgments about the behavior's appropriateness and whether it deserved a reprimand. The fMRI results showed that social norm violation behavior, relative to normative behavior, led to greater activation in multiple neural circuits, including those involved in mentalizing others (i.e., superior medial frontal gyrus, superior temporal gyrus) (Berthoz et al., 2002), emotional processing and emotional regulation (i.e., insula and inferior frontal gyrus) (Berthoz et al., 2002; Wager et al., 2008), and motivation (i.e., supplemental motor area and medial prefrontal area) (Mathur et al., 2010), regardless of judgment types. More importantly, reprimand judgments, relative to appropriateness judgments, elicited greater neural activation related to punishment motivation (in, e.g., the medial frontal gyrus and supplementary motor area). In sum, the fMRI findings provide a more elaborative understanding of psychological processes such as theory of mind, emotion, and motivation. They extend our knowledge of how processing social norms is modulated by other factors, such as intentionality and type of judgment being made.

Neural Mechanisms Involved in Norm Enforcement

Humans are expert not only in detecting norm violations but also in punishing norm violators in order to maintain social norms (Buckholtz & Marois, 2012). Punishments can be formal (e.g., through sanctions) or informal (e.g., nonverbal communication cues), and neuroimaging techniques have been increasingly used to help understand their underlying mechanisms. The most commonly used paradigms for testing punishment and its underlying neural mechanisms are economic games, including the ultimatum game (Sanfey et al., 2003), public goods game (Fehr & Rockenbach, 2004), dictator game (Strobel et al., 2011), third-party punishment game (Buckholtz et al., 2008), and trust game (de Quervain et al., 2004). Together, these studies show that specific brain networks are activated when engaging in punishment.

Research has shown that punishment involves the *emotional network*: subcortical and cortical brain regions that support emotional processing, such as the anterior insula, the anterior cingulate, and the right dorsolateral prefrontal cortex. In an fMRI study, Sanfey et al. (2003) scanned participants' brains while they decided whether to accept or reject proposed fair or unfair splits of a sum of money in an ultimatum game. Rejecting unfair offers, which led to economic loss for the proposer and bore a cost without a benefit, was operationalized as a form of altruistic punishment in this study. The fMRI results showed that unfair offers elicited activity in the anterior insula (AI), as well as in the right dorsolateral prefrontal cortex (DLPFC) and anterior cingulate cortex (ACC). In addition, participants with stronger AI activation to unfair offers accepted them at lower rates, suggesting recruitment of emotion regions (Calder et al., 2001) in their evaluation and negative emotional response. Further evidence supports the view that the AI is related to representations of emotional states in economic decision-making (Singer et al., 2009), which, in turn, drives the motivation of rejecting unfair offers and punishing norm violation behaviors (Montague & Lohrenz, 2007).

Punishment involves the *reward network*, a collection of brain structures and neural pathways that are responsible for reward-related processing (i.e., reward anticipation and feedback). De Quervain et al. (2004) used positron emission tomography (PET) to examine the neural basis for altruistic punishment of defectors in a trust game involving real monetary payoffs. During this game, subjects were able to punish defectors who kept all the money, either symbolically (i.e., there was no actual reduction in the defectors' payoff) or effectively (i.e., they reduced the defectors' actual payoffs). They found that activity in the caudate area, which is implicated in the reward network, was greater in the effective punishment conditions relative to the symbolic ones where there was no deduction from the defectors' payoff. Greater activation in the caudate was associated with participants' investments in punishment. The caudate has been shown to be involved in reward anticipation (Benningfield et al., 2014), reflecting these individuals' anticipated satisfaction from punishing violators. The study further demonstrated that effective punishment, relative to symbolic punishment, led to greater activation in the ventromedial prefrontal cortex (VMPFC) and the medial orbitofrontal cortex (MOFC). These two regions are involved in integrating separate cognitive operations and decision-making (Krawczyk, 2002; Miller & Cohen, 2001) and pursuing higher behavioral goals that require the integration of distinct operations (i.e., retrieval itself and a comparison between the retrieved item and a stimulus) (Ramnani & Owen, 2004), suggesting they help to weigh the benefits and costs of altruistic punishment (de Quervain et al., 2004). This scientific evidence has shed light on the proximate neural mechanisms underlying altruistic punishment, particularly the involvement of the reward system, which reflects the anticipated satisfaction from punishing defectors.

Punishment also involves the *emotion regulation network*. Emotion regulation is often critical for adaptive decision-making, and researchers have examined whether it also plays a causal role in decisions about punishment. This question was clearly addressed by a lesion study of patients with brain damage that investigated whether emotion regulation defects following focal prefrontal brain damage were associated with exceptionally irrational economic decision-making in situations of unfair treatment (Koenigs & Tranel, 2007). The researchers found that, compared to a control group, individuals with lesions in the VMPFC exhibited exaggerated irrational economic decisions in the ultimatum game (i.e., a higher rejection rate of unfair offers). This area is critical for emotion regulation in emotion-guided decision-making (Bechara et al., 2000), supporting the hypothesis that emotion regulation processes made possible by the VMPFC are a critical component of making rational punishment decisions.

Punishment also involves *the cognitive control network* that comprises the brain regions associated with the cognitive control of behavior (i.e., attentional control, conflict processing, and assessment of responsibility). Studies have noted differences in neural patterns underlying first-party and third-party punishment. First-party punishment is subjectively beneficial via satisfaction through revenge. Third-party punishment is less likely to be driven by anger and revenge-like motives, and it requires more cognitive control to make a rational decision. Strobel et al. (2011) compared a first-party punishment condition, where participants received unfair offers and were given the opportunity to punish the violators, to a third-party punishment condition, where they were "watching" unfair assignments between two other players and had the choice of punishing the violators at the cost of reducing their own payoff. They found differences between these two types of punishment at the neural level. In particular, reward-related areas (i.e., nucleus accumbens) were more strongly activated in the first-person perspective, and cognitive control areas, including the DLPFC and ACC, showed stronger activation in the third-party perspective. These findings support less revenge-like emotional responses and more cognitive control demands and cognitive–affective conflict accompanying the decision to punish defectors in the third-party perspective.

The involvement of the DLPFC in third-party punishment has been supported by other researchers. Buckholtz et al. (2008), for example, scanned subjects using fMRI while they determined the appropriate punishment for crimes that varied in perpetrator responsibility and crime severity (responsibility, diminished responsibility, or no crime). They found that neural activation in the right dorsolateral prefrontal cortex (rDLPFC) varied on the basis of criminal responsibility, showing greater activity in the responsibility condition compared to the two diminished responsibility conditions. The overlap of DLPFC activity between studies of economic decision-making and the examination of legal decision-making suggests that this region plays a key role in third-party punishment and is involved in the assessment of responsibility.

In all, neuroimaging research on punishment has highlighted the involvement of complex neural systems in tasks including emotional response (AI, amygdala), reward processing (caudate), emotion regulation (VMPFC), and cognitive control processing (DLPFC). Understanding the psychological processes and their underlying neural mechanisms is important for the development of stable social norms in human societies.

The Neural Underpinnings of Norm Compliance

People often follow what the majority do in order to be accepted in human groups. In the classic Asch line experiments, one-third of the participants conformed to the majority view even when the majority claimed incorrectly that two lines differing by several inches were the same length; this speaks to how powerful normative influences can be (Asch, 1956). In most cases, to conform with human groups, people comply with many norms, even when these no longer appear to have a function and compliance appears to go against their own subjective opinions about the truth. Accordingly, it is possible that human beings may have evolved specialized neural circuits that are responsible for compliance with norms.

Given that social punishment compels norm compliance, it is possible that norm compliance activates brain regions related to punishment processing. This is supported by empirical evidence from several fMRI studies. For example, Spitzer et al. (2007) used fMRI to study the neural circuitry behind social norm compliance by comparing a condition in which norm violations could be punished with a control condition in which punishment was impossible. They found that individuals' norm compliance behaviors (i.e., money units transferred as the monetary measure of norm compliance) increased when punishment was possible. Norm compliance induced greater neural activation in the lateral orbitofrontal cortex and right dorsal lateral prefrontal cortex. As discussed above, these two regions, which are involved in punishment processing (Buckholtz et al., 2008; Strobel et al., 2011), may reflect an evaluative and cognitive control mechanism under the threat of social punishment.

Research by Ruff et al. (2013) tested the role of the right lateral prefrontal cortex (rLPFC) in norm compliance. They experimentally altered neural excitability in this brain area while participants played an economic exchange game, using a double-blind, placebo-controlled transcranial direct current stimulation (tDCS) design. The tDCS technique, a noninvasive, painless brain stimulation treatment, can increase or decrease neural excitability in the stimulated region (Nitsche & Paulus, 2000). The researchers randomly assigned participants to three stimulation groups in which neural excitability in the rLPFC was enhanced with anodal tDCS, reduced with cathodal tDCS, or left unaltered by sham/placebo tDCS as a control for the possible non-neural effects of stimulation. During the economic exchange game, one participant (Player A) received a certain amount of money and could decide how much they wanted to transfer to another randomly assigned anonymous participant

(Player B). In the baseline voluntary condition, only transfers could be made. However, in the punishment condition, Player B could punish Player A by deducting their money. The results showed that participants' norm compliance behavior (i.e., following the fairness norm to split equally) in the baseline and punishment conditions could be altered by varying the neural excitability of this brain region with tDCS. Voluntary transfers decreased during anodal tDCS and increased during cathodal tDCS relative to the sham condition, while sanction-induced transfers increased during anodal tDCS and decreased during cathodal tDCS. These findings confirm that the lateral prefrontal regions, such as the DLPFC and rLPFC, serve as key biological prerequisites for norm compliance during social interaction.

Culture Influences on the Neurological Mechanisms Underlying Social Norms

An exciting new set of cultural neuroscience studies has begun to examine how brain mechanisms related to norm processing vary as a function of cultural tightness–looseness (TL), or the strength of norms, at the neural level. Next, we will review recent neuroscience research illuminating how cultural TL affects the neural mechanisms associated with social norm processing, such as a culture-specific N400 effect in social norm violation.

Cultural Differences in Social Norm Violation Detection. Integrating cultural neuroscience theory with research on cultural TL, Mu et al. (2015) recorded ERPs while Chinese and American participants read sentences that described people either following norms ("Sally is dancing at a tango lesson") or deviating from them ("Sally is dancing in the art museum"). Consistent with TL theory, the behavioral results demonstrated that Chinese participants, compared with American participants, exhibited greater tightness, including perceiving more behaviors as strongly inappropriate, reporting more constraint in their daily lives, having stronger beliefs about the importance of territorial defense, and evidencing more cultural superiority and less creativity. The ERP results showed that the N400 effect, which was related to the detection of social norm violations, appeared to be stronger in the central and parietal regions for both Chinese and US participants when they witnessed someone violating a social norm, suggesting a general neural component of social norm violation detection across cultures. Furthermore, they found that the N400 effect in the frontal and temporal regions was significantly stronger among Chinese participants (see Figure 10.2). Of note, the culture-specific N400 mediated cultural differences in attitudes and behaviors associated with the strength of social norms, including higher self-control but also lower levels of creativity and openness among Chinese relative to American participants. The authors argue that it is possible that the tightness of a culture (which is likely fostered by various historical threats)

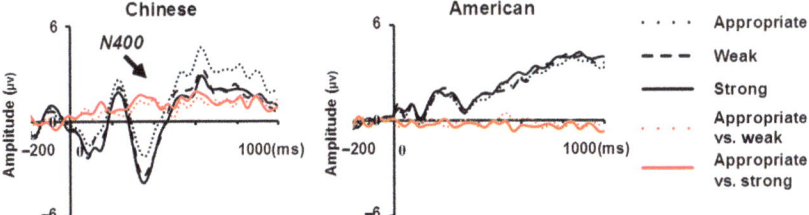

Figure 10.2 Culture-specific N400 effects of social norm violations. Grand average ERPs (black lines) for the strong violation, weak violation, and appropriate conditions and differential ERPs (red lines) for the contrasts between appropriate and strong/weak violation conditions at the frontal regions in Chinese and American participants.
Adapted from "How Culture Gets Embrained: Cultural Differences in Event-Related Potentials of Social Norm Violations," by Y. Mu, S. Kitayama, S. Han, and M. J. Gelfand, 2015, *Proceedings of the National Academy of Sciences of the United States of America*, *112*(50), 15351 (https://doi.org/10.1073/pnas.1509839112)

sensitizes individuals in tight cultures to norm violations and their associated affordances.

Using a modified social norm task, a follow-up EEG study by Salvador et al. (2020) aimed to further address whether the effect of cultural tightness on the neural response to social norm violations (i.e., N400) could be modulated by motivation to affiliate with others. To manipulate the affiliation goals, participants received either a subliminal affiliation prime (with words such as "friendship") or a neural prime as control (with neutral words). Their EEG results support that individuals become more reactive to norm violations (thereby showing increases in the norm violation N400) when they are prepared to affiliate with others relative to as well as reporting high levels of normative tightness. These findings suggest that the neural sensitivity to norm violations is jointly modulated by a person's psychological readiness to affiliate with others and perceived tightness.

Cultural Differences in the Neural basis of Self-Control. Self-control is the ability to control one's behavior. This has far-reaching consequences, from eating healthy food to getting good grades to avoiding aggressive impulses (Bandura, 1991). While self-control is universal, cross-cultural observations have demonstrated variation in different domains of this ability, such as impulsive buying (Kacen & Lee, 2002), emotion regulation (Eisenberg & Zhou, 2000; Kitayama et al., 2004), gambling (Gelfand, 2018), and alcohol consumption (Harrington & Gelfand, 2014; Zhang & Shrum, 2009). Cultural tightness–looseness theory posits that people who live in tight cultures develop more self-regulation and higher cognitive control behaviors to fit into a much stronger normative environment, as compared to people in loose cultures, who exhibit more self-regulation failures.

To examine how culture influences self-control and its underlying neurobiological mechanisms, Mu, Kitayama, et al. (2020) conducted a cross-cultural EEG study in which American and Chinese participants were instructed to close their eyes and relax, but stay awake while their EEG signals were recorded. As compared to task-induced neural activity where people are required to engage in self-control – which activates a more domain-specific and task-dependent process – the resting-state EEG approach illuminates a more spontaneous, domain-general, and largely automatic neural mechanism of self-control processes. The researchers examined the alpha band oscillations during a five-minute resting-state session and compared this neural activity between cultural groups. Their results showed that, relative to US participants, Chinese participants exhibited enhanced resting-state alpha activity in the parietal area. Moreover, the increased parietal alpha activity was associated with individual differences in a variety of self-control related measurements, including higher self-control, more self-regulation in eating behaviors, increased ability to resist temptations, and better performance on a Stroop task. Further mediation models demonstrated the mediational role of resting-state alpha activity, through which cultural tightness affects generalized self-control ability, regulation in eating behaviors, and temptation inhibition. This study extends previous work on the functional role of alpha activity in supporting inhibitory top-down control (Klimesch et al., 2007; Sauseng et al., 2005). It is also consistent with the neural evidence that resting-state parietal alpha activity is greater when individuals are with others (as compared to being alone), as they may need more social regulation because they feel they are being watched (Verbeke et al., 2014). The resting-state EEG study offers a novel cultural neuroscience perspective on cultural differences in inhibition ability and its underlying mechanisms.

The Neural Basis of Group Coordination. According to TL theory, people in tight cultures need to coordinate more than people in loose cultures, as they need to cope with more ecological threats such as natural disasters, resource scarcity, and pathogens, as well as human-made threats such as territorial invasions. Roos et al. (2015) modeled the evolutionary emergence of social norms by integrating research in cross-cultural psychology with evolutionary game theory. The simulation results show that groups that face a high degree of threat evolve to have stronger norms of coordination and punishment as compared to groups with fewer threats. This evolutionary game theoretic work suggests the ability of humans to effectively coordinate their actions under threat confers an important survival advantage (Roos et al., 2015).

Inspired by the results of the evolutionary game modeling, Mu et al. (2017) provided further empirical evidence on the effects of societal threat on human coordination at both the neural and behavioral levels. They combined state-of-the-art hyperscanning EEG techniques with exposure to real-world threat.

Hyperscanning techniques, which record multiple brains' neural activity simultaneously with great precision as humans interact over time (Dumas et al., 2011; Montague et al., 2002), are well suited for elucidating the interbrain mechanisms underlying social coordination under high societal threat. In this study, two participants were randomly assigned to read one of three articles on in-group threat (i.e., their own country was facing a serious external threat from its neighbor), out-group threat (i.e., another country was facing serious external threats from its neighbors), and no threat (i.e., nonthreatening events were occurring on their own soil). They then participated in a coordination game where two participants cooperatively counted time (e.g., eight seconds) either with a human partner in the coordination condition or with a computer partner in the control task. The interpersonal time lag between the two participants was used as a behavioral synchronization index for assessing coordination performance (Mu et al., 2016). The behavioral results showed that dyads exposed to an in-group threat exhibited greater coordination (i.e., lower interpersonal time lags) as compared to dyads in the out-group threat and no threat control conditions. Estimating the interbrain synchrony (i.e., interbrain phase-locking-value) between two interacting individuals (Dumas et al., 2010; Mu et al., 2016), they further illustrate that interbrain synchrony of gamma band oscillations is enhanced when people are under high threat, and that increased gamma interbrain synchrony mediates threat's effect on social coordination (Figure 10.3). In sum, the sharing of gamma activity plays a role in this collective ability among human groups, which provides the first evidence for how humans in tight cultures respond quickly and coordinate effectively in the face of societal and ecological threats.

Taken together, cultural variation in the strength of social norms modulates individuals' brain mechanisms involved in norm detection (e.g., N400), influences task-independent neural activity during resting states (i.e., alpha band activity), and affects interbrain neural oscillatory activity of social coordination (i.e., gamma interbrain synchrony). These findings expand the current theoretical framework of cultural tightness–looseness by adding neural-level patterns, and they help us understand how the human brain has evolved to support adaptation to sociocultural contexts within a variety of social norms.

How Do Genetic Factors Influence Social Norm Processing? Converging scientific evidence supports the notion that the human brain and behavior have been markedly influenced by the interaction of cultural and genetic inheritance systems (Chiao & Blizinsky, 2010; Mrazek et al., 2013). Gene–culture evolutionary theory, a branch of theoretical population genetics that models the transmission of genes and cultural traits from one generation to the next, posits that culture has shaped the human genome by driving the evolution of both our brains and bodies along trajectories not available to other species (Laland et al., 2010). Thus, it is necessary to take the interaction between culture and genes

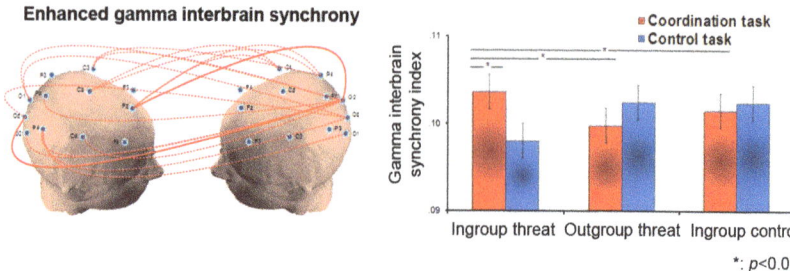

Figure 10.3 Cultural modulations of gamma interbrain synchrony during group coordination. The plot in the left panel shows enhanced gamma interbrain synchrony of the coordination task (cooperating with a human partner) compared with the control task (cooperation with a computer partner) is observed under the in-group threat (threats to one's own country) compared with the out-group (threats to another country) and in-group control (no threat) conditions. The bar chart in the right panel shows increased gamma interbrain synchrony index at 2000–3000 ms of the coordination (vs. control) task under the in-group threat and not the other two low-threat conditions.
From Y. Mu, S. Han, and M. J. Gelfand, "The Role of Gamma Interbrain Synchrony in Social Coordination When Humans Face Territorial Threats," *Social and Affective Neuroscience*, 2017, *12*(10), 1614–23 (https://doi.org/10.1093/scan/nsx093), by permission of Oxford University Press

into consideration when we try to understand human behavior that requires understanding culturally transmitted norms and the evolved cognitive mechanisms that generate them, such as social norms (Chudek & Henrich, 2011).

Two candidate genotypes, namely the serotonin transporter polymorphism (5-HTTLPR) and the dopamine D4 receptor gene (DRD4), have already been shown to be implicated in social norm processing. For example, 5-HTTLPR is a degenerate repeat polymorphic region in the serotonin transporter gene (SLC6A4). The two common variations of this polymorphism in humans are a short (S) allele and a long (L) allele that result in differential expressions and functions (Lesch et al., 1996). Previous behavioral evidence has shown that relative to long-allele carriers, short-allele carriers have more negative emotions, such as anxiety (Sen et al., 2004) and neuroticism traits (Lesch et al., 1996), and they show more sensitivity to emotional information in the environment (Beevers et al., 2010). For instance, the short-allele carriers selectively shift their attention to threatening stimuli (e.g., a picture of spiders), suggesting an involvement of 5-HTTLPR in processing threats (Osinsky et al., 2008). In line with this, neuroimaging evidence indicates that the threat-related network, namely the amygdala, varies as a function of 5-HTTLPR, showing greater activation in the short-allele carriers (Hariri et al., 2002; Munafò et al., 2008). Research highlights the relationship between threats, the serotonin transporter polymorphism (5-HTTLPR), and cultural variation in the strength of social norms, showing that increased vulnerability to ecological and human-made threat predicts increased strength in social norms via heightened frequency of S-allele carriers across nations (Mrazek et al., 2013). This supports the notion that ecological and human-made threats increase the selection for S-allele carriers, as these individuals are more likely to detect such environmental threats and avoid them; they are also more inclined to develop strong norms that help them to coordinate their behavior in order to deal with these threats.

The dopamine receptor D4 (*DRD4*) gene, located near the telomere of chromosome 11p, exhibits an unusual amount of expressed polymorphism and has also been implicated in social norm processing. It contains a 48-bp variable number tandem repeat (VNTR) polymorphism in the third exon, repeated between two and eleven times, with the most frequent versions being 2 (2R), 4 (4R) and 7 (7R) repeat alleles (Van Tol et al., 1992). Prior research has demonstrated associations between the *DRD4* 7R allele and certain behavioral patterns, including increased novelty- or sensation-seeking (Ebstein et al., 1996), financial risk taking (Kuhnen & Chiao, 2009), higher attention control (Sheese et al., 2007), and greater prosocial orientations (Sasaki et al., 2013).

According to the norm sensitivity hypothesis, the acquisition of global behavioral patterns and cultural norms is influenced by learning processes such as reinforcement-mediated social learning, which is associated with the dopamine system (Kitayama et al., 2016). Drawing on the role of *DRD4* in cultural norm learning, Kitayama et al. (2014) found that carriers of the 7R and 2R alleles, relative to noncarriers, were more sensitive to cultural norms and showed greater differences in social orientation. In particular, people with the 7R and 2R alleles in interdependent cultures are more interdependent, but those in independent cultures behave more independently. This suggests an interesting culture–gene interaction that should be explored with other phenomena in future research.

Conclusions and Future Directions

While substantial neural evidence has demonstrated cultural differences in brain activity underlying social norm-related processing, this field is still in its infancy. Many intriguing questions have yet to be addressed. For example, cultural variation in the strength of social norms has been proven to shape brain activity associated with detecting social norm violations. Future research should directly test how ecological and historical threats as well as social affiliation affect the detection of norm violations and its neural substrates. Future research could also address the influence of socioecological factors on the neural mechanisms underlying the punishment of social norm violators. For example, do people punish more frequently and/or severely in the face of collective as compared to personal threats, and what are the neural mechanisms underlying such effects?

Moreover, given the frequency with which people move between cultures in our increasingly globalized world, research should investigate how bicultural and expatriate individuals navigate norm differences in the brain and with what consequences. In particular, how might the brain change when people travel between tight and loose cultures? How would such neural changes affect psychological adaptation and behavioral outcomes? Do people who use different acculturation styles show different neural patterns in support of adaptation? By addressing these questions, research can unfold how cultural influences on the neural systems underlying processing social norms change as a function of time and social factors.

There is also a limited understanding of how culture interacts with genetic factors to influence the brain. For instance, a critical question for future researchers will be to identify whether or not certain genes, such as *DRD4*, are sensitive to cultural variation in the strength of social norms. In particular, in tight cultures, the 7R and 2R alleles might exhibit more traits that are characteristic of tightness, whereas in loose cultures, they might show more features associated with looseness (cf. Kitayama et al., 2014). In addition, given previous work showing that threat increases selection for the 5-HTTLPR S-alleles, it would be interesting to test whether the S-alleles, relative to the L-alleles, show greater neural activity associated with detecting social norm violations in individuals who face conditions of high threat. Research has also demonstrated that oxytocin serves as a neuromodulator in the modulation of complex social behaviors (Shamay-Tsoory & Abu-Akel, 2016) such as prosocial temperament (Tost et al., 2010), trust (Krueger et al., 2012), and in-group favoritism (De Dreu et al., 2011; Han et al., 2020). However, little is known about how oxytocin influences norm-related processes and their brain mechanisms. Given that the neural networks related to social information processing are sensitive to oxytocin modulations (Kanat et al., 2014), it is possible that oxytocin plays a key role in social norm processing and its underlying brain mechanisms to help individuals adapt to social environments. It would be interesting to test, for example, whether oxytocin increases the neural substrates underlying altruistic punishment motivation, and if this process varies as a function of whether an in-group or out-group member is performing the violation. Addressing these questions could help improve our understanding of how cultural and genetic factors interact to affect social norm processing.

While much work has examined the individual brain mechanisms underlying social norm-related processes, future research should study potential group-level neural mechanisms that are related to the detection and enforcement of social norms. Human groups that have been subjected to a long history of collective threats evolve to be tight. However, little is known about the group-level brain mechanisms of processing ecological and societal threats. Research on this topic would benefit from EEG and fMRI hyperscanning methods to understand how collective threats, relative to personal threats, affect interbrain threat-related functions (e.g., amygdala–amygdala interbrain coupling) and whether these mechanisms play a mediational role in various group behavioral outcomes, such as group coordination. Hyperscanning techniques can provide unique insights into the interbrain neural circuits and mechanisms that show sensitivity to cultural differences in the strength of social norms.

In conclusion, social norms are a human universal. They have facilitated large-scale cooperation and coordination among human groups for millennia. By integrating neuroscience techniques with cultural psychology theory, the new field of cultural neuroscience has the potential to give us deep insight into one of the most important human inventions: social norms.

Acknowledgments

We thank Sarah Michelle Gordon for her very helpful suggestions and comments. This work was funded in part by US Air Force Grant FA9550-14-1-0020, the US Army Research Laboratory, the US Army Research Office Grant W911NF-08-1-0144, and an Annaliese Maier Research Award to M.J.G. (principal investigator) from the Alexander von Humboldt Foundation.

REFERENCES

Aplin, L. M., Farine, D. R., Morand-Ferron, J., Cockburn, A., Thornton, A., & Sheldon, B. C. (2015). Experimentally induced innovations lead to persistent culture via conformity in wild birds. *Nature*, *518*(7540), 538–41. https://doi.org/10.1038%2Fnature13998

Asch, S. E. (1956). Studies of independence and conformity: I. A minority of one against a unanimous majority. *Psychological Monographs: General and Applied*, *70*(9), 1–70. https://doi.org/10.1037/h0093718

Balzer, M. M. (1980). The route to eternity: Cultural persistence and change in Siberian Khanty burial ritual. *Arctic Anthropology*, *17*(1), 77–89. www.jstor.org/stable/40315968

Bandura, A. (1991). Social cognitive theory of self-regulation. *Organizational Behavior and Human Decision Processes*, *50*(2), 248–87. https://doi.org/10.1016/0749-5978(91)90022-L

Bechara, A., Tranel, D., & Damasio, H. (2000). Characterization of the decision-making deficit of patients with ventromedial prefrontal cortex lesions. *Brain*, *123*(11), 2189–202. https://doi.org/10.1093/brain/123.11.2189

Beevers, C. G., Ellis, A. J., Wells, T. T., & McGeary, J. E. (2010). Serotonin transporter gene promoter region polymorphism and selective processing of emotional images. *Biological Psychology*, *83*(3), 260–5. https://doi.org/10.1016/j.biopsycho.2009.08.007

Benningfield, M. M., Blackford, J. U., Ellsworth, M. E., Samanez-Larkin, G. R., Martin, P. R., Cowan, R. L., & Zald, D. H. (2014). Caudate responses to reward anticipation associated with delay discounting behavior in healthy youth. *Developmental Cognitive Neuroscience*, *7*, 43–52. https://doi.org/10.1016/j.dcn.2013.10.009

Berthoz, S., Armony, J. L., Blair, R. J. R., & Dolan, R. J. (2002). An fMRI study of intentional and unintentional (embarrassing) violations of social norms. *Brain*, *125*(8), 1696–708. https://doi.org/10.1093/brain/awf190

Blair, R. J. R., Morris, J. S., Frith, C. D., Perrett, D. I., & Dolan, R. J. (1999). Dissociable neural responses to facial expressions of sadness and anger. *Brain*, *122*(5), 883–93. https://doi.org/10.1093/brain/122.5.883

Boesch, C., Marchesi, P., Marchesi, N., Fruth, B., & Joulian, F. (1994). Is nut cracking in wild chimpanzees a cultural behaviour? *Journal of Human Evolution*, *26*(4), 325–38. https://doi.org/10.1006/jhev.1994.1020

Buckholtz, J. W., Asplund, C. L., Dux, P. E., Zald, D. H., Gore, J. C., Jones, O. D., & Marois, R. (2008). The neural correlates of third-party punishment. *Neuron*, *60*(5), 930–40. http://doi.org/10.1016/j.neuron.2008.10.016

Buckholtz, J. W., & Marois, R. (2012). The roots of modern justice: Cognitive and neural foundations of social norms and their enforcement. *Nature Neuroscience*, *15*(5), 655–61. https://doi.org/10.1038/nn.3087

Calder, A. J., Lawrence, A. D., & Young, A. W. (2001). Neuropsychology of fear and loathing. *Nature Reviews Neuroscience*, *2*(5), 352–63. https://doi.org/10.1038/35072584

Ceballos, N. A., Houston, R. J., Smith, N. D., Bauer, L. O., & Taylor, R. E. (2005). N400 as an index of semantic expectancies: Differential effects of alcohol and cocaine dependence. *Progress in Neuro-Psychopharmacology and Biological Psychiatry*, *29*(6), 936–43. http://doi.org/10.1016/j.pnpbp.2005.04.036

Chiao, J. Y. (2009). Cultural neuroscience: A once and future discipline. *Progress in Brain Research*, *178*, 287–304. https://doi.org/10.1016/S0079-6123(09)17821-4

Chiao, J. Y., & Blizinsky, K. D. (2010). Culture-gene coevolution of individualism-collectivism and the serotonin transporter gene. *Proceedings of the Royal Society B: Biological Sciences*, *277*(1681), 529–37. http://doi.org/10.1098/rspb.2009.1650

Chudek, M., & Henrich, J. (2011). Culture-gene coevolution, norm-psychology and the emergence of human prosociality. *Trends in Cognitive Sciences*, *15*(5), 218–26. https://doi.org/10.1016/j.tics.2011.03.003

De Dreu, C. K. W., Greer, L. L., Van Kleef, G. A., Shalvi, S., & Handgraaf, M. J. J. (2011). Oxytocin promotes human ethnocentrism. *Proceedings of the National Academy of Sciences of the United States of America*, *108*(4), 1262–6. http://doi.org/10.1073/pnas.1015316108

de Quervain, D. J.-F., Fischbacher, U., Treyer, V., Schellhammer, M., Schnyder, U., Buck, A., & Fehr, E. (2004). The neural basis of altruistic punishment. *Science*, *305*(5688), 1254–8. http://doi.org/10.1126/science.1100735

Dellinger, K. (2002). Wearing gender and sexuality "on your sleeve": Dress norms and the importance of occupational and organizational culture at work. *Gender Issues*, *20*(1), 3–25. https://doi.org/10.1007/s12147-002-0005-5

Dixon, R. B. (1971). Explaining cross-cultural variations in age at marriage and proportions never marrying. *Population Studies*, *25*(2), 215–33. https://doi.org/10.1080/00324728.1971.10405799

Dumas, G., Lachat, F., Martinerie, J., Nadel, J., & George, N. (2011). From social behaviour to brain synchronization: Review and perspectives in hyperscanning. *IRBM*, *32*(1), 48–53. http://doi.org/10.1016/j.irbm.2011.01.002

Dumas, G., Nadel, J., Soussignan, R., Martinerie, J., & Garnero, L. (2010). Inter-brain synchronization during social interaction. *PLoS ONE*, *5*(8), e12166. http://doi.org/10.1371/journal.pone.0012166

Ebstein, R. P., Novick, O., Umansky, R., Priel, B., Osher, Y., Blaine, D., Bennett, E. R., Nemanov, L., Katz, M., & Belmaker, R. H. (1996). Dopamine D4 receptor (D4DR) exon III polymorphism associated with the human personality trait of novelty seeking. *Nature Genetics*, *12*(1), 78–80. https://doi.org/10.1038/ng0196-78

Eisenberg, N., & Zhou, Q. (2000). Regulation from a developmental perspective. *Psychological Inquiry*, *11*(3), 166–71. www.jstor.org/stable/1449796

Elster, J. (1989). *The cement of society: A study of social order*. Cambridge University Press.

Fehr, E., & Fischbacher, U. (2004a). Social norms and human cooperation. *Trends in Cognitive Sciences*, *8*(4), 185–90. http://doi.org/10.1016/j.tics.2004.02.007

Fehr, E., & Fischbacher, U. (2004b). Third-party punishment and social norms. *Evolution and Human Behavior*, *25*(2), 63–87. http://doi.org/10.1016/S1090-5138(04)00005-4

Fehr, E., & Rockenbach, B. (2004). Human altruism: Economic, neural, and evolutionary perspectives. *Current Opinion in Neurobiology*, *14*(6), 784–90. https://doi.org/10.1016/j.conb.2004.10.007

Frith, C. D., & Frith, U. (2006). The neural basis of mentalizing. *Neuron*, *50*(4), 531–4. http://doi.org/10.1016/j.neuron.2006.05.001

Galef, B. G., & Whiskin, E. E. (2008). "Conformity" in Norway rats? *Animal Behaviour*, *75*(6), 2035–9. https://doi.org/10.1016/j.anbehav.2007.11.012

Gelfand, M. J. (2018). *Rule makers, rule breakers: How tight and loose cultures wire our world*. Scribner.

Gelfand, M. J., Harrington, J. R., & Jackson, J. C. (2017). The strength of social norms across human groups. *Perspectives on Psychological Science*, *12*(5), 800–9. https://doi.org/10.1177/1745691617708631

Gelfand, M. J., Raver, J. L., Nishii, L., Leslie, L. M., Lun, J., Lim, B. C., Duan, L., Almaliach, A., Ang, S., Arnadottir, J., Aycan, Z., Boehnke, K., Boski, P., Cabecinhas, R., Chan, D., Chhokar, J., D'Amato, A., Ferrer, M., Fischlmayr, I. C., ... Yamaguchi, S. (2011). Differences between tight and loose cultures: A 33-nation study. *Science*, *332*(6033), 1100–4. http://doi.org/10.1126/science.1197754

Goto, S. G., Ando, Y., Huang, C., Yee, A., & Lewis, R. S. (2009). Cultural differences in the visual processing of meaning: Detecting incongruities between background and foreground objects using the N400. *Social Cognitive and Affective Neuroscience*, *5*(2–3), 242–53. http://doi.org/10.1093/scan/nsp038

Hagoort, P., Hald, L., Bastiaansen, M., & Petersson, K. M. (2004). Integration of word meaning and world knowledge in language comprehension. *Science*, *304*(5669), 438–41. http://doi.org/10.1126/science.1095455

Han, X., Gelfand, M. J., Wu, B., Zhang, T., Li, W., Gao, T., Pang, C., Wu, T., Zhou, Y., Zhou, S., & Wu, X. (2020). A neurobiological association of revenge propensity during intergroup conflict. *ELife*, *9*, e52014. https://doi.org/10.7554/eLife.52014

Han, S., Northoff, G., Vogeley, K., Wexler, B. E., Kitayama, S., & Varnum, M. E. W. (2013). A cultural neuroscience approach to the biosocial nature of the human brain. *Annual Review of Psychology*, *64*, 335–59. https://doi.org/10.1146/annurev-psych-071112-054629

Hariri, A. R., Mattay, V. S., Tessitore, A., Kolachana, B., Fera, F., Goldman, D., Egan, M. F., & Weinberger, D. R. (2002). Serotonin transporter genetic variation and the response of the human amygdala. *Science*, *297*(5580), 400–3. https://doi.org/10.1126/science.1071829

Harrington, J. R., & Gelfand, M. J. (2014). Tightness-looseness across the 50 United States. *Proceedings of the National Academy of Sciences of the United States of America*, *111*(22), 7990–5. http://doi.org/10.1073/pnas.1317937111

Harrington, J. R., & Gelfand, M. J. (2020). *A world unto themselves: Tightness-looseness and social class* [Unpublished manuscript]. Department of Psychology, University of Maryland.

Haun, D. B. M., Rekers, Y., & Tomasello, M. (2014). Children conform to the behavior of peers; other great apes stick with what they know. *Psychological Science*, *25*(12), 2160–7. https://doi.org/10.1177/0956797614553235

Heeger, D. J., & Ress, D. (2002). What does fMRI tell us about neuronal activity? *Nature Reviews Neuroscience*, *3*(2), 142–51. https://doi.org/10.1038/nrn730

Higgs, S. (2015). Social norms and their influence on eating behaviours. *Appetite*, *86*, 38–44. https://doi.org/10.1016/j.appet.2014.10.021

Hoehl, S., Keupp, S., Schleihauf, H., McGuigan, N., Buttelmann, D., & Whiten, A. (2019). 'Over-imitation': A review and appraisal of a decade of research. *Developmental Review*, *51*, 90–108. https://doi.org/10.1016/j.dr.2018.12.002

Hofstede, G. (1980). Culture and organizations. *International Studies of Management & Organization*, *10*(4), 15–41. https://doi.org/10.1080/00208825.1980.11656300

Kacen, J. J., & Lee, J. A. (2002). The influence of culture on consumer impulsive buying behavior. *Journal of Consumer Psychology*, *12*(2), 163–76. https://doi.org/10.1207/S15327663JCP1202_08

Kanat, M., Heinrichs, M., & Domes, G. (2014). Oxytocin and the social brain: Neural mechanisms and perspectives in human research. *Brain Research*, *1580*, 160–71. https://doi.org/10.1016/j.brainres.2013.11.003

Kitayama, S., Karasawa, M., & Mesquita, B. (2004). Collective and personal processes in regulating emotions: Emotion and self in Japan and the United States. In P. Philippot & R. S. Friedman (Eds.), *The regulation of emotion* (pp. 251–73). Lawrence Erlbaum Associates.

Kitayama, S., King, A., Hsu, M., Liberzon, I., & Yoon, C. (2016). Dopamine-system genes and cultural acquisition: The norm sensitivity hypothesis. *Current Opinion in Psychology*, *8*, 167–74. https://doi.org/10.1016%2Fj.copsyc.2015.11.006

Kitayama, S., King, A., Yoon, C., Tompson, S., Huff, S., & Liberzon, I. (2014). The dopamine D4 receptor gene (DRD4) moderates cultural difference in independent versus interdependent social orientation. *Psychological Science*, *25*(6), 1169–77. https://doi.org/10.1177/0956797614528338

Kitayama, S., & Uskul, A. K. (2011). Culture, mind, and the brain: Current evidence and future directions. *Annual Review of Psychology*, *62*, 419–49. https://doi.org/10.1146/annurev-psych-120709-145357

Klimesch, W., Sauseng, P., & Hanslmayr, S. (2007). EEG alpha oscillations: The inhibition-timing hypothesis. *Brain Research Reviews*, *53*(1), 63–88. https://doi.org/10.1016/j.brainresrev.2006.06.003

Koenigs, M., & Tranel, D. (2007). Irrational economic decision-making after ventromedial prefrontal damage: Evidence from the Ultimatum Game. *Journal of Neuroscience*, *27*(4), 951–6. http://doi.org/10.1523/JNEUROSCI.4606-06.2007

Krawczyk, D. C. (2002). Contributions of the prefrontal cortex to the neural basis of human decision-making. *Neuroscience & Biobehavioral Reviews*, *26*(6), 631–64. https://doi.org/10.1016/S0149-7634(02)00021-0

Krueger, F., Parasuraman, R., Iyengar, V., Thornburg, M., Weel, J., Lin, M., Clarke, E., McCabe, K., & Lipsky, R. H. (2012). Oxytocin receptor genetic variation promotes human trust behavior. *Frontiers in Human Neuroscience*, *6*, 4. https://doi.org/10.3389/fnhum.2012.00004

Kuhnen, C. M., & Chiao, J. Y. (2009). Genetic determinants of financial risk taking. *PLoS ONE*, *4*(2), e4362. https://doi.org/10.1371/journal.pone.0004362

Kutas, M., & Federmeier, K. D. (2011). Thirty years and counting: Finding meaning in the N400 component of the event-related brain potential (ERP). *Annual Review of Psychology*, *62*, 621–47. http://doi.org/10.1146/annurev.psych.093008.131123

Laland, K. N., Odling-Smee, J., & Myles, S. (2010). How culture shaped the human genome: Bringing genetics and the human sciences together. *Nature Reviews Genetics*, *11*(2), 137–48. https://doi.org/10.1038/nrg2734

Lesch, K.-P., Bengel, D., Heils, A., Sabol, S. Z., Greenberg, B. D., Petri, S., Benjamin, J., Müller, C. R., Hamer, D. H., & Murphy, D. L. (1996). Association of anxiety-related traits with a polymorphism in the serotonin transporter gene regulatory region. *Science*, *274*(5292), 1527–31. https://doi.org/10.1126/science.274.5292.1527

Luncz, L. V, Mundry, R., & Boesch, C. (2012). Evidence for cultural differences between neighboring chimpanzee communities. *Current Biology*, *22*(10), 922–6. https://doi.org/10.1016/j.cub.2012.03.031

Markus, H. R., & Kitayama, S. (1991). Culture and the self: Implications for cognition, emotion, and motivation. *Psychological Review*, *98*(2), 224–53. https://doi.org/10.1037/0033-295X.98.2.224

Mathur, V. A., Harada, T., Lipke, T., & Chiao, J. Y. (2010). Neural basis of extraordinary empathy and altruistic motivation. *NeuroImage*, *51*(4), 1468–75. http://doi.org/10.1016/j.neuroimage.2010.03.025

Miller, E. K., & Cohen, J. D. (2001). An integrative theory of prefrontal cortex function. *Annual Review of Neuroscience*, *24*, 167–202. https://doi.org/10.1146/annurev.neuro.24.1.167

Montague, P. R., Berns, G. S., Cohen, J. D., McClure, S. M., Pagnoni, G., Dhamala, M., Wiest, M. C., Karpov, I., King, R. D., Apple, N., & Fisher, R. E. (2002). Hyperscanning: Simultaneous fMRI during linked social interactions. *NeuroImage*, *16*(4), 1159–64. http://doi.org/10.1006/nimg.2002.1150

Montague, P. R., & Lohrenz, T. (2007). To detect and correct: Norm violations and their enforcement. *Neuron*, *56*, 14–18. http://doi.org/10.1016/j.neuron.2007.09.020

Mrazek, A. J., Chiao, J. Y., Blizinsky, K. D., Lun, J., & Gelfand, M. J. (2013). The role of culture-gene coevolution in morality judgment: Examining the interplay between tightness-looseness and allelic variation of the serotonin transporter gene. *Culture and Brain*, *1*(2–4), 100–17. https://doi.org/10.1007%2Fs40167-013-0009-x

Mu, Y., Guo, C., & Han, S. (2016). Oxytocin enhances inter-brain synchrony during social coordination in male adults. *Social Cognitive and Affective Neuroscience*, *11*(2), 1882–93. https://doi.org/10.1093/scan/nsw106

Mu, Y., Han, S., & Gelfand, M. J. (2017). The role of gamma interbrain synchrony in social coordination when humans face territorial threats. *Social Cognitive and Affective Neuroscience*, *12*(10), 1614–23. https://doi.org/10.1093%2Fscan%2Fnsx093

Mu, Y., Han, S., & Gelfand, M. J. (2020). *An fMRI study on social norm violation detection and punishment* [Unpublished manuscript]. Department of Psychology, University of Maryland.

Mu, Y., Kitayama, S., Han, S., & Gelfand, M. J. (2015). How culture gets embrained: Cultural differences in event-related potentials of social norm violations. *Proceedings of the National Academy of Sciences of the United States of America*, *112*(50), 15348–53. https://doi.org/10.1073/pnas.1509839112

Mu, Y., Kitayama, S., Han, S., & Gelfand, M. J. (2020). *Do we rest differently?: Cultural variation in neural markers of self-control* [Unpublished manuscript]. Department of Psychology, University of Maryland.

Munafò, M. R., Brown, S. M., & Hariri, A. R. (2008). Serotonin transporter (5-HTTLPR) genotype and amygdala activation: A meta-analysis. *Biological Psychiatry*, *63*(9), 852–7. https://doi.org/10.1016/j.biopsych.2007.08.016

Na, J., & Kitayama, S. (2011). Spontaneous trait inference is culture-specific: Behavioral and neural evidence. *Psychological Science*, *22*(8), 1025–32. http://doi.org/10.1177/0956797611414727

Nitsche, M. A., & Paulus, W. (2000). Excitability changes induced in the human motor cortex by weak transcranial direct current stimulation. *Journal of Physiology*, *527*(3), 633–9. https://doi.org/10.1111/j.1469-7793.2000.t01-1-00633.x

Osinsky, R., Reuter, M., Küpper, Y., Schmitz, A., Kozyra, E., Alexander, N., & Hennig, J. (2008). Variation in the serotonin transporter gene modulates selective attention to threat. *Emotion*, *8*(4), 584–8. https://doi.org/10.1037/a0012826

Pelto, P. J. (1968). The differences between "tight" and "loose" societies. *Society*, *5*(5), 37–40. https://doi.org/10.1007/BF03180447

Ramnani, N., & Owen, A. M. (2004). Anterior prefrontal cortex: Insights into function from anatomy and neuroimaging. *Nature Reviews Neuroscience*, *5*(3), 184–94. https://doi.org/10.1038/nrn1343

Reher, D. S. (1998). Family ties in Western Europe: Persistent contrasts. *Population and Development Review*, *24*(2), 203–34. https://doi.org/10.2307/2807972

Röder, B., Rösler, F., & Neville, H. J. (2000). Event-related potentials during auditory language processing in congenitally blind and sighted people. *Neuropsychologia*, *38*(11), 1482–502. http://doi.org/10.1016/S0028-3932(00)00057-9

Roos, P., Gelfand, M. J., Nau, D., & Lun, J. (2015). Societal threat and cultural variation in the strength of social norms: An evolutionary basis. *Organizational Behavior and Human Decision Processes*, *129*, 14–23. https://doi.org/10.1016/j.obhdp.2015.01.003

Ruff, C. C., Ugazio, G., & Fehr, E. (2013). Changing social norm compliance with noninvasive brain stimulation. *Science*, *342*(6157), 482–4. https://doi.org/10.1126/science.1241399

Salvador, C. E., Mu, Y., Gelfand, M. J., & Kitayama, S. (2020). When norm violations are spontaneously detected: An electrocortical investigation. *Social Cognitive and Affective Neuroscience, 15*(3), 319–27. https://doi.org/10.1093/scan/nsaa035

Sanfey, A. G., Rilling, J. K., Aronson, J. A, Nystrom, L. E., & Cohen, J. D. (2003). The neural basis of economic decision-making in the Ultimatum Game. *Science, 300* (5626), 1755–8. http://doi.org/10.1126/science.1082976

Sanz, C., Call, J., & Morgan, D. (2009). Design complexity in termite-fishing tools of chimpanzees (*Pan troglodytes*). *Biology Letters, 5*(3), 293–6. https://doi.org/10.1098/rsbl.2008.0786

Sasaki, J. Y., Kim, H. S., Mojaverian, T., Kelley, L. D. S., Park, I. Y., & Janušonis, S. (2013). Religion priming differentially increases prosocial behavior among variants of the dopamine D4 receptor (DRD4) gene. *Social Cognitive and Affective Neuroscience, 8*(2), 209–15. https://doi.org/10.1093/scan/nsr089

Sauseng, P., Klimesch, W., Doppelmayr, M., Pecherstorfer, T., Freunberger, R., & Hanslmayr, S. (2005). EEG alpha synchronization and functional coupling during top-down processing in a working memory task. *Human Brain Mapping, 26*(2), 148–55. https://doi.org/10.1002/hbm.20150

Schwartz, S. H. (1992). Universals in the content and structure of values: Theoretical advances and empirical tests in 20 countries. *Advances in Experimental Social Psychology, 25*, 1–65. https://doi.org/10.1016/S0065-2601(08)60281-6

Sen, S., Burmeister, M., & Ghosh, D. (2004). Meta-analysis of the association between a serotonin transporter promoter polymorphism (5-HTTLPR) and anxiety-related personality traits. *American Journal of Medical Genetics Part B: Neuropsychiatric Genetics, 127B*(1), 85–9. https://doi.org/10.1002/ajmg.b.20158

Shamay-Tsoory, S. G., & Abu-Akel, A. (2016). The social salience hypothesis of oxytocin. *Biological Psychiatry, 79*(3), 194–202. https://doi.org/10.1016/j.biopsych.2015.07.020

Sheese, B. E., Voelker, P. M., Rothbart, M. K., & Posner, M. I. (2007). Parenting quality interacts with genetic variation in dopamine receptor D4 to influence temperament in early childhood. *Development and Psychopathology, 19*(4), 1039–46. https://doi.org/10.1017/S0954579407000521

Singelis, T. M. (1994). The measurement of independent and interdependent self-construals. *Personality and Social Psychology Bulletin, 20*(5), 580–91. http://doi.org/10.1177/0146167294205014

Singer, T., Critchley, H. D., & Preuschoff, K. (2009). A common role of insula in feelings, empathy and uncertainty. *Trends in Cognitive Sciences, 13*(8), 334–40. https://doi.org/10.1016/j.tics.2009.05.001

Spitzer, M., Fischbacher, U., Herrnberger, B., Grön, G., & Fehr, E. (2007). The neural signature of social norm compliance. *Neuron, 56*(1), 185–96. https://doi.org/10.1016/j.neuron.2007.09.011

Spring, J. H. (2008). *Wheels in the head: Educational philosophies of authority, freedom, and culture from Confucianism to human rights* (3rd ed.). Routledge.

Strobel, A., Zimmermann, J., Schmitz, A., Reuter, M., Lis, S., Windmann, S., & Kirsch, P. (2011). Beyond revenge: Neural and genetic bases of altruistic punishment. *NeuroImage, 54*(1), 671–80. http://doi.org/10.1016/j.neuroimage.2010.07.051

Suitor, J. J., & Carter, R. S. (1999). Jocks, nerds, babes and thugs: A research note on regional differences in adolescent gender norms. *Gender Issues, 17*(3), 87–101. https://doi.org/10.1007/s12147-999-0005-9

Tomasello, M., Kruger, A. C., & Ratner, H. H. (1993). Cultural learning. *Behavioral and Brain Sciences*, *16*(3), 495–511. https://doi.org/10.1017/S0140525X0003123X

Tost, H., Kolachana, B., Hakimi, S., Lemaitre, H., Verchinski, B. A., Mattay, V. S., Weinberger, D. R., & Meyer-Lindenberg, A. (2010). A common allele in the oxytocin receptor gene (OXTR) impacts prosocial temperament and human hypothalamic-limbic structure and function. *Proceedings of the National Academy of Sciences of the United States of America*, *107*(31), 13936–41. https://doi.org/10.1073/pnas.1003296107

Triandis, H. C. (1989). The self and social behavior in differing cultural contexts. *Psychological Review*, *96*(3), 506–20. https://doi.org/10.1037/0033-295X.96.3.506.

Triandis, H. C., & Gelfand, M. J. (1998). Converging measurement of horizontal and vertical individualism and collectivism. *Journal of Personality and Social Psychology*, *74*(1), 118–28. http://doi.org/10.1037/0022-3514.74.1.118

van de Waal, E., Borgeaud, C., & Whiten, A. (2013). Potent social learning and conformity shape a wild primate's foraging decisions. *Science*, *340*(6131), 483–5. https://doi.org/10.1126/science.1232769

Van Tol, H. H. M., Wu, C. M., Guan, H.-C., Ohara, K., Bunzow, J. R., Civelli, O., Kennedy, J., Seeman, P., Niznik, H. B., & Jovanovic, V. (1992). Multiple dopamine D4 receptor variants in the human population. *Nature*, *358*(6382), 149–52. https://doi.org/10.1038/358149a0

Varnum, M. E. W., Na, J., Murata, A., & Kitayama, S. (2012). Social class differences in N400 indicate differences in spontaneous trait inference. *Journal of Experimental Psychology: General*, *141*(3), 518–26. http://doi.org/10.1037/a0026104

Verbeke, W. J. M. I., Pozharliev, R., Van Strien, J. W., Belschak, F., & Bagozzi, R. P. (2014). "I am resting but rest less well with you." The moderating effect of anxious attachment style on alpha power during EEG resting state in a social context. *Frontiers in Human Neuroscience*, *8*, 486. https://doi.org/10.3389%2Ffnhum.2014.00486

Wager, T. D., Davidson, M. L., Hughes, B. L., Lindquist, M. A., & Ochsner, K. N. (2008). Prefrontal-subcortical pathways mediating successful emotion regulation. *Neuron*, *59*(6), 1037–50. https://doi.org/10.1016/j.neuron.2008.09.006

White, K. R., Crites, S. L., Jr., Taylor, J. H., & Corral, G. (2009). Wait, what? Assessing stereotype incongruities using the N400 ERP component. *Social Cognitive and Affective Neuroscience*, *4*(2), 191–8. http://doi.org/10.1093/scan/nsp004

Whiten, A. (2019). Conformity and over-imitation: An integrative review of variant. In M. Naguib, L. Barrett, S. D. Healy, J. Podos, L. W. Simmons, & M. Zuk (Eds.), *Advances in the study of behavior* (Vol. 51, pp. 31–75). Elsevier Academic Press. https://doi.org/10.1016/bs.asb.2018.12.003

Whiten, A., Horner, V., & de Waal, F. B. M. (2005). Conformity to cultural norms of tool use in chimpanzees. *Nature*, *437*(7059), 737–40. https://doi.org/10.1038/nature04047

Zhang, Y., & Shrum, L. J. (2009). The influence of self-construal on impulsive consumption. *Journal of Consumer Research*, *35*(5), 838–50. https://doi.org/10.1086/593687.

11 Ritual and Religion as Social Technologies of Cooperation

Christopher Kavanagh, Jonathan Jong, and Harvey Whitehouse

Introduction

This chapter takes as its point of departure the influential French sociologist Émile Durkheim's view that religion and ritual are inherently *social* phenomena (Durkheim, 1912/1965). Although we emphasize the social aspects of religion and ritual in this chapter, this is not to deny the value of approaches that focus on the individual as the unit of analysis.[1] We focus on the role that collective rituals and religious beliefs play in fostering and maintaining cooperation and coordination. This seems to put us once again on Durkheim's side, insofar as his theory of religion and ritual is functionalist and thus presents them as playing a role in maintaining social order in society. However, we do not seek to defend a functionalist *explanation* of religion and ritual here. Rather, we aim to consider the effects of these cultural technologies. Our focus is empirical, however, rather than just theoretical. We examine the effects that collective rituals can have on cooperation and coordination by reviewing recent work from experimental and developmental psychology, as well as the fields of cognitive anthropology and cultural evolution.

By "ritual," we mean a culturally sanctioned, collectively performed set of actions that are characterized by such traits as normative rigidity, repetitive redundancy, and functional or causal opacity (Boyer & Liénard, 2006; Liénard & Boyer, 2006; Rappaport, 1999; Rossano, 2012; Whitehouse, 2011). By "religion," we mean the social and psychological phenomena associated with culturally shared beliefs in supernatural agents or forces (Boyer, 2001; Guthrie, 1993; Jong, 2015; Pyysiäinen, 2003, 2009; Sutherland, 2012)[2]

---

[1] Idiosyncratic supernatural beliefs and experiences are topics of investigation in their own right, as are rigid, repetitive, and non-functional behaviors. Furthermore, there is increasing evidence for a panoply of psychological effects of religious belief and ritual participation at the individual level, such as the alleviation of grief (Norton & Gino, 2014), the mitigation of death anxiety (Jong & Halberstadt, 2016), the bolstering of feelings of control (Kay et al., 2010), and the provision of a sense of life's meaningfulness (Park, 2005, 2011).

[2] Without denying that religious beliefs and ritual behaviors can and often do interact, we treat them separately and emphasize that rituals can and do occur frequently outside of religious contexts (see, for example, state rituals: Kapitány et al., 2019; Verkaaik, 2010).

and entailing social, collectively performed behaviors (Rossano, 2012).[3] Given these definitions, rituals may or may not make reference to supernatural agents, and insofar as they do, they count as *religious* rituals.

We begin our chapter with a discussion of rituals and their relationship with cooperation, examining them both inside and outside of religious contexts. We then proceed to examine the associations between cooperation and religious beliefs and consider whether this corresponds to what we found with rituals. Finally, we consider the role of religions in cultural evolution and thus the potential interactive effect of rituals and religious beliefs.

Ritual Processes That Promote Coordination

Causal Opacity and Social Learning

Two exemplars of ritual processes are the Roman Catholic mass and the Shinto *misogi*. The Catholic mass is centered around a sacrificial meal, in which participants consume bread and wine consecrated by a priest. *Misogi* is a type of Japanese purification ritual in which participants cleanse themselves – usually with water, including under running waterfalls. These two culturally distinct phenomena have much in common, including the recitation of predetermined prayers, repetition of words and actions, donning of special garments, and collective participation.[4]

They are also characterized by what cognitive anthropologists and psychologists are increasingly recognizing as a defining property of ritualized behavior: causal opacity. Rituals are causally opaque in that the relationship between actions and stated goals cannot *in principle* be specified in physical–causal terms (Humphrey & Laidlaw, 1994; Whitehouse, 2011). To seek out a practical rationale is to misunderstand the very nature of ritualized behavior. Thus, social anthropologists have often observed that ritual participants are powerless to explain why they carry out the particular procedures that constitute any given ritual, appealing only to tradition or the authority of ancestors.

For example, why the particular liturgical formulas used in a Catholic mass can evince transubstantiation of bread and wine into the body and blood of Christ is difficult even for professional theologians to explain. Similarly, for many *misogi* participants, the specific *kami* (Shinto deities) that are evoked in the chants or venerated at specific shrines remain largely unknown; they are singing to gods, but they do not know which ones. Even for the minority of

---

[3] We recognize that rituals may also be enacted in solitude but our interest here is in collective performances and their social consequences.
[4] *Misogi* rituals can also be an individual ascetic practice; and there is also a provision for Catholic priests to celebrate the mass *sine populo*.

practitioners who can identify the relevant *kami*, few would be able to provide doctrinal details about what individual elements of the *misogi* signify. Indeed, some have argued that participating in ritual practices with pragmatic goals and a lack of theological articulation is a defining characteristic of Japanese religion (Kavanagh, 2016b; Kavanagh & Jong, 2020; Reader & Tanabe, 1998). This corresponds to a wider distinction (Bell, 1997; Berling, 1987) between religions and cultures that are *orthodoxic*, meaning they place "an emphasis on belief, on the assent to propositions and on Doctrinal conformity," and those that are *orthopraxic*, which in contrast place "greater stress on external behaviour rather than internal belief" (Szerszynski, 2002, p. 61).

The Ritual Stance and Overimitation

Causally opaque actions are not amenable to instrumental interpretation. They do not make sense in physical–causal terms and instead assume that whatever it is that requires us to observe this particular sequence of actions in this particular way derives from an altogether different way of reasoning. The reasoning is seldom transparent; the actions may be regarded as symbolic, the product of divine or supernatural forces, or simply part of tradition (Whitehouse, 2012, pp. 266–7). In any case, when we consider actions in this way, we have abandoned the *instrumental* stance and adopted the *ritual* stance toward them (Whitehouse, 2011). This point may be illustrated by the different ways in which swords can be used. Historically, swords have been used instrumentally as effective weapons by many military forces, but swords are also regularly used in rituals, including to confer a knighthood by tapping the flat edge of the blade on the candidate's shoulders.

But why would behaviors not thought to have any rational causal structure spread across human populations and become culturally entrenched? It may relate to our species' tendency to "overimitate" others' actions, that is, imitate actions that make no obvious contributions to intended end-goals. Recent psychological research suggests that overimitation, if not unique to our species, plays a far greater role in human learning as compared with other primates (Hoehl et al., 2019; Hoppitt & Laland, 2013; Horner & Whiten, 2005; McGuigan et al., 2011; Whiten et al., 2009). Studies have shown that from a very young age children copy modeled behaviors in their entirety, even when the procedures include superfluous elements that they have been told to exclude (Lyons et al., 2011, 2007).

These studies have employed a variety of methods, but the most common procedure involves participants attempting to retrieve a reward from a "puzzle box" after observing a model do so. To extract the reward from the box the model performs some actions that are instrumental and some that are superfluous. Experimental conditions vary by how salient the superfluous actions are made, for instance by using a transparent puzzle box to reveal that certain actions have no impact on the box unlocking mechanism, and then measuring the degree to which casually superfluous actions are imitated. Studies using similar procedures have demonstrated the tendency to "overimitate" superfluous actions to be cross-culturally recurrent (Clegg & Legare, 2016; Corriveau et al., 2017; Nielsen & Tomaselli, 2010; Nielsen et al., 2014; Taniguchi & Sanefuji, 2017) and to persist into adulthood (Flynn & Smith, 2012; McGuigan et al., 2011; McGuigan, 2012; Whiten et al., 2016). Indeed, counter to expectations, results to date suggest that adults are more, not less, prone to overimitation than children.

Similarly, recent studies have demonstrated that young children seem to be sensitive to the difference between opportunities for ritual (i.e., group-specific conventional behavior) and instrumental learning in a modeled imitation task (Clegg & Legare, 2015; Herrmann et al., 2013). The basic paradigm in the studies comparing ritual and instrumental actions (Legare et al., 2015) is to present novel objects to young children with which the model then demonstrates a series of arbitrary actions. In the ritualistic condition, the end state of the action sequence is identical to its beginning. Nothing has been achieved, and so it makes little sense to look for an overarching goal of the actions performed. Conversely, in the instrumental condition, a change is introduced at the end of the same sequence, suggesting the actions served some purpose. These studies have generally found that children copy the ritualistic actions more rigidly than they do the instrumental actions. One interpretation of these results is that overimitation is driven by social concerns, and especially the desire to affiliate, rather than concerns about practical outcomes (Kenward et al., 2010; Nielsen & Blank, 2011). Indeed, depending on the context and the characteristics of the model, goals can vary between focusing on social versus learning goals and this can impact overimitation tendencies (Over & Carpenter, 2009; Schleihauf et al., 2018; Wood et al., 2016). This kind of social learning may be a vital part of acquiring and maintaining membership of groups, defined by arbitrary rituals that range from distinctive styles of greeting and address to more elaborated forms of etiquette, attire, and ceremony (Whitehouse, 2011).

Building on this, recent studies have set out to explore what kinds of social conditions encourage children to engage in ritualistic behaviors. If rituals are about belonging to a group, children might be more eager to copy ritualistic actions after being primed with an ostracism threat, such as when they are made to feel excluded by their peers. In two studies using the Cyberball paradigm – an ostensibly online ball-tossing game used to manipulate feelings of social ostracism via the exclusionary actions of other "players" (Williams & Jarvis, 2006) – Watson-Jones et al. (2014, 2016) experimentally manipulated children's feelings of ostracism or social exclusion, and found that the advantage of ritual imitation over instrumental imitation was greater under those conditions. These findings imply that the adoption of the ritual stance serves as a social reinclusion strategy.

If the ritual stance is about affiliation to a group, then children should also be sensitive to *social* cues suggesting that a causally opaque behavior is shared by a group, which should in turn motivate high-fidelity imitation. Herrmann et al. (2013) compared identical actions in a group of preschool children that were verbally framed in a ritualistic (e.g., they are "always done this way") or instrumental manner (i.e., where the outcomes of the actions were described) and found that imitative fidelity was higher with the ritual framing and was also higher when two models performed the actions synchronously (i.e., simultaneously) than when the actions were performed individually. Thus, rituals do not have to differ in form from instrumental actions (e.g., in terms of start–end states); social cues alone can increase the likelihood of adopting the ritual stance and its behavioral consequences.

Synchronous Rituals as Bonding Activities

Having considered what we think of as an essential trait of rituals – causal opacity – we now turn to one that is merely extremely widespread. Almost all collective rituals, whether in religious or in secular contexts, involve some degree of synchronized behavior – the matching of actions in time, examples of which include speaking, singing, and marching. This is, we believe, no accident; rather, collective rituals often involve synchrony because it is an effective means to bond individuals within groups. The experimental evidence for this has grown rapidly in the past decade. The study by Herrmann et al. (2013) described above, for instance, found that synchrony enhances imitation fidelity. Other studies have shown that synchrony also increases positive attitudes and prosocial behaviors toward in-group members, both among adults (Hove & Risen, 2009; Reddish et al., 2013; Valdesolo & DeSteno, 2011; Wiltermuth & Heath, 2009) and children (Cirelli et al., 2014a, 2014b, 2016; Kirschner & Tomasello, 2010; Rabinowitch & Knafo-Noam, 2015; Tunçgenç & Cohen, 2016; Tunçgenç et al., 2015). Meta-analyses of the available research have confirmed the general conclusion that synchrony increases prosocial attitudes and behaviors (Mogan et al., 2017; Rennung & Göritz, 2016).

The cultural prevalence of ritualized synchrony might reflect a leveraging of intuitive behaviors that manifest in early infancy as there is some evidence that newborns readily match adult behavior, though true imitative behavior probably only emerges toward the child's second year of life (see Jones, 2009, for a critical review). Some psychologists have even argued that this tendency to mimic others' behavior is foundational for the development of social cognitive abilities (Meltzoff, 2007) and is likely linked to the function of "mirror neurons" (Iacoboni, 2009). Adults also automatically mimic others during normal social interactions, and there is increasing evidence that this behavior increases positive feelings between both mimicker and mimickee (Chartrand & Bargh, 1999; Stel & Vonk, 2010). Synchronous rituals may, therefore, be a form of culturally constructed mimicry.

Currently research has focused on the mechanisms underlying the relationship between synchrony and social bonding. One promising theory is that synchrony and related forms of behavioral matching produce social benefits by increasing feelings of similarity between actors or within groups, perhaps even to the extent that the boundary between self and other is blurred. Consistent with this theory, several experiments have found that synchrony increases perceived similarity (Rabinowitch & Knafo-Noam, 2015; Valdesolo & DeSteno, 2011) as well as feelings of the group's unity or "oneness" (Lakens, 2010; Lakens & Stel, 2011; Reddish et al., 2016), though Mogan et al.'s (2017) meta-analysis found that such self-report measures generally evinced weaker and less robust results than did behavioral measures.

Finally, there is also some evidence from both the mimicry and the synchrony literature that these effects extend beyond the dyad or group in question. Experiments have shown that participants who were subtly mimicked were subsequently more likely to help others absent from the mimicry situation; these effects have been found in the laboratory (van Baaren et al., 2004), on the streets (Fischer-Lokou et al., 2011), and among eighteen-month-old infants (Carpenter et al., 2013). Similarly, experiments on synchrony have found prosocial effects on nonperformers, including even out-groups and out-group members (Reddish et al., 2014, 2016). This suggests that, as a social technology, collective synchrony may be leveraged in rituals to promote widespread cooperation.

Costly Rituals as Persuasive Signals

All rituals, as we have defined them, involve causal opacity, which is important for social learning; most rituals involve synchronous behaviors, which fosters cooperative and prosocial behavior. Some rituals are also *costly* in some way, for example because they involve physical or psychological pain. Earlier we discussed Japanese *misogi* rituals, extreme versions of which entail immersion in freezing water while wearing little clothing during the coldest months of winter, and these are far from an isolated case. Consider, for instance, the mass public spectacles of bloody self-flagellation practiced by Shia devotees during the Islamic celebration of *Ashura* (Norton, 2005) or the multiple piercings endured by Tamil Hindus as part of the *kavadi attam* ritual practiced annually as part of the *Thaipusam* festival (Jegindø et al., 2013; Xygalatas et al., 2013).

The costliness of rituals like these raise questions for evolutionary anthropologists about their functions and benefits, both at the individual and group level. In recent theorizing on this question, two mutually consistent proposals have arisen. First, costly rituals might serve as *credibility-enhancing displays* (CREDs) that help to foster trust and also to produce ideological – and theological – consensus within the group, particularly by persuading nonparticipants (Henrich, 2009; Irons, 2001; Sosis, 2003; Sosis & Alcorta, 2003). Second, collective participation in costly or *dysphoric* rituals might serve as a potent means of generating strong relational bonds between co-participants, particularly when the ritual is personally consequential and leads those involved to feel that they have collectively shared a self-defining experience (Swann et al., 2012; Whitehouse & Lanman, 2014). We discuss this second proposal a little later; in the next section, we focus on the role that costly rituals can play as "hard-to-fake" social signals.

Rituals' Effects on Observers

From the social-psychological literature on persuasion, we know that source credibility is an important factor in persuasiveness (see Pornpitakpan, 2004, for a critical review), and that the credibility of the source is not merely dependent on their actual expertise. Rather, people tend to attribute credibility to sources based on indirect cues like similarity (Bandura et al., 1961), group membership (Clark & Maass, 1988; Simons et al., 1970), prestige (Hovland & Weiss, 1951), and even physical attractiveness (DeBono & Harnish, 1988; Patzer, 1983). Most relevant to the role of rituals in persuasion is the research on the effects of various forms of costliness. For example, Walster et al. (1966) found that a source is more persuasive when arguing for a position opposed to their own self-interest; the message itself can therefore be the costly signal of trustworthiness. Similarly, on literal financial costliness, Willard et al. (2016) found that participants judged a counterintuitive story as more believable when they witnessed someone else bet money on its truth.

Consistent with costly signaling theory, field experiments on costly rituals suggest that they affect observers as well as performers. Xygalatas et al.'s (2013) study of the *Thaipusam* in Mauritius, for instance, found that both performers of the *kavadi attam* and related observers displayed greater generosity to a local temple than those performing less onerous ritual prayers. This accords with the hypothesis that costly rituals serve as potent illustrations of genuine commitment to a group and thus are able to serve as effective signals to other members and encourage progroup actions.

In another field experiment conducted at a *kavadi* festival, Mitkidis et al. (2017) found evidence that related observers were more honest in reporting results in a dice rolling task after witnessing the rituals, whereas no such change was found with the performers themselves. Mitkidis et al. suggest this implies that "observers chose to cleanse themselves by acting more morally" (Mitkidis et al., 2017, p. 5) in response to observing the prosocial moral signal provided by the endurance of a physical ordeal by performers. Similarly, in the context of a Mauritian firewalking ritual, Fischer et al. (2014) found a divergence in the emotional response to the ritual between performers and related observers: Compared to baseline, firewalkers reported increased happiness and decreased fatigue – a "fire-walker's high" – whereas related observers reported no change in happiness but an increase in fatigue. This finding, again, suggests that while performers may receive a psychological "payoff" for their suffering in terms of feeling morally cleansed, purified, or having demonstrated their devotion; a corresponding psychological "debt" may be generated among group members who observe such events. That observers can be strongly physiologically impacted by watching others perform rituals has been demonstrated in a study of a Spanish firewalking festival by Konvalinka et al. (2011). They found that performers' and their relatives' heart rates synchronized during the ritual; whereas no such synchrony was observed for unrelated observers.

Recent research has also examined the effects of exposure to CREDs on religious belief itself. Lanman and Buhrmester (2017) reported two retrospective correlational studies on American participants which found that childhood exposure to religious CREDs – including caregivers' religious observance – was a better predictor of current belief in god than were caregivers' verbal emphasis on religion or even participants' own childhood religious observance. Willard and Cingl (2017), similarly, found that exposure to CREDs explained much of the difference in religious belief and participation between two historically and culturally comparable but religiously divergent countries: the societally secular Czech Republic and unrepentantly Catholic Slovakia.

Rituals and Self-Persuasion

Social-psychological research also suggests that costly behavior might serve as a signal to oneself (Bem, 1972) or as a means of reducing a "dissonance" induced by the performance of an unpleasant act (Festinger, 1957). For example, in a classic study by Aronson and Mills (1959), participants – who were led to believe that they were volunteers for a discussion group – were first asked to read aloud in front of the experimenter a list of words, as part of their initiation into the group. The list could either contain mildly sexual words or highly sexual words. The participants who were assigned the highly sexual words – an embarrassing task, especially in the 1950s –subsequently rated the discussion group, which was by design rather boring, to be more positive. Gerard and Mathewson's (1966) conceptual replication of the study, which replaced the reading task with the endurance of electric shocks of varying intensity, also found that unpleasant initiations increased progroup attitudes. In their study of college hazing activities, Keating et al. (2005) found that the harshness of the initiation predicted how important members thought their group was to them; in an experiment comparing humiliating induction activities against innocuous ones, they found that the severe initiation promoted conformity and social dependency. More recent attempts at replication have produced mixed results (Hautaluoma & Spungin, 1974; Lodewijkx & Syroit, 1997; Van Raalte et al., 2007), but insofar as the effect holds, both dissonance reduction and self-signaling accounts provide reasonable explanations.

In the classic dissonance account, enduring painful or unpleasant events introduce a subsequent need to justify the actions to decrease any psychological inconsistency (Festinger, 1957). Later formulations of the theory emphasized the importance of personal responsibility (Cooper & Fazio, 1984) and the central role of dissonance within self-concepts (Aronson, 1968, 1999). Another development, relevant to the effects we described on observers in the preceding section, is the theory of "vicarious dissonance" (Cooper & Hogg, 2007). Cooper and Hogg suggest that "under conditions of intersubjectivity," such as being a member of the same group, "observers are able to experience the actor's inner states as their own" and thus can "experience cognitive dissonance vicariously" (Cooper & Hogg, 2007, p. 395).

A self-perception account (Bem, 1972) would suggest that initiates infer from their willingness to undergo severe rituals that they are committed to the group, which in turn increases their commitment. The precise relationship between dissonance and self-perception accounts has been a long-enduring and still unresolved controversy, but notably advocates of cognitive dissonance theories also recognize the importance of self-persuasion processes (Aronson, 1999).

Another more recent model, that could also account for the results discussed above, is the "biosocial model of affective decision making" proposed by Kitayama and Tompson (2015). Their model argues that when facing a conflicting choice between two behaviors, such as participating in a painful ritual vs. avoidance, people feel compelled to find a positive incentive to choose between the options. If participation is selected, then they suggest that the ritual will be experienced affectively more positively and thus regarded as being more valued, pleasant, or important.

Alongside research focusing on individual psychology, there has also been research conducted on hazing and other initiation rituals that interprets them as an evolutionary mechanism that enables current members to test and thus better assess the intentions and relevant qualities of incoming members. In two studies, Cimino (2011, 2013) found that when asked to imagine strongly cooperative, enduring coalitions, people tended to desire more severe initiation practices than those who were asked to imagine less cooperative groups. In other words, people designed more severe initiations for higher quality groups. Relatedly, Young's (1965) study of male initiation rites found that societies with more powerful coalitions tended to have more dramatic initiation practices, and a similar pattern was reported for mystery cults in Melanesia (Allen, 1967; Strathern, 1970).

There has also been research on the group-level effects of costly demands and other CREDs – not limited to painful rituals or severe hazing activities – in religious contexts. Iannaccone (1994, p. 1181), for example, found that strict churches – those that demand "complete loyalty, unwavering belief, and rigid adherence to a distinctive lifestyle" – tend to grow faster than lax ones. Similarly, in their study of nineteenth-century American communes, Sosis and Bressler (2003) found that the communes that imposed costlier requirements were able to survive for longer than those whose membership were less demanding. Notably, this relationship was only observed for religious and not for secular communes.

These studies converge on the finding that costly rituals – college hazing, Hindu Tamil *kavadi*, Spanish firewalking, and so forth – have effects beyond the performers themselves. However, more work still needs to be done to disentangle the *signaling* effects of costly rituals from other mechanisms that produce social cohesion. For example, the fact that in some studies only those related to ritual performers were affected complicates the view that costly rituals serve as signals to observers as a general category: Not all observers are created equal. Emotional investment and a shared social identity are likely to be key contributing factors to producing significant effects on observers (Cooper & Hogg, 2007; Kitayama & Tompson, 2015). Finally, there are a variety of possibilities regarding the content of the signals themselves: Rituals may advertise fitness to potential partners (Zahavi & Zahavi, 1997), or commitment to other group members (Cimino, 2011, 2013), or the benefits of a group relative to others (Bulbulia & Sosis, 2011). These are unlikely to be mutually exclusive propositions, but we are still at the early stages of establishing how they fit together.

Costly Rituals and Collective Effervescence

The previous section surveyed the evidence that costly rituals serve as social signals, focusing primarily on how those receiving the signal respond. This section focuses on the psychological effects that participation has on the ritual performers themselves. Durkheim (1912/1965) theorized that taking part in emotionally arousing collective rituals helped to generate a sense of collective unity, which he referred to as a "collective effervescence" (Durkheim, 1912/1965). Yet in the decades that followed, despite insightful ethnographic work (Turner, 1969, 1985; Van Gennep, 1909/1960), there was very little empirical exploration of collective rituals. Recently, this has begun to change as cognitive anthropologists and psychologists have started to employ field- and lab-based experimental methodologies to examine the physiological and psychological effects of collective rituals.

The field experiments introduced in the preceding section on *kavadi* and firewalking rituals are from this new wave and were primarily intended to test hypotheses inspired by Durkheim. As such, they focused on whether these dramatic ritual events evoked a shared physiological and emotional response among performers and observers. As summarized, there is now some evidence for shared physiological arousal, but crucially this is restricted to ritual performers and *related* observers (Fischer et al., 2014; Konvalinka et al., 2011). Hence, a recent field study conducted at four Shinto and Buddhist firewalking festivals in Japan found that patterns of inclusive vs. exclusive social identification and identity fusion diverged between nonlocal observers and local observers (Kavanagh, 2016a). Collectively, results from field experiments at ritual events demonstrate that simply observing an arousing ritual is insufficient to generate a collectively shared response; to produce such effects, it seems clear that "observers must share membership in the group and have a (preexisting) relationship" (Konvalinka et al., 2011, p. 8518).

Alongside the differential impacts on observers, questions remain concerning the effects on the ritual performers and the extent to which, through their participation, they establish an independent shared "effervescence" with the other performers. We have already discussed the growing evidence that synchronous activities, including rituals, generate social bonds, but independently there is also emerging evidence for the affiliative properties of shared pain. The suggestion of an affiliative role for pain may seem counterintuitive given that pain typically serves as a reliable threat-signal that should encourage individuals to withdraw from whatever is causing the pain. However, this fundamental desire to escape from pain also serves to motivate individuals to increase their relational focus, as they search for sources of social support to aid their escape or provide comfort. In support of this, perceived social support was found to predict pain adjustment among patients suffering from chronic pain (López-Martínez et al., 2008) and to correlate with lower self-reported labor pain during childbirth (Cogan & Spinnato, 1986; Lidderdale & Walsh, 1998). Moreover, laboratory-based studies that ask participants to endure various types of experimentally induced pain (for an in-depth review, see Bastian et al., 2014) have found that participants report less pain when they are reminded of partners (Master et al., 2009; Younger et al., 2010), salient group identities (Jones & Jetten, 2011; Platow et al., 2007), when they are provided with social support (Brown et al., 2003), or when they are allowed to hold a partner's hand (Coan et al., 2006). One study also found that religious images were capable of reducing the perception of pain for religious believers (Wiech et al., 2008). These results illustrate that pain is not purely an individual experience and can be significantly modulated by reminders of social affiliation. However, it remains less clear whether the reverse is true, that is: Do shared painful experiences, such as those involved with costly rituals, induce social cohesion?

Attempting to address this question, Bastian et al. (2014) reported three experiments examining the effects of shared painful experiences on cooperation and social bonds. All three experiments demonstrated a consistent pattern of participants in the pain conditions reporting stronger bonds (Study 1) with other group members and more cooperation in an economic task (Study 2 and Study 3). The authors note that since the painful tasks were framed as individual rather than group tasks, "the enhanced bonding and cooperation ... emerged from the (shared) experience of the pain rather than ... (in enduring) pain for the group" (Bastian et al., 2014, p. 84).

A real-world correlation with these findings was provided by Xygalatas et al. (2013) in the previously discussed study of the Mauritian *Thaipusam* piercing festival. Donations to an in-group temple were positively correlated with the perceived pain of the task for both participants and observers. These two results offer preliminary evidence that collectively experienced pain can increase progroup behavior and group solidarity. However, countervailing evidence also exists with no relationship being found between perceived pain and in-group donations in data collected from Japanese firewalking festivals (Kavanagh, 2016a) and a similar lack of correlation between pain and social cohesion measures found in Kavanagh et al.'s (2018) study of Brazilian jujitsu belt promotion experiences (which often involve painful belt whipping). Given the current small numbers of studies, especially those collected from actual ritual events, the existence of a relationship between pain and social bonding or progroup behavior requires further investigation to confirm.

Ritual Modes and Different Types of "Social Glue"

We have now seen how different kinds of rituals can lead to similar outcomes, describable as increases in social bonding or cohesion. Nevertheless, the costliness of rituals like the *kavadi* raises the question about what added social value they might provide over less arduous rituals. Costly signaling theories offer one possibility: Unlike mere synchrony, emotionally and physiologically demanding rituals serve as good signals. Another possibility is that different kinds of ritual produce different kinds of social bonding. According to

Whitehouse's *divergent modes of religiosity* (henceforth, Modes) theory, there is an important "divergence in modalities of religious experience and practice" (Whitehouse, 2004, p. 63) between small-scale *imagistic* traditions and larger, more hierarchical *doctrinal* ones. The imagistic mode refers to "small scale local traditions, with loosely defined doctrines and highly arousing but rarely performed rituals" (Whitehouse, 2004, p. 63). The doctrinal mode refers to "larger, more hierarchical doctrinal traditions that contain explicit doctrines, transmitted through frequently repeated low arousal rituals" (Whitehouse, 2004, p. 63).

Early evidence for the distinction between doctrinal and imagistic modes of religiosity came from ethnographic fieldwork conducted in Papua New Guinea with followers of the *Pomio Kivuing* religious movement that had developed into a large, hierarchical organization (Whitehouse, 1995). Despite its stable mainstream form, however, the *Pomio Kivung* also spawned a series of a small-scale, localized splinter movements. These splinter groups encouraged novel interpretations of the *Pomio Kivung* religious doctrine and developed distinctive rituals that were dramatic and emotional. These divergent modes of religiosity, Whitehouse argued, conformed to a recurrent global pattern (Whitehouse, 1995, 2000, 2004; Whitehouse & Laidlaw, 2004, 2007; Whitehouse & McCauley, 2005). Accordingly, a large cross-cultural coding study of 645 rituals by Atkinson and Whitehouse (2011) found that rituals do cluster around these expected divergent modes: intense and rare rituals on one hand, and mild and frequent ones on the other. Here it should be noted that the divergent modes do not represent a dichotomous typology but rather a ritual spectrum with two cognitively attractive clusters (Atkinson & Whitehouse, 2011). These clusters, in turn, appear to be constituted by cross-culturally statistical recurrent factors, which include positive and negative arousal, physical and psychological pageantry, kin, frequency, and "viscera" (Kapitany et al., 2020). Modes theory does not argue there will never be groups that have ritual practices combining imagistic and doctrinal elements but rather that such groups are unlikely to be as stable or successful as groups that adhere *predominately* to one of the two modes or in which the modes are associated with distinct domains within the tradition (e.g., mainstream movement versus splinter group or monastic tradition versus local cult).

Modes theory also posits distinctive forms of social bonding commensurate with imagistic and doctrinal practices, respectively (Whitehouse, 2013; Whitehouse & Lanman, 2014). In the doctrinal mode, the bonds created between ritual members are diffuse and extend across a large "imagined community" (Anderson, 1983) based on shared identity markers, whereas in the imagistic mode the bonds are localized and directed at specific individuals who share intense ritual experiences. This model parallels a raft of recent research in social psychology advocating for important distinctions between the categorical and depersonalized group bonds described in classic social identity theory (Abrams & Hogg, 1988; Hogg, 2006; Hornsey, 2008; Tajfel & Turner, 1985) and a more recently postulated form of group bonding termed *identity fusion* (Gómez et al., 2011; Swann et al., 2009, 2010, 2012, 2014). Identity fusion is argued to be distinct from group identification because it involves retaining "a highly agentic personal-self" alongside "a visceral feeling of oneness with the group" and relies on forming relational, rather than categorical (Brewer & Gardner, 1996), bonds with fellow group members (Swann et al., 2012).

Identity fusion has thus been proposed as a potential mechanism generating the intense bonds created in collective imagistic rituals (Swann et al., 2012; Whitehouse & Lanman, 2014). More specifically, Modes theory proposes that imagistic rituals generate rich autobiographical memories that invite long-enduring reflection (Whitehouse, 2002). This is important because "the perception that one shares with others' episodic memories that are essential components of one's autobiographical self-concept" (Whitehouse & Lanman, 2014, p. 677) can create a sense of psychological kinship (Bressan & Kramer, 2015; DeBruine, 2005; Krupp et al., 2012).

Some evidence consistent with this model has been provided by a set of studies which indicate that shared highly arousing experiences, including traumatic events, are associated with higher levels of identity fusion with relevant groups. Among revolutionary fighters during the 2011 Libyan civil war, for instance, nearly half of frontline combat troops reported being more strongly fused with their battalion than they were with their biological family (Whitehouse et al., 2014). Jong et al. (2015) also provided correlational and experimental evidence linking reflection on shared negative experiences (viz., of the Northern Irish Troubles and the Boston Bombing) to levels of identity fusion. Similarly, Whitehouse et al. presented a diverse array of evidence that sharing painful experiences produces identity fusion and that this in turn can motivate self-sacrifice, including a mathematical evolutionary model showing that cooperation conditioned on past negative experiences increases the overall fitness of groups and their members (Whitehouse et al., 2017).

Focusing specifically on ritual settings, a study by Páez et al. (2015) examined both negatively and positively valenced ritualized gatherings and found that participation in such events "consistently strengthened collective identity, identity fusion, and social integration" and that "perceived emotional synchrony (collective effervescence) with others mediated these effects." Finally, a study that examined the experience of promotional rituals of over 600 Brazilian jujitsu practitioners (Kavanagh et al., 2018) found that subjective positive assessment of promotion rituals, including painful events with belt whipping ordeals, was associated with greater levels of identity fusion with the training group.

In contrast to the intense relational bonds generated by costly imagistic rituals, Modes theory conversely suggests that the routinized rituals of doctrinal traditions serve to enhance the categorical ties of group identification, by providing repeated reinforcement of beliefs and practices that serve as group identity markers in semantic memory. The key distinction here is that group identification enables the bonding of "larger assemblages of more distantly related individuals" (Whitehouse & Lanman, 2014, p. 678) as the relationship is with an abstract social category as opposed to individual group members.

There has been comparatively little direct empirical research into the connection between doctrinal rituals and group identification as the research literature has remained focused primarily on studies of costly rituals. Nevertheless, the previously reviewed literature on the affiliative effects of synchronous ritual and evidence from developmental studies that even simple ritual action sequences can foster group identities suggest that repeated participation in culturally salient ritual performances is likely to serve as an effective reinforcer of relevant social identities.

Religion's Role in Promoting Coordination

The previous section outlined the important role that rituals play in promoting cooperation and coordination, highlighting some potential mechanisms underpinning this association. Accepting that collective rituals are a means of reinforcing and inducing cooperation and that they feature prominently in religious contexts, one could reasonably anticipate that religion might promote the same outcomes. However, religion is not entirely reducible to rituals and, as we stressed in the introduction to this chapter, our intention is to treat religion by focusing particularly on the impacts of supernatural beliefs. In so doing we critically interrogate widespread assumptions that religion inevitably begets cooperation.

The social and cultural units that people commonly refer to as religions – Christianity, Islam, Judaism, Buddhism, Shintoism, Hinduism, Melanesian cargo cults, and so forth – are each complexes of beliefs, practices, and social structures too diverse for conceptual reduction and unification. Thus, attempts to generate necessary and sufficient criteria for religion tend either to exclude or include too many characteristics (for further critical discussions of definitional issues, see Arnal & McCutcheon, 2012; Boyer, 2011; Jong, 2015; McCutcheon, 1997). Fortunately, such criteria are unnecessary for our purposes. It is sufficient to stipulate a provisional definition, deferring questions of universal generalizability for the future. Our definition of religion, as stated in the introduction, is reminiscent of the early anthropologist E. B. Tylor's (1871, p. 383) "belief in Spiritual beings," but this ought not saddle us with Tylor's particular brand of evolutionism and intellectualism (Jong, 2017). Rather, we recruit Tylor's definition for Durkheimian purposes, asking how beliefs in supernatural agents – gods, ghosts, angels, demons, souls, ancestral and shamanic spirits, and so forth – contribute to or detract from social coordination and cooperation. This approach does privilege one aspect of religion, which we consider the most distinctive, but it does not deny that other features of religion – social identity, structures of authority, collective rituals – might also play important roles.

Religion as a Harmful Social Virus

The role that religion plays in society has been an enduring topic of scholarly interest (Durkheim, 1912/1965; Freud, 1961; Weber, 1930) with earlier accounts tending to represent the religious traditions observed around the world as fitting into a linear evolutionary hierarchy. E. B. Tylor is illustrative of this approach. He argued that all religions were ultimately based on *animist* beliefs that objects, places, animals, and people possess a distinct spiritual essence and that this represented a prescientific effort to explain the world and cope with mortality. Tylor's evolutionary framework presented polytheism and later monotheism as emerging from animism, but he conceived these later religious systems as elaborations of an animist core (Tylor, 1871). This led Tylor to disparage religious systems as providing "primitive" systems of thought that would inevitably be replaced by science and rationalism (Strenski, 2006).

A modern descendant of this kind of rationalist critique of religion can be found in the popular works of the writers collectively known as the "New Atheists" (Dawkins, 2007; Dennett, 2006; Harris, 2006; Hitchens, 2008). The evolutionary theorist Richard Dawkins is perhaps the most prominent member of this group and has famously argued that religions represent a pathological "virus of the mind" generating self-replicating and harmful "meme-complexes" (Dawkins, 2004). Religious meme-complexes in Dawkins's view are like an infective virus that exploit the evolved features of human cognition to generate delusional beliefs (and eventually religious institutions) that enable them to replicate and spread further but that are harmful to both their host's intellect and to societal progress more generally, increasing intolerance and out-group prejudice (Dawkins, 2017, Section IV).

In summary, then, for both the New Atheist and Tylorian models, religions are vestigial social organs from our evolutionary past that in the modern era are, at best, unnecessary and, at worst, active and dangerous impediments to social progress. Such a uniformly negative assessment of the role of religion faces strong challenges from contemporary research on the evolution of religion and morality, which tends to argue that rather than being an obstacle to progress, supernatural agent beliefs represent a critical cultural invention that enabled humans to achieve levels of cooperation and social living with non-kin that is unprecedented in the animal kingdom (Bellah, 2011; Henrich, 2009; Johnson, 2015; Norenzayan, 2013; Purzycki et al., 2016, 2017; West et al., 2006; Wilson, 2010).

Gods and the Evolution of Cooperation

There are two dominant theoretical views about the role of supernatural agent beliefs in the evolution of human cooperation. In both cases, gods are presented as cultural technologies that solve two related social challenges: first, of promoting culturally normative (e.g., cooperative) behavior and, second, of outsourcing punishment and reward. According to the *big gods* hypothesis, a particular form of religion – that which involves morally interested high or "big" gods (Norenzayan, 2013) – enabled cooperation to extend more effectively to strangers, contributing to the cultural evolution of large-scale societies. On this view, big gods are the supreme third-party punishers, because they can detect every norm violation by virtue of their omniscience and are able, due to their omnipotence, to issue penalties in this life and the next. The *supernatural punishment* hypothesis (Johnson, 2015; Piazza et al., 2011) downplays the necessity of big gods, and posits that even small gods – ancestral or shamanic spirits, for example – can be morally interested, and have sufficient access to knowledge and power to serve effectively as moral police in local contexts. As we shall see later, these two theories posit rather different histories of the evolution of religion and morality, but both assume that belief in gods promotes prosocial behavior.

Do Religious Believers Behave More Prosocially? Many attempts have been made to ascertain whether religious believers behave more prosocially than unbelievers; however, this research literature has produced mixed results (Bloom, 2012; Galen, 2012; McKay & Whitehouse, 2015; Saroglou, 2006). For example, while self-reported religiosity (e.g., religious affiliation, service attendance, and orthodox belief) has generally been found to predict self-reported charitable giving, volunteering, and other acts of kindness (for review, see Brooks, 2006; Putnam & Campbell, 2012), this relationship is rarely reflected in studies that measure actual behavior (Annis, 1976; Darley & Batson, 1973; Grossman & Parrett, 2011; Hofmann et al., 2014; Smith et al., 1975). There is also evidence that certain forms of religiosity predict prejudice against ethnic, sexual, and religious others (Johnson et al., 2012; Scheepers et al., 2002; Siegman, 1962; Whitley, 2012).

The inconclusiveness of the literature is further exacerbated by the multiple interpretability of the findings: Prejudice may be damaging to the out-group while being beneficial to the in-group. In other words, it may represent the flipside of loyalty by being prosocial, albeit in a very narrow sense. In this regard, from a moral foundations theoretic (Graham & Haidt, 2010; Graham et al., 2009, 2013) perspective, religiosity is associated with group-focused "binding" moral emphases on attributes such as authority, loyalty, and purity, rather than "individuating" ones such as care and fairness. Therefore, what has conventionally been defined as *moral* concerns may reflect a restrictive liberal bias that excludes the kind of moral issues prevalent in religions, such as concerns about the preservation of traditions or the respect for authority. There is some evidence for this claim, but so far, only at the level of self-report (Johnson et al., 2016; LaBouff et al., 2017).

To date, most research on this topic has been conducted on Western Christians. Nevertheless, two recent attempts to go beyond this convenient sample have provided some support for the big gods hypothesis. First, Henrich et al. (2010) reported that across fifteen societies – including communities in Colombia, Kenya, and Papua New Guinea – participants who were involved with world religions, which all posit morally concerned high gods, were more generous toward anonymous strangers. Second, Purzycki et al. (2016) found that the more individuals rated their moralistic gods as punitive and knowledgeable about human thoughts and actions, the more generous they were to geographically distant co-religionists.

Overall, the evidence for a relationship between religious traits and prosocial behaviors is weak, but this may be unsurprising from a social-psychological perspective, which has long given us reason to doubt the predictive power of self-reported attitudes (Fishbein & Ajzen, 1975; Mischel, 1968). Rather, behaviors are the product of interactions between personalities and situations (Ross & Nisbett, 1991). We might, therefore, expect religious situations to promote prosocial behaviors, even if religious traits prove to be poor predictors. This raises the possibility that religious *reminders* are necessary, even for moralizing religions, to increase prosociality.

Does Religious Priming Promote Prosociality? Whether because of fears of supernatural punishment, belief in moralizing high gods, or other alternative mechanisms, recent experimental and quasi-experiment findings suggest that religious priming – the making salient of religious concepts – does increase prosocial behavior. For example, actual religious environments (e.g., chapels, temples) stimulate greater levels of cooperation than similar secular environments (Ahmed & Salas, 2013; Johnson et al., 2012; Ruffle & Sosis, 2010; Xygalatas, Klocová, et al., 2016; Xygalatas, Mitkidis, et al., 2013). Furthermore, following an influential paper by Shariff and Norenzayan (2007), which found that implicit priming of god concepts increased "prosocial behavior in an anonymous economic game" regardless of stated religiosity, a substantial body of laboratory-based priming studies suggests that the priming of religious concepts promotes a range of prosocial behaviors, such as honesty

(Randolph-Seng & Nielsen, 2007), obedience (Saroglou et al., 2009), and third-party punishment (McKay et al., 2011). A recent meta-analysis of this literature examined ninety-three religion priming studies (Shariff et al., 2015; but see Van Elk et al., 2015 for a critical view) and concluded that the effects of religious priming on prosocial behavior is robust, based on a subanalysis of twenty-five studies, but only for religious participants; effects on nonreligious participants were unreliable. This suggests that both religious belief and religious priming are necessary.

However, as with the correlational research reviewed earlier, a closer look at the research provides a more complicated picture. It is not a simple matter to interpret whether the motivations producing the effects observed (McKay & Whitehouse, 2015, pp. 458–60) are due to the reminder of supernatural punishment, teachings that promote compassion for the disadvantaged, or a more general aversion to inequity (Fehr & Schmidt, 1999). Moreover, studies have shown that in addition to prosociality, religious priming can elicit aggressive or prejudicial responses. For instance, Bushman et al. (2007) found that after reading a violent passage, participants who were told it came from the Bible displayed greater aggression than those who were told it came from an ancient scroll. Similarly, Saroglou et al. (2009) found that after being primed with religious concepts, participants indicated more willingness to take revenge on an individual who had criticized them, although this effect was restricted to those who scored high in personal submissiveness. Finally, Johnson et al. (2010) found that priming Christian concepts in ethnically diverse samples increased racial prejudice (see also Ginges et al., 2009; LaBouff et al., 2012; Van Tongeren et al., 2013). The current results from the literature taken collectively then suggest a more nuanced relationship in which religious priming can elicit both "prosocial" and "non-prosocial" or parochial outcomes, depending on contextual factors (see Galen, 2012, and McKay & Whitehouse, 2015, for reviews).

In addition to the interpretive issues and parochial outcomes observed there are also questions about the validity of the effects observed. In particular, a large-scale preregistered attempt at replicating Shariff and Norenzayan's (2007) experiment failed to reproduce their findings (Gomes & McCullough, 2015), as did a preregistered cross-cultural replication attempt in Japan (Miyatake & Higuchi, 2017). Furthermore, Purzycki et al. (2016, Supplementary Material) reported finding "no overall effect beyond chance" for religious primes in a five-country sample – including Mauritius, Brazil, Fiji, Russia, and Tanzania. In general, the current preponderance of samples from Western populations, and the reliance on references drawn from Abrahamic religious traditions, make it uncertain how far the priming results, if they are indeed replicable, are generalizable outside of such contexts – a point acknowledged even in positive reviews (Shariff et al., 2015, p. 42).

Big Gods or Supernatural Punishment?

Overall, we lack sufficient cross-cultural evidence to adjudicate between the two theoretical approaches on the evolution of religion and morality. The distinction between them may seem minor, but they posit different historical trajectories. Moralizing high gods would appear to be a relatively recent cultural innovation (Baumard et al., 2014). Outside the Abrahamic faiths, supernatural agents are reported to vary significantly in their levels of knowledge and power, and the extent to which they care about moral activity (Purzycki, 2013; Purzycki & Sosis, 2011). The spirits and deities of smaller societies, including hunter-gatherers and foragers, are argued to display more limited moral concern and powers of enforcement, with "intermediate" forms found in chiefdoms and early states (Norenzayan et al., 2016, p.9). This would seem to be consistent with the prediction that big gods are only needed in big societies.

While big gods could be one way of enforcing cooperation among relative strangers, the same effect could be achieved through beliefs in broad forms of supernatural punishment not requiring agents, for example by positing instead impersonal forces such as karma. Accordingly, a recent study by Watts et al., (2015) used a Bayesian phylogenetic approach to analyze beliefs in ninety-six Austronesian societies and predict their likely historical emergence. Watts et al.'s (2015, p. 1) analysis found that "broad supernatural punishment drove political complexity, whereas moralizing high gods *follow* political complexity." Moreover, recent analyses of data from 414 societies over 10 000 years from *Seshat* – a newly constructed historical database (Turchin et al., 2015; Turchin et al., 2020.) – to examine relationships between social complexity and supernatural enforcement of morality found that "moralizing gods follow – rather than precede – large increases in social complexity" (Whitehouse et al., 2019, p. 226).

To date the evidence thus appears to run counter to the idea that big gods helped to drive the emergence of big societies and raises questions about whether beliefs in moralizing high gods – strongly associated with the Abrahamic religions – are as significant as has been proposed to systems of cooperation. This remains an active area of research, and there is no established consensus but the growing emphasis on cross-cultural samples, historical analysis, and more nuanced measures of religious belief, ritual practices, and "prosociality" offer cause for optimism that progress is being made.

Conclusion

Our overview is far from exhaustive, but it touches on several key topics and active areas of research relating to both ritual and religion in promoting cooperation. As we have emphasized, rituals are not solely the province of groups espousing religious beliefs (as defined here); many of the potential mechanisms discussed in the first section are likely to have broad relevance across a wide range of activities. Indeed, it is hard to think of an area of social life that does not involve rituals and ritualized behavior. Overall we find the evidence for a link to prosocial behavior is stronger for ritual than for religion.

To end on a cautious note of optimism, we would emphasize that many of the studies we consider are from the last ten years, reflecting a surge of recent interest in empirical research on ritual and religion. We welcome this but also note that the majority of findings remain in need of high-quality replications and more substantial cross-cultural investigations before strong generalizable conclusions can be drawn. This remains the case even for topics that have been studied for decades, such as the disputed link between prosociality and religion.

This is not to deny that progress has been made; there is now a broad consensus among relevant researchers that both rituals and religions play an important role in promoting social coordination, at least within in-group boundaries (Bulbulia et al., 2013). However, it is essential to take insights about methodological reforms, derived from the "replication crisis" in social psychology, seriously (Nosek et al., 2015; Open Science Collaboration, 2015; Simmons et al., 2011). That is, studies should be appropriately powered to answer the questions they ask, preregister their models and predictions where appropriate, and adhere to open science practices with regard to data sharing and transparency. Taking the potential impact of these methodological reforms seriously means that the current era presents exciting new opportunities for scholars interested in religion and ritual to make genuine discoveries that can help resolve some of the longstanding theoretical debates discussed in this chapter.

Acknowledgments

This work was funded by a grant from the Templeton World Charity Foundation entitled "Cognitive and Cultural Foundations of Religion and Morality" (TWCF0164; C.K., J.J., & H.W.), and an Advanced Grant from the European Research Council (ERC) under the European Union's Horizon 2020 Research and Innovation Programme (grant agreement no. 694986; C.K & H.W.).

REFERENCES

Abrams, D., & Hogg, M. A. (1988). Comments on the motivational status of self-esteem in social identity and intergroup discrimination. *European Journal of Social Psychology*, *18*(4), 317–34. https://doi.org/10.1002/ejsp.2420180403

Ahmed, A., & Salas, O. (2013). Religious context and prosociality: An experimental study from Valparaíso, Chile. *Journal for the Scientific Study of Religion*, *52*(3), 627–37. https://doi.org/10.1111/jssr.12045

Allen, M. R. (1967). *Male cults and secret initiations in Melanesia*. Melbourne University Press.
Anderson, B. (1983). *Imagined communities: Reflections on the origin and spread of nationalism*. Verso.
Annis, L. V. (1976). Emergency helping and religious behavior. *Psychological Reports*, *39*(1), 151–8. https://doi.org/10.2466%2Fpr0.1976.39.1.151
Arnal, W., & McCutcheon, R. T. (2012). *The sacred is the profane: The political nature of "religion."* Oxford University Press. https://doi.org/10.1093/acprof:oso/9780199757114.001.0001
Aronson, E. (1968). Dissonance theory: Progress and problems. In R. Abelson, E. Aronson, W. McGuire, T. Newcomb, M. Rosenberg, & P. Tannebaum (Eds.), *The cognitive consistency theories: A source book* (pp. 5–27). Rand McNally.
Aronson, E. (1999). The power of self-persuasion. *American Psychologist*, *54*(11), 875–84. https://doi.org/10.1037/h0088188
Aronson, E., & Mills, J. (1959). The effect of severity of initiation on liking for a group. *Journal of Abnormal and Social Psychology*, *59*(2), 177–81. https://doi.org/10.1037/h0047195
Atkinson, Q. D., & Whitehouse, H. (2011). The cultural morphospace of ritual form: Examining modes of religiosity cross-culturally. *Evolution and Human Behavior*, *32*(1), 50–62. https://doi.org/10.1016/j.evolhumbehav.2010.09.002
Bandura, A., Ross, D., & Ross, S. A. (1961). Transmission of aggression through imitation of aggressive models. *Journal of Abnormal and Social Psychology*, *63*(3), 575–82. https://doi.org/10.1037/h0045925
Bastian, B., Jetten, J., & Ferris, L. J. (2014). Pain as social glue: Shared pain increases cooperation. *Psychological Science*, *25*(11), 2079–85. https://doi.org/10.1177/0956797614545886
Baumard, N., Hyafil, A., Morris, I., & Boyer, P. (2014). Increased affluence explains the emergence of ascetic wisdoms and moralizing religions. *Current Biology*, *25*(1), 10–15. https://doi.org/10.1016/j.cub.2014.10.063
Bell, C. (1997). *Ritual: Perspectives and dimensions*. Oxford University Press.
Bellah, R. N. (2011). *Religion in human evolution: From the Paleolithic to the Axial Age*. Belknap Press.
Bem, D. J. (1972). Self-perception theory. In L. Berkowitz (Ed.), *Advances in experimental social psychology* (Vol. 6, pp. 1–62). Academic Press.
Berling, J. A. (1987). Orthopraxy. In M. Eliade (Ed.), *The encyclopedia of religion* (Vol. 11, pp. 129–32). Macmillan.
Bloom, P. (2012). Religion, morality, evolution. *Annual Review of Psychology*, *63*, 179–99. https://doi.org/10.1146/annurev-psych-120710-100334
Boyer, P. (2001). *Religion explained: The evolutionary origins of religious thought*. Basic Books.
Boyer, P. (2011, February 2). Why would (otherwise intelligent) scholars believe in "religion"? [Blog post]. https://cognitionandculture.net/blog/pascals-blog/why-would-otherwise-intelligent-scholars-believe-in
Boyer, P., & Liénard, P. (2006). Why ritualized behavior? Precaution systems and action parsing in developmental, pathological and cultural rituals. *Behavioral and Brain Sciences*, *29*(6), 595–613. https://doi.org/10.1017/S0140525X06009332
Bressan, P., & Kramer, P. (2015). Human kin detection. *Wiley Interdisciplinary Reviews: Cognitive Science*, *6*(3), 299–311. https://doi.org/10.1002/wcs.1347

Brewer, M. B., & Gardner, W. (1996). Who is this "we"? Levels of collective identity and self representations. *Journal of Personality and Social Psychology*, *71*(1), 83–93. https://doi.org/10.1037//0022-3514.71.1.83

Brooks, A. C. (2006). *Who really cares: The surprising truth about compassionate conservatism—America's charity divide—who gives, who doesn't, and why it matters*. Basic Books.

Brown, J. L., Sheffield, D., Leary, M. R., & Robinson, M. E. (2003). Social support and experimental pain. *Psychosomatic Medicine*, *65*(2), 276–83. https://doi.org/10.1097/01.PSY.0000030388.62434.46

Bulbulia, J., Geertz, A. W., Atkinson, Q. D., Cohen, E., Evans, N., François, P., Gintis, H., Gray, R. D., Henrich, J., Jordon, F. M., Norenzayan, A., Richerson, P. J., Slingerland, E., Turchin, P., Whitehouse, H., Widlok, T., & Wilson, D. S. (2013). The cultural evolution of religion. In P. J. Richerson & M. H. Christiansen (Eds.), *Cultural evolution: Science, technology, language, and religion* (pp. 381–404). MIT Press. https://doi.org/10.7551/mitpress/9780262019750.003.0020

Bulbulia, J. A., & Sosis, R. (2011). Signalling theory and the evolution of religious cooperation. *Religion*, *41*(3), 363–88. https://doi.org/10.1080/0048721X.2011.604508

Bushman, B. J., Ridge, R. D., Das, E., Key, C. W., & Busath, G. L. (2007). When God sanctions killing: Effect of scriptural violence on aggression. *Psychological Science*, *18*(3), 204–7. https://doi.org/10.1111/j.1467-9280.2007.01873.x

Carpenter, M., Uebel, J., & Tomasello, M. (2013). Being mimicked increases prosocial behavior in 18-month-old infants. *Child Development*, *84*(5), 1511–18. https://doi.org/10.1111/cdev.12083

Chartrand, T. L., & Bargh, J. A. (1999). The chameleon effect: The perception–behavior link and social interaction. *Journal of Personality and Social Psychology*, *76*(6), 893–910. https://doi.org/10.1037/0022-3514.76.6.893

Cimino, A. (2011). The evolution of hazing: Motivational mechanisms and the abuse of newcomers. *Journal of Cognition and Culture*, *11*(3–4), 241–67. https://doi.org/10.1163/156853711X591242

Cimino, A. (2013). Predictors of hazing motivation in a representative sample of the United States. *Evolution and Human Behavior*, *34*(6), 446–52. https://doi.org/10.1016/j.evolhumbehav.2013.08.007

Cirelli, L. K., Einarson, K. M., & Trainor, L. J. (2014a). Interpersonal synchrony increases prosocial behavior in infants. *Developmental Science*, *17*(6), 1003–11. https://doi.org/10.1111/desc.12193

Cirelli, L. K., Wan, S. J., & Trainor, L. J. (2014b). Fourteen-month-old infants use interpersonal synchrony as a cue to direct helpfulness. *Philosophical Transactions of the Royal Society B: Biological Sciences*, *369*(1658), 20130400. https://doi.org/10.1098/rstb.2013.0400

Cirelli, L. K., Wan, S. J., & Trainor, L. J. (2016). Social effects of movement synchrony: Increased infant helpfulness only transfers to affiliates of synchronously moving partners. *Infancy*, *21*(6), 807–21. https://doi.org/10.1111/infa.12140

Clark, R. D., III, & Maass, A. (1988). The role of social categorization and perceived source credibility in minority influence. *European Journal of Social Psychology*, *18*(5), 381–94. https://doi.org/10.1002/ejsp.2420180502

Clegg, J. M., & Legare, C. H. (2015). Instrumental and conventional interpretations of behavior are associated with distinct outcomes in early childhood. *Child Development*, *87*(2), 527–42. https://doi.org/10.1111/cdev.12472.

Clegg, J. M., & Legare, C. H. (2016). A cross-cultural comparison of children's imitative flexibility. *Developmental Psychology*, *52*(9), 1435–44. https://doi.org/10.1037/dev0000131

Coan, J. A., Schaefer, H. S., & Davidson, R. J. (2006). Lending a hand: Social regulation of the neural response to threat. *Psychological Science*, *17*(12), 1032–9. https://doi.org/10.1111/j.1467-9280.2006.01832.x

Cogan, R., & Spinnato, J. A. (1986). Pain and discomfort thresholds in late pregnancy. *Pain*, *27*(1), 63–8. https://doi.org/10.1016/0304-3959(86)90223-X

Cooper, J., & Fazio, R. H. (1984). A new look at dissonance theory. In L. Berkowitz (Ed.), *Advances in experimental social psychology* (Vol. 17, pp. 229–66). Academic Press. https://doi.org/10.1016/S0065-2601(08)60121-5

Cooper, J., & Hogg, M. A. (2007). Feeling the anguish of others: A theory of vicarious dissonance. In M. P. Zanna (Ed.), *Advances in experimental social psychology* (Vol. 39, 359–403). Academic Press. https://doi.org/10.1016/S0065-2601(06)39007-7

Corriveau, K. H., DiYanni, C. J., Clegg, J. M., Min, G., Chin, J., & Nasrini, J. (2017). Cultural differences in the imitation and transmission of inefficient actions. *Journal of Experimental Child Psychology*, *161*, 1–18. https://doi.org/10.1016/j.jecp.2017.03.002

Darley, J. M., & Batson, C. D. (1973). " From Jerusalem to Jericho": A study of situational and dispositional variables in helping behavior. *Journal of Personality and Social Psychology*, *27*(1), 100–8. https://doi.org/10.1037/h0034449

Dawkins, R. (2004). *A devil's chaplain: Reflections on hope, lies, science, and love.* Houghton Mifflin Harcourt.

Dawkins, R. (2007). *The God delusion.* Black Swan.

Dawkins, R. (2017). *Science in the soul: Selected writings of a passionate rationalist.* (G. Somerscales, Ed.). Penguin Random House.

DeBono, K. G., & Harnish, R. J. (1988). Source expertise, source attractiveness, and the processing of persuasive information: A functional approach. *Journal of Personality and Social Psychology*, *55*(4), 541–6. https://doi.org/10.1037/0022-3514.55.4.541

DeBruine, L. M. (2005). Trustworthy but not lust-worthy: Context-specific effects of facial resemblance. *Proceedings of the Royal Society B: Biological Sciences*, *272*(1566), 919–22. https://doi.org/10.1098/rspb.2004.3003

Dennett, D. C. (2006). *Breaking the spell: Religion as a natural phenomenon.* Viking.

Durkheim, É. (1912/1965). *The elementary forms of the religious life* (J.W. Swain, Trans.). Free Press. (Original work published 1912)

Fehr, E., & Schmidt, K. M. (1999). A theory of fairness, competition, and cooperation. *Quarterly Journal of Economics*, *114*(3), 817–68. https://doi.org/10.1162/003355399556151

Festinger, L. (1957). *A theory of cognitive dissonance.* Stanford University Press.

Fischer, R., Xygalatas, D., Mitkidis, P., Reddish, P., Tok, P., Konvalinka, I., & Bulbulia, J. A. (2014). The fire-walker's high: Affect and physiological responses in an extreme collective ritual. *PLoS ONE*, *9*(2), e88355. https://doi.org/10.1371/journal.pone.0088355

Fischer-Lokou, J., Martin, A., Guéguen, N., & Lamy, L. (2011). Mimicry and propagation of prosocial behavior in a natural setting. *Psychological Reports*, *108*(2), 599–605. https://doi.org/10.2466/07.17.21.PR0.108.2.599-605

Fishbein, M., & Ajzen, I. (1975). *Belief, attitude, intention, and behavior: An introduction to theory and research*. Addison-Wesley Pub. Co.

Flynn, E., & Smith, K. (2012) Investigating the mechanisms of cultural acquisition: How pervasive is overimitation in adults? *Social Psychology*, *43*(4), 185–95. https://doi.org/10.1027/1864-9335/a000119

Freud, S. (1961). Obsessive actions and religious practices. In J. Strachey (Ed.), *The standard edition of the complete psychological works of Sigmund Freud* (Vol. 9, pp. 167–75). Hogarth Press.

Galen, L. W. (2012). Does religious belief promote prosociality? A critical examination. *Psychological Bulletin*, *138*(5), 876–906. https://doi.org/10.1037/a0028251

Gerard, H. B., & Mathewson, G. C. (1966). The effects of severity of initiation on liking for a group: A replication. *Journal of Experimental Social Psychology*, *2*(3), 278–87. https://doi.org/10.1016/0022-1031(66)90084-9

Ginges, J., Hansen, I., & Norenzayan, A. (2009). Religion and support for suicide attacks. *Psychological Science*, *20*(2), 224–30. https://doi.org/10.1111%2Fj.1467-9280.2009.02270.x

Gomes, C. M., & McCullough, M. E. (2015). The effects of implicit religious primes on dictator game allocations: A preregistered replication experiment. *Journal of Experimental Psychology: General*, *144*(6), e94–e104. https://doi.org/10.1037/xge0000027

Gómez, Á., Brooks, M. L., Buhrmester, M. D., Vázquez, A., Jetten, J., & Swann, W. B., Jr. (2011). On the nature of identity fusion: Insights into the construct and a new measure. *Journal of Personality and Social Psychology*, *100*(5), 918–33. https://doi.org/10.1037/a0022642

Graham, J., & Haidt, J. (2010). Beyond beliefs: Religions bind individuals into moral communities. *Personality and Social Psychology Review*, *14*(1), 140–50. https://doi.org/10.1177/1088868309353415

Graham, J., Haidt, J., Koleva, S., Motyl, M., Iyer, R., Wojcik, S. P., & Ditto, P. H. (2013). Moral foundations theory: The pragmatic validity of moral pluralism. In P. Devine & A. Plant (Eds.), *Advances in experimental social psychology* (Vol. 47, pp. 55–130). Academic Press. https://doi.org/10.1016/B978-0-12-407236-7.00002-4

Graham, J., Haidt, J., & Nosek, B. A. (2009). Liberals and conservatives rely on different sets of moral foundations. *Journal of Personality and Social Psychology*, *96*(5), 1029–46. https://doi.org/10.1037/a0015141

Grossman, P. J., & Parrett, M. B. (2011). Religion and prosocial behaviour: A field test. *Applied Economics Letters*, *18*(6), 523–6. https://doi.org/10.1080/13504851003761798

Guthrie, S. E. (1993). *Faces in the clouds: A new theory of religion*. Oxford University Press.

Harris, S. (2006). *The end of faith: Religion, terror, and the future of reason*. Free Press.

Hautaluoma, J. E., & Spungin, H. (1974). Effects of initiation severity and interest on group attitudes. *Journal of Social Psychology*, *93*(2), 245–9. https://doi.org/10.1080/00224545.1974.9923159

Henrich, J. (2009). The evolution of costly displays, cooperation and religion: Credibility enhancing displays and their implications for cultural evolution. *Evolution and Human Behavior*, *30*(4), 244–60. https://doi.org/10.1016/j.evolhumbehav.2009.03.005

Henrich, J., Ensminger, J., McElreath, R., Barr, A., Barrett, C., Bolyanatz, A., Cardenas, J. C., Gurven, M., Gwako, E., Henrich, N., Lesorogol, C., Marlowe, F., Tracer, D., & Ziker, J. (2010). Markets, religion, community size, and the evolution of fairness and punishment. *Science*, *327*(5972), 1480–4. https://doi.org/10.1126/science.1182238

Herrmann, P. A., Legare, C. H., Harris, P. L., & Whitehouse, H. (2013). Stick to the script: The effect of witnessing multiple actors on children's imitation. *Cognition*, *129*(3), 536–43. https://doi.org/10.1016/j.cognition.2013.08.010

Hitchens, C. (2008). *God is not great: How religion poisons everything*. McClelland & Stewart.

Hoehl, S., Keupp, S., Schleihauf, H., McGuigan, N., Buttelmann, D., & Whiten, A. (2019). 'Over-imitation': A review and appraisal of a decade of research. *Developmental Review*, *51*, 90–108. https://doi.org/10.1016/j.dr.2018.12.002

Hofmann, W., Wisneski, D. C., Brandt, M. J., & Skitka, L. J. (2014). Morality in everyday life. *Science*, *345*(6202), 1340–3. https://doi.org/10.1126/science.1251560

Hogg, M. A. (2006). Social identity theory. In P. J. Burke (Ed.), *Contemporary social psychological theories* (pp. 111–36). Stanford University Press.

Hoppitt, W., & Laland, K. N. (2013). *Social learning: An introduction to mechanisms, methods, and models*. Princeton University Press.

Horner, V., & Whiten, A. (2005). Causal knowledge and imitation/emulation switching in chimpanzees (Pan troglodytes) and children (Homo sapiens). *Animal Cognition*, *8*(3), 164–81. https://doi.org/10.1007/s10071-004-0239-6

Hornsey, M. J. (2008). Social identity theory and self-categorization theory: A historical review. *Social and Personality Psychology Compass*, *2*(1), 204–22. https://doi.org/10.1111/j.1751-9004.2007.00066.x

Hove, M. J., & Risen, J. L. (2009). It's all in the timing: Interpersonal synchrony increases affiliation. *Social Cognition*, *27*(6), 949–60. https://doi.org/10.1521/soco.2009.27.6.949

Hovland, C. I., & Weiss, W. (1951). The influence of source credibility on communication effectiveness. *Public Opinion Quarterly*, *15*(4), 635–50. https://doi.org/10.1086/266350

Humphrey, C., & Laidlaw, J. (1994). *The archetypal actions of ritual: A theory of ritual illustrated by the Jain rite of worship*. Oxford University Press.

Iacoboni, M. (2009). Imitation, empathy, and mirror neurons. *Annual Review of Psychology*, *60*, 653–70. https://doi.org/10.1146/annurev.psych.60.110707.163604

Iannaccone, L. R. (1994). Why strict churches are strong. *American Journal of Sociology*, *99*(5), 1180–211. https://doi.org/10.1086/230409

Irons, W. (2001). Religion as a hard-to-fake sign of commitment. In R. M. Nesse (Ed.), *Vol. 3 in the Russell SAGE Foundation series on trust. Evolution and the capacity for commitment* (pp. 292–309). Russell SAGE Foundation.

Jegindø, E.-M. E., Vase, L., Jegindø, J., & Geertz, A. W. (2013). Pain and sacrifice: Experience and modulation of pain in a religious piercing ritual. *International*

Journal for the Psychology of Religion, *23*(3), 171–87. https://doi.org/10.1080/10508619.2012.759065

Johnson, D. (2015). *God is watching you: How the fear of God makes us human*. Oxford University Press.

Johnson, K. A., Hook, J. N., Davis, D. E., Van Tongeren, D. R., Sandage, S. J., & Crabtree, S. A. (2016). Moral foundation priorities reflect U. S. Christians' individual differences in religiosity. *Personality and Individual Differences*, *100*, 56–61. https://doi.org/10.1016/j.paid.2015.12.037

Johnson, M. K., Rowatt, W. C., & LaBouff, J. (2010). Priming Christian religious concepts increases racial prejudice. *Social Psychological and Personality Science*, *1*(2), 119–26. https://doi.org/10.1177%2F1948550609357246

Johnson, M. K., Rowatt, W. C., & LaBouff, J. P. (2012). Religiosity and prejudice revisited: In-group favoritism, out-group derogation, or both? *Psychology of Religion and Spirituality*, *4*(2), 154–68. https://doi.org/10.1037/a0025107

Jones, S. S. (2009). The development of imitation in infancy. *Philosophical Transactions of the Royal Society B: Biological Sciences*, *364*(1528), 2325–35. https://doi.org/10.1098/rstb.2009.0045

Jones, J. M., & Jetten, J. (2011). Recovering from strain and enduring pain: Multiple group memberships promote resilience in the face of physical challenges. *Social Psychological and Personality Science*, *2*(3), 239–44. https://doi.org/10.1177/1948550610386806

Jong, J. (2015). On (not) defining (non)religion. *Science, Religion & Culture*, *2*(3), 15–24. https://doi.org/10.17582/journal.src/2015/2.3.15.24

Jong, J. (2017). "Belief in spiritual beings": E. B. Tylor's (primitive) cognitive theory of religion. In P.-F. Tremlett, G. Harvey, & L. T. Sutherland (Eds.), *Edward Burnett Tylor, religion and culture* (pp. 47–61). Bloomsbury Publishing.

Jong, J., & Halberstadt, J. (2016). *Death anxiety and religious belief: An existential psychology of religion*. Bloomsbury Academic.

Jong, J., Whitehouse, H., Kavanagh, C. M., & Lane, J. (2015). Shared negative experiences lead to identity fusion via personal reflection. *PLoS ONE*, *10*(12), e0145611. https://doi.org/10.1371%2Fjournal.pone.0145611

Kapitány, R., Kavanagh, C., Buhrmester, M. D., Newson, M., & Whitehouse, H. (2019). Ritual, identity fusion, and the inauguration of president Trump: A pseudo-experiment of ritual modes theory. *Self and Identity*. Advance online publication. https://doi.org/10.1080/15298868.2019.1578686

Kavanagh, C. (2016a). *Individual pain & social gain: The personal and social consequences of collective dysphoric rituals* [doctoral dissertation]. University of Oxford. https://ora.ox.ac.uk/objects/uuid:e2e0f4de-ccf1-4962-87fe-4d7fa48faf75

Kavanagh, C. (2016b, September 15) Religion without belief. *Aeon*. https://aeon.co/essays/can-religion-be-based-on-ritual-practice-without-belief

Kavanagh, C. M., & Jong, J. (2020). Is Japan religious? *Journal for the Study of Religion, Nature and Culture*, *14*(1). https://doi.org/10.31234/osf.io/qyt95

Kavanagh, C. M., Jong, J., McKay, R., & Whitehouse, H. (2018). Positive experiences of high arousal martial arts rituals are linked to identity fusion and costly pro-group actions. *European Journal of Social Psychology*, *49*(3), 461–81. https://doi.org/10.1002/ejsp.2514

Kay, A. C., Gaucher, D., McGregor, I., & Nash, K. (2010). Religious belief as compensatory control. *Personality and Social Psychology Review*, *14*(1), 37–48. https://doi.org/10.1177/1088868309353750

Keating, C. F., Pomerantz, J., Pommer, S. D., Ritt, S. J. H., Miller, L. M., & McCormick, J. (2005). Going to college and unpacking hazing: A functional approach to decrypting initiation practices among undergraduates. *Group Dynamics: Theory, Research, and Practice*, *9*(2), 104–26. https://doi.org/10.1037/1089-2699.9.2.104

Kenward, B., Karlsson, M., & Persson, J. (2010). Over-imitation is better explained by norm learning than by distorted causal learning. *Proceedings of the Royal Society B: Biological Sciences*, *278*(1709), 1239–46. https://doi.org/10.1098/rspb.2010.1399

Kirschner, S., & Tomasello, M. (2010). Joint music making promotes prosocial behavior in 4-year-old children. *Evolution and Human Behavior*, *31*(5), 354–64. https://doi.org/10.1016/j.evolhumbehav.2010.04.004

Kitayama, S., & Tompson, S. (2015). A biosocial model of affective decision making: Implications for dissonance, motivation, and culture. In J. M. Olson & M. P. Zanna (Eds.), *Advances in experimental social psychology* (Vol. 52, pp. 71–137). Academic Press.

Konvalinka, I., Xygalatas, D., Bulbulia, J., Schjødt, U., Jegindø, E.-M., Wallot, S., Van Orden, G., & Roepstorff, A. (2011). Synchronized arousal between performers and related spectators in a fire-walking ritual. *Proceedings of the National Academy of Sciences of the United States of America*, *108*(20), 8514–19. https://doi.org/10.1073/pnas.1016955108

Krupp, D. B., DeBruine, L. M., Jones, B. C., & Lalumière, M. L. (2012). Kin recognition: Evidence that humans can perceive both positive and negative relatedness. *Journal of Evolutionary Biology*, *25*(8), 1472–8. https://doi.org/10.1111/j.1420-9101.2012.02553.x

LaBouff, J. P., Humphreys, M., & Shen, M. J. (2017). Religiosity and group-binding moral concerns. *Archive for the Psychology of Religion*, *39*(3), 263–82. https://journals.sagepub.com/doi/10.1163/15736121-12341343?icid=int.sj-abstract.similar-articles.2; https://doi.org/10.1163/15736121-12341343

Lakens, D. (2010). Movement synchrony and perceived entitativity. *Journal of Experimental Social Psychology*, *46*(5), 701–8. https://doi.org/10.1016/j.jesp.2010.03.015

Lakens, D., & Stel, M. (2011). If they move in sync, they must feel in sync: Movement synchrony leads to attributions of rapport and entitativity. *Social Cognition*, *29*(1), 1–14. https://doi.org/10.1521/soco.2011.29.1.1

LaBouff, J. P., Rowatt, W. C., Johnson, M. K., & Finkle, C. (2012). Differences in attitudes toward outgroups in religious and nonreligious contexts in a multinational sample: A situational context priming study. *International Journal for the Psychology of Religion*, *22*(1), 1–9. https://doi.org/10.1080/10508619.2012.634778

Lanman, J. A., & Buhrmester, M. D. (2017). Religious actions speak louder than words: Exposure to credibility-enhancing displays predicts theism. *Religion, Brain & Behavior*, *7*(1), 3–16. https://doi.org/10.1080/2153599X.2015.1117011

Legare, C. H., Wen, N. J., Herrmann, P. A., & Whitehouse, H. (2015). Imitative flexibility and the development of cultural learning. *Cognition*, *142*, 351–61. https://doi.org/10.1016/j.cognition.2015.05.020

Lidderdale, J. M., & Walsh, J. J. (1998). The effects of social support on cardiovascular reactivity and perinatal outcome. *Psychology & Health*, *13*(6), 1061–70. https://doi.org/10.1080/08870449808407450

Liénard, P., & Boyer, P. (2006). Whence collective rituals? A cultural selection model of ritualized behavior. *American Anthropologist*, *108*(4), 814–27. https://doi.org/10.1525/aa.2006.108.4.814

Lodewijkx, H. F. M., & Syroit, J. E. M. M. (1997). Severity of initiation revisited: Does severity of initiation increase attractiveness in real groups? *European Journal of Social Psychology*, *27*(3), 275–300. https://doi.org/10.1002/(SICI)1099-0992(199705)27:3<275::AID-EJSP822>3.0.CO;2-S

López-Martínez, A. E., Esteve-Zarazaga, R., & Ramírez-Maestre, C. (2008). Perceived social support and coping responses are independent variables explaining pain adjustment among chronic pain patients. *Journal of Pain*, *9*(4), 373–9. https://doi.org/10.1016/j.jpain.2007.12.002

Lyons, D. E., Damrosch, D. H., Lin, J. K., Macris, D. M., & Keil, F. C. (2011). The scope and limits of overimitation in the transmission of artefact culture. *Philosophical Transactions of the Royal Society B: Biological Sciences*, *366* (1567), 1158–67. https://doi.org/10.1098/rstb.2010.0335

Lyons, D. E., Young, A. G., & Keil, F. C. (2007). The hidden structure of overimitation. *Proceedings of the National Academy of Sciences of the United States of America*, *104*(50), 19751–6. https://doi.org/10.1073/pnas.0704452104

Master, S. L., Eisenberger, N. I., Taylor, S. E., Naliboff, B. D., Shirinyan, D., & Lieberman, M. D. (2009). A picture's worth: Partner photographs reduce experimentally induced pain. *Psychological Science*, *20*(11), 1316–18. https://doi.org/10.1111/j.1467-9280.2009.02444.x

McCutcheon, R. T. (1997). *Manufacturing religion: The discourse on sui generis religion and the politics of nostalgia*. Oxford University Press.

McGuigan, N. (2012). The role of transmission biases in the cultural diffusion of irrelevant actions. *Journal of Comparative Psychology*, *126*(2), 150–60. https://doi.org/10.1037/a0025525

McGuigan, N., Makinson, J., & Whiten, A. (2011). From over-imitation to super-copying: Adults imitate causally irrelevant aspects of tool use with higher fidelity than young children. *British Journal of Psychology*, *102*(1), 1–18. https://doi.org/10.1348/000712610X493115

McKay, R., Efferson, C., Whitehouse, H., & Fehr, E. (2011). Wrath of God: Religious primes and punishment. *Proceedings of the Royal Society B: Biological Sciences*, *278*(1713), 1858–63. https://doi.org/10.1098/rspb.2010.2125

McKay, R., & Whitehouse, H. (2015). Religion and morality. *Psychological Bulletin*, *141*(2), 447–73. https://doi.org/10.1037/a0038455

Meltzoff, A. N. (2007). "Like me": A foundation for social cognition. *Developmental Science*, *10*(1), 126–34. https://doi.org/10.1111/j.1467-7687.2007.00574.x

Mischel, W. (1968). *Personality and assessment*. Lawrence Erlbaum Associates.

Mitkidis, P., Ayal, S., Shalvi, S., Heimann, K., Levy, G., Kyselo, M., Wallot, S., Ariely, D., & Roepstorff, A. (2017). The effects of extreme rituals on moral behavior: The performers-observers gap hypothesis. *Journal of Economic Psychology, 59,* 1–7. https://doi.org/10.1016/j.joep.2016.12.007

Miyatake, S., & Higuchi, M. (2017). Does religious priming increase the prosocial behaviour of a Japanese sample in an anonymous economic game? *Asian Journal of Social Psychology, 20*(1), 54–9. https://doi.org/10.1111/ajsp.12164

Mogan, R., Fischer, R., & Bulbulia, J. A. (2017). To be in synchrony or not? A meta-analysis of synchrony's effects on behavior, perception, cognition and affect. *Journal of Experimental Social Psychology, 72,* 13–20. https://doi.org/10.1016/j.jesp.2017.03.009

Nielsen, M., & Blank, C. (2011). Imitation in young children: When who gets copied is more important than what gets copied. *Developmental Psychology, 47*(4), 1050–3. https://doi.org/10.1037/a0023866

Nielsen, M., Mushin, I., Tomaselli, K., & Whiten, A. (2014). Where culture takes hold:"Overimitation" and its flexible deployment in Western, Aboriginal, and Bushmen children. *Child Development, 85*(6), 2169–84. https://doi.org/10.1111/cdev.12265

Nielsen, M., & Tomaselli, K. (2010) Overimitation in Kalahari Bushman children and the origins of human cultural cognition. *Psychological Science, 21*(5), 729–36. https://doi.org/10.1177/0956797610368808

Norenzayan, A. (2013). *Big gods: How religion transformed cooperation and conflict.* Princeton University Press.

Norenzayan, A., Shariff, A. F., Gervais, W. M., Willard, A. K., McNamara, R. A., Slingerland, E., & Henrich, J. (2016). The cultural evolution of prosocial religions. *Behavioral and Brain Sciences, 39,* e1. https://doi.org/10.1017/S0140525X14001356

Norton, A. R. (2005). Ritual, blood, and Shiite identity: Ashura in Nabatiyya, Lebanon. *TDR/The Drama Review, 49*(4), 140–55. https://doi.org/10.1162/105420405774762880

Norton, M. I., & Gino, F. (2014). Rituals alleviate grieving for loved ones, lovers, and lotteries. *Journal of Experimental Psychology: General, 143*(1), 266–72. https://doi.org/10.1037/a0031772

Nosek, B. A., Alter, G., Banks, G. C., Borsboom, D., Bowman, S. D., Breckler, S. J., Buck, S., Chambers, C. D., Chin, G., Christensen, G., Contestabile, M., Dafoe, A., Eich, E., Freese, J., Glennerster, R., Goroff, D., Green, D. P., Hesse, B., Humphreys, M., Ishiyama, J., ... Yarkoni, T. (2015). Promoting an open research culture. *Science, 348*(6242), 1422–5. https://doi.org/10.1126/science.aab2374

Open Science Collaboration. (2015). Estimating the reproducibility of psychological science. *Science, 349*(6251), aac4716. https://doi.org/10.1126/science.aac4716

Over, H., & Carpenter, M. (2009). Priming third-party ostracism increases affiliative imitation in children. *Developmental Science, 12*(3), F1–F8. https://doi.org/10.1111/j.1467-7687.2008.00820.x

Páez, D., Rimé, B., Basabe, N., Wlodarczyk, A., & Zumeta, L. (2015). Psychosocial effects of perceived emotional synchrony in collective gatherings. *Journal of Personality and Social Psychology, 108*(5), 711–29. https://doi.org/10.1037/pspi0000014

Park, C. L. (2005). Religion as a meaning-making framework in coping with life stress. *Journal of Social Issues, 61*(4), 707–29. https://doi.org/10.1111/j.1540-4560.2005.00428.x

Park, C. L. (2011). Meaning and growth within positive psychology: Toward a more complete understanding. In K. M. Sheldon, T. B. Kashdan, & M. F. Steger (Eds.), *Designing positive psychology: Taking stock and moving forward* (pp. 324–34). Oxford University Press. https://doi.org/10.1093/acprof:oso/9780195373585.003.0021

Patzer, G. L. (1983). Source credibility as a function of communicator physical attractiveness. *Journal of Business Research*, *11*(2), 229–41. https://doi.org/10.1016/0148-2963(83)90030-9

Piazza, J., Bering, J. M., & Ingram, G. (2011). "Princess Alice is watching you": Children's belief in an invisible person inhibits cheating. *Journal of Experimental Child Psychology*, *109*(3), 311–20. https://doi.org/10.1016/j.jecp.2011.02.003

Platow, M. J., Voudouris, N. J., Coulson, M., Gilford, N., Jamieson, R., Najdovski, L., Papaleo, H., Pollard, C., & Terry, L. (2007). In-group reassurance in a pain setting produces lower levels of physiological arousal: Direct support for a self-categorization analysis of social influence. *European Journal of Social Psychology*, *37*(4), 649–60. https://doi.org/10.1002/ejsp.381

Pornpitakpan, C. (2004). The persuasiveness of source credibility: A critical review of five decades' evidence. *Journal of Applied Social Psychology*, *34*(2), 243–81. https://doi.org/10.1111/j.1559-1816.2004.tb02547.x

Purzycki, B. G. (2013). The minds of gods: A comparative study of supernatural agency. *Cognition*, *129*(1), 163–79. https://doi.org/10.1016/j.cognition.2013.06.010

Purzycki, B. G., Apicella, C., Atkinson, Q. D., Cohen, E., McNamara, R. A., Willard, A. K., Xygalatas, D., Norenzayan, A., & Henrich, J. (2016). Moralistic gods, supernatural punishment and the expansion of human sociality. *Nature*, *530*(7590), 327–30. https://doi.org/10.1038/nature16980

Purzycki, B. G., Henrich, J., Apicella, C., Atkinson, Q. D., Baimel, A., Cohen, E., McNamara, R. A., Willard, A. K., Xygalatas, D., & Norenzayan, A. (2017). The evolution of religion and morality: A synthesis of ethnographic and experimental evidence from eight societies. *Religion, Brain and Behavior*, *8*(2), 101–32. https://doi.org/10.1080/2153599X.2016.1267027

Purzycki, B. G., & Sosis, R. (2011). Our gods: Variation in supernatural minds. In U. J. Frey, C. Störmer, & K. P. Willführ (Eds.), *Essential building blocks of human nature* (pp. 77–93). Springer. https://doi.org/10.1007/978-3-642-13968-0_5

Putnam, R. D., & Campbell, D. E. (2012). *American grace: How religion divides and unites us*. Simon & Schuster.

Pyysiäinen, I. (2003). Buddhism, religion and the concept of "God." *Numen International Review for the History of Religions*, *50*(2), 147–71. https://doi.org/10.1163/156852703321506141

Pyysiäinen, I. (2009). *Supernatural agents: Why we believe in souls, gods, and Buddhas*. Oxford University Press. https://doi.org/10.1093/acprof:oso/9780195380026.001.0001

Rabinowitch, T. C., & Knafo-Noam, A. (2015). Synchronous rhythmic interaction enhances children's perceived similarity and closeness towards each other. *PLoS ONE*, *10*(4), e0120878 https://doi.org/10.1371/journal.pone.0120878

Randolph-Seng, B., & Nielsen, M. E. (2007). Honesty: One effect of primed religious representations. *International Journal for the Psychology of Religion*, *17*(4), 303–15. https://doi.org/10.1080/10508610701572812

Rappaport, R. A. (1999). *Ritual and religion in the making of humanity*. Cambridge University Press.
Reader, I., & Tanabe, G. J., Jr. (1998). *Practically religious: Worldly benefits and the common religion of Japan*. University of Hawai'i Press.
Reddish, P., Bulbulia, J. A., & Fischer, R. (2014). Does synchrony promote generalized prosociality? *Religion, Brain and Behavior, 4*(1), 3–19. https://doi.org/10.1080/2153599x.2013.764545
Reddish, P., Fischer, R., & Bulbulia, J. A. (2013). Let's dance together: Synchrony, shared intentionality and cooperation. *PLoS ONE, 8*(8), e71182. https://doi.org/10.1371/journal.pone.0071182
Reddish, P., Tong, E. M. W., Jong, J., Lanman, J. A., & Whitehouse, H. (2016). Collective synchrony increases prosociality towards non-performers and outgroup members. *British Journal of Social Psychology, 55*(4), 722–38. https://doi.org/10.1111/bjso.12165
Rennung, M., & Göritz, A. S. (2016). Prosocial consequences of interpersonal synchrony: A meta-analysis. *Zeitschrift für Psychologie/Journal of Psychology, 224*, 168–89. https://doi.org/10.1027/2151-2604/a000252
Ross, L., & Nisbett, R. (1991). *McGraw-Hill series in social psychology. The person and the situation*. McGraw-Hill Book Company.
Rossano, M. J. (2012). The essential role of ritual in the transmission and reinforcement of social norms. *Psychological Bulletin, 138*(3), 529–49. https://doi.org/10.1037/a0027038
Ruffle, B., & Sosis, R. (2010). Do religious contexts elicit more trust and altruism? An experiment on Facebook. *Discussion Paper No. 10–02, Department of Economics: Ben-Gurion University*, (860), 1–30. https://doi.org/10.2139/ssrn.1566123
Saroglou, V. (2006). Religion's role in prosocial behavior: Myth or reality? *Psychology of Religion Newsletter: American Psychological Association Division 36, 31*(2), 1–8. https://cdn.uclouvain.be/public/Exports reddot/psyreli/documents/Newsletter.pdf
Saroglou, V., Corneille, O., & Van Cappellen, P. (2009). "Speak, Lord, your servant is listening": Religious priming activates submissive thoughts and behaviors. *International Journal for the Psychology of Religion, 19*(3), 143–54. https://doi.org/10.1080/10508610902880063
Scheepers, P., Gijsberts, M., & Hello, E. (2002). Religiosity and prejudice against ethnic minorities in Europe: Cross-national tests on a controversial relationship. *Review of Religious Research, 43*(3), 242–65. https://doi.org/10.2307/3512331
Schleihauf, H., Graetz, S., Pauen, S., & Hoehl, S. (2018). Contrasting social and cognitive accounts on overimitation: The role of causal transparency and prior experiences. *Child Development, 89*(3), 1039–55. https://doi.org/10.1111/cdev.12780
Shariff, A. F., & Norenzayan, A. (2007). God is watching you: Priming God concepts increases prosocial behavior in an anonymous economic game. *Psychological Science, 18*(9), 803–9. https://doi.org/10.1111/j.1467-9280.2007.01983.x
Shariff, A. F., Willard, A. K., Andersen, T., & Norenzayan, A. (2015). Religious priming: A meta-analysis with a focus on prosociality. *Personality and Social Psychology Review, 20*(1), 27–48. https://doi.org/10.1177/1088868314568811

Siegman, A. W. (1962). Personality and socio-cultural variables associated with religious behavior. *Archiv für Religionspsychologie/Archive for the Psychology of Religion, 7*(1), 96–104. www.jstor.org/stable/23919300

Simmons, J. P., Nelson, L. D., & Simonsohn, U. (2011). False-positive psychology: Undisclosed flexibility in data collection and analysis allows presenting anything as significant. *Psychological Science, 22*(11), 1359–66. https://doi.org/10.1177/0956797611417632

Simons, H. W., Berkowitz, N. N., & Moyer, R. J. (1970). Similarity, credibility, and attitude change: A review and a theory. *Psychological Bulletin, 73*(1), 1–16. https://doi.org/10.1037/h0028429

Smith, R. E., Wheeler, G., & Diener, E. (1975). Faith without works: Jesus people, resistance to temptation, and altruism. *Journal of Applied Social Psychology, 5*(4), 320–30. https://doi.org/10.1111/j.1559-1816.1975.tb00684.x

Sosis, R. (2003). Why aren't we all Hutterites? Costly signaling theory and religious behavior. *Human Nature, 14*(2), 91–127. https://doi.org/10.1007/s12110-003-1000-6

Sosis, R., & Alcorta, C. S. (2003). Signalling, solidarity, and the sacred: The evolution of religious behavior. *Evolutionary Anthropology, 12*(6), 264–74. https://doi.org/10.1002/evan.10120

Sosis, R., & Bressler, E. R. (2003). Cooperation and commune longevity: A test of the costly signaling theory of religion. *Cross-Cultural Research, 37*(2), 211–39. https://doi.org/10.1177/1069397103037002003

Stel, M., & Vonk, R. (2010). Mimicry in social interaction: Benefits for mimickers, mimickees, and their interaction. *British Journal of Psychology, 101*(2), 311–23. https://doi.org/10.1348/000712609X465424

Strathern, A. (1970). Male initiation in New Guinea highlands societies. *Ethnology, 9*(4), 373–9. https://doi.org/10.2307/3773043

Strenski, I. (2006). *Thinking about religion: An historical introduction to theories of religion*. Blackwell Publishing.

Sutherland, L. (2012). Tylor and Neo-Tylorian approaches to the study of religion: Re-evaluating an important lineage in the theorisation of religion. *Paranthropology: Journal of Anthropological Approaches to the Paranormal, 3*(3), 47–57.

Swann, W. B., Jr., Buhrmester, M. D., Gómez, A., Jetten, J., Bastian, B., Vázquez, A., Ariyanto, A., Besta, T., Christ, O., Cui, L., Finchilescu, G., González, R., Goto, N., Hornsey, M., Sharma, S., Susianto, H., & Zhang, A. (2014). What makes a group worth dying for? Identity fusion fosters perception of familial ties, promoting self-sacrifice. *Journal of Personality and Social Psychology, 106*(6), 912–26. https://doi.org/10.1037/a0036089

Swann, W. B., Jr., Gómez, Á., Huici, C., Morales, J. F., & Hixon, J. G. (2010). Identity fusion and self-sacrifice: Arousal as a catalyst of pro-group fighting, dying, and helping behavior. *Journal of Personality and Social Psychology, 99*(5), 824–41. https://doi.org/10.1037/a0020014

Swann, W. B., Jr., Gómez, Á., Seyle, D. C., Morales, J. F., & Huici, C. (2009). Identity fusion: The interplay of personal and social identities in extreme group behavior. *Journal of Personality and Social Psychology, 96*(5), 995–1011. https://doi.org/10.1037/a0013668

Swann, W. B., Jr., Jetten, J., Gómez, Á., Whitehouse, H., Bastian, B., Gómez, A., & Bastian, B. (2012). When group membership gets personal: A theory of identity fusion. *Psychological Review, 119*(3), 441–56. https://doi.org/10.1037/a0028589

Szerszynski, B. (2002). Ecological rites: Ritual action in environmental protest events. *Theory, Culture & Society, 19*(3), 51–69. https://doi.org/10.1177/026327602401081521

Tajfel, H., & Turner, J. C. (1985). The social identity theory of intergroup behavior. In S. Worchel & W. G. Austin (Eds.), *Psychology of intergroup relations* (2nd ed., Vol. 2, pp. 7–24). Nelson-Hall.

Taniguchi, Y., & Sanefuji, W. (2017). The boundaries of overimitation in preschool children: Effects of target and tool use on imitation of irrelevant actions. *Journal of Experimental Child Psychology, 159*, 83–95. https://doi.org/10.1016/j.jecp.2017.01.014

Tunçgenç, B., & Cohen, E. (2016). Interpersonal movement synchrony facilitates pro-social behavior in children's peer-play. *Developmental Science, 21*(1), e12505. https://doi.org/10.1111/desc.12505

Tunçgenç, B., Cohen, E., & Fawcett, C. (2015). Rock with me: The role of movement synchrony in infants' social and nonsocial choices. *Child Development, 86*(3), 976–84. https://doi.org/10.1111/cdev.12354

Turchin, P., Brennan, R., Currie, T. E., Feeney, K. C., François, P., Hoyer, D., Manning, J. G., Marciniak, A., Mullins, D., Palmisano, A., Peregrine, P., Turner, E. A. L., & Whitehouse, H. (2015). Seshat: The global history databank. *Cliodynamics, 6*, 77–107.

Turchin, P., Whitehouse, H., François, P., Hoyer, D., Nugent, S., Larson, J., Covey, A., Altaweel, M., Peregrine, P., Carballo, D., Feinman, G., Wallace, V., Bol, P., Korotayev, A., Kradin, N., Anderson, E., Savage, P., Cioni, E., Levine, J., ... Brandl, E. (2019, November 20). Explaining the rise of moralizing religions: A test of competing hypotheses using the Seshat Databank. SocArXiv. https://doi.org/10.31235/osf.io/2v59j

Turner, V. (1969). *The ritual process: Structure and anti-structure.* Transaction Publishers.

Turner, V. (1985). Betwixt and between: The liminal period in *rites de passage*. In A. C. Lehmann & J. E. Myers (Eds.), *Magic, witchcraft, and religion: An anthropological study of the supernatural* (pp. 46–55). Mayfield Publishing Company.

Tylor, E. B. (1871). *Primitive culture: Researches into the development of mythology, philosophy, religion, language, art, and custom.* John Murray.

Valdesolo, P., & DeSteno, D. (2011). Synchrony and the social tuning of compassion. *Emotion, 11*(2), 262–66. https://doi.org/10.1037/a0021302

van Baaren, R. B., Holland, R. W., Kawakami, K., & van Knippenberg, A. (2004). Mimicry and prosocial behavior. *Psychological Science, 15*(1), 71–4. https://doi.org/10.1111/j.0963-7214.2004.01501012.x

Van Elk, M., Matzke, D., Gronau, Q. F., Guan, M., Vandekerckhove, J., & Wagenmakers, E.-J. (2015). Meta-analyses are no substitute for registered replications: A skeptical perspective on religious priming. *Frontiers in Psychology, 6*, 1365. https://doi.org/10.3389/fpsyg.2015.01365

Van Gennep, A. (1960). *The rites of passage* (M. B. Vizedom & G. L. Caffee, Trans.). University of Chicago Press. (Original work published 1909)

Van Raalte, J. L., Cornelius, A. E., Linder, D. E., & Brewer, B. W. (2007). The relationship between hazing and team cohesion. *Journal of Sport Behavior*, *30*(4), 491–507.

Van Tongeren, D. R., Raad, J. M., McIntosh, D. N., & Pae, J. (2013). The existential function of intrinsic religiousness: Moderation of effects of priming religion on intercultural tolerance and afterlife anxiety. *Journal for the Scientific Study of Religion*, *52*(3), 508–23. https://doi.org/10.1111/jssr.12053

Verkaaik, O. (2010). The cachet dilemma: Ritual and agency in new Dutch nationalism. *American Ethnologist*, *37*(1), 69–82. https://doi.org/10.1111/j.1548-1425.2010.01242.x

Walster, E., Aronson, E., & Abrahams, D. (1966). On increasing the persuasiveness of a low prestige communicator. *Journal of Experimental Social Psychology*, *2*(4), 325–42. https://doi.org/10.1016/0022-1031(66)90026-6

Watson-Jones, R. E., Legare, C. H., Whitehouse, H., & Clegg, J. M. (2014). Task-specific effects of ostracism on imitative fidelity in early childhood. *Evolution and Human Behavior*, *35*(3), 204–10. https://doi.org/10.1016/j.evolhumbehav.2014.01.004

Watson-Jones, R. E., Whitehouse, H., & Legare, C. H. (2016). In-group ostracism increases high-fidelity imitation in early childhood. *Psychological Science*, *27*(1), 34–42. https://doi.org/10.1177/0956797615607205

Watts, J. A., Greenhill, S. J., Atkinson, Q. D., Currie, T. E., Bulbulia, J. A., & Gray, R. D. (2015). Broad supernatural punishment but not moralizing high gods precede the evolution of political complexity in Austronesia. *Proceedings of the Royal Society B: Biological Sciences*, *282*(1804), 20142556. https://doi.org/10.1098/rspb.2014.2556

Weber, M. (1930). *The Protestant work ethic and the spirit of capitalism*. George Allen and Unwin.

West, S. A., Gardner, A., Shuker, D. M., Reynolds, T., Burton-Chellow, M., Sykes, E. M., Guinnee, M. A., & Griffin, A. S. (2006). Cooperation and the scale of competition in humans. *Current Biology*, *16*(11), 1103–6. https://doi.org/10.1016/j.cub.2006.03.069

Whitehouse, H. (1995). *Inside the cult: Religious innovation and transmission in Papua New Guinea. Oxford studies in social and cultural anthropology*. Oxford University Press.

Whitehouse, H. (2000). *Arguments and icons: Divergent modes of religiosity*. Oxford University Press.

Whitehouse, H. (2002). Religious reflexivity and transmissive frequency. *Social Anthropology*, *10*(1), 91–103. https://doi.org/10.1111/j.1469-8676.2002.tb00048.x

Whitehouse, H. (2004). *Modes of religiosity: A cognitive theory of religious transmission*. AltaMira Press.

Whitehouse, H. (2011). The coexistence problem in psychology, anthropology, and evolutionary theory: Commentary on Evans & Lane, Harris, Legare & Visala, and Subbotsky. *Human Development*, *54*(3), 191–9. https://doi.org/10.1159/000329149

Whitehouse, H. (2012). Ritual, cognition, and evolution. In R. Sun (Ed.), *Grounding the social sciences in the cognitive sciences* (pp. 265–84). MIT Press.
Whitehouse, H. (2013). Religion, cohesion and hostility. In S. Clarke, R. Powell, & J. Savulescu (Eds.), *Religion, intolerance and conflict: A scientific and conceptual investigation* (pp. 36–47). Oxford University Press. https://doi.org/10.1093/acprof: oso/9780199640911.003.0002
Whitehouse, H., François, P., Savage, P. E., Currie, T. E., Feeney, K. C., Cioni, E., Purcell, R., Ross, R. M., Larson, J., Baines, J., ter Haar, B., Covey, A., & Turchin, P. (2019). Complex societies precede moralizing gods throughout world history. *Nature*, 568, 226–229.
Whitehouse, H., Jong, J., Buhrmester, M. D., Gómez, Á., Bastian, B., Kavanagh, C. M., Newson, M., Matthews, M., Lanman, J. A., McKay, R., & Gavrilets, S. (2017). The evolution of extreme cooperation via shared dysphoric experiences. *Scientific Reports*, 7, 44292. https://doi.org/10.1038/srep44292
Whitehouse, H., & Laidlaw, J. (Eds.). (2004). *Ritual and memory: Towards a comparative anthropology of religion*. AltaMira Press.
Whitehouse, H., & Laidlaw, J. (Eds.). (2007). *Religion, anthropology and cognitive science*. Carolina Academic Press.
Whitehouse, H., & Lanman, J. A. (2014). The ties that bind us: Ritual, fusion, and identification. *Current Anthropology*, 55(6), 674–95. https://doi.org/10.1086/678698
Whitehouse, H., & McCauley, R. N. (Eds.). (2005). *Mind and religion: Psychological and cognitive foundations of religiosity*. AltaMira Press.
Whitehouse, H., McQuinn, B., Buhrmester, M. D., & Swann, W. B., Jr. (2014). Brothers in arms: Libyan revolutionaries bond like family. *Proceedings of the National Academy of Sciences of the United States of America*, 111(50), 17783–5. https://doi.org/10.1073/pnas.1416284111
Whiten, A., McGuigan, N., Marshall-Pescini, S., & Hopper, L. M. (2009). Emulation, imitation, over-imitation and the scope of culture for child and chimpanzee. *Philosophical Transactions of the Royal Society B: Biological Sciences*, 3641(1528), 2417–28. https://doi.org/10.1098/rstb.2009.0069
Whiten, A., Allan, G., Devlin, S., Kseib, N., Raw, N., & McGuigan, N. (2016). Social learning in the real-world: 'Over-imitation' occurs in both children and adults unaware of participation in an experiment and independently of social interaction. *PLoS ONE*, 11(7), e0159920. https://doi.org/10.1371/journal.pone.0159920
Whitley, R. (2012). "Thank you God": Religion and recovery from dual diagnosis among low-income African Americans. *Transcultural Psychiatry*, 49(1), 87–104. https://doi.org/10.1177/1363461511425099
Wiech, K., Farias, M., Kahane, G., Shackel, N., Tiede, W., & Tracey, I. (2008). An fMRI study measuring analgesia enhanced by religion as a belief system. *Pain*, 139(2), 467–76. https://doi.org/10.1016/j.pain.2008.07.030
Willard, A. K., & Cingl, L. (2017). Testing theories of secularization and religious belief in the Czech Republic and Slovakia. *Evolution and Human Behavior*, 38(5), 604–15. https://doi.org/10.1016/j.evolhumbehav.2017.01.002
Willard, A. K., Henrich, J., & Norenzayan, A. (2016). Memory and belief in the transmission of counterintuitive content. *Human Nature*, 27(3), 221–43. https://doi.org/10.1007/s12110-016-9259-6

Williams, K. D., & Jarvis, B. (2006). Cyberball: A program for use in research on interpersonal ostracism and acceptance. *Behavior Research Methods*, *38*(1), 174–80. https://doi.org/10.3758/BF03192765

Wilson, D. S. (2010). *Darwin's cathedral: Evolution, religion, and the nature of society*. University of Chicago Press.

Wiltermuth, S. S., & Heath, C. (2009). Synchrony and cooperation. *Psychological Science*, *20*(1), 1–5. https://doi.org/10.1111/j.1467-9280.2008.02253.x

Wood, L. A., Harrison, R. A., Lucas, A. J., McGuigan, N., Burdett, E. R. R., & Whiten, A. (2016). "Model age-based" and "copy when uncertain" biases in children's social learning of a novel task. *Journal of Experimental Child Psychology*, *150*, 272–84. https://doi.org/10.1016/j.jecp.2016.06.005

Xygalatas, D., Klocová, E. K., Cigán, J., Kundt, R., Maňo, P., Kotherová, S., Mitkidis, P., Wallot, S., & Kanovsky, M. (2016). Location, location, location: Effects of cross-religious primes on prosocial behavior. *International Journal for the Psychology of Religion*, *26*(4), 304–19. https://doi.org/10.1080/10508619.2015.1097287

Xygalatas, D., Mitkidis, P., Fischer, R., Reddish, P., Skewes, J., Geertz, A. W., Roepstorff, A., & Bulbulia, J. (2013). Extreme rituals promote prosociality. *Psychological Science*, *24*(8), 1602–5. https://doi.org/10.1177/0956797612472910

Young, F. W. (1965). *Initiation ceremonies: A cross-cultural study of status dramatization*. Bobbs-Merrill.

Younger, J., Aron, A., Parke, S., Chatterjee, N., & Mackey, S. (2010). Viewing pictures of a romantic partner reduces experimental pain: Involvement of neural reward systems. *PLoS ONE*, *5*(10), e13309. https://doi.org/10.1371/journal.pone.0013309

Zahavi, A., & Zahavi, A. (1997). *The handicap principle: A missing piece of Darwin's puzzle*. Oxford University Press.

Part II
Applications

Introduction

The first part of this book offers theories and models that advance an interactional ecosocial view of the dynamics of culture, mind, and brain. Contributors to this second part discuss the application of these innovative models to a wide range of topics. Compelling theory is "good to think with" because it defines a set of phenomena and delineates explanatory mechanisms or processes that help us understand, predict, and act on things that matter. Good scientific theory has several key features: it is coherent, fitting what we already know; adequate, subsuming and unifying existing observations; causal, identifying cause or causal mechanisms; and parsimonious, providing the simplest account. Importantly, useful theory and explanation are selective: they direct our gaze, help us identify salient information, cast new light on prior knowledge and beliefs, and generate new insights and hypotheses that prompt quests for confirmation or refutation. While initially formulated as a *post hoc* account, good explanations are generative, providing a basis for new questions or hypotheses that stimulate further inquiry and discovery.

The applications presented in the chapters that follow aim to tap the power of culture–mind–brain frameworks to contribute new insights to major areas of study (history, cognition, education, music, literature, film) and contemporary concerns (mental illness, urbanization, social media, diversity). Some chapters focus on the impacts of neuroscience in different domains of popular culture while others emphasize the impact on academic work of new understandings about brain. The themes that cut across these analyses point to especially generative ideas.

One cross-cutting theme considers the value of models that clarify how social context informs our functioning, experience, and behavior. Taking context sensitivity and dynamic plasticity a step further, the 4E view integrates brain, mind, and behavior by viewing cognition as embodied, embedded, enacted, and extended. Perhaps the past really is a foreign country, for an enactivist view suggests that brains are cultural artifacts embedded in particular times and places (see Chapter 12) such that experience is shaped by distinctive configurations of emotions, even those considered basic or "universal" like anger or fear.

A view of the brain as dynamic and plastic, developing experience-dependent models of the world, and engaging actively with local affordances, emphasizes the direct links of culture to mind and brain. Thus, habits of mind such as differences in spatial navigation strategies alter the volume of relevant brain structures and may also influence the impact of aging on cognition (see Chapter 13). The concept of a predictive brain that constantly anticipates the world through cycles of active inference and expectations, error detection, and embodied simulation can be applied to understand the great emotional power that music holds for humans (see Chapter 15) and the imaginative process of reading literature (see Chapter 16).

An understanding of neuroplasticity can provide critical insight into the mechanisms and consequences of online social behavior with smartphones and social media (see Chapter 20). But widespread uptake of the notion of brain plasticity in popular culture has led to exaggerated claims of unbounded possibility through "hacking the brain," which can prove corrosive and stigmatizing in educational settings and beyond (see Chapter 14).

These analyses emphasize the brain's predictive processing, which links processes "inside" and "outside" the individual in cycles of co-construction. Indeed, this cyclical process supports our ability to see the world through others' eyes and appreciate embodied aspects of their experience. Hence, skillful ethnographic film can evoke embodied experiences and narrative understanding to provide insights that go well beyond verbal content (see Chapter 17). Similarly, viewing PhotoVoice stories of recovery produced by former patients dramatically can improve empathy and the competence of mental healthcare providers (see Chapter 18). Predictive and enactive models show how dynamics linking concepts and emotions are built into processing and provide explanations for the power of narrative. Narratives represent arcs of experience propelled by sensory stimulation, perceptual content, and emotion dynamics (stigma/aversion, surprise, empathy, craving, pride, or shame). Narrative structures can create a sense of progression and motivation through sequences of tension and resolution with associated feelings of arousal and reward. The importance of these narrative processes is manifest in many of the following chapters, which seek to demonstrate how meaning and lived experiential worlds are made.

Both neuroplasticity and enactivist cognition contribute to an ecological perspective that understands diversity as products of common mechanisms operating with and through local cultural niches. Ecosocial models of culture, mind, and brain as mutually constitutive insist that the historical contingency of human experience goes all the way down. That is, my brain, mind, and experience are different now than they might have been had I lived in another, even slightly different, time and place. Twin studies show how important small contingencies can be even when genomes and environments ostensibly are identical (Spector, 2013). This perspective also accords with the massive evidence for the impact of social inequality on health disparities. Further, it prompts hypotheses about the impact of changes in human ecology such as ongoing global processes of urbanization (see Chapter 19).

If diversity is ubiquitous, how do we find common ground? Here is where culture plays essential roles in developing shared narratives, models, and conditions, while also shaping perceptions, meanings, and consequences of diversity. Exposure to diversity and shifting grounds for negotiating difference may be behind the rise of identity as a dominant theme of our current moment (see Chapter 14). Importantly, social categories and ascriptions of identity – even those that claim to be rooted in biology – are always motivated and situated: they have social, cultural, political, and existential roots. Explanatory frameworks for human difference and diversity can be instruments of control that reflect particular interests or needs, though they also can be strategically deployed to meet counter interests, as seen in current identity politics (see Chapter 21). We hope the reflections on culture–mind–brain interactions in this volume provide the reader with some critical lenses to reflect on the issues raised in these essays and in the wider debates in which concepts of culture, mind, and brain are deployed to address our most pressing ethical and pragmatic challenges.

REFERENCE

Spector, T. D. (2013). *Identically different: Why we can change our genes*. Overlook Press.

12 The Cultural Brain as Historical Artifact

Rob Boddice[1]

This volume asks, collectively, how "context" can be studied in a scientifically rigorous fashion, in order to get at local contingencies and the inherent instability of the constructed worlds in which humans live and have lived. It asks how we should investigate culture as a vital and dynamic part of mind and experience, of the biological formation of the plurally plastic, situated, contingent human brain–body system. Here I will briefly sketch how historians have been addressing precisely these questions for more than two decades, approaching the human from the outside in. The more recent turn of the social neurosciences in particular, but also of social psychology and transcultural psychiatry, to the importance of culture in human formation and experience has, to a large extent, overlooked historical work in this field. The human sciences have arrived at the importance of culture from the inside-out. Between us, we meet at a common point, at the unstable boundary between biology and culture, between interior and exterior, that defines the human. Recent historiographical trends, just as with recent neuroscientific trends, promise to collapse dualistic ways of thinking, to remove the space between biology and culture, nature and nurture, and to fully embrace the human as a dynamic biocultural entity. For their part, some historians are actively reaching out to make use of scientific work on the contingent interior, but we see little traffic in the opposite direction. Yet if historians' claims that the cultural brain is, by logical extension, understood also to be an historical artifact, then historical insight must become an essential element in brain research. It offers the kind of critical cultural reflection that is required in order to transform vague references to "the exterior" or to "social input" or to "the world" into major complicating factors in the study of the human interior and the brain.

Historians have always asked what it means to be human and how this meaning comes to change. Their attempts, in recent times, to answer these questions impose historical scholarship on the human sciences. In particular, historians have become direct contributors to emotion and sensory knowledge.

---

[1] This project has received funding from the European Union's Horizon 2020 research and innovation programme under the Marie Sklodowska-Curie grant agreement No. 742470.

Both the history of emotions and the history of the senses have a common origin point in the Annaliste work of Lucien Febvre (1938/1992, 1941) in the 1930s and 1940s, based on a critical reception of psychological attempts to fix, both rhetorically and biologically, categories of human experience. Yet it was not until the late 1990s that the history of emotions acquired something like a mature methodology, coming on the back of innovative explorations of the emotional past from the mid-1980s (Stearns & Stearns, 1985) and via a close working relationship with cultural anthropologists (Reddy, 1997). In the first two decades of this century the history of emotions and the history of the senses have witnessed an explosion of scholarship (Boddice, 2016; Bourke, 2005; Eustace, 2008; Frevert, 2011; Gross, 2006; Lanzoni, 2018; Rosenwein, 2002; Sullivan, 2016), a refinement of theoretical approach and methodological application (Reddy, 2001), and a number of moves toward interdisciplinary engagement on the terms of bioculture, opening up a new front on the question of "experience" (Boddice, 2018a, 2019; Boddice & Smith, 2020; Plamper, 2015).

William Reddy in particular, who transitioned to the discipline of history via cultural anthropology, put the history of emotions on the map. In his 1997 article, "Against Constructionism," Reddy put the brain–body and the world in dynamic relation through his concept of "emotives." Put simply, an "emotive" defines the dynamic relation of expressive "utterances" (bound by cultural scripts) and inward feelings. To emote is at once to try to give voice to what one feels, but also a translation of that feeling into an available expression. The act of translation also feeds back on to the feeling itself, the act of expression being a modifier of experience. To the extent that an individual finds an available expression for an inward feeling, there is emotive success, and a degree of experiential satisfaction; to the extent that an individual fails to match expression to feeling, there is emotional suffering. By this theory Reddy implicated the brain–body in cultural worlds and demonstrated their interrelation. There were no "authentic" or "basic" emotions because there was no place or space outside of a culture in which to experience such things. Reddy saw "emotives" as part of human efforts at conscious self-management (even where the effort was, as it were, invisible), where all bodily feelings were culturally mediated and all cultural expressions were bodily situated.

The insights of affective neuroscientist Lisa Feldman Barrett (2006a, 2006b, 2017; Hoemann et al., 2019; see also Chapter 6) have been particularly appealing to historians because they confirm, from the opposite direction, Reddy's findings, closely mirroring his theoretical innovations from 1997 and 2001. Barrett is one of the architects of a schism in the discipline of psychology between Barrett's bioconstructionist side and the universalists of the Ekman, Tomkins schools. Barrett argues that emotion "concepts" such as anger or fear are more or less ephemeral constructions that arise from the culturally situated brain's multiple (and multipurpose) moving parts; the universalists of the Ekman, Tomkins schools argue that core emotions like fear and anger are hardwired into neural circuitry that is dedicated to the task and more or less universal. A thorough appraisal of historical scholarship on the emotions and senses ought to settle this debate, however, since historians have amassed empirical evidence of the contingency of human affective experiences from three millennia of historical data. Moving on from what appear, from within psychological practice, to be intractable arguments would do more than save time and paper. The insights of historians ought also to change the kind of questions that scientists like Barrett ask. Since concepts play such an important role in her work (just as language is central to Reddy's work), it ought to be of significant consequence that concepts themselves are historically contingent. Thomas Dixon (2003) has pointed out that the word "emotion" itself is of relatively recent usage in its signification of a category of psychological investigation, and that its linguistic forebears, especially the "passions," entailed entirely different ways of both knowing about human experience and of experiencing being human per se. In extending this view (Boddice, 2019), looking at affective categories in Greek, Latin, Italian, German, French, and English, over time, I drew upon a massive body of scholarship that together demonstrates the error of translating historical categories into contemporary English master categories (such as "anger" or "love" or "disgust"). To do so undermines and overwrites the situated significance of the original terms. I take seriously Barrett's claims that concept development is culturally contingent and that emotional experience is hitched to this contingency. By exploring such concepts across time and space, where "emotions" as we know them do not exist, I posit the logical extension of her claims. The variability of human "emotional" development and experience is bigger, I suspect, than even Barrett realizes.

Moreover, since Reddy's (1997, 2001) interventions, his "emotives" theory has been developed and extended by those of us who questioned the limited focus on linguistic utterances and upon conscious self-management. Monique Scheer (2012), in particular, pushed historians to think about emotions as a kind of practice – things that humans *do* in the world – that involve not just words and concepts, but also physical expressions, gestures, and postures, and which are connected both to distinct epistemologies and the ways in which such epistemologies are performed. Historians of emotion are increasingly persuaded that once cultural scripts are understood to be running, there is no place, no private space nor unconscious realm, where they can be avoided. Experience is mediated all the time, always filtered and translated according to local contexts of possibility. The insight leads to a collapse of hard distinctions between culture and biology, conscious and unconscious, nature and nurture, because there are simply no functions that can be isolated from a context.

Whatever structural similarities in the human brain and body might be appealed to, it is inescapable that the *experience* of the brain–body–world dynamic is always situated, always practiced (Reckwitz, 2012; Vallgårda et al., 2015). We might, looking at the past one way, seek to emphasize similarities and commonalities in experience over time and across cultures. The risk, and something to which the historical mind is highly attuned, is that seeking continuity overlooks that which is lost or changed and with it, the causes of such. Given that the impetus of research into the relation of culture, mind, and brain is heavily focused on disruption, plasticity, development, and transformation, it seems germane that those of us who see the cultural brain as historical artifact emphasize change over time.

Sensory history tends in the same direction (Smith, 2007) and accords with a body of interdisciplinary research on interoception – the perception of one's own interior – that is attempting to integrate models of "awareness of the self from outside and from within" (Allen & Tsakiris, 2018, p. 41). An implication about interior sensation and homeostasis follows. If interiority is dynamically involved with exteriority, then what happens and the feeling of what happens inside the body are no less situated than stimuli from the outside. They cannot, in any meaningful sense, be isolated as entirely "natural" or fixed "biological" functions or states. Once we head toward integration, once we head toward biocultural understandings of the human, then we cannot parcel off bits of biological functioning that sit outside of the model. The most basic of "automatic" functions and sensations become, in a meaningful sense, as contingent as the most obviously constructed. Philosopher Drew Leder (2018, p. 307) has pointed in this direction, by reference to the "exterior interior," but I see no reason for the semantic ordering here, or even the space in between. We are dealing, simply, with an element of bioculture. Barrett herself has noted the ways in which interoception has to be translated through situated conceptual repertoires in order to become meaningful as experience, and this accords with much of the latest research on interoception from a variety of disciplines. Cognitive and developmental neuroscientists Mariana von Mohr and Katerina Fotopoulou (2018, p. 116) go so far as to say that even the most fundamental of "core subjective feelings," things like "hunger and satiation, pain and relief, cold or warmth," homeostasis itself, have cultural origins. Historians are well placed to confirm this, and indeed have gone to some lengths already in doing so. But they also go beyond confirmation of a scientific insight. By stressing the mutability of cultural configurations, that is, the contingency and situatedness of human beings, the category of "core subjective feelings" becomes unstable. Hunger and satiation, pain and relief, cold and warmth are all historical, experienced according to junctures of time and place, following no set path or repertoire of significance, meaning, or value. There is already a large and growing body of historical evidence, for example, on the importance of cultural contingency in the experience of pain (Boddice, 2014; Bourke, 2014; Cohen, 2009; Moscoso, 2012; van Dijkhuizen & Enenkel, 2009), and an emerging historiography on the historical contingency of homeostasis (Geroulanos & Meyers, 2018).

These trends converge with a separate historical project that has attempted to foreground the historical brain in cultural context. Daniel Lord Smail (2008) coined the term "neurohistory" in his book, *On Deep History and the Brain*, to try to demonstrate the myriad ways in which culture writes to nature, as it were, such that the psychological condition of an individual in another time might radically differ from that of a contemporary actor. Neurohistory embraces research in neuroplasticity to explore past contexts of brain development, where now lost cultural influences and scripts of experience must have played formative roles. The actual brains, of course, are missing, but the neurohistorian works by piecing context, practices, and historical dynamics of power together with testimony, description, and depiction of experience in historical terms. The picture that emerges is one of historical brains constructing historical cultures and historical cultures forming historical brains: a dynamic relationship. Moreover, neurohistory examines historically specific psychotropic influences on brain development, brain chemistry, and perceptions of reality to show the extent to which the culturally mediated brain is temporally situated. Such psychotropic influences include the introduction of obvious brain changers, such as alcohol, coffee, tobacco, or narcotics, into various historical theaters. But it also explores what might be thought of as less obviously psychotropic factors, such as disease, new technology, atmospheric pollutants, or new cultural practices. One might think about the introduction of syphilis to South America, the effect on the brain of the invention of movable type and of the sudden rise of mass literacy, of the spike in lead in the atmosphere after the industrial revolution, and of the cultural brain in the age of the Internet. That human brains underwent sudden changes in development, concomitant with acute changes in the perception of reality, seems beyond doubt. More historical investigation is required, but there is enough already to suggest that brain researchers need to think in historical time and not simply in evolutionary time.

While Smail's project hinged on an attachment to a fundamental biological structure that transcended humanity both in the present and in the historical past, the implications of his innovative study nonetheless pointed to the collapse of the culture/biology dyad. Recent attempts at revision of neurohistory's aims have pursued this collapse more pointedly (Boddice, 2018b; Burman, 2012; McGrath, 2017). They ask what value remains in thinking about "ancient" parts of the brain, or "hardwired" processes, when such parts and processes are nonetheless always culturally situated and where experience is always culturally mediated. Historians are exploring the implications and potential of epigenetics to explain changes in historical contexts of possibility, and borrowing the vocabulary of situated or local biology from anthropologists in order to give full credence to historical evidence of bodily mutability (Lock & Kaufert, 2001; Lock & Palsson, 2016; Meloni, 2016). What is emerging from this strand of biocultural historicism is evidence of a plurally plastic human, irreducible to biology or culture, to brain or to body, but rather caught up in a dynamic of formation that entangles brain, body, and world.

This chapter provides a sketch of scholarship that already exists. I refer readers to *The History of Emotions* (Boddice, 2018a) for a more thorough appraisal of where we are. Where we are going remains an open question. As psychology and the neurosciences turn toward culture, they inevitably turn toward questions that have long preoccupied the humanities. As yet, there is little cross-pollination of ideas across disciplinary boundaries between those sciences and the humanities, but this is not a sustainable situation. The study of mind and brain increasingly recognizes that culture cannot be parceled off or reduced, any more than biology can be isolated or rendered deterministic. Such a recognition builds a bridge across the disciplines, changing research questions and methods on both sides as it does so.

REFERENCES

Allen, M., & Tsakiris, M. (2018). The body as first prior: Interoceptive predictive processing and the primacy of self–models. In M. Tsakiris & H. De Preester (Eds.), *The interoceptive mind: From homeostasis to awareness* (pp. 27–45). Oxford University Press. https://doi.org/10.1093/oso/9780198811930.003.0002

Barrett, L. F. (2006a). Are emotions natural kinds? *Perspectives on Psychological Science*, *1*(1), 28–58. https://doi.org/10.1111/j.1745-6916.2006.00003.x

Barrett, L. F. (2006b). Solving the emotion paradox: Categorization and the experience of emotion. *Personality and Social Psychology Review*, *10*(1), 20–46. https://doi.org/10.1207/s15327957pspr1001_2

Barrett, L. F. (2017). *How emotions are made: The secret life of the brain*. Houghton Mifflin Harcourt.

Boddice, R. (Ed.). (2014). *Pain and emotion in modern history*. Palgrave Macmillan. https://doi.org/10.1057/9781137372437

Boddice, R. (2016). *The science of sympathy: Morality, evolution and Victorian civilization*. University of Illinois Press. www.jstor.org/stable/10.5406/j.ctt1hfr069

Boddice, R. (2018a). *The history of emotions*. Manchester University Press.

Boddice, R. (with Daniel Lord Smail). (2018b). Neurohistory. In M. Tamm & P. Burke (Eds.), *Debating new approaches to history* (pp. 301–25). Bloomsbury.

Boddice, R. (with Daniel Lord Smail). (2019). *A history of feelings*. Reaktion Books Ltd.

Boddice, R., & Smith, M. (2020). *Emotion, sense, experience*. Cambridge University Press.

Bourke, J. (2005). *Fear: A cultural history*. Virago.

Bourke, J. (2014). *The story of pain: From prayer to painkillers*. Oxford University Press.

Burman, J. T. (2012). History from within? Contextualizing the new neurohistory and seeking its methods. *History of Psychology*, *15*(1), 84–99. https://doi.org/10.1037/a0023500

Cohen, E. (2009). *The modulated scream: Pain in late medieval culture*. University of Chicago Press.

Dixon, T. (2003). *From passions to emotions: The creation of a secular psychological category*. Cambridge University Press.

Eustace, N. (2008). *Passion is the gale: Emotion, power, and the coming of the American Revolution*. University of North Carolina Press.

Febvre, L. (1941). La sensibilité et l'histoire: Comment reconstituer la vie affective d'autrefois? *Annales D'histoire Sociale (1939–1941)*, *3*(1–2), 5–20. http://www.jstor.org/stable/27574143

Febvre, L. (1992). Une vue d'ensemble: Histoire et psychologie. In R. Toussaint & J.-M. Simonet (Eds.), *Combats pour l'histoire* (pp. 207–20). Armand Colin. (Original work published 1938)

Frevert, U. (2011). *Emotions in history: Lost and found*. Central European University Press. www.jstor.org/stable/10.7829/j.ctt1281z9

Geroulanos, S., & Meyers, T. (2018). *The human body in the age of catastrophe: Brittleness, integration, science and the Great War*. University of Chicago Press.

Gross, D. M. (2006). *The secret history of emotion: From Aristotle's rhetoric to modern brain science*. University of Chicago Press.

Hoemann, K., Xu, F., & Barrett, L. F. (2019). Emotion words, emotion concepts, and emotional development in children: A constructionist hypothesis. *Developmental Psychology*, *55*(9), 1830–49. https://doi.org/10.1037/dev0000686

Lanzoni, S. (2018). *Empathy: A history*. Yale University Press.

Leder, D. (2018). Inside insight: A phenomenology of interoception. In M. Tsakiris & H. De Preester (Eds.), *The interoceptive mind: From homeostasis to awareness* (pp. 307–22). Oxford University Press. https://doi.org/10.1093/oso/9780198811930.003.0017

Lock, M., & Kaufert, P. (2001). Menopause, local biologies, and cultures of aging. *American Journal of Human Biology*, *13*(4), 494–504. https://doi.org/10.1002/ajhb.1081

Lock, M., & Palsson, G. (2016). *Can science resolve the nature/nurture debate?* Polity Press.

McGrath, L. S. (2017). Historiography, affect, and the neurosciences. *History of Psychology*, *20*(2), 129–47. https://doi.org/10.1037/hop0000047

Meloni, M. (2016). *Political biology: Science and social values in human heredity from eugenics to epigenetics*. Palgrave Macmillan. https://doi.org/10.1057/9781137377722

Moscoso, J. (2012). *Pain: A cultural history* (S. Thomas & P. House, Trans.). Palgrave Macmillan. https://doi.org/10.1057/9781137284235

Plamper, J. (2015). *The history of emotions: An introduction* (K. Tribe, Trans.). Oxford University Press.

Reckwitz, A. (2012). Affective spaces: A praxeological outlook. *Rethinking History*, *16*(2), 241–58. https://doi.org/10.1080/13642529.2012.681193

Reddy, W. M. (1997). Against constructionism: The historical ethnography of emotions. *Current Anthropology*, *38*(3), 327–51. https://doi.org/10.1086/204622

Reddy, W. M. (2001). *The navigation of feeling: A framework for the history of emotions*. Cambridge University Press.

Rosenwein, B. H. (2002). Worrying about emotions in history. *The American Historical Review*, *107*(3), 821–45. https://doi.org/10.1086/ahr/107.3.821

Scheer, M. (2012). Are emotions a kind of practice (and is that what makes them have a history)? A Bourdieuian approach to understanding emotion. *History and Theory*, *51*(2), 193–220. https://doi.org/10.1111/j.1468-2303.2012.00621.x

Smail, D. L. (2008). *On deep history and the brain*. University of California Press. www.jstor.org/stable/10.1525/j.ctt1pp7mz

Smith, M. M. (2007). *Sensing the past: Seeing, hearing, smelling, tasting, and touching in history*. University of California Press.

Stearns, P. N., & Stearns, C. Z. (1985). Emotionology: Clarifying the history of emotions and emotional standards. *The American Historical Review*, *90*(4), 813–36. https://doi.org/10.1086/ahr/90.4.813

Sullivan, E. (2016). *Beyond melancholy: Sadness and selfhood in renaissance England*. Oxford University Press. https://doi.org/10.1093/acprof:oso/9780198739654.001.0001

Vallgårda, K., Alexander, K., & Olsen, S. (2015). Emotions and the global politics of childhood. In S. Olsen (Ed.), *Childhood, youth and emotions in modern history: National, colonial and global perspectives* (pp. 12–34). Palgrave Macmillan. https://doi.org/10.1057/9781137484840_2

van Dijkhuizen, J. F., & Enenkel, K. A. E. (Eds.). (2009). *The sense of suffering: Constructions of physical pain in early modern culture*. Brill. https://doi.org/10.1163/ej.9789004172470.i-520

von Mohr, M., & Fotopoulou, A. (2018). The cutaneous borders of interoception: Active and social inference of pain and pleasure on the skin. In M. Tsakiris & H. De Preester (Eds.), *The interoceptive mind: From homeostasis to awareness* (pp. 102–20). Oxford University Press. https://doi.org/10.1093/oso/9780198811930.003.0006

13 Experience-Dependent Plasticity in the Hippocampus

Greg L. West and Véronique D. Bohbot

Life experiences have been associated with significant changes in the brain's structure and functioning. This experience-dependent plasticity is thought to reflect the capacity of our nervous systems to adapt to environmental demands, and ultimately shape cognition. Our essay focuses on how such experiences and environment can specifically impact the hippocampus, a structure important for learning, memory, and healthy cognition. We will outline how the hippocampal memory system maintains a competitive relationship with other memory systems in the brain and what specific types of behavior can influence this system both positively and negatively.

Neuroplasticity in the Hippocampus

The hippocampus (HPC) is a structure located in the medial temporal lobe, adjacent to the amygdala, entorhinal, perirhinal, and parahippocampal cortices. A rich body of neuroscience research suggests that the hippocampus is centrally involved in both episodic and spatial memory (O'Keefe & Nadel, 1978; Tulving & Markowitsch, 1998). The hippocampus is also critical for healthy cognition across the lifespan (Amico et al., 2011; Apostolova et al., 2006; Gilbertson et al., 2002; Pantelis et al., 2003). Because of this, a large amount of research has focused on how this structure can be impacted both positively and negatively by a variety of factors. There is evidence that the hippocampus undergoes experience-dependent neuroplastic changes in both nonhuman animals (Kempermann, Brandon, et al., 1998; Kempermann, Kuhn, et al., 1998; Lerch et al., 2011; Pinaud et al., 2002) and humans (Maguire et al., 2003; West et al., 2018). For example, birds that rely on precise knowledge of the geographic layout of a region in order to locate food or to migrate from one location to another have increased HPC volumes relative to non-food-storing birds (Lee et al., 1998; Smulders et al., 1995). In the former species, the HPC decreases in size over a period of time when navigation is not required, suggesting that the HPC is a labile, use-dependent structure affected by external demands. Rodents who were trained on the Morris Water Maze using place navigation (i.e., reliance on multiple extramaze landmarks) to locate a submerged platform were found to display increased volume in the hippocampus. In contrast, rodents trained to use local cues to find the platform (i.e., reliance on a single visual "beacon" stimulus) were found to display increased volume in the striatum (which includes the caudate nucleus; Lerch et al., 2011). The caudate nucleus of the striatum is located within the basal ganglia, a centrally located group of nuclei that connect the brain's cerebral cortex to brain systems involved in movement and a wide range of behaviors including habit formation (McDonald & White, 1993; Packard et al., 1989; Packard & McGaugh, 1992, 1996).

It is also possible to measure learning-induced morphological changes in the HPC of young and older adults using structural magnetic resonance imaging (sMRI). This form of neuroimaging indirectly visualizes brain anatomy primarily based on the distribution of gray matter and white matter. Briefly, "gray matter" is made up of the cell bodies of neurons as well as dendrites and axon terminals, which together comprise the brain's synapses. "White matter" is primarily composed of bundles of myelinated axons, the threadlike nerve-cell projections that carry electrical impulses from one neuron to another. Using sMRI, Maguire and colleagues showed a positive correlation between HPC gray matter volume and taxi-driving experience (Maguire et al., 2003), and even showed growth in HPC volume after a three-year study of London roads needed to obtain a taxi-driving permit called "The Knowledge" (Woollett & Maguire, 2011). Interestingly, only those who successfully completed "The Knowledge" showed growth in the hippocampus. Other studies have demonstrated increased gray matter in the HPC of both young and older human adults as a function of training (Filippi et al., 2010; Lustig et al., 2009). Students were scanned before and after studying for medical school exams, as well as three months following the examination. Structural changes were observed in the HPC and the parietal cortex between the first and second scans (Draganski et al., 2006). Older adult volunteers who learned to juggle showed increases in gray matter in the left HPC and in the nucleus accumbens of the striatum bilaterally (Boyke et al., 2008). Further, aerobic exercise has also been shown to increase gray matter in the HPC of older adults (Bherer et al., 2006; Erickson et al., 2011).

Research aimed at increasing gray matter of the hippocampus is becoming more common because the hippocampus has been identified as one of the best-known biomarkers for risk of neuropsychiatric illness across the lifespan. For example, reduced gray matter in the hippocampus of healthy individuals is associated with an increased risk of schizophrenia (Pantelis et al., 2003), posttraumatic stress disorder (Gilbertson et al., 2002), and depression (Amico et al., 2011). Furthermore, older adults with lower volume in the hippocampus are at increased risk of having cognitive deficits in normal aging (Lupien et al., 1998) and later developing Alzheimer's disease (Apostolova et al., 2006;

Swan & Lessov-Schlaggar, 2007). Further, the first brain regions to show Alzheimer's disease pathology are the entorhinal cortex and hippocampus (Apostolova et al., 2006; de Toledo-Morrell, et al., 2000). The entorhinal cortex (EC) is the main input to the hippocampus and plays a key role in the coding of spatial relationships between objects in the environment, supporting spatial navigation. Only later does the disease progress to include other brain regions in the neocortex. Reduction in HPC and EC volumes are therefore strong predictors of Alzheimer's disease (Apostolova et al., 2006; de Toledo-Morrell, et al., 2000). Furthermore, reduction in HPC volume has also been observed in people with mild cognitive impairment, a syndrome intermediate between normal aging and dementia for approximately 50 percent of patients (Haroutunian et al., 1998; Price & Morris, 1999), and even at an earlier stage classified as subjective cognitive impairment, where healthy individuals subjectively report a decline in cognition (Sánchez-Benavides et al., 2018).

Importantly, the hippocampus shows signs of neurogenesis across the entire life span in rodents and in primates (Gould, Beylin, et al., 1999). Learning and memory increase the rate of survival of newborn cells in the adult primate HPC (Gould, Reeves, et al., 1999). Memory-based spatial learning also increases the cellular organization of existing HPC neurons (Lerch et al., 2011). Because of this, it has been argued that memory-based learning has the potential to increase gray matter in the HPC of people at risk of associated neuropsychiatric disorders (e.g., mild cognitive impairment patients) by focusing on the very region in which this pathology emerges.

Competition between Multiple Memory Systems

Memory is governed by multiple brain systems that support distinct types of memory processes that are either hippocampus-dependent or non-hippocampus-dependent (O'Keefe & Nadel, 1978; Packard et al., 1989; Packard & McGaugh, 1992). The hippocampus memory system is centrally involved in relational memory, considered to be a flexible memory system for past events (Cohen et al., 1997; Eichenbaum et al., 1990; Squire & Zola, 1996). The hippocampus is critical for allocentric spatial learning and memory, and the formation of cognitive maps (i.e., learning and memory for the relationships between environmental landmarks) irrespective of the position of the observer (Bohbot et al., 2007; Hartley et al., 2003; Lee et al., 1998; Lerch et al., 2011; Packard et al., 1989; Packard & McGaugh, 1992, 1996). In contrast, procedural memories, such as stimulus–response relationships, do not rely on the hippocampus, but instead rely on the striatum within the basal ganglia (McDonald & White, 1993; Packard et al., 1989; Packard & McGaugh, 1992). The striatum, which contains the caudate nucleus in humans, also plays a role in the brain's reward pathway and is involved in the formation of habits by supporting rigid stimulus–response associations (Alvarez et al., 1995; McDonald & White, 1993; Mishkin & Petri, 1984; Packard et al., 1989; Packard & McGaugh, 1996; Wolbers et al., 2004).

These neural systems also support navigation. Navigation involves accurately identifying and monitoring one's position in order to plan and follow a route from one place to another. The hippocampus and striatum support distinct navigation strategies in humans (Etchamendy & Bohbot, 2007) and rodents (Packard et al., 1989; Packard & McGaugh, 1992). Specifically, the *spatial strategy*, which relies on the hippocampus (O'Keefe & Nadel, 1978), involves building relationships between the positions of various landmarks in an environment to create a cognitive map. In contrast, the *response strategy*, which relies on the striatum (Packard & McGaugh, 1992), entails learning a series of movements (e.g., left and right turns) in response to locations that act as stimuli (e.g., the post office). When these series of movements are learned, they become part of a non-hippocampal or procedural memory system. Spatial navigational strategies are associated with increased gray matter and activity in the hippocampus, while response-based navigational strategies are associated with increased gray matter and activity in the striatum (Bohbot et al., 2007; Etchamendy et al., 2012; Iaria et al., 2003; Konishi & Bohbot, 2013; Lerch et al., 2011; Lin et al., 2012). For example, when tested in a dual-solution task that allows for the use of both spatial and response navigational strategies, rodent studies have demonstrated increased basal levels of the neurotransmitter acetylcholine, an indicator of increased neural activity, in the hippocampus prior to the spontaneous use of the spatial strategy. In contrast, rodents that spontaneously used a response strategy in the dual-solution task had increased basal levels of acetylcholine in the striatum (Chang & Gold, 2003). In humans, it has been shown that hippocampal volume positively correlates with peoples' ability to rely on an internal cognitive representation of space (i.e., a cognitive map) during navigation. Conversely, lower levels of accuracy in this task were associated with higher volume in the caudate nucleus (Schinazi et al., 2013). Another study found that the "wayfinding" performance of participants using the relationship between landmarks (i.e., spatial learning) and route memorizing (i.e., response learning) was positively correlated with baseline hippocampal and caudate nucleus volumes, respectively (Head & Isom, 2010). When participants navigated in a dual-solution virtual maze that allows for the use of both spatial or response navigation strategies, those who navigated using spatial strategies showed greater functional MRI activity (Iaria et al., 2003) and gray matter (Bohbot et al., 2007) in the hippocampus. Conversely, participants who used response strategies showed increased fMRI activity (Iaria et al., 2003) and gray matter (Bohbot et al., 2007) in the caudate nucleus of the striatum. These findings were also replicated in older adults where spatial strategy use was associated with greater fMRI activity (Konishi et al., 2013) and gray matter (Konishi & Bohbot, 2013) in the hippocampus compared to those using the response strategy.

Analysis of navigation strategies and their underlying neural structures also reveals a competitive nature between hippocampus-dependent and non-hippocampus memory systems. Healthy individuals can flexibly use both memory systems depending on which is best suited for the situation, and they are used in balance. An imbalance between the two, however, appears to occur in aging and in neuropathology. This is characterized by an increased reliance on the non-hippocampal memory system supported by the striatum and a decreased reliance on the hippocampal memory system. The age-related decreased reliance was observed in a sample of 599 healthy participants. Only 15 percent of eight-year-old children used response strategies to navigate a virtual maze as opposed to 50 percent of young adults and 65 percent of participants over the age of sixty (Bohbot et al., 2012). Neuroimaging data in humans further demonstrates the existence of a competitive, "use-it-or-lose-it" relationship between memory systems whereby increased striatal volume and activity is also associated with decreased volume and activity in the hippocampus (Bohbot et al., 2004, 2007; Iaria et al., 2003). Together, these results suggest that the use of non-hippocampus-dependent response navigational strategies is associated with increased development and activation of the striatum and a reduction in hippocampus volume and activity across the lifespan (Bohbot et al., 2012).

Recent results from the rodent literature further support this hypothesis. As in humans, aging rodents move away from relying on the hippocampus-dependent memory system in favor of using response strategies to remember targets within a maze (Barnes et al., 1980). Interestingly, preliminary results showed that when the striatum of older rats was inactivated with lidocaine, they instead favored the use of hippocampus-dependent spatial strategies in a dual-solution task. These results further suggest that the downregulation of striatal processing during aging can effectively reintroduce balance of use between the hippocampus-dependent non-hippocampus-dependent memory systems (Gardner et al., 2018). In other words, experience-dependent training that promotes the use of the hippocampal memory system holds promise in restoring function within this system even in populations that display pathology associated with aging and disease.

In healthy individuals, acute experience can also create an imbalance of use between memory systems. For example, stressed rats display reduced long-term potentiation (LTP), or excitatory postsynaptic potentials (EPSPs), in the hippocampus that results in impaired spatial memory performance and intact striatum-dependent response learning. This effect was shown to be mediated through the connections between the hippocampus and amygdala. When the amygdala of rats were lesioned, the stress response did not reduce hippocampal LTP or spatial memory performance (Kim et al., 2001). Furthermore, the promotion of response strategies with stress relied on an intact amygdala (Leong and Packard, 2014). In humans, being placed in a stressful situation before completing a spatial memory task led to decreased use of spatial strategies in favor of response strategies (Schwabe et al., 2007). Further, chronic stress in both rodents and humans is associated with reduced hippocampus-dependent spatial strategies (Schwabe et al., 2008). Together, these findings suggest that stress can cause shifting away from using the hippocampal memory system in favor of the caudate nucleus and could, in part, be responsible for the imbalance between both systems.

Genetic variation also appears to play an important role in the preferential use of one memory system over another. An allelic variant of the apolipoprotein E gene (*APOE4*), which is present in approximately 10–15 percent of people, increases the risk for Alzheimer's, lowers the age of onset, and is also associated with less gray matter in the hippocampus (O'Dwyer et al., 2012; Pievani et al., 2011). On the other hand, the *APOE2* variant is protective against Alzheimer's disease (Conejero-Goldberg et al., 2014). *APOE2* carriers were found to adopt hippocampus-dependent spatial strategies at a higher rate compared to people who carried an *APOE4* allele (Konishi et al., 2016).

Competition between hippocampus-dependent and non-hippocampus memory systems is influenced by a number of factors that are thought to lead to long-term neuroplastic changes. Future work is still needed to further elucidate how to restore balance between the usage of hippocampus-dependent and non-hippocampus-dependent systems.

Human–Computer Interactions and Plastic Changes in the Hippocampus

To date, little is known about how modern human–computer interactions (HCIs), such as video games and virtual reality, can impact our brains. While some positive effects related to video game consumption have been observed, specifically 3D-platform video games such as *Super Mario 64* (Nintendo, 1996) and increased hippocampal gray matter (Kühn & Gallinat, 2014; Kühn et al., 2014; West et al., 2017, 2018), recent research has shown that other types of video games can have a damaging effect on this system. Previous research from our team demonstrated, for the first time, a causal relationship between video games and reduced gray matter in the hippocampus. Specifically, ninety hours of in-lab action video game training (e.g., first-person shooting games such as *Call of Duty* [Infinity Ward, 2003]) either increased or decreased gray matter in the hippocampus depending on individual differences in "navigational learning" (Bohbot et al., 2007, 2013; Iaria et al., 2003;

Konishi & Bohbot, 2013). People who navigate using *response strategies* (a rigid series of turns from a given stimuli, ignoring other landmarks, Bohbot et al., 2007) experience reduced hippocampal gray matter after action video game training (West et al., 2018). As previously stated, reduced gray matter in the hippocampus is a known risk factor for many neurological disorders across people's lifespan (Amico et al., 2011; Apostolova et al., 2006; Gilbertson et al., 2002; Pantelis et al., 2003; Swan & Lessov-Schlaggar, 2007). Conversely, people who navigate with hippocampus-dependent *spatial strategies* (learning relationships between environmental landmarks; Bohbot et al., 2007) showed increased hippocampal gray matter at post-video game training. Further, reduced gray matter was specific to *action* video games, as the same dose of ninety hours of in-lab training on an active control 3D-platform video game (e.g., *Super Mario 64* [Nintendo, 1996]) led to increases in gray matter within the hippocampal memory system across all participants (West et al., 2018). A second replication study further demonstrated that a different group of action video games (e.g., *Borderlands* [Gearbox, 2009] and *Dead Island* [Techland, 2011]) caused reduced gray matter in the hippocampus among response learners and increased gray matter in the hippocampus in spatial learners. Further, these changes in hippocampal gray matter were tied to changes in hippocampus-dependent navigation behavior: Decreased reliance on landmarks during navigation correlated with decreased gray matter in the hippocampus after the 90-hour training period (West et al., 2018).

Why are neuroplastic changes related to video game consumption dependent on people's navigational strategies? We hypothesize that this is due to the fact that people's navigational strategies (i.e., spatial and response learning which relies on different memory systems; Lerch et al., 2011; Packard et al., 1989) interact with specific aspects of a virtual environment's design that cause a differential impact on the hippocampus: Spatial learners spontaneously learn relationships between landmarks to build cognitive maps of virtual environments that they explore while playing video games (Andersen et al., 2012; Lerch et al., 2011), leading to growth within the hippocampus (Bohbot et al., 2015). In contrast, response learners ignore the relationships between landmarks while they navigate using stimulus–response relationships (Lerch et al., 2011; Packard et al., 1989), such as in-game GPS, which promote caudate nucleus activity (Bohbot et al., 2007; Iaria et al., 2003; Lerch et al., 2011), resulting in reduced activity in the hippocampus and gray matter loss. Moreover, stress and immediate reward associated with first-person shooting games may promote caudate nucleus activity (Shohamy & Adcock, 2010). In fact, direct electrical stimulation of the caudate nucleus in cats leads to a reduction in unit activity of neurons in the hippocampus (La Grutta et al., 1988), proving the competitive nature of the two memory systems. Additional evidence is obtained from a study involving deep brain stimulation of the subthalamic nucleus in patients with Parkinson's disease where a reduction in hippocampal volume was measured in the span of 15 months (Sankar et al., 2016). Interestingly, deep brain stimulation of the subthalamic nucleus led to increased volume of the putamen, a region of the brain connected to the caudate nucleus (Sankar et al., 2016). Altogether, these studies show that a direct reduction in neural activity in the hippocampus as well as a reduction in hippocampal gray matter volume occurs as a result of stimulating the caudate nucleus or putamen directly, indirectly, or with response learning. In summary, the type of content consumed in human–computer interactions such as video games can be a factor in creating an imbalance between hippocampus-dependent and non-hippocampus-dependent memory systems.

Future Directions

Further study is needed to better understand how imbalances between multiple memory systems occurs and how this can be mitigated. Several factors have been identified to contribute to the overuse of non-hippocampal-dependent memory systems in favor of more efficient response-based learning. In short, as cultural beings, our particular ways of thinking, repetitive behaviors, and practices – including our use of devices such as GPS, smartphones, and video games – may promote certain neural connections at the expense of others (for in-depth discussion, see Chapter 3). Emerging research is now pointing to the wide use of such devices as a contributing factor to greater reliance on non-hippocampus-dependent memory. This warrants further study as use of these devices and virtual environments are growing at an exponential rate. Further, their impacts on the developing and aging brain are practically unknown. Given the limited, but concerning evidence that certain human–computer interactions can interact with already established factors related to underuse of the hippocampal memory system to cause further atrophy in this system, future work should focus on how this negative impact can be mitigated.

REFERENCES

Alvarez, P., Zola-Morgan, S., & Squire, L. R. (1995). Damage limited to the hippocampal region produces long-lasting memory impairment in monkeys. *Journal of Neuroscience*, *15*(5 Pt 2), 3796–807. https://doi.org/10.1523/JNEUROSCI.15-05-03796.1995

Amico, F., Meisenzahl, E., Koutsouleris, N., Reiser, M., Möller, H. J., & Frodl, T. (2011). Structural MRI correlates for vulnerability and resilience to major depressive disorder. *Journal of Psychiatry and Neuroscience*, *36*(1), 15–22. https://doi.org/10.1503/jpn.090186

Andersen, N. E., Dahmani, L., Konishi, K., & Bohbot, V. D. (2012). Eye tracking, strategies, and sex differences in virtual navigation. *Neurobiology of Learning and Memory*, *97*(1), 81–9. https://doi.org/10.1016/j.nlm.2011.09.007

Apostolova, L. G., Dutton, R. A., Dinov, I. D., Hayashi, K. M., Toga, A. W., Cummings, J. L., & Thompson, P. M. (2006). Conversion of mild cognitive impairment to Alzheimer disease predicted by hippocampal atrophy maps. *Archives of Neurology*, *63*(5), 693–9. https://doi.org/10.1001/archneur.63.5.693

Barnes, C. A., Nadel, L., & Honig, W. K. (1980). Spatial memory deficit in senescent rats. *Canadian Journal of Psychology/Revue canadienne de psychologie*, *34*(1), 29–39. https://doi.org/10.1037/h0081022

Bherer, L., Kramer, A. F., Peterson, M. S., Colcombe, S., Erickson, K., & Becic, E. (2006). Testing the limits of cognitive plasticity in older adults: Application to attentional control. *Acta Psychologica*, *123*(3), 261–78. https://doi.org/10.1016/j.actpsy.2006.01.005

Bohbot, V. D., Del Balso, D., Conrad, K., Konishi, K., & Leyton, M. (2013). Caudate nucleus-dependent navigational strategies are associated with increased use of addictive drugs. *Hippocampus*, *23*(11), 973–84. https://doi.org/10.1002/hipo.22187

Bohbot, V. D., Iaria, G., & Petrides, M. (2004). Hippocampal function and spatial memory: Evidence from functional neuroimaging in healthy participants and performance of patients with medial temporal lobe resections. *Neuropsychology*, *18*(3), 418–25. https://doi.org/10.1037/0894-4105.18.3.418

Bohbot, V. D., Konishi, K., Sodums, D., Dahmani, L., & Bherer, L. (2015, October). Hippocampus and cortical plasticity following a virtual spatial memory intervention program promote spontaneous hippocampus-dependent navigation strategies in healthy older adults [Paper presentation]. Society for Neuroscience, 45th Annual Meeting, Chicago, IL, United States.

Bohbot, V. D., Lerch, J., Thorndycraft, B., Iaria, G., & Zijdenbos, A. P. (2007). Gray matter differences correlate with spontaneous strategies in a human virtual navigation task. *Journal of Neuroscience*, *27*(38), 10078–83. https://doi.org/10.1523/JNEUROSCI.1763-07.2007

Bohbot, V. D., McKenzie, S., Konishi, K., Fouquet, C., Kurdi, V., Schachar, R., Boivin, M., & Robaey, P. (2012). Virtual navigation strategies from childhood to senescence: Evidence for changes across the life span. *Frontiers in Aging Neuroscience*, *4*, 28. https://doi.org/10.3389/fnagi.2012.00028

Boyke, J., Driemeyer, J., Gaser, C., Büchel, C., & May, A. (2008). Training-induced brain structure changes in the elderly. *Journal of Neuroscience*, *28*(28), 7031–5. https://doi.org/10.1523/JNEUROSCI.0742-08.2008

Chang, Q., & Gold, P. E. (2003). Switching memory systems during learning: Changes in patterns of brain acetylcholine release in the hippocampus and striatum in rats. *Journal of Neuroscience*, *23*(7), 3001–5. https://doi.org/10.1523/JNEUROSCI.23-07-03001.2003

Cohen, N. J., Poldrack, R. A., & Eichenbaum, H. (1997). Memory for items and memory for relations in the procedural/declarative memory framework. *Memory*, *5*(1–2), 131–78. https://doi.org/10.1080/741941149

Conejero-Goldberg, C., Gomar, J. J., Bobes-Bascaran, T., Hyde, T. M., Kleinman, J. E., Herman, M. M., Chen, S., Davies, P., & Goldberg, T. E. (2014). APOE2 enhances neuroprotection against Alzheimer's disease through multiple molecular mechanisms. *Molecular Psychiatry*, *19*(11), 1243–50. https://doi.org/10.1038/mp.2013.194

de Toledo-Morrell, L., Goncharova, I., Dickerson, B., Wilson, R.S., & Bennett, D.A. (2000). From healthy aging to early Alzheimer's disease: In vivo detection of entorhinal cortex atrophy. *Annals of the New York Academy of Sciences*, *911*, 240–53. https://nyaspubs.onlinelibrary.wiley.com/doi/abs/10.1111/j.1749-6632.2000.tb06730.x?sid=nlm%3Apubmed

Draganski, B., Gaser, C., Kempermann, G., Kuhn, H. G., Winkler, J., Büchel, C., & May, A. (2006). Temporal and spatial dynamics of brain structure changes during extensive learning. *Journal of Neuroscience*, *26*(23), 6314–17. https://doi.org/10.1523/JNEUROSCI.4628-05.2006

Eichenbaum, H., Stewart, C., & Morris, R. G. (1990). Hippocampal representation in place learning. *Journal of Neuroscience*, *10*(11), 3531–42. https://doi.org/10.1523/JNEUROSCI.10-11-03531.1990

Erickson, K. I., Voss, M. W., Prakash, R. S., Basak, C., Szabo, A., Chaddock, L., Kim, J. S., Heo, S., Alves, H., White, S. M., Wojcicki, T. R., Mailey, E., Vieira, V. J., Martin, S. A., Pence, B. D., Woods, J. A., McAuley, E., & Kramer, A. F. (2011). Exercise training increases size of hippocampus and improves memory. *Proceedings of the National Academy of Sciences of the United States of America*, *108*(7), 3017–22. https://doi.org/10.1073/pnas.1015950108

Etchamendy, N., & Bohbot, V. D. (2007). Spontaneous navigational strategies and performance in the virtual town. *Hippocampus*, *17*(8), 595–9. https://doi.org/10.1002/hipo.20303

Etchamendy, N., Konishi, K., Pike, G. B., Marighetto, A., & Bohbot, V. D. (2012). Evidence for a virtual human analog of a rodent relational memory task: A study of aging and fMRI in young adults. *Hippocampus*, *22*(4), 869–80. https://doi.org/10.1002/hipo.20948

Filippi, M., Ceccarelli, A., Pagani, E., Gatti, R., Rossi, A., Stefanelli, L., Falini, A., Comi, G., & Rocca, M. A. (2010). Motor learning in healthy humans is associated to gray matter changes: A tensor-based morphometry study. *PLoS ONE*, *5*(4), e10198. https://doi.org/10.1371/journal.pone.0010198

Gardner, R. S., Gold, P. E., & Korol, D. L. (2018, November). A multiple memory systems approach to understanding cognitive aging: Not all aging is equal [Paper presentation]. Society for Neuroscience, 48th Annual Meeting, San Diego, CA, United States.

Gearbox Software. (2009). *Borderlands* [Video game]. 2K Games. https://borderlands.com/en-US/

Gilbertson, M. W., Shenton, M. E., Ciszewski, A., Kasai, K., Lasko, N. B., Orr, S. P., & Pitman, R. K. (2002). Smaller hippocampal volume predicts pathologic vulnerability to psychological trauma. *Nature Neuroscience*, *5*(11), 1242–7. https://doi.org/10.1038/nn958

Gould, E., Beylin, A., Tanapat, P., Reeves, A., & Shors, T. J. (1999). Learning enhances adult neurogenesis in the hippocampal formation. *Nature Neuroscience*, *2*(3), 260–5. https://doi.org/10.1038/6365

Gould, E., Reeves, A. J., Fallah, M., Tanapat, P., Gross, C. G., & Fuchs, E. (1999). Hippocampal neurogenesis in adult Old World primates. *Proceedings of the*

National Academy of Sciences of the United States of America, 96(9), 5263–7. https://doi.org/10.1073/pnas.96.9.5263

Haroutunian, V., Perl, D. P., Purohit, D. P., Marin, D., Khan, K., Lantz, M., Davis, K. L., & Mohs, R. C. (1998). Regional distribution of neuritic plaques in the nondemented elderly and subjects with very mild Alzheimer disease. *Archives of Neurology, 55*(9), 1185–91. https://jamanetwork.com/journals/jamaneurology/fullarticle/774252

Hartley, T., Maguire, E. A., Spiers, H. J., & Burgess, N. (2003). The well-worn route and the path less traveled: Distinct neural bases of route following and wayfinding in humans. *Neuron, 37*(5), 877–88. https://doi.org/10.1016/S0896-6273(03)00095-3

Head, D., & Isom, M. (2010). Age effects on wayfinding and route learning skills. *Behavioural Brain Research, 209*(1), 49–58. https://doi.org/10.1016/j.bbr.2010.01.012

Iaria, G., Petrides, M., Dagher, A., Pike, B., & Bohbot, V. D. (2003). Cognitive strategies dependent on the hippocampus and caudate nucleus in human navigation: Variability and change with practice. *Journal of Neuroscience, 23*(13), 5945–52. https://doi.org/10.1523/JNEUROSCI.23-13-05945.2003

Infinity Ward. (2003). *Call of Duty* [Video game]. Activision. https://www.callofduty.com/

Kempermann, G., Brandon, E. P., & Gage, F. H. (1998). Environmental stimulation of 129/SvJ mice causes increased cell proliferation and neurogenesis in the adult dentate gyrus. *Current Biology, 8*(16), 939–42. https://doi.org/10.1016/S0960-9822(07)00377-6

Kempermann, G., Kuhn, H. G., & Gage, F. H. (1998). Experience-induced neurogenesis in the senescent dentate gyrus. *Journal of Neuroscience, 18*(9), 3206–12. https://doi.org/10.1523/JNEUROSCI.18-09-03206.1998

Kim, J. J., Lee, H. J., Han, J. S., & Packard, M. G. (2001). Amygdala is critical for stress-induced modulation of hippocampal long-term potentiation and learning. *Journal of Neuroscience, 21*(14), 5222–8. https://doi.org/10.1523/JNEUROSCI.21-14-05222.2001

Konishi, K., Bhat, V., Banner, H., Poirier, J., Joober, R., & Bohbot, V. D. (2016). APOE2 is associated with spatial navigational strategies and increased gray matter in the hippocampus. *Frontiers in Human Neuroscience, 10*, 349. https://doi.org/10.3389/fnhum.2016.00349

Konishi, K., & Bohbot, V. D. (2013). Spatial navigational strategies correlate with gray matter in the hippocampus of healthy older adults tested in a virtual maze. *Frontiers in Aging Neuroscience, 5*, 1. https://doi.org/10.3389/fnagi.2013.00001

Konishi, K., Etchamendy, N., Roy, S., Marighetto, A., Rajah, N., & Bohbot, V. D. (2013). Decreased functional magnetic resonance imaging activity in the hippocampus in favor of the caudate nucleus in older adults tested in a virtual navigation task. *Hippocampus, 23*(11), 1005–14. https://doi.org/10.1002/hipo.22181

Kühn, S., & Gallinat, J. (2014). Amount of lifetime video gaming is positively associated with entorhinal, hippocampal and occipital volume. *Molecular Psychiatry, 19*(7), 842–7. https://doi.org/10.1038/mp.2013.100

Kühn, S., Gleich, T., Lorenz, R. C., Lindenberger, U., & Gallinat, J. (2014). Playing Super Mario induces structural brain plasticity: Gray matter changes resulting from training with a commercial video game. *Molecular Psychiatry, 19*(2), 265–71. https://doi.org/10.1038/mp.2013.120

La Grutta, V., Sabatino, M., Gravante, G., Morici, G., Ferraro, G., & La Grutta, G. (1988). A study of caudate inhibition on an epileptic focus in the cat hippocampus. *Archives Internationales de Physiologie et de Biochimie, 96*(2), 113–20. https://doi.org/10.3109/13813458809079632

Lee, D. W., Miyasato, L. E., & Clayton, N. S. (1998). Neurobiological bases of spatial learning in the natural environment: Neurogenesis and growth in the avian and mammalian hippocampus. *NeuroReport, 9*(7), R15–R27. https://doi.org/10.1097/00001756-199805110-00076

Leong, K. C., & Packard, M.G. (2014). Exposure to predator odor influences the relative use of multiple memory systems: Role of basolateral amygdala. *Neurobiology of Learning and Memory, 109*, 56–61. www.sciencedirect.com/science/article/pii/S1074742713002438?via%3Dihub

Lerch, J. P., Yiu, A. P., Martínez-Canabal, A., Pekar, T., Bohbot, V. D., Frankland, P. W., Henkelman, R. M., Josselyn, S. A., & Sled, J. G. (2011). Maze training in mice induces MRI-detectable brain shape changes specific to the type of learning. *NeuroImage, 54*(3), 2086–95. https://doi.org/10.1016/j.neuroimage.2010.09.086

Lin, S. Y., Calcott, R., Germann, J., Konishi, K., Bohbot, V. D., & Lerch, J. P. (2012, October). Decreased use of hippocampus-dependent spatial strategy in favor of caudate nucleus-dependent response strategy from childhood to adolescence [Poster presentation]. Society for Neuroscience, 42nd Annual Meeting, New Orleans, LA, United States.

Lupien, S. J., de Leon, M., de Santi, S., Convit, A., Tarshish, C., Nair, N. P. V., Thakur, M., McEwen, B. S., Hauger, R. L., & Meaney, M. J. (1998). Cortisol levels during human aging predict hippocampal atrophy and memory deficits. *Nature Neuroscience, 1*(1), 69–73. https://doi.org/10.1038/271

Lustig, C., Shah, P., Seidler, R., & Reuter-Lorenz, P. A. (2009). Aging, training, and the brain: A review and future directions. *Neuropsychology Review, 19*(4), 504–22. https://doi.org/10.1007/s11065-009-9119-9

Maguire, E. A., Spiers, H. J., Good, C. D., Hartley, T., Frackowiak, R. S., & Burgess, N. (2003). Navigation expertise and the human hippocampus: A structural brain imaging analysis. *Hippocampus, 13*(2), 250–9. https://doi.org/10.1002/hipo.10087

McDonald, R. J., & White, N. M. (1993). A triple dissociation of memory systems: Hippocampus, amygdala, and dorsal striatum. *Behavioral Neuroscience, 107*(1), 3–22. https://doi.org/10.1037/0735-7044.107.1.3

Mishkin, M., & Petri, H. L. (1984). Memories and habits: Some implications for the analysis of learning and retention. In L. R. Squire & N. Butters (Eds.), *Neuropsychology of memory* (pp. 287–96). Guilford Press.

Nintendo. (1996). *Super Mario 64* [Video game]. Nintendo.

O'Dwyer, L., Lamberton, F., Matura, S., Tanner, C., Scheibe, M., Miller, J., Rujescu, D., Prvulovic, D., & Hampel, H. (2012). Reduced hippocampal volume in healthy young ApoE4 carriers: An MRI study. *PLoS ONE, 7*(11), e48895. https://doi.org/10.1371/journal.pone.0048895

O'Keefe, J., & Nadel, L. (1978). *The hippocampus as a cognitive map*. Oxford University Press. www.cognitivemap.net/

Packard, M. G., Hirsh, R., & White, N. M. (1989). Differential effects of fornix and caudate nucleus lesions on two radial maze tasks: Evidence for multiple memory systems. *Journal of Neuroscience*, *9*(5), 1465–72. https://doi.org/10.1523/JNEUROSCI.09-05-01465.1989

Packard, M. G., & McGaugh, J. L. (1992). Double dissociation of fornix and caudate nucleus lesions on acquisition of two water maze tasks: Further evidence for multiple memory systems. *Behavioral Neuroscience*, *106*(3), 439–46. https://doi.org/10.1037/0735-7044.106.3.439

Packard, M. G., & McGaugh, J. L. (1996). Inactivation of hippocampus or caudate nucleus with lidocaine differentially affects expression of place and response learning. *Neurobiology of Learning and Memory*, *65*(1), 65–72. https://doi.org/10.1006/nlme.1996.0007

Pantelis, C., Velakoulis, D., McGorry, P. D., Wood, S. J., Suckling, J., Phillips, L. J., Yung, A. R., Bullmore, E. T., Brewer, W., Soulsby, B., Desmond, P., & McGuire, P. K. (2003). Neuroanatomical abnormalities before and after onset of psychosis: A cross-sectional and longitudinal MRI comparison. *Lancet*, *361*(9354), 281–8. https://doi.org/10.1016/S0140-6736(03)12323-9

Pievani, M., Galluzzi, S., Thompson, P. M., Rasser, P. E., Bonetti, M., & Frisoni, G. B. (2011). APOE4 is associated with greater atrophy of the hippocampal formation in Alzheimer's disease. *NeuroImage*, *55*(3), 909–19. https://doi.org/10.1016/j.neuroimage.2010.12.081

Pinaud, R., Tremere, L. A., Penner, M. R., Hess, F. F., Robertson, H. A., & Currie, R. W. (2002). Complexity of sensory environment drives the expression of candidate-plasticity gene, nerve growth factor induced-A. *Neuroscience*, *112*(3), 573–82. https://doi.org/10.1016/S0306-4522(02)00094-5

Price, J. L., & Morris, J. C. (1999). Tangles and plaques in nondemented aging and "preclinical" Alzheimer's disease. *Annals of Neurology*, *45*(3), 358–68. https://doi.org/10.1002/1531-8249(199903)45:3<358::AID-ANA12>3.0.CO;2-X

Sánchez-Benavides, G., Grau-Rivera, O., Suárez-Calvet, M., Minguillon, C., Cacciaglia, R., Gramunt, N.; ALFA Study, Falcon, C., Gispert, J. D., & Molinuevo, J. L. (2018). Brain and cognitive correlates of subjective cognitive decline-plus features in a population-based cohort. *Alzheimer's Research & Therapy*, *10*(1), 123. https://doi.org/10.1186/s13195-018-0449-9

Sankar, T., Li, S. X., Obuchi, T., Fasano, A., Cohn, M., Hodaie, M., Chakravarty, M. M., & Lozano, A. M. (2016). Structural brain changes following subthalamic nucleus deep brain stimulation in Parkinson's disease. *Movement Disorders*, *31*(9), 1423–5. https://doi.org/10.1002/mds.26707

Schinazi, V. R., Nardi, D., Newcombe, N. S., Shipley, T. F., & Epstein, R. A. (2013). Hippocampal size predicts rapid learning of a cognitive map in humans. *Hippocampus*, *23*(6), 515–28. https://doi.org/10.1002/hipo.22111

Schwabe, L., Dalm, S., Schächinger, H., & Oitzl, M. S. (2008). Chronic stress modulates the use of spatial and stimulus-response learning strategies in mice and man. *Neurobiology of Learning and Memory*, *90*(3), 495–503. https://doi.org/10.1016/j.nlm.2008.07.015

Schwabe, L., Oitzl, M. S., Philippsen, C., Richter, S., Bohringer, A., Wippich, W., & Schachinger, H. (2007). Stress modulates the use of spatial versus stimulus-response learning strategies in humans. *Learning & Memory*, *14*(1), 109–16. https://doi.org/10.1101/lm.435807

Shohamy, D., & Adcock, R. A. (2010). Dopamine and adaptive memory. *Trends in Cognitive Sciences*, *14*(10), 464–72. https://doi.org/10.1016/j.tics.2010.08.002

Smulders, T. V., Sasson, A. D., & DeVoogd, T. J. (1995). Seasonal variation in hippocampal volume in a food-storing bird, the black-capped chickadee. *Journal of Neurobiology*, *27*(1), 15–25. https://doi.org/10.1002/neu.480270103

Squire, L. R., & Zola, S. M. (1996). Structure and function of declarative and nondeclarative memory systems. *Proceedings of the National Academy of Sciences of the United States of America*, *93*(24), 13515–22. https://doi.org/10.1073/pnas.93.24.13515

Swan, G. E., & Lessov-Schlaggar, C. N. (2007). The effects of tobacco smoke and nicotine on cognition and the brain. *Neuropsychology Review*, *17*(3), 259–73. https://doi.org/10.1007/s11065-007-9035-9

Tang, Y. Y., Lu, Q., Geng, X., Stein, E. A., Yang, Y., & Posner, M. I. (2010). Short-term meditation induces white matter changes in the anterior cingulate. *Proceedings of the National Academy of Sciences of the United States of America*, *107*(35), 15649–52. https://doi.org/10.1073/pnas.1011043107

Techland. (2011). *Dead Island* [Video game]. Deep Silver. https://www.deepsilver.com/us/games/dead-island/

Tulving, E., & Markowitsch, H. J. (1998). Episodic and declarative memory: Role of the hippocampus. *Hippocampus*, *8*(3), 198–204. https://doi.org/10.1002/(SICI)1098-1063(1998)8:3<198::AID-HIPO2>3.0.CO;2-G

West, G. L., Konishi, K., Diarra, M., Benady-Chorney, J., Drisdelle, B. L., Dahmani, L., Sodums, D. J., Lepore, F., Jolicoeur, P., & Bohbot, V. D. (2018). Impact of video games on plasticity of the hippocampus. *Molecular Psychiatry*, *23*(7), 1566–74. https://doi.org/10.1038/mp.2017.155

West, G. L., Zendel, B. R., Konishi, K., Benady-Chorney, J., Bohbot, V. D., Peretz, I., & Belleville, S. (2017). Playing Super Mario 64 increases hippocampal grey matter in older adults. *PLoS ONE*, *12*(12), e0187779. https://doi.org/10.1371/journal.pone.0187779

Wolbers, T., Weiller, C., & Büchel, C. (2004). Neural foundations of emerging route knowledge in complex spatial environments. *Cognitive Brain Research*, *21*(3), 401–11. https://doi.org/10.1016/j.cogbrainres.2004.06.013

Woollett, K., & Maguire, E. A. (2011). Acquiring "the knowledge" of London's layout drives structural brain changes. *Current Biology*, *21*(24), 2109–14. https://doi.org/10.1016/j.cub.2011.11.018

14 Liminal Brains in Uncertain Futures
Critical Neuroscience and the Cultural Contexts of Neuroeducation

Suparna Choudhury and Joshua Berson

Introduction: The Developing Brain in Digital Culture

In December 2017, the *New York Times* reported that the Esalen Institute, the Big Sur retreat at the epicenter of the "human potential" movement, had emerged from a year of landslides, flooding, and closures with a new mission: to help Silicon Valley entrepreneurs discover a deeper sense of purpose. "The CEOs," then-executive director Ben Tauber explained, "inside they're hurting" (Bowles, 2017). Indeed, this had been a year in which media technology industries had lost their luster, with Facebook and Twitter widely blamed for the triumph of right-wing populism in the United States. Among the changes at Esalen is the planned closure of its preschool – in operation for some four decades, but now lacking a sufficient number of affluent families with young children to warrant its continuance. The demographic shift at Big Sur may be unsurprising. Still, there is something ironic in Esalen's closing its preschool just as the institute turns its attention to the spiritual growth of media technology unicorns. For many in Esalen's new target demographic, schools represent the next frontier.

Children, of course, are the next generation of users, and as Facebook and its competitors and symbiotes begin to roll out services expressly designed for under-thirteens, it is no surprise that they should view schools as a key touchpoint. Schools may in fact be a key place to cultivate brand goodwill and user familiarity for the next generation of social media services. But more than that, schools represent the place where many in Esalen's new clientele hope to maximize their impact on the broader trajectory of the culture they have helped bring into being. Schools, and more specifically the redesign of primary school curricula, offer the hurting CEOs the opportunity to remake society in their image (Singer & Ivory, 2017).

Across the United States, Canada, and the United Kingdom, schoolchildren represent a population of minds at the nexus of competing sets of values. Adolescents on the one hand are thought of as the highest consumers and most proficient users of digital media for communication and entertainment, and on the other hand as the population most at risk to the dangers of digital addiction and hyperconnectedness (see Choudhury & McKinney, 2013, and Orben & Przybylski, 2019, for reviews that complicate the debate). Increasingly understood through the lens of neuroscience to be a particularly vulnerable group in terms of mental health, they are also paradoxically seen as an unmissable opportunity by media giants seeking target audiences and consumers, and simultaneously by educators, clinicians, and spiritual teachers aiming to remedy the consequences of these digital dangers.

Children's minds and brains have become the somewhat surprising terrain on which the social conscience and consumption pragmatics of the digital technology world are playing out. Meanwhile, scientists and educators – amid an expanding galaxy of philanthropists, Hollywood actors, and spiritual leaders – are calling for urgent interventions into developing brains through mindfulness meditation in schools, hospitals, and detention centers. The adolescent brain is now a space on which to project a multitude of moral panics, and with them social and medical interventions. At the same time, these biomedicalized concerns about adolescents reflect the cognitive styles, cultural values, and kinds of adult characters a society aims to cultivate, and the ways in which neuroscience has become part of these wider projects.

The recent imperative to apply data about the adolescent brain to mainstream educational curricula provides a lens onto the cultural logics by which the brain is made salient in various domains in society. It also allows us to reflect on the appeal of neuroscience in contemporary cultural settings: How is it that a science of brain structure and function serves to bridge worlds as seemingly divergent as Buddhist contemplation and tech entrepreneurialism? How do children and adolescents, and their real and imagined brains, become the canvas on which these cultural connections are made? Finally, how should we as researchers at the intersection between cognitive neuroscience and anthropology understand, and critique, the entanglements between neuroscience and culture? In this chapter, we begin with an outline of new understandings of adolescence, including mindfulness meditation as a newly conceived evidence-based tool to cultivate resilience among young people. We then introduce critical neuroscience, a multidisciplinary approach we use to analyze the uptake and appeal of mindfulness. We focus on the concept of neuroplasticity and examine its role in translation between neuroscience and education, demonstrating in particular the cultural appeal of the plastic adolescent brain as a site to direct social anxieties and their hoped-for solutions.

The Adolescent Brain: Plasticity, Potential/Vulnerability, Risk

Soon after the advent of neuroimaging in the 1980s, a large body of longitudinal MRI data revealed that brain development is far more protracted than previously thought: The brain was shown to undergo considerable structural change beyond middle childhood, through adolescence and into young adulthood (see Blakemore & Choudhury, 2006). Jay Giedd and his colleagues at the National Institute of Mental Health (NIMH) demonstrated gray and white matter changes, thought to correspond to earlier small-scale postmortem studies showing synaptic pruning and axonal myelination, particularly in the prefrontal cortex (Giedd et al., 1999). Since this discovery, the adolescent brain has become a prominent object of study by cognitive neuroscientists investigating the cognitive correlates and mental health implications of these structural developments (Blakemore, 2018), and as a result of this and the many scientific outreach initiatives related to the developing brain, the "teenage brain" has come into view in the popular imagination. Neuroscience of the adolescent brain has been used to explain the anecdotal behaviors associated with teenagers in everyday ("Western") culture, such as risk taking, addiction, and impulsivity. Although the data remain preliminary – in the sense that many of the studies draw on small samples from particular populations, relationships between behavior and brain activity are correlational rather than causal, and the role of social and cultural context is rarely incorporated into the experimental studies – there has been swift application into health and social policy. Health recommendations geared toward doctors, parents, educators, and young people themselves convey how plastic or malleable the developing adolescent brain is, and emphasizing adolescence as at once a sensitive period of vulnerability (to substance addiction, risky behaviors, poor decision-making) and opportunity (for interventions through education, psychiatry, and the law; Fuhrmann et al., 2015). Positioned at the threshold of childhood and adulthood, adolescents are understood through the lens of neuroscience to be liminal, in a state of becoming, and capable of transformation in multiple directions. Knowledge of the liminal state of the brain is thought by neuroscientists and policy makers to be important for adolescents, parents, and practitioners to help steer behaviors toward healthy futures (Fricke & Choudhury, 2011).

Neuroeducation and the Developing Brain

The field of "neuroeducation" has emerged in response to the drive for translational neuroscience in conjunction with a trend toward evidence-based education, and provides a rich site to explore how developmental brain data are transferred toward practical goals geared to young people. Increasingly institutionalized through highly funded multidisciplinary centers, programs, academic journals, and books, neuroeducation brings together researchers and educators to try to create new pathways between scientific research and educational practice based on a rigorous "learning science" (Battro et al., 2008; Goswami, 2006). A key goal of this research agenda is to build effective strategies of education that improve the academic achievement and social–emotional development of young people, reframing curricula in terms of research on the developing brain. These strategies are presented as science-based and make strong claims about what can be accomplished through programs that capitalize on brain plasticity. Although the science is relatively new, recently established high-profile graduate centers for neuroeducation in the United States, research centers in the United Kingdom, and schools and programs for children in Canada have been set up to develop skills and capacities to bridge neuroscience and educational policy and to respond to varying degrees of concern that education is in crisis.

Despite the preliminary nature of research data, findings from neuroeducation have begun to trickle directly into schools in the form of new customized teaching methods built around interpretations of data about social cognitive development and neurocognitive plasticity. These methods aim predominantly to improve the ability of children and adolescents to regulate actions, impulses, and emotions, and to provide a biological foundation for working with developmental disorders such as dyslexia in the classroom (Howard-Jones, 2009; Thomson et al., 2013). This expeditious translation is not without controversy. Earlier attempts to bridge brain science and education through high-profile commercial projects such as Baby Einstein, Baby Mozart, and educational programs premised on left brain/right brain lateralization have been widely discredited (Fischer, 2009; Maxwell & Racine, 2012), raising the need for greater scrutiny in the transfer of research to policy and educational practice. Critics highlight the commercialization and oversimplification of neuroscientific results and the emergence of "neuromyths," a term that refers to "a misconception generated by a misunderstanding, a misreading, or a misquoting of facts scientifically established (by brain research) to make a case for use of brain research in education and other contexts" (Organization for Economic Cooperation and Development; OECD, 2002). While we are attentive to the current privileged status of neuroscience in explanations of human behavior, our aim is not to undermine the validity of neuroeducation. Rather, it is to explore the values, motivations, and vehicles of communication facilitating and underlying the imperative for knowledge translation between neuroscience researchers, policy makers, and teachers.

In recent years, mindfulness-based education in particular has become a central focus in neuroeducation, with researchers setting out to analyze long-term impacts of mindfulness practices on children and adolescents and non-profit organizations contending with poverty and behavioral problems among youth, using mindfulness and yoga. Funding agencies and policy makers have invested enormous hope and investment in the outcomes of these projects, with the goal of realizing "human potential across the lifespan ... [by employing] rigorous science" (http://oxfordmindfulness.org). New curricula have been designed with the goal of equipping children and teenagers with the ability to practice mindfulness as a tool to improve self-regulation, attentional focus, emotional resilience, and symptoms of depression and anxiety, many of which are thought to be adversely impacted by the growing use of digital technology, and more broadly by the effects of growing up in an "unsustainable and disharmonious" modern world (www.blueschool.org). Teachers involved in programs in the United States and United Kingdom are increasingly training in secular forms of mindfulness meditation and using these teachings in their classes, drawing on the brain to substantiate their approach. Critics within neuroscience have cautioned against the "seductive allure" (Weisberg et al., 2008) of "neuromythology" (Rose, 2005; Tallis, 2004) and the risks of applying preliminary findings to education too soon. Social scientists have also drawn attention to the ways in which neuroscientific evidence is being leveraged toward new forms of psychological governance (Whitehead et al., 2017), with the authority of neuroscience – which tends to address questions of achievement, cognitive capacities, and developmental challenges within the brain – being used to obfuscate more pressing social and economic contexts of young people (Blakemore, 2012; Pitts-Taylor 2010). While we are attentive to the current privileged status of neuroscience in explanations of human behavior, our aim is not to undermine the validity of neuroeducation. Rather, it is to explore the values, motivations, and vehicles of communication facilitating and underlying the imperative for knowledge translation between neuroscience researchers, policy makers, and teachers, and as such to study one instance of how neuroscience has come to impose specific claims on us in our everyday lives.

Critical Neuroscience: A Tool to Analyze the Adolescent Brain in Its Cultural Contexts

Critical neuroscience offers a useful vantage point and a set of tools to understand the limits and potentials of applying neuroscience to education, as well as the political and cultural contexts in which the translation of this form of evidence is favored. Established a decade ago by philosophers, anthropologists, and psychiatrists engaged with cognitive neuroscientists, the label "critical neuroscience," was coined to capture a productive tension. The title represented the need to respond to the surge of the neurosciences and the surrounding revolutionary rhetoric, without either celebrating the field uncritically or undermining it wholesale. Rather, one objective has been to open up a space of reflexive, unconstrained inquiry for researchers from multiple backgrounds to be able to scrutinize methodological problems, translational trends, and controversies, while remaining alert to the political contexts of the institution of neuroscience itself (Choudhury & Slaby, 2012).

The other objective has been to draw from the methods and perspectives of several disciplines in the human sciences to attend to the many layers of behavioral phenomena, categories of personhood, development, or mental disorder that are studied through neuroscience and to widen the lens beyond the location of neural correlates or association with particular brain networks (Choudhury et al., 2009). By maintaining close engagement with neuroscience and developing new modes of interdisciplinary collaboration, critical neuroscience researchers have attempted to bring into view the social and cultural contexts in which behaviors, developmental trajectories, and disorders occur; to nuance the ways in which the social context of the person is operationalized in the laboratory; and to begin to investigate how "meaning and mechanism" interact to give rise to behaviors (Kirmayer & Gold, 2012).

Critical neuroscience constitutes a heterogeneous set of conceptual and methodological tools, and does not apply one particular mode of "critique." However, it does make explicit, in common with the Frankfurt School, for example, a spirit of historico-political mission, in the sense that it acknowledges that scientific inquiry into human reality tends to mobilize specific values and often works in the service of interests that come to shape construals of nature or "naturalness." These notions of nature or of what counts as natural, whether referring to constructs of gender, emotion, mental disorder, normal brain development, or other key human traits or capacities, require unpacking. Without reflective scrutiny, they can appear as inevitable givens, universal and below history, and are seen as a form of "normative facticity," imposing specific demands on us and our conduct in everyday life (see Hartmann, 2012). Maintaining close engagement with neuroscience is on the one hand crucial for building accurately informed analyses of the societal implications of neuroscience, while on the other hand, providing a connection, a reflexive interface, through which historical, anthropological, philosophical, and sociological analysis can feed back into research practice and provide critical as well as creative potential for experimental research in the laboratory. The metaphor of the *looping journey* – of that which is taken to be a "brain fact" – can help to operationalize critique, opening up possibilities for layering, or assembling, a given brain-based phenomenon (see Figure 14.1). Whether we focus on the neural basis of addiction, depression, adolescence, culture, gender, morality, or violence, the journey can be traced using multiple methodologies, from the point of a theme's entry into – and treatment in – the lab, through various experimental and technical practices, to the interaction with the media and policy, to its engagement with various publics. What we mean by a "brain fact" is not a thing-in-itself, but a specifically conceptualized phenomenon or "local resistance" that emerges from the collective practices and directed cognition of neuroscientists working in a community at a given time and in a given context (Choudhury et al., 2009).

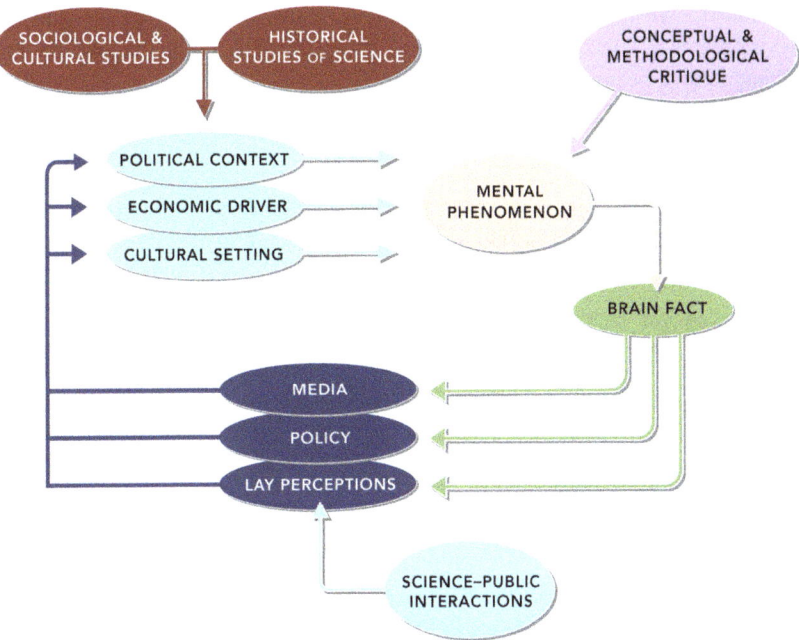

Figure 14.1 Critical neuroscience and the looping journey of the "brain fact." Adapted with permission from Springer Nature Customer Service Centre GmbH: Springer Nature, *BioSocieties*, "Critical neuroscience: Linking neuroscience and society through critical practice," S. Choudhury, S. K. Nagel, and J. Slaby. Copyright 2009 by the London School of Economics and Political Science

One particular objective for critical neuroscience has been to investigate the epistemological dilemmas and ethical questions surrounding the translation of new brain data into areas of society involved in mental health and social policy and to scrutinize "the subtle relationship and feedback loops between popular opinion or ideologies about the brain and findings in neuroscience" (Slaby & Choudhury, 2018, p. 357). The area of neuroeducation provides an opportunity to explore the ways in which changing conceptions of the brain embedded in new forms of everyday practice and policies regarding young people are influencing how medicalized societies view development, health, and illness during adolescence, and to understand the tensions and dilemmas surrounding the translation of neuroscience in society.

Over the past decades, brain-based explanations have become increasingly salient beyond neuroscience, in social theory, public policy, and everyday lay parlance. We suggest that *neuroplasticity* has been the most powerful enabling concept in the "neuro-turn" and the movement of "neuro-talk" beyond the laboratory. We argue that adolescent brains, understood through the lens of developmental cognitive neuroscience to be particularly plastic during the lifespan, have become mirrors which reflect societal anxieties about the future and simultaneously canvases on which we can project hopes about remedies and reinvention, and concretely, a locus of social and medical intervention. Positioned between a critical stance and optimism about the potential of neuroscience, our aim is to understand the cultural contexts in which the mobilization of (interpretations of) neuroplasticity are made possible.

Plastic Brains, Liminal Lives

Plasticity is the dominant enabling concept for the neuroeducation movement. In the broadest sense, plasticity refers to any capacity on the part of a living thing to experience enduring change in response to signals from its milieu. The change in question could be behavioral, physiological, morphological, or neurological, and the plastic changes that unfold in humans over the course of development and continue throughout adulthood encompass all four dimensions. Plasticity is a pervasive feature of the living world, but plasticity as the term is used in developmental neuroscience and neuroeducation has a more specific sense: the capacity for synaptic remodeling in the central nervous system and above all in the brain. In principle, synaptic plasticity is value-neutral: It can be adaptive or maladaptive. But for proponents of neuroeducation, plasticity is, if not free of dangers, then at least intrinsically positive. It is synaptic plasticity that makes it possible to mitigate the developmental and social effects of poverty, inequality, marginalization, and violence with interventions that target the individual child and maintain the hope that these changes will backpropagate to society at large.

In the popular imagination, plasticity is an exuberant tendency toward excitatory synaptogenesis, an uncontrolled proliferation of neural connectivity. Metaphors of trees, hedges, and bushes are frequently used by neuroscientists to convey the processes of cellular changes in the developing brain (e.g., Blakemore & Frith, 2004). In reality, of course, things are more complex. "Brain plasticity," as Sherwood and Gómez-Robles put it, "refers to the way synaptic connections, axon fiber pathways, and the mapping of the cerebral cortex can change during the lifespan in response to the environment and experience" (Sherwood & Gómez-Robles, 2017, p. 401). It encompasses excitatory and inhibitory synaptogenesis, along with synaptic pruning, complex developmental arcs that incorporate widespread synaptogenesis followed by pruning, axon pathfinding and myelination, the formation of secondary and tertiary gyri and sulci, and the epigenetic modulation of gene complexes implicated in synapse turnover, neuro- and gliogenesis, and motor development, including *FOX2*, *SRGAP2*, and *BDNF* (Raichlen & Polk, 2013;

Sherwood & Gómez-Robles, 2017). Humans exhibit markedly greater post-gestational brain plasticity relative both to other primates and to eutherians broadly. This is partly an evolutionary response to anatomical and energetic constraints on hominin encephalization – obstetrically and metabolically it is not possible for brain development to unfold in utero to the same degree in humans as in other mammals. But it also represents part of a broader adaptive complex for an elongated life history with an extended period of social and motor development in childhood and adolescence. That is, human brains continue to develop well past sexual maturity not simply because they are so big and energetically expensive, but because postponing development is adaptive. To an uncommon degree, the human nervous system is shaped by social contact and sensorimotor exploration. The brain (or rather, the body including the nervous system) "builds itself to be enculturated" (Sherwood & Gómez-Robles, 2017, p. 400). Plasticity is not uniform across the developmental arc. Synaptogenesis peaks early, while myelination accelerates in late adolescence and continues into adulthood, perhaps supporting the development of executive control and perspective-taking (Blakemore & Choudhury, 2006). Observations of social and motor development in foraging communities, where the pace of skills acquisition is not imposed via schooling, suggest that cognitive development is punctuated (MacDonald, 2007), a view that has been corroborated by longitudinal imaging studies.

Of course, we must be careful not to think of cognitive development as unfolding in a vacuum – bodies are not vessels for brains, rather brains are instruments of bodily adaptation to environmental change over epochs too short for the kinds of plastic strategies outlined above (Berson, 2015; Cosmelli & Thompson, 2010; Ingold, 2004). The punctuated nature of developmental sensitivity, whether to the acquisition of motor or of social skills, is driven not simply by innate neurodevelopmental schemas but by developmentally salient changes in a young person's body and environment. As such, adolescence has come to be viewed as a "sensitive window" for social cognitive development (Blakemore, 2018) as well as for biological embedding of culture (Worthman & Trang, 2018). The fact that brain development is shaped by cultural ecology is amply demonstrated by the case of sleep strategies, which vary widely with features of the social and sensorikinetic environments (Worthman, 2011).

It is not difficult to see how a basic awareness of neural altriciality and the significance of plasticity for development, even (or especially) if wrong in the details, would inspire educators to see their role as one of shaping brains. Adolescence in particular, the period when executive control and perspective-taking come to the fore in social development, has acquired a status as a delicate liminal time. In an evolutionary sense, adolescence *is* a liminal period, an elongated transition from juvenility to maturity whose benefits – the enhanced social cognition and group-orientedness that are essential to cooperative provision and cooperative childrearing – are accompanied by new risks including those of mental disorder such as schizophrenia, which is now increasingly understood as a disorder of developmental plasticity (Miller et al., 2012).

The model of the "teen brain" serves to reinforce the cultural view of adolescence as a moment of becoming, a transitional period at the threshold, characterized by heightened sensitivity to the surrounding world, susceptibility to risk, but also potency and potential for undoing and remaking. Neuroplasticity brings a material layer to this liminal window of life, fusing the temporal frames of what was, what is, and what could be, in the adolescent's life, through the highly flexible cortex. Located at the threshold between the body and world, the adolescent cortex is defined – in line with how bodies of certain populations including children, women, and colonized peoples have been viewed through biology as "porous" since the nineteenth century (Choudhury & McKinney, 2013; Otis, 2000) – in terms of a "permeable" cortical boundary, open to environmental infiltration and subsequent neural changes. The adolescent brain is therefore simultaneously a target for social media start-ups looking to hook the most "vulnerable" and impressionable population of digital consumers and also a group of greatest potential to be steered back "on track" through educational interventions such as mindfulness practices.

Conclusion

Mindfulness, with its goal to sculpt the developing brain toward resiliency and moral/ethical development, stands as one neuroeducational antidote to the risks of the unstable real and virtual worlds in which adolescents are maturing. In earlier work, we have proposed that the phenomenon of brain-based mindfulness programs in schools arises as one instance of a wider cultural dissatisfaction and moral panic about social ills from digital addiction to loneliness, in which "Eastern" ideas have found new resonance in the "West" and in particular within Western biomedicine (Harrington, 2008; Sánchez-Allred & Choudhury, 2016). The appeal of secular, neuroscience-backed mindfulness meditation as an educational intervention lies in its prioritizing of compassion and self-regulation over academic achievement and competition. These virtues are understood as visualizable, measurable, and fundamental processes in the seat of self-control in the brain, which serves as a plastic, material substrate on which to project these hopes and goals for the lives of young people and a site on which to effect the necessary changes. In a cultural context in which it has become an ethical imperative to deploy one's brain in ways that preserve psychological health (Malabou, 2005/2010; Pitts-Taylor, 2010; Rees, 2010), the adolescent brain and the goals for its metamorphosis reflect both social anxieties about our futures as well as the ways in which we orient ourselves toward science to structure our everyday lives.

REFERENCES

Battro, A. M., Fischer, K. W., & Léna, P. J. (Eds.). (2008). *The educated brain: Essays in neuroeducation.* Cambridge University Press. https://doi.org/10.1017/CBO9780511489907

Berson, J. (2015). *Computable bodies: Instrumented life and the human somatic niche.* Bloomsbury.

Blakemore, S.-J. (2012). Development of the social brain in adolescence. *Journal of the Royal Society of Medicine, 105*(3), 111–16. https://doi.org/10.1258/jrsm.2011.110221

Blakemore, S.-J. (2018). Avoiding social risk in adolescence. *Current Directions in Psychological Science, 27*(2), 116–22. https://doi.org/10.1177/0963721417738144

Blakemore, S.-J., & Choudhury, S. (2006). Development of the adolescent brain: Implications for executive function and social cognition. *Journal of Child Psychology and Psychiatry, 47*(3–4), 296–312. https://doi.org/10.1111/j.1469-7610.2006.01611.x

Blakemore, S.-J., & Frith, U. (2004). How does the brain deal with the social world? *NeuroReport, 15*(1), 119–28. https://doi.org/10.1097/00001756-200401190-00024

Bowles, N. (2017, December 4). Where Silicon Valley is going to get in touch with its soul. *The New York Times.* www.nytimes.com/

Choudhury, S., & McKinney, K. A. (2013). Digital media, the developing brain and the interpretive plasticity of neuroplasticity. *Transcultural Psychiatry, 50*(2), 192–215. https://doi.org/10.1177/1363461512474623

Choudhury, S., Nagel, S. K., & Slaby, J. (2009). Critical neuroscience: Linking neuroscience and society through critical practice. *BioSocieties, 4*(1), 61–77. https://doi.org/10.1017/S1745855209006437

Choudhury, S., & Slaby, J. (Eds.). (2012). *Critical neuroscience: A handbook of the social and cultural contexts of neuroscience.* Wiley-Blackwell. https://doi.org/10.1002/9781444343359

Cosmelli, D., & Thompson, E. (2010). Embodiment or envatment? Reflections on the bodily basis of consciousness. In J. Stewart, O. Gapenne, & E. A. Di Paolo (Eds.), *Enaction: Toward a new paradigm for cognitive science* (pp. 361–85). MIT Press. https://doi.org/10.7551/mitpress/9780262014601.003.0014

Fischer, K. W. (2009). Mind, brain, and education: Building a scientific groundwork for learning and teaching. *Mind, Brain, and Education, 3*(1), 3–16. https://doi.org/10.1111/j.1751-228X.2008.01048.x

Fricke, L., & Choudhury, S. (2011). Neuropolitik und plastische Gehirne. Eine Fallstudie des adoleszenten Gehirns. *Deutsche Zeitschrift für Philosophie Zweimonatsschrift der internationalen philosophischen Forschung, 59*(3), 391–402. https://doi.org/10.1524/dzph.2011.0032

Fuhrmann, D., Knoll, L. J., & Blakemore, S. J. (2015). Adolescence as a sensitive period of brain development. *Trends in Cognitive Sciences, 19*(10), 558–66. https://doi.org/10.1016/j.tics.2015.07.008

Giedd, J. N., Blumenthal, J., Jeffries, N. O., Castellanos, F. X., Liu, H., Zijdenbos, A., Paus, T., Evans, A. C., & Rapoport, J. L. (1999). Brain development during childhood and adolescence: A longitudinal MRI study. *Nature Neuroscience, 2*(10), 861–3. https://doi.org/10.1038/13158

Goswami, U. (2006). Neuroscience and education: From research to practice? *Nature Reviews Neuroscience, 7*(5), 406–13. https://doi.org/10.1038/nrn1907

Harrington, A. (2008). *The cure within: A history of mind-body medicine.* W.W. Norton.

Hartmann, M. (2012). Against first nature: Critical theory and neuroscience. In S. Choudhury & J. Slaby (Eds.), *Critical neuroscience: A handbook of the social and cultural contexts of neuroscience* (pp. 67–84). Wiley-Blackwell.

Howard-Jones, P. A. (2009). Scepticism is not enough. *Cortex, 45*(4), 550–1. https://doi.org/10.1016/j.cortex.2008.06.002

Ingold, T. (2004). Culture on the ground: The world perceived through the feet. *Journal of Material Culture, 9*(3), 315–40. https://doi.org/10.1177%2F1359183504046896

Kirmayer, L. J., & Gold, I. (2012). Re-socializing psychiatry: Critical neuroscience and the limits of reductionism. In S. Choudhury & J. Slaby (Eds.), *Critical neuroscience: A handbook of the social and cultural contexts of neuroscience* (pp. 307–30). Wiley-Blackwell.

MacDonald, K. (2007). Cross-cultural comparison of learning in human hunting: Implications for life history evolution. *Human Nature, 18*(4), 386–402. https://doi.org/10.1007/s12110-007-9019-8

Malabou, C. (2010). *Plasticity at the dusk of writing: Dialectic, destruction, deconstruction* (C. Shread, Trans.). Columbia University Press. (Original work published 2005) https://doi.org/10.7312/mala14524

Maxwell, B., & Racine, E. (2012). The ethics of neuroeducation: Research, practice and policy. *Neuroethics, 5*(2), 101–3. https://doi.org/10.1007/s12152-012-9156-6

Miller, D. J., Duka, T., Stimpson, C. D., Schapiro, S. J., Baze, W. B, McArthur, M. J., Fobbs, A. J., Sousa, A. M. M., Šestan, N., Wildman, D. E., Lipovich, L., Kuzawa, C. W., Hof, P. R., & Sherwood, C. C. (2012). Prolonged myelination in human neocortical evolution. *Proceedings of the National Academy of Sciences of the United States of America, 109*(41), 16480–5. https://doi.org/10.1073/pnas.1117943109

Orben, A., & Przybylski, A. K. (2019). The association between adolescent well-being and digital technology use. *Nature Human Behaviour, 3*, 173–82. https://doi.org/10.1016/j.jaac.2019.06.017

Organisation for Economic Co-operation and Development (OECD). (2002). *Understanding the brain: Towards a new learning science.* OECD. https://doi.org/10.1787/9789264174986-en

Otis, L. (2000). *Membranes: Metaphors of invasion in nineteenth-century literature, science, and politics.* Johns Hopkins University Press.

Pitts-Taylor, V. (2010). The plastic brain: Neoliberalism and the neuronal self. *Health, 14*(6), 635–52. https://doi.org/10.1177/1363459309360796

Raichlen, D. A., & Polk, J. D. (2013). Linking brains and brawn: Exercise and the evolution of human neurobiology. *Proceedings of the Royal Society B: Biological Sciences, 280*(1750), 20122250. https://doi.org/10.1098/rspb.2012.2250

Rees, T. (2010). Being neurologically human today: Life and science and adult cerebral plasticity (An ethical analysis). *American Ethnologist, 37*(1), 150–66. https://doi.org/10.1111/j.1548-1425.2010.01247.x

Rose, S. (2005). *The future of the brain: The promise and perils of tomorrow's neuroscience.* Oxford University Press.

Sánchez-Allred, A., & Choudhury, S. (2016). The imperative to shape young brains: Mindfulness as a neuroeducational intervention. In J. Pykett, R. Jones & M. Whitehead (Eds.), *Psychological governance and public policy: Governing the mind, brain and behaviour* (pp. 116–35). Routledge.

Sherwood, C. C., & Gómez-Robles, A. (2017). Brain plasticity and human evolution. *Annual Review of Anthropology, 46*, 399–419. https://doi.org/10.1146/annurev-anthro-102215-100009

Singer, N., & Ivory, D. (2017, November 3). How Silicon Valley plans to conquer the classroom. *The New York Times.* www.nytimes.com/2017/11/03/technology/silicon-valley-baltimore-schools.html

Slaby, J., & Choudhury, S. (2018). Proposal for a critical neuroscience. In M. Meloni, J. Cromby, D. Fitzgerald, & S. Lloyd (Eds.), *The Palgrave handbook of biology and society* (pp. 341–70). Palgrave Macmillan. https://doi.org/10.1057/978-1-137-52879-7_15

Tallis, R. (2004). *Why the mind is not a computer: A pocket lexicon of neuromythology.* Imprint Academic.

Thomson, J. M., Leong, V., & Goswami, U. (2013). Auditory processing interventions and developmental dyslexia: A comparison of phonemic and rhythmic approaches. *Reading and Writing, 26*(2), 139–61. https://doi.org/10.1007/s11145-012-9359-6

Weisberg, D. S., Keil, F. C., Goodstein, J., Rawson, E., & Gray, J. R. (2008). The seductive allure of neuroscience explanations. *Journal of Cognitive Neuroscience, 20*(3), 470–77. https://doi.org/10.1162/jocn.2008.20040

Whitehead, M., Jones, R., Lilley, R., Pykett, J., & Howell, R. (2017). *Neuroliberalism: Behavioural government in the twenty-first century.* Routledge.

Worthman, C. M. (2011). Developmental cultural ecology of sleep. In M. El-Sheikh (Ed.), *Sleep and development: Familial and socio-cultural considerations* (pp. 167–94). Oxford University Press. https://doi.org/10.1093/acprof:oso/9780195395754.003.0008

Worthman, C. M., & Trang, K. (2018). Dynamics of body time, social time and life history at adolescence. *Nature, 554*(7693), 451–7. https://doi.org/10.1038/nature25750

15 The Reward of Musical Emotions and Expectations

Benjamin P. Gold and Robert J. Zatorre

Across millennia of coexistence and coevolution, humans have discovered and developed a lot to love about music. We include it in social gatherings, important life events, sports games, advertisements, and more, associating it with the social cohesion, memories, and identities they offer. But why include it in the first place? Out of the many valuable aspects of music for humans, there must be a fundamental one that accounts for its existence independently of its association with other rewarding experiences.

The predominant reason people give for listening to music is to express and manage emotions, both one's own and those of others (Lonsdale & North, 2011; Saarikallio & Erkkilä, 2007; Sloboda & O'Neill, 2001). Music is remarkably capable of eliciting strong emotional responses, even when unfamiliar, and despite the absence of any explicit reference to external emotion-provoking events (Bogert et al., 2016; Brattico & Pearce, 2013; Brattico et al., 2016; Huron, 2006; Juslin & Laukka, 2004; Mas-Herrero et al., 2013; Meyer, 1956; North et al., 2000; Salimpoor et al., 2009; Vuoskoski et al., 2011). These responses tend to be highly pleasurable, even for nominally negative emotions like sadness (Brattico et al., 2016; Vuoskoski et al., 2011).

But how to explain the pleasure induced by abstract patterns of sounds which need not have any external referent to generate their strong sensations? One of the major neuroscientific findings pertaining to music in the last few years has been the demonstration that much of the pleasure derived from it is mediated by the brain's reward system. This system includes the ventral tegmental area in the brainstem, the nucleus accumbens, caudate, amygdala, orbitofrontal cortex, and other structures (Koelsch, 2014), and has been extensively characterized in various animal species as well as in humans (Berridge & Kringelbach, 2008). Dopamine transmission within these structures is known to mediate responses to biologically significant inputs such as food and sexual stimuli, as well as certain drugs (e.g., cocaine, amphetamine, nicotine). The reward system's engagement in music was first demonstrated in a study in which listeners were exposed to music that they selected as inducing highly pleasurable chills (Blood et al., 1999). Subsequent studies confirmed not only that the reward system was active during musical pleasure, but also that it involves dopamine (Salimpoor et al., 2011), and that it unfolds in two phases: one during anticipation of peak pleasure, and a second one during the experience of the peak pleasure itself. In addition, the response of the reward system to music has now been shown to be coupled to the response of perceptual areas of the brain, including the auditory cortex (Salimpoor et al., 2013), leading to the idea that perceptual analysis, and computation of expectancies carried out in these cortical areas, interacts with the reward system's computation of the value of a stimulus. When reward-system activity is directly manipulated, using either brain stimulation techniques (Mas-Herrero et al., 2018) or pharmacology (Ferreri et al., 2019), musical pleasure can be affected. That is, when the reward system is stimulated it leads to greater pleasure experiences, and greater physiological arousal, whereas when it is inhibited, people report less pleasure and experience less arousal. Thus, there is a direct, causal link between dopaminergic activity in the reward system and both subjective and objective indicators of musical pleasure.

Emotions often emerge from expectations, like the excitement of anticipation or the disappointment of a worse-than-expected outcome (Burgdorf & Panksepp, 2006; Wilson et al., 1989). Expectations are therefore central to several forms of cultural and aesthetic practices, such as humor (Franklin and Adams, 2011), visual art (Van de Cruys & Wagemans, 2011), and poetry (Wassiliwizky et al., 2017). Yet out of all of these, music is perhaps the most suited to elicit and exploit expectations. Unconstrained by linguistic or visual semantics, it relies instead on purely abstract structures like melody or rhythm, and manipulating them as it unfolds over time. Even newborns have musical expectations, evident from their neural "mismatch" responses when those expectations are violated (Partanen et al., 2013; Virtala et al., 2013), and converging evidence suggests that such violations are often responsible for music's most emotional and pleasurable moments (Egermann et al., 2013; Gold et al., 2019a; Grewe et al., 2007; Huron, 2006; Meyer, 1956; Sloboda, 1991; Steinbeis et al., 2006).

In addition to emotional reactions, surprises can also induce strong physiological responses such as shivers down the spine, or "chills" (Egermann et al., 2013; Grewe et al., 2007; Sloboda, 1991; Steinbeis et al., 2006), which are characterized by intense pleasure, increased sweat gland activity (i.e., skin conductance), faster and shallower heart beats, faster breathing, and lower skin temperatures (Salimpoor et al., 2009), all of which may be considered signs of emotional arousal.

While pleasurable music generally increases dopamine transmission in the nucleus accumbens, caudate, and putamen, chills do so to a greater extent, commensurate with their peak physiological and emotional effects (Salimpoor et al., 2011). Similarly, two recent studies show the specific engagement of the nucleus accumbens after pleasurable musical surprises (Gold et al., 2019b; Shany et al., 2019). Even anticipating such peak moments in music elicits physiological and dopaminergic caudate activity (Salimpoor et al., 2011). Together, these findings demonstrate how effectively music can exploit expectations to rewarding, emotional, and pleasurable effect, implicating this mechanism as the central reward of music listening.

The Power of Predictions and Their Errors

When music manipulates our expectations, it acts on a fundamental neural process. Across many brain networks, processes as diverse as perception, language comprehension, memory, cognitive control, goal orientation, and decision-making rely on making, evaluating, and updating predictions (reviewed in den Ouden et al., 2012). Recent theories posit that this "predictive coding" allows us to represent the world around us efficiently by maintaining and refining an internal model of it, rather than responding to every stimulus at every time devoid of any context (Clark, 2013; Friston, 2005). Our specific predictions are thus model-derived hypotheses such that we can engage in specific model updates based on their errors.

Electrophysiological recordings of nonhuman animals evince prediction errors in the dopamine neurons projecting from the ventral tegmental area to the nucleus accumbens, especially when the predictions concern an adaptive goal like obtaining food (Fiorillo et al., 2003; Schultz et al., 1997), that ultimately modulate the strengths of local and long-range connections (den Ouden et al., 2010; Frank et al., 2004). These signals are often accompanied by activity in the brain's reward system, especially the nucleus accumbens (Chase et al., 2015), and strong emotional and physiological arousal (Menon et al., 2007; Seymour et al., 2005). If the cue that triggered the prediction reoccurs but its outcome remains uncertain, the same neurons ramp up their activity in anticipation, apparently driving attention and motivation toward learning about potential rewards and their antecedents (Anselme, 2013; Fiorillo et al., 2003; Pearce & Hall, 1980).

Consistent with the adaptiveness of learning about one's surroundings, people are willing to pay considerable amounts of money to learn how likely they are to receive a reward – even when that knowledge has no effect on the reward delivery (Bennett et al., 2016; Brydevall et al., 2018). These findings suggest that information is valuable in and of itself; accordingly, both anticipating and receiving information – even about nonrewards such as neutral or unpleasant stimuli – elicits dopamine transmission and motivates decision-making (Bromberg-Martin & Hikosaka, 2009; Bromberg-Martin et al., 2010;

Brydevall et al., 2018; Jepma et al., 2012; Kang et al., 2009; Oudeyer et al., 2016; Ripollés et al., 2014).

This type of learning is a constant process, not just because the environment is constantly changing but also because it behooves us to incorporate new information gradually, rather than rapidly adapting to every new event. In the predictive coding framework, this occurs through precision weighting, wherein the strength of a prediction error is modulated by its precision, or confidence (Friston, 2008). We therefore exhibit larger prediction errors when more confident predictions are thwarted, and smaller prediction errors when more uncertain ones are, even if the predictions themselves are identical (Kanai et al., 2015; Koelsch et al., 2019; Lumaca et al., 2019). As a result, correct but uncertain predictions also yield prediction errors, updating the validity of the prediction to improve one's world model.

Prediction Errors in Music: Learning, Reward, and Optimization

An ever-changing environment – like the world around us, or the microcosm of music – offers ample opportunities to improve incorrect predictions and validate uncertain-but-correct ones. As musical structures repeat, evolve, and interconnect, we can continuously predict, evaluate, and learn. We might have only imprecise predictions about the first motif in an unfamiliar piece of music, experiencing relatively small prediction errors as a result. Yet when it repeats, our predictions are more confident. This second motif could be a play on the first, as in the call-and-response pattern typical across many musical genres, likely causing a larger prediction error than the first one in the process. Or it could repeat exactly and then change, as in the "AAB" structure of blues music, and validate the motivic prediction that was just updated. And how will the rhythm and harmony interact with it? Similar manipulations often occur over other timescales, too, as in the exposition–development–recapitulation form of a classical sonata, or the verse–chorus–verse–chorus–bridge form of a pop song. In each case, as the piece progresses, so do our predictions, enabling the music to guide and (sometimes) misguide us as we listen.

Like language, every musical system has statistical regularities, or likelihoods and rules about which events can follow others and with what probability. By gradually updating precision-weighted prediction errors, our brains become remarkably sensitive to such musical syntax (Barascud et al., 2016; Bigand et al., 2003; Partanen et al., 2013; Virtala et al., 2013). Listeners exhibit neural mismatch responses to contextually unusual notes or chords even in the absence of explicit attention (Omigie et al., 2013; Partanen et al., 2013; Pearce et al., 2010; Virtala et al., 2013); they also report stronger expectations for likelier chords (Bigand et al., 2003; Hansen & Pearce, 2014). Befitting the learning process, listeners can even internalize the structure of a novel artificial musical syntax within as little as an hour (Loui & Wessel, 2008; Loui et al., 2009). Once they do so, they can identify beyond chance which novel musical sequences are emblematic of the artificial grammar, they have better memory for musical sequences that follow it, and they come to exhibit neural mismatch responses that distinguish syntactically likely versus unlikely notes just as during naturalistic music listening (Loui et al., 2009).

Statistical learning is the means by which we learn the statistical structure of sensory environments, and by extension, musical regularities (Perruchet & Pacton, 2006; Saffran et al., 1999). This mechanism is thought to be a basic and implicit ability of the human mind, applicable to language as well as to music, and expressing itself even in infancy (Perruchet & Pacton, 2006; Saffran et al., 1999). Statistical learning can also help to explain cross-cultural differences in music processing. Listeners best remember and best understand the statistical regularities in music of their own culture, and are also more knowledgeable about music from a familiar foreign culture than that from an unfamiliar one (Demorest et al., 2008; Krumhansl, 2000; Wong et al., 2009). When experimenters disrupt musical structures, this within-culture expertise corresponds to enhanced detection and greater neural mismatch responses for deviations from one's own culture's regularities (Hannon et al., 2012a; Haumann et al., 2018). That this is a causal effect is evident from seven-month-olds, who show no such cultural biases, and one-year-olds, who do, indicating that acculturation may take some time, even if it starts comparatively early. However, the culture specificity can disappear after two weeks of exposure to the foreign musical system (Hannon & Trehub, 2005; Hannon et al., 2012b), showing that a great deal of flexibility still exists, at least at this early age. Moreover, adults undergoing the same procedure as the one-year-olds do not detect disruptions to structures different from those of their own culture after the same amount of exposure as young children, reflecting the many years of experience that make their internal models more robust, but also less flexible – that is, less susceptible to information from the recent past.

Our expectations of music therefore develop over long and short timescales, depending on both our cultural/syntactic knowledge and the particular structure of the piece at hand (Hargreaves & North, 2010). Since we bring a lifetime of musical statistics to every listening experience, even familiar music can surprise us, simply by differing from the rest of the music we have heard. In fact, familiarity allows us to anticipate our favorite musical moments, engaging the dopaminergic reward system (Salimpoor et al., 2011) and building pleasurable excitement (cf. Gebauer et al., 2012; Huron, 2006). Listeners often prefer familiar music, but also that which is prototypical – i.e., in keeping with their existing expectations (Hargreaves & North, 2010; Martindale & Moore, 1989). Yet with very high levels of predictability, music can essentially become boring and lose its appeal (Chmiel & Schubert, 2017; Szpunar et al., 2004). This pattern suggests that musical preferences rely on a balance between validating correct predictions (like the anticipation of an exciting key change that is about to occur) and updating incorrect ones: a sweet spot for learning between the tedium of predictability and the chaos of unpredictability (cf. Berlyne, 1960, 1974; Chmiel & Schubert, 2017; Oudeyer et al., 2016). While the content of these predictions depends on the listener's musical experience, making the same piece subjectively simple to some listeners and complex to others, this interpretation implies that whenever music facilitates our learning of the musical environment, it also evokes the reward value and dopamine transmission associated with anticipating and receiving information (Bromberg-Martin & Hikosaka, 2009; Bromberg-Martin et al., 2010; Brydevall et al., 2018; Jepma et al., 2012; Kang et al., 2009; Oudeyer et al., 2016; Ripollés et al., 2014).

Research on the relationship between musical complexity and pleasure has been mixed, hampered by arbitrary and differing measures of complexity (Chmiel & Schubert, 2017). Using a well-validated computational model of long- and short-term statistical learning (Pearce, 2005), in a recent study we formally represented the predictability of several musical excerpts by computing the likelihood of each note based on the preceding context and the regularities of Western tonal music (Gold et al., 2019a). For a related measure of complexity, we also represented the uncertainty of each piece, based on the precision of the model's predictions. This computational approach allowed us to uncover reliable preferences for music that balanced either predictability or uncertainty. More specifically, we found that listeners particularly liked more surprising music in the context of greater certainty – i.e., larger precision-weighted prediction errors. And they were less fond of equally surprising music during uncertainty, when precision weighting resulted in smaller prediction errors. These findings support the view that musical pleasure capitalizes on the reward of learning, but also point to the critical impact of prior exposure: The model used was first trained on a corpus of music from a particular cultural background; its predictions thus represent those of a listener with a similar background, but not necessarily those with different cultural exposure. This approach, however, suggests an excellent way to formally test the role of knowledge and exposure by manipulating the similarity of the model vs. the listener's training.

Considering the reward of music in terms of learning could explain the emotional impact of musical surprises (Grewe et al., 2007; Huron, 2006; Meyer, 1956; Sloboda, 1991) as powerful learning signals, and the distinct dopaminergic activity before and during peak pleasure moments (Salimpoor et al., 2011) as curious anticipation and evaluation. Although there is considerable evidence that listening to music is in part a learning process

(Barascud et al., 2016; Bigand et al., 2003; Hannon & Trehub, 2005; Hannon et al., 2012b; Loui & Wessel, 2008; Loui et al., 2009), and growing evidence for the intrinsic reward of learning (Bromberg-Martin & Hikosaka, 2009; Bromberg-Martin et al., 2010; Brydevall et al., 2018; Jepma et al., 2012; Kang et al., 2009; Oudeyer et al., 2016; Ripollés et al., 2014), there remains a lot to uncover about the mechanisms linking musical learning and reward. If this learning account is correct, we would expect surprises to elicit rewarding prediction error signals when they facilitate the listener's understanding of the musical environment, as in a sudden resolution of long-brewing tension for instance (cf. Grewe et al., 2007; Sloboda, 1991), but not when they obstruct understanding (see Gebauer et al., 2012; Hansen et al., 2017; Zald & Zatorre, 2011), as in an abrupt new tonality during a short excerpt lacking context (Brattico et al., 2010; Koelsch et al., 2008). Accordingly, we recently revealed that participants experienced negative subjective responses and decreased reward-system activity when listening to music that unexpectedly became scrambled and incomprehensible, whereas they experienced positive subjective responses and positive reward-system activity when music that they expected to become scrambled instead retained its structure (Gold et al., 2019b). This finding is consistent with other research which suggests that surprises are more likely to be pleasant when the context is stable enough for them to be informative and unpleasant otherwise (e.g., Brattico et al., 2010; Egermann et al., 2013; Grewe et al., 2005, 2007; Koelsch et al., 2008; Sloboda, 1991). While these findings are a promising start, there are still many aspects of this account requiring further exploration and validation.

In the context of understanding the interplay between culture, learning, aesthetics, and neural function, we believe that the kind of approach described in this essay provides a means both to generate precise, even quantifiable, testable hypotheses, as well as the means to evaluate them. There are no doubt many other approaches that could also provide meaningful insights into such complex questions. No matter the paradigm, though, it will ultimately be necessary to bridge the gap between biological and cultural influences on human aesthetic judgments, and we believe that the reward-prediction/statistical learning account has much to recommend itself toward this end.

REFERENCES

Anselme, P. (2013). Dopamine, motivation, and the evolutionary significance of gambling-like behaviour. *Behavioural Brain Research*, 256, 1–4. https://doi.org/10.1016/j.bbr.2013.07.039

Barascud, N., Pearce, M. T., Griffiths, T. D., Friston, K. J., & Chait, M. (2016). Brain responses in humans reveal ideal observer-like sensitivity to complex acoustic patterns. *Proceedings of the National Academy of Sciences of the United States of America*, *113*(5), E616–E625. https://doi.org/10.1073/pnas.1508523113

Bennett, D., Bode, S., Brydevall, M., Warren, H., & Murawski, C. (2016). Intrinsic valuation of information in decision making under uncertainty. *PLoS Computational Biology*, *12*(7), e1005020. https://doi.org/10.1371/journal.pcbi.1005020

Berlyne, D. E. (1960). *McGraw-Hill series in psychology. Conflict, arousal, and curiosity*. McGraw-Hill Book Company. https://doi.org/10.1037/11164-000

Berlyne, D. E. (Ed.). (1974). *Studies in the new experimental aesthetics: Steps toward an objective psychology of aesthetic appreciation*. Hemisphere.

Berridge K. C., & Kringelbach, M. L. (2008). Affective neuroscience of pleasure: Reward in humans and animals. *Psychopharmacology*, *199*(3), 457–80. https://doi.org/10.1007/s00213-008-1099-6

Bigand, E., Poulin, B., Tillmann, B., Madurell, F., & D'Adamo, D. A. (2003). Sensory versus cognitive components in harmonic priming. *Journal of Experimental Psychology: Human Perception and Performance*, *29*(1), 159–71. https://doi.org/10.1037/0096-1523.29.1.159

Blood, A. J., Zatorre, R. J., Bermudez, P., & Evans, A. C. (1999). Emotional responses to pleasant and unpleasant music correlate with activity in paralimbic brain regions. *Nature Neuroscience*, *2*(4), 382–7. https://doi.org/10.1038/7299

Bogert, B., Numminen-Kontti, T., Gold, B., Sams, M., Numminen, J., Burunat, I., Lampinen, J., & Brattico, E. (2016). Hidden sources of joy, fear, and sadness: Explicit versus implicit neural processing of musical emotions. *Neuropsychologia*, *89*, 393–402. https://doi.org/10.1016/j.neuropsychologia.2016.07.005

Brattico, E., Bogert, B., Alluri, V., Tervaniemi, M., Eerola, T., & Jacobsen, T. (2016). It's sad but I like it: The neural dissociation between musical emotions and liking in experts and laypersons. *Frontiers in Human Neuroscience*, *9*, 676. https://doi.org/10.3389/fnhum.2015.00676

Brattico, E., Jacobsen, T., De Baene, W., Glerean, E., & Tervaniemi, M. (2010). Cognitive vs. affective listening modes and judgments of music: An ERP study. *Biological Psychology*, *85*(3), 393–409. https://doi.org/10.1016/j.biopsycho.2010.08.014

Brattico, E., & Pearce, M. (2013). The neuroaesthetics of music. *Psychology of Aesthetics, Creativity, and the Arts*, *7*(1), 48–61. https://doi.org/10.1037/a0031624

Bromberg-Martin, E. S., & Hikosaka, O. (2009). Midbrain dopamine neurons signal preference for advance information about upcoming rewards. *Neuron*, *63*(1), 119–26. https://doi.org/10.1016/j.neuron.2009.06.009

Bromberg-Martin, E. S., Matsumoto, M., & Hikosaka, O. (2010). Dopamine in motivational control: Rewarding, aversive, and alerting. *Neuron*, *68*(5), 815–34. https://doi.org/10.1016/j.neuron.2010.11.022

Brydevall, M., Bennett, D., Murawski, C., & Bode, S. (2018). The neural encoding of information prediction errors during non-instrumental information seeking. *Scientific Reports*, *8*(1), 6134. https://doi.org/10.1038/s41598-018-24566-x

Burgdorf, J., & Panksepp, J. (2006). The neurobiology of positive emotions. *Neuroscience & Biobehavioral Reviews*, *30*(2), 173–87. https://doi.org/10.1016/j.neubiorev.2005.06.001

Chase, H. W., Kumar, P., Eickhoff, S. B., & Dombrovski, A. Y. (2015). Reinforcement learning models and their neural correlates: An activation likelihood estimation meta-analysis. *Cognitive, Affective, & Behavioral Neuroscience, 15*(2), 435–59. https://doi.org/10.3758/s13415-015-0338-7

Chmiel, A., & Schubert, E. (2017). Back to the inverted-U for music preference: A review of the literature. *Psychology of Music, 45*(6), 886–909. https://doi.org/10.1177%2F0305735617697507

Clark, A. (2013). Whatever next? Predictive brains, situated agents, and the future of cognitive science. *Behavioral and Brain Sciences, 36*(3), 181–204. https://doi.org/10.1017/S0140525X12000477

Demorest, S. M., Morrison, S. J., Jungbluth, D., & Beken, M. N. (2008). Lost in translation: An enculturation effect in music memory performance. *Music Perception, 25*(3), 213–23. https://doi.org/10.1525/mp.2008.25.3.213

den Ouden, H. E. M., Daunizeau, J., Roiser, J., Friston, K. J., & Stephan, K. E. (2010). Striatal prediction error modulates cortical coupling. *Journal of Neuroscience, 30*(9), 3210–19. https://doi.org/10.1523/JNEUROSCI.4458-09.2010

den Ouden, H. E. M., Kok, P., & de Lange, F. P. (2012). How prediction errors shape perception, attention, and motivation. *Frontiers in Psychology, 3*, 548. https://doi.org/10.3389/fpsyg.2012.00548

Egermann, H., Pearce, M. T., Wiggins, G. A., & McAdams, S. (2013). Probabilistic models of expectation violation predict psychophysiological emotional responses to live concert music. *Cognitive, Affective, & Behavioral Neuroscience, 13*(3), 533–53. https://doi.org/10.3758/s13415-013-0161-y

Ferreri, L., Mas-Herrero, E., Zatorre, R. J., Ripollés, P., Gomez-Andres, A., Alicart, H., Olivé, G., Marco-Pallarés, J., Antonijoan, R. M., Valle, M., Riba, J., & Rodriguez-Fornells, A. (2019). Dopamine modulates the reward experiences elicited by music. *Proceedings of the National Academy of Sciences of the United States of America, 116*(9), 3793–8. https://doi.org/10.1073/pnas.1811878116

Fiorillo, C. D., Tobler, P. N., & Schultz, W. (2003). Discrete coding of reward probability and uncertainty by dopamine neurons. *Science, 299*(5614), 1898–902. https://doi.org/10.1126/science.1077349

Frank, M. J., Seeberger, L. C., & O'Reilly, R. C. (2004). By carrot or by stick: Cognitive reinforcement learning in parkinsonism. *Science, 306*(5703), 1940–3. https://doi.org/10.1126/science.1102941

Franklin, R. G., Jr., & Adams, R. B., Jr. (2011). The reward of a good joke: Neural correlates of viewing dynamic displays of stand-up comedy. *Cognitive, Affective, & Behavioral Neuroscience, 11*(4), 508–15. https://doi.org/10.3758/s13415-011-0049-7

Friston, K. (2005). A theory of cortical responses. *Philosophical Transactions of the Royal Society B: Biological Sciences, 360*(1456), 815–36. https://doi.org/10.1098/rstb.2005.1622

Friston, K. (2008). Hierarchical models in the brain. *PLoS Computational Biology, 4*(11), e1000211. https://doi.org/10.1371/journal.pcbi.1000211

Gebauer, L., Kringelbach, M. L., & Vuust, P. (2012). Ever-changing cycles of musical pleasure: The role of dopamine and anticipation. *Psychomusicology: Music, Mind, and Brain, 22*(2), 152–67. https://doi.org/10.1037/a0031126

Gold, B. P., Mas-Herrero, E., Zeighami, Y., Benovoy, M., Dagher, A., & Zatorre, R. J. (2019b). Musical reward prediction errors engage the nucleus accumbens and motivate learning. *Proceedings of the National Academy of Sciences of the United States of America, 116*(8), 3310–15. https://doi.org/10.1073/pnas.1809855116

Gold, B. P., Pearce, M. T., Mas-Herrero, E., Dagher, A., & Zatorre, R. J. (2019a). Predictability and uncertainty in the pleasure of music: A reward for learning? Journal of Neuroscience, 39(47), 9397–409. https://doi.org/10.1523/JNEUROSCI.0428-19.2019

Grewe, O., Nagel, F., Kopiez, R., & Altenmüller, E. (2005). How does music arouse "chills"? Investigating strong emotions, combining psychological, physiological, and psychoacoustical methods. Annals of the New York Academy of Sciences, 1060(1), 446–9. https://doi.org/10.1196/annals.1360.041

Grewe, O., Nagel, F., Kopiez, R., & Altenmüller, E. (2007). Listening to music as a re-creative process: Physiological, psychological, and psychoacoustical correlates of chills and strong emotions. Music Perception, 24(3), 297–314. https://doi.org/10.1525/mp.2007.24.3.297

Hannon, E. E., Soley, G., & Ullal, S. (2012a). Familiarity overrides complexity in rhythm perception: A cross-cultural comparison of American and Turkish listeners. Journal of Experimental Psychology: Human Perception and Performance, 38(3), 543–8. https://doi.org/10.1037/a0027225

Hannon, E. E., & Trehub, S. E. (2005). Tuning in to musical rhythms: Infants learn more readily than adults. Proceedings of the National Academy of Sciences of the United States of America, 102(35), 12639–43. https://doi.org/10.1073/pnas.0504254102

Hannon, E. E., Vanden Bosch der Nederlanden, C. M., & Tichko, P. (2012b). Effects of perceptual experience on children's and adults' perception of unfamiliar rhythms. Annals of the New York Academy of Sciences, 1252(1), 92–9. https://doi.org/10.1111/j.1749-6632.2012.06466.x

Hansen, N. C., Dietz, M. J., & Vuust, P. (2017). Commentary: Predictions and the brain: How musical sounds become rewarding. Frontiers in Human Neuroscience, 11, 168. https://doi.org/10.3389/fnhum.2017.00168

Hansen, N. C., & Pearce M. T. (2014). Predictive uncertainty in auditory sequence processing. Frontiers in Psychology, 5, 1052. https://doi.org/10.3389/fpsyg.2014.01052

Hargreaves, D. J., & North, A. C. (2010). Experimental aesthetics and liking for music. In P. N. Juslin & J. A. Sloboda (Eds.), Series in affective science. Handbook of music and emotion: Theory, research, applications (pp. 515–46). Oxford University Press. https://doi.org/10.1093/acprof:oso/9780199230143.003.0019

Haumann, N. T., Vuust, P., Bertelsen, F., & Garza-Villarreal, E. A. (2018). Influence of musical enculturation on brain responses to metric deviants. Frontiers in Neuroscience, 12, 218. https://doi.org/10.3389/fnins.2018.00218

Huron, D. (2006). Sweet anticipation: Music and the psychology of expectation. MIT Press.

Jepma, M., Verdonschot, R. G., van Steenbergen, H., Rombouts, S. A. R. B., & Nieuwenhuis, S. (2012). Neural mechanisms underlying the induction and relief of perceptual curiosity. Frontiers in Behavioral Neuroscience, 6, 5. https://doi.org/10.3389/fnbeh.2012.00005

Juslin, P. N., & Laukka, P. (2004). Expression, perception, and induction of musical emotions: A review and a questionnaire study of everyday listening. Journal of New Music Research, 33(3), 217–38. https://doi.org/10.1080/0929821042000317813

Kanai, R., Komura, Y., Shipp, S., & Friston, K. (2015). Cerebral hierarchies: Predictive processing, precision and the pulvinar. *Philosophical Transactions of the Royal Society B: Biological Sciences, 370*(1668), 20140169. https://doi.org/10.1098/rstb.2014.0169

Kang, M. J., Hsu, M., Krajbich, I. M., Loewenstein, G., McClure, S. M., Wang, J. T.-Y., & Camerer, C. F. (2009). The wick in the candle of learning. *Psychological Science, 20*(8), 963–73. https://doi.org/10.1111/j.1467-9280.2009.02402.x

Koelsch, S. (2014). Brain correlates of music-evoked emotions. *Nature Reviews Neuroscience, 15*(3), 170–80. https://doi.org/10.1038/nrn3666

Koelsch, S., Fritz, T., & Schlaug, G. (2008). Amygdala activity can be modulated by unexpected chord functions during music listening. *NeuroReport, 19*(18), 1815–19. https://doi.org/10.1097/WNR.0b013e32831a8722

Koelsch, S., Vuust, P., & Friston, K. (2019). Predictive processes and the peculiar case of music. *Trends in Cognitive Sciences, 23*(1), 63–77. https://doi.org/10.1016/j.tics.2018.10.006

Krumhansl, C. L. (2000). Rhythm and pitch in music cognition. *Psychological Bulletin, 126*(1), 159–79. https://doi.org/10.1037/0033-2909.126.1.159

Lonsdale, A. J., & North, A. C. (2011). Why do we listen to music? A uses and gratifications analysis. *British Journal of Psychology, 102*(1), 108–34. https://doi.org/10.1348/000712610X506831

Loui, P., & Wessel, D. (2008). Learning and liking an artificial musical system: Effects of set size and repeated exposure. *Musicae Scientiae, 12*(2), 207–30. https://doi.org/10.1177%2F102986490801200202

Loui, P., Wu, E. H., Wessel, D. L., & Knight, R. T. (2009). A generalized mechanism for perception of pitch patterns. *Journal of Neuroscience, 29*(2), 454–9. https://doi.org/10.1523/JNEUROSCI.4503-08.2009

Lumaca, M., Haumann, N. T., Brattico, E., Grube, M., & Vuust, P. (2019). Weighting of neural prediction error by rhythmic complexity: A predictive coding account using mismatch negativity. *European Journal of Neuroscience, 49*(12), 1597–609. https://doi.org/10.1111/ejn.14329

Martindale, C., & Moore, K. (1989). Relationship of musical preference to collative, ecological, and psychophysical variables. *Music Perception, 6*(4), 431–45. https://doi.org/10.2307/40285441

Mas-Herrero, E., Dagher, A., & Zatorre, R. J. (2018). Modulating musical reward sensitivity up and down with transcranial magnetic stimulation. *Nature Human Behavior, 2*, 27–32. https://doi.org/10.1038/s41562-017-0241-z

Mas-Herrero, E., Marco-Pallares, J., Lorenzo-Seva, U., Zatorre, R. J., & Rodriguez-Fornells, A. (2013). Individual differences in music reward experiences. *Music Perception, 31*(2), 118–38. https://doi.org/10.1525/mp.2013.31.2.118

Menon, M., Jensen, J., Vitcu, I., Graff-Guerrero, A., Crawley, A., Smith, M. A., & Kapur, S. (2007). Temporal difference modeling of the blood-oxygen level dependent response during aversive conditioning in humans: Effects of dopaminergic modulation. *Biological Psychiatry, 62*(7), 765–72. https://doi.org/10.1016/j.biopsych.2006.10.020

Meyer, L. B. (1956). *Emotion and meaning in music*. University of Chicago Press.

North, A. C., Hargreaves, D. J., & Mckendrick, J. (2000). The effects of music on atmosphere in a bank and a bar. *Journal of Applied Social Psychology*, *30*(7), 1504–22. https://doi.org/10.1111/j.1559-1816.2000.tb02533.x

Omigie, D., Pearce, M. T., Williamson, V. J., & Stewart, L. (2013). Electrophysiological correlates of melodic processing in congenital amusia. *Neuropsychologia*, *51*(9), 1749–62. https://doi.org/10.1016/j.neuropsychologia.2013.05.010

Oudeyer, P. Y., Gottlieb, J., & Lopes, M. (2016). Intrinsic motivation, curiosity, and learning: Theory and applications in educational technologies. In B. Studer & S. Knecht (Eds.), *Progress in brain research. Motivation: Theory, neurobiology and applications* (Vol. 229, pp. 257–84). Academic Press. https://doi.org/10.1016/bs.pbr.2016.05.005

Partanen, E., Kujala, T., Tervaniemi, M., & Huotilainen, M. (2013). Prenatal music exposure induces long-term neural effects. *PLoS ONE*, *8*(10), e78946. https://doi.org/10.1371/journal.pone.0078946

Pearce, J. M., & Hall, G. (1980). A model for Pavlovian learning: Variations in the effectiveness of conditioned but not of unconditioned stimuli. *Psychological Review*, *87*(6), 532–52. https://doi.org/10.1037/0033-295X.87.6.532

Pearce, M. T. (2005). *The construction and evaluation of statistical models of melodic structure in music perception and composition* [Unpublished doctoral dissertation]. City University London. http://openaccess.city.ac.uk/8459/

Pearce, M. T., Müllensiefen, D., & Wiggins, G. A. (2010). The role of expectation and probabilistic learning in auditory boundary perception: A model comparison. *Perception*, *39*(1), 1365–89. https://doi.org/10.1068%2Fp6507

Perruchet, P., & Pacton, S. (2006). Implicit learning and statistical learning: One phenomenon, two approaches. *Trends in Cognitive Sciences*, *10*(5), 233–8. https://doi.org/10.1016/j.tics.2006.03.006

Ripollés, P., Marco-Pallarés, J., Hielscher, U., Mestres-Missé, A., Tempelmann, C., Heinze, H.-J., Rodríguez-Fornells, A., & Noesselt, T. (2014). The role of reward in word learning and its implications for language acquisition. *Current Biology*, *24*(21), 2606–11. https://doi.org/10.1016/j.cub.2014.09.044

Saarikallio, S., & Erkkilä, J. (2007). The role of music in adolescents' mood regulation. *Psychology of Music*, *35*(1), 88–109. https://doi.org/10.1177%2F0305735607068889

Saffran, J. R., Johnson, E. K., Aslin, R. N., & Newport, E. L. (1999). Statistical learning of tone sequences by human infants and adults. *Cognition*, *70*(1), 27–52. https://doi.org/10.1016/S0010-0277(98)00075-4

Salimpoor, V. N., Benovoy, M., Larcher, K., Dagher, A., & Zatorre, R. J. (2011). Anatomically distinct dopamine release during anticipation and experience of peak emotion to music. *Nature Neuroscience*, *14*(2), 257–62. https://doi.org/10.1038/nn.2726

Salimpoor, V. N., Benovoy, M., Longo, G., Cooperstock, J. R., & Zatorre, R. J. (2009). The rewarding aspects of music listening are related to degree of emotional arousal. *PLoS ONE*, *4*(10), e7487. https://doi.org/10.1371/journal.pone.0007487

Salimpoor, V. N., van den Bosch, I., Kovacevic, N., McIntosh, A. R., Dagher, A., & Zatorre, R. J. (2013). Interactions between the nucleus accumbens and auditory cortices predict music reward value. *Science, 340*(6129), 216–19. https://doi.org/10.1126/science.1231059

Schultz, W., Dayan, P., & Montague, P. R. (1997). A neural substrate of prediction and reward. *Science, 275*(5306), 1593–9. https://doi.org/10.1126/science.275.5306.1593

Seymour, B., O'Doherty, J. P., Koltzenburg, M., Wiech, K., Frackowiak, R., Friston, K., & Dolan, R. (2005). Opponent appetitive-aversive neural processes underlie predictive learning of pain relief. *Nature Neuroscience, 8*(9), 1234–40. https://doi.org/10.1038/nn1527

Shany, O., Singer, N., Gold, B. P., Jacoby, N., Tarrasch, R., Hendler, T., & Granot, R. (2019). Surprise-related activation in the nucleus accumbens interacts with music-induced pleasantness. *Social Cognitive and Affective Neuroscience, 14*(4), 459–70. https://doi.org/10.1093/scan/nsz019

Sloboda, J. A. (1991). Music structure and emotional response: Some empirical findings. *Psychology of Music, 19*(2), 110–20. https://doi.org/10.1177%2F0305735691192002

Sloboda, J. A., & O'Neill, S. A. (2001). Emotions in everyday listening to music. In P. N. Juslin & J. A. Sloboda (Eds.), *Series in affective science. Music and emotion: Theory and research* (pp. 415–29). Oxford University Press.

Steinbeis, N., Koelsch, S., & Sloboda, J. A. (2006). The role of harmonic expectancy violations in musical emotions: Evidence from subjective, physiological, and neural responses. *Journal of Cognitive Neuroscience, 18*(8), 1380–93. https://doi.org/10.1162/jocn.2006.18.8.1380

Szpunar, K. K., Schellenberg, E. G., & Pliner, P. (2004). Liking and memory for musical stimuli as a function of exposure. *Journal of Experimental Psychology: Learning, Memory, and Cognition, 30*(2), 370–81. https://doi.org/10.1037/0278-7393.30.2.370

Van de Cruys, S., & Wagemans, J. (2011). Putting reward in art: A tentative prediction error account of visual art. *i-Perception, 2*(9), 1035–62. https://doi.org/10.1068/i0466aap

Virtala, P., Huotilainen, M., Partanen, E., Fellman, V., & Tervaniemi, M. (2013). Newborn infants' auditory system is sensitive to Western music chord categories. *Frontiers in Psychology, 4*, 492. https://doi.org/10.3389/fpsyg.2013.00492

Vuoskoski, J. K., Thompson, W. F., McIlwain, D., & Eerola, T. (2011). Who enjoys listening to sad music and why? *Music Perception, 29*(3), 311–17. https://doi.org/10.1525/mp.2012.29.3.311

Wassiliwizky, E., Koelsch, S., Wagner, V., Jacobsen, T., & Menninghaus, W. (2017). The emotional power of poetry: Neural circuitry, psychophysiology and compositional principles. *Social Cognitive and Affective Neuroscience, 12*(8), 1229–40. https://doi.org/10.1093/scan/nsx069

Wilson, T. D., Lisle, D. J., Kraft, D., & Wetzel, C. G. (1989). Preferences as expectation-driven inferences: Effects of affective expectations on affective experience. *Journal of Personality and Social Psychology, 56*(4), 519–30. https://doi.org/10.1037/0022-3514.56.4.519

Wong, P. C. M., Roy, A. K., & Margulis, E. H. (2009). Bimusicalism: The implicit dual enculturation of cognitive and affective systems. *Music Perception*, *27*(2), 81–8. https://doi.org/10.1525/mp.2009.27.2.81

Zald, D. H., & Zatorre, R. J. (2011). Music. In J. A. Gottfried (Ed.), *Neurobiology of sensation and reward* (pp. 405–28). CRC Press. www.ncbi.nlm.nih.gov/books/NBK92781/

16 Literary Analysis and Weak Theories

Omri Moses

On a basic level, literature can be said to uncover the importance of context to the way we think. This is true whether we are speaking of narrative fiction, poetry, or drama and whether the context is described or merely implied. Literary texts give us a *mise en scène* in which to apply concepts, understand actions, and evaluate situations and behaviors, helping to reinforce what cultural neuroscience has proven experimentally: that human reasoning is context sensitive. Emerging work in embodied, extended, enactive, and embedded cognition (the so-called 4Es) gives a great deal of weight to the way bodies are oriented and the environment is structured to support and constrain thought. Such work argues that context is not merely a supplement to more basic, abstract conceptual operations that our brains perform innately. We are organisms whose cognitive development depends on the naturally situated way we learn to reason. Researchers promoting this new science inevitably focus more attention than classical neuroscience on cultural and social practices – on the rituals, patterns, and routines that help configure how brains and bodies work together with their environments. Because literature is itself a cultural practice, the 4Es seem particularly well set up to investigate it. Its researchers are simply encouraged to present the literary arts as "tools" that supply us with the naturally situated context we need to practice solving problems that are important to us. Such tools help us get a "grip" on the social world, test our social reasoning skills, practice mind-reading, extend conceptual abstractions to new scenarios, anticipate the direction of thoughts and actions, and enhance other skills that require us to come to terms with changing environments and constantly changing information about them.

The close fit between these new embodied models of mind and the literary-critical emphasis on the pragmatic value of literature is to be celebrated. My sense is that this approach to literary cognition, which examines the forms of inference and sensorimotor awareness we need to understand literary texts, will lead to years of interdisciplinary collaboration and research between scientists and literary critics. But we run into a number of snags when we apply quite general theories of mind to understand literary reading and writing. Many of these candidate theories – some of which I will examine below – such as Gibson's affordance theory and emergent research on predictive processing, are put forward as bridge concepts that capture the broad dynamics of the embodied mind across multiple domains. While such theories are exciting and important – in part because they show how the brain is built to work in local contexts – they are "weak theories," to borrow a phrase from Terence Cave (2016, p. 61), offering breadth and inclusiveness, purchased at the expense of depth. It is not always clear what "applying" them to a domain, such as literature, accomplishes, except as further confirmation of the theory. To my mind, they have not yet succeeded in revealing very interesting things about literature as an object of study.

When used badly or crudely, these theories also misconstrue how we read literature and why. Proponents wielding them often treat reading literature as a cognitive puzzle, not as an emotionally engaging or ethically challenging way of reconstructing the ecology in which we think. This is partly because of the underlying epistemic assumptions that cognitive literary critics borrow from neuroscience as a field and the priority researchers give to functional explanations. Also, because scientists and critics fall back on the cognitive predilections and interpretive dispositions that readers in general might be expected to have, they tend to ignore the shaping force that specific literary objects have on our thinking. Quite simply, they are not culturally specific enough. What we need, then, is a way of using these theories to explore how texts, as artworks, help us extend or redefine the purposes of reading in individual cases.

The results will help us honor the conceptual resources that the 4Es offer, which allow us to treat literature as a culturally and historically variable object with multiple and sometimes indeterminate functions, which are only created through the dynamic encounter between individual readers and individual texts. In this short piece, I would like first to outline some of the ways neuroscientific theories have been applied to literature. Then I will consider how literature might serve as a provocation to cultural neuroscience by helping researchers of the 4Es assess the role that affects and emotions play in our mental lives; understand better how cognitive tasks may alter our value schemes, not just implement them; and consider more accurately the role of aesthetic experience. Literary critics can, in turn, expect to inherit cognitive theories that help us intervene in interpretive controversies, where the question is not only why an average reader might naturally prefer one kind of reading to another (based on general cognitive predispositions, associated brain architecture, or whatever), but also how a specific reader can go about choosing from a variety of plausible readings based on interpretive protocols that are shaped, in part, by the text itself. The goal is to strengthen the bidirectionality of cultural neuroscience's interdisciplinary focus. Instead of approaching the literary arts the way the field of neuroaesthetics does, as reducible to a set of generalized cognitive tasks that our brains need to solve,[1] we can begin to study the way specific literary texts configure our cognitive environment and shape our reading experience by training us to read them in culturally distinctive ways. Thus, we place the brain within a cultural ecosystem that organizes our mental activity, even as we research the brain structures that support such cognitive flexibility and interactiveness in the first place.

Already in the short years since the 4Es have taken off, the field of cognitive literary criticism has begun to apply theories of predictive processing and affordance theory to reflect on narrative handling and genre theory, the literary devices and codes that shape our expectations about how a text will unfold.[2] The assumption is that literary texts are inherently filled with gaps that present obstacles to our understanding, and readers navigate these gaps in part by anticipating the direction of thought and action. Neuroscientists, such as Karl Friston and his colleagues, treat the brain as a hypothesis-tester that uses Bayesian prediction coding or an analogous neurological approximation to process the ongoing supply of information (Friston, 2003). They argue that we make guesses about a situation, coupled with predictions about the likely accuracy of those guesses. For example, as we negotiate uncertainty about what is happening in a text, we adjust the predictions so that they accord with the incoming data. By this account, literary training, like other forms of understanding, is pattern oriented. We create predictive models that can be built to order to help account for individual situations, and we use disruptions to patterns to help us learn more about those very situations. The resulting changes to patterns are received as error signals and mismatch, which help us adjust the starting model. The theory of predictive processing can lend itself to different emphases. We can treat these prediction models that our brains construct in more cognitive terms, as something like representational slices or pictures of a changing situation, or we can take our cues from the 4Es, which emphasize that our perceptions – which are always anticipatory – are less like descriptions of a state of affairs than a fillip to action, where our models of the world depend on our bodily states, and action includes the adjustments involved in changing up our interpretive procedures.

---

[1] For an account of how the field of neuroaesthetics has developed by linking general aesthetic responses "to the neuroscience of visual and affective processing as well as reward systems and decision-making," see Chatterjee (2010, p. 57). For an exponent of neuroaesthetics in the literary realm, see Hogan (2010): "a theory of literary universals would describe a repertoire of techniques available to authors and a range of nontechnical correlations derived from broad statistical patterns" (p. 43), where the correlations at issue bear on cognitive responses.

[2] For a sharp discussion of the usefulness of affordance theory for literary analysis, see Cave's (2016) chapter, "Literary Affordances" in *Thinking with Literature*. For a cognitive literary critic who applies predictive processing to novel reading, see Kukkonen (2014b); see also Kukkonen (2014a) on Bayesian narrative.

While the theory of predictive processing concerns itself with the mechanisms of prediction, affordance theory tells us that we construe objects and environments on the basis of their general uses, the pattern of responses they tend to elicit from us. Those patterns, in turn, help us gauge the relative importance of different details within the text and anticipate their possible relevance. The genre of a text itself conveys certain affordances, meaning that we know what interpretive acts to perform on the basis of the clues that genre provides. So, for example, the playwright Anton Chekhov famously asserts that "if you say in the first chapter that there is a rifle hanging on the wall, in the second or third chapter it absolutely must go off. If it's not going to be fired, it shouldn't be hanging there" (Bill, 1986, p. 79). Commonly, a gun affords us the possibility of displaying it, but also grasping it, taking it down from the wall, aiming at a target, and firing it. And the genre norms of narrative fiction sometimes (but not always) require us to anticipate how details of plot will come to be meaningful later in the story. Note that Chekhov's narrative advice is not put forward as a universal feature of stories, but as a culturally specific practice that he is endorsing for certain dramatic effects, such as creating suspense. Such protocols help us interpret plot in culturally appropriate ways.

At the same time, we can acknowledge other competing narrative protocols that texts sometimes invoke, such as those that cultural theorist Roland Barthes associates with the "reality effect" (1967–1980/1986). They concern superfluous details that remain in the narrative for no apparent narrative or symbolic reason, merely asserting themselves as signs that reality is replete and filled to the brim with minutiae we cannot possibly make use of. For example, in Gustav Flaubert's story, "A Simple Heart," a barometer hangs over a piano in someone's parlor (Flaubert, 1877/2005). In this case, the narrative forces the reader to navigate the detail without knowing in advance whether it is important. These two details, a gun and a barometer, refer to protocols that are in tension with each other. Individual texts signal their reliance on such protocols to construct specific cognitive challenges. And we get a sense of the stylistic and cognitive effects the text wants to encourage through the patterns it generates, which we can confirm or disconfirm by making predictions and continuously gauging their accuracy.

Importantly, affordance theory does not presume that our perceptions of the world bear directly upon a mind-independent reality. Instead, we construe specific actions, images, and settings – including the language we use to describe them – according to the customary ways our bodies perceive our environment and respond to it. As David Herman construes this enactivist idea, "cognition is not the representation of a pregiven world by a pregiven mind but is rather the enactment of a world and a mind on the basis of a history of the variety of actions that a being in the world performs" (2011, p. 256).

From this point of view, literary genres are not instruments that give us a more or less accurate picture of the world. Instead they are conventions that help writers and readers align expectations about a text so that readers know which actions and cognitive tests they are supposed to perform on it. They are not fixed, but profoundly flexible and various, and they underscore that the uses of a text are not necessarily specified in advance. Instead we might measure the value of a text at least in part by its generativity in producing new possibilities to continue interacting with it. This includes but is not limited to discovering new ways of perceiving and conceiving the meaning of its details – broadly what we would refer to as the interpretation of the text.

By taking for granted that the affordances of any given thing are underspecified, we can avoid presuming that genres are utterly fixed as forms, stable interpretive structures, or codes that are passed on across time. Just as a chair affords more than one possible use – and can occasionally be used in unconventional ways (for example to support a hot mug of coffee) – so too a poem, play, or novel can inspire multiple uses. In a moment, I will even suggest that it *invites* alternate uses. By uses, I mean the uses that writers have when they rework a genre for their own purposes, or the uses that readers make of a text when they invent new interpretive paradigms for reading it. These general uses co-occur with the ritualistic, institutional, and performative functions that texts are called on to enact (e.g., commemorating a scene, elegizing a person, inaugurating an event, organizing an entertainment, structuring a classroom discussion).

Here, even the conventional associations triggered by a text or its genre are use and context dependent. Moreover, interpretation can also hinge on the inclinations of a specific interpreter. Rather than presupposing that minds all work in the same way, embodied cognition and other postcognitivist models of mind take for granted that there can be multiple strategies for resolving a cognitive problem and that brains are built to make use of various localized strategies, so long as they are reasonably competent. Andy Clark puts forward a model in which "Solutions are 'soft assembled' out of multiple heterogeneous components including bodily mechanics, neural states and processes, and environmental conditions" (Clark, 1997, p. 155). In such an instance, there would be no hardwired biological basis for our cognitive inferences or approaches to interpretation. But nor would we be forced to follow fixed cultural norms and scripts, top-down rules and codes that are discursively promulgated. Instead, as Karin Kukkonen and Marco Caracciolo would have it, we rely on feedback loops through which our embodied consciousness and resulting "experience shapes cultural practices" (Caracciolo, 2014, p. 45), even as "cultural practices help the mind make sense of bodily experience" (Kukkonen & Caracciolo, 2014, p. 267).

For many years, literary critics and narratologists were in the habit of searching for the structures that regulate and standardize everything from genre interpretation to narrative processing. This structuralist approach is still at work in Barthes's idea of the "reality effect." He thinks Flaubert's meaningless details are "justified, if not by the work's logic, at least by the laws of literature [... and] the cultural rules of representation" (Barthes, 1986, p. 145). The trouble is, do we know which rules? The rules that suggest that apparently throwaway details, such as the placement of a barometer, create the feeling of verisimilitude? The rules that imply that details have symbolic or aesthetic value? The rules of plotting and suspense? The indefinite and changeable rules that ask us to assess the veracity or, indeed, the psychological import of the details by asking us to consider who the narrator is, what relationship that person maintains to the story, and how she or he measures up to other model observers? Other yet unnamable rules? In Paul Armstrong's view, second-generation cognitive science is poised to disrupt structuralists' critical aims: "The formalist goal of identifying orderly, universal structures of mind, language, and narrative does not match up well with the unstable equilibrium of the temporally decentered brain or the probabilistic processes through which cognitive connections develop and dissolve" (Armstrong, 2019). Armstrong presupposes that the brain is not manipulating symbols according to fixed, preset principles, but training itself on wobbly, complex, unstable probabilistic processes. To cope with these probabilistic processes, we do not simply discover rule-driven patterns and obey them, but sometimes actively disrupt them, inviting deviations in our interpretive approach to test our models. Our brain's pattern-generating system is built for a world that is constantly changing, with models that are constructed and dissolved for specific uses.

So far, we have vaguely presumed that literature allows us to use the same underlying brain architecture to support our problem-solving that we use to make real-world inferences and solve problems. When construed the wrong way, however, the idea comes with a host of unhelpful emphases. First, researchers are encouraged to instrumentalize literature by assuming that it evolved as a tool to help us practice quite general or universal human cognitive problems. Here theories abound concerning which cognitive skills to focus on, from social reasoning and interpretations of behavior to conceptual blending and action sequencing. All are thought to help us cope with our physical and social environments or draw meaning from them. As I already stated, these concerns share one thing in common: they view the scene of reading as a cognitive puzzle with a distinct solution. This orientation has been generative for cognitive literary criticism, in part, because it offers a contained and suitably "reductive" approach to analysis. But it also has the unfortunate effect of promoting a view of literary reading that is basically purposeful and end-directed. At best we are encouraged to think of such reading as a model for cognitive work of a more important sort we perform elsewhere, with a few added curlicues thrown into the account for the particularities of genre and literary reading activities as such.

Second, researchers tend to sideline questions of pleasure in reading. Or more precisely, they presume that the pleasures involved are similar to those we feel when we are practicing a skill or accomplishing a task important to our general functioning and social cognition as a species. By this account, literature works toward the optimization of our cognitive machinery (the pursuit of the fastest route or the most reliable or efficient prediction) or the prescriptive implementation of values that we take for granted as good for us. What happens when we are invited to imagine a scene in a story or fill out an unspoken thought in a poem but – despite our curiosity – reluctant or averse to doing so because it makes us uncomfortable, feels emotionally difficult, or conflicts with other desires we have? How do literary texts help us negotiate such emotional double binds? How do they enable us to imagine scenarios that test the reach and validity of socially accepted attitudes? For example, they may force us to test those attitudes against complex situations that overwhelm rules-based responses with particulars that seem difficult to square with general norms. Sometimes literature inspires imaginative activities that assist us in suspending customary instrumental or rational responses to environments so that we can interact with those environments in new ways. Yet researchers tend to ignore such possibilities – namely, that literature might help us challenge our presumed value schemes, explore contradictions, or discover alternate values through the structured thought processes of a literary narrative, dialogue, or lyric meditation.

Third, researchers assume that authors intend to raise specific interpretive problems in their works for readers to solve. While on some level, this is indisputable, it leads quickly to an intentionalist understanding of artistic process, in which the author is seen to be in control of the interpretive questions at issue. Instead of focusing on the author's intentions for the work, we may be interested in examining the ways that authors collaborate with readers in a joint process that accords more distributed roles to all participants. In this account, readers have the freedom to raise interpretive controversies, discover or create value in a text, and extend or reimagine the purposes of reading in the absence of very precise instructions for how to do so.

To give some substance to these general remarks, I will wind down my discussion with a brief example taken from the annals of modernist poetry. William Carlos Williams crafted a charming short poem, "The Red Wheelbarrow" (Tomlinson, 1985, p. 56), which has gained considerable fame for the manner in which it provokes expansive, sometimes unaccountable, responses from readers. It does so by disrupting common protocols associated with lyric poetry:

so much depends
upon

a red wheel
barrow

glazed with rain
water

beside the white
chickens.

The speaker of this poem claims that "so much" depends on an object, even though he fails to specify exactly what. A wheelbarrow is, of course, a functional implement on a farm, one whose uses may be obvious to anyone who has the competence and background to understand it, but in this case, it is hard to figure out what advantage we may gain from a poem that does little more than raise such an object into view. Readers may choose to go down the path of hunting for "deeper" symbolic meanings to pin to the image. Like other forms of story projection or conceptual blending, this is a customary cognitive operation most novice poetry readers are familiar with. For example, we might wonder what is the customary symbolic significance of the colors red and white. However, the unexpected curtness of the poem seems to derail this pattern of meaning-making. The poet offers few further details that might corroborate such an approach, and the details do not readily point toward conventional associations. What is going on?

Without getting into too much interpretive complexity here, I would propose that the poem here creates a space for imagining an object as well as constructing an occasion or reading activity that suspends our conviction that we know what affordances the object represents. The gesture, which frames the object in a certain light or takes it out of its embedded everyday context, is not wholly different from Williams's friend Marcel Duchamp's gesture of putting a urinal upside down on a pedestal and signing it as an artwork. Presenting a functional object in a state of disuse asks individual readers to figure out what other associations, emotional orientations, and feeling states they may wish to attach to the wheelbarrow or the poem as a whole, which project new meanings or discover new affordances for either or both. Here, the aesthetic task of the literary text is to suspend instrumental ways of interacting with a thing so that we are free to play with the assorted connections its image awakens in us. We cannot presume that Williams intended us to solve the mystery of the poem in a specific way. Nor can we presume that there is just one way to react to the speaker's claim that "so much depends / upon" a mundane object. But we are invited to align ourselves with the speaker's state of mind. We do this not simply by agreeing with him (e.g., "yes, so much *does* depend on a red wheelbarrow"), but by dwelling with the implied pleasures or satisfactions that the image arouses once it is displaced into a new cognitive environment. In so doing, we rely on the uncertainty or vagueness of his claim to explore or locate satisfactions of our own choosing.

Many cognitive theories take uncertainty in the world for granted. We do not have access to what other people think; things have uncertain functions; events have uncertain ramifications. I began by invoking affordance theory and predictive processing as "weak" theories because they transcend the particularities of literary reading to speak to the way we manage uncertainty in various spheres of life. What reading Williams's poem shows is that our cognitive activities are not always aimed at achieving greater certainty so that we can smooth our progress toward goals. In this respect, the relative "weakness" of affordance theory and predictive processing is a strength because neither insists on specifying the cognitive ends or aims of our activities as such. Some cultural activities, such as reading a poem by Williams, create a cognitive space in which to experiment with new affordances for things by keeping their functions and purposes intentionally underspecified. They also disorganize the customary interpretive procedures entailed in reading. As Alva Noë might put it, framing an object or putting it on a pedestal are ways of putting our social practices into view in order to reorganize those practices (Noë, 2015, p. 16). The cognitive tasks that a poem constructs depend on the particular ways it refines or reinvents the challenges that we face when reading it. Such challenges are not simply cognitive in nature, but bear on the larger social, ethical, and emotional effects of the text. For cultural neuroscience to be truly helpful in understanding practices, such as literature, it would need to absorb from disciplines, such as literary studies, a richer sense of the possible affordances of the objects of its inquiry.

REFERENCES

Armstrong, P. B. (2019). Neuroscience, narrative, and narratology. *Poetics Today*, 40(3), 395–428.

Barthes, R. (1986). *The rustle of language* (R. Howard, Trans.). Hill and Wang. (Original work published 1967–1980)

Bill, V. T. (1986). *Chekhov: The silent voice of freedom*. Allied Books.

Caracciolo, M. (2014). *The experientiality of narrative: An enactivist approach*. De Gruyter.

Cave, T. (2016). *Thinking with literature: Towards a cognitive criticism*. Oxford University Press. https://doi.org/10.1093/acprof:oso/9780198749417.001.0001

Chatterjee, A. (2010). Neuroaesthetics: A coming of age story. *Journal of Cognitive Neuroscience*, 23(1), 53–62. https://doi.org/10.1162/jocn.2010.21457

Clark, A. (1997). *Being there: Putting brain, body, and world together again*. MIT Press.

Flaubert, G. (2005). *Three tales* (R. Whitehouse, Trans.). Penguin. (Original work published 1877)

Friston, K. (2003). Learning and inference in the brain. *Neural Networks*, *16*(9), 1325–52. https://doi.org/10.1016/j.neunet.2003.06.005

Herman, D. (2011). 1880–1945: Re-minding modernism. In D. Herman (Ed.), *The emergence of mind: Representations of consciousness in narrative discourse in English* (pp. 243–72). University of Nebraska Press.

Hogan, P. C. (2010). Literary universals. In L. Zunshine (Ed.), *Introduction to cognitive cultural studies* (pp. 37–60). Johns Hopkins University Press.

Kukkonen, K. (2014a). Bayesian narrative: Probability, plot and the shape of the fictional world. *Anglia*, *132*(4), 720–39. https://doi.org/10.1515/ang-2014-0075

Kukkonen, K. (2014b). Presence and prediction: The embodied reader's cascades of cognition. *Style*, *48*(3), 367–84. http://www.jstor.org/stable/10.5325/style.48.3.367

Kukkonen, K., & Caracciolo, M. (2014). Introduction: What is the "second generation?" *Style*, *48*(3), 261–74. www.jstor.org/stable/10.5325/style.48.3.261

Noë, A. (2015). *Strange tools: Art and human nature*. Hill and Wang.

Tomlinson, C. (Ed.). (1985). *William Carlos Williams: Selected poems*. New Directions.

17 Capturing Context Is Not Enough
The Embodied Impact of Story and Emotion in Ethnographic Film

Robert Lemelson and Annie Tucker

Biocultural methods have been used in fruitful projects measuring biomarkers related to brain and behavior (Dressler, 2017), assessing gene expression profiles (Kohrt et al., 2015), tracking neurological activity associated with culturally inflected roles, behaviors, and self-construals with neuroimaging (Kitayama & Park, 2014; Rilling & Mascaro, 2017), and exploring the role of plasticity alleles in environmental susceptibility (Silveira et al., 2016). Methodological contributions from cultural anthropology typically seem less directly applicable to neuroscience. Still, classic qualitative methods in cultural anthropology such as survey instruments, participant observation, and interviews have their place in providing potential conceptual frameworks and research directions; their result, typically an ethnographic monograph, can provide contextualized information to frame, provide meaning for, or elaborate upon more discrete or particularistic research.

This chapter argues that visual ethnography, a research method in cultural anthropology, and its narrative and pedagogical endpoint, ethnographic film, can also be productive for qualitative research collection, presentation, and teaching. While ethnographic film *qua* ethnographic film may not be directly applied in interdisciplinary research per se, connections can be drawn to this volume's main focus on culture, mind, and brain interactions when accounting for the embodied aspects of the film experience. In the course of the chapter, we sketch out some ideas on how embodied aspects relating specifically to story and emotion may be more effective at not just capturing context but sharing this context than others.

Uses of Video and Ethnographic Film in Anthropological and Interdisciplinary Research

Visual documentation, including film, is a traditional ethnographic tool (Banks & Ruby, 2011; Edwards, 2001; Muybridge, 1979). Early "salvage" filming sought to archive purportedly dying cultures (Curtis & Hodge, 1907–1930/1970; Gruber, 1970), but pedagogical and interpretive approaches quickly assumed prominence (Asch & Chagnon, 1975; Gardner, 1963).

Classic examples of film being used to enhance data collection and extraction include Mead and Bateson's work in Bali, which linked photography, film, and ethnographic analysis to suggest a "schizoid" configuration of Balinese character (Bateson & Mead, 1942); Robert Gardner's work exploring tribal warfare among the Highland Dani in collaboration with a team of anthropologists (Gardner, 1963); Timothy Asch's collaborations with Napoleon Chagnon on aspects of Yanamamo (Asch & Chagnon, 1968–1971) and Balinese (Connor et al., 1979–1983) life; and John Marshall's 50-year work among Ju/'Hoansi (Marshall & Ritchie, 1951–2002). There is a similar history of transforming video materials into quantitative data via coding (Angelillo et al., 2007).

The ways in which visual material can complement and extend other research methods in cultural and psychological anthropology have multiplied, from earlier "sequencing" approaches aiming to record "integral" events or "whole single units of behavior" (Asch et al., 1973; Heider, 1976) to sensory immersion (Grimshaw & Ravetz, 2009), autoethnography (Scott, 2013), and participatory visual ethnography (Gubrium & Harper, 2013); these and more have been discussed at length (Barbash & Taylor, 1997; Heider, 1997; Marion & Crowder, 2013). However, with the high associated costs, for years film documentation was not typically in the armamentarium of anthropologists without a strikingly visual component to their research (MacDougall, 1992).

With the digital and miniaturization revolution, which has made video increasingly affordable, accessible, and easily stored, visual methods have been used to explore a range of topics and foci in cultural anthropology using a variety of approaches. One of the primary utilizations of visual material is to code for behavioral analysis. The extraction of visual data from film or video is useful for cultural research in the neurosciences. Such research often uses coded video data in ethological recordings of animals (Suomi, 2004), human interactive and proxemics studies (McCall & Singer, 2015), burgeoning facial recognition research, and related biometrics (Rilling et al., 2017). Some use video prompts in fMRI scans (Zadbood et al., 2017).

Beyond its utility in data analysis, another longstanding rationale for film recording in anthropology is the creation of ethnographic films. Ethnographic film is generally made for one of three broad purposes. The first is to document cultural practices. This has included agriculture and foodways (Smith & Reichline, 1974); traditional architecture, technologies, and trade (Heider, 1974); arts, crafts, and material culture (Fruzetti et al., 2005); ritual and ceremonial life (Hoskins & Whitney, 1991); performance traditions (Lomax & Paulay, 1974–2008); festivals (Willis, 2009); and more. The second is to create materials that will support or enhance the teaching of anthropology; for example, *The Ax Fight* (Asch & Chagnon, 1975) explicitly addresses ethnographic concepts such as emic versus etic interpretations of events, kinship, conflict, and ethnographer subjectivity. The third purpose goes beyond the documentary or the pedagogical to create stories about the various domains, filtered through individualized and subjectively oriented accounts. These narratives can illustrate key points in anthropological theory, and help fulfill the general anthropological goals of holism and making the unknowable or previously unexplored knowable and understandable. Sometimes, of course, all three purposes are addressed within the same film.

Capturing Context with Ethnographic Film

No matter their topic or scope, ethnographic films can be powerful tools in cultural research because they capture collective behavior and individual stories alike *in context*. While documenting cultural and social behavior, ethnographic film simultaneously records sensory, textural, material, and environmental surroundings. Most importantly, ethnographic film records all of these – along with social interactions and nonverbal communications such as body mechanics, affect, and embodied habitus – as they occur naturally in the "real world" as opposed to laboratory settings. The ability of film to convey, more than written ethnography, some of the sensorial richness and naturally occurring and culturally specific everyday "affordances" (possibilities for engagement with the environment, see, e.g., Ramstead et al., 2016) may be its key contribution to the interests of cultural neuroscience, which has been challenged to better illustrate how findings might appear and impact experience or behavior in people's everyday lives (Immordino-Yang, 2013). For those concerned with reflexivity, film can capture the research setting itself (Lutz, 1988) for scrutiny. While of course never a purely objective observation (Brand, 1976), ethnographic film comes close to depicting or illustrating various emotions, sensations, behaviors, and so forth in their lived contexts.

Still, while succeeding in more holistically documenting different aspects of diverse cultures, many didactic and educational filmic representations have lacked a focus on the emotions of the subjects portrayed, and certainly not evoked emotion in viewers. This is in part due to visual anthropology's original intention to be objective and scientific (Michaelis, 1955) in capturing others' realities, but also to avoid imposing a Western framework onto the experience of non-Western peoples (Worth & Adair, 1972). A psychological visual anthropological approach, exploring the subjectivity of its characters and exploring issues that are important and salient to this subjectivity, almost invariably requires an exploration and display of emotion and its meaning and modulations.

It was only with the birth of modern ethnographic film that narrative and character began to be developed, following broader trends in anthropological research that acknowledged the personal and not just cultural contexts for data (Lemelson & Tucker, 2017). As researchers began to attend to individuals as having unique life stories and subjectivities rather than as generic cultural actors, some filmmakers followed suit. For example, while most of Marshall's *The Hunters* (1957) focuses on the ecological and cultural contexts of a giraffe hunt, it also renders the personal experiences and compelling life concerns of the hunt's leader, Tsoma Tsamko, with a degree of poignant, restrained emotion.

Still, much academic ethnographic film has retained a documentary and explanatory focus that privileges an "objective" stance, rather than telling the dramatic or emotional stories of individual characters. This is unfortunate; if one pedagogical goal is to help viewers empathetically understand what they are witnessing in a film, a more emotionally resonant, story-oriented, character-based focus is more likely to evoke an engaged response. One way to understand different reactions to different kinds of ethnographic film comes from neuroscience inquiry into film viewing, in particular the embodied effects of story and emotion on brain activity.

The Embodied Impact of Story and Emotion

Stories package and convey information to listeners in a way that makes the content accessible, meaningful, and memorable. Our capacity to tell stories is considered a universal trait, one that putatively evolved to strengthen social and cultural bonds (Boyd, 2009; Smith et al., 2017). According to anthropologist Polly Wiessner, stories by firelight may have had a particularly influential effect. Among the Ju/'hoansi (!Kung Bushmen), contemporary hunter-gathers living in parts of Namibia and Botswana, she describes how "imagination soars" while "body language" and perceptual "awareness of self and others" falls away by the fireside (Wiessner, 2014). Furthermore, the act of listening to the same "real-life spoken stories" activates the same subcortical and cortical brain regions across listeners, from early auditory and speech processing areas to the default mode network (DMN; Honey et al., 2012; Suzuki et al., 2018).[1] Hasson et al. (2012) link the similar activations in the latter, high-order network to a shared understanding of the narrative (Honey et al., 2012; Suzuki et al., 2018), although this effect may be limited to people who share the same beliefs and values more generally (Yeshurun et al., 2017). Film viewing seems to have a similar effect. In a series of functional neuroimaging experiments, a significant percentage of brain activity was highly correlated across viewers

---

[1] The DMN has been implicated in self-oriented tasks, such as mind wandering, self-reflection, remembering the past, and thinking about the future, as well as the mental states of others (Buckner et al., 2008). Hasson et al. (2012) hypothesize more broadly that the DMN is a high-level "global integrator" of information from many lower-level networks (Margulies et al., 2016; Vatansever et al., 2015; Vidaurre et al., 2017; cited in Nguyen et al., 2019).

watching a spaghetti western, *The Good, the Bad, and the Ugly*, but not across viewers of an unedited, one-shot video clip of a concert (Hasson et al., 2008).

Given these neural mechanisms, stories broadly conceived are an effective way for individuals or communities to share important information and values. But, as Hasson et al.'s research has demonstrated, some stories are more effective than others. Effective stories, such as the Sergio Leone film, may be defined first as those that best engage and hold attention, so that complex material can be absorbed and hence retained; and secondly as those that elicit an empathetic response – in other words, those that move the listener or observer to some kind of action. Some have suggested that emotionally compelling stories about individuals that follow a dramatic arc, particularly one that starts with a surprising new idea, introduces a character who is in crisis or facing difficulties that must be overcome, and leads up to a climax where the character ultimately transforms and resolves this crisis, is an effective mechanism for illustrating themes and ideas the filmmaker is trying to convey (Zak, 2013) – this is commonly known among professional storytellers in various genres as the "three-act" structure. Some scholars think that the emotional salience of this dramatic arc is a transcultural and transhistorical human universal closely linked to fundamental human neurobiology (Young & Saver, 2001). This is of course not to say that it is the only salient narrative structure, given the vast array of extant oratory and other narrative forms, and genres, and many anthropologists have long been skeptical of such a universalist approach (Worth & Adair, 1972).

Narrative and Character-Driven Films Are Effective at Telling Stories

However, for urban Americans at least, emotional stories following a dramatic arc have a greater impact than dispassionate ones, and this impact seems to be amplified when they are presented in the form of a *character-driven film*.

In lab conditions, subjects displayed more sustained attention and empathetic activation when watching an emotional film about a father whose son has cancer than when they simply read what the father had to say; similarly, viewers displayed greater heightened activation when this story was presented onscreen in the familiar dramatic arc rather than other filmic formats (Zak, 2013).

Torben Grodal proposes an evolutionary, biocultural, embodied model that suggests how films can influence brain activity, particularly our emotions. According to Grodal's model, there is a predictable flow in brain activation when we watch a film, from *perception, emotion, and cognition* to *motor action* (PECMA), with bottom-up, top-down, and feedback components (Grodal, 2006, 2009). According to the PECMA flow model, incoming sensory information is matched with previous experience and memories, which have an emotional valence, and subject to cognitive appraisal. Grodal assumes, with Frijda (1986; see also Damasio, 2018), that emotions are action tendencies or, more specifically, "tendencies to establish, maintain, or disrupt a relationship with the environment" (Frijda, 1986, p. 71). Instead of willing us to action, however, the experience of film viewing affords an opportunity for emotional attunement to or sensory-motor resonance with the characters we encounter onscreen, putatively via mirror neurons (Grodal & Kramer, 2010), which "map the action of others on the observers' motor representations of the same action" (Gallese, 2017, p. 43; see also Gallese & Guerra, 2019, on embodied simulation theory and the film-viewing experience).

Bitter Honey

Despite our more nuanced understanding that certain kinds of character-based films "move" viewers, the conventions of ethnographic film have thus far not supported the development of an "effective" emotional approach to making films. This is not to say that there is not significant emotional content in ethnographic films. Classics such as *The Ax Fight* clearly illustrate anger and rage; *Dead Birds* illustrates mourning, and many other classic films have some aspect of emotional expression and display in viewers. Yet having taught these films for over twenty years, the first author can attest that students rarely empathize with the emotions displayed, in that the students rarely comment on the emotional impact these films have on them. This is perhaps perplexing; there has, of course, been a longstanding interest in stories and storytelling in anthropology and an investment in the efficacy, impact, and function of narrative construction and performance within the experience of illness and healing (Kleinman, 1988; Mattingly & Garro, 2000). Scholars working in the field honor and study the impact of stories in peoples' lives but somewhat ironically have not tended to use the repertory of storytelling techniques at their disposal to impact the way they impart data or theory – avoiding film stories in particular (Taylor, 1998), and dramatic or emotional filmed stories about individuals that follows this purportedly "universal" narrative trajectory of a main character struggling to address a conflict even more so (Lemelson & Tucker, 2015). Therefore, despite their shared origins (Ruby, 2000) over the course of the twentieth century, visual ethnography has moved quite far away from mainstream documentary film, which remains invested in and associated with emotional and dramatic narrative arcs.

The first author's film work has not followed these familiar conventions. His approach (visual psychological anthropology) involves a more embodied and subjectively oriented form of storytelling, one that attempts to address more holistically his subjects' complex emotions and compelling life stories and their emergence from an interplay of multiple forces – developmental, relational, and familial issues; intrapsychic drives and conflicts; work, community, and local politics; and larger macrostructural issues of gender, ethnicity, national identity, and power (Lemelson & Tucker, 2017). *Bitter Honey* (Lemelson, 2015), which was shot over a seven-year period in Bali, exemplifies the first author's use of a three-part narrative structure highlighting strong emotional components. The film explores the complexities of polygamous unions in Bali through the experiences of three families. In Bali, power dynamics of such unions support infidelity on the part of the men and restrict women's ability to leave given the potential loss of inheritance and custody of their children. During the course of the film, the wives share intense narratives imbued with strong emotions around common themes of infidelity, domestic violence, and altered or even shattered hopes and dreams. Following the three-act structure, at the end of the second "act" of the film, an intervention is staged to stop one of the husbands from beating his wife. Throughout the film, the women's pain, isolation, and sense of confinement is also conveyed non-narratively. *Bitter Honey* ends by invoking narratives of resilience as the wives emphasize their close and satisfying relationships with their children, and draw strength from Balinese idioms of fate and acceptance to cope with those aspects of their lives they cannot change, while taking advantage of the different opportunities they each still have.

Telling such emotional stories involves an iterative process of understanding multiple contexts and situated perspectives, and then placing these within storylines that coherently unfold within the confines of a film. The vast bulk of interviews and other footage lies "on the cutting room floor," but through clarifying salient themes and presenting distinct and relatable characters, both an honest account of the subjects and a clear development of significant themes do emerge.

Several of the first author's other Indonesian films also share a general concern with the effects of violence, trauma, and stigma, and the disruption of moral worlds on the emotions of their characters. They simultaneously provide windows into how these larger issues influence individual lives over time and contextual material that can frame and inform other forms of research documenting these processes from a different perspective. Emotionally resonant, character-driven narratives deepen our engagement with the subject matter by making us "care" more about the material.

It is important to note that the narrative arc in *Bitter Honey* was crafted by the filmmaker in the process of editing. The content itself arises naturally through listening to what the subjects themselves say over the course of longitudinal ethnographic interviews and observations. The film edit adheres as closely as possible to their experiences and evolving life concerns, albeit with a focus toward those specific themes the filmmaker most wants to explore in any project. But there are certain trade-offs to this form of deeply engaged anthropology, especially with respect to ending the film with a narrative evoking resilience or recovery (Woods et al., 2019).

Keeping these trade-offs in mind, emotionally resonant, story-oriented, character-driven ethnographic films can be useful tools for elucidating context, helping students and others absorb relevant information in a way they might not be able to through simply reading. Again, Zak's research has shown that "character-driven stories with emotional content result in a better understanding of the key points a speaker wishes to make and enable better recall of these points weeks later" (Zak, 2014). Within the fields of transcultural psychiatry and psychology in particular, character-based films can also convey cultural and clinical information and impart key concepts in a novel, more engaged, or immersive way, one that makes judicious use of the power of visual storytelling.

REFERENCES

Angelillo, C., Rogoff, B., & Chavajay, P. (2007). Examining shared endeavors by abstracting video coding schemes with fidelity to cases. In R. Goldman, R. Pea, & S. J. Derry (Eds.), *Video research in the learning sciences* (pp. 189–206). Erlbaum.

Asch, T., & Chagnon, N. (1968–1971). *Yanomamö series*. 7 hrs, 8 min. Documentary Educational Resources. https://store.der.org/yanomam-series-p970.aspx

Asch, T., & Chagnon, N. (1975). *The ax fight*. 30 min. [Documentary]. Documentary Educational Resources. https://store.der.org/the-ax-fight-p180.aspx

Asch, T., Marshall, J., & Spier, P. (1973). Ethnographic film: Structure and function. *Annual Review of Anthropology*, *2*, 179–87. https://doi.org/10.1146/annurev.an.02.100173.001143

Banks, M., & Ruby, J. (Eds.). (2011). *Made to be seen: Perspectives on the history of visual anthropology*. University of Chicago Press.

Barbash, I., & Taylor, L. (1997). *Cross-cultural filmmaking: A handbook for making documentary and ethnographic films and videos*. University of California Press.

Bateson, G., & Mead, M. (1942). *Balinese character: A photographic analysis*. The New York Academy of Sciences.

Boyd, B. (2009). *On the origin of stories: Evolution, cognition, and fiction*. Belknap Press.

Brand, S. (1976). For God's sake, Margaret [Conversation between Stewart Brand, Gregory Bateson, and Margaret Mead]. *CoEvolutionary Quarterly*, *10*(21), 32–44. www.wholeearth.com/issue/2010/article/361/for.god's.sake.margaret

Buckner, R. L., Andrews-Hanna, J. R., & Schachter, D. L. (2008). The brain's default mode network: Anatomy, function, and relevance to disease. *Annals of the New York Academy of Sciences*, *1124*(1), 1–38. https://doi.org/10.1196/annals.1440.011

Connor, L., Asch, T., & Asch, P. (1979–1983). *The Jero Tapakan series*. 2 hrs, 26 min. Documentary Educational Resources. https://store.der.org/the-jero-tapakan-series-p967.aspx

Curtis, E. S., & Hodge, F. W. (Ed.). (1970). *The North American Indian, being a series of volumes picturing and describing the Indians of the United States and Alaska* (20 Vols.). Johnson Reprint Corp. (Original work published 1907–1930).

Damasio, A. (2018). *The strange order of things: Life, feeling, and the making of cultures.* Pantheon Books.

Dressler, W. W. (2017). *Culture and the individual: Theory and method of cultural consonance.* Routledge. https://doi.org/10.4324/9781315164007

Edwards, E. (2001). *Raw histories: Photographs, anthropology and museums.* Berg.

Frijda, N. H. (1986). *The emotions.* Cambridge University Press.

Fruzetti, L., Ostor, A., & Sarkar, A. N. (2005). *Singing pictures.* 40 min. [Documentary]. Documentary Educational Resources. https://store.der.org/singing-pictures-p422.aspx

Gallese, V. (2017). Visions of the body. Embodied simulation and aesthetic experience. *Aisthesis, 10*(1), 41–50. https://doi.org/10.13128/Aisthesis-20902

Gallese, V., & Guerra, M. (2019). *The empathic screen: Cinema and Neuroscience* (F. Anderson, Trans.). Oxford University Press. (Original work published 2015)

Gardner, R. (1963). *Dead birds.* 1 hr, 23 min. [Documentary]. Documentary Educational Resources. https://store.der.org/dead-birds-p858.aspx

Grimshaw, A., & Ravetz, A. (2009). Rethinking observational cinema. *Journal of the Royal Anthropological Institute, 15*(3), 538–56. https://doi.org/10.1111/j.1467-9655.2009.01573.x

Grodal, T. (2006). The PECMA flow: A general model of visual aesthetics. *Film Studies, 8*(1), 1–11. http://doi.org/10.7227/FS.8.3

Grodal, T. (2009). *Embodied visions: Evolution, emotion, culture, and film.* Oxford University Press. https://doi.org/10.1093/acprof:oso/9780195371314.001.0001

Grodal, T., & Kramer, M. (2010). Empathy, film, and the brain. *Recherches semiotiques/Semiotic Inquiry, 30*(1–3), 19–35. https://doi.org/10.7202/1025921ar

Gruber, J. W. (1970). Ethnographic salvage and the shaping of anthropology. *American Anthropologist, 72*(6), 1289–99. https://doi.org/10.1525/aa.1970.72.6.02a00040

Gubrium, A., & Harper, K. (2013). *Participatory visual and digital methods.* Left Coast Press.

Hasson, U., Ghazanfar, A. A, Balantucci, B., Garrod, S., & Keysers, C. (2012). Brain-to-brain coupling: A mechanism for creating and sharing a social world. *Trends in Cognitive Sciences, 16*(2), 113–20. https://doi.org/10.1016%2Fj.tics.2011.12.007

Hasson, U., Landesman, O., Knappmeyer, B., Vallines, I., Rubin, N., & Heeger, D. J. (2008). Neurocinematics: The neuroscience of film. *Projections, 2*(1), 1–26. https://doi.org/10.3167/proj.2008.020102

Heider, K. (1974). *Dani houses.* 35 min, 9 min extras. [Documentary]. Documentary Educational Resources. https://store.der.org/dani-films-p855.aspx

Heider, K. G. (1976). *Ethnographic film.* University of Texas Press.

Heider, K. G. (1997). *Seeing anthropology: Cultural anthropology through film.* Allyn and Bacon.

Honey, C. J., Thompson, C. R., Lerner, Y., & Hasson, U. (2012). Not lost in translation: Neural responses shared across languages. *Journal of Neuroscience, 32*, 15277–82. https://doi.org/10.1523/JNEUROSCI.1800-12.2012

Hoskins, J., & Whitney, L. (1991). *Horses of life and death.* 28 min. [Documentary]. Center for Visual Anthropology. https://store.der.org/horses-of-life-and-death-p787.aspx

Immordino-Yang, M. H. (2013). Studying the effects of culture by integrating neuroscientific with ethnographic approaches. *Psychological Inquiry*, *24*(1), 42–6. https://doi.org/10.1080/1047840X.2013.770278

Kitayama, S., & Park, J. (2014). Error-related brain activity reveals self-centric motivation: Culture matters. *Journal of Experimental Psychology: General*, *143*(1), 62–70. https://doi.org/10.1037/a0031696

Kleinman, A. (1988). *The illness narratives: Suffering, healing, and the human condition*. Basic Books.

Kohrt, B. A., Worthman, C. M., Ressler, K. J., Mercer, K. B., Upadhaya, N., Koirala, S., Nepal, M. K., Sharma, V. D., & Binder, E. B. (2015). Cross-cultural gene-environment interactions in depression, post-traumatic stress disorder, and the cortisol awakening response: *FKBP5* polymorphisms and childhood trauma in South Asia. *International Review of Psychiatry*, *27*(3), 180–96. https://doi.org/10.3109/09540261.2015.1020052

Lemelson, R. (2015). *Bitter honey*. 1 hr, 21 min. [Documentary]. Documentary Educational Resources. https://store.der.org/bitter-honey-p198.aspx

Lemelson, R., & Tucker, A. (2015). Steps toward an integration of psychological and visual anthropology: Issues raised in the production of the film series *Afflictions: Culture and mental illness in Indonesia*. *Ethos*, *43*(1), 6–39. https://doi.org/10.1111/etho.12070

Lemelson, R., & Tucker, A. (2017). *Afflictions: Steps towards a visual psychological anthropology*. Palgrave Macmillan. https://doi.org/10.1007/978-3-319-59984-7

Lomax, A., & Paulay, F. (1974–2008). *Rhythms of the earth*. 1 hr, 36 min. [Documentary]. Documentary Educational Resources. https://store.der.org/rhythms-of-earth-p478.aspx

Lutz, C. A. (1988). *Unnatural emotions: Everyday sentiments on a Micronesian atoll & their challenge to Western theory*. University of Chicago Press.

MacDougall, D. (1992). "Photo wallahs": An encounter with photography. *Visual Anthropology Review*, *8*(2), 96–100. https://doi.org/10.1525/var.1992.8.2.96

Margulies, D. S., Ghosh, S. S., Goulas, A., Falkiewicz, M., Huntenburg, J. M., Langs, G., Bezgin, G., Eickhoff, S. B., Castellanos, F. X., Petrides, M., Jefferies, E., & Smallwood, J. (2016). Situating the default-mode network along a principal gradient of macroscale cortical organization. *Proceedings of the National Academy of Sciences of the United States of America*, *113*(44), 12574–9. https://doi.org/10.1073/pnas.1608282113

Marion, J. S., & Crowder, J. W. (2013). *Visual research: A concise introduction to thinking visually*. Bloomsbury Academic.

Marshall, J. (1957). *The hunters*. 1 hr, 12 min. [Documentary]. Documentary Educational Resources. https://store.der.org/the-hunters-p798.aspx

Marshall, J., & Ritchie, C. (1951–2002). *A Kalahari family*. 6 hrs. [Documentary]. Kalfam Productions and Documentary Educational Resources. https://store.der.org/a-kalahari-family-p937.aspx

Mattingly, C., & Garro, L. (Eds.). (2000). *Narrative and the cultural construction of illness and healing*. University of California Press.

McCall, C., & Singer, T. (2015). Facing off with unfair others: Introducing proxemic imaging as an implicit measure of approach and avoidance during social interaction. *PLoS ONE*, *10*(2), e0117532. https://doi.org/10.1371/journal.pone.0117532

Michaelis, A. (1955). *Research films in biology, anthropology, psychology and medicine*. New York Academic Press. https://doi.org/10.1016/B978-0-12-395693-4.X5001-4

Muybridge, E. (1979). *Muybridge's complete human and animal locomotion: All 781 plates from the 1887 "animal locomotion"* (Vol. 3). Dover Publications.

Nguyen, M., Vanderwal, T., & Hasson, U. (2019). Shared understanding of narratives is correlated with shared neural responses. *NeuroImage*, *184*, 161–70. https://doi.org/10.1016/j.neuroimage.2018.09.010

Ramstead, M. J. D., Veissière, S. P. L, & Kirmayer, L. J. (2016). Cultural affordances: Scaffolding local worlds through shared intentionality. *Frontiers in Psychology*, *7*, 1090. https://doi.org/10.3389/fpsyg.2016.01090

Rilling, J. K., Li, T., Chen, X., Gautam, P., Haroon, E., & Thompson, R. R. (2017). Arginine vasopressin effects on subjective judgments and neural responses to same and other-sex faces in men and women. *Frontiers in Endocrinology*, *8*, 200. https://doi.org/10.3389/fendo.2017.00200

Rilling, J. K., & Mascaro, J. S. (2017). The neurobiology of fatherhood. *Current Opinion in Psychology*, *15*, 26–32. https://doi.org/10.1016/j.copsyc.2017.02.013

Ruby, J. (2000). *Picturing culture: Explorations of film and anthropology*. University of Chicago Press.

Scott, J.-A. (2013). Problematizing a researcher's performance of "insider status": An autoethnography of "designer disabled" identity. *Qualitative Inquiry*, *19*(2), 101–15. https://doi.org/10.1177/1077800412462990

Silveira, P. P., Gaudreau, H., Atkinson, L., Fleming, A. S., Sokolowksi, M. B., Steiner, M., Kennedy, J. L., Meaney, M. J., Levitan, R. D., & Dubé, L. (2016). Genetic differential susceptibility to socioeconomic status and childhood obesogenic behavior: Why targeted prevention may be the best societal investment. *JAMA Pediatrics*, *170*(4), 359–64. https://doi.org/10.1001/jamapediatrics.2015.4253

Smith, H., & Reichline, N. (1974). *Potato planters*. 17 min. [Documentary]. Documentary Educational Resources. https://store.der.org/potato-planters-p524.aspx

Smith D., Schlaepfer, P., Major, K., Dyble, M., Page, A. E., Thompson, J., Chaudhary, N., Salali, G. D., Mace, R., Astete, L., Ngales, M., Vinicius, L., & Migliano, A. B. (2017). Cooperation and the evolution of hunter-gatherer storytelling. *Nature Communications*, *8*, 1853. https://doi.org/10.1038/s41467-017-02036-8

Suomi, S. J. (2004). How gene-environment interactions shape biobehavioral development: Lessons from studies with rhesus monkeys. *Research in Human Development*, *1*(3), 205–22. https://doi.org/10.1207/s15427617rhd0103_5

Suzuki, W. A., Feliú-Mójer, M. I., Hasson, U., Yehuda, R., & Zarate, J. M. (2018). Dialogues: The science and power of storytelling. *Journal of Neuroscience*, *38* (44), 9468–70. https://doi.org/10.1523/JNEUROSCI.1942-18.2018

Taylor, L. (1998). "Visual anthropology is dead, long live visual anthropology!" *American Anthropologist*, *100*(2), 534–7. https://doi.org/10.1525/aa.1998.100.2.534.

Vatansever, D., Menon, D. K., Manktelow, A. E., Sahakian, B. J., & Stamatakis, E. A. (2015). Default mode dynamics for global functional integration. *Journal of*

Neuroscience, *35*(46), 15254–62. https://doi.org/10.1523/JNEUROSCI.2135-15.2015

Vidaurre, D., Smith, S. M., & Woolrich, M. W. (2017). Brain network dynamics are hierarchically organized in time. *Proceedings of the National Academy of Sciences of the United States of America*, *114*(48), 12827–32. https://doi.org/10.1073/pnas.1705120114

Wiessner, P. W. (2014). Embers of society: Firelight talk among the Ju/'hoansi Bushmen. *Proceedings of the National Academy of Sciences of the United States of America*, *111*(39), 14027–35. https://doi.org/10.1073/pnas.1404212111

Willis, A. (2009). *Da feast!* 22 min. [Documentary]. Documentary Educational Resources. https://store.der.org/da-feast-p851.aspx

Woods, A., Hart, A., & Spandler, H. (2019). The recovery narrative: Politics and possibilities of a genre. *Culture, Medicine, and Psychiatry*, 1–27. https://doi.org/10.1007/s11013-019-09623-y

Worth, S., & Adair, J. (1972). *Through Navajo eyes: An exploration in film communication and anthropology*. Indiana University Press.

Yeshurun, Y., Swanson, S., Simony, E., Chen, J., Lazaridi, C., Honey, C. J., & Hasson, U. (2017). Same story, different story: The neural representation of interpretive frameworks. *Psychological Science*, *28*(3), 307–19. https://doi.org/10.1177%2F0956797616682029

Young, K., & Saver, J. L. (2001). The neurology of narrative. *SubStance*, *30*(94/95), 72–84. https://doi.org/10.2307/3685505

Zadbood, A., Chen, J., Leong, Y. C., Norman, K. A, & Hasson, U. (2017). How we transmit memories to other brains: Constructing shared neural representations via communication. *Cerebral Cortex*, *27*(10), 4988–5000. https://doi.org/10.1093/cercor/bhx202

Zak, P. J. (2013). How stories change the brain. *Greater Good Magazine*. https://greatergood.berkeley.edu/article/item/how_stories_change_brain

Zak, P. J. (2014). Why your brain loves good storytelling. *Harvard Business Review*. https://hbr.org/2014/10/why-your-brain-loves-good-storytelling

18 Social Neuroscience in Global Mental Health
Case Study on Stigma Reduction in Nepal

Brandon Kohrt

Namita stood in front of a group of eighteen health workers from nearby primary care health centers in southern Nepal. The health workers had been told by their managers that they needed to attend a nine-day training course in recognizing and treating mental illness. This was part of an initiative of the World Health Organization (WHO) to increase availability of mental health services in primary care. However, this training was different from the standard format outlined by WHO for training the primary care workers. In a typical training, the health workers would be listening to a psychiatrist or other mental health specialists as they outlined the diagnostic criteria for depression, psychosis, or another condition. But, these health workers, instead, were listening to Namita tell her story of living with mental illness.

Namita was in her early twenties. A few years ago, after her father suffered a serious health problem, she began to have problems sleeping, she lost interest in going to school or spending time with friends, and at one point she began to have thoughts of dying. One day, she had taken her mother to a primary care center for a check-up. While there, she noticed a pamphlet about depression and talked about this with her mother's health worker. He then referred her to a local counselor who began treating her with psychotherapy. Now, a few years into the treatment, Namita has enrolled in college, she has an active social life, and she provides support for her mother and father.

Namita's gradual recovery led her to be enrolled in a program to train persons living with mental illness in photography and visual storytelling (a technique known as PhotoVoice). After a few months' training in PhotoVoice, Namita and other persons living with mental illness became part of the team of trainers for primary care workers. They joined up with psychiatrists and other mental health experts to conduct the WHO trainings.

Why does Namita's participation in such training matter? Why go through all the effort to identify, train, and pay persons living with mental illness to take part in these trainings when a psychiatrist has all the expertise to deliver the content? The answer to that lies in social neuroscience and medical anthropology theories of human behavior – in particular stigma and discrimination. Knowledge alone is inadequate to change human behavior. But when attitudes and emotional responses are also addressed, there is much greater potential to change behavior and make programs such as WHO trainings considerably more effective. In this chapter, the social neuroscience and medical anthropology theories of stigma are discussed so that one can understand why and how participation of Namita and others like her is so vital to effective behavioral change.

Stigma against Persons with Mental Illness in Primary Care

Attitudes among primary care workers toward persons with mental, neurological, and substance abuse (MNS) disorders in low- and middle-income countries (LMICs) are of particular concern. The majority of the world's population live in LMICs, and these countries have the least access to mental healthcare. Only one out of twenty-seven persons with depression in lower to middle income countries receives minimally adequate care (Thornicroft et al., 2017), and treatment coverage is even more limited for persons with psychotic and substance use disorders. Persons with MNS disorders typically die twenty-five years earlier than the general population, often as a result of discrimination within the medical establishment and associated poor medical treatment (Tiihonen et al., 2009). Initiatives such as the WHO's mental health Gap Action Programme (mhGAP) are designed to address this treatment gap by training primary care workers to deliver MNS care (World Health Organization; WHO, 2010). Increasing knowledge, however, may be insufficient to produce changes in clinical care. Evidence from both LMICs and high-income settings has shown that efforts solely targeting MNS knowledge among healthcare professionals and the general public are inadequate for sustained attitudinal and behavioral change (Henderson et al., 2014).

In contrast, interventions focused on contact among different groups, rather than just the dissemination of knowledge, more consistently have shown greater benefit for reducing stigma and discrimination in health fields (Pescosolido & Manago, 2017). For example, interventions in which health workers spend time interacting with persons with MNS disorders in recovery and hearing their personal stories are associated with positive attitudinal changes and behavioral predispositions, at least in the short term (Corrigan et al., 2012). Although social contact interventions hold promise, some studies report neutral or even negative results. Further, among studies with positive outcomes the duration of the benefit is variable. There is also debate about which are the active ingredients in these interventions that lead to positive change (Thornicroft et al., 2015). And finally, there is limited evidence about what works cross-culturally, with few studies conducted in LMICs. For example, a review of the literature on stigma research in LMICs identified only nineteen studies with primary care staff, of which just seven included a control condition, and only one included a patient with a recovery story (Heim et al., 2018). Results were mixed within this subgroup of studies, and cultural adaptation often was lacking.

Such limitations highlight the need for revisiting the theoretical foundations for stigma and discrimination so that conceptually grounded interventions can be developed to meet the need for preparing primary care workers now expected to treat persons with MNS disorders, especially in LMICs. Theories and research from social neuroscience can provide useful information, as well as elucidate the mechanism of how and in what contexts stigma reduction is effective. Our goal is therefore to draw upon social neuroscience to develop an intervention to improve health workers' attitudes when treating MNS disorders that would be feasible, acceptable, and effective in LMICs.

Social Neuroscience and Medical Anthropology Frameworks of Discrimination

Empathy is an important component of the clinical encounter (Kirmayer, 2015). Among health workers, the failure of empathy – "the natural capacity to share, understand, and respond with care to the affective states of others" (Decety, 2012, p. vii) – suggests that there are mechanisms in place to justify not responding to another person's suffering. Specifically, persons in distress are stigmatized and identified as members of an out-group. Out-group members in pain, their distress calls, and visual images of their suffering do not appear to elicit the same neurobiological empathic reaction, and under some circumstances, the suffering of out-groups may even trigger pleasure responses (Cikara & Fiske, 2013; Cikara, Bruneau, et al., 2014; Cikara, Jenkins et al., 2014). Therefore, the behavioral disposition to help is not triggered substantially with out-group members. Whereas "eudaimonia" is the pleasure felt through meaning, purpose, and helping others, the same is not the case when helping out-groups: social out-grouping effectively moderates the pain and other negative emotions associated with not helping others.

Social psychology underpins most current models of intergroup behavior in social neuroscience. Almost a century ago, social psychologists introduced theories of intergroup contact to explain why we support some individuals and reject others based on group identities (Pettigrew et al., 2011). In the 1930s and 1940s, the field of social psychology became interested in intergroup relations and the role of intergroup contact. During the civil rights era in the United States, the social psychologist Floyd Allport focused on group contact in the context of changing racial relations. Allport evaluated approaches such as the "jigsaw classroom" in which racially mixed student groups worked together toward common goals, and saw the reduction of between-group differences (Allport, 1954). Allport eventually hypothesized four requisite elements for effective intergroup contact: (1) equal status for the groups; (2) common goals; (3) intergroup cooperation; and (4) support of authorities, law, or custom. Since development of the intergroup contact theory, there have been over 500 experimental and observational studies, with the majority supporting intergroup contact to reduce prejudice (Pettigrew et al., 2011). This holds for health and mental health stigma, which can be reduced through intergroup contact (Corrigan et al., 2012).

Since Allport, social psychologists have come to the realization that not all four elements are needed (Pettigrew et al., 2011). Moreover, although Allport postulated that knowledge about the other group mediates positive change, this has turned out to play a minor role. More important are affective mediators that reduce threat and anxiety and promote empathy (Pettigrew et al., 2011). Additional developments in social psychology – which have subsequently influenced social neuroscience – are important for understanding behavioral change. For example, fear leads to inaction, whereas increasing hope leads to motivation and more action (Berridge, 2004).

Social neuroscience has contributed a brain-based perspective to understanding prejudice and discrimination, which have been associated with the threat response in Pavlovian fear conditioning (Mattan et al., 2018). Importantly, perceived threat tends to shut down empathic experiences and caregiving behavioral responses. This tendency has been related to reduced activity in the ventral medial prefrontal cortex, thought to be associated with empathy and theory of mind, underpinning the ability to attribute mental states to oneself and others (Amodio, 2014; Montag et al., 2011). Further, activation of the amygdala and anterior cingulate communicates two behavioral cues: (1) this stimulus is putting me at risk in some form; and (2) this stimulus is different from me in some way (Amodio, 2014). The threat that triggers stigmatization may be survival-based, for example, a certain individual represents an immediate threat through violence or a longer-term threat through contagion. Equally important are threats to one's social membership or status. If engagement with a certain group could lead to loss of one's social inclusion in their primary social group, that is tantamount to a survival risk as well.

Frameworks from medical anthropology can be used to extend the findings of social neuroscience. The concept of "what matters most" is important from a cultural and occupational perspective. "What matters most" has been used to explain why stigma associated with mental illness differs across cultural groups (Yang et al., 2007). For example, different priorities on social relationships, behavior, and livelihood lead to varied profiles with regard to what types of MNS conditions are stigmatized and the impact of that stigma. Similarly, an individual's professional identity also influences "what matters most" within an occupational context. For example, the reasons for stigmatizing persons with MNS conditions may take different forms in law enforcement, healthcare,

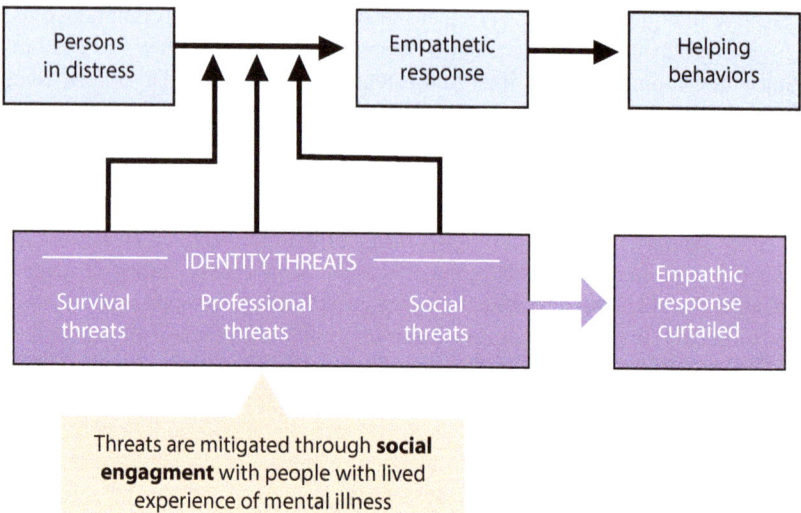

Figure 18.1 Identity threat model of stigmatization in healthcare settings and social engagement intervention elements to combat stigmatization rooted in medical anthropology, social neuroscience, and social psychology.

educational, religious, and military professional settings. Medical anthropology also can guide our understanding of attitudinal, behavioral, and role change, specifically symbolic transformation in rituals (Kirmayer, 2004; Turner, 1967). Rituals are not only important for healing but also for role transitions at different life stages and for professions. This is done through emotional manipulation facilitated by symbolic transformation (Dow, 1986). It also informs group inclusion and exclusion.

Identity Threat Model of Discrimination

All of the above can be combined into an "identity threat model" of discrimination in healthcare settings. The model depicted in Figure 18.1 addresses three specific threats – survival, professional, and social – and sheds light on how to mitigate them:

1. **Survival threats**. Because certain conditions may be associated with risk of contagion and violence, healthcare professionals feel threatened by patients with conditions such as leprosy, HIV/AIDS, schizophrenia, and substance abuse disorders. The perception of threat is associated with amygdala activation, which dampens empathic responses. Even in the absence of observed pathways of contagion or behavioral markers suggesting threat

of violence, patients may still be ostracized. Moreover, patients adequately treated and bearing low risks of contagion or violence often continue to be stigmatized by healthcare workers.
2. **Professional threats**. These threats are related to such issues as burdensomeness and perceived competence to fulfill one's professional obligations. A healthcare professional who cannot improve a patient's condition may feel incompetent. Social neuroscience has shown that subjective incompetence is associated with pain centers in the brain (de Figueiredo & Griffith, 2016). To protect against the feeling of subjective incompetence, healthcare professionals often blame the patient for lack of recovery, "dump" the patient on other health facilities or providers, and fail to invest their full medical expertise for diagnoses and treatment implementation.
3. **Social threats**. The third series of threats are those related to the feared exclusion from one's own social group, including professional and personal social networks. If the group norm is to disregard persons with MNS disorders because they are violent, then health workers who engage with them are excluded from their own group. Similarly, if the group norm is to not provide care for persons with MNS disorders because they are not treatable, then healthcare professionals who spend time with them are threatening to the rest of the group because of potential loss of productivity to the group. As a group, the healthcare professionals may blame the conditions on the patient's behavior, personal choices, moral infractions, poor character, and laziness. The social impacts of association may extend to one's personal social network resulting in ostracism by one's family and friends.
4. **Burnout.** Burnout is another aspect of the phenomenon described above. Burnout may be associated with feeling unable to achieve one's desired level of self-efficacy and thus inducing occupational threats.

According to the proposed social neuroscience-informed approach, an effective intervention to reduce stigma among primary care workers would need to target beliefs related to survival, professional obligations, and social norms.

Development of Stigma Reduction Intervention for Healthcare Workers

The above model was used to formulate an intervention for primary care workers which was designed to be incorporated into MNS trainings for primary care workers that would reduce stigma and feasibly be implemented in both high- and low-resource settings (Kohrt et al., 2020). Nepal was selected as the site for piloting the intervention because it represents the conditions – lack of access to specialist mental health services– under which the majority of the world's population with MNS disorders live. In these settings, the WHO mhGAP and other initiatives have advocated for delivery of MNS care in primary care settings.

In southern Nepal, the UK AID/Department for International Development-sponsored PRogramme for Improving Mental health carE (PRIME) took place from 2012 to 2019 (Jordans et al., 2016). The goal of PRIME is to increase the coverage of treatment for priority mental disorders by implementing and evaluating a comprehensive mental healthcare package, integrated into primary healthcare in five LMICs (Nepal, India, South Africa, Ethiopia, and Uganda) (De Silva et al., 2015; Hanlon et al., 2014, 2015; Lund et al., 2012, 2016; Makan et al., 2015; Mendenhall et al., 2014). Primary care workers with legal authority to prescribe medicine (hereafter referred to as "prescribers") were trained in a ten-day curriculum roughly divided between basic psychosocial skills and mhGAP content for four MNS disorders (depression, psychosis, alcohol use disorder, and epilepsy). Primary care workers who provide care but do not manage medications (hereafter referred to as "nonprescribers") were all trained for five days on basic psychosocial support skills. PRIME is implemented by Transcultural Psychosocial Organization (TPO) Nepal, a Nepali nongovernmental mental health research and training organization (Upadhaya et al., 2014).

We developed the REducing Stigma among HealthcAre ProvidErs (RESHAPE) intervention to add attitude improvement components to the nonprescriber and prescriber versions of the PRIME trainings in Nepal (Kohrt et al., 2018, 2020). For the nonprescriber training, on Day 2, two nonprescribers who were selected and trained as aspirational figures (see below for aspiration figure selection and training) presented recovery stories and discussed common myths about MNS disorders. On Day 3, two persons with lived experience of MNS disorders who had been trained on PhotoVoice presented recovery stories, participated in question-and-answer sessions, and spent time with primary care worker trainees during tea breaks and lunch. PhotoVoice is a qualitative research technique that asks participants to take photos related to a certain theme in order to provide insight into community needs and experiences (Wang & Burris, 1997). It is often used in participatory action research and at times is used to generate compelling narratives to influence policy makers (Catalani & Minkler, 2010). PhotoVoice has been used to reduce stigma among persons living with mental illness and facilitate peer support in the United States. However, it has not previously been used as a tool to facilitate mental health service users engaging with health workers.

A one-hour didactic session on stigma and discrimination also occurred on Day 3. On Day 4, two persons with lived experience of MNS disorders participated in communication role plays and interacted with primary care workers during tea breaks and mealtimes. On Day 5, two aspirational figures and two persons with lived experience participated in a collaborative problem-solving session with the primary care worker trainees. For the 10-day prescriber training, comparable RESHAPE elements were included with recovery narratives from persons with lived experience paired to specific mhGAP modules.

Working with primary care health workers and psychosocial workers in the region for the study, we identified persons living with mental illness who had received treatment in the prior year and were currently in recovery. In addition, we trained the persons with lived experience in PhotoVoice so that they were able to use a PowerPoint presentation to tell recovery stories with photographs they had taken (Rai et al., 2018). This helped them to claim some of the symbolic authority held by the other trainers.

Given the arc of symbolic healing as well as ritual structure in general, we worked with persons with lived experience to craft their recovery narratives in a three-act story structure. The first act described their lives with MNS disorders before treatment. Local photographs and experiences would help primary care workers connect and invest in the subsequent narrative. In addition, the first act highlighted the impact on family members of the untreated MNS disorder. This helped build empathy for the individual and their family. In the second act of the story structure, the persons with lived experience showed photos of receiving treatment from local primary care workers. This helped the primary care workers connect with providing care by seeing their colleagues able to do this effectively. From a "what matters most" perspective, primary care workers hearing the story and viewing the photos could see that the MNS training would help them be even more effective healthcare workers rather than seeing MNS care as interfering with other professional obligations. The third act showed what life was like after recovery. The persons with lived experience often framed this phase in terms of economic productivity (e.g., being able to farm, raise goats), educational achievement (returning to school), and family functioning (caring for children, playing with grandchildren). We encouraged these indicators of recovery from a "what matters most" perspective, i.e., what matters most to both patients and healthcare providers is quality of life and social, family, and economic functioning rather than simply focusing on symptom reduction.

This story structure was designed to mobilize empathy and hope among the primary care workers at the training. With regard to violence and threat, we encouraged persons with lived experience to describe how their MNS disorder contributed to violence when appropriate. We predicted that it would be helpful to primary care workers to have specific examples of violence and the impact of treatment on violence. Persons with lived experience of substance use disorders were most likely to describe violence before treatment and how treatment led to preventing future violence. In addition, the person-to-person contact between persons with lived experience and primary care worker trainees during tea breaks and lunches was intended to dispel primary care worker expectations that persons with MNS disorders are typically difficult and violent. After presenting their stories, the persons with lived experience participated in a question-and-answer session in which the primary care trainees were given the opportunity to ask questions about living with mental illness, receiving treatment, and the life in recovery.

Ultimately, impact of the intervention mapped onto our three domains in the Identity Threat Model. In qualitative interviews, primary care workers described changes in perceptions of violence and the ability to effectively treat MNS disorders. Quantitative measurements demonstrated improvement in attitudes from pretraining to 16-month follow-up (54 percent willing to spend time with persons with MNS disorders to 81 percent willing), knowledge (63 percent accurate MNS knowledge to 76 percent accuracy), and clinical competency (49 percent achieving minimal competency to 93 percent competency). Implicit association test scores did not change. This proof of concept demonstration suggests that social neuroscience theories can play an important role in the conceptualization of global mental health training programs intended to improve both clinical skills and attitudes toward persons living with mental, neurological, and substance use disorders.

REFERENCES

Allport, F. H. (1954). The structuring of events: Outline of a general theory with applications to psychology. *Psychological Review*, *61*(5), 281–303. https://doi.org/10.1037/h0062678

Amodio, D. M. (2014). The neuroscience of prejudice and stereotyping. *Nature Reviews Neuroscience*, *15*(10), 670–82. https://doi.org/10.1038/nrn3800

Berridge, K. C. (2004). Motivation concepts in behavioral neuroscience. *Physiology & Behavior*, *81*(2), 179–209. https://doi.org/10.1016/j.physbeh.2004.02.004

Catalani, C., & Minkler, M. (2010). Photovoice: A review of the literature in health and public health. *Health Education & Behavior*, *37*(3), 424–51. https://doi.org/10.1177/1090198109342084

Cikara, M., Bruneau, E., Van Bavel, J. J., & Saxe, R. (2014). Their pain gives us pleasure: How intergroup dynamics shape empathic failures and counter-empathic responses. *Journal of Experimental Social Psychology*, *55*, 110–25. https://doi.org/10.1016/j.jesp.2014.06.007

Cikara, M., & Fiske, S. T. (2013). Their pain, our pleasure: Stereotype content and schadenfreude. *Annals of the New York Academy of Sciences*, *1299*(1), 52–9. https://doi.org/10.1111/nyas.12179

Cikara, M., Jenkins, A. C., Dufour, N., & Saxe, R. (2014). Reduced self-referential neural response during intergroup competition predicts competitor harm. *NeuroImage*, *96*, 36–43. https://doi.org/10.1016/j.neuroimage.2014.03.080

Corrigan, P. W., Morris, S. B., Michaels, P. J., Rafacz, J. D., & Rüsch, N. (2012). Challenging the public stigma of mental illness: A meta-analysis of outcome studies. *Psychiatric Services*, *63*(10), 963–73. https://doi.org/10.1176/appi.ps.201100529

de Figueiredo, J. M., & Griffith, J. L. (2016). Chronic pain, chronic demoralization, and the role of psychotherapy. *Journal of Contemporary Psychotherapy*, *46*(3), 167–77. https://doi.org/10.1007/s10879-016-9331-x

De Silva, M. J., Rathod, S. D., Hanlon, C., Breuer, E., Chisholm, D., Fekadu, A., Jordans, M., Kigozi, F., Petersen, I., Shidhaye, R., Medhin, G., Ssebunnya, J., Prince, M., Thornicroft, G., Tomlinson, M., Lund, C., & Patel, V. (2015). Evaluation of district mental healthcare plans: The PRIME consortium methodology. *British Journal of Psychiatry*, *208*(s56), s63–s70. https://doi.org/10.1192/bjp.bp.114.153858

Decety, J. (Ed.). (2012). *Empathy: From bench to bedside*. MIT Press.

Dow, J. (1986). Universal aspects of symbolic healing – A theoretical synthesis. *American Anthropologist*, *88*(1), 56–69. https://doi.org/10.1525/aa.1986.88.1.02a00040

Hanlon, C., Fekadu, A., Jordans, M., Kigozi, F., Petersen, I., Shidhaye, R., Honikman, S., Lund, C., Prince, M., Raja, S., Thornicraft, G., Tomlinson, M., & Patel, V. (2015). District mental healthcare plans for five low- and middle-income countries: Commonalities, variations and evidence gaps. *British Journal of Psychiatry*, *208*(s56), s47–s54. https://doi.org/10.1192/bjp.bp.114.153767

Hanlon, C., Luitel, N. P., Kathree, T., Murhar, V., Shrivasta, S., Medhin, G., Ssebunnya, J., Fekadu, A., Shidhaye, R., Petersen, I., Jordans, M., Kigozi, F., Thornicroft, G., Patel, V., Tomlinson, M., Lund, C., Breuer, E., De Silva, M., & Prince, M. (2014). Challenges and opportunities for implementing integrated mental health care: A district level situation analysis from five low- and middle-income countries. *PLoS ONE*, *9*(2), e88437. https://doi.org/10.1371/journal.pone.0088437

Heim, E., Kohrt, B. A., Koschorke, M., Milenova, M., & Thornicroft, G. (2018). Reducing mental health related stigma in primary health care settings in low- and middle-income countries: A systematic review. *Epidemiology and Psychiatric Sciences*, *4*, 1–10. https://doi.org/10.1017/S2045796018000458

Henderson, C., Noblett, J., Parke, H., Clement, S., Caffrey, A., Gale-Grant, O., Schulze, B., Druss, B., & Thornicroft, G. (2014). Mental health-related stigma in health care and mental health-care settings. *Lancet Psychiatry*, *1*(6), 467–82. https://doi.org/10.1016/S2215-0366(14)00023-6

Jordans, M. J. D., Luitel, N. P., Pokhrel, P., & Patel, V. (2016). Development and pilot testing of a mental healthcare plan in Nepal. *British Journal of Psychiatry*, *208*(s56), s21–s28. https://doi.org/10.1192/bjp.bp.114.153718

Kirmayer, L. J. (2004). The cultural diversity of healing: Meaning, metaphor and mechanism. *British Medical Bulletin*, *69*, 33–48. https://doi.org/10.1093/bmb/ldh006

Kirmayer, L. J. (2015). Empathy and alterity in psychiatry. In L. J. Kirmayer, R. Lemelson, & C. A. Cummings (Eds.), *Re-visioning psychiatry: Cultural phenomenology, critical neuroscience and global mental health* (pp. 141–67). Cambridge University Press. https://doi.org/10.1017/CBO9781139424745.009

Kohrt, B. A., Jordans, M. J. D., Turner, E. L., Sikkema, K. J., Luitel, N. P., Rai, S., Singla, D. R., Lamichhane, J., Lund, C., & Patel, V. (2018). Reducing stigma among healthcare providers to improve mental health services (RESHAPE): Protocol for a pilot cluster randomized controlled trial of a stigma reduction intervention for training primary healthcare workers in Nepal. *Pilot and Feasibility Studies, 4*(1), 36. https://doi.org/10.1186/s40814-018-0234-3

Kohrt, B. A., Turner, E. L., Rai, S., Bhardwaj, A, Sikkema, K. J., Adelekun, A., Dhakal, M., Luitel, N. P., Lund, C., Patel, V., & Jordans, M. J. D. (2020). Reducing mental illness stigma in healthcare settings: Proof of concept for a social contact intervention to address what matters most for primary care providers. Social Science & Medicine, *250*, 112852. https://doi.org/10.1016/j.socscimed.2020.112852

Lund, C., Tomlinson, M., De Silva, M., Fekadu, A., Shidhaye, R., Jordans, M., Petersen, I., Bhana, A., Kigozi, F., Prince, M., Thornicroft, G., Hanlon, C., Kakuma, R., McDaid, D., Saxena, S., Chisholm, D., Raja, S., Kippen-Wood, S., Honikman, S., ... Patel, V. (2012). PRIME: A programme to reduce the treatment gap for mental disorders in five low- and middle-income countries. *PLoS Medicine, 9*(12), e1001359. https://doi.org/10.1371/journal.pmed.1001359

Lund, C., Tomlinson, M., & Patel, V. (2016). Integration of mental health into primary care in low- and middle-income countries: The PRIME mental healthcare plans. *British Journal of Psychiatry, 208*(s56), s1–s3. https://doi.org/10.1192/bjp.bp.114.153668

Makan, A., Fekadu, A., Murhar, V., Luitel, N., Kathree, T., Ssebunya, J., & Lund, C. (2015). Stakeholder analysis of the Programme for Improving Mental health carE (PRIME): Baseline findings. *International Journal of Mental Health Systems, 9*, 27. https://doi.org/10.1186/s13033-015-0020-z

Mattan, B. D., Wei, K. Y., Cloutier, J., & Kubota, J. T. 2018. The social neuroscience of race-based and status-based prejudice. *Current Opinion in Psychology, 24*, 27–34. https://doi.org/10.1016/j.copsyc.2018.04.010

Mendenhall, E., De Silva, M. J., Hanlon, C., Petersen, I., Shidhaye, R., Jordans, M., Luitel, N., Ssebunnya, J., Fekadu, A., Patel, V., Tomlinson, M., & Lund, C. (2014). Acceptability and feasibility of using non-specialist health workers to deliver mental health care: Stakeholder perceptions from the PRIME district sites in Ethiopia, India, Nepal, South Africa, and Uganda. *Social Science & Medicine, 118*, 33–42. https://doi.org/10.1016/j.socscimed.2014.07.057

Montag , C., Dziobek, I., Richter, I. S., Neuhaus, K., Lehmann, A., Sylla, R., Heekeren, H. R., Heinz, A., & Gallinat, J. (2011). Different aspects of theory of mind in paranoid schizophrenia: Evidence from a video-based assessment. *Psychiatry Research, 186*(2–3), 203–209. https://doi.org/10.1016/j.psychres.2010.09.006

Pescosolido, B. A., & Manago, B. (2017). Getting underneath the power of "contact": Revisiting the fundamental lever of stigma as a social network phenomenon. In B. Major, J. F. Dovidio, & B. G. Link (Eds.), *The Oxford handbook of stigma, discrimination, and health* (pp. 397–411). Oxford University Press. https://doi.org/10.1093/oxfordhb/9780190243470.013.16

Pettigrew, T. F., Tropp, L. R., Wagner, U., & Christ, O. (2011). Recent advances in intergroup contact theory. *International Journal of Intercultural Relations, 35*(3), 271–80. https://doi.org/10.1016/j.ijintrel.2011.03.001

Rai, S., Gurung, D., Kaiser, B. N., Sikkema, K. J., Dhakal, M., Bhardwaj, A., Tergesen, C., & Kohrt, B. A. (2018). A service user co-facilitated intervention to reduce mental illness stigma among primary healthcare workers: Utilizing perspectives of family members and caregivers. *Families, Systems, & Health, 36*(2), 198–209. https://doi.org/10.1037/fsh0000338

Thornicroft, G., Chatterji, S., Evans-Lacko, S., Gruber, M., Sampson, N., Aguilar-Gaxiola, S., Al-Hamzawi, A., Alonso, J., Andrade, L., Borges, G., Bruffaerts, R., Bunting, B., Caldas de Almeida, J. M., Florescu, S., de Girolamo, G., Gureje, O., Haro, J. M., He, Y., Hinkov, H., ... Kessler, R. C. (2017). Undertreatment of people with major depressive disorder in 21 countries. *British Journal of Psychiatry, 210*(2), 119–24. https://doi.org/10.1192/bjp.bp.116.188078

Thornicroft, G., Mehta, N., Clement, S., Evans-Lacko, S., Doherty, M., Rose, D., Koschorke, M., Shidhaye, R., O'Reilly, C., & Henderson, C. (2015). Evidence for effective interventions to reduce mental-health-related stigma and discrimination. *Lancet, 387*(10023), 1123–32. https://doi.org/10.1016/S0140-6736(15)00298-6

Tiihonen, J., Lönnqvist, J., Wahlbeck, K., Klaukka, T., Niskanen, L., Tanskanen, A., & Haukka, J. (2009). 11-year follow-up of mortality in patients with schizophrenia: A population-based cohort study (FIN11 study). *Lancet, 374*(9690), 620–7. https://doi.org/10.1016/S0140-6736(09)60742-X

Turner, V. W. (1967). *The forest of symbols: Aspects of Ndembu ritual.* Cornell University Press.

Upadhaya, N., Luitel, N. P., Koirala, S., Adhikari, R. P., Gurung, D., Shrestha, P., Tol, W. A., Kohrt, B. A., & Jordans, M. J. D. (2014). The role of mental health and psychosocial support nongovernmental organizations: Reflections from post-conflict Nepal. *Intervention: International Journal of Mental Health, Psychosocial Work & Counselling in Areas of Armed Conflict, 12*(Supplement 1), 113–28. https://doi.org/10.1097/WTF.0000000000000064

Wang, C., & Burris, M. A. (1997). Photovoice: Concept, methodology, and use for participatory needs assessment. *Health Education & Behavior, 24*(3), 369–87. https://doi.org/10.1177/109019819702400309

World Health Organization. (2010). *mhGAP Intervention Guide for mental, neurological and substance-use disorders in non-specialized health settings: Mental health Gap Action Programme (mhGAP).* www.who.int/mental_health/publications/mhGAP_intervention_guide/en/

Yang, L. H., Kleinman, A., Link, B. G., Phelan, J. C., Lee, S., & Good, B. (2007). Culture and stigma: Adding moral experience to stigma theory. *Social Science & Medicine, 64*(7), 1524–35. https://doi.org/10.1016/j.socscimed.2006.11.013

19 Cities, Psychosis, and Social Defeat

Firrhaana Sayanvala, Lisa Bornstein, Suparna Choudhury, Jai Shah, Daniel Weinstock, and Ian Gold

Cities and Psychosis

Nowhere perhaps are the interactions among mind, brain, and culture clearer than in psychosis. "Psychosis" refers to a family of neurodevelopmental illnesses characterized most dramatically by auditory voice hallucinations and the bizarre beliefs known as delusions. Schizophrenia is the most devastating of the psychotic illnesses; it inflicts decades-long suffering on the patient, places an enormous burden on the family, and takes a tremendous economic toll on society at large. As of 2013, schizophrenia was among the top twenty-five causes of disability worldwide (Chong et al., 2016). In that same year, the cost of schizophrenia to the United States alone was $155.7 billion (Cloutier et al., 2016). Although psychosis is a manifestation of brain dysfunction, its distal causes are social as well as biological. The "social determinants" of psychosis (Akdeniz et al., 2014) include childhood adversity (Misiak et al., 2017), being an immigrant or the child of an immigrant (Bourque et al., 2012), and – perhaps most surprisingly – urban living. The last of these has been known since 1939 when two sociologists, Robert Faris and Warren Dunham, published a study of psychosis across Chicago neighborhoods (Faris & Dunham, 1939). The authors reported higher rates of psychosis in socially fragmented neighborhoods but found no such difference for bipolar disorder. In the intervening years, psychiatric epidemiology has repeatedly confirmed Faris and Dunham's finding; a recent review found an incidence rate ratio for psychotic disorders of 1.64 in urban compared with rural areas (Castillejos et al., 2018). A meta-analysis carried out by Vassos et al. in 2012 concluded that the effect of urban living was nearly linear: the bigger the city (both in terms of population and population density), the bigger the risk (Vassos et al., 2012). Recent evidence, however, has cast doubt on whether the urban effect is universal. Although the effect is robust in developed countries, the same may not be true of low- and middle-income countries (DeVylder et al., 2018).

The cause of the urban effect in psychosis remains unknown, but it is widely believed to be a function of the social environment. Although infections spread more rapidly in cities than in rural areas, for example, rates of psychosis vary within cities as a function of social conditions (Kirkbride et al., 2007); and while drugs known to raise the risk of psychosis are more common in cities, the urban effect is not fully explained by drug abuse (Krabbendam & van Os, 2005). There is also good evidence that the urban effect is causal and not a result of a movement into cities of those already at higher risk of psychosis; a large Danish study (Pedersen & Mortensen, 2001) found that moving from rural to urban environments raised the risk of psychosis, and movement in the other direction lowered it (for a contrasting view, see Sariaslan et al., 2016). Finally, there is evidence for an effect of population size on brain function. A 2011 fMRI study (Lederbogen et al., 2011) found that under conditions of stress, amygdala activity in healthy individuals varied as a function of the population of their current city, and perigenual anterior cingulate cortex activation varied with the population of their city of birth.

Even if the urban effect in psychosis is indeed a social one, it is an open question which of the myriad social phenomena characteristic of urbanicity interact with psychosis. To address this question, Selten and Cantor-Graae (2005; see also Selten & Cantor-Graae, 2007; Selten et al., 2013, 2016) developed the "social defeat" hypothesis of psychosis. Their hypothesis has been widely endorsed, although a variety of different interpretations of it have been proposed. The purpose of this essay is to review the versions of the social defeat hypothesis and to make some remarks about its limitations. Our review suggests that to properly understand mind–brain–culture interactions, we need better and more nuanced social science as much as we do theories of the mind and brain.

Social Defeat

"Social defeat" refers to a class of animal models of the stress associated with social conflict (Toyoda, 2017). In one popular paradigm – the resident–intruder test – a strange male is introduced into the cage of a dominant male. The intruder is attacked and, if it cannot escape, will exhibit characteristic submissive behavior (Hollis & Kabbaj, 2014) as well as alterations in physiology, immune function, cognition, and neurological activity. In particular, neurotransmitter systems, including dopamine, are affected (Hammels et al., 2015).

Although social defeat is commonly thought to provide a model for depression and anxiety, the effect on dopamine opens up the possibility of a role for social stress in the etiology of psychosis (Howes & Kapur, 2009). Selten and Cantor-Graae (2005, p. 101) originally proposed that "a chronic and long-term experience of social defeat may lead to sensitization of the mesolimbic dopamine system ... and thereby increase the risk for schizophrenia," and they characterize the experience of social defeat as one of occupying "a subordinate position" or having "outsider status." Revisiting the hypothesis in 2013, Selten et al. (2013, p. 1180) describe social defeat as the "negative experience of being excluded from the majority group."

Four interpretations of the social defeat hypothesis can be found in the literature: social defeat as (1) objective experience; (2) sensitization; (3) social disadvantage; and (4) thwarted aspirations. We consider each below.

1. **Social defeat as objective experience.** In her ethnographic study of homelessness and schizophrenia in the United States, Luhrmann (2007, p. 151) characterizes social defeat as an "actual social encounter in which one person physically or symbolically loses to another one"; a person "loses" in this sense when someone "demeans them, humiliates them, subordinates them." This conception of social defeat thus construes it as an objective, competitive encounter. For someone living on the streets, for example, defeat can mean losing a physical fight, or being refused a safe place to sleep. Racial minorities can undergo social defeat by being denied employment regardless of qualifications, or by being racially profiled by law enforcement. In these scenarios, a real interaction between two people results in one having lost in a way that would be clear to an observer: a "social defeat," Luhrmann says, "is not so much an idea that someone holds but a human encounter" (2007, p. 152). While understanding social defeat in this way makes it relatively easy to identify, it does not account for the effect of the experience itself or the anticipation of defeat – learned with repeated exposure to humiliating encounters – without which social defeat could never get "under the skin." As a result, some investigators have focused on the *phenomenology* of defeat rather than the encounter itself. One such account focuses on sensitization.

2. **Social defeat as sensitization.** Anglin et al. (2016) investigated the effect on psychotic symptoms of repeated exposure to experiences of race-related rejection sensitivity (RS-race) – "an outlook characterized by an anxious expectation of rejection that develops when an individual's desires to belong are repeatedly unrealized" (2016, p. 2). They report a positive relationship between RS-race and total number of "attenuated positive psychotic symptoms" that are experienced as distressing (APPS-distress) and suggest that levels of RS-race "partially mediates the relationship between racial discrimination and APPS-distress" (2016, p. 5). Collip et al. (2008) suggest that sensitization of this kind leads over time to an increased dopaminergic response to the same stressor, and particularly traumatic stressors may lead to sensitization that increases the behavioral response to less acute stressors. Further, the frequency of exposure one has

had to racial discrimination may contribute to a heightened anticipation of future encounters and thus a greater vulnerability to the effects of such encounters. The potential role of sensitization in social defeat points up the importance of understanding defeat as an experience. In individuals with a long history of exposure to discrimination or other forms of social subordination, relatively minor encounters – including those that might not be easily identified as humiliating – may nonetheless contribute to the development of psychosis.

3. **Social defeat as social disadvantage.** In an effort to quantify social defeat and better evaluate the effect of environmental factors in schizophrenia, some investigators have focused on social disadvantage as a proxy for social defeat (Marwaha et al., 2007; Morgan et al., 2008). Moreover, it has been proposed that "intersectionality" – falling into more than one category of disadvantage – may enhance social defeat (Haarmans et al., 2016). This approach makes it possible to measure the risk of psychosis by means of demographic data and may suggest methods of prevention or intervention. However, it does not explain *why* particular factors constitute risks for psychosis, and Selten et al. (2013) suggest that this version of the social defeat hypothesis fails to identify a putative mechanism through which disadvantage is translated into risk. Nor does the approach take account of an individual's interpretation of disadvantage which, as we have just noted, may be directly relevant to assessing risk. For example, while long-term unemployment is a form of disadvantage that might plausibly be thought to constitute a form of social defeat, those who attribute their unemployment to a poor economy are unlikely to experience being unemployed in the same way as someone who takes it to be the result of racial discrimination (Cantor-Graae, 2007).

4. **Social defeat as thwarted aspirations.** Finally, social defeat has been conceptualized as the result of thwarted aspirations (Maraj et al., 2018) – a discrepancy between the expectations of an individual in a marginalized position and the reality of what they can achieve (Li et al., 2012). This proposal is a particularly useful one when applied to the risk of psychosis associated with immigration. Immigrants and their children are at about twice the risk of psychosis compared to the general population (Bourque et al., 2012); indeed, dark-skinned children are at four times the risk. Why would second-generation immigrants be more vulnerable than their parents? One possibility is that while first-generation immigrants anticipate being perceived as the "other" in their adopted country, second-generation immigrants expect to be treated like everyone else. Visible minorities, however, may find that their opportunities do not match their self-conception, and this gap between expectation and reality may explain the increased risk of illness; indeed it may be a more accurate predictor of

psychosis risk than measures of absolute deprivation (Cantor-Graae, 2007; Kirkbride et al., 2014; Li et al., 2012).

Social Defeat and the City

Social defeat is, on the face of it, a plausible hypothesis both about childhood adversity and immigration as determinants of psychosis insofar as both of these social factors can quite naturally, if vaguely, be thought to involve distressing social experiences or interactions. The role of the city in psychosis presents a greater explanatory challenge. Although one cannot deny that cities shape social interactions in unique ways, it is not obvious how to link increased population with greater social defeat. Further, different theoretical accounts will have to be formulated to fit the various interpretations of social defeat. However, there are some apparent obstacles to such accounts.

If we take social defeat to mean encounters leading to social subordination, then some forms of social defeat may correlate with city size. Crime, for example, increases in large cities, and being the victim of crime seems like a form of subordination. In general, however, social subordination is more likely to depend on individual psychological factors, and socioeconomic or cultural conditions than on population per se. Similar remarks apply to social sensitization. One might anticipate humiliation or rejection more frequently in an environment with more individuals (especially strangers) in it. Nevertheless, one would have to show that social anxiety of the relevant sort will continue to rise with population. Again, it seems likely that a range of factors independent of city size will play a more important role than population. The gap between aspiration and achievement may also be heightened in cities where the manifestations of other people's socioeconomic status may bring one's own limitations into relief. Here too, however, the particular socioeconomic structure of a city and a range of cultural factors are likely to be highly relevant to experiences of social defeat of this kind. Finally, social defeat construed as social disadvantage raises different theoretical questions that will depend in part on the ways of measuring disadvantage. Unemployment, for example, is likely to be on most lists of significant disadvantage, but whether urban and rural differences will mirror the epidemiology of psychosis is likely to differ across countries. In Canada, for example, one measure of unemployment finds rural areas better off (4.8 percent unemployment compared to 5.7 percent in metropolitan areas according to Statistics Canada[1]). Rural unemployment is also lower in Latin America and the Caribbean, (3.1 percent as against 6.9 percent),

---

[1] Statistics Canada Table 14-10-0106-01. Employment and unemployment rate, annual, population centres and rural areas (https://www150.statcan.gc.ca/t1/tbl1/en/tv.action?pid=1410010601).

but 56 percent of rural workers experience "vulnerable employment" – associated with lower wages and fewer protections – compared to 27 percent of workers in cities.[2] Is unemployment or vulnerable employment the greater stressor with respect to psychosis?

One cannot answer this question, and many others like it, because the social defeat hypothesis is not only equivocal but underspecified. The various interpretations of social defeat make use of notions of social stress that are conceptually broad and not uncommon in one form or another in most people's lives. Moreover, the social structure of cities is complex, and the paths linking the properties of a city and unpleasant social experiences are likely to be long and winding. Finally, cities are cultural objects, and if we are to identify the effects of cities on the mind and brain, we need a nuanced theory of the city just as we do a theory of the mind and brain. If the social defeat hypothesis is to prove useful in the long run, research will have to be devoted to all of these concerns as well as to developing methods to test the detailed hypotheses that research throws up. In the next section, we provide a brief illustration of the latter.

Social Networks and City Size

Although the nature of urban social life has been a research theme for decades, new communication technologies are now producing fine-grained data relating city size to social interactions. Schläpfer et al. (2014; see also Bettencourt, 2013) analyzed a large dataset consisting of several million cellular phone calls made in Portugal over a fifteen-month period. In order to use the data to reveal patterns in social interactions, only reciprocal phone contacts were included – a restriction that eliminates business phones, telemarketing calls, wrong numbers, and the like (Miritello et al., 2013). Further, because phone calls have been shown to correlate with face-to-face encounters (Calabrese et al., 2011; Saramäki et al., 2014), these data may provide insight into social interactions more broadly. For our purposes, Schläpfer et al.'s central finding is that as city size increases, phone contacts also rise: with a doubling of population, contacts increase by 12 percent. Call frequency, as well as volume (i.e., time spent on the phone), show a similar pattern of change.

How could these data be used to clarify the social defeat hypothesis? Notice, to begin with, that they are at odds with the exclusion interpretation of the hypothesis because people living in heavily populated areas, compared to sparsely populated ones, are *more* socially connected rather than less. Of course, it is possible to *feel* excluded in a crowd – more acutely, perhaps, in

---

[2] UN report reveals stark gap between urban and rural employment in Latin America and the Caribbean. *UN News*, October 20, 2016, (https://news.un.org/en/story/2016/10/543332-un-report-reveals-stark-gap-between-urban-and-rural-employment-latin america).

a big crowd than a small one. One can thus envisage yet another interpretation of the social defeat hypothesis that focuses on the subjective sense of exclusion rather than actual isolation. While this idea might be worth exploring, in the absence of further details, it is no more susceptible of useful experimental investigation than the views already on offer.

These findings also have a bearing on the interpretation of social defeat as social subordination. The hypothesis predicts that experiences of subordination will grow with population size. One could argue that the presence of more people leads to more frequent social interactions, and more social interactions create more opportunities for subordination. While Schläpfer et al.'s study supports the first of these conditions, evaluating the second is more difficult. More people do indeed lead to a greater number of social interactions both by means of technology and, presumably, in face-to-face encounters (Saramäki et al., 2014). Since the increase in encounters is due to a larger social network, however, the overall *quality* of the encounters remains to be determined. Indeed, there is considerable evidence that social relationships and social support *enhance* physical and psychological well-being in healthy individuals (Kawachi & Berkman, 2001) and in those with psychosis in particular (Degnan et al., 2018; Priebe et al., 2019). As a result, the Schläpfer et al. data provide only partial support for the subordination interpretation. Whether other interpretations fare better will require other datasets or novel analytic methods.

Future Directions

Progress on understanding the nature of the social determinants of psychosis and the mechanisms of their action should be a priority for research. The social defeat hypothesis is important in that it provides a framework to link social interactions with the neurophysiology of psychosis, but, as we have suggested, the hypothesis is insufficiently developed to be tested as it applies to urban environments. To make progress we must find ways to begin to address a number of questions including these: Which version of social defeat seems most plausible? How can we fractionate the complex concept of social defeat (of whichever variety) to make it experimentally tractable? What sorts of social interaction typically lead to experiences of social defeat, and how should we characterize those experiences? In parallel with this articulation of the social defeat hypothesis, we must develop qualitative and quantitative evidence about the patterns of social interaction that emerge in more and less populous environments that can make contact with more refined interpretations of the hypothesis. This latter effort will have to be carried out largely by social scientists; computational social science (Lazer et al., 2009) involving the analysis of very large datasets is likely to be of particular use.

Finally, the investigation of the effect of city living on psychosis provides a telling illustration of a blindspot in research on the relations among mind, brain, and culture. Culture is part of the environment of the behaving agent and is often taken as a given. An adequate account of the effects of culture on the mind or brain, however, requires a *theory* of the cultural phenomenon at issue. A successful account of mind, brain, and culture, then, will have to be a multidisciplinary effort in which social science is treated as an equal partner to psychology and neuroscience.

REFERENCES

Akdeniz, C., Tost, H., & Meyer-Lindenberg, A. (2014). The neurobiology of social environmental risk for schizophrenia: An evolving research field. *Social Psychiatry and Psychiatric Epidemiology*, *49*(4), 507–17. https://doi.org/10.1007/s00127-014-0858-4

Anglin, D. M., Greenspoon, M., Lighty, Q., & Ellman, L. M. (2016). Race-based rejection sensitivity partially accounts for the relationship between racial discrimination and distressing attenuated positive psychotic symptoms. *Early Intervention in Psychiatry*, *10*(5), 411–18. https://doi.org/10.1111/eip.12184

Bettencourt, L. M. A. (2013). The origins of scaling in cities. *Science*, *340*(6139), 1438–41. https://doi.org/10.1126/science.1235823

Bourque, F., van der Ven, E., Fusar-Poli, P., & Malla, A. (2012). Immigration, social environment and onset of psychotic disorders. *Current Pharmaceutical Design*, *18*(4), 518–26. https://doi.org/10.2174/138161212799316028

Calabrese, F., Smoreda, Z., Blondel, V. D., & Ratti, C. (2011). Interplay between Telecommunications and face-to-face interactions: A study using mobile phone data. *PLoS ONE*, *6*(7), e20814. https://doi.org/10.1371/journal.pone.0020814

Cantor-Graae, E. (2007). The contribution of social factors to the development of schizophrenia: A review of recent findings. *Canadian Journal of Psychiatry*, *52*(2), 277–86. https://doi.org/10.1177/070674370705200502

Castillejos, M. C., Martin-Pérez, C., & Moreno-Küstner, B. (2018). A systematic review and meta-analysis of the incidence of psychotic disorders: The distribution of rates and the influence of gender, urbanicity, immigration and socio-economic level. *Psychological Medicine*, *48*(13), 2101–15. https://doi.org/10.1017/S0033291718000235

Chong, H. Y., Teoh, S. L., Wu, D. B., Kotirum, S., Chiou, C. F., & Chaiyakunapruk, N. (2016). Global economic burden of schizophrenia: A systematic review. *Neuropsychiatric Disease and Treatment*, *12*, 357–73. https://doi.org/10.2147/NDT.S96649.

Cloutier, M., Aigbogun, M. S., Guerin, A., Nitulescu, R., Ramanakumar, A. V., Kamat, S. A., DeLucia, M., Duffy, R., Legacy, S. N., Henderson, C., Francois, C., & Wu, E. (2016). The economic burden of schizophrenia in the United States in 2013. *Journal of Clinical Psychiatry*, *77*(6), 764–71. https:// doi.org/10.4088/JCP.15m10278.

Collip, D., Myin-Germeys, I., & Van Os, J. (2008). Does the concept of "sensitization" provide a plausible mechanism for the putative link between the environment and schizophrenia? *Schizophrenia Bulletin, 34*(2), 220–5. https://doi.org/10.1093/schbul/sbm163

Degnan, A., Berry, K., Sweet, D., Abel, K., Crossley, N., & Edge, D. (2018). Social networks and symptomatic and functional outcomes in schizophrenia: A systematic review and meta-analysis. *Social Psychiatry and Psychiatric Epidemiology, 53*(9), 873–88. https://doi.org/10.1007/s00127-018-1552-8

DeVylder, J. E., Kelleher, I., Lalane, M., Oh, H., Link, B. G., & Koyanagi, A. (2018). Association of urbanicity with psychosis in low- and middle-income countries. *JAMA Psychiatry, 75*(7), 678–86. https://doi.org/10.1001/jamapsychiatry.2018.0577

Faris, R. E. L., & Dunham, H. W. (1939). *Mental disorders in urban areas: An ecological study of schizophrenia and other psychoses*. University of Chicago Press.

Haarmans, M., Vass, V., & Bentall, R. P. (2016). Voices' use of gender, race and other social categories to undermine female voice-hearers: Implications for incorporating intersectionality within CBT for psychosis. *Psychosis, 8*(3), 203–13. https://doi.org/10.1080/17522439.2015.1131323

Hammels, C., Pishva, E., De Vry, J., van den Hove, D. L. A., Prickaerts, J., van Winkel, R., Selten, J.-P., Lesch, K.-P., Daskalakis, N. P., Steinbusch, H. W. M., van Os, J., Kenis, G., & Rutten, B. P. F. (2015). Defeat stress in rodents: From behavior to molecules. *Neuroscience & Biobehavioral Reviews, 59*, 111–40. https://doi.org/10.1016/j.neubiorev.2015.10.006

Hollis, F., & Kabbaj, M. (2014). Social defeat as an animal model for depression. *ILAR J, 55*(2), 221–32. https://doi.org/10.1093/ilar/ilu002

Howes, O. D., & Kapur, S. (2009). The dopamine hypothesis of schizophrenia: Version III – The final common pathway. *Schizophrenia Bulletin, 35*(3), 549–62. https://doi.org/10.1093/schbul/sbp006

Kawachi, I., & Berkman, L. F. (2001). Social ties and mental health. *Journal of Urban Health, 78*(3), 458–67. https://doi.org/10.1093/jurban/78.3.458

Kirkbride, J. B., Jones, P. B., Ullrich, S., & Coid, J. W. (2014). Social deprivation, inequality, and the neighborhood-level incidence of psychotic syndromes in East London. *Schizophrenia Bulletin, 40*(1), 169–80. https://doi.org/10.1093/schbul/sbs151

Kirkbride, J. B., Morgan, C., Fearon, P., Dazzan, P., Murray, R. M., & Jones, P. B. (2007). Neighbourhood-level effects on psychoses: Re-examining the role of context. *Psychological Medicine, 37*(10), 1413–25. https://doi.org/10.1017/S0033291707000499

Krabbendam, L., & van Os, J. (2005). Schizophrenia and urbanicity: A major environmental influence – conditional on genetic risk. *Schizophrenia Bulletin, 31*(4), 795–9. https://doi.org/10.1093/schbul/sbi060

Lazer, D., Pentland, A., Adamic, L., Aral, S., Barabási, A.-L., Brewer, D., Brewer, D., Christakis, N., Contractor, N., Fowler, J., Gutmann, M., Jebara, T., King, G., Macy, M., Roy, D., & Van Alstyne, M. (2009). Computational social science. *Science, 323*(5915), 721–3. https://doi.org/10.1126/science.1167742

Lederbogen, F., Kirsch, P., Haddad, L., Streit, F., Tost, H., Schuch, P., Wüst, S., Pruessner, J. C., Rietschel, M., Deuschle, M., & Meyer-Lindenberg, A. (2011). City living and urban upbringing affect neural social stress processing in humans. *Nature, 474*(7352), 498–501. https://doi.org/10.1038/nature10190

Li, D., Law, S., & Andermann, L. (2012). Association between degrees of social defeat and themes of delusion in patients with schizophrenia from immigrant and ethnic minority backgrounds. *Transcultural Psychiatry*, *49*(5), 735–49. https://doi.org/10.1177/1363461512464625

Luhrmann, T. M. (2007). Social defeat and the culture of chronicity: Or, why schizophrenia does so well over there and so badly here. *Culture, Medicine and Psychiatry*, *31*(2), 135–72. https://doi.org/10.1007/s11013-007-9049-z

Maraj, A., Veru, F., Morrison, L., Joober, R., Malla, A, Iyer, S., & Shah, J. (2018). Disengagement in immigrant groups receiving services for a first episode of psychosis. *Schizophrenia Research*, *193*, 399–405. https://doi.org/10.1016/j.schres.2017.07.054

Marwaha, S., Johnson, S., Bebbington, P., Stafford, M., Angermeyer, M. C., Brugha, T., Azorin, J.-M., Kilian, R., Hansen, K., & Toumi, M. (2007). Rates and correlates of employment in people with schizophrenia in the UK, France and Germany. *British Journal of Psychiatry*, *191*(1), 30–7. https://doi.org/10.1192/bjp.bp.105.020982

Miritello, G., Lara, R., Cebrian, M., & Moro, E. (2013). Limited communication capacity unveils strategies for human interaction. *Scientific Reports*, *3*, 1950. https://doi.org/10.1038/srep01950

Misiak, B., Krefft, M., Bielawski, T., Moustafa, A. A., Sąsiadek, M. M., & Frydecka, D. (2017). Toward a unified theory of childhood trauma and psychosis: A comprehensive review of epidemiological, clinical, neuropsychological and biological findings. *Neuroscience & Biobehavioral Reviews*, *75*, 393–406. https://doi.org/10.1016/j.neubiorev.2017.02.015

Morgan, C., Kirkbride, J., Hutchinson, G., Craig, T., Morgan, K., Dazzan, P., Boydell, J., Doody, G. A., Jones, P. B., Murray, R. M., Leff, J., & Fearon, P. (2008). Cumulative social disadvantage, ethnicity and first-episode psychosis: A case-control study. *Psychological Medicine*, *38*(12), 1701–15. https://doi.org/10.1017/S0033291708004534

Pedersen, C. B., & Mortensen, P. B. (2001). Evidence of a dose-response relationship between urbanicity during upbringing and schizophrenia risk. *Archives of General Psychiatry*, *58*(11), 1039–46. https://doi.org/10.1001/archpsyc.58.11.1039

Priebe, S., Chevalier, A., Hamborg, T., Golden, E., King, M., & Pistrang, N. (2019). Effectiveness of a volunteer befriending programme for patients with schizophrenia: Randomised controlled trial. *British Journal of Psychiatry*. Advance online publication. https://doi.org/10.1192/bjp.2019.42

Saramäki, J., Leicht, E. A., López, E., Roberts, S. G. B., Reed-Tsochas, F., & Dunbar, R. I. M. (2014). Persistence of social signatures in human communication. *Proceedings of the National Academy of Sciences of the United States of America*, *111*(3), 942–7. https://doi.org/10.1073/pnas.1308540110

Sariaslan, A., Fazel, S., D'Onofrio, B. M., Långström, N., Larsson, H., Bergen, S. E., Kuja-Halkola, R., & Lichtenstein, P. (2016). Schizophrenia and subsequent neighborhood deprivation: Revisiting the social drift hypothesis using population, twin and molecular genetic data. *Translational Psychiatry*, *6*, e796. https://doi.org/10.1038/tp.2016.62

Schläpfer, M., Bettencourt, L. M. A., Grauwin, S., Raschke, M., Claxton, R., Smoreda, Z., West, G. B., & Ratti, C. (2014). The scaling of human interactions with city size. *Journal of the Royal Society Interface, 11*(98), 20130789. https://doi.org/10.1098/rsif.2013.0789

Selten, J.-P., & Cantor-Graae, E. (2005). Social defeat: Risk factor for schizophrenia? *British Journal of Psychiatry, 187*(2), 101–2. https://doi.org/10.1192/bjp.187.2.101

Selten, J.-P., & Cantor-Graae, E. (2007). Hypothesis: Social defeat is a risk factor for schizophrenia? *British Journal of Psychiatry,* (S51), s9–s12. https://doi.org/10.1192/bjp.191.51.s9

Selten, J.-P., van der Ven, E., Rutten, B. P. F., & Cantor-Graae, E. (2013). The social defeat hypothesis of schizophrenia: An update. *Schizophrenia Bulletin, 39*(6), 1180–6. https://doi.org/10.1093%2Fschbul%2Fsbt134

Selten, J.-P., van Os, J., & Cantor-Graae, E. (2016). The social defeat hypothesis of schizophrenia: Issues of measurement and reverse causality. *World Psychiatry, 15*(3), 294–5. https://doi.org/10.1002/wps.20369

Statistics Canada. (2014–2018). *Employment and unemployment rate, annual, population centres and rural areas.* Table 14-10-0106-01. [Data file]. www150.statcan.gc.ca/t1/tbl1/en/tv.action?pid=1410010601

Toyoda, A. (2017). Social defeat models in animal science: What we have learned from rodent models. *Animal Science Journal, 88*(7), 944–52. https://doi.org/10.1111/asj.12809

Vassos, E., Pedersen, C. B., Murray, R. M., Collier, D. A., & Lewis, C. M. (2012). Meta-analysis of the association of urbanicity with schizophrenia. *Schizophrenia Bulletin, 38*(6), 1118–23. https://doi.org/10.1093/schbul/sbs096

20 Internet Sociality

Moriah Stendel, Maxwell J. D. Ramstead, and Samuel P. L. Veissière

Introduction: An Evo–Devo Epidemiological Approach to the Study of (Internet) Sociality

The Puzzle of Sociality and "Society"

Human sociality refers to our species' unique ability to form joint goals, engage in joint action, and develop shared ways of doing things (Tomasello, 2009). In more phenomenological terms, it also refers to our ability to feel similar things. In anthropology, sociality is characterized by culturally specific ways of "inhabiting one's body" (Bourdieu, 1977; Mauss, 1973). It is precisely because we can identify stable differences between groups on all these levels – differences which can be attributed to social learning and not merely to biological hardwiring – that we can speak of "culture" per se (Tomasello, 2009; Veissière, 2016). "Culture" here is understood as fundamental facts about the general ecological niche for humans; "cultural differences," in turn, point to observable behavioral differences between groups of the same species that arise through largely implicit forms of social learning (Constant et al., 2019; Veissière, 2016; Veissière et al., 2019).

Some have theorized that, over phylogeny (the evolutionary timeline of a species), human sociality arose through cognitive adaptations for perspective-taking and shared intentionality – that is, the ability to attune oneself to the "invisible" intentions, thoughts, feelings, and needs of others (Hrdy, 2011; Tomasello & Rakoczy, 2003). How cultural forms of life are passed on without much explicit instruction is still open for debate (see Henrich, 2016; Ingold, 2001; Ramstead et al., 2016; Sperber, 1996 for different positions).

The study of large-scale sociality (across phylogeny and ontogeny) presents further challenges. As most human groups started to transition into large societies and civilizations twelve thousand years ago, they began to form integrated communities that became increasingly abstract and "imagined." Nowadays, most humans implicitly acquire culturally specific tastes, values, implicit biases, and ways of doing and desiring things with only limited opportunities for face-to-face interaction with, and imitation of, those in the vast network of "peers" that constitute their societies.

The evolutionary anthropologist Robin Dunbar (1992) famously argued that, for the most part, humans cannot maintain stable relationships with more than 150 of their conspecifics. Beyond this, human relations become increasingly abstract and social cohesion will require intense forms of "social grooming" and specific social pressures.

Hypernatural Monitoring: Society Is Like the Internet (Not the Other Way Around)

Internet communities are imagined, invisible, and have populations many times Dunbar's number. They thus provide a compelling example of the workings of societies. The point is not so much that the Internet is like society, but rather that societies themselves are like the Internet (Veissière, 2016). We propose internet culture as a case study on human sociality, giving us a further window into ordinary mechanisms of human social cognition.

Human worlds can be viewed as organized landscapes of "cultural affordances" grounded in mutual, recursively nested expectations – especially expectations about standards of behavior (Ramstead et al., 2016). On this view, humans learn to see the world through the perspective of other people, and intuitively imagine context-relevant agents to guide them through many of their everyday actions. From context to context and moment to moment, we outsource a large part of our thinking, feeling, and decision-making to sometimes explicit, most often implicit, scenarios of the "what would so-and-so think, feel, or expect me to do" variety.

This feeling of being watched and guided by imaginary others might have played an important role in the evolution of cooperation, morality, large-scale social life, and even organized religion. According to this view, often called the "supernatural monitoring hypothesis," we humans fashioned our gods and spirits to better flesh out the imaginary agents that guide our ordinary cognition, consciousness, and action (Atran & Norarenzayan, 2004; Gervais & Norenzayan, 2012; reviewed in Chapter 11).

Internet communities and social media satisfy the human need to be connected, but also the need to monitor others, and better still, the need to be seen, thought about, and appraised by others. We might call this the "hypernatural monitoring hypothesis" (Veissière & Stendel, 2018).

Cyber-Mediation: Mediating the Experience of Human Embodiment through the Internet

In this chapter, we discuss how human sociality takes shape on the Internet. First, we situate the Internet in the ecological–enactivist approach, considering *cyberspace* as an emergent ecological niche within which virtual communities form. Online communities and social media platforms serve as hubs for the constitution of shared ways-of-being, allowing for the emergence of online cultures that function much like subcultures "in real life," albeit subcultures that spread virally with faster feed-forward potential in cultural epidemiology.

Second, we argue that the communities of cyberspace, too, can constitute distinct cultures, with their own characteristic forms of shared attention, expectations, and experience, and with communities forming through collectively mediated expectations. We suggest that these communities, like those in real life, are formed and remain cohesively bound through the enactment of shared rituals.

After examining the formation of online communities, we turn to the diverse mechanisms by which online communities transmit and share their ways-of-being in this world. This section will uncover the affordances of digital technology that enable distinct forms of attention and embodiment. We argue that the Internet functions to amplify our tendency toward sociality; or, in other words, that cyberspace can be regarded as an "absorption matrix" that leverages the human tendency to surrender attention under particular, culturally prescribed, ritualized circumstances.

The final section of this chapter comprises a typology of thriving online communities. We illustrate how the aforementioned processes interact to mediate distinct shared embodied experiences.

The Internet and the Ecological–Enactivist Approach

Ecological Systems and Affordances

We can model the Internet as a biologically diverse ecosystem – a community of organisms that stand in relations of dense interaction with one another and with their physical environment. Such a picture of the Internet fits well with "enactive" views of biological systems wherein the organism and the environment effectively produce one another in a process of mutual constitution (Thompson, 2007; Varela et al., 1991). In cyberspace, users simultaneously produce and consume content; the Internet constitutes the user in part by providing platforms whereby content can be accessed, and is constituted by the users and their own provision of content. In other words, there is no ontological gulf between the users and the space they inhabit.

Unlike a terrestrial ecosystem, delimited in space and time as they are, the architecture of cyberspace is comprised of bits (boyd, 2011), a fundamental difference that enables certain possibilities. The Internet as a virtual cyberspace is scalable and has proven able to accommodate and foster massive growth (Karakas, 2009). This scalability has fostered a shift from the earlier, more passive web, based primarily on viewing of preexisting content, to the establishment of the web as we know it today, a highly interactive and collaborative platform running mostly on user-generated content. This platform, Web 2.0 or World 2.0 (Karakas, 2009; O'Reilly, 2007) signals a move away from a static surface picture, toward that of a dynamic ecosystem. Web 2.0 can be considered as a landscape of affordances, whereby possibilities for action and perception endow users with similar sets of shared expectations and experiences (Bruineberg & Rietveld, 2014; Chemero, 2003, 2009; Ramstead et al., 2016; Rietveld & Kiverstein, 2014).

The Formation of Internet Cultures: Imagined Communities and Technological Revolutions

There is nothing paradigmatically different between a large-scale society bounded by international borders (or diasporically spread across multiple nation states) and an Internet community. Both are in a sense "virtual," in that their large, anonymous makeup prevents face-to-face interaction between members; both, however, enable the large-scale spread of ideas that guide the goals of their members and shape their expectations, identities, and experiences. Following Anderson (1983), one might argue that these communities are largely *imagined*. The concept of imagined communities was originally introduced to explain the spread of nationalism in the early modern period, despite the relative paucity of personal relationships between all members. For Anderson, the nation is a sociocognitive construct that exists in the imaginations of its inhabitants, fueled notably by the advent of print-culture (Anderson, 1983).

The advent of digital culture has fueled the proliferation of imagined Internet communities that conform to nation-like structures with specific vernacular, rules, rituals, and expectations. Members have accounts and usernames, holding a digital "nationality" of sorts. Etiquette and communication vary from one site to the next. However, most importantly, few users will ever meet "IRL" (in real life) – in cyberspace, nearly all communities are imagined ones. The unique affordances of cyberspace – like replicability, persistence, and searchability (boyd, 2011) – allow for communities to exist in temporally and spatially extended ways that would not be feasible in physical environments. This tandem of spatiotemporal fragmentation and dynamic integration means that the unity of a community rests on the collective imagination and shared expectations of the Internet users that constitute it.

Ritualistic Bonding in Cyberspace

How does the collective "we" form in the first place? One explanation may lie in the fundamental human craving for shared experiences and a structured worldview.

This need can be satiated through cultural groups such as families, religious groups, or other communities that disseminate systemic knowledge that might respond to such needs. However, if the structured world order we inherit fails us, we may search for a new preexisting order that seems more rational, or at least better able to account for those failings (Veissière & Gibbs-Bravo 2016; Whitehouse, 2001). This sheds light on diverse phenomena such as cults, music festivals, artistic subcultures, born-again Christians, ex-Mormons, and of course, Internet communities, which are a natural extension of these phenomena into the digital sphere. Online communities share systems of beliefs, expectations, and attention, and like offline communities, they are also bound by rites of passage (Veissière & Gibbs-Bravo, 2016).

Though rites of passage are evolutionarily expensive – they tend to be challenging, uncomfortable, or dangerous – they are present in nearly all cultures, religions, and communities (Xygalatas et al., 2013). Given that humans form bonds after intense shared experiences (Fischer & Xygalatas, 2014; Xygalatas et al., 2013), the near-universality of extreme rituals might serve as an evolved social technology that strengthens group cohesion and cooperation (Xygalatas et al., 2013).

Harvey Whitehouse's seminal work on modes of religiosity (2001, 2004; see also Chapter 11) provides a framework to understand how different types of rituals facilitate the spread and maintenance of different forms of sociality. "Imagistic rituals" – those rarely performed and highly arousing – tend to build and consolidate episodic memory, create strong social bonds in small groups, and confer a sense of choice, agency, and privilege on those who partake in the experience. "Doctrinal rituals," conversely, are those characterized by frequently repeated actions and low arousal, and typically relate to semantic memory, which in turn facilitates the large-scale spread of anonymous communities. Entering a new subculture usually entails imagistic rites of passages that facilitate bonding to a new group. Subcultural identities, in turn, tend to be reinforced and maintained through frequently repeated doctrinal rituals, usually entailing new restrictions and group-specific ways of doing things (Veissière & Gibbs-Bravo, 2016).

As social networks migrate to the Internet, imagistic and doctrinal modes of ritual action are preserved, allowing members to form secure bonds and attribute meaning to their experience. Online communities tend to form group identities around shared suffering or salient emotional experiences – perhaps bonding over loneliness or illness in a support group. However, even seemingly happy digital communities have rites of passage. Health-nuts, meditators, and lucid dreamers pleasantly convene in cyberspace to bond over challenging rituals like juice cleanses, laborious dream journals, or vows of celibacy. Through esoteric, challenging, and highly embodied experiences, members of these communities cohere to a shared identity while also, by the very same fact, warranting their membership.

The Mechanisms of Cyber-Mediation

Joint Attention, Second-Order Learning, and the Ontology of Screens

Our world contains an unfathomable amount of information. To navigate this myriad data, humans develop second-order learning – rather than just learning, we learn from whom to learn (Henrich, 2016). It seems that human beings implicitly and automatically evaluate salient attentional cues in order to select sources of information and label them as relevant (Constant et al., 2019; Ramstead et al., 2016; Veissière et al., 2020).

Now that most of human knowledge is available on the Internet, knowing from where and from whom to learn is of massive importance; indeed, second-order learning may be one of the most useful skills to have in the twenty-first century. As we navigate the Internet, we secure cues and learn heuristics that guide us through immense amounts of data. Our epistemic "antennae" survey cyberspace for contextual cues that indicate reliability: Perhaps it is easier to submit oneself to a .org web address than a flashy site with explicit pop-up ads, although the readiness of surrender would depend on the information one seeks. Second-order cues are constantly revived, with "likes," "views," and "comments" as indices of collective attention.

Due to the rise of Web 2.0. and its seamless integration into daily life, screens have become a prevalent target of joint attention. Joint attention mediates second-order learning from screens, especially in the era of digital natives. With videogames, movie theaters, social media, televised sports, or massive multiplayer online role-playing games, screens are a common object of joint attention with which we engage in scripted narratives, suspending disbelief to what we see. Second-order learning is dependent on the social cues that guide our intention, and a lifetime of learning to automatically attend to screens imbue them with epistemic power.

On the Internet, joint attention and second-order learning facilitate an epistemic preference for culturally and subculturally relevant information. In doing so, these mechanisms allow the individual to join in on collective intentions, entering a shared system of knowledge, conventions, and ways-of-being – that is, they enable *enculturation*.

Mind, Body, and Internet

Once a novelty, the Internet is now seamlessly integrated with life, mind, and body (Clark, 2003). The integration of our sensory systems and our digital ecologies is evident in the design of technological devices, which is highly interwoven with the human perceptual system (as evidenced by the emergent science of ergonomics). Tapping a touchscreen device is a feat of multisensory integration, our typing rhythm congruent with the visual, sonic, and haptic stimuli of the interface. Despite the claims that the digital age fosters disembodiment, clearly, the navigation of technology is fundamentally embodied. Internet culture is not disembodied; it is differently embodied.

Conceptions of cognition as extended (Clark & Chalmers, 1998) or extensive (Hutto et al., 2014) become increasingly relevant in a digital context. In the case of the Internet, the human brain is actively coupled with an external entity, arguably forming a distinct, integrative system beyond the individual human body. However, this line of argument pertains most clearly to the myriad relationships between an agent and an artifact. The Internet is a collective artifact, and as such, the lines between organism and environment are blurred even further. When one interacts in the digital sphere, the coupling is not limited to human and computer, but rather encompasses multiple agents and artifacts, including the agency of the collective, or collective intentionality. In the Internet era, extensive mind–body processes mesh with the digital landscape, each constituting one another. This conception of the embodied co-construction of user and interface is supported in empirical studies that reveal the potential of cyber-mediated social contagion (Ferrara & Yang, 2015; Kramer et al., 2014; Mueller & Abrutyn, 2015).

In nondigital social networks, the spread of affect is a validated effect, and has long-lasting impacts (Fowler & Christakis, 2008; Kramer et al., 2014). Though often explained with simulative theories like spontaneous mimicking of facial expressions and neural mirror systems (Colombetti, 2013; Fuchs & De Jaegher, 2009), this effect occurs online too, where in-person contact is limited. In a massive ($N = 689\ 003$) experiment, Kramer et al. (2014) manipulated the content of Facebook user's newsfeed, titrating the posts to tend toward either positive or negative expressions. The result of this manipulation was emotional contagion that corresponded with the valence of the content: If negative content was reduced, users produced more positive posts and vice versa. This study exhibits the power of the Internet to modulate highly embodied experiences, such as emotions, and reveals the enactive and extensive manner in which users inhabit online social spaces.

Another mechanism that may account for the cyber-mediation of bodily experiences is *somatic amplification* – the selective focus on bodily sensations. Absorption may render individuals more likely to somatically amplify (Kirmayer et al., 1994), and engaging in cyberspace is a highly absorptive experience. Digital media is stimulating and rewarding: we surrender our attention to screens, and individuals with a propensity for cognitive absorption are more likely to use the Internet in the first place (Bozoglan et al., 2014). These factors may further account for the role online communities can play in the modulation of embodiment.

A Brief Anthropological Survey of Cyber-Mediated Bodily Experiences

To illustrate the ways in which the Internet harnesses and accentuates basic human proclivities for socially mediated embodiment, we now turn to a brief survey of "extreme" human experiences that can be partially – in some cases entirely – attributed to the online spread of ideas.

The examples described below, although by no means exhaustive, review novel forms of cyber-mediated human organization and experience that span from the wonderfully weird to the possibly dangerous. Our aims in sketching out a brief anthropological account of these communities, in keeping with the generalist aims of our niche construction account, is to better understand the co-constructive dynamics of personhood, embodiment, and technology.

Cyberchondria

Cyberchondria is a distinct condition of the digital era, characterized by excessive and repetitive online searches for information about health-related information. A popular online source of health information is the website WebMD which features news articles, videos, and proxy diagnoses. Its simple web design mimics the hygiene of a hospital and the website title includes "MD," insinuating credentials. This generalized lab coat effect (Milgram, 1963) increases the likelihood of epistemic surrender. A notorious feature of the website is the symptom checker, a tool that uses algorithms to calculate possible diagnoses given the inputted symptoms. To use this feature, an individual scans through a proxy body in the interface while also scanning their own, checking off the boxes that correspond with their symptoms. The design of this tool affords the highly embodied experience of a body scan framed in the semantics of pathology. In tandem with the absorptive nature of Internet use, the symptom checker could render one susceptible to potentially harmful or dangerous somatic amplification. Although there is valid medical information available online, studies suggest that searching behaviors can be harmful, indicating that this activity often leads to increased health anxiety (Aiken & Kirwan, 2012; Starcevic & Aboujaoude, 2015).

Empty Nose Syndrome

Empty nose syndrome (ENS) is somewhat of a medical mystery – weeks to years after a nasal surgery, often to the turbinates but not always, a minute percentage of patients experience debilitating symptoms including sensations of suffocation, pain, nasal dryness, sleep problems, anxiety, and depression (Lemogne et al., 2015; Saafan et al., 2016). The intensity of these symptoms has driven many to suicide, one patient even stabbing their otolaryngologist to death. Despite the severity of ENS, its etiology remains enigmatic to doctors; a consistent anatomical cause has yet to be identified and there are no validated diagnostic tests. Moreover, there appears to be a significant level of comorbidity between ENS and psychiatric conditions, suggesting that there may be a psychosomatic component to the distress (Payne, 2009).

Many ENS sufferers turn to the Internet to seek answers and comfort, and in doing so they enter an affordance landscape that may shape their phenomenological experience of the syndrome itself. ENS has a huge online presence with prolific blogs, forums, and articles devoted to discussing the syndrome. Sufferers can form intense bonds over their shared rite of passage into the ENS online community – namely, an elective surgery gone wrong. Given the capacity of social, emotional, and somatic contagion via cyberspace, ENS forums may be doing more harm than good.

In exploring these psychosocial factors, we are in no way discounting the extreme phenomenological suffering of those with ENS. However, reframing the condition may actually improve the course of treatment. Lemogne et al. (2015) describe a case study of a thirty-seven-year-old male ENS patient with extreme functional impairment; the patient had withdrawn from all social activities to isolate himself in his bedroom with an air humidifier. Following a normal physical examination, a psychiatrist diagnosed him with a typically presenting somatic symptom disorder (SSD) – a condition characterized by excessive thoughts and catastrophizing about somatic symptoms that may or may not be associated with an organic etiology (Lemogne et al., 2015). Following standard treatment for SSD, which includes cognitive therapy that targets core dysfunctional beliefs and avoidance behavior, the patient reported substantial functional improvement. This case study suggests that a comprehensive understanding of ENS may be imperative to successful treatment.

Erowid Experience Vaults

Erowid is a nonprofit, educational resource with information about drugs, plants, and altered states of consciousness, with an overall mission of harm reduction. Their website hosts an experience vault with over 23 000 user-submitted "experience reports" of personal psychoactive experiences that range from illuminating to frightening.

The placebo effect has proven to be very robust when it is used in the medical contexts involving pharmaceuticals, and can actually cause changes in pathophysiology (Assefi & Garry, 2003; Medoff & Colloca, 2015; Parker et al., 2011; Raz et al., 2008). Of course, drugs have a chemical effect on the brain, regardless of mindset, however these findings on the placebo effect inform us that our response to psychoactives is influenced by expectations, context, and sociality. This compounds with the generalized lab coat effect (Milgram, 1963) of pharmaceuticals, or the shared societal expectations that drugs change us in a biological, physical, or sensory way. An Erowid review holds the power to transform an individual's expectation of their experience, and subsequently, the experience itself.

Erowid displays epistemic power through their .org web address and the sheer mass of information they possess. Every experience published was selected, reviewed, and edited, earning it a second-order epistemic stamp of approval. Finally, the intensity of psychoactive experiences strengthens the bond between users, promoting in-group identity and social contagion.

Online Meditation

Meditation is increasingly popular in Western life and science, with a particularly expansive digital presence, through apps, websites, and online communities. One group of interest is the Zen Buddhist community of Second Life®. Second Life is an immersive, digital world in which millions of people participate in a rich affordance landscape that allows for gestural and verbal communication, as well as a more complex representation of self through an online avatar. Residents of the Zen Buddhist community come together in cyberspace to engage in talks, silent meditations, and other activities. Their physical bodies are geographically separate, but their avatars are present with one another, engaging in *virtual embodiment*, Grieve's (2010) term for immersed, embodied performances that occur in cyberspace. When these groups unite to sit a silent meditation together, they engage in an embodied and challenging ritual that reinforces the group cohesion and fosters collective intentionality.

Otherkin

Otherkins ontologically define themselves as partially or entirely nonhuman along a spectrum (O'Callaghan, 2015). The subculture arose online in the mid-1990s, and cyberspace has continued to be the primary arena for discussion, communication, and interaction, although there are gatherings in "real life" (Laycock, 2012). While the label is nebulous and encompasses a broad range of experiences, there is consensus among Otherkin that their interphenomenal experience is highly embodied. Otherkin describe unusual bodily characteristics, like minor deformities, phantom limb/wing/tail sensations, or subtle physical powers (Laycock, 2012; O'Callaghan, 2015). The process of discovering one's Otherkin identity is called *awakening*, and for many this manifests itself in a somatic manner. The physical process of *awakening* is a rite of passage that all members of the community go through, a second puberty that secures group cohesion. The oppositional "other" – entitled "nonkin," "mundanes," or "muggles" – magnify the group bond and create an in-group boundary to maintain (Laycock, 2012). As the Otherkin title represents an extensive variety of experience, it would be impossible to paint a comprehensive picture. The community negotiates identity in a diverse manner, narrating through myth, the occult, spirituality, reincarnation, and more.

r/NoFap

r/NoFap is a sub-Reddit community of around 300 000 primarily male users that abstain from masturbation. The reasons for abstinence vary from one member to the next, from promoting health, improving appearance, or gaining confidence. Many of the users engage in the community and its rituals to overcome a pornography addiction. The community has an eclectic epistemology drawing from a variety of sources, such as Alcoholics Anonymous, behaviorism, Daoism, neuroscience, and humoral theory.

In participating as a member of the NoFap community, users engage in an affordance landscape that guides their perception and actions, and thus, they encounter and enact radical shifts in their embodied phenomenology. Users report the embodied benefits of their practice, claiming quite profound changes like the breeze feeling better, increased dexterity, a more masculine appearance, quicker wit, thicker facial hair, richer color perception, synesthetic experiences, new talents, and regaining the ability to feel the whole spectrum of human emotion.

These shared dramatic embodied experiences occur in part through our proposed mechanisms of cyber-mediation. For instance, on Reddit, there exist highly tangible and measurable indices of social approval in the form of comments and upvotes, which create intergroup pressure but also promote a hivemind mentality by rendering the most popular posts the most visible. Constant exposure to the benefits of the practice amplifies certain somatic sensations in turn reinforcing their actions and strengthening the group bond. The ritual context bestows authority to the group's system of knowledge and expectations, creating a context where physiological sensations are emphasized or muted.

Tulpamancy

Tulpamancy is the practice of conjuring sentient imaginary companions (tulpas) through "thoughtform" meditative practice (Veissière, 2016). This practice is esoteric and challenging, marked by a set of shared rituals. The most important of these rituals may be "forcing," whereby one mentally conjures, then interacts with their tulpa in order to develop and sustain them. "Forcing" is a challenging, exciting, and elusive process – the perfect ingredients for ritualistic bonding. As members of the community work toward this hard-to-reach common goal, they become a closer-knit group. Tulpa communities may also be bonded through shared "real-life" experiences, as many report struggling with mental health problems and extreme loneliness (Isler, 2016). From these shared experiences emerges a unified culture with prescribed ontologies, taboos, and a unique lexicon of terminology.

The act of tulpamancy is sensory at the core, wherein hosting human or nonhuman tulpas in a single body involves auditory, tactile, visual, olfactory, and (more controversially) sexual sensations. These shared sensory experiences may arise from a heightened state of absorption that Tulpamancers have a proclivity for (or have cultivated) as evidenced by high scores on the Tellegen Absorption Scale (Veissière, 2016). The absorptive affordance of cyberspace may further encourage these experiences. By harnessing jointly mediated absorption in a virtual context that invites, expects, and frames the experience of conjuring tulpas, members of the community can develop similar ways-of-being.

Xenomelia

Xenomelia, literally "foreign limb," is a condition where an individual does not recognize one or more healthy limbs as their own, and thus, possesses a strong desire for paralysis or amputation (McGeoch et al., 2011). Neurological findings may indicate that such a disturbance in body schema originates in the brain (Brugger et al., 2013; McGeoch et al., 2011); however, a purely neuroscientific approach has its limits. For instance, there are instances where an individual's foreign limb switches to the opposite side of the body, or desires more amputations over time (Brugger et al., 2013). Alternatively, years of hostility directed toward a limb may cause neuroplastic changes to the cortex (Brugger et al., 2013).

Regardless of origin, the Internet plays a role in the incidence and manifestation of xenomelia (Charland, 2004; Davis, 2012). Our body is in constant negotiation with its cultural backdrop that structures the matrix of normality. In Davis' phenomenological account of transabled.org members (2012), she explores the complex co-construction of identity that occurs in cyberspace. The identity of xenomelia simultaneously shapes and is shaped by digital content in the form of narratives, experiences, and questions, which stabilize the identity as a category available for consumption (Davis, 2012). Connecting over shared suffering also acts as a social technology that strengthens the bond of the group as well as their identity. In these online communities, language is a powerful mediator of intersubjective representations, and may be a mechanism that amplifies somatic symptoms.

Conclusion

In this chapter, we sketched out a cultural ecological epidemiology and phenomenology of Internet sociality. We argued that online communities, though seemingly novel and often "strange," give us a window into invariant mechanisms of shared intentionality, distributed attention, and embodied joint expectations through which all human experiences arise. We have argued that if a paradigmatic shift in ways of being social beings can be detected through this increased digitalization of cultural epidemiology, it may simply be on a level of *speed* and *scale* of distribution. As the drastic examples of "new" Internet-mediated forms of embodiment described above show, new levels of affective *intensity* (in pain and pleasure, wellness and distress) may also be emerging. As we have insisted throughout this chapter, however, the collective (that is, contagious, "anonymous," language-dependent, culturally situated) nature of experience (Internet or not) remains the most fundamental characteristic of human life.

REFERENCES

Aiken, M., & Kirwan, G. (2012). Prognoses for diagnoses: Medical search online and "cyberchondria". *BMC Proceedings, 6*(Suppl. 4), P30. https://doi.org/10.1186/1753-6561-6-S4-P30

Anderson, B. (1983). *Imagined communities: Reflections on the origin and spread of nationalism.* Verso.

Assefi, S. L., & Garry, M. (2003). Absolut® memory distortions: Alcohol placebos influence the misinformation effect. *Psychological Science, 14*(1), 77–80. https://doi.org/10.1111/1467-9280.01422

Atran, S., & Norenzayan, A. (2004). Religion's evolutionary landscape: Counterintuition, commitment, compassion, communion. *Behavioral and Brain Sciences, 27*(6), 713–30. https://doi.org/10.1017/S0140525X04000172

Bourdieu, P. (1977). *Outline of a theory of practice* (R. Nice, Trans.). Cambridge University Press. https://doi.org/10.1017/CBO9780511812507

Boyd, d. (2011). Social network sites as networked publics: Affordances, dynamics, and implications. In Z. Papacharissi (Ed.), *A networked self: Identity, community, and culture on social network sites* (pp. 39–58). Routledge.

Bozoglan, B., Demirer, V., & Sahin, I. (2014). Problematic Internet use: Functions of use, cognitive absorption, and depression. *Computers in Human Behavior, 37*, 117–23. https://doi.org/10.1016/j.chb.2014.04.042

Brugger, P., Lenggenhager, B., & Giummarra, M. J. (2013). Xenomelia: A social neuroscience view of altered bodily self-consciousness. *Frontiers in Psychology, 4*, 204. https://doi.org/10.3389/fpsyg.2013.00204

Bruineberg, J., & Rietveld, E. (2014). Self-organization, free energy minimization, and optimal grip on a field of affordances. *Frontiers in Human Neuroscience, 8*, 599. https://doi.org/10.3389/fnhum.2014.00599

Charland, L. C. (2004). A madness for identity: Psychiatric labels, consumer autonomy, and the perils of the Internet. *Philosophy, Psychiatry, & Psychology, 11*(4), 335–49. https://doi.org/10.1353/ppp.2005.0006

Chemero, A. (2003). An outline of a theory of affordances. *Ecological Psychology, 15*(2), 181–95. https://doi.org/10.1207/S15326969ECO1502_5

Chemero, A. (2009). *Radical embodied cognitive science*. MIT Press.

Clark, A. (2003). *Natural-born cyborgs: Minds, technologies, and the future of human intelligence*. Oxford University Press.

Clark, A., & Chalmers, D. (1998). The extended mind. *Analysis, 58*(1), 7–19. https://doi.org/10.1093/analys/58.1.7

Colombetti, G. (2013). Psychopathology and the enactive mind. In K. W. M. Fulford, M. Davies, R. G. T. Gipps, G. Graham, J. Z. Sadler, G. Stanghellini, & T. Thornton (Eds.), *The Oxford handbook of philosophy and psychiatry* (pp. 1083–1102). Oxford University Press.

Constant, A., Ramstead, M. J., Veissière, S. P., & Friston, K. (2019). Regimes of expectations: An active inference model of social conformity and human decision making. *Frontiers in Psychology, 10*, 679. https://doi.org/10.3389/fpsyg.2019.00679

Davis, J. (2012). Prosuming identity: The production and consumption of transableism on transabled.org. *American Behavioral Scientist, 56*(4), 596–617. https://doi.org/10.1177/0002764211429361

Dunbar, R. I. M. (1992). Neocortex size as a constraint on group size in primates. *Journal of Human Evolution, 22*(6), 469–93. https://doi.org/10.1016/0047-2484(92)90081-J

Ferrara, E., & Yang, Z. (2015). Measuring emotional contagion in social media. *PLoS ONE, 10*(11), e0142390. https://doi.org/10.1371/journal.pone.0142390

Fischer, R., & Xygalatas, D. (2014). Extreme rituals as social technologies. *Journal of Cognition and Culture, 14*(5), 345–55. https://doi.org/10.1163/15685373-12342130

Fowler, J. H., & Christakis, N. A. (2008). Dynamic spread of happiness in a large social network: Longitudinal analysis over 20 years in the Framingham Heart Study. *The BMJ, 337*, a2338. https://doi.org/10.1136/bmj.a2338

Fuchs, T., & De Jaegher, H. (2009). Enactive intersubjectivity: Participatory sense-making and mutual incorporation. *Phenomenology and the Cognitive Sciences, 8*(4), 465–86. https://doi.org/10.1007/s11097-009-9136-4

Gervais, W. M., & Norenzayan, A. (2012). Like a camera in the sky? Thinking about God increases public self-awareness and socially desirable responding. *Journal of Experimental Social Psychology, 48*(1), 298–302. https://doi.org/10.1016/j.jesp.2011.09.006https://doi.org/10.1016/j.jesp.2011.09.006

Grieve, G. (2010). Virtually embodying the field: Silent online Buddhist meditation, immersion, and the Cardean ethnographic method. *Online: Heidelberg Journal of Religions on the Internet, 4*(1), 35–62. https://doi.org/10.11588/rel.2010.1.9384.

Henrich, J. (2016). *The secret of our success: How culture is driving human evolution, domesticating our species, and making us smarter*. Princeton University Press.

Hrdy, S. B. (2011). *Mothers and others: The evolution of mutual understanding*. Harvard University Press.

Hutto, D. D., Kirchhoff, M. D., & Myin, E. (2014). Extensive enactivism: Why keep it all in? *Frontiers in Human Neuroscience, 8*, 706. https://doi.org/10.3389/fnhum.2014.00706

Ingold, T. (2001). From the transmission of representations to the education of attention. In H. Whitehouse (Ed.), *The debated mind: Evolutionary psychology versus ethnography* (pp. 113–53). Berg Publishers.

Isler, J. J. (2016). *Tulpamancy: Transcending the assumption of singularity in the human mind.* Paper presented at the meeting of GRACLS, "The extra-human," The University of Texas at Austin, TX, United States of America.

Karakas, F. (2009). Welcome to World 2.0: The new digital ecosystem. *Journal of Business Strategy*, *30*(4), 23–30. https://doi.org/10.1108/02756660910972622

Kirmayer, L. J., Robbins, J. M., & Paris, J. (1994). Somatoform disorders: Personality and the social matrix of somatic distress. *Journal of Abnormal Psychology*, *103*(1), 125–36. https://doi.org/10.1037/0021-843X.103.1.125

Kramer, A. D. I., Guillory, J. E., & Hancock, J. T. (2014). Experimental evidence of massive-scale emotional contagion through social networks. *Proceedings of the National Academy of Sciences of the United States of America*, *111*(24), 8788–90. https://doi.org/10.1073/pnas.1320040111

Laycock, J. P. (2012). "We are spirits of another sort": Ontological rebellion and religious dimensions of the otherkin community. *Nova Religio*, *15*(3), 65–90. https://doi.org/10.1525/nr.2012.15.3.65

Lemogne, C., Consoli, S. M., Limosin, F., & Bonfils, P. (2015). Treating empty nose syndrome as a somatic symptom disorder. *General Hospital Psychiatry*, *37*(3), 273.e9–10273.e10. https://doi.org/10.1016/j.genhosppsych.2015.02.005

Mauss, M. (1973). Techniques of the body. *Economy and Society*, *2*(1), 70–88. https://doi.org/10.1080/03085147300000003

McGeoch, P. D., Brang, D., Song, T., Lee, R. R., Huang, M., & Ramachandran, V. S. (2011). Xenomelia: A new right parietal lobe syndrome. *Journal of Neurology, Neurosurgery & Psychiatry*, *82*(12), 1314–19. https://doi.org/10.1136/jnnp-2011-300224

Medoff, Z. M., & Colloca, L. (2015). Placebo analgesia: Understanding the mechanisms. *Pain Management*, *5*(2), 89–96. https://doi.org/10.2217/pmt.15.3

Milgram, S. (1963). Behavioral study of obedience. *Journal of Abnormal and Social Psychology*, *67*(4), 371–8. https://doi.org/10.1037/h0040525

Mueller, A. S., & Abrutyn, S. (2015). Suicidal disclosures among friends: Using social network data to understand suicide contagion. *Journal of Health and Social Behavior*, *56*(1), 131–48. https://doi.org/10.1177/0022146514568793

O'Callaghan, S. (2015). Navigating the 'other' world: Cyberspace, popular culture and the realm of the otherkin. *Culture and Religion*, *16*(3), 253–68. https://doi.org/10.1080/14755610.2015.1083454

O'Reilly, T. (2007). What is Web 2.0: Design patterns and business models for the next generation of software. *Communications & Strategies*, *65*, 17–37. https://mpra.ub.uni-muenchen.de/4580/1/MPRA_paper_4580.pdf

Parker, S., Garry, M., Einstein, G. O., & McDaniel, M. A. (2011). A sham drug improves a demanding prospective memory task. *Memory*, *19*(6), 606–12. https://doi.org/10.1080/09658211.2011.592500

Payne, S. C. (2009). Empty nose syndrome: What are we really talking about? *Otolaryngologic Clinics of North America*, *42*(2), 331–7. https://doi.org/10.1016/j.otc.2009.02.002

Ramstead, M. J. D., Veissière, S. P. L., & Kirmayer, L. J. (2016). Cultural affordances: Scaffolding local worlds through shared intentionality and regimes of attention. *Frontiers in Psychology*, *7*, 1090. https://doi.org/10.3389/fpsyg.2016.01090

Raz, A., Raikhel, E., & Anbar, R. D. (2008). Placebos in medicine: Knowledge, beliefs, and patterns of use. *McGill Journal of Medicine*, *11*(2), 206–11. www.ncbi.nlm.nih.gov/pmc/articles/PMC2582662/

Rietveld, E., & Kiverstein, J. (2014). A rich landscape of affordances. *Ecological Psychology*, *26*(4), 325–52. https://doi.org/10.1080/10407413.2014.958035

Saafan, M. E., Hegazy, H. M., & Albirmawy, O. A. (2016). Empty nose syndrome: Etiopathogenesis and management. *The Egyptian Journal of Otolaryngology*, *32*(3), 119–29. https://doi.org/10.4103/1012-5574.186540

Sperber, D. (1996). *Explaining culture: A naturalistic approach*. Blackwell Publishers.

Starcevic, V., & Aboujaoude, E. (2015). Cyberchondria, cyberbullying, cybersuicide, cybersex: "New" psychopathologies for the 21st century? *World Psychiatry*, *14*(1), 97–100. https://doi.org/10.1002/wps.20195

Thompson, E. (2007). *Mind in life: Biology, phenomenology, and the sciences of mind*. Belknap Press.

Tomasello, M. (2009). *Why we cooperate*. MIT Press.

Tomasello, M., & Rakoczy, H. (2003). What makes human cognition unique? From individual to shared to collective intentionality. *Mind & Language*, *18*(2), 121–47. https://doi.org/10.1111/1468-0017.00217

Varela, F. J., Thompson, E., & Rosch, E. (1991). *The embodied mind: Cognitive science and human experience*. MIT Press.

Veissière, S. (2016). Varieties of Tulpa experiences: The hypnotic nature of human sociality, personhood, and interphenomenality. In A. Raz & M. Lifshitz (Eds.), *Hypnosis and meditation: Towards an integrative science of conscious planes* (pp. 55–76). Oxford University Press.

Veissière, S., & Gibbs-Bravo, L. (2016). Juicing: Language, ritual, and placebo sociality in a community of extreme eaters. In K. Cargill (Ed.), *Food cults: How fads, dogma, and doctrine influence diet* (pp. 63–86). Rowman & Littlefield.

Veissière, S. P. L., & Stendel, M. (2018). Hypernatural monitoring: A social rehearsal account of smartphone addiction. *Frontiers in Psychology*, *9*, 141. https://doi.org/10.3389/fpsyg.2018.00141

Veissière, S. P., Constant, A., Ramstead, M. J., Friston, K. J., & Kirmayer, L. J. (2020). Thinking through other minds: A variational approach to cognition and culture. *Behavioral and Brain Sciences*, *43*, e90, 1–75. https://doi.org/10.1017/S0140525X19001213

Whitehouse, H. (2001). Transmissive frequency, ritual, and exegesis. *Journal of Cognition and Culture*, *1*(2), 167–81. https://doi.org/10.1163/156853701316931399

Whitehouse, H. (2004). *Modes of religiosity: A cognitive theory of religious transmission*. Rowman Altamira.

Xygalatas, D., Mitkidis, P., Fischer, R., Reddish, P., Skewes, J., Geertz, A.W., Roepstorff, A., & Bulbulia, J. (2013). Extreme rituals promote prosociality. *Psychological Science*, *24*(8), 1602–5. https://doi.org/10.1177/0956797612472910

21 Neurodiversity as a Conceptual Lens and Topic of Cross-Cultural Study

M. Ariel Cascio

Introduction

When I was conducting my ethnographic fieldwork on autism-focused services in Italy in 2012–2013, there was little talk about "neurodiversity" (*neurodiversità*) among my participants (Cascio, 2015; Cascio et al., 2018). A handful of interviewees used adjectives like neurodiverse (*neurodiversa*) and neurotypical (*neurotipici*) to describe people with and without autism, respectively, but explicit conversation about autism-related social movements rested more on "autism pride." Advocates I heard talk about autism pride retained the English word "pride" to name the movement, but described it in terms of the Italian concepts of *orgoglio* (pride) and *vergogna* (shame, about which much has been written and contested in the literature on the anthropology of the Mediterranean region, see, e.g., Coombe, 1990). At an introduction to a self-advocacy event, one self-advocate explained the meaning of "pride." 'It's like this: if I'm Calabrese, and I come to Milan, I'm not ashamed (*non mi vergogno*). I'm Calabrese, I'm proud (*ho orgoglio*). I don't mean that we are better, but I am not ashamed to have this Asperger's syndrome or high functioning autism.'[1] However, pride is not always the straightforward opposite of shame. At another point, a parent advocate told me that autism or Asperger Pride did not mean *orgoglio* but acknowledged that 'there are many good sides but also problems. It isn't right to be this prideful (*fare questa orgoglio*).' Debates and different interpretations over the nature and uses of pride occur in a context, like Italy, where self-advocates and parent advocates often work together but may have quite different perspectives. They also allude to high-profile differences between self-advocacy and parent advocacy groups in places like the United States and Canada. This chapter explores cross-cultural differences in the uptake (or lack thereof) of neurodiversity discourses in autism social movements, as well as the potential use of neurodiversity as a conceptual lens for scholarship.

---

[1] Single quotes indicate an indirect quotation taken from written fieldnotes or interviews that were not audio-recorded.

The neurodiversity movement is an area in which broader trends in the relationship between culture, mind, and brain are rendered especially visible through the interaction of neuroscience, self-understanding, and social action. In a variety of contexts, neuroscientific ideas and neuroscientistic language are used in individual and collective understandings of selfhood, including broad concepts such as brainhood (Vidal, 2009), the cerebral subject (Vidal & Ortega, 2017), cerebral subjectivation (Ortega, 2009), and neurochemical selfhood (Rose, 2003), as well as specific examples such as neurostructural selfhood (Fein, 2011) among people with autism. Such individual understandings of brain-based selfhood also have implications for collective identification, in social movements such as the neurodiversity movement, which asserts that autism is a type of human neurological diversity, a different way of thinking, perceiving, and being in the world that should not necessarily be understood as a disorder (Cascio, 2012). These concepts lie at the intersection of culture, mind, and brain – as mind/brain discourses are taken up as cultural practices used in individual and collective identity formation as well as social and political action.

In this chapter, I offer insights into the role of neurodiversity as both a lens to inform scholarship and a topic of cross-cultural research, informed by my own work as an anthropologist with a focus on bioethics. I begin by describing neurodiversity and then discuss the way it can inform bioethics as a conceptual lens. I then summarize some cross-cultural research on neurodiversity movements, grounded within and contributing to neurodiversity-informed empirical bioethics questions regarding respect and justice for neurodivergent people and within neurodiverse societies. Beyond bioethics, these questions have relevance for self-understanding and social group formation through the language of the brain, and for societal debates about the changing realities of brain, culture, and their interrelations. Am I my brain, and if so, how? Is it a good thing or a bad thing? What are the implications for my social life and possibilities for political action?

Neurodiversity

One area in which brainhood has been rendered particularly visible in the late twentieth and early twenty-first centuries is in social movements (formal or informal) that are organized around an idea of self-as-brain, explicitly draw on the language of neuroscience, and have implications for personal identity. The neurodiversity movement is perhaps the most well documented of these new ways of talking and thinking about self and identity (e.g., Fenton & Krahn, 2007; Orsini, 2009; Ortega, 2009). In the language of neurodiversity advocates, neurodiversity is a specific type of human diversity that has to do with the brain. All people are neurodiverse insofar as we each have our own unique brains. People whom scientists and clinicians have labeled as "normal" or "typically developing" may be called neurotypical, whereas people with autism or other forms of neurological difference are called neurodivergent. The neuro- prefix also figures prominently in journalist Steve Silberman's (2016) well-received book on autism, which introduced readers to the term "neurotribes," referring especially to the social affinity component of the neurodiversity movement as a way of finding one's own "tribe" to belong to.

The neurodiversity movement is anchored firmly in the experiences of autistic people (who generally prefer identity-first, rather than person-first, language), but it has never been exclusive to autism. The early neurodiversity movement welcomed "cousins," people who were not autistic but also not neurotypical and shared some social and communication characteristics that enabled a mutual identification with autistic people – conditions like dyslexia, attention-deficit/hyperactivity disorder (ADHD), and so on (Baggs, 2016; Silberman, 2016). An association with these other forms of neurodivergence is an important part of the neurodiversity movement and, more recently, neuroqueer theory (Graby, 2015; Yergeau, 2018). Neuroqueer is a new concept at the intersection of neurodiversity and queer studies that includes understanding neurodivergence as a form of queerness, being both neurodivergent and queer, and "queering" (in the queer theory sense) performance of gender and other identities through neurodivergence (Walker, 2015). In short, neuroqueer means "queering our neurodivergence, neurodiversifying our queer" (Grace, 2013).

Neurodiversity and Bioethics

In outlining a research agenda for "autism ethics," Hens et al. (2019) foreground the conceptual heterogeneity of autism, including the claims of the neurodiversity movement that autism is primarily a neurological reality and identity. Such claims are often contrasted with perspectives on autism used by more parent- and professional-oriented advocacy movements, which tend to use more of a deficit model, framing autism primarily as a problem to be solved (Antze, 2010; Orsini, 2009). Conceptualizations of autism are highly contested, and a case of what Ian Hacking calls "making up people" – the category of "an autistic person" changes through a looping effect in which more or different people identify or are identified as autistic, thereby little by little changing the definition, which changes who is identified, which changes the definition, and so on (Hacking, 1995, 2006). Conceptualizations of autism are also influenced by metaphors and stories (Hacking, 2009a, 2009b, 2009c, 2010; Waltz, 2003). While the neurodiversity movement draws on neuroscience and brainhood discourses, the neurological reality and identity of autism is by no means a top-down determination from neuroscience to culture and identity. Rather, conceptualizations of autism, culture, mind, brain (and autistic cultures, minds, and brains) are agentively contested, constructed, and negotiated within neurodiversity communities which may assert neuro- discourses while resisting "neuro-hegemonies" (Yergeau, 2018).

How autism (and culture, and mind, and brain) is conceptualized raises important considerations for bioethics. Bioethics literature has considered neurodiversity arguments in debates about the ethics of researching a cure (Barnes & McCabe, 2012) or using gene therapy (Hens et al., 2019), who has the right to provide informed consent for children on the autism spectrum (Perry, 2012), what is the nature of a good life (Rodogno et al., 2016), and how to promote epistemic justice by appropriately valuing autistic self-report and self-knowledge (Hens et al., 2019, Jongsma et al., 2017).This chapter extends these considerations, looking at the influence of neurodiversity perspectives on the core questions of bioethics. Bioethics is generally considered to be centrally about values or principles at both the individual level (like respect for persons) and the collective level (like justice). The neurodiversity movement posits particular views on respect and justice that can lead to neurodiversity-informed bioethics questions.

At the individual level, the neurodiversity movement asserts ethical positions about respect and the worth of neurodivergent individuals. A neurodiversity perspective stresses the worth and value of neurodivergent lives. Central ethical questions for neurodiversity-informed bioethics address issues of respect such as autonomy, self-determination, and freedom from coercion, including: How can people with autism be respected as persons? What are the characteristics of an (un)ethical treatment or intervention strategy or goal?

At the collective level, neurodiversity-informed bioethics questions address how societies should account for the neurological diversity of their members. A neurodiversity perspective stresses the importance of autistic rights as human rights, and the disability rights assertion "nothing about us, without us." Central bioethical questions at the community level therefore address issues of justice, such as fairness, distribution of resources, and representation of autistic perspectives, including: How can people with autism be treated fairly, as members of society and endowed with human rights? How can the perspectives of autistic people be represented in deliberations about autism (be they regarding policy, education, healthcare, research, and so on)?

For the remainder of this chapter, I will overview how neurodiversity can serve as a useful conceptual lens for bioethics, and how the empirical cross-cultural study of neurodiversity can enrich discussions about bioethical questions – especially about treatment ethics and political representation – by presenting multiple proposed solutions that vary in different contexts.

Neurodiversity as a Conceptual Lens

Neurodiversity advocates assert several propositions that can serve as a conceptual lens for bioethics scholarship on neurological disability and diversity. Several tenets of a neurodiversity approach could inform bioethics scholarship, from formulating the questions listed above to developing strategies to answer those questions in ways that may be meaningful to autistic people themselves. Not all tenets may be useful in all bioethics projects – for example, scholars may want to investigate the experiences and perspectives of people (with or without autism) who do not support a neurodiversity approach, and therefore may find adopting too much of a neurodiversity approach to be alienating to such participants. However, key tenets could provide a starting point for scholarship that respects autistic research subjects, researchers, and research consumers. These tenets include:

1. A nondeficit approach, in line with critical autism studies (Orsini & Davidson, 2013), which challenges degrading deficit-focused constructions of autism such as dramatic and dehumanizing language used in cure-seeking campaigns (see Kras, 2010) and functioning labels ("high- or low functioning").
2. A diversity mindset, which entails being flexible and open to difference. This flexibility is an important part of the neurodiversity movement, which often seeks to represent people across the autism spectrum and people who are very different from one another in many ways despite having a common diagnosis.
3. A focus on the experiences of autistic people. The neurodiversity movement emerged in part from autistic people who were frustrated with being marginalized within broader autism communities, which focused on parents and professionals to the exclusion of autistic people. While parents and professionals can provide important insight, it is important not to exclude the perspectives of autistic people.
4. Transparency and openness about one's needs, by asserting them clearly and not relying on the unwritten rules of social niceties.
5. Including autistic perspectives in the development of research questions, research design, write-up, and dissemination, again following the disability rights movement mantra of "nothing about us without us."
6. Pursuing topics of interest to autistic people in the here and now, informed by neurodiversity advocacy as well as surveys of autistic people more broadly that will capture a range of experiences and concerns (e.g., Pellicano et al., 2014).

Using some or all of these strategies allows scholars to be aligned with some key neurodiversity perspectives, even if neurodiversity as such is not their topic of inquiry. It provides a starting point for considering neurodiversity-informed bioethics questions, with potentially broader implications for engaging with other kinds of human diversity.

Cross-Cultural Study of Neurodiversity

Neurodiversity is not just a conceptual lens that researchers can take, it can also be a topic of study in and of itself with its own unique history. The term neurodiversity is often attributed to anthropology and sociology student Judy Singer, who used the term in her sociology undergraduate thesis in 1998, as a shorthand for "neurological diversity." Singer aimed to create a minority empowerment model for autistic people, modeled on feminism, gay rights, and Deaf Culture (Silberman, 2016). While Singer did not have an autism diagnosis, her daughter did and she identified similar traits in herself. Early studies of neurodiversity describe the history of an emerging movement that only became possible in the Internet age, when autistic people could more easily find and communicate with each other in more accessible ways online (Antze, 2010; Bagatell, 2010; Chamak, 2008, 2010). While some nonautistic stakeholders in the autism community, such as some parents and professionals, argued that neurodiversity was only applicable to so-called high-functioning individuals on the spectrum, even the early literature recognized that neurodiversity has never been limited to people with lower levels of support needs (Fenton & Krahn, 2007). Moreover, neurodiversity advocates often reject notions of high or low functioning as reductive and incomplete (Silberman, 2016).

While social science research on neurodiversity – both as a movement and as an ideology – has been growing, much of this research at least in the English language literature has been limited to the United States (Bagatell, 2007, 2010; Cascio, 2012; Kapp et al., 2013; Silverman, 2011; Tan, 2018), Canada (Orsini, 2009), and the UK (Belek, 2018; Kapp et al., 2013). Explicitly cross-cultural research and research in non-English-dominant contexts has been limited, likely reflecting the parallel English language genesis of the neurodiversity movement (and term), described in more detail below. However, there have been some notable exceptions. Neurodiversity politics have been contrasted between North America and France (Chamak, 2008, 2009, 2010; Chamak & Bonniau, 2013, 2014), as well as between Israel and Germany (Raz et al., 2018). There has been substantial literature on neurodiversity and autistic self-advocacy in Sweden (e.g., Bertilsdotter-Rosqvist, 2012) and some literature on such movements in the Netherlands (van den Bosch et al., 2018; Waltz et al., 2015) and Germany (Jongsma et al., 2017). There have also been studies addressing the role of neurodiversity perspectives in parent movements and daily life in Brazil (Rios & Andrada, 2015) and Morocco (Hart, 2014).

A full review is beyond the scope of this chapter, but I will highlight some examples, specifically ethnographic or interview-based studies of autistic advocacy groups in different parts of the world, and how those groups do or do not use neurodiversity perspectives. In these studies, the researchers may use a neurodiversity lens, but neurodiversity is not taken for granted; the central question is – how, if at all, does neurodiversity play out in these local contexts? Exploring this question reveals differences linked to broader sociocultural context, and can inform bioethics researchers on the variety of proposed solutions to neurodiversity-informed bioethical questions.

Significant work has been done on neurodiversity in Sweden by Hanna Bertilsdotter-Rosqvist et al. While this research does not take an explicitly cross-cultural perspective, Bertilsdotter-Rosqvist links one group's focus on openness and "coming out" with "a more general ideal of openness in Sweden, according to which the members of subordinate groups are expected to come out and be open about their differences to gain access to various societal support services" (Bertilsdotter-Rosqvist, 2012, p. 126). Bertilsdotter-Rosqvist and participants see the Swedish self-advocacy movement as a neurodiversity movement, and autism as a brain-based form of diversity, very similar to the anglophone activism discourse on the matter, with identity politics and coming out as a key form of social advocacy.

There has also been substantial work on autistic advocacy movements in France, specifically on the organization SAtedI. Brigitte Chamak explicitly contrasts this French autistic self-advocacy group with the international neurodiversity movement, especially the US-based Autism Network International (ANI) and the UK-based Aspies for Freedom (which was started by a Dutch self-advocate), but making reference also to neurodiversity in Australia and Sweden. SAtedI members do not adopt a neurodiversity perspective, at least insofar as they do not resist as strongly the deficit narratives of autism used by parent groups (Chamak, 2008, 2009, 2010; Chamak & Bonniau, 2013). Chamak argues that SAtedI is not part of the broader autism rights movement, because it focuses not on social critique but rather on information, awareness, organizing social meetings, taking a stand on political questions, and influencing research.[2] SAtedI works closely with French parent advocacy groups related to autism, in contrast to tensions between self-advocacy and parent groups in the United States and Canada (Chamak, 2008). Chamak links these differences to several sources, including the French ethos of anti-communitarianism, an opposition to political action on the basis of community membership such as identity politics, in favor of "universalism" in which all

---

[2] Chamak argues that the neurodiversity movement was not involved with research in 2008, although at the time of this writing in 2019 groups like the Autistic Self Advocacy Network in the United States do have a greater involvement in directing research.

individuals are treated the same by virtue of their position as citizens (Chamak, 2009; Chamak & Bonniau, 2013). Self-advocacy and parent advocacy groups share a rejection of psychoanalysis, which has had a strong influence in the professional approach to autism in France (Chamak, 2008). Finally, many services for people with autism in France are run by parent associations, so SAtedI and parent advocates work together to ensure their continued existence (Chamak, 2009, 2010).

Similarly, Silke Schicktanz et al. explicitly compare autism self-advocacy movements in Germany and Israel (Jongsma et al., 2017; Raz et al., 2018). They also compare organizations "*for* autism" (generally run by parents and professionals) with organizations "*of* autism" that are run by autistic people, and report that the latter group in Germany take a neurodiversity approach as a contrast to the "patient" and "illness" oriented language of groups *for* autism (Jongsma et al., 2017). In both Germany and Israel, the logos for groups *of* autism represent diversity whereas the logos for the organizations *for* autism use puzzle piece logos (Raz et al., 2018), which is very much in line with iconography in North America and the division between neurodiversity advocacy which focuses on autism as human diversity and much parent advocacy which focuses on autism as a confusing puzzle of a condition in need of solving (Figures 21.1 and 21.2).

Both German and Israeli associations of autistic people were also important for peer groups, identity formation, and social interaction more than political activism (Raz et al., 2018). Relationships with associations *for* autism differed between the two countries, with more involvement of autistic people in these associations in Germany as well as more political action within associations *of* autism, due to the stronger history of British and US social models of disability following the disability activism in West Germany in the 1970s, which put forth this social model. In Israel, no such parallel movement challenged the medical model of disability, which is more influential in Israeli associations *for* autism. In both countries, members of Israeli associations *of* autism lamented lack of recognition by parents' associations (Raz et al., 2018).

My own research in Italy certainly sought to engage with the ideas of the neurodiversity movement, particularly in the everyday lives of autistic people, their families, and professionals. However, on the ground, the movement was not important to most of my participants, and only one interviewee tentatively used the term "neurotypical," using the vocabulary of the movement (Cascio, 2015; Cascio et al., 2018; see also Cola, 2012; Cola & Crocetti, 2011). The neurodiversity movement does have a presence in Italy, for example through the group Asperger Pride, but the major autism self-advocacy group is characterized more by partnership with parents and professionals than occurs in North America (or Germany or Israel), similar to the situation described in France (Cascio, 2015; Cascio et al., 2018; see also Cola & Crocetti, 2011).

Figure 21.1 Logos for Autistics United Canada and Autistic Self Advocacy Network. The logos for (A) Autistics United Canada (AUC) and (B) Autistic Self Advocacy Network (ASAN) integrate rainbow motifs with variations on a Möbius strip or an infinity symbol.
AUC logo designed by Chantal Snazel. Copyright by Autistics United Canada, all rights reserved. ASAN logo is licensed material trademarked by ASAN. Copyright by Autistic Self-Advocacy Network, all rights reserved

Figure 21.2 Logo for Autism Support Network. The logo for Autism Support Network (ASN) prominently features puzzle pieces.
Copyright by Autism Support Network, all rights reserved

This small body of cross-cultural research shows that neurodiversity concepts have begun to spread throughout the globe. Given that the neurodiversity movement largely emerged online, the Internet has been an important force for globalization of neurodiversity concepts. However, there are important local variations in the way autistic self-advocacy movements play out in different contexts, shaped by the local history of political action and broader political notions about diversity, inclusion, and civil society, as well as broader scientific and medical cultures. These differences include a limited influence of some of the more social critique-oriented aspects of neurodiversity in the French setting, greater partnership between parents and self-advocates in France, some greater involvement of self-advocates within German parent associations, and a distinctly Swedish focus on openness and "coming out" as political action. These comparisons suggest an important axis of difference. In North America, the UK, and Sweden, a strong neurodiversity movement incorporates some neuroscience discourse while rejecting "neuro-hegemonies" (Yergeau, 2018, p. 88) and a deficit approach to autism, in contexts where parents' and professionals' advocacy movements often embrace that deficit. In France and Italy, on the other hand, self-advocacy movements involve more partnership with parents and select professionals, allied in a joint project of searching for services and rejecting the dominant psychoanalytic models of autism. While some of this literature, especially in France, can be read as demonstrating that the neurodiversity movement is not influential, I would argue instead that it demonstrates that neurodiversity is a multivocal movement and that intersections of neuroscience discourses, identity, and political action are complex and related to interactions between facets of scientific and treatment cultures (like institutionalization, psychoanalysis, and behavioral psychology) and political cultures (like identity politics, Swedish openness about minority experiences, and anti-communitarianism).

Implications for Bioethics

This cross-cultural study of neurodiversity can provide insight into core bioethics issues. Insofar as the neurodiversity movement is a political movement, the focus of the cross-cultural literature reviewed here, it makes claims and calls to action that are directly relevant to the ethical sphere, especially on the topics of respect and justice. How are neurodiversity-informed bioethics questions of respect and justice handled differently cross-culturally?

Respect

How can people with autism be respected as persons? What are the characteristics of an (un)ethical treatment or intervention strategy or goal?

Neurodiversity advocates around the world are engaged in conversations about what treatments are ethical or unethical. Research on autistic advocacy in France details the influence of psychoanalysis in this setting and finds self-advocates and parents are aligned in opposition to psychoanalytic views of autism (Chamak, 2008, 2009, 2010; Chamak & Bonniau, 2013, 2014). Aspies for Freedom as well as advocates in Canada like Michelle Dawson argue against Applied Behavior Analysis (Cascio, 2012; Orsini, 2009), a commonly proposed intervention for autism that many autistic adults argue is abusive and manipulative (Sparrow, 2016). However, many parents and professionals in North America advocate *for* Applied Behavior Analysis (Cascio, 2012; Orsini, 2009), and in this way self-advocates and parents can often be opposed. Attention to the nuances of self-advocates' arguments for or against different treatments in different contexts can help bioethicists understand what broad characteristics make a diagnostic and treatment approach ethical or unethical by identifying common themes as well as structural, economic, and institutional factors related to differences in perspectives on specific interventions.

Justice

How can people with autism be treated fairly, as members of society and endowed with human rights? How can the perspectives of autistic people be represented in deliberations about autism? Research comparing advocacy organizations within Germany and between Germany and Israel is especially instructive on this point, especially in comparison with the other literature on advocacy movements in France, Italy, and elsewhere. Schicktanz et al. (Jongsma et al., 2017; Raz et al., 2018) explicitly place their study of these movements within an ethics of representation framework, particularly concerned with *epistemic injustice* – the notion that a special kind of injustice occurs when people's ability to assert knowledge claims is blocked or discounted (Fricker, 2007). Their work focuses on autistic advocacy organizations as patient organizations specifically for contributions to the representation of patient perspectives in healthcare. Schicktanz's research group asks how well patient organizations represent the population of people with autism, and how autistic people can best have their perspectives considered in deliberations about healthcare. They consider the limited role of autistic people in organizations run by parents and professionals – although how limited this role is varies in different countries due to local histories of activism – as well as the limited role of autistic-run organizations in various political spheres. This question ties into broader concerns about who should represent people with autism who do not communicate in ways that neurotypical people easily understand (such as speaking or writing; Hens et al., 2019) – is it autistic people who do speak and write about their experiences who might best be able to empathize with other autistic people? Is it parents, siblings, or other friends or family who know that individual person closely? Is it professionals, clinicians, or researchers who know large numbers of people on the spectrum and can apply their familiarity and credentialed expertise?

These questions of justice apply to a range of situations within and beyond the political and medical spheres.

Literature explicitly contrasting different neurodiversity or autistic self-advocacy movements provides a welcome complement to literature comparing autistic self-advocacy movements with parent movements (e.g., Orsini, 2009) and with other movements such as Deaf Culture (Davidson & Henderson, 2010). It also informs broader literature on health social movements and the different models – identity politics and otherwise – such as biosociality, the social model of disability, and embodied health movements (Brown et al., 2004; Hughes, 2009). Health social movements and disability rights movements are an area in which the intersection of culture, mind, and brain is at the forefront as groups negotiate the role of neuroscience research and discourse in both personal identity and politics, namely the potential for identity politics that, while common in the United States especially, is not a cross-cultural universal.

Conclusion

Recent scientific and social developments that have supported a neurodiversity approach to advocacy for people with autism have implications for the central concerns of bioethics, as well as broader questions of individual and collective identity and social organization. Notions of personhood as rooted in the brain – or indeed, in a diversity of human brains – raise implications for how to honor the bioethics principle of respect for personhood. Discourses that frame autism as an integral part of one's self that rests in the brain (as well as counter-discourses that challenge this notion) tie into long-standing concerns in transcultural psychiatry, the social sciences, and humanities regarding identity and self-understanding. The use of such brain-based personhood concepts in social advocacy and identity politics raise implications for how to honor the bioethics principle of justice, and relate to broader scholarship of social movements and health advocacy as well as the role of diversity of any kind within and between societies. This chapter has provided a brief overview of cross-cultural research on neurodiversity, proposed a neurodiversity-informed bioethics, outlined core questions for such bioethics inquiry, and highlighted the ways that neurodiversity can be used as a lens to inform scholarship in bioethics and likely also other fields. Neurodiversity posits particular views on ethical issues, focusing on neurological difference understood as a form of diversity within societies. Empirical research on neurodiversity movements, the influence of neurodiversity ideas, and the interactions between different stakeholders can advance bioethics theory around these questions. Cross-cultural research in particular highlights how ethical issues are addressed differently based on local professional perspectives, politics, and traditions of activism, revealing cultural, institutional, and structural factors that influence the value of different ethical arguments.

Neurodiversity, as a lens and a topic of cross-cultural study, provides a key example of changing notions of culture, mind, and brain. The neurodiversity movement implicitly draws from the broad turn toward a neuroscientific view on autism, while not necessarily wholesale embracing all neuroscience perspectives on the matter (Yergeau, 2018). It draws also from changing notions of the person and the role of diversity in society, and rests within different local models of political action and recognition for marginalized groups. Moreover, it interfaces with changing trends in academia, such as the "critical" turn reflected in critical autism studies. These ideas about neuroscience, politics, and scholarly approaches may continue to change along with changing communities and evolving global and local biologies (Lock & Kaufert, 2001). Neurodiversity serves as an important area for scholarly attention as a site in which these changing ideas are rendered especially salient.

Acknowledgments

I would like to acknowledge the participants in the Society for Psychological Anthropology/Lemelson Workshop, "Autism Spectrum Disorders in Global, Local and Personal Perspective: A Cross-Cultural Workshop," especially organizers Clarice Rios and Elizabeth Fein. It was at this 2015 conference in Brazil that I first articulated the idea of the dual role of neurodiversity as a lens and neurodiversity as a topic of study. I would also like to thank John Aspler for feedback on an earlier draft of this chapter. Any errors or lack of clarity remain my own.

REFERENCES

Antze, P. (2010). On the pragmatics of empathy in the neurodiversity movement. In M. Lambek (Ed.), *Ordinary ethics: Anthropology, language, and action* (pp. 310–27). Fordham University Press. www.jstor.org/stable/j.ctt13x07p9.20

Bagatell, N. (2007). Orchestrating voices: Autism, identity and the power of discourse. *Disability & Society*, 22(4), 413–26. https://doi.org/10.1080/09687590701337967

Bagatell, N. (2010). From cure to community: Transforming notions of autism. *Ethos*, 38(1), 33–55. https://doi.org/10.1111/j.1548-1352.2009.01080.x

Baggs, M. (2016, November 1). Reviving the concept of cousins [Blog post]. https://ballastexistenz.wordpress.com/2016/11/01/cousins/

Barnes, R. E., & McCabe, H. (2012). Should we welcome a cure for autism? A survey of the arguments. *Medicine Health Care and Philosophy*, 15(3), 255–69. https://doi.org/10.1007/s11019-011-9339-7

Belek, B. (2018). Autism and the proficiency of social ineptitude: Probing the rules of "appropriate" behavior. *Ethos*, *46*(2), 161–79. https://doi.org/10.1111/etho.12202

Bertilsdotter-Rosqvist, H. (2012). Normal for an Asperger: Notions of the meanings of diagnoses among adults with Asperger syndrome. *Journal of Intellectual and Developmental Disabilities*, *50*(2), 120–8. https://doi.org/10.1352/1934-9556-50.2.120

Brown, P., Zavestoski, S., McCormick, S., Mayer, B., Morello-Frosch, R., & Altman, R. G. (2004). Embodied health movements: New approaches to social movements in health. *Sociology of Health & Illness*, *26*(1), 50–80. https://doi.org/10.1111/j.1467-9566.2004.00378.x

Cascio, M. A. (2012). Neurodiversity: Autism pride among mothers of children with autism spectrum disorders. *Intellectual and Developmental Disabilities*, *50*(3), 273–83. https://doi.org/10.1352/1934-9556-50.3.273

Cascio, M. A. (2015). Biopolitics and subjectivity: The case of autism spectrum conditions in Italy [Doctoral dissertation]. Case Western Reserve University. https://etd.ohiolink.edu/pg_10?::NO:10:P10_ETD_SUBID:102221

Cascio, M. A., Andrada, B. C., & Bezerra, B. (2018). Psychiatric reform and autism services in Italy and Brazil. In E. Fein & C. Rios (Eds.), *Autism in translation: An intercultural conversation on autism spectrum conditions* (pp. 53–87). Springer International Publishing. https://doi.org/10.1007/978-3-319-93293-4_3

Chamak, B. (2008). Autism and social movements: French parents' associations and international autistic individuals' organisations. *Sociology of Health and Illness*, *30*(1), 76–96. https://doi.org/10.1111/j.1467-9566.2007.01053.x

Chamak, B. (2009). Autisme et militantisme: De la maladie à la différence. *Quaderni*, *68*, 61–70. https://doi.org/10.4000/quaderni.268

Chamak, B. (2010). Autisme, handicap et mouvements sociaux. *ALTER-European Journal of Disability Research/Revue Européenne de Recherche sur le Handicap*, *4*(2), 103–15. https://doi.org/10.1016/j.alter.2010.02.001

Chamak, B., & Bonniau, B. (2013). Autism and social movements in France: A comparative perspective. In J. Davidson & M. Orsini (Eds.), *Worlds of autism: Across the spectrum of neurological difference* (pp. 239–57). University of Minnesota Press. https://doi.org/10.5749/minnesota/9780816688883.003.0011

Chamak, B., & Bonniau, B. (2014). Neurodiversité: Une autre façon de penser. In B. Chamak & B. Moutaud (Eds.), *Neurosciences et société: Enjeux des savoirs et pratiques sur le cerveau* (pp. 211–30). Armand Colin.

Cola, M. (2012). *Ragionevolmente differenti: Una riflessione antropologica su sindrome di Asperger e disturbo dello spettro autistico*. I libri di Emil.

Cola, M., & Crocetti, D. (2011). Negotiating normality: Experiences from three Italian patient support groups. *Kroeber Anthropological Society Papers*, *99*(1), 214–36. https://kas.berkeley.edu/documents/Issue_99-100/15-Negotiating.pdf

Coombe, R. J. (1990). Barren ground: Re-conceiving honour and shame in the field of Mediterranean ethnography. *Anthropologica*, *32*(2), 221–38. www.jstor.org/stable/25605579

Davidson, J., & Henderson, V. L. (2010). 'Coming out' on the spectrum: Autism, identity and disclosure. *Social & Cultural Geography*, *11*(2), 155–70. https://doi.org/10.1080/14649360903525240

Fein, E. (2011). Innocent machines: Asperger's syndrome and the neurostructural self. In M. Pickersgill & I. Van Keulen (Eds.), *Sociological reflections on the neurosciences* (pp. 27–49). Emerald Group Publishing. https://doi.org/10.1108/S1057-6290(2011)0000013006

Fenton, A., & Krahn, T. (2007). Autism, neurodiversity, and equality beyond the 'normal'. *Journal of Ethics in Mental Health*, *2*(2), 1–6. https://jemh.ca/issues/v2n2/documents/JEMH_V2N2_Theme_Article2_Neurodiversity_Autism.pdf

Fricker, M. (2007). *Epistemic injustice: Power & the ethics of knowing*. Oxford University Press. https://doi.org/10.1093/acprof:oso/9780198237907.001.0001

Graby, S. (2015). Neurodiversity: Bridging the gap between the disabled people's movement and the mental health system survivors' movement? In H. Spandler, J. Anderson, & B. Sapey (Eds.), *Madness, distress and the politics of disablement* (pp. 231–44). Bristol University Press. https://doi.org/10.2307/j.ctt1t898sg.21

Grace, I. (2013). NeuroQueer. http://neuroqueer.blogspot.com

Hacking, I. (1995). The looping effects of human kinds. In D. Sperber, D. Premack, & A. J. Premack (Eds.), *Symposia of the Fyssen Foundation. Causal cognition: A multidisciplinary debate* (pp. 351–94). Clarendon Press. https://doi.org/10.1093/acprof:oso/9780198524021.003.0012

Hacking, I. (2006). Making up people. *London Review of Books*, *28*(16), 23–6. www.lrb.co.uk/v28/n16/ian-hacking/making-up-people

Hacking, I. (2009a). Autistic autobiography. *Philosophical Transactions of the Royal Society B: Biological Sciences*, *364*(1522), 1467–73. https://doi.org/10.1098/rstb.2008.0329

Hacking, I. (2009b). How we have been learning to talk about autism: A role for stories. *Metaphilosophy*, *40*(3–4), 499–516. https://doi.org/10.1111/j.1467-9973.2009.01607.x

Hacking, I. (2009c). Humans, aliens, & autism. *Daedalus*, *138*(3), 44–59. https://doi.org/10.1162/daed.2009.138.3.44

Hacking, I. (2010). Autism fiction: A mirror of an internet decade? *University of Toronto Quarterly*, *79*(2), 632–55. https://doi.org/10.3138/utq.79.2.632

Hart, B. (2014). Autism parents & neurodiversity: Radical translation, joint embodiment and the prosthetic environment. *BioSocieties*, *9*(3), 284–303. https://doi.org/10.1057/biosoc.2014.20

Hens, K., Robeyns, I., & Schaubroeck, K. (2019). The ethics of autism. *Philosophy Compass*, *14*(1), e12559. https://doi.org/10.1111/phc3.12559

Hughes, B. (2009). Disability activisms: Social model stalwarts and biological citizens. *Disability & Society*, *24*(6), 677–88. https://doi.org/10.1080/09687590903160118

Jongsma, K., Spaeth, E., & Schicktanz, S. (2017). Epistemic injustice in dementia and autism patient organizations: An empirical analysis. *AJOB Empirical Bioethics*, *8*(4), 221–33. https://doi.org/10.1080/23294515.2017.1402833

Kapp, S. K., Gillespie-Lynch, K., Sherman, L. E., & Hutman, T. (2013). Deficit, difference, or both? Autism and neurodiversity. *Developmental Psychology*, *49*(1), 59–71. https://doi.org/10.1037/a0028353

Kras, J. F. (2010). The "ransom notes" affair: When the neurodiversity movement came of age. *Disability Studies Quarterly*, *30*(1). www.dsq-sds.org/article/view/1065/1254

Lock, M., & Kaufert, P. (2001). Menopause, local biologies, and cultures of aging. *American Journal of Human Biology*, *13*(4), 494–504. https://doi.org/10.1002/ajhb.1081

Orsini, M. (2009). Contesting the autistic subject: Biological citizenship and the autism/autistic movement. In S. J. Murray & D. Holmes (Eds.), *Critical interventions in the ethics of healthcare: Challenging the principle of autonomy in bioethics* (pp. 115–30). Ashgate Publishing Company.

Orsini, M., & Davidson, J. (2013). Critical autism studies: Notes on an emerging field. In J. Davidson & M. Orsini (Eds.), *Worlds of autism: Across the spectrum of neurological difference* (pp. 1–28). University of Minnesota Press. https://doi.org/10.5749/minnesota/9780816688883.003.0001

Ortega, F. (2009). The cerebral subject and the challenge of neurodiversity. *BioSocieties, 4*(4), 425–45. https://doi.org/10.1017/S1745855209990287

Pellicano, E., Dinsmore, A., & Charman, T. (2014). What should autism research focus upon? Community views and priorities from the United Kingdom. *Autism, 18*(7), 756–70. https://doi.org/10.1177/1362361314529627

Perry, A. (2012). Autism beyond pediatrics: Why bioethicists ought to rethink consent in light of chronicity and genetic identity. *Bioethics, 26*(5), 236–41. https://doi.org/10.1111/j.1467-8519.2011.01952.x

Raz, A., Jongsma, K. R., Rimon-Zarfaty, N., Späth, E., Bar-Nadav, B., Vaintropov, E., & Schicktanz, S. (2018). Representing autism: Challenges of collective representation in German and Israeli associations for and of autistic people. *Social Science & Medicine, 200*, 65–72. https://doi.org/10.1016/j.socscimed.2018.01.024

Rios, C., & Andrada, B. C. (2015). The changing face of autism in Brazil. *Culture, Medicine and Psychiatry, 39*(2), 213–34. https://doi.org/10.1007/s11013-015-9448-5

Rodogno, R., Krause-Jensen, K., & Ashcroft, R. E. (2016). 'Autism and the good life': A new approach to the study of well-being. *Journal of Medical Ethics, 42*(6), 401–8. https://doi.org/10.1136/medethics-2016-103595

Rose, N. (2003). Neurochemical selves. *Society, 41*(1), 46–59. https://doi.org/10.1007/BF02688204

Silberman, S. (2016). *NeuroTribes: The legacy of autism and the future of neurodiversity*: Penguin Publishing Group.

Silverman, C. (2011). *Understanding autism: Parents, doctors, and the history of a disorder*. Princeton University Press.

Sparrow, M. (2016, October 26). ABA [Blog post]. http://unstrangemind.com/aba/

Tan, C. D. (2018). "I'm a normal autistic person, not an abnormal neurotypical": Autism spectrum disorder diagnosis as biographical illumination. *Social Science & Medicine, 197*, 161–7. https://doi.org/10.1016/j.socscimed.2017.12.008

van den Bosch, K. E., Krzeminska, A., Song, E. Y., van Hal, L. B. E., Waltz, M. M., Ebben, H., & Schippers, A. P. (2018). Nothing about us, without us: A case study of a consumer-run organization by and for people on the autism spectrum in the Netherlands. *Journal of Management & Organization*, 1–17. https://doi.org/10.1017/jmo.2018.54

Vidal, F. (2009). Brainhood, anthropological figure of modernity. *History of the Human Sciences, 22*(1), 5–36. https://doi.org/10.1177%2F0952695108099133

Vidal, F., & Ortega, F. (2017). *Being brains: Making the cerebral subject*. Fordham University Press. https://doi.org/10.2307/j.ctt1xhr6bn

Walker, N. (2015, May 4). Neuroqueer: An introduction [Blog post]. http://neuroqueer.blogspot.com/2015/05/neuroqueer-introduction-by-nick-walker.html

Waltz, M. (2003, July). Metaphors of autism, and autism as metaphor: An exploration of representation [Paper presentation]. Inter-Disciplinary.net Second Global Conference – Making Sense of: Health, Illness and Disease, Mansfield College, Oxford, England.

Waltz, M., van den Bosch, K., Ebben, H., van Hal, L., & Schippers, A. (2015). Autism self-advocacy in the Netherlands: Past, present and future. *Disability & Society*, *30*(8), 1174–91. https://doi.org/10.1080/09687599.2015.1090954

Yergeau, M. (2018). *Authoring autism: On rhetoric and neurological queerness*. Duke University Press.

22 Epilogue
Interdisciplinarity in the Study of Culture, Mind, and Brain

Laurence J. Kirmayer, Carol M. Worthman, and Shinobu Kitayama

Advancing an integrated understanding of culture, mind, and brain depends on fostering meaningful exchanges between diverse disciplines, each of which holds a piece of the puzzle. In this epilogue, we reflect on the prospects for advancing interdisciplinarity in the sciences of culture, mind, and brain and in the translation of research into social policy and practice. We come to this colloquy from the perspective of our respective disciplines: cultural psychiatry, biocultural and psychological anthropology, and cultural psychology. Over the last several decades, we have each participated in efforts to develop interdisciplinary programs and draw from this experience in our remarks. We also revisit some issues raised in the first edited volume based on the interdisciplinary conferences of the Foundation for Psychocultural Research (Kirmayer et al., 2007).

Varieties of Interdisciplinary Collaboration

Multidisciplinarity involves researchers from several disciplines working in parallel, with a clear division of labor, to address different aspects of a shared question or object of concern. *Interdisciplinarity* aims to go beyond this by promoting dialogue, knowledge exchange, and synthesis to create new frameworks and methodologies (Efstathiou & Mirmalek, 2014, p. 234). This can take many forms and result in hybrid methodologies, theory, and applications (Frodeman et al., 2017). Forms of interdisciplinarity are evident within neuroscience in current efforts to develop multilevel systems biology that integrates genomics, proteomics, metabolomics, and connectomics (the organization of brain circuitry, Alivisatos et al., 2012). As Sporns notes:

> The "omics" revolution that is still unfolding within the biological sciences is fueled by a paradigm shift away from reducing biological systems to individual parts (be they genes, proteins, neurons, or organisms) and towards considering all their parts and interactions at once. This paradigm shift requires the adoption of new models for representing, explaining and predicting complex biological functions, and these models draw heavily on the theoretical frameworks of system dynamics and network science.

In a sense, connectomics is an extension of systems biology to neuroscience. The role of networks in systems biology is paralleled by the strong links that have formed, even at this early stage, between the emerging field of connectomics and the science of complex networks. These links are likely to grow even stronger in the future, and they will help in overcoming the many challenges connectomics currently faces. (Sporns, 2013, p. 56)

In terms of current work at the intersection of neuroscience and social science, we can distinguish several ways in which interdisciplinary collaboration is organized.

Neuroscience is increasingly being applied to address questions of central concern to the social sciences. There are two broad lines of work of this type: (1) using neuroscience to explore underlying mechanisms, constraints, or interactions in social cognition and behavior (which is a major focus of work presented in Part I of this volume); and (2) applying the insights of neuroscience to practical domains of social life (as seen in many of the contributions to Part II). Whole new hybrid fields have emerged based on employing neuroscientific models, methods, and modes of explanation to study social phenomena, including social, cultural, and affective neuroscience, as well as applied domains like neuroeducation, neuropolitics, neuroeconomics, neurophilosophy, and neurolaw. Of course, simply tacking the prefix "neuro" onto the name of a field may reflect the current fad for brain-centric explanations (so-called neuroenchantment; see Ali et al., 2014); but it may also signal meaningful engagements with cutting-edge research that can creatively reshape theory and practice in particular domains. Cognitive science, which began as an amalgam of psychology, computer science, linguistics, anthropology, neuroscience, and philosophy (Dawson, 2013), never gelled as a single discipline (Núñez et al., 2019), but has given rise to more deeply interdisciplinary approaches to mechanistic explanation in cognitive neuroscience that consider multiple levels of organization (Boone & Piccinini, 2016; Cooper & Peebles, 2015). When extended to social cognition, this framework recognizes social processes as additional mechanistic levels (Cacioppo et al., 2000). The methods and insights of neuroscience have contributed to social science by making it possible to examine some of the underlying processes that contribute to sociality, decision-making, and the response to a wide variety of social contextual features. The neurosciences can provide measures that do not depend on self-report, and apparent discrepancies between brain activity and self-report may yield important insights into processes like self-awareness, self-deception, coping, and communication.

Social sciences in turn can contribute to neuroscience research in a variety of ways. For our present purposes, it is useful to distinguish four broad approaches: (1) the study of social factors that influence the brain; (2) the translation of neuroscience research beyond the laboratory into applications in clinical and other social settings; (3) the critical social analysis of the cultural, conceptual, and institutional framing and constraints on neuroscience research and its applications; and (4) the integration of all three in an ecosocial view of the brain (Laliberté et al., 2019).

Social Determinants. Work on social determinants examines social factors that influence brain development and functioning. For example, there is a wealth of evidence for the effects of early exposures to social adversity on subsequent brain structure and functioning (Hanson et al., 2010; Labonté et al., 2015). The timing of adversity is a crucial determinant of its impact on the epigenome (Dunn et al., 2019). Such work can help identify environmental factors that promote healthy brain development and resilience as well as those that cause vulnerability and illness (Paus, 2013).

Social Impacts, Applications, and Outcomes. The application of neuroscience in clinical or other settings requires translating knowledge into practical techniques informed by social context. While laboratory studies require a high degree of standardization and control over parameters that could affect the reproducibility of results, real-world applications must contend with the myriad changes of a world in flux. Applications must therefore respond to these larger, unpredictable dynamics. Sensitivity to context is essential to the skills that allow experts to translate generic knowledge into effective action.

Social Critique of Neuroscience. Critical neuroscience, an offshoot of science and technology studies, aims to analyze the production of neuroscientific knowledge and the ways it is applied by using the conceptual tools and frameworks of philosophy, social science, and political economy (Choudhury & Slaby, 2016). This includes examining the political economy of knowledge production (Robinson, 2019), as well as exploring how modes of self-understanding that are produced by neuroscience influence subsequent social processes (Rose & Abi-Rached, 2013; Vidal & Ortega, 2017). Practical applications of neuroscience research may have unforeseen and unintended consequences that need to be explored. Some of this may be subtle: for example, changes in the ways that people view agency, sense of self, emotion, and illness (Choudhury et al., 2015; Kirmayer & Gómez-Carrillo, 2019). Critical neuroscience itself can foster interdisciplinarity by exposing the hidden assumptions of current disciplinary practices and opening up a space for discussion, debate, and creative "entanglement" (Choudhury & Slaby, 2011; Fitzgerald & Callard, 2015).

Ecosocial View of the Brain. The preceding three modes of collaborative work can be brought together in an integrative view of the brain in environmental context. This includes dynamic links between the networks of the brain, the person as cognitive agent, and the social networks of the world (Fuchs, 2017). Cognition and experience then can be understood as arising from circuits that include the networks of the brain but that extend into the world to become part of a social–cultural ecology of mind (Kirmayer, 2015, 2019).

Challenges to Interdisciplinarity

While disciplinary specialization makes scientific progress possible, it can also create barriers to collaboration. The obstacles stem from institutional structures, methodological strategies, epistemic commitments, and implicit ontologies.

Disciplines themselves are the products of intellectual activities built around certain questions, bodies of knowledge, and methodologies, but they also reflect the institutional history of academia (Turner, 2017). This has resulted in different metrics of productivity, success, and reward. The guild-like nature of academic disciplines results in active efforts to police boundaries, which guard against hybrid or heterodox forms of activity that would undermine the core identity of the discipline. In this process, economic and power differentials skew the process of collaboration, spurring defensive postures and sometimes heated rivalries.

Despite frequent calls for interdisciplinarity to tackle urgent priorities in health and social policy, some evidence suggests that interdisciplinary research is less likely to be funded than projects that fall squarely within disciplinary boundaries (Bromham et al., 2016). Indeed, presenting interdisciplinary work in grant proposals and publications poses practical challenges. The description of theory and methods must adhere to conventional standards, providing sufficient detail to determine the rigor of multiple facets of the work, usually within the same space than would be allotted to a narrower study. This increases the risk that peer reviewers will identify gaps or weaknesses in the presentation. Similarly, publications presenting mixed methods research using both qualitative and quantitative methods often require more space than is available and thus expose themselves to critique from multiple angles in the peer-review process.

More substantive issues have to do with the nature of disciplinary interests. What counts as an interesting question and what is a satisfying, adequate, or productive answer varies from discipline to discipline. Objects of study are framed in terms of particular concepts and levels of description that constitute the domain of study for a discipline. These descriptions reflect an underlying ontology – that is, a set of commitments about the kinds of things that exist, which identifies objects, dimensions, metrics, measures, and domains that motivate the development of specific theories and methodologies (Bhaskar et al., 2018; Smith & Ceusters, 2010).

Methodologies provide specific ways of posing and answering questions, and these, in turn, serve to consolidate disciplinary boundaries, defined in terms of styles of reasoning, forms of evidence, strategies for validation, and bodies of cumulative knowledge. Measurement itself serves ontological purposes: what can be measured is real – in the sense that it points to (a fact about or property of) an object in the world. Methodologies thus give rise to and support particular scientific ontologies (Smith & Ceusters, 2010; Larsen & Hastings, 2018). Once a methodology is developed, therefore, it can itself become a way to define a discipline. For example, development of brain imaging technologies enabled the emergence of cognitive neuroscience as a new discipline (Bennett & Hacker, 2003; Raichle, 2009).

To the extent that disciplines differ in their ontologies, and in what counts as an interesting question and a productive answer, they constitute distinct communities with their own practices, codes of conduct, and culture – not all of which converge easily. Each community of practice, then, may find another's framing of problems and everyday practices unclear, obtuse, or beside the point. For example, there have been sharp critiques from across the disciplinary divides of social science and neuroscience that reflect these differences, some of which may block the meaningful exchange of information, let alone active collaboration (DeVos & Pluth, 2015). Yet there is wide recognition that meaningful translation of neuroscientific knowledge into practice requires an appreciation of the technical limitations of specific methods and paradigms, and adequate contextualization of findings – work that requires engagement with social science perspectives (Pykett, 2015).

We suggest that the way forward in the sciences of culture, mind, and brain will involve a multilevel, ecosocial systems view. Such a view recognizes mechanisms at multiple levels of biological, psychological, and social organization (Badcock et al., 2019; Bechtel, 2012; Craver, 2009; O'Malley et al., 2014). These levels of organization involve different spatial and temporal scales and composition of components (Eronen, 2015), but give rise to emergent processes, which, in turn, result in new kinds of structures or objects, requiring that we expand our ontologies (Bhaskar et al., 2018; Kauffman, 2019; Noble, 2016). Each of these levels may have its own dynamics that constitute a field of study. This is the practical and methodological origin of disciplinary ontologies. But there are dynamics across levels and this in turn requires methodological pluralism and interdisciplinarity. Indeed, neuroscience itself requires interdisciplinarity to study the multiple levels of organization within the brain, and it faces many of the same conceptual and methodological challenges as work that aims to understand the brain in its larger ecosocial environment, as illustrated in Figure 22.1 (Kotchoubey et al., 2016).

Building Interdisciplinary Bridges

There are strategies to address each of these obstacles to effective interdisciplinary collaboration. Table 22.1 summarizes some of these strategies at institutional, conceptual, and methodological levels. While institutional support is essential for long-term and large-scale work, steps toward interdisciplinarity can occur through conceptual and methodological exchange.

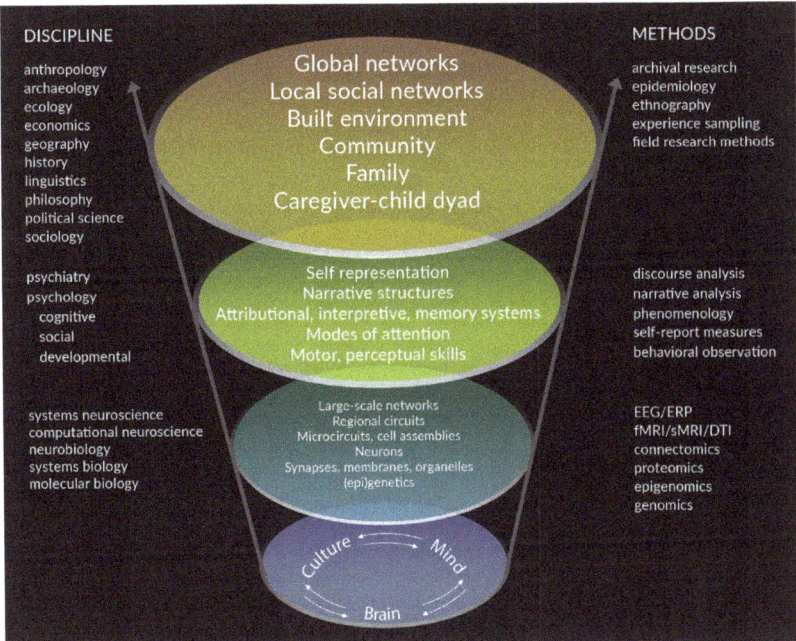

Figure 22.1 The co-construction of culture, mind, and brain on multiple levels. The domain of culture, mind, and brain is composed of multiple levels of organization, each with its own structure, dynamics, and descriptive vocabularies and methods.

Institutionally, interdisciplinarity requires creating places for work, training programs with appropriate mentoring, employment, and funding opportunities. Such institutional structures could equitably distribute economic and human resources (in terms of funded research projects and hiring), reward meaningful collaboration, and respect multiple metrics of success. This would including recognizing the value of process rather than just outcome as a necessary step toward productive interdisciplinary work. This demands that scholars familiar with the current exigencies of research in each domain have a hand in shaping institutional policy and practice. But this must occur in a larger context in which the importance of multiple levels of explanation is widely accepted.

Interdisciplinarity begins with recognition of its importance for tackling *multilevel problems* – since human systems span multiple scales, from cells to societies (Coen, 2012). To realize its potential, however, there must be personal and institutional commitments to open collaboration, working together to address hurdles. These include changes in funding priorities, the

Table 22.1 *Strategies for interdisciplinary collaboration*

Level	Strategy
Institutional	Create spaces and places for interdisciplinary exchange
	Fund interdisciplinary teams
	Establish metrics and sustained support for interdisciplinary work
Conceptual	Use cross-domain metaphors and expand conceptual vocabularies
	Establish common questions, objects of concern, or boundary objects
	Enlarge the dimensional space
	Develop shared ontologies
	Populate systems diagrams
Methodological	Correlate multiple methods for convergent validity
	Adapt methods to new objects
	Hybridize methods
	Develop new methods
	Create shared databases for access to methods and data

creation of spaces and adequate time to develop collaborations, and sustained support. Forms of recognition and reward of academic work need to take into account the time needed to develop truly meaningful collaborations and recognize that knowledge production in social science and neuroscience tend to operate on different timescales and with different metrics of success.

Involvement of stakeholders is vital first and foremost for ethical and political reasons. But the stakeholder perspective "on the ground" also can serve to challenge or upend conventional disciplinary boundaries and hierarchies, compelling meaningful collaboration to find ways to address relevant problems. Indeed, interdisciplinarity has been seen as a partial solution to the problem of equitable engagement and accountability in public science in so far as the bridge building makes contact with the concerns of everyday knowledge users and citizens (Barry & Born, 2013).

Enlarging the Conceptual Universe

The multilevel picture of mind, brain, and culture that we have sketched in Chapter 1 of this volume makes it clear that we need active dialogue and engagement among the humanities, social sciences, and biological sciences – each captures only some facets of being human, and the best picture we are likely to get of human functioning will come from interactional models. To do this, research must employ social science models and methods that are as sophisticated as those of neuroscience, and neuroscience, in turn, needs to be centered on (or at least open to) the study of the varieties of human experience. But these disciplines all involve levels of organization that are more or less familiar. Existentially, everyday activities and experience seem to be located closer to social and psychological than to neurobiological phenomena. Hence, people tend to think that they already understand these processes intuitively through folk psychology or social background knowledge, even though they actually may be unable to see much of what actually undergirds their cognition and social behavior.

This blindness to the underpinnings of human cognition and social reality has a dual basis in individual psychology and social process. Self-awareness is like the tip of an iceberg, maintained (and sometimes subverted) by myriad non-conscious processes (of which the Freudian unconscious reflects only one subset). In fact, efforts to introspect often produce accounts that reveal neither the underlying machinery nor the external influences on individuals' actions, but a post hoc, conventional narrative that conforms to cultural models and expectations (Mercier & Sperber, 2017; Nisbett & Wilson, 1977; Schwitzgebel, 2011). This blindness extends to the understanding of others, since people often appreciate neither their inner psychological workings (which reflect not just their biology and psychology but also their personal history) nor the impact of their lifeworlds (which reflect not just current circumstances, but also collective history – both of which are refracted by cultural meaning). Hence, neither first-person accounts nor third-person "heterophenomenology" (that is, understanding the structure of another's experience by building bridges from their accounts to underlying mechanisms through natural science and experiment; Dennett, 2007) can give us a clear picture of human nature and its constitutive mechanisms – which involve processes located not just in the brain, but in the world also. These processes include interpersonal interaction, engagements with environmental affordances, and narrative practices of self-depiction and presentation (Di Paolo et al., 2018; Veissière et al., 2020).

When researchers approach the social world from the perspective of what they already know about the brain, they are led to focus on certain features that are relevant to current theories, constructs, and available measures in neuroscience. If instead we start from the social world, and ask what might be important about the brain given what is known about social processes, we may be led in different directions. The social world has its own structure and dynamics and does not present itself to the brain in terms of isolated factors or parameters but as meaningful wholes.

This poses a challenge to contemporary social and cultural neuroscience, which tend to operationalize culture in terms of individual traits or discrete social factors. Experimental cognitive social neuroscience tends to be single-brain neuroscience that examines the impact of social stimuli (such as the presentation of a threatening face) on the individual or as a way to probe neural functioning. In focusing on the brain, the structure and dynamics of the social world may be grossly oversimplified or entirely lost. Ways to capture some of the dynamics of the social world include hyperscanning, ecological studies, and the use of big data to examine the interactions of multiple social dimensions through multivariate statistics, dynamical system theory, or agent-based modeling.

Conceptual and Methodological Pluralism

To engage with diverse methods, it is vital to begin with an ecumenical view that recognizes the strengths and limitations of specific methods. Methods are ways of taking hold of specific aspects of the world in particular ways (Krieger, 2012). The use of a method involves not simply a laboratory procedure, but participation in a community of practice with its own measures of conceptual relevance, fidelity, and validity (Collins, 2017; Collins & Evans, 2019). Learning a new method is learning a way of engaging the world – one that necessarily brings certain features or relationships into sharp relief while letting other aspects fall into shadow.

Methods can be brought into alignment by identifying common objects of concern, bridging concepts, and vocabularies. This process can also clarify the relationships among diverse methods. Each method exposes some facets of an object, situation, or event. When understood as revealing part of a whole, diverse methods can be correlated or compared to clarify the relationships between methods and models derived from different traditions. Triangulation of methods, then, is not simply a way to validate observations or see the object in multiple aspects, but to rethink the meaning and uses of each method.

The actual process of interdisciplinary engagement depends on identifying common interests, questions, and concerns. Considering the questions raised by specific disciplinary perspectives and the available methodological strategies allows us to identify what may be feasible to study at a given moment and what new methods need to be developed. Existing disciplinary work provides bridging for building an integrative view, in which each line of work finds its place in relation to others. The conceptual work can be seen as a kind of multidisciplinary puzzle solving, in which the validity of findings comes not only from their correspondence to reality but also from the ways the puzzle pieces fit together (Haack, 2005). Indeed, this fit can reveal new forms of coherence as it builds up a more detailed picture of the whole. This potential value of diverse methods does not amount to a blanket endorsement of every approach, but calls for a careful reflection on the virtues and limitations of different methodologies, clarifying their complementarity. The result is a rich, iterative exchange in which particular kinds of questions are elaborated and addressed from multiple angles, and the answers that are obtained stimulate new questions, some of which will be better addressed from another disciplinary perspective. Seen from a distance, what is at play is more than the sum of multiple disciplines. Rather, it is an emergent field centered on the object of interest, which helps to define the relationships among seemingly disparate lines of inquiry, with corresponding epistemic resources and commitments (Anderson, 2016).

Methodological and explanatory pluralism therefore are not ends in themselves, but necessary responses to the complexity of phenomena. In the case of the interaction of social science and neuroscience, where the common objects of interest are human cognition and behavior – and the multiscale, multilevel coordination of structures from molecule to society – what is required is the development of multiple levels of description and coordinated methodological strategies. Integrating this hierarchy of structures and processes involves cross-level translation which demands thoroughgoing interdisciplinary collaboration.

From Systems Theory to the Ecology of Mind

Over the last 60 years, systems theory has emerged as a powerful way to identify commonalities in the dynamics of different scales and levels of structure in biological and social phenomena (Capra & Luisi, 2014; Krakauer, 2019; Siskin, 2016; West, 2017). The challenge is how to locate culture, mind, and brain within the same dynamical system. Systems theory offers a picture of how behavior and experience can emerge from interactions among many processes over the timespan of development and across the spatial networks of many individuals and aspects of the environment. The elaborate, multilevel systems that underwrite human action and experience have great complexity owing to their scale, but they also show recurrent patterns that follow from their organization and regulatory processes. While these recurring patterns do not allow us to identify a simple set of "laws" of behavior and culture, they do make it possible to recognize organizational principles, particular system dynamics, and their likely consequences (Badcock et al., 2019). Capturing these dynamic processes requires thinking about mind, brain, and culture in ecological terms.

Brain, mind, and culture each can be thought of as constituting complex systems that are open, nonlinear, and generally irreducible to simple component subsystems. Even simple systems can be exquisitely sensitive to initial or boundary conditions and display complex dynamics (Feldman, 2019). For an organism to survive, however, it must dampen or control some of this complexity. A key insight from cybernetics (the study of [self-]regulatory systems) is the importance of *feedback loops* in organizing goal-directed behavior. Crucially, the higher-order levels or scales of structure feed back into lower-level processes by configuring relationships within and between individuals in new ways. As systems get larger, they may become more sensitive to conditions far away (think of the Internet) and long ago (think of the dependence of culture on history) and so require consideration of ever-widening cycles of interaction (Prigogine & Stengers, 1997).

The ubiquity of such circular causality, in which cause and effect are linked in cycles over time, has implications for how to do meaningful research and also for the prospects for making predictions – since some dynamic systems have stable attractors or final common pathways they arrive at no matter where they start, while others exhibit extreme sensitivity to initial conditions, with widely divergent trajectories or chaos (Kellert, 1993; Mitchell, 2009). Complexity theory provides tools for thinking about emergent system dynamics through mathematical models that can be simulated on computers (Byrne & Callaghan, 2013; Thurner et al., 2018). Multiple models can be compared to identify design principles that may have influenced evolutionary selection or adaptive fit (Gao & Ganguli, 2015).

While systems may exhibit similar dynamics, it remains that biological, psychological, and sociocultural systems each have their own unique properties, requiring specific methods to explore. What distinguishes human systems from most others is their self-referentiality and embedding in a human-designed environment that allows individuals to think with and through each other's experience (Veissière et al., 2020). This cooperative activity constitutes local cultural worlds. Through language and symbol systems, humans are able to think about their own constitution and modify it both from within and by taking action in the social world (Bateson, 1972). As a result of this capacity for self-description and ability to organize individual and collective action under these descriptions, human activities exhibit cognitive and sociocultural looping effects (Hacking, 1996, 1999, 2002). As people articulate and enact a way of being, it becomes a new social form and possibility for others. And as institutions and practices grow up around this way of being, it becomes a social fact, something that is taken for granted and that becomes the background to subsequent actions and gives them meaning (Searle, 2011). This background is not simply a matter of cognitive representations but of ways of actively engaging with social–environmental affordances (De Jaegher et al., 2016; Kirmayer & Ramstead, 2017; Ramstead et al., 2016).

Putting Culture at the Center

The contributions to this volume emphasize the co-construction of culture, mind, and brain. Cultural histories and forms of cooperative social activity are central to the unique reach and scope of human cognition. Interdisciplinary research methods encourage a back and forth between frameworks that can throw new facets of mind, brain, and culture into relief. In particular, ethnographic methods that capture the material, sensory, and affective qualities of local worlds help us to appreciate the phenomenology of experience, but also point to the crucial features, dimensions, or components involved in system-level cultural processes that constitute human minds.

In anthropology and psychology, culture often has been approached in terms of types, traits, and characteristics of individuals and groups. In much health and social research, culture is conflated with social categories like race and ethnicity. These categories are produced by culture – or, more accurately, at and by the interface of cultures. They are important because of the ways they organize and rationalize social structures that may produce enormous disparities of health, wealth, and power. Their study requires close examination of how the categories are constructed, and their consequences for individual development, functioning, and interactions with others including larger social structures. But culture stands for more than these ways of partitioning human groups.

More contemporary views understand culture as providing knowledge, skills, and dispositions to respond to particular situational affordances in the environment. Culture guides the construction of these environments and niches, as well as the development of individuals more or less competent to engage with the resulting possibilities for action or affordances. Individuals then have agency in the ways they engage or attempt to disengage, rebel against, or transform these collectively maintained resources. Individuals are influenced by multiple cultural strands depending on their connections to others, and, in the contemporary world, these influences range far and wide and can be presented with a speed and intensity that upends habitual patterns, rapidly recruiting emotional responses to create new forms of transient social groups. The technologies of the Internet, information and telecommunications devices, and, especially, social media are changing the nature and dynamics of culture. These changing configurations call for new models and methods of research on culture, mind, and brain.

Evolutionary history, historical accident, choices based on partial knowledge, and local idiosyncrasy all contribute to a world in which the fit between specific behaviors and intermediate outcomes or long-term survival is always uncertain and which, given current impacts on the climate, may lead to our own extinction. By 2050, most of the global population will be living in urban environments (United Nations, 2018) – spending increasing amounts of time in large-scale virtual worlds and communities. The pace of change threatens to exceed human adaptive capacities. And there are increasing signs of strain in both individual physiology and psychology as well as in the dynamics of communities.

The world holds traps and challenges for the human brain: our hunger and satiety regulatory systems were not designed to deal with refined sugar or fast food (Lowe et al., 2019); our sleep–wake cycles were never intended for a world online 24/7 (Crary, 2013); our attentional systems were not optimized for a world saturated with screens and social media (Veissière & Stendel, 2018); our social affiliation system never anticipated a world in which individuals are connected not to 150 people in their in-group but to thousands or millions who can all push the levers of social approval or attack (Dunbar, 2016). Can an ecosocial understanding of the human brain contribute to human survival and our eventual posthuman evolution?

Cultural Diversity as Challenge and Promise

There are some 7000 cultures in the world, each with its own languages, social structures, and ways of life. Despite the effects of globalization, with mass migration, rapid telecommunications, and popular media promoting cultural exchange, there is little sign that cultural diversity is disappearing. Instead, there is an ongoing process of cultural hybridization and invention. New technologies are also reconfiguring the social world in ways that give new meanings to the notion of culture. In particular, engagements with communities through social media and the opportunities for living in virtual or augmented reality encourage us to use our brains in new ways. If these become more prevalent, there likely will be corresponding changes in our neurocognitive functioning.

In addition to addressing cultural diversity as a reality that needs exploration in its own right, cultural systems of knowledge can present radically different ways of thinking about ourselves. For example, the work on interdependence discussed in this volume speaks to an important shift in how we might conceive the person – not as an individual autonomous organism, as is common in Euro-American psychology, but as inherently relational, embedded in webs of shared meaning and interpersonal ties that are constitutive of both self and other. This interdependent view fits well with more relational or ecological understandings of the person that can be formalized and studied empirically.

But there are still other cultural views that can provoke a rethinking of human functioning (Kirmayer et al., 2018). Emerging work in Indigenous psychologies considers the impact on views of human dynamics of starting from fundamentally different premises about the nature of human personhood and experience (Allwood, 2018). Many Indigenous Peoples, for example, regard the person as deeply connected to the environment in ways that acknowledge nonhuman forms of agency. This radical shift in perspective raises challenging ethical and pragmatic issues, but it can interrogate and clarify the interplay between the normative claims that underwrite our life choices and the cultural, historical, and political systems we inhabit. Western folk psychology underlies a lot of theory building and examining its assumptions opens up a space for fresh thinking and creative innovations.

Cultures provide flexible toolkits, and the diversity of cultures represents a kind of cognitive diversity that may prove adaptive in the face of rapid change (Page, 2010). Indigenous psychologies encourage us to rethink our place in the world from one of dominion to coexistence. The years to come will tell whether this new thinking will provide us with the flexibility and innovation needed to survive the catastrophic consequences of our own "success."

Conclusion

Over the next decades, innovations in brain research will lead to significant advances in our understanding of social and contextual influences on human cognition, emotion, and behavior. The emerging view of the brain in terms of dynamic networks that are plastic and adaptable across the lifespan points to new ways to think about the role of social context in individual development. This can help us understand ourselves and address human vulnerability and resilience in new ways. However, to realize this promise, neuroscience must be brought into more active dialogue with the social sciences and humanities, including anthropology, and cultural psychology and psychiatry. This exchange can illuminate how contextual differences at multiple scales affect human consciousness, cognition, behavior, and sociality. The social sciences have the potential to enliven, enrich, and redirect theory, research, and applications of neuroscience by providing salient examples of variation, refined notions of the meanings of context, and novel methodologies to study action and experience. In addition to guiding and interpreting experimental work, critical social science perspectives can play an essential role in the interpretation of research findings that often have important ethical, social, and political implications.

If this book were a Shakespearean comedy, the *finale* might include a marriage, bringing together all of the opposites in some form of celebratory union. Neuroscience, psychological and social sciences, and the humanities are essential partners in any picture of the human condition. As a step toward this integration, the contributors to this book show how the brain must be understood as plastic and dynamic, part of a predictive/enactive – rather than passive/responsive – system that gives rise to individual psychology and cultural worlds. The brain is inherently social, an "organ of culture," shaped across the lifespan by social interactions and dependent on social and cultural contexts for its development and functioning. The circuits of the mind connect the brain and social world. The disciplines present in this book – and many others not represented – must work in concert to describe these interacting networks. Neuroscience reveals how the brain engages the world; the social sciences show us how and why the various kinds of events in the world matter; and the humanities provide the language needed to speak truth to power. Each can contribute to our imaginative capacity to invent new ways of thinking, new forms of culture, and new possibilities for our lives.

REFERENCES

Ali, S. S., Lifshitz, M., & Raz, A. (2014). Empirical neuroenchantment: From reading minds to thinking critically. *Frontiers in Human Neuroscience, 8*, 357. https://doi.org/10.3389/fnhum.2014.00357

Alivisatos, A. P., Chun, M., Church, G. M., Greenspan, R. J., Roukes, M. L., & Yuste, R. (2012). The brain activity map project and the challenge of functional connectomics. *Neuron, 74*(6), 970–74. https://doi.org/10.1016/j.neuron.2012.06.006

Allwood, C. M. (2018). *The nature and challenges of Indigenous psychologies*. Cambridge University Press.

Andersen, H. (2016). Collaboration, interdisciplinarity, and the epistemology of contemporary science. *Studies in History and Philosophy of Science Part A, 56*, 1–10.

Badcock, P. B., Friston, K. J., Ramstead, M. J. D., Ploeger, A., & Hohwy, J. (2019). The hierarchically mechanistic mind: An evolutionary systems theory of the human brain, cognition, and behavior. *Cognitive, Affective, & Behavioral Neuroscience*. Advance online publication. https://doi.org/10.3758/s13415-019-00721-3

Barry, A., & Born, G. (Eds.). (2013). *Interdisciplinarity: Reconfigurations of the social and natural sciences*. Routledge.

Bateson, M. C. (1972). *Our own metaphor: A personal account of a conference on the effects of conscious purpose on human adaptation*. Knopf.

Bechtel, W. (2012). *Mental mechanisms: Philosophical perspectives on cognitive neuroscience*. Psychology Press. https://doi.org/10.4324/9780203810095

Bennett, M., & Hacker, P. (2003). *Philosophical foundations of neuroscience*. Blackwell.

Bhaskar, R., Danermark, B., & Price, L. (2018). *Interdisciplinarity and wellbeing: A critical realist general theory of interdisciplinarity*. Routledge. https://doi.org/10.4324/9781315177298

Boone, W., & Piccinini, G. (2016). The cognitive neuroscience revolution. *Synthese, 193*(5), 1509–34. https://doi.org/10.1007/s11229-015-0783-4

Bromham, L., Dinnage, R., & Hua, X. (2016). Interdisciplinary research has consistently lower funding success. *Nature, 534*(7609), 684. https://doi.org/10.1038/nature18315

Byrne, D. S., & Callaghan, G. (2013). *Complexity theory and the social sciences: The state of the art*. Routledge.

Cacioppo, J. T., Berntson, G. G., Sheridan, J. F., & McClintock, M. K. (2000). Multilevel integrative analyses of human behavior: Social neuroscience and the complementing nature of social and biological approaches. *Psychological Bulletin*, *126*(6), 829–43. https://doi.org/10.1037/0033-2909.126.6.829

Capra, F., & Luisi, P. L. (2014). *The systems view of life: A unifying vision*. Cambridge University Press.

Choudhury, S., McKinney, K. A., & Kirmayer, L. J. (2015). "Learning how to deal with feelings differently": Psychotropic medications as vehicles of socialization in adolescence. *Social Science & Medicine*, *143*, 311–19.

Choudhury, S., & Slaby, J. (Eds.). (2011). *Critical neuroscience: A handbook of the social and cultural contexts of neuroscience*. Wiley Blackwell.

Coen, E. (2012). *Cells to civilizations: The principles of change that shape life*. Princeton University Press.

Collins, H. (2017). *Gravity's kiss: The detection of gravitational waves*. MIT Press.

Collins, H., & Evans, R. (2017). *Why democracies need science*. John Wiley & Sons.

Cooper, R. P., & Peebles, D. (2015). Beyond single-level accounts: The role of cognitive architectures in cognitive scientific explanation. *Topics in Cognitive Science*, *7*(2), 243–58. https://doi.org/10.1111/tops.12132

Crary, J. (2013). *24/7: Late capitalism and the ends of sleep*. Verso Books.

Craver, C. F. (2009). *Explaining the brain: Mechanisms and the mosaic unity of neuroscience*. Oxford University Press. https://doi.org/10.1093/acprof:oso/9780199299317.003.0007

Dawson, M. R. (2013). *Mind, body, world: Foundations of cognitive science*. Athabasca University Press.

De Jaegher, H., Di Paolo, E., & Adolphs, R. (2016). What does the interactive brain hypothesis mean for social neuroscience? A dialogue. *Philosophical Transactions of the Royal Society B: Biological Sciences*, *371*(1693), 20150379. https://doi.org/10.1098/rstb.2015.0379

Dennett, D. (2007). Heterophenomenology reconsidered. *Phenomenology and the Cognitive Sciences*, *6*, 247–70.

De Vos, J., & Pluth, E. (2015). *Neuroscience and critique: Exploring the limits of the neurological turn*. Routledge.

Di Paolo, E. A., Cuffari, E. C., & De Jaegher, H. (2018). *Linguistic bodies: The continuity between life and language*. MIT Press. https://doi.org/10.7551/mitpress/11244.001.0001

Dunbar, R. I. (2016). Do online social media cut through the constraints that limit the size of offline social networks? *Royal Society Open Science*, *3*(1), 150292. https://doi.org/10.1098/rsos.150292

Dunn, E. C., Soare, T. W., Zhu, Y., Simpkin, A. J., Suderman, M. J., Klengel, T., Smith, A. D. A. C., Ressler, K. J., & Relton, C. L. (2019). Sensitive periods for the effect of child adversity on DNA methylation: Results from a prospective, longitudinal study. *Biological Psychiatry*, *85*, 838–49. https://doi.org/10.1016/j.biopsych.2018.12.023

Efstathiou, S., & Mirmalek, Z. (2014). Interdisciplinarity in action. In N. Cartwright & E. Montuschi (Eds.), *Philosophy of social science: A new introduction* (pp. 233–48). Oxford University Press.

Eronen, M. I. (2015). Levels of organization: A deflationary account. *Biology & Philosophy*, *30*(1), 39–58. https://doi.org/10.1007/s10539-014-9461-z

Feldman, D. (2019). *Chaos and dynamical systems.* Princeton University Press. https://doi.org/10.1515/9780691189390

Fitzgerald, D., & Callard, F. (2015). Social science and neuroscience beyond interdisciplinarity: Experimental entanglements. *Theory, Culture & Society, 32*(1), 3–32. https://doi.org/10.1177%2F0263276414537319

Frodeman, R., Klein, J. T., & Pacheco, R. C. S. (Eds.). (2017). *The Oxford handbook of interdisciplinarity* (2nd ed.). Oxford University Press. https://doi.org/10.1093/oxfordhb/9780198733522.001.0001

Fuchs, T. (2017). *Ecology of the brain: The phenomenology and biology of the embodied mind.* Oxford University Press. https://doi.org/10.1093/med/9780199646883.001.0001

Gao, P., & Ganguli, S. (2015). On simplicity and complexity in the brave new world of large-scale neuroscience. *Current Opinion in Neurobiology, 32,* 148–55. https://doi.org/10.1016/j.conb.2015.04.003

Haack, S. (2005). The unity of truth and the plurality of truths. *Principia: An International Journal of Epistemology, 9*(1–2), 87–109.

Hacking, I. (1996). The looping effects of human kinds. In D. Sperber, D. Premack, & A. J. Premack (Eds.), *Symposia of the Fyssen Foundation. Causal cognition: A multidisciplinary debate* (pp. 351–94). Oxford University Press. https://doi.org/10.1093/acprof:oso/9780198524021.003.0012

Hacking, I. (1999). *The social construction of what?* Harvard University Press.

Hacking, I. (2002). *Historical ontology.* Harvard University Press. https://doi.org/10.1007/978-94-017-0475-5_13

Hanson, J. L., Chung, M. K., Avants, B. B., Shirtcliff, E. A., Gee, J. C., Davidson, R. J., & Pollak, S. D. (2010). Early stress is associated with alterations in the orbitofrontal cortex: a tensor-based morphometry investigation of brain structure and behavioral risk. *Journal of Neuroscience, 30*(22), 7466–7472.

Kauffman, S. A. (2019). *A world beyond physics: The emergence and evolution of life.* Oxford University Press.

Kellert, S. H. (1993). *In the wake of chaos: Unpredictable order in dynamical systems.* University of Chicago Press. https://doi.org/10.7208/chicago/9780226429823.001.0001

Kirmayer, L. J. (2015). Re-visioning psychiatry: Toward an ecology of mind in health and illness. In L. J. Kirmayer, R. Lemelson, & C. A. Cummings (Eds.). *Re-visioning psychiatry: Cultural phenomenology, critical neuroscience, and global mental health* (pp. 622–60). Cambridge University Press. https://doi.org/10.1017/CBO9781139424745

Kirmayer, L. J. (2019). Toward an ecosocial psychiatry. *World Social Psychiatry, 1*(1), 30–32.

Kirmayer, L. J., Adeponle, A., & Dzokoto, V. A. A. (2018). Varieties of global psychology: Cultural diversity and constructions of the self. In S. Fernando and R. Moodley (eds.) *Global psychologies* (pp. 21–37). Palgrave Macmillan.

Kirmayer, L. J., & Gómez-Carrillo, A. (2019). Agency, embodiment and enactment in psychosomatic theory and practice. *Medical Humanities, 45*(2), 169–182.

Kirmayer, L. J., Lemelson, R., & Barad, M. (2007). Epilogue: Trauma and the vicissitudes of interdisciplinary integration. In L. J. Kirmayer, R. Lemelson, & M. Barad (Eds.), *Understanding trauma: Integrating biological, clinical, and cultural perspectives* (pp. 475–89). Cambridge University Press.

Kirmayer, L. J., & Ramstead, M. J. D. (2017). Embodiment and enactment in cultural psychiatry. In C. Durt, T. Fuchs, & C. Tewes (Eds.), *Embodiment, enaction, and culture: Investigating the constitution of the shared world* (pp. 397–422). MIT Press.

Kotchoubey, B., Tretter, F., Braun, H. A., Buchheim, T., Draguhn, A., Fuchs, T., Hasler, F., Hastedt, H., Hinterberger, T., Northoff, G., Rentschler, I., Schleim, S., Sellmaier, S., van Elst, L. T., & Tschacher, W. (2016). Methodological problems on the way to integrative human neuroscience. *Frontiers in Integrative Neuroscience, 10*, 41. https://doi.org/10.3389/fnint.2016.00041

Krakauer, D. C. (Ed.). (2019). *Worlds hidden in plain sight: The evolving idea of complexity at the Santa Fe Institute, 1984–2019*. SFI Press.

Krieger, M. H. (2012). *Doing physics: How physicists take hold of the world*. Indiana University Press.

Labonté, B., Farah, A., & Turecki, G. (2015). Early-life adversity and epigenetic changes: Implications for understanding suicide. In L. J. Kirmayer, R. Lemelson, & C. A. Cummings (Eds.). *Re-visioning psychiatry: Cultural phenomenology, critical neuroscience, and global mental health* (pp. 206–35). Cambridge University Press. https://doi.org/10.1017/CBO9781139424745.012

Laliberté, V., Ramstead, M. J. D., Langlois-Therien, T., Choudhury, S., & Kirmayer, L. J. (2019). *How can the social sciences contribute to the neurosciences? Challenges and opportunities in the era of big data* [Manuscript in preparation]. Department of Psychiatry, McGill University.

Larsen, R. R., & Hastings, J. (2018). From affective science to psychiatric disorder: Ontology as a semantic bridge. *Frontiers in Psychiatry, 9*. https://doi.org/10.3389/fpsyt.2018.00487

Lowe, C. J., Reichelt, A. C., & Hall, P. A. (2019). The prefrontal cortex and obesity: A health neuroscience perspective. *Trends in Cognitive Sciences, 23*(4), 349–61. https://doi.org/10.1016/j.tics.2019.01.005

Mercier, H., & Sperber, D. (2017). *The enigma of reason*. Harvard University Press.

Mitchell, S. D. (2009). *Unsimple truths: Science, complexity, and policy*. University of Chicago Press. https://doi.org/10.7208/chicago/9780226532653.001.0001

Nisbett, R. E., & Wilson, T. D. (1977). Telling more than we can know: Verbal reports on mental processes. *Psychological Review, 84*(3), 231. https://doi.org/10.1037/0033-295X.84.3.231

Noble, D. (2016). *Dance to the tune of life: Biological relativity*. Cambridge University Press. https://doi.org/10.1017/9781316771488

Núñez, R., Allen, M., Gao, R., Rigoli, C. M., Relaford-Doyle, J., & Semenuks, A. (2019). What happened to cognitive science? *Nature Human Behaviour, 3*(8), 782–91.

O'Malley, M. A., Brigandt, I., Love, A. C., Crawford, J. W., Gilbert, J. A., Knight, R., Mitchell, S. D., & Rohwer, F. (2014). Multilevel research strategies and biological systems. *Philosophy of Science, 81*(5), 811–28. https://doi.org/10.1086/677889

Page, S. E. (2010). *Diversity and complexity*. Princeton University Press. https://doi.org/10.1515/9781400835140

Paus, T. (2013). *Population neuroscience*. Springer Science & Business Media. https://doi.org/10.1007/978-3-642-36450-1

Prigogine, I., & Stengers, I. (1997). *The end of certainty*. Simon & Schuster.
Pykett, J. (2015). *Brain culture: Shaping policy through neuroscience*. Policy Press. https://doi.org/10.2307/j.ctt1t89jbm
Raichle, M. E. (2009). A brief history of human brain mapping. *Trends in Neurosciences, 32*(2), 118–26.
Ramstead, M. J., Veissière, S. P., & Kirmayer, L. J. (2016). Cultural affordances: Scaffolding local worlds through shared intentionality and regimes of attention. *Frontiers in Psychology, 7*, 1090. https://doi.org/10.3389/fpsyg.2016.01090
Robinson, M. D. (2019). *The market in mind: How financialization is shaping neuroscience, translational medicine, and innovation in biotechnology*. MIT Press. https://doi.org/10.7551/mitpress/11726.001.0001
Rose, N., & Abi-Rached, J. M. (2013). *Neuro: The new brain sciences and the management of the mind*. Princeton University Press. https://doi.org/10.1515/9781400846337
Schwitzgebel, E. (2011). *Perplexities of consciousness*. MIT Press. https://doi.org/10.7551/mitpress/8243.001.0001
Searle, J. R. (2011). Wittgenstein and the Background. *American Philosophical Quarterly, 48*(2), 119–28.
Siskin, C. (2016). *System: The shaping of modern knowledge*. MIT Press.
Smith, B., & Ceusters, W. (2010). Ontological realism: A methodology for coordinated evolution of scientific ontologies. *Applied Ontology, 5*(3–4), 139–88. https://doi.org/10.3233/AO-2010-0079
Sporns, O. (2013). The human connectome: Origins and challenges. *NeuroImage, 80*, 53–61. https://doi.org/10.1016/j.neuroimage.2013.03.023
Thurner, S., Hanel, R., & Klimek, P. (2018). *Introduction to the theory of complex systems*. Oxford University Press. https://doi.org/10.1093/oso/9780198821939.001.0001
Turner, S. (2017). Knowledge formations: An analytic framework. In R. Frodeman, J. T. Klein, & R. C. S. Pacheco (Eds.), *The Oxford handbook of interdisciplinarity* (2nd ed.). Oxford University Press. https://doi.org/10.1093/oxfordhb/9780198733522.001.0001
United Nations, Population Division of the Department of Economic and Social Affairs. (2018). *2018 Revision of world urbanization prospects*. https://population.un.org/wup/
Veissière, S. P., Constant, A., Ramstead, M. J., Friston, K. J., & Kirmayer, L. J. (2020). Thinking through other minds: A variational approach to cognition and culture. *Behavioral and Brain Sciences, 43*, e90, 1–75. https://doi.org/10.1017/S0140525X19001213
Veissière, S. P., & Stendel, M. (2018). Hypernatural monitoring: a social rehearsal account of smartphone addiction. *Frontiers in Psychology, 9*, 141.
Vidal, F., & Ortega, F. (2017). *Being brains: Making the cerebral subject*. Fordham University Press. https://doi.org/10.5422/fordham/9780823276073.001.0001
West, G. (2017). *Scale: The universal laws of growth, innovation, sustainability, and the pace of life in organisms, cities, economies, and companies*. Penguin Press.

Index

"A Simple Heart" (Flaubert), 419
Abrahamic religions, 343–4
absorption, 467, 472
absorption matrix, 463
abstinence, 471
abstractions, 208
academic disciplines
  boundaries, 497, 500
  collaboration, 500
  ontologies, 497
ACC. *See* anterior cingulate cortex (ACC)
accidental events, 260
acculturation
  concept learning, 210
  defined, 190
  engagement with culture, 210
acculturative stress, 209
acetylcholine, 378
action preparation, 249
action selection, 249
action-outcome prediction, 249
actions, agency, 255
actions, agentic, 246
actions, automatic, 246
actions, habitual, 246
actions, non-agentic, 257
actions, voluntary
  sequence of steps, 263
active inference, 9, 201, 274, 282–3, 291, 364
active perception, 58
adaptation
  timescales, 123
ADHD (attention-deficit/hyperactivity disorder), 479
adolescence
  brain plasticity, 390–1
  ethnographic studies, 127
  liminal period, 397–8
  parental intervention, 138
  risk-taking and implusivity, 391
adolescents
  digital media use, 389

  health and social policy, 391
  social and economic contexts, 393
  social cognitive development, 397
adverse life events, 205
aerobic exercise, 376
affect
  allostasis, 193
  intensity, 473
  spread of, 467
  valence dimension, 208
affective categories, 369
affective niche, 198
  caregiving, 200–1
  defined, 198
  emotion concepts, 205
affiliation goals, 311
affordance theory, 419–20
  narrative handling, 418
  weak theory, 417, 424
affordances
  cooperative behavior, 273
  cultural meaning and participation, 261–3
  culturally specific, 428
  culture, 176
  cyberspace, 464, 472
  environment, 175
  genre, 419
  internal model, 189
  social norm violations, 311
  underspecification, 420
Africa, emotion words vs. behaviors, 206
AG (angular gyrus), 249
agency, 505
  anticipatory adaptation, 160
  attribution, 260
  bottom-up models, 249, 251
  brain regions, 248
  cognitive biases, 248
  comparator models, 249, 251
  decrease in, 265
  defined, 246–7
  ecosocial, 245

513

agency (cont.)
  feeling of vs. judgment of, 251
  intention, action and response, 266
  interplay of types, 264–5
  mental causation models, 249, 251
  models, 268
  modulation of, 247, 264
  multidimensional models, 249–50
  non-human forms, 506
  ontology, 259
  reason, 245
  self-construal, 259
  sense of, 26
  top-down models, 249, 251
agent-based modeling, 502
agents
  competitive views of consensus, 284
  expectations, 283
aging
  cognitive deficits in, 376
  navigation memory system competition, 379
alcohol dehydrogenase 1B, 18
alcohol use and abuse, 17, 303, 311
alcohol use disorder
  training, 444
alloparenting, 67
allostasis, 188–9
  acculturation, 210
  affective niche, 198
  age-related increase, 197
  maintenance of, 58
  social regulation, 204, 210
allostatic overload, 199n3
allostatic support, 197, 200–1
Allport, Floyd, 440
alpha activity, 312–13
altruistic behavior, 235
Alzheimer's disease, 376, 380
Americans
  agency, 260–1
  alpha activity, 312
  CTRA, 144
  emotions, 205
  social norm violation protections, 310
  stories, emotional, 430
amygdala, 285, 308
  decreased empathy, 442
  migraines, 169n2
  population effect on, 451
  reward system, 402
  risk-detection, 441
  stress and spatial memory performance, 379
anger, 204n7
angular gyrus (AG), 249
animism, 340

Annaliste work, 368
anterior cingulate cortex (ACC), 231, 307–8, 441, 451
anterior insula (AI), 307–8
anterior supramarginal gyrus (aSMG), 73
anterior temporal pole, 305
anthropology
  biological vs. cultural frameworks, 127
  differences, 130
  ethnographic participation, 120
  focus of, 127
  observer effects, 129
anticipation, 403–4
anti-communitarianism, 483
anxiety, 209
  affective mediators, 441
  allostatic load, 209
  children and adolescents, 393
  5-HTTLPR, 314
  social defeat, 451, 454
apolipoprotein E gene, 380
Applied Behavior Analysis, 487
APPS-distress (attenuated positive psychotic symptoms), 452
Arabs
  holistic attention, 100
  self-assertive interdependence, 91
  situational inference, 102
archaeology
  behavior, 57
archaeology, cognitive, 58
archaeology, experimental, 69
argumentation, 92
art, technology vs., 60
artifacts, 55, 58
Ashura, 330
Asian flush response, 17–18
Asians
  attitude inferences, 99–101
  dispositional vs. situational factor attribution, 101
  DRD4 7/2-R allele, 108–9
  holistic attention, 98–100
  interdependent self-construal, 105, 108
  mPFC volume, 105
  orbitofrontal cortex, 108
  positive affect, 108
  prefrontal cortex, 104–5
  self-construal priming, 97–8
aSMG (anterior supramarginal gyrus), 73
Asperger Pride, 484
Asperger's syndrome, 477
Aspies for Freedom, 483, 487
aspirational figures, 444
aspirations, thwarted, 453–4

Index

assimilation, 211
association cortex, 66–7
attention, absolute vs. relative judgment, 99
attention, holistic, 98–100
attention, shared, 274
attentional cues, 466
attentional focus, 393
attentional mechanisms, 286
attentional systems, 72, 506
attention-deficit/hyperactivity disorder (ADHD), 479
attenuated positive psychotic symptoms (APPS-distress), 452
attribution, 251
attunement, 181
auditory cortex, 403
augmented reality, 506
Austrians, 260
authorial intent, 422
authority, symbolic, 445
autism. *See* autistic people
autism ethics, 479
autism narratives, non-deficit approach, 483
autism pride, 477
autism research
 diversity mindset, 481
 focus on experiences, 481
 non-deficit approach, 481
 transparency about needs, 481
autistic people
 bioethics, 480
 conceptualization, 479–80
 deficit model, 479
 focus on experiences, 481
 functioning labels, 481, 482
 identity, 479
 justice, 487–8
 perspectives, 481
 psychoanalysis, 484, 486
 respect, 487
 self-advocacy vs. parent advocacy, 477, 483–4, 487–8
 topics of interest, 481
automaticity, 258
autonomy, 480
autopoiesis, 58
avatars, online, 470
awakening, 470
Ax Fight, The, 427, 431
axon myelination, 396

Baby Einstein, 392
Baby Mozart, 392
bacteria, 177

Bali
 Bitter Honey, 432
Balinese, 260–1, 427
barometer, 419
Barrett, Lisa Feldman, 368
Barthes, Roland, 419, 421
basal ganglia, 376–7
Bayes's rule, 282
Bayesian brain, 201
Bayesian hierarchical levels, 167n1
Bayesian predictions, 282
behavior
 dispositional vs. situational factors, 100
 model-free vs. model-driven, 177
behavioral analysis, 427
behavioral change, 230, 441
behavioral goals, 307
behavioral sciences, representation in, 131
being there
 formal research contrasted with, 145
 interventions, 139
 limitations, 145
 as method, 128
 practical requirement, 129
 re-humanization, 132
belief propagation, 201
beliefs, values, and practices, 188, 223–6, 228, 230, 237–8, *See also* parental beliefs, religious beliefs
 brain, 230, 274
 cultural relativism, 130, 160
 delusions, 450, 469
 egocentric projection, 29
 expectations, 253, 274, 283
 false beliefs, 75
 knowledge, xvii, 59, 169
 narrative bond, 429
 online communities, 465
 social norms, 310, 443
 top-down beliefs, 164, 171
biases
 academic bias, 280
 dispositional inferences, 101
 egocentric projection, 29
 embodied, 280
 in-group/out-group, 235, 274
 investigator subjectivity, 131
 observability, 145
 perceptual content, 164
 reflexivity, 145
biculturalism
 cultural priming, 226, 234
 social adaptation, 211
 social norm differences, 316
big data, 502

big gods hypothesis, 341–2, 344
Big Sur, 389
biocultural historicism, 372
biocultural perspective, 22, 370, 426
  adaptations, 53, 273, 281
  embodied model, 280, 367, 430
  embrained model, 277
biocultural reproduction, 67
bioecocultural view, 123, 133–6
bioethics, 480
biological processes, context sensitive, 134
biology, reductionist, 494
biology, shaped by culture, 127
biomarkers
  CTRA, 141, 143
  social science research, 135
biosocial model of affective decision making, 333
bipedalism, 14
bipolar disorder, 450
birds, 301, 375
birth spacing, 133–6
Bitter Honey, 432
blind individuals, 289
blue, 181
bodily spatial awareness, 73
body
  anticipation of needs, 196
  brain, coupled to, 180
  mind, 143
  ownership, 255
body–mind dualism, 143, 159
Borderlands, 381
Boston Bombing, 338
Bourdieu, P., 60, 280–1
brain
  allostasis, 190
  anatomy, 34
  architecture and social life, 285
  association networks, 66
  attunement to environment, 165
  body, coupled to, 180
  cultural shaping of, 68, 89, 160, 188
  default mode subnetwork, 192
  defined, 3
  development, 65, 197
  distributed processing, 159
  dynamic concept construction, 189
  ecosocial view, 496
  evolution, 53, 65, 166, 180
  information flow, 197
  intrinsic activity, 191
  learning, 202
  models for, 8, 159, 193
  niche construction, 122
  prediction error, 202
  predictive framework, 58, 60, 188, 201, 203
  size, 14, 55, 57, 65
  top-down effects, 11
brain activity
  cultural differences, 223
  motivation-related, 95–7
  temporal variance, 225
  theory of mind, 306
brain fact, 394
brain framework, expensive, 68
brain imaging
  cross-cultural studies, 223
  cultural priming, 226
brain lateralization, 392
brain lesions, 265
brain plasticity, 5
  adolescence, 390–1
  culturally mediated, 6
  development, 65
  mechanisms, 396
brain stem, 305, 402
brain synchrony, 274, 288
brain–body–environment, 166
brainhood, 478
Brazil, 302, 343
breastfeeding and birth spacing, 133–6
Buddhism firewalking festivals, 335
burnout, 443

CAAFAG (children associated with armed forces and groups). *See* child soldiers
cab drivers, London, 103, 376
Call of Duty, 380
Canada, 454
canalization, 66, 77, 281
  development, 287, 289
  scaffolding, 24
cancer, 209
caregiving, 200–1
Caribbean, 454
caste discrimination, 141
categorical perception, 171
cats, 381
cattle herding, 17
caudate nucleus
  music, 403
  navigation, 376, 378, 381
  punishment, 307–8
  reward system, 308, 377, 402
  video games, 381
causal agents, 259
causal opacity, 326–7
causality, 26
causality, circular, 504

Index

causation, for action, 254
causation, reciprocal, 64
causes, proximate vs. ultimate, 64
cellular phone calls, 455
cerebellum, 249
cerebral subject, 478
cerebral subjectivation, 478
challenges, environmental, 123–5
character-driven stories, 430, 432–3
Chekhov, Anton, 419
child development and parent beliefs, 137–9
child impulsivity, 107
child mortality, 132
child soldiers, 140–4
childhood
   ethnographic studies, 127
   neurodevelopment, 197
   psychobehavioral development, 128
childhood adversity, 450
children
   social and economic contexts, 393
   social media, 389
children associated with armed forces and groups (CAAFAG). *See* child soldiers
chimpanzees, 16, 73, 301
Chinese
   alpha activity, 312
   biculturalism, 227
   cultural priming, 233
   empathic neural responses, 235
   ERP, 231
   interdependent self-construal, 105
   mPFC volume, 105
   neural representations, overlapping, 233
   pain processing, 231
   self-construal priming, 238
   self-relevant information, 233
   social norm violation detection, 310
Christianity, 342–3, 465
chronic illness and agency, 259
circuitry, neural, 7
city size and phone contacts, 455
Clark, Andy, 287, 420
classical conditioning, 199
classification, semantic vs. thematic, 99
climate instability and brain size, 14
code-switching, 211, 225
coevolution, 35
cognition
   bacteria, 177
   contentful, 168–9
   context, 166
   cultural values/beliefs, 230
   digital context, 467
   distributed, 12
   distributed cognition, 58
   ecosocial view, 496
   embedding, 12
   embodied, 11
   enaction, 11, 419
   extensiveness, 12
   free energy view, 282
   grounded cognition, 58
   language impact on, 164
   linguistic syntax model, 57
   lived experience, 58
   modular-interactionism, 171–2
   modularism, 167
   neurocomputational models, 176
   non-representational, 165
   organismic activity, 165
   shipboard navigation as, 287
   top-down, 288
cognition, numerical, 76
cognition, situated, 224
cognition, social
   brain regions, 285
   extended mind, 287
cognitive control network, 308
cognitive development, 397
cognitive impairment, 377
cognitive maps, 377–8
cognitive models, 178
cognitive neuroscience, interdisciplinary approaches, 495
cognitive penetration, 168–9
cognitive programs, 57
cognitive science, 495
cognitive therapy, 469
cognitivism, 58, 164, 166, 168, 182
collective effervescence, 335, 338
collective identity, 20
collectivism. *See also* interdependence
   Asia, 33
   cultural priming, 227–8, 238
   empathic neural responses, 235
   mPFC activity, 234
   sense of self, 260
   social cooperation, 33
colonialism, 129–30
colonization, 21
color, lack of universality, 163
coming out, 483, 486
communes, 334
communication, para-linguistic, 92
communities, imagined, 464
communities, multilingual, 92
community of practice, 498
competence, embodied, 180
complexity theory, 504

computational neuroscience
  active inference approach, 291
  cultural foundation, 287
concept construction, dynamic, 189
concepts, 203
  abstract, 11
  allostatically relevant events, 212
  binding process, 171
  emotional, 368
conceptual systems
  secondary acculturation, 210
  upcoming states, 203
conditioning, classical, 9
conflict avoidance, 91–2
conflicts in business, 91
conformity, 284
connectomics, 7, 495
consciousness, 16, 195
conserved transcriptional response to adversity (CTRA), 142–3
consonance
  active inference approach, 291
  cultural fit, 274, 282–3
  multiple domains, 285
  social interaction, 284
  stress, 284–5
construction, niche, 64
constructive development, 64
contents, representational, 165
context
  cognition and, 12
  congruous vs. incongruous, 100
  ethnographic films, 428
  focus and, 98, 100
  intellectualism, 166
  recursive mechanisms, 123
  rice vs. wheat farming, 32
  social behavior, 26–7
  ulterior motives, 181
continuity, 237, 239, 370
cooperation
  alcohol metabolism, 18
  brain systems, 286
  cognition, 12
  evolution, 462
  games, 228
  in-group/out-group bias, 274
  pain, 336
  Prisoner's Dilemma, 227
  religion, 342
  rice farming, 18, 32
  rituals, 325
  shared cultural frames, 274
  social affiliation, 75
  variation, 273

coordination vs. synchronization, 288
cortical midline structures
  hypnotism, 258
  self-consciousness, 239
  self-construal priming, 237
cortical morphology, heritability, 66
cortico-striatal-amygdala subnetwork, 209
costliness, 331–2, 334, 336
courtroom, neuroscience images, 265
credibility enhancing displays (CREDs), 331–2, 334
critical neuroscience, 395, 496
CTRA (conserved transcriptional response to adversity), 141, 143
Cubeo, 302
cultural accumulation, 55, 68
cultural affordances, 462
cultural anthropology, 291, 426–7
cultural biases, embodiment, 280
cultural consonance, 283
cultural constructs, 21
cultural context, 204
cultural dissonance, 284
cultural diversity, 506–7
cultural ecology, 128
cultural evolution, 74, 208
cultural feedback, 93
cultural genocide, 21
cultural knowledge systems, 230
cultural learning, 224
cultural mindset, 224
cultural models and dissonance, 284–5
cultural neuroscience, 131, 277
cultural priming
  brain activity modulation, 230
  brain imaging, 226
  defined, 224
  implementation, 230
  neural differentiation, 233
  neuronal mechanisms, 238
  personality trait reflection, 233
  Western vs. Chinese, 227
cultural psychology, 131
cultural relativism, 127, 130, 160
cultural transmission, 160, 189
cultural values/beliefs, 230, 238
culture
  abstract symbol system, 56
  acquisition of, 24
  collective construction, 93
  computational neuroscience, 287
  concept transmission, 204
  defined, 4, 59, 160, 188
  dynamic system, 224
  encounter between peoples, 21

Index   519

idiosyncratic adoption, 93, 111
information system, 59
information transmission, 59
music, 406–7
niches, 35
not a manipulated variable, 223
pattern perception, 292
patterned practices, 60, 164, 167, 174
physical manifestation, 59, 130
reproducibility, 112
selection force, 53
social structures, 505
surprise minimization, 283
technology and, 60
variation in time and space, 130
culture, enactive, 60
cuneus, 305
curriculum, helical, 61
Cyberball paradigm, 328
cyberchondria, 468
cybernetics, 503
cyberspace
  absorption, 467
  affordances, 464
  bonding, 464–5
  contagion, 469
  ecological niche, 462
  identity, 470, 472
  reliability, 466
  scalability, 463
  virtual embodiment, 470
Czech Republic, 332

D'Andrade, R., 59
Dalit, 141
dancing, 304
dang-ki, 244, 261–3
Dawkins, Richard, 340
Dead Birds, 431
Dead Island, 381
Deaf Culture, 488
decision-making
  adolescence, 391
  biosocial model, 333
  cultural mindset, 224
  dorsolateral prefrontal cortex (DLPFC), 308
  emotion regulation, 307
  emotions in, 159
  free will, 254
  information anticipation, 404
  operation integration, 307
  outsourced, 462
de-colonization, 54
default mode network (DMN), 192, 202, 286, 429

deities, ontology of, 262
deliberate practice, 72
deoxyribonucleic acid (DNA). *See* DNA
depression, 209
  children and adolescents, 393
  hippocampal GM volume, 376
  personal story, 438
  social defeat, 451
  training, 444
development as adaptive process, 64
development, constructive, 64
developmental inflection, 74
developmental influences, 279
developmental neuroplasticity, 278
developmental niches, 281, 283
developmental timescale, 22–5
diabetes, 209
digital addiction, 389
disability education system, 289
disability rights, 480–1
disciplinary ontologies, 498
disciplinary specialization, 497
discourse, 3–4, 477–8
discrimination, 441
discursive practices, 20, 420
dishabituation, 178
dissociation, 143, 258
dissonance
  cultural fit, 284
  models, 284–5
  outcome mismatch, 264
  priming, 28
  reduction, 332
  self-concepts, 25
  self-signaling, 333
  surprisal, 274
  vicarious dissonance, 333
distributed cognition, 12, 58
divergent modes of religiosity (Modes) theory, 337
diversity, 54, *See also* neurodiversity
diversity mindset, 481
division of labor, coordinated, 288
DLPFC. *See* dorsolateral prefrontal cortex (DLPFC)
DMN. *See* default mode network (DMN)
DNA
  computer science and, 63
  information-holding system, 56, 59, 63
  junk DNA, 123
  methylation, 123
  replication, 122
  self-modulation, 5
doctrinal rituals, 337, 339
domain specificity, 167

dopamine
  allostasis, 209
  increased response to stressor, 452
  information anticipation and reception, 404
  music, 403–4, 406
  prediction errors, 404
  prevalence, 106
  resident–intruder test, 451
  reward system, 402–3
  reward-based learning, 282
dopamine receptor gene D4 (DRD4), 18–19
  environmental effect on, 107
  hub, 106
  inhibitory effect, 106
  7/2-R (7- or 2-repeat allele), 107
  social norms, 314–16
dorsal stream, 72
  across species, 73
  gesture production, 75
  token streams, 76
  toolmaking skills, 77
dorsolateral prefrontal cortex (DLPFC), 248, 307–9
dramatic arc, 430
DRD4. *See* dopamine receptor gene D4 (DRD4)
drug abuse, 303, 451
dualism, 120, 143, 159
Duchamp, Marcel, 423
Dunbar number, 15, 462, 506
Durkheim, Émile, 325, 334
dyadic interactions, 8, 274, 313, 330
dynamic networks, 507
dynamical system theory, 502
dyslexia, 392, 479
dysphoric rituals, 331

Early Stone Age (ESA), 55
East Asians
  attenuation of self-serving tendencies, 104
  emotions and cultural contexts, 207
  self-effacing interdependence, 91
EC (entorhinal cortex), 377
echolocation, 289
ecological analysis, 146
ecological niche, 199
ecological studies, 502
ecology
  defined, 123
  ecological–constructivist view, 127
  sensitivity to, 54
  shared humanity, 130
economic games, 306
ecosocial systems view, 498
education, mindfulness-based, 392–3

EEA (environment of evolutionary adaptedness), 57
EEG. *See* electroencephalography (EEG)
EES. *See* extended evolutionary synthesis (EES)
effortful choice, 247
Ekman, Tomkins schools, 368
electroencephalography (EEG), 7
  alpha activity, 312
  cross-cultural studies, 223
  gamma activity, 313
  hyperscanning technique, 312
  perceptual processing, 231
  readiness potential, 253
  semantic incongruity testing, 102
  social coordination, 313
  social norm violations, 304, 311
  visual mismatch negativity, 163
embodied activity, 165
embodied capital theory, 67
embodied cognition, 167
embodied simulation theory, 431
embodiment
  bodily grounding, 11
  culture, 160
  generational, 280
  habitus, 280–1
  social divisions, 280
emergent processes, 498
emergent properties, 64
emotion concepts, untranslatable, 206
emotion regulation network, 307
emotional arousal, 403
emotional network, 306
emotional social resonance, 92
emotions
  action tendencies, 431
  affective categories, 369
  allostasis, 205
  allostatically relevant events, 212
  behaviors vs. words, 207
  causal mechanisms, 206
  constructions of, 27
  core subjective feelings, 370
  cultural artifacts, 190
  cultural values/beliefs, 230
  ephemeral constructions, 368
  ethnographic films, 428
  expectations, 403
  4E cognition, 159
  hard-wired, 369
  homeostasis, 88
  as interaction, 207
  minority vs. majority, 210
  music, 402

musical surprises, 407–8
  as noise, 159
  as practice, 369
  translation to expression, 368
  Western model, 206
emotives, 368–9
empathic neural responses, 235
empathy
  affective mediators, 441
  clinical encounters, 440
  mobilization, 445
  narrative, 430
  VMPFC, 441
employment, vulnerable, 455
empty nose syndrome (ENS), 468–9
emulator theories, 253
enactive approach, 12, 60, 74, 168, 176, 419
encapsulation
  information, 167, 170
  perception, 170–1
enculturation in Internet communities, 466
energy allocation, 191
energy regulation, 198
English, 260
ENS (empty nose syndrome), 468–9
entorhinal cortex (EC), 377
entrainment with music, 286
environment
  embodied activity, 165
  selection pressure, 122
environment of evolutionary adaptedness (EEA), 57
environmental challenges, 123–5
environmental stressors, 126
environments
  development, 125
  niche construction, 199
epigenetics
  adversity, 496
  anatomical variation, 197
  brain plasticity, 396
  contexts of possibility, 372
  mechanisms as context, 122
epilepsy, 444
epistemic injustice, 487
epistemic justice, 480
EPSPs (excitatory post-synaptic potentials), 379
ergonomics, 467
Erowid, 469–70
ERPs. *See* event-related potentials (ERPs)
error-related negativity (ERN), 95
ESA (Early Stone Age), 55
Esalen Institute, 389
ethanol metabolism, 18

ethics of representation framework, 487
ethics, reflexive, 146
Ethiopia, 444
ethnicity, 4
ethnographer, 129, 427
ethnographic films
  character-driven narratives, 432
  cultural practice documentation, 427
  emotional impact, lack of, 431
  life stories, unique, 429
  lived context, 428
  objective stance, 429
  story creation, 428
  teaching anthropology, 427
  trade-offs, 433
ethnographic methods, 505
ethnography
  being there, 129, 145
  bias and subjectivity, 131
eudaimonia, 440
European Americans
  attitude inferences, 101
  dispositional vs. situational factor attribution, 101
  DRD4 7/2-R alleles, 107–8
  focused attention, 98–100
  independent self-construal, 108
  orbitofrontal cortex, 108
  positive affect, 108
  prefrontal cortex, 104
  self-construal priming, 97–8
Europeans, 102, 205
event-related potentials (ERPs), 7
  error-related negativity, 95
  global/local letters, 231
  N130, 231
  N400, 100, 102, 304, 310–11, 313
  N60, 231
  P1, 232
  P300, 231
  P90, 231
  pain processing, 231
events, allostatically relevant
  concepts, 212
  convergence, 207–9
  culturally variant, 206
  emotions, 205, 212
  predictability, 207
evolution, behavior-led, 65
evolutionary biology, 56, 63
evolutionary game theory, 312
ex-child soldiers, 140–4
excitatory post-synaptic potentials (EPSPs), 379
exclusion, 455

executive control, 397
expatriates, 316
expectations
  agents, 283
  embodiment, 253
  shared sets of, 176
experience
  contexts of possibility, 369
  ecosocial view, 496
  perceptual processing, 181
experience-dependent training, 379
experimental design, 132
extended evolutionary synthesis (EES), 29, 64
  brain evolution, 65, 67
  cross-disciplinary approach, 67
extended mind, 58, 61, 287, 467
extended nervous system, 288–9, 291
exterior interior, 370
exteroception, 3
extrastriate cortex, 231

Facebook content manipulation, 467
face-to-face interaction, 288
facial recognition, 171
failure of empathy, 440
fairness for autistic people, 487–8
farming, rice vs. wheat, 32
feedback loops, 395, 420
  cultural affordances, 176
  importance of, 504
  intended outcomes and goals, 263
feedback positivity, 98
feedback-related negativity (FRN), 98
feelings. *See also* emotions
  consciousness, 193
  defined, 193
  outsourced, 462
Fiji, 343
film
  brain activation, 430
  emotional attunement, 431
  ethnographic tool, 426
  shared understanding, 429
firewalking rituals, 332, 335–6
first thousand days, 136–40
first-person accounts, 501
5-HTTLPR (serotonin transporter polymorphism), 314–16
Flaubert, Gustav, 419, 421
fMRI. *See* functional magnetic resonance imaging (fMRI)
focus and context, 98, 100
food regulatory systems, 506
foraging, 67
forcing, 471

4E cognition, 159, 363, 416
4E cognitive science
  agents, 178
  definition, 11
  literature, 417
  reconstructive processes, 123
  world model, 178, 418
framed line test, 99–100
France and neurodiversity, 483–4, 486
free energy, 282–4
free will, 245, 253–4
freedom of choice, 264
Freesurfer, 104
Friston, Karl, 178, 282, 418
FRN (feedback-related negativity), 98
frontal regions, intentional actions, 249
frontoparietal action system, 70
frontoparietal control network, 72–3
functional magnetic resonance imaging (fMRI), 7
  description of, 304
  in-group/out-group perception, 235
  navigation strategies, 378
  personality trait reflection, 233
  self-relevant information processing, 233
  senses of ownership and agency, 258
  stress effects, 451
  ventral striatum, 97
functional movement disorders, 257
functioning labels, 481–2
functions, psychological, 89
fundamental attribution error, 101

gambling task, 97
gamma band oscillations, 313
gender discrimination, 141
gender neurologies, local, 281
gendered difference, 281
gene complexes and epigenetic modulation, 396
gene therapy, 480
gene–culture coevolution, 18–19, 68
gene–culture evolutionary theory, 313
genetic polymorphisms, 105
genome, functional, 5
genotype, phenotype vs., 64
genre theory, 418
genres, 419–20
Germany, self-advocacy movements, 484
giraffe hunt, 429
global/local letters
  event-related potentials (ERPs), 231
  self-construal priming, 229
globalization emergence, 130
glucocorticoid receptor methylation, 24

Index 523

GM. *See* gray matter (GM)
goal-directed behavior, 504
goal-seeking behaviors, 104
good life, nature of, 480
Good, the Bad, and the Ugly, The, 430
governance, psychological, 393
gray matter (GM)
  hippocampus volume increase, 103
  independence vs. interdependence, 223
  orbitofrontal cortex, 108
  prefrontal cortex variation, 104
  sMRI, 376
  volume, 226
Greek blue, 163
Greek city-states, 92
grounded cognition, 58
group loyalty, 90
group membership, 328
gun, Chekhov's, 419

habit formation, 378
habits vs. knowledge, 59
habituation, 178
habitus, 60, 280, 291
hacking the brain, 364
Hacking, Ian, 479
Hanno, 302
happiness, predictors of, 94–8
hardship, 281
hazing, 333
HCIs (human–computer interactions), 380
healer, traditional, 244, 261–3
heart disease, 209
helical curriculum, 72, 74
helping behaviors, 228
heterophenomenology, 501
hierarchy of control, 258
Highland Dani, 427
Hindu, *kavadi attam*, 330–1
hippocampus (HPC), 376
  cognitive maps, 378
  competition with striatum, 379
  experience-dependent training, 375, 379
  gray matter volume, 376
  London cab drivers, 103, 376
  memory-based spatial learning, 377
  neurogenesis, 377
  neuropsychiatric illness, 376
  relational memory, 377
  spatial navigation strategies, 378
  video games and gray matter, 380
history and languages, 20
hivemind mentality, 471
homeostasis
  context, 121

cultural origins, 370
emotions, 88
historical contingency, 371
hope, 445
HPC. *See* hippocampus (HPC)
human capital, 146
human development
  course across cultures, 128
  ecological approaches, 278
  embodiment culture, 160
human diversity
  cultural variation, 127
  culture under-representation, 146
  ecological frameworks, 146
  neurological correlates, 277
human ecology, 127
human, becoming, 54
human–computer interactions (HCIs), 380
humanities, 372
humans
  learning transmission, 204
  niche construction, 122
  self-referentiality, 504
  social animals, 189
Hunters, The, 429
Hutterites, 302
hygge, 206
hyperconnectedness, 390
hyper-natural monitoring hypothesis, 462
hyperscanning, 8, 312, 317, 502
hypnotic catalepsy, 257
hypnotic suggestion, 257

IBH (interactive brain hypothesis), 288
identification, collective, 478
identities, subcultures, 465
identity fusion, 338
identity politics, 365, 488
  France, 483
  neurodiversity, 483
  personhood concepts, 488
identity threat model, 442, 446
identity, co-construction, 472
imagistic rituals, 337–8
imitation, 16, 55
immigrant paradox, 211
immigrants
  emotional fit, 210
  first-generation health, 210
  physical differences, 130
  psychosis, 450
  thwarted aspirations, 453
immigration
  acculturative stress, 209
  cultural value/belief changes, 225

in real life (IRL), 463–4, 470
inclusive fitness, 198
incompetence, subjective, 443
independence. *See also* individualism
  cultural priming, 228
  interdependence vs., 27–8
  priming of, 34
  rewards, 235
  self-construal priming, 228–9
  sense of self, 260
  Western cultures, 33, 89
independent tasks, prefrontal functions, 104
index of similarity for happiness, 94
India, 92, 444
Indigenous Peoples, 21, 26
Indigenous psychologies, 506
individual fitness, 198
individualism. *See also* independence
  agency, 245
  cultural priming, 227–8
  mPFC activity, 234
  sense of self, 260
individualism–collectivism framework, 228
inertia, cultural, 20
infant brain
  affective niche, 200–1
  cultural models, 196
inferior prefrontal cortex, 305
inflammation and negative emotion states, 144
information
  anticipation and reception, 404
  encapsulation, 167
  encoding, 176
  relevance, 466
  storage and transmission, 63
information transmission, intergenerational, 125–6
informed consent, 480
in-group identity, 470
in-group protection, 91–2
in-group/out-group bias, 274
in-group/out-group perception, 235
initiation rituals, 333
instructions, top-down cognition, 287
instrumental actions, 328
insula, 235
intellectualism, 166
intentional binding effect, 248, 251
intentionality, 245, 254, 461, 467
interactive brain hypothesis (IBH), 288
interbirth interval, 133–6
interbrain synchrony, 313
interdependence. *See also* collectivism
  argumentative form, 91
  Asia, 33

  expressive form, 92
  independence vs., 27–8
  interpersonal ties, 506
  loyalty to groups, 90
  non-Western cultures, 90
  priming, 27, 34, 228
  rewards, 235
  rice farming, 33
  self-assertive form, 91
  self-construal, 96
  self-construal priming, 228–9
  self-effacing form, 91
  sense of self, 260
  socio-ecology, 111
interdisciplinarity, 494
interdisciplinary collaboration
  barriers to, 497–8
  institutional structures, 499
  multilevel problems, 499
  stakeholder involvement, 500
interdisciplinary research funding, 497
intergroup contact theory, 441
interiority, 370
Internet as ecosystem model, 463
interoception, 3, 193, 206, 370
interoceptive sensations, 203
interoceptive system, 208
interpretation, 251
intersectionality, 453
intersubjectivity, 286
interventions, 139, 141
intraparietal sulcus, 73
intrinsic activity, 191
invasion, 21
IRL (in real life), 463–4, 470
Islam, *Ashura*, 330
Israel, self-advocacy movements, 484
Israelis (European background), 102
Italy, neurodiversity, 477, 484

Japan
  firewalking festivals, 335–6
  misogi, 326, 330
  social norm strength, 302
Japanese
  agentic language, 260
  attitude inferences, 99–101
  CTRA, 144
  interdependent self-construal, 105
  prefrontal cortex, 105
joint attention, 286, 466
Ju/'hoansi, 427, 429, *See also* !Kung
judgment, value-based, 104
juggling and gray matter changes, 103
jujitsu, 288, 336, 338

Index

junk DNA, 123
justice for autistic people, 487–8

kami (Shinto deities), 326
karma, 344
kavadi attam, 330–1
keyboard players and gray matter changes, 103
kinship, affinal and fictive, 75
knapping
  model system, 69
  technique acquisition, 70–2
knowledge, 203
  competence, 180
  embodiment, 11
  storage, 178–80
knowledge production, 496
!Kung
  birth spacing, 133–6
  social norms, 302
  stories, 429

lab coat effect, 468, 470
lactation. *See* breastfeeding
lactose tolerance, 17
language
  acquisition, 125
  combinatorial and generative, 76
  EEA, 57
  identity-first vs. person-first, 479
  natural selection, 57
  shifts in internal model, 210
  theory of mind, 75
languages and history, 20
lateral orbitofrontal cortex, 309
lateral prefrontal cortex (LPFC), 309
Latin America, 454
Latin Americans
  holistic attention, 100
  interdependence, 92
  situational inference, 102
lead in the atmosphere, 371
learning, 202
  intrinsic activity, 191
  motor resonance, 72
  prediction errors, 408
  predictions vs., 189
  prosociality, 67
  simulation and, 71
  social and asocial, 72
learning ability, 225
learning reinforcement, 19
learning, error-driven, 282
learning, memory-based, 377
learning, second-order, 466
learning, statistical, 406

lesion studies on economic decision-making, 307
Libyan civil war, 338
lidocaine, 379
life history
  self-determined, 281
  strategy, 15
  trade-offs, 134
life history theory, 126
lifeworlds, 501
linguistic stimuli, 304
linguistic syntax, 57
linguistics, 75
literacy, 66, 125, 371
literature
  cognitive puzzle, 417–18, 421
  pleasure, 422
  reading experience, 418
  structuralism, 421
  symbolic meaning, 423
  tools, 416
lived experience, 58
LMICs. *See* low- and middle-income countries (LMICs)
long-term potentiation (LTP), 379
looping, 479, 504
looping journey, 394
loss, experience of, 209
low- and middle-income countries (LMICs), 439, 444, 450
LPFC (lateral prefrontal contex), 309
LTP (long-term potentiation), 379
Lubara, 302

macaques, 16, 73, 77, 199
magnetic resonance imaging (MRI), 7, 223, *See also* functional magnetic resonance imaging (fMRI), structural magnetic resonance imaging (sMRI)
manual labor, 53
Markov blankets, 167n1
mass, Roman Catholic, 326
masturbation, abstinence from, 471
maternal time, demands on, 139
Mauritius
  firewalking ritual, 332
  religious priming, 343
  Thaipusam, 331, 336
measurement and reality, 497
medial frontal gyrus, 306
medial orbitofrontal cortex (MOFC), 181, 307
medial prefrontal cortex (mPFC), 233, 305
  cross-cultural differences, 104
  mental state representation, 305
  self-construal priming, 238

medial prefrontal cortex (mPFC) (cont.)
  sense of self, 104
medical anthropology, 131, 438, 441
medical school exams, 376
meditation, 390, 392–3, 470–1
Melanesia, 334
meme-complexes, 340
memes, 56, 59, 64
memories, procedural, 377
memory system imbalances, 382
mental health, 390
mental health Gap Action Programme (mhGAP), 439, 444–5
mental, neurological, and substance abuse disorders (MNS)
  attitudes toward, 439, 441
  lack of access to services, 443
  not treating, 443
  three-act stories, 445–6
mentalizing, 61, 306
  brain networks, 285
  definition, 14
  language, 75
  modular framework, 171
  motor resonance, 74
  neurological assemblies, 286
  other species, 16
  VMPFC, 441
mentor mothers, 137
meta-cognition, 250
metaplasticity, 166
methods
  circumscribed nature, 502
  multiple viewpoints, 502–3
methylation
  DNA, 123
  glucocorticoid receptors, 24
  hippocampus, 24
mhGAP. *See* mental health Gap Action Programme (mhGAP)
micro-culture, 211
mid-cingulate, 235
migraine auras, 169n2
migration, 20
mimicry, 329
mind
  as computer, 166
  definition, 3
  enactive approach, 288
  gap with world, 177
  localization, 11
  modular model, 279
mind, extended, 58, 61, 287, 467
mind–body dualism, 3
mind–body dualism, 143

mind–body dualism, 159
mindfulness practices, 390, 392–3, 398
mind-reading, 286, 416, *See also* mentalizing
minorities, visible, 453
mirror neurons, 330, 431
Mirror Self-Recognition (MSR) Test, 73
mirror system, 286, 467
misattribution theory, 257
misogi, 326, 330
mixed-methods research, 497
mnemotechnologies, 20
MNS. *See* mental, neurological, and substance abuse disorders (MNS)
model, internal, 191, 404
  biculturalism, 211
  contact with new culture, 210
  cultural dependence, 196
  default mode network, 192
  default mode subnetwork, 193
  infant brain, 200–1
  language, 210
  multiple predictions, 202
  predictive, 201
  salience system subnetwork, 193
  sociocultural context fit, 209
models
  agency, 249, 251
  knowledge storage, 178–9
  range of internal, 212
  recurrent situations, 188
modern synthesis (MS)
  brain evolution, 65, 67
  evolutionary biology, 63
Modes theory, 337
  imagistic rituals, 338
  stable groups, 337
modular-interactionism, 171–2
modularism
  cognition, 167
  early perception, 170–1
  PPC vs., 174
MOFC (medial orbitofrontal cortex), 181, 307
Mongolians, 260
monotheism, 340
moral culpability, 265
moral implications, 251
moral responsibility, 245, 261
Morris Water Maze, 375
motor areas and action preparation, 249
motor resonance, 72, 74
movable type, 371
movement synchronization, 286
mPFC. *See* medial prefrontal cortex (mPFC)
MS (modern synthesis)

brain evolution, 65, 67
evolutionary biology, 63
MSR (Mirror Self-Recognition) Test, 73
multiculturalism, 211, 225, 239
multidisciplinarity, defined, 494
multilevel problems, 499
multisensory integration, 467
multivariate statistics, 502
music
 anticipation, 403–4
 chills, 403–4
 cultural background, 407
 expectation violation, 403–4
 prediction errors, 408
 reward value, 407
 statistical learning, 406
 surprises, 403–4, 407–8
music motifs, 405
musical complexity, 407
musical systems, 405
myelination, 397
mystery cults, 334

narrative
 action and, 12
 agency, 259
 cultural bonds, 429, 501
narrative handling, 418
narrative practice hypothesis (NPH), 175
narrative structures, 364, 430
nationalism, 464
natural selection
 derived features, 66
 information processing adaptations, 57
 organism vs. genes, 64
 variation and change, 62
navigation strategies, 378–9
navigational learning in video games, 380
neighborhood as context, 121
neoteny, 22
Nepal, 140–4, 443
 local collaboration, 146
 mental illness treatment, 438
nervous system, extended, 288–9, 291
Netherlands, social norm strength, 302
network theory, 2, 5
neural accommodation, 181
neural activity and phase synchrony, 171
neural circuitry and cultural feedback, 93
neural development and social interaction, 288
neuroaesthetics, 417
neuroanatomy and toolmaking training, 70
neuroanthropology, 278
neuroarchaeology, 69
neurochemical selfhood, 478

neurodivergent, defined, 479
neurodiversity
 defined, 478
 France, 483–4, 486
 Germany, 484
 global perspectives, 485–6
 Israel, 484
 Italy, 477, 484
 multivocal movement, 486
 Sweden, 483, 486
neurodiversity politics, 482
neuroeducation, 391
neuroenchantment, 495
neurogenesis in hippocampus, 377
neuro-hegemonies, 480, 486
neurohistory, 371
neuroimaging, 131, 277
 statistical fabrication, 266
neuroimaging techniques, 7, *See also specific techniques*
neurologies, local, 281
neurome, 5
neuromyths, 392–3
neuropathology, 379
neuroplasticity
 popular interpretations of, 395
 short-term changes, 226
 social contexts, 225
neuroqueer theory, 479
neuroscience
 applications, 496
 interactions with social science, 495–6
neurostructural selfhood, 478
neuroticism, 314
neurotribes, 479
neurotypical, defined, 479
New Atheists, 340
New Zealand, social norm strength, 302
newborns and musical expectations, 403
niche availability, 121
niche construction, 31, 122, 199
 ecological approaches, 278
 literacy, 66
niches
 culturally mediated, 35
 technological, 68–9
niches, developmental, 281, 283
niches, ecological, 462
non-deficit approach, 481, 483
non-representationalism. *See* radically enactive accounts of cognition (REC)
normative behavior, 33, 306
Northern Irish Troubles, 338
Norway rats, 301
novelty-seeking, 9, 19, 315

NPH (narrative practice hypothesis), 175
nucleus accumbens
  learning, 376
  music, 403
  prediction errors, 404
  reward system, 308, 402
numbers, tokenization, 76

object manipulation, 74
object recognition, 171
occipital cortex, 232, 305
OFC. *See* orbitofrontal cortex (OFC)
omics revolution, 494–5
ontology and agency, 259
ontology of dieties, 262
operant learning, 9
oral history, transmission of, 21
orbitofrontal cortex (OFC)
  aversive emotional reactions, 305
  cross-cultural differences, 104, 108
  experience modulation, 109
  reward system, 402
  social cognition, 285
  value-based judgment, 104
orgoglio (pride), 477
orthodoxy, 327
orthopraxy, 327
ostracism, 328
Other(s), 130, 161, 280
Otherkin, 470–1
out of body experiences, 256
out-group members, 440
outsider status, 452
overimitation, 327
oxytocin, 316

package of care, 22
pain, 231
  affiliative role, 335
  cooperation, 336
  cultural contingency, 371
  empathic neural responses, 235
  firewalking, 336
  jujitsu, 336
  mutual support, 336
  social affiliation, 335
  social instruction, 288
  subjective incompetence, 443
pain perception, 286
Pakistan, social norm strength, 302
Papua New Guinea, 337
parent advocacy (*for* autism), 477, 483–4, 487–8
parental beliefs, 24, 137–9, 144
parenting, 107

parietal cortex, 376
parietal regions, 249
Parkinson's disease, 382
passions, 369
patterned practices
  culture, 164, 166, 174
  enactive, 60
  narrative practices, 175
  neuroanthropology, 279
Pavlovian fear conditioning, 441
PCC (posterior cingulate cortex), 238
PECMA flow model (perception, emotion, and cognition to motor action), 430
peers, 461
perception
  embodied activity, 165
  recognition, 181
  top-down effects, 164, 170
perception, active, 58
perceptual abstraction, 75
perceptual analysis, 403
personhood, 488, 506
perspective-taking, 397
persuasiveness, 331
Pesqueriro, 343
PET (positron emission tomography), 307
phantom limb/wing/tail, 470
phenotypes
  genotypes vs., 64
  intergenerational transmission, 24
phoebes, 199
PhotoVoice, 438, 444–5
physiological dependency, 189
piercings, 330, 336
place navigation, 375
placebo effect, 469
plasticity
  brain development, 65
  defined, 396
  synaptic remodeling, 396
plasticity alleles, 105
polygamous unions, 432
polytheism, 340
Pomio Kivuing, 337
population size, effect on brain function, 451
population-statistical genetics, 63
Portugal, 455
positive emotions, engaging vs. disengaging, 94–5
positron emission tomography (PET), 307
posterior cingulate cortex (PCC), 238
posterior fusiform gyrus, 305
posterior parietal cortex (PPC), 249
post-immigration cranial dimensions, 127
post-traumatic stress disorder (PTSD)

child soldiers, 142
CTRA, 142, 144
hippocampal GM volume, 376
resilience, 142, 144
PPC (posterior parietal cortex), 249
precision weighting, 405
precuneus, 258
prediction errors
  abstractions, 208
  dopamine, 282, 404
  encoding, 11, 203
  free energy view, 282
  generation, 405
  learning, 284, 408
  minimization, 202, 253
  music motifs, 405
  precision-weighted musical syntax, 405, 407
prediction patterns
  concepts, 203
  incomplete patterns, 202
  priors, 203
  upcoming states, 203
predictions
  coding, 201, 404–5, 418
  content influence, 173
  corrections, 193
  interoception, 209
  learning vs., 189
predictive coding, 201, 404–5, 418
predictive models, literature, 418
predictive processing
  narrative handling, 418
  weak theory, 417
predictive processing accounts of cognition (PPC)
  conservative enactive account, 176
  defined, 172, 174
  inner models, 168
  modularism vs., 174
  preferred model, 167
  top-down predictions, 174
predictive processing theories, 253
prejudice
  racial prejudice, 343
  religiosity, 340–1
  threat response, 441
premotor areas and action preparation, 249
prescribers, 444
primary motor cortex and hypnotism, 258
PRIME (UK AID/Department for International Development-sponsored PRogramme for Improving Mental health carE), 444–5
priors, 188, 203, 282
Prisoner's Dilemma, 227
probability distributions, 176

procedural memory system, 378
process over context, 166
processes, impenetrable, 169
processes, probabilistic, 421
processing hierarchy, 10, 172
processing, predictive, 9
professional threats, 443
program, culture as, 59
prosociality, 67
  religions, 341–2
  religious priming, 342–3
  ritual vs. religion, 345
  self-report, 341
proximate causes, 64
psychoanalysis and autism, 484, 486–7
psychological reactance, 264
psychology and WEIRD societies, 131, 279–80
psychosis
  defined, 450
  social defeat hypothesis, 451
  social determinants, 450
  training, 444
psychosis rates, 451
psychotropic influences, 371
PTSD. See post-traumatic stress disorder (PTSD)
puberty
  brain maturation, 126
  Otherkin, 471
  parental intervention, 138
  timing, 125
punishment, 306–9
  first-party vs. third-party, 308
  religion, 341
  threats, collective vs. personal, 315
punishment motivation, 306
putamen, 382, 403

queer theory, 479

r/NoFap, 471
race, cultural construction of, 21–2
race-related rejection sensitivity (RS-race), 452
radically enactive accounts of cognition (REC), 165, 182
reader preferences, 417
readiness potential, 249
reading. See literature
reality effect, 419, 421
REC (radically enactive accounts of cognition), 165, 182
reciprocal causation, 64
recovery, 205, 433
"The Red Wheelbarrow" (Williams), 422–4
reddit, 471

Reddy, William, 368
REducing Stigma among HealthcAre ProvidErs (RESHAPE) intervention, 444–5
reductionism, 3, 494
relational memory, 377
relationships, identity and, 90
reliability, 466
religion
  big gods hypothesis, 341, 344
  defined, 325
  doctrinal mode, 337
  evolutionary hierarchy, 340
  imagistic mode, 337
  individual level, 325n1
  orthodoxy vs. orthopraxy, 327
  prosocial behavior, 341–2
  prosociality, 345
  social cooperation, 340
  splinter groups, 337
  strictness of, 334
  supernatural punishment hypothesis, 341, 344
religiosity
  prejudice, 340–1
  self-report, 341
religious beliefs, 325–7, 339, 341–3
  credibility enhancing displays (CREDs), 332
  supernatural beliefs, 339–40, 344
  unwavering belief, 334
religious priming and prosociality, 342–3
replication crisis, 345
reproduction, biocultural, 67
reproductive ecology, 125, 135
research
  being there vs. formal research, 145
  de-colonization, 146
  non-deficit approach, 481
research biases, 280
research participants, 132
RESHAPE (REducing Stigma among HealthcAre ProvidErs) intervention, 444–5
resident–intruder test, 451
resignation syndrome, 244, 264–5
resilience, 393, 398
  Balinese wives, 432
  child soldiers, 141
  CTRA, 142
  environmental factors, 496
  mindfulness meditation, 390
  narratives, 433
  PTSD, 142
resistance as other, 246
resource availability, 121, 126

respect, autistic people, 486–7
response-based navigational strategies
  striatum, 378
  video game training, 381
responses, environmental, 125
revolutionary fighters, 338
reward anticipation, 307
reward measurement, 97–8
reward network, 307
reward processing, 19
reward system and music, 402–3, 406
rewards
  religion, 341
  video games, 381
rewards, vicarious, 235
Rhesus macaques, 199
rice farming, 18, 32, 91
rites of passage, 465
ritual action and expectations, 262
ritual adoption, 328
  overimitation, 328
  social cues, 329
ritualistic actions, 328
rituals
  bonding, 465
  causal opacity, 326–7
  collective participation, 331
  commitment, 334
  defined, 325
  effects on observers, 332, 335
  individual level, 325n1
  online communities, 463
  online meditation, 470
  prosociality, 345
  symbolic transformations, 442
rituals, doctrinal, 465
rituals, imagistic, 465
rodents
  hippocampal volume, 376
  memory system and age, 379
Roman Catholic mass, 326
rubber-hand illusion, 255
rules, 179–80

sadness, 206, 209
salience subnetwork, 192, 202
Sapir–Whorf hypothesis, 163
Satedi, 483
scaffolding, 24, 61, 74, 175, 230
schizophrenia, 398, 450
  hippocampal GM volume, 376
  social defeat, chronic, 452
schoolchildren. See children
scientific theory, 363
Second Life Zen Buddhist community, 470

Index

segregation, 211
selection, frequency-dependent, 19
selective pressure, 29
self
  independence, 89
  relational, 90
self, cultural construction of, 26
self, production of, 161
self-advocacy (*of* autism), 477, 483–4, 487–8
self-as-brain, 478
self-assembly, 64
self-awareness, 501
  adaptive value of, 16
  neural correlates, 233
self-concept, 227
self-construal
  agency, 259
  independent, 232
  independent vs. interdependent, 34, 97–8
  independent vs. interdependent self-construal, 105
  interdependent, 232
  temporary shifts, 231
self-construal priming, 228
  cortical midline structures, 237
  global/local letters, 229, 231
  independence, 231
  independent, 235
  in-group/out-group perception, 235
  interdependent, 231, 235
  intergroup relationships, 237
  self-relevant information, 233
  social emotion, 235
  visual perception and attention, 229
  visual perceptual processing, 232
self-continuity, 237
self-control, 247, 398
  alpha activity, 312
  free will, 254
self-determination, 281, 480
self-efficacy, 443
self-experience, 256
self-flagellation, 330
self-focus, 231–2
selfhood, brain-based, 478
selfish gene, 64
self-organization, 282
self-perception accounts, 333
self-regulation, 393
self-representation narrative, 25
self-sacrifice, 338
self-understanding, 496
semantic incongruity testing, 102
sense of agency, 256
  cognitive-attributional processes, 250
  connectivity, 249
  influence of expectations, 257
  prediction, 251
  reconstruction, 251
sense of ownership, 256
sense of self, 104
sensitization, 452–3
sensorimotor control feedback loop, 245, 254
sensorimotor regions, bilateral, 257
sensorimotor systems, 72
sensory experiences, 11
sensory input, embodied, 189
sensory processing, 161
serotonin transporter polymorphism (5-HTTLPR), 314–16
SES (socioeconomic status), 197
Shia, *Ashura*, 330
Shinto firewalking festivals, 335
Shinto *misogi*, 326, 330
shipboard navigation, 287
Similarities and Differences with Family and Friends task, 227, 234
simulation, 15
  attentional system, 72
  linguistic meaning, 75
  sensorimotor systems, 72
  skilled actions, 72
Singapore, 92, 244, 262, 302
Singaporean Chinese prefrontal cortex, 104
Singer, Judy, 482
skills, embodied, 74
Skolt Lapps, 302
sleep strategies, 397
sleep–wake cycles, 506
SLFIII. *See* superior longitudinal fasciculus (SLFIII)
Slovakia, 332
sMRI (structural magnetic resonance imaging), 376
social adaptation and immigration, 209
social adversity, 496
social affiliation system, 75, 506
social agency, 247
social cognition
  brain regions, 285
  dispositional vs. situational inference, 100–2
  extended mind, 287
  self-construal priming, 229
social connection
  patterns of interaction, 456
  phone calls, 455
  quality of encounters, 456
social constraints, 99–101
social construction, 277
social contact interventions, 439

social contagion, 467, 470
social contract, 90
social defeat
  intersectionality, 453
  objective experience, 452
  sensitization, 452–3
  social disadvantage, 453
  thwarted aspirations, 453–4
social defeat hypothesis, 456
social dependency, 190
social determinants, 496
social disadvantage, 453
social ecology
  community perceptions, 141
  interventions, 142
social emotion and self-construal priming, 235
social exclusion, 328
social groups and neocortex size, 15
social identity theory, 338
social interaction, 165
  cultural consonance, 284
  default mode, 287
  without mind-reading, 286
social judgment task, 228
social media, 398, 506
social network, 15, 455–6
social norm violations
  fMRI, 304
  intentional vs. unintentional, 305
  punishment, 306–9
  reprimand judgment, 306
social norms
  compliance, 310
  defined, 300
  ecological and societal threats, 302–3
  strength, 302–3
  symbolic reasons, 301
  tightness vs. looseness, 302–3, 310–11
  transmission systems, 301
social practices, reorganization, 424
social science interactions with neuroscience, 495–6
social structures, embodiment, 280
social subordination, 454, 456
social support and well-being, 456
social world as starting point, 501
societies, multicultural, 225
societies, traditional, 302
sociocultural factors, patterned practices, 174
sociocultural scaffolding, 175
socioecology, 111
socioeconomic status (SES), 197
somatic amplification, 467–8
somatic symptom disorder (SSD), 469
somatosensory cortex, 231

songbirds, affective niches, 199
source credibility, 331
South Africa
  intervention with mothers, 137–9
  local collaboration, 146
  mental health care, 444
spatial and temporal contiguity, 253
spatial learning, 377
spatial navigation strategies, 364
  entorhinal cortex, 377
  hippocampus, 378
  hippocampus volume increase, 103, 376
  video game training, 381
SSD (somatic symptom disorder), 469
states, US, social norms, 303
statistical learning, 406
stigmatization, triggering threats, 441
stimulus–response associations, 378
stone toolmaking, 55
stories, 429–30
storytelling, 431
storytelling, visual, 438
stress
  cultural learning, 284
  hippocampus-dependent spatial strategy reduction, 380
  neuroendocrine response, 281
  video games, 381
stress response system regulation, 24
stressors, 199n3, 452
striatum
  competition with hippocampus, 379
  procedural memories, 377
  response-based navigational strategies, 378
structural magnetic resonance imaging (sMRI), 376
structuration, 60
student engagement, 288
subcultures, 463, 465
subjectivity, 161
subliminal priming, 28, 248, 311
subthalamic nucleus, 382
suicide
  empty nose syndrome, 469
  Indigenous peoples, 21
Sumerian Warrior Story task, 226, 234
Super Mario 64, 380–1
superior longitudinal fasciculus (SLFIII)
  action plans, 73
  MSR performance, 73
  toolmaking, 77
superior parietal lobule, 73
superior prefrontal cortex, 305
supernatural agents, belief in, 340
supernatural monitoring hypothesis, 462

Index

supernatural punishment hypothesis, 341, 344
supplementary motor area, 235, 306
surface-based analysis, 104
surprisal, 274, 282
survival threats, 442
suspense, creation of, 419
Sweden and neurodiversity, 483, 486
symbol manipulation, 57
symbolic operations, 58
symbols, amodal, 57
symbols, external, 175
symptom checker as embodied experience, 468
synaptic plasticity, 396
synaptic pruning, 396
synaptogenesis, 396–7
synchronization vs. coordination, 288
synchrony
   cooperative behavior, 330
   emotional, 338
   imitation fidelity, 329
   perceived similarity, 330
   prosocial attitudes, 329
   prosocial effects, 330
syphilis, 371
system learning, 178–9
system of systems, 129
systems theory, 503

Tamil, *kavadi attam*, 330
Taoist worldview, 262
tasks
   context sensitive meaning, 225
   culturally specific, 226
   Similarities and Differences with Family and Friends, 227, 234
   social Simon, 229
   Sumerian Warrior Story, 226, 234
Tauber, Ben, 389
taxi drivers, London, 103, 376
tDCS (transcranial direct current stimulation), 309
teaching, 16, 61
   prosociality, 67
   stone toolmaking, 55
technological niche
   knapping, 69
   social affiliation, 74
technology and culture, 60
teenagers. *See* adolescents
teleonomy, 63
Tellegen Absorption Scale, 472
temporal contiguity, 260
temporal cortex, 285
temporoparietal junction
   comparator models, 249
   mental state representation, 305
   movement self-agency, 257
tethering hypothesis, 65–6
Thaipusam, 331, 336
theory of mind, 61, 306
   brain networks, 285
   definition, 14
   language, 75
   modular framework, 171
   motor resonance, 74
   neurological assemblies, 286
   other species, 16
   VMPFC, 441
thinking
   action and, 12
   outsourced, 462
third-person observation, 274
thoughtform, 471
threat response, 441
three-act story structure, 430, 432, 445–6
thrushes, 199
tightness–looseness (TL) in social norms, 302–3, 310–11
time as context, 121
timeline, developmental, 62
timeline, historical, 62
timescales
   autobiographical, 25–6
   coconstruction, 13
   coevolutionary, 17–19
   developmental, 22–5
   evolutionary, 14–17
   historical, 19–22
   real-time context, 26–9
TL (tightness–looseness) in social norms, 302–3, 310–11
tokens, externalized, 75
tool use, 14
toolmaking, 53, 86
top-down effects
   actions, 188
   control, 16
   error signals, 11
   perception, 164, 170
   PPC, 174
   vision, 171
TPO (Transcultural Psychosocial Organization)
   Nepal, 146, 444
trade routes, 91
tradition, 20
transabled.org, 472
transcranial direct current stimulation (tDCS), 309
Transcultural Psychosocial Organization (TPO)
   Nepal, 146, 444

534   Index

transmission, cultural, 16
transparency about needs, 481
transubstantiation, 326
trauma in society, 142
traumatic events, 338
tribes, 479
Tsamko, Tsoma, 429
tulpamancy, 472–5
tulpas, 471–2
Tylor, E. B., 340
Tyva, 343

Uganda, 444
UK AID/Department for International Development-sponsored PRogramme for Improving Mental health carE (PRIME), 444–5
ultimate causes, 64
uncertainty, 209, 424
unemployment, 453–4
unity, 330
upward mobility, 285
urban living and psychosis, 450
US Navy, 287

VBM (voxel-based morphometry), 104
ventral stream and object recognition, 73
ventral striatum (VS), 97
ventral tegmental area, 402, 404
ventromedial prefrontal cortex (VMPFC), 307–8, 441
vergogna (shame), 477
vervet monkeys, 301
vicarious reward, 235
video games and hippocampal gray matter, 380
video, cultural research uses, 427
violence, 445–6
virtual embodiment, 470
virtual reality, 256, 506
visceromotor regulation, 193
vision
    cognitive penetration, 168, 171
    information encapsulation, 170
    top-down effects, 171
vision-impaired individuals, 289
visual anthropology, 428
visual cortex, 65, 181
visual mismatch negativity (vMMN), 163, 172
visual perception, 229, 232
visual processing of colors, 163

visual psychological anthropology, 431
vMMN (visual mismatch negativity), 163, 172
VMPFC. *See* ventromedial prefrontal cortex (VMPFC)
volition, 249
volitional competency, 260–1
voxel-based morphometry (VBM), 104
VS (ventral striatum), 97

weak theories, 417, 424
Web 2.0, 464, 466
WebMD, 468
WEIRD societies, 131, 143, 279–80
West Germany, disability activism, 484
Western contexts, 245
Western cultural symbols, 226
Western independence, 89, 110
Western, educated, industrial, rich, democratic (WEIRD) societies. *See* WEIRD societies
Westerners
    neural representations, overlapping, 233
    self-serving tendencies, 104
    traits, 279
what matters most, 445
white matter, 376
WHO. *See* World Health Organization (WHO)
will, mind vs. brain, 261
Williams, William Carlos, 422–4
willpower, 247
Wittgenstein's rules, 179–80
words
    allostasis, 204
    semantic distinctions, 76
    tokens, 75
working class social norms, 303
world
    brain-based representations, 12
    construction of models, 174
    gap with mind, 177
    own model, 178
World Health Organization (WHO), 438–9, 444–5
world order, structured, 465

xenomelia, 472

Yanamamo, 427
yoga, 392

Zen Buddhism, 470